ZAGAT®

New York City
Restaurants
2008

EDITORS
Kurt Gathje and Carol Diuguid
COORDINATOR
Larry Cohn

Published and distributed by
Zagat Survey, LLC
4 Columbus Circle
New York, NY 10019
212.977.6000
newyork@zagat.com
www.zagat.com

ACKNOWLEDGMENTS

We thank Caren Weiner Campbell, Leigh Crandall, Mikola De Roo, Lynn Hazlewood, Bernard Onken, Mary Phillips-Sandy, Blake Royer, Laura Siciliano-Rosen, Miranda Van Gelder, as well as the following members of our staff: Josh Rogers (assistant editor), Rachel McConlogue (assistant editor), Sean Beachell, Maryanne Bertollo, Amy Cao, Sandy Cheng, Reni Chin, Bill Corsello, Deirdre Donovan, Caitlin Eichelberger, Alison Flick, Jeff Freier, Shelley Gallagher, Michelle Golden, Randi Gollin, Caroline Hatchett, Karen Hudes, Roy Jacob, Natalie Lebert, Mike Liao, Christina Livadiotis, Allison Lynn, Dave Makulec, Chris Miragliotta, Andre Pilette, Becky Ruthenburg, Troy Segal, Robert Seixas, Carla Spartos, Kelly Stewart, Kilolo Strobert, Donna Marino Wilkins, Liz Borod Wright, Yoji Yamaguchi, Sharon Yates and Kyle Zolner.

The reviews published in this guide are based on public opinion surveys, with numerical ratings reflecting the average scores given by all survey participants who voted on each establishment and text based on direct quotes from, or fair paraphrasings of, participants' comments. Phone numbers, addresses and other factual information were correct to the best of our knowledge when published in this guide; any subsequent changes may not be reflected.

Contents

Ratings & Symbols

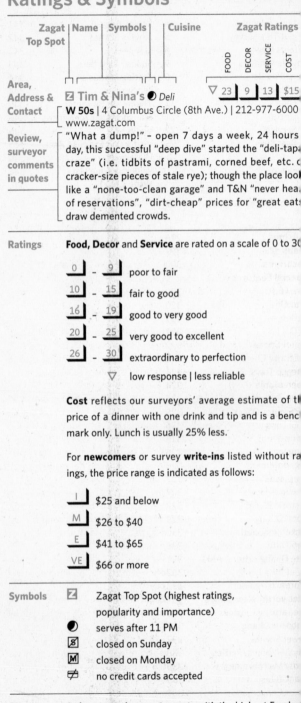

Zagat Top Spot	Name	Symbols	Cuisine	Zagat Ratings

| | | | | FOOD | DECOR | SERVICE | COST |

Area, Address & Contact

☑ **Tim & Nina's** ◗ *Deli* ▽ 23 | 9 | 13 | $15
W 50s | 4 Columbus Circle (8th Ave.) | 212-977-6000
www.zagat.com

Review, surveyor comments in quotes

"What a dump!" – open 7 days a week, 24 hours day, this successful "deep dive" started the "deli-tapa craze" (i.e. tidbits of pastrami, corned beef, etc. c cracker-size pieces of stale rye); though the place look like a "none-too-clean garage" and T&N "never hea of reservations", "dirt-cheap" prices for "great eats draw demented crowds.

Ratings

Food, Decor and **Service** are rated on a scale of 0 to 30

0	–	9	poor to fair
10	–	15	fair to good
16	–	19	good to very good
20	–	25	very good to excellent
26	–	30	extraordinary to perfection
▽			low response	less reliable

Cost reflects our surveyors' average estimate of th price of a dinner with one drink and tip and is a benc mark only. Lunch is usually 25% less.

For **newcomers** or survey **write-ins** listed without ra ings, the price range is indicated as follows:

I	\$25 and below
M	\$26 to \$40
E	\$41 to \$65
VE	\$66 or more

Symbols

☑	Zagat Top Spot (highest ratings, popularity and importance)
◗	serves after 11 PM
Ⓢ	closed on Sunday
Ⓜ	closed on Monday
≠	no credit cards accepted

Maps

Index maps show restaurants with the highest Food ra ings in those areas.

About This Survey

Here are the results of our 2008 New York City Restaurants Survey, which covers 2,069 establishments throughout the five boroughs. Like all of our guides, it's based on the collective opinions of thousands of savvy local consumers who have been there before you.

WHO PARTICIPATED: Input from 34,678 frequent diners forms the basis for the ratings and reviews in this guide (their comments are shown in quotation marks within the reviews). Of these surveyors, 52% are women, 48% men; the breakdown by age is 11% in their 20s; 25%, 30s; 19%, 40s; 22%, 50s; and 23%, 60s or above. Collectively they bring roughly six million annual meals' worth of experience to this Survey. We sincerely thank each of these participants – this book is really "theirs."

HELPFUL LISTS: Whether you're looking for a celebratory meal, a hot scene or a bargain bite, our lists can help you find exactly the right place. See Key Newcomers (page 9), Most Popular (page 10), Top Ratings (pages 11-22) and Best Buys (page 23-26). We've also provided 47 handy indexes; especially check our Sleepers and Critic-Proof indexes.

OUR TEAM: We especially thank our editors, Curt Gathje and Carol Diuguid, for their hard work over the years; this is the seventh edition of this guide that they have collaborated on. Thanks also to Larry Cohn, who coordinated the data collection for this book and has been ensuring our accuracy since 1994.

ABOUT ZAGAT: This marks our 29th year reporting on the shared experiences of consumers like you. What started in 1979 as a hobby involving 200 of our friends has come a long way. Today we have over 300,000 surveyors and now cover dining, entertaining, golf, hotels, movies, music, nightlife, resorts, shopping, spas, theater and tourist attractions worldwide.

SHARE YOUR OPINION: We invite you to join any of our upcoming surveys – just register at **zagat.com,** where you can rate and review establishments year-round. Each participant will receive a free copy of the resulting guide when published.

AVAILABILITY: Zagat guides are available in all major bookstores, by subscription at **zagat.com** and for use on a wide range of Web-enabled mobile devices via **Zagat To Go** or **zagat.mobi.** Either of the latter two products will allow you to contact any restaurant by phone with one click.

FEEDBACK: There is always room for improvement, thus we invite your comments and suggestions about any aspect of our performance. Just contact us at newyork@zagat.com.

New York, NY
October 10, 2007

Nina and Tim Zagat

What's New

The NYC restaurant scene showed remarkable strength over the past year, continuing to grow and diversify with 234 new openings vs. 88 closings. This year's crop of newcomers (see page 9), fueled by a young, upwardly mobile clientele, represents a vast range of cuisines and styles, with increasing informality and very little change in overall pricing.

DRESSING DOWN: The move toward more casual dining sans tablecloths and dress codes persisted with the arrival of a wide variety of inexpensive newcomers. Intimacy was the word at hot boîtes like Maze, Morandi, Wakiya and Waverly Inn. In contrast, 2006 was highlighted by a mega-restaurant invasion, e.g. Buddakan, Buddha Bar, Craftsteak, Del Posto and Morimoto.

DOLLARS AND SENSE: Although NYC restaurant prices remain the most expensive of any American city at $39.46 per dinner, they are virtually unchanged from last year's $39.43. This represents a multiyear pattern, with an average annual inflation of 0.97% since 2001; credit for this goes to a slew of inexpensive newcomers for keeping the cost average steady. Indeed, NYC continues to be a place where good cheap meals are abundant – this Survey includes 697 restaurants offering dinners for less than $30.

HIGH-PRICED DINING: Inflation among the 20 most expensive eateries has been far higher. Since 2001, the average price at these places has jumped an average of 11.6% a year, i.e. from $84.45 to $143.06. The arrival of restaurants such as L'Atelier de Joël Robuchon, Masa and Per Se contributed to this sea change.

SMALL PLATES ARE BIG: One of the phenomena noted this year is the growing number of restaurants offering small-plate menus. Though the cost per plate is lower, the catch is it takes twice as many of them to fill you up. Consumers remain wary, however, with 75% reporting that traditional menus offer better value.

HIGH TIMES FOR LOW FOOD: In keeping with this year's casual mood, some less-than-sophisticated food groups got haute spins. The lowly hamburger was reinterpreted at BLT Burger, brgr, Five Guys, 67 Burger and Stand (with rumors of California's In-N-Out Burger on the way). And BBQ caught its second wind with the arrivals of Fette Sau, Georgia's Eastside BBQ, Hill Country, Johnny Utah's, Smoke Joint and Southern Hospitality.

AVERAGE EATING: NYers report eating out an average of 3. times per week – which, they might be surprised to learn, puts them squarely in the average ranks, behind leaders such as Houston and Dallas/Ft. Worth (4.2 and 4.0 times per week, respectively) and ahead of the likes of Boston and Philly (both 2.7 times per week).

WEB DINING: The Internet's influence on dining out made itself felt: 66% of surveyors report consulting online menus before selecting restaurant – we have over 10,000 menus on zagat.com – while 17% make their reservations online or via e-mail (up from just 7% in 2005).

THE GREENING OF NY: Diners continue to express concern about the healthfulness of what they eat: 52% of surveyors report they're willing to pay more for sustainably raised food. The NYC Health Department's banning of trans fat–heavy frying oils similarly won the support of over two-thirds of our voters. And a notorious video of a rat-infested Taco Bell caused an uproar, triggering stepped-up inspections and a record number of (temporary) shutterings; 65% of respondents called the closings warranted.

NEW RESTAURANT ROWS: The South Street Seaport's Front Street was the city's latest Restaurant Row, where an international mix of newcomers arrived: Il Brigante (Italian), Nelson Blue (New Zealand), Stella Maris (European) and Suteishi (Japanese). On the horizon, the Meatpacking District's Gansevoort Street looks hot thanks to Sue Torres' new Mexican cantina, Los Dados, soon to be followed by Merkato 55 from Marcus Samuelsson.

THE SCENE IN A NUTSHELL: Rating NYC's overall dining scene, surveyors gave it a 27 (out of a possible 30 points) for choice/diversity and a 24 for creativity, but a mere 13 for table availability and 15 for hospitality. This huge discrepancy is confirmed by the fact that service remains the industry's weak link, with 50% calling it the most irritating part of the dining experience, followed by noise/crowds (34%) and prices (11%).

CASE CLOSED: Gone but not forgotten were such notables as Alain Ducasse, Brasserie LCB, Ité, Devi, En Plo, 50 Carmine, Honmura An, aside, Jerry's, Jezebel, Kitchen 22, Lenox Room, March and 66. Happily, some of the restaurateurs behind these establishments (among them Alain Ducasse, Tony Fortuna and Alan Stillman) are working on projects for the coming year.

RANDOM NOTES: Survey winners this year included Daniel for Food, Asiate for Decor, Per Se for Service and Union Square Cafe for Most Popular; Gordon Ramsay was voted Top Newcomer . . . Haute Chinese cooking, still struggling to assert itself, got a big boost with the arrival of Wakiya in the Gramercy Park Hotel, headed up by the re-nowned toque Yuji Wakiya . . . Reclaimed wood was the design feature du jour, turning up at BLT Market, Borough Food & Drink, The E.U., Johnny Utah's and Spitzer's Corner . . . Tipping continues to edge up, with this year's average rising to 19% (compared to 18.1% in 2001) . . . Italian (at 30%) held its lead as diners' favorite cuisine, fol-lowed by French, Japanese, American and Thai . . . Finally, after years of critiquing the looks of others, we thought it time for a face-lift of our own. In this redesigned edition you'll find new fonts, easier-to-use in-dexes and, by popular demand, our first dining map of Brooklyn.

New York, NY
October 10, 2007

Nina and Tim

Nina and Tim Zagat

KEY NEWCOMERS

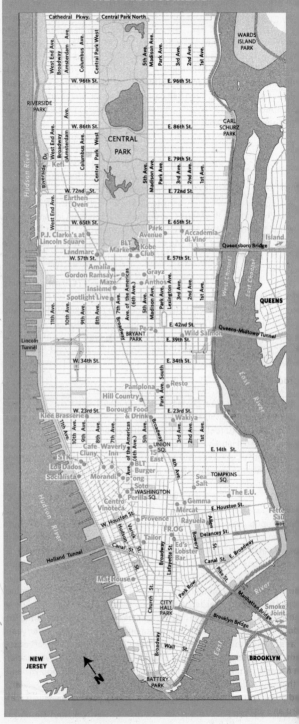

Key Newcomers

ur take on the most notable new arrivals of the past year. For a full
st, see the Noteworthy Newcomers index on page 334.

ccademia di Vino | *Italian*	Los Dados | *Mexican*
malia | *Mediterranean*	Mai House | *Vietnamese*
nthos | *Greek*	Maze | *French*
T Burger | *Hamburgers*	Mercat | *Spanish*
T Market | *American*	Morandi | *Italian*
orough Food/Drink | *American*	Pamplona | *Spanish*
afe Cluny | *American/French*	Park Avenue . . . | *American*
entro Vinoteca | *Italian*	Pera | *Med./Turkish*
arthen Oven | *Indian*	Perilla | *American*
d's Lobster Bar | *Seafood*	P.J. Clarke's/Lincoln Sq. | *Pub*
U., The | *European*	p*ong | *Dessert*
ette Sau | *BBQ*	Provence | *French*
5 East | *Japanese*	Rayuela | *Pan-Latin*
R.OG | *Eclectic/French*	Resto | *Belgian*
emma | *Italian*	Sea Salt | *Med./Seafood*
ordon Ramsay | *French*	Smoke Joint | *BBQ*
rayz | *Eclectic*	Socialista | *Cuban*
ill Country | *BBQ*	Soto | *Japanese*
sieme | *Italian*	Spotlight Live | *American*
land | *Mediterranean*	STK | *Steak*
efi | *Greek*	Tailor | *Dessert*
lee Brasserie | *Amer./Euro.*	Wakiya | *Chinese*
obe Club | *Steak*	Waverly Inn | *American*
andmarc (TWC) | *French*	Wild Salmon | *Seafood*

he year to come shows plenty of potential with a number of big-name
rojects on tap: Daniel Boulud is cooking up **Bar Boulud** near Lincoln
enter as well as **DBGB** on the Bowery; Alain Ducasse plans to open
dour in the former Lespinasse space, plus a spin-off of his Parisian
rasserie **Benoît** in La Côte Basque's previous digs; Marcus
amuelsson will bring African cuisine to the Meatpacking District
a **Merkato 55;** the Bromberg brothers' empire continues to expand
ith a new **Blue Ribbon Sushi** off Columbus Circle; and the legendary
nd Avenue Deli** will be reborn – the name notwithstanding – at
3rd and 3rd.

Most Popular

Each surveyor has been asked to name his or her five favorit places. This list reflects their choices (also see the gatefold map in th back of the book).

1. Union Square Cafe
2. Gramercy Tavern
3. Le Bernardin
4. Babbo
5. Jean Georges
6. Daniel
7. Gotham Bar & Grill
8. Peter Luger
9. Bouley
10. Balthazar
11. Blue Water Grill
12. Eleven Madison Park
13. Nobu
14. Per Se*
15. Rosa Mexicano
16. Modern, The
17. Aureole
18. Del Posto
19. Four Seasons
20. Café Boulud
21. Atlantic Grill
22. Spice Market
23. Buddakan
24. Picholine
25. Artisanal
26. Il Mulino
27. Telepan
28. Chanterelle
29. Tabla
30. Aquavit
31. Palm
32. Carmine's
33. Becco
34. Café des Artistes
35. davidburke/donatella
36. Del Frisco's
37. Aquagrill
38. Lupa
39. Bar Americain
40. Pastis
41. Felidia
42. Mesa Grill
43. Craft
44. One if by Land
45. Blue Hill
46. L'Impero
47. Sparks
48. Nobu 57
49. db Bistro Moderne
50. Ouest*

It's obvious that many of the above restaurants are among NYC's mo. expensive, but if popularity were calibrated to price, we suspect th. a number of other places would join their ranks. Given the fact th. both our surveyors and readers love to discover dining bargains, w. have added several lists of Best Buys on pages 23-26. These a. restaurants that give real quality at extremely reasonable prices.

---

* Indicates a tie with restaurant above

Top Food Ratings

Ratings are to the left of names. Lists exclude places with low votes.

28 Daniel
Sushi Yasuda
Le Bernardin
Per Se
Peter Luger (Brooklyn)
Jean Georges
Bouley

27 Chanterelle
Sushi Seki
L'Atelier de Joël Robuchon
Nobu
Gotham Bar & Grill
Café Boulud
Gramercy Tavern
Di Fara (Brooklyn)
La Grenouille
Babbo
Saul (Brooklyn)
Annisa
Il Mulino
Aureole
Masa
Picholine
Roberto (Bronx)

26 Union Square Cafe

Blue Hill
Gari/Sushi
Pearl Oyster Bar
Aquagrill
Veritas
Eleven Madison Park
Cru
Al Di La (Brooklyn)
Sripraphai (Queens)
Nobu 57
Scalini Fedeli
Danube
Poke
Il Tinello
Milos
Grocery, The (Brooklyn)
Modern, The
Trattoria L'incontro (Queens)
River Café (Brooklyn)
Yakitori Totto
L'Impero
Bouley, Upstairs
Tomoe Sushi
Il Giglio
Tocqueville

BY CUISINE

AMERICAN

28 Per Se
27 Gotham Bar & Grill
Gramercy Tavern
Saul
Annisa
Aureole

AMERICAN (REGIONAL)

26 Pearl Oyster Bar/NE
25 Roy's NY/Hawaiian
22 Carl's Steaks/Philly
21 Michael's/CA
19 Great Jones Cafe/Cajun
Delta Grill/Cajun

BARBECUE

24 Daisy May's
23 Smoke Joint
22 Dinosaur BBQ
Blue Smoke
20 RUB BBQ
Virgil's Real BBQ

CARIBBEAN

23 Don Pedro's/Carib.
22 Café Habana/Cuban
Sofrito/Puerto Rican
21 Cuba/Cuban
El Malecon/Dominican
Victor's Cafe/Cuban

CHINESE

25 Tse Yang
24 Oriental Garden
Phoenix Garden
Shun Lee Palace
23 Mr. K's
Tang Pavilion

COFFEEHOUSES

22 Ferrara
Once Upon a Tart
19 Le Pain Quotidien
Cafe Lalo
Omonia Cafe
18 Edgar's Cafe

DELIS

23	Barney Greengrass
	Katz's Deli
21	Carnegie Deli
	Mill Basin Deli
20	Stage Deli
19	Pastrami Queen

DESSERT

25	Chocolate Room
24	ChikaLicious
	La Bergamote
	Payard Bistro
23	Veniero's
22	L & B Spumoni

DIM SUM

24	Oriental Garden
22	Ping's Seafood
21	Shun Lee Cafe
	Excellent Dumpling
	Chinatown Brasserie
20	Mandarin Court

FRENCH

28	Daniel
	Le Bernardin
	Jean Georges
	Bouley
27	Chanterelle
	L'Atelier de Joël Robuchon
	Café Boulud
	La Grenouille
26	Eleven Madison Park
	Modern, The
	Tocqueville
25	Fleur de Sel

FRENCH (BISTRO)

25	db Bistro Moderne
24	Raoul's
	Tournesol
	JoJo
	Le Gigot
	Le Tableau

GREEK

26	Milos
25	Taverna Kyclades
	Pylos
24	Avra
	Agnanti
23	Periyali

HAMBURGERS

| 24 | burger joint/Parker M. |
| 23 | DuMont Burger |

	Shake Shack
22	Corner Bistro
	Island Burgers
21	Rare B&G

HOTEL DINING

28	Jean Georges (Trump Intl. Hotel)
27	L'Atelier de Joël Robuchon (Four Seasons Hotel)
	Café Boulud (Surrey Hotel)
25	Gordon Ramsay (London NYC)
	Norma's (Le Parker Meridien)
	db Bistro Moderne (City Club Hotel)

INDIAN

25	Tamarind
24	Amma
23	Chola
	Dawat
	Adä
	Banjara

ITALIAN

27	Babbo
	Il Mulino
	Roberto
26	Al Di La
	Scalini Fedeli
	Il Tinello
	Trattoria L'incontro
	L'Impero
	Il Giglio
	Alto
	Aurora
25	Spigolo

JAPANESE/SUSHI

28	Sushi Yasuda
27	Sushi Seki
	Nobu
	Sugiyama
	Kanoyama
	Masa
26	Gari/Sushi
	Nobu 57
	Poke
	Yakitori Totto
	Tomoe Sushi
25	Blue Ribbon Sushi

subscribe to zagat.com

KOREAN

23 Hangawi
   Woo Lae Oak
21 Do Hwa
   Kum Gang San
20 Mandoo Bar
19 Mill Korean

KOSHER

22 Prime Grill
21 Chennai Garden
   Mill Basin Deli
   Pongal
20 Le Marais
19 Abigael's

MEDITERRANEAN

27 Picholine
25 Convivium Osteria
   Tempo
   Il Buco
24 Savoy
   Red Cat

MEXICAN

25 Pampano
23 Mexicana Mama
   Hell's Kitchen
   Itzocan
   Maya
   Sueños

MIDDLE EASTERN

27 Tanoreen
24 Taboon
23 Hummus Place
22 Zaytoons
21 Miriam
   Moustache

NEWCOMERS

25 Gordon Ramsay
23 Kefi
   Maze
   Smoke Joint
22 Pera
21 Earthen Oven
   Mai House
   Klee Brasserie

NOODLE SHOPS

24 Momofuku Noodle Bar
   Soba-ya
22 Great NY Noodle
21 Pho Bang
20 Bao Noodles
   Menchanko-tei

PIZZA

27 Di Fara
25 Denino's
   Grimaldi's
24 Lombardi's
   Nick's
23 Adrienne's Pizza

RAW BARS

26 Aquagrill
25 Blue Ribbon
23 Blue Water Grill
   Lure Fishbar
   Balthazar
   BLT Fish

SEAFOOD

28 Le Bernardin
26 Pearl Oyster Bar
   Aquagrill
   Milos
   Oceana
25 Esca

SMALL PLATES

27 L'Atelier de Joël Robuchon
26 Degustation
24 Perbacco
   Frankies Spuntino
23 Alta
   'inoteca

SOUTH AMERICAN

26 Caracas
23 Churrascaria
   Pio Pio
22 Tierras Colombianas
21 Porcão Churrascaria
   Hacienda de Argentina

SOUTHERN/SOUL

22 Amy Ruth's
   Maroons
20 Pink Tea Cup
   Rack & Soul
19 Kitchenette
   B. Smith's

SOUTHWESTERN

24 Mesa Grill
21 Los Dos Molinos
19 Canyon Road
18 Miracle Grill
   Agave
17 Cilantro

SPANISH/TAPAS

25 Casa Mono
24 Tía Pol
   Bolo
23 Sevilla
   Boqueria
   El Faro

STEAKHOUSES

28 Peter Luger
25 Sparks
   Del Frisco's
   Strip House
   Wolfgang's
24 Jake's
   Dylan Prime
   BLT Steak
   BLT Prime
   Quality Meats
   Palm
   Keens

THAI

26 Sripraphai
24 Song
23 Land
   Kittichai

   Joya
22 Erawan

TURKISH

23 Ali Baba
22 Turkish Kitchen
   Pera
21 Beyoglu
   Pasha
20 Turkish Cuisine

VEGETARIAN

23 Candle
   Hangawi
   Vatan
   Hummus Place
22 Pure Food & Wine
   Counter

VIETNAMESE

23 Omai
22 Nam
   Sapa
   Saigon Grill
21 Pho Bang
   Nha Trang

BY SPECIAL FEATURE

BREAKFAST

Balthazar
Barney Greengrass
Bubby's
Café Sabarsky
Clinton St. Baking
Good Enough to Eat
Jean Georges
Norma's
Payard Bistro
Popover Cafe
Regency
Sarabeth's

BRUNCH DOWNTOWN

Aquagrill
Balthazar
Bubby's
Clinton St. Baking
Essex
Félix
Five Points
Jane
Odeon
Pastis
Prune
Schiller's

BRUNCH MIDTOWN

Artisanal
Blue Water Grill
Cafeteria
Cafe Un Deux Trois
Eatery
elmo
Friend of a Farmer
L'Express
Norma's
Penelope
Rainbow Room
Water Club

BRUNCH UPTOWN

Annie's
Arté Café
Atlantic Grill
Carlyle
Good Enough to Eat
Isabella's
JoJo
Miss Mamie's/Maude's
Ocean Grill
Ouest
Popover Cafe
Sarabeth's

subscribe to zagat.com

BUSINESS LUNCH/ DOWNTOWN

- Bouley
- City Hall
- Delmonico's
- Dylan Prime
- fresh
- Gotham Bar & Grill
- Harry's
- Les Halles
- MarkJoseph
- Nobu
- Provence
- Wolfgang's

BUSINESS LUNCH/ MIDTOWN

- Alto
- Amma
- Anthos
- Aquavit
- Bar Americain
- BLT Steak
- Felidia
- Four Seasons
- Le Bernardin
- Lever House
- Modern, The
- Sparks

CELEBRATIONS

- Aureole
- Bouley
- Cru
- Daniel
- FireBird
- Four Seasons
- Le Bernardin
- Le Cirque
- Rainbow Room
- River Café
- Tavern on the Green
- Water's Edge

CELEBRITY SCENES

- Balthazar
- Cipriani Downtown
- Da Silvano
- Elaine's
- Fresco
- Joe Allen
- Nobu
- Per Se
- Rao's
- Spotted Pig
- Wakiya
- Waverly Inn

CHILD-FRIENDLY

- American Girl Place
- Bubby's
- Cowgirl
- EJ's Luncheonette
- ESPN Zone
- Hard Rock Cafe
- Ninja
- Peanut Butter & Co.
- Serendipity 3
- Soda Shop
- Spotlight Live
- Two Boots

DINING AT THE BAR

- Aquagrill
- Babbo
- Centro Vinoteca
- Four Seasons (lunchtime)
- Gotham Bar & Grill
- Gramercy Tavern
- Hearth
- Perry Street
- Picholine
- Red Cat
- Tabla (Bread Bar)
- Union Square Cafe

GROUP DINING

- Asia de Cuba
- Buddakan
- Carmine's
- China Grill
- Churrascaria Plataforma
- Hill Country
- Rosa Mexicano
- Ruby Foo's
- Sambuca
- Stanton Social
- Tao
- Tony's Di Napoli

HIPSTER HANGOUTS

- Cafe Gitane
- Employees Only
- Five Points
- Freemans
- La Esquina
- Orchard, The
- Public
- Schiller's
- Spitzer's Corner
- Stanton Social
- wd-50
- Zum Schneider

HOTTEST SERVERS

Asia de Cuba
Brother Jimmy's
Cafeteria
Coffee Shop
Del Frisco's
Food Bar
44 & X Hell's Kit.
Hawaiian Tropic Zone
Indochine
Pastis
Spice Market
Tao

LATE DINING

Balthazar
Baraonda
Blue Ribbon
Blue Ribbon Sushi
Frank
'ino
Mas
Pastis
Raoul's
Spotted Pig
West Bank Cafe
Wollensky's

MEET FOR A DRINK/ DOWNTOWN

Balthazar
Bond Street
Buddha Bar
City Hall
Employees Only
Gotham Bar & Grill
Harry's
Morimoto
Odeon
Rayuela
Spice Market
Stanton Social

MEET FOR A DRINK/ MIDTOWN

Barbounia
Blue Fin
Country, Café at
Django
Grayz
Houston's
Koi
Maze
Michael Jordan's
Modern, The
Nobu 57
Town

MEET FOR A DRINK/ UPTOWN

Aix Brasserie
Atlantic Grill
Café Gray
Cafe Luxembourg
Compass
Daniel
Demarchelier
Geisha
Jean Georges
Landmarc
Ouest
212

MILESTONES

100th	Barney Greengrass
75th	Patsy's Pizzeria (Harlem)
25th	Cafe Luxembourg
	Jackson Diner
	Orso
	Paola's
	Tomoe Sushi
20th	Aureole
	Isabella's
	Rocking Horse Cafe
	San Domenico
	Trattoria Dell'Arte

POWER SCENES

Coco Pazzo
Daniel
Elio's
Four Seasons
Jean Georges
Le Bernardin
Lever House
Michael's
Regency
Sant Ambroeus
Smith & Wollensky
21 Club

SINGLES SCENES

Baraonda
Buddakan
Buddha Bar
Butter
Coffee Shop
Employees Only
'inoteca
La Esquina
STK
SushiSamba
Tao
Thor

24-HOUR

Bereket
Cafeteria
Cozy Soup/Burger
Empire Diner
Florent
Gold St.
Gray's Papaya
Kum Gang San
L'Express
Maison
Sarge's Deli
WonJo

VISITORS ON EXPENSE ACCOUNT

Bouley
Chanterelle
Craft
Daniel
Four Seasons

Gordon Ramsay
Jean Georges
Le Cirque
Masa
Megu
Nobu
Per Se

WINNING WINE LISTS

Alto
Babbo
Cru
Daniel
Del Posto
Landmarc
Modern, The
Per Se
Sparks
Tribeca Grill
21 Club
Veritas

BY LOCATION

CHELSEA

25 Da Umberto
   Del Posto
24 Tía Pol
   Momoya
   Morimoto
   Red Cat

CHINATOWN

24 Oriental Garden
22 Peking Duck
   New Green Bo
   Big Wong
   Great NY Noodle
   Grand Sichuan

EAST 40s

28 Sushi Yasuda
26 L'Impero
25 Sparks
   Sushiden
   Pampano
24 Sakagura

EAST 50s

27 L'Atelier de Joël Robuchon
   La Grenouille
26 Alto
   Oceana
25 Four Seasons
   Felidia

EAST 60s

28 Daniel
27 Sushi Seki
   Aureole
25 davidburke/donatella
   Scalinatella
24 JoJo

EAST 70s

27 Café Boulud
26 Gari/Sushi
24 Lusardi's
   Payard Bistro
23 Candle
   Campagnola

EAST 80s

26 Poke
25 Spigolo
   Erminia
   Sushi Sen-nin
   Etats-Unis
24 Sistina

EAST 90s & EAST 100s

24 Nick's
23 Itzocan
   Sfoglia
   Don Pedro's
   Pio Pio
22 El Paso Taqueria

EAST VILLAGE

- 27 Kanoyama
- 26 Degustation
-    Caracas
- 25 Jewel Bako
-    Hearth
-    Pylos

FINANCIAL DISTRICT

- 25 Roy's NY
- 24 MarkJoseph
- 23 Adrienne's Pizza
- 22 Bridge Cafe
-    Harry's
-    Bobby Van's

FLATIRON/ UNION SQUARE

- 27 Gramercy Tavern
- 26 Union Square Cafe
-    Veritas
-    Tocqueville
- 25 Tamarind
-    Craft

GARMENT DISTRICT

- 24 Keens
-    Osteria Gelsi
- 23 Uncle Jack's
- 22 Nick & Stef's
- 21 Frankie & Johnnie's
-    Kum Gang San

GRAMERCY/ MADISON PARK

- 26 Eleven Madison Park
- 25 Tabla
-    Casa Mono
-    A Voce
- 24 Yama
-    BLT Prime

GREENWICH VILLAGE

- 27 Gotham Bar & Grill
-    Babbo
-    Annisa
-    Il Mulino
- 26 Blue Hill
-    Pearl Oyster Bar

HARLEM

- 22 Dinosaur BBQ
-    Amy Ruth's
-    Rao's
- 21 Mo-Bay
- 20 Papaya King
-    Patsy's Pizzeria

LITTLE ITALY

- 23 Angelo's of Mulberry St.
-    Il Cortile
- 22 Pellegrino's
-    Ferrara
-    Nyonya
- 21 Da Nico

LOWER EAST SIDE

- 25 Falai
- 24 Clinton St. Baking
-    Orchard, The
-    ápizz
-    Frankies Spuntino
- 23 Stanton Social

MEATPACKING DISTRICT

- 24 Valbella
- 23 Old Homestead
- 22 Spice Market
- 21 Ono
-    Son Cubano
-    Macelleria

MURRAY HILL

- 25 Sushi Sen-nin
-    Wolfgang's
- 23 Mishima
-    Rossini's
-    Artisanal
-    Asia de Cuba

NOHO

- 25 Bond Street
-    Il Buco
- 22 Five Points
-    Sala
- 21 Chinatown Brasserie
- 19 Great Jones Cafe

NOLITA

- 24 Lombardi's
-    Peasant
- 23 Public
- 22 Tasting Room
-    Café Habana
- 20 Cafe Gitane

SOHO

- 26 Aquagrill
- 25 Blue Ribbon Sushi
-    Blue Ribbon
-    Fiamma Osteria
- 24 Raoul's
-    Savoy

TRIBECA

28 Bouley
27 Chanterelle
    Nobu
26 Scalini Fedeli
    Danube
    Bouley, Upstairs

WEST 40s

26 Gari/Sushi
25 Sushiden
    Esca
    Del Frisco's
    db Bistro Moderne
    Sushi Zen

WEST 50s

28 Le Bernardin
27 Sugiyama
26 Nobu 57
    Il Tinello
    Milos
    Modern, The

WEST 60s

28 Per Se
    Jean Georges
27 Masa
    Picholine
25 Telepan
    Café Gray

WEST 70s

26 Gari/Sushi
23 Tenzan
    Ocean Grill
    Hummus Place
    Kefi
    'Cesca

WEST 80s

25 Ouest
24 Celeste
23 Barney Greengrass
    Land
22 Neptune Room
    Nëo Sushi

WEST 90s & UP

25 Gennaro
23 Max SoHa
    Pisticci
    Indus Valley
    Pio Pio
22 Awash

WEST VILLAGE

26 Wallsé
25 Piccolo Angolo
    Mary's Fish Camp
24 Da Andrea
    Little Owl
    Perry Street

OUTER BOROUGHS

BRONX

27 Roberto
24 Jake's
    Riverdale Garden
23 Enzo's
    Pasquale's Rigoletto
    Pio Pio

BROOKLYN: BAY RIDGE

27 Tanoreen
25 Areo
24 Tuscany Grill
    Agnanti
23 Pearl Room
22 Chadwick's

BROOKLYN: HTS/DUMBO

26 River Café
25 Grimaldi's
    Henry's End
24 Noodle Pudding
    Queen
21 Five Front

BROOKLYN: CARROLL GARDENS/BOERUM HILL/COBBLE HILL

27 Saul
26 Grocery, The
24 Frankies Spuntino
23 Chestnut
    Fragole
    Joya

BROOKLYN: PARK SLOPE

26 Al Di La
25 Blue Ribbon Sushi
    Chocolate Room
    Convivium Osteria
    Blue Ribbon
    Tempo

BROOKLYN: WILLIAMSBURG

28 Peter Luger
26 Aurora
24 Dressler

23 DuMont
    Bamonte's
22 Fornino

BROOKLYN: OTHER

27 Di Fara (Midwood)
    Garden Cafe (Prospect Hts.)
26 Good Fork (Red Hook)
23 Franny's (Prospect Hts.)
    Tenzan (Bensonhurst)
    Farm on Adderley (Ditmas Pk.)

QUEENS: ASTORIA/L.I.C.

26 Trattoria L'incontro
25 Piccola Venezia
    Taverna Kyclades
24 Tournesol (LIC)
    Agnanti
23 Water's Edge (LIC)

QUEENS: OTHER

26 Sripraphai (Woodside)
25 Sapori D'Ischia (Woodside)
    Don Peppe (Ozone Park)
24 Park Side (Corona)
    Nick's (Forest Hills)
23 Uncle Jack's (Bayside)

STATEN ISLAND

25 Denino's
24 Da Noi
    Trattoria Romana
20 South Fin Grill
    American Grill
19 China Chalet

subscribe to zagat.com

Top Decor Ratings

Ratings are to the left of names.

28 Asiate
Daniel
Per Se
River Café
La Grenouille

27 Four Seasons
Buddakan
Danube
Rainbow Room
Kittichai
Tao*
Le Bernardin

26 Spice Market
Megu
Buddha Bar
Chanterelle
Eleven Madison Park
Del Posto
Cávo
Matsuri*
Modern, The
One if by Land
Water's Edge
Bouley
Café des Artistes

Carlyle
Public
Morimoto
Suba
Kings' Carriage House
Jean Georges

25 Aureole
EN Japanese
FireBird
Piano Due
Gramercy Tavern
Sapa
Russian Tea Room
Tabla
Dressler
Thalassa
Porter House NY
Terrace in the Sky*
Boathouse
Alto
Scalini Fedeli
Gotham Bar & Grill
Le Cirque

24 Sea Grill
Tavern on the Green

GARDENS

Barbetta
Battery Gardens
Bottino
Cávo
Da Nico
Farm on Adderley
Five Front
Gascogne
Gnocco Caffe
Grocery, The
I Coppi
I Trulli

Jolie
L & B Spumoni
Le Jardin Bistro
Paradou
Park, The
Patois
Pure Food & Wine
Revel
Riverdale Garden
Sripraphai
Surya
Tavern on the Green

PRIVATE PARTIES

(max. capacity)

Barbetta (120)
Buddakan (800)
Café Gray (300)
City Hall (180)
Country (60)
Del Frisco's (85)
Del Posto (200)
Fiamma Osteria (50)
Four Seasons (350)

Le Cirque (80)
Oceana (60)
Patroon (60)
Per Se (60)
Picholine (22)
River Café (100)
Spice Market (30)
Tavern on the Green (1,000)
21 Club (150)

ROMANCE

Aureole
Bouley
Café des Artistes
Chanterelle
Convivium Osteria
Daniel
Danube
Erminia
Gascogne
Il Buco
Kings' Carriage House
Le Refuge

L'Impero
Mas
One if by Land
Petrossian
Piccola Venezia
Rainbow Room
Raoul's
River Café
Scalini Fedeli
Suba
Wallsé
Water's Edge

VIEWS

Alma
Asiate
Battery Gardens
Boathouse
Café Gray
Gigino (Wagner Park)
Modern, The
Per Se

Porter House NY
River Café
River Room
Sea Grill
Terrace in the Sky
View, The
Water Club
Water's Edge

Top Service Ratings

Ratings are to the left of names.

<u>28</u> Per Se
Daniel
Le Bernardin

<u>27</u> Chanterelle
La Grenouille
Jean Georges
Bouley
Gramercy Tavern

<u>26</u> Masa
Il Tinello
Café Boulud
Aureole
Union Square Cafe
Danube
Four Seasons
L'Atelier de Joël Robuchon
Eleven Madison Park
Gotham Bar & Grill
River Café
Cru
Annisa

<u>25</u> Veritas
Picholine
Blue Hill
Asiate

Scalini Fedeli
Erminia
Degustation
Tocqueville
Mas
Tabla
Alto
Babbo
Gordon Ramsay

<u>24</u> Grocery, The
One if by Land
Piano Due
Del Posto
Le Perigord
Trattoria L'incontro
Aquavit
Modern, The
21 Club
Capsouto Frères
Sushi Yasuda
Hearth
Carlyle
Oceana
Saul
Craft

subscribe to zagat.com

Best Buys

Everyone loves a bargain, and NYC offers plenty of places that fill the bill. Three things to bear in mind: lunches typically cost 25 to 30% less than dinners, outer-borough restaurants are less costly than those in Manhattan and biannual Restaurant Weeks (usually in January and July) offer the chance to sample some of the city's finest at greatly reduced prices.

ALL YOU CAN EAT

23	Chola
	Churrascaria
	Vatan
22	Becco
	Turkish Kitchen
21	Chennai Garden
	Porcão Churrascaria
	Yuka
	Utsav
20	Mangia
	East Buffet
19	Green Field

BYO/MANHATTAN

26	Poke
24	Kuma Inn∇
	Phoenix Garden
23	Hummus Place
22	Peking Duck
	Nook
	Tartine
	Amy Ruth's
	Wondee Siam
21	Cube 63
	Pho Bang
	Angelica Kit.
20	Meskerem
19	Zen Palate
18	La Taza de Oro
	X.O.
	Bereket

BYO/OUTER BOROUGHS

27	Di Fara
	Tanoreen
	Lucali∇
22	Zaytoons
21	Pho Bang
	Sweet Melissa
20	Babouche∇

FAMILY-STYLE

27	Roberto
25	Don Peppe
	Piccolo Angolo
24	Supper
	Oriental Garden
	Phoenix Garden
	Frank
	Nick's
23	Posto
	Pisticci
22	Dominick's
	China Grill

PRIX FIXE LUNCH

28	Jean Georges ($24)
	Bouley ($38)
27	Gotham Bar & Grill ($31)
	Aureole ($38)
26	Milos ($24)
	Tocqueville ($24)
25	Tabla ($32)
	Fleur de Sel ($29)
	Pampano ($25)
24	Perry Street ($24)
	Petrossian ($28)
	Duane Park Cafe ($24)

PRIX FIXE DINNER

28	Sushi Yasuda ($21)
27	Garden Cafe ($32)
26	Poke ($20)
25	Henry's End ($23)
	Aki ($28)
	Ouest ($33)
24	Duane Park Cafe ($35)
	Caviar Russe ($30)
23	L'Ecole ($40)
	Artisanal ($35)
	ViceVersa ($35)
	Hangawi ($38)

BEST BUYS: FULL MENU

Alice's Tea Cup | tearoom
Bereket | Turkish
Big Wong | Chinese
Brennan & Carr | sandwiches
Chickpea | Middle Eastern
Chipotle | Mexican
Congee | Chinese
Cubana Café | Cuban
Doyers | Vietnamese
El Malecon | Dominican
Energy Kitchen | health food
Excellent Dumpling | Chinese
Goodies | Chinese
Great NY Noodle | noodles
Hope & Anchor | American
Hummus Place | Israeli
Joya | Thai
Land | Thai
L & B Spumoni | Italian
La Taqueria | Mexican
La Taza de Oro | Puerto Rican
Mama's Food | American
Mandoo Bar | Korean
Mill Basin Deli | deli

Mill Korean | Korean
Momofuku Noodle | noodles
Nha Trang | Vietnamese
Nyonya | Malaysian
Pepe . . . To Go | Italian
Pho Bang | Vietnamese
Pho Pasteur | Vietnamese
Pho Viet Huong | Vietnamese
Pio Pio | Peruvian
Pump | health food
Rice | Eclectic
Saigon Grill | Vietnamese
SEA | Thai
Smoke Joint | BBQ
Song | Thai
Sripraphai | Thai
Sweet-n-Tart | Chinese
teany | vegetarian
Thai Pavilion | Thai
Tierras | Colombian
Whole Foods | Eclectic
Wo Hop | Chinese
X.O. | Chinese
Zaytoons | Middle Eastern

BEST BUYS: SPECIALTY SHOPS

Amy's Bread | baked goods
Better Burger | burgers
Blue 9 Burger | burgers
brgr | burgers
burger joint/P.M. | burgers
Burritoville | Mexican
Caracas | arepas
Carl's | cheese steaks
ChikaLicious | desserts
Chipotle | Mexican
Chocolate Room | desserts
Chop't Creative | salads
Coals | pizza
Corner Bistro | burgers
Cozy Soup | burgers
Denino's | pizza
Di Fara | pizza
Dishes | sandwiches
Dumpling Man | dumplings
Empanada Mama | empanadas
Ess-a-Bagel | deli
F & B | European hot dogs
Ferrara | Italian pastry
goodburger | burgers

Gray's Papaya | hot dogs
Grimaldi's | pizza
Hale & Hearty | soup
Hampton Chutney | Indian
Joe's Pizza | pizza
Kati Roll Co. | Indian
La Bergamote | bakery
Lenny's | sandwiches
New York Burger Co. | burgers
Nicky's | Vietnamese sandwiches
99 Miles to Philly | cheese steaks
Once Upon a Tart | baked goods
Papaya King | hot dogs
Peanut Butter | sandwiches
Pizza 33 | pizza
Press 195 | sandwiches
Rickshaw | dumplings
Roll-n-Roaster | sandwiches
Shake Shack | burgers
S'mac | mac 'n' cheese
Sweet Melissa | pastry
Veniero's | Italian pastry
Waldy's | pizza
Zip Burger | burgers

LUNCH

Abboccato	$28	La Petite Auberge	20
Adä	17	L'Ecole	27
Al Bustan	25	Le Perigord	32
Alto	30	Le Veau d'Or	20
Angelo & Maxie's	21	Le Zie 2000	15
Anthos	28	L'Impero	35
Aquavit	39	Mercer Kitchen	24
Artisanal	25	Michael Jordan's	24
Asiate	24	Milos	24
Atlantic Grill	24	Molyvos	25
Avra	28	Morimoto	24
Baldoria	28	Mr. K's	28
Beacon	32	Oceana	33
Becco	17	Ocean Grill	24
Bistro du Nord	18	Olives	24
Bouley	38	Orsay	26
Brasserie 8½	25	Osteria del Circo	25
Café Boulud	32	Pampano	25
Cafe Luxembourg	30	Patroon	27
Capsouto Frères	24	Patsy's	34
Carlyle	24	Periyali	26
Chin Chin	24	Perry Street	24
Churrascaria	33	Petrossian	28
Cibo	28	Post House	25
davidburke/donatella	24	Remi	24
Dawat	16	René Pujol	24
Del Frisco's	30	Roc	25
Demarchelier	25	Roy's NY	30
Django	24	San Domenico	38
Duane Park Cafe	24	Shun Lee Palace	20
etcetera etcetera	24	Solera	26
Felidia	30	Spice Market	17
FireBird	30	Sushi Yasuda	21
Fleur de Sel	29	Tabla	32
Gallagher's	20	Tamarind	24
Gascogne	20	Tao	24
Gavroche	20	Tavern on the Green	38
Giorgio's/Gramercy	20	Thalassa	24
Gotham Bar & Grill	31	Thalia	17
Gusto	20	Tía Pol	15
Hangawi	20	Tocqueville	24
I Trulli	28	Trata Estiatorio	22
Inagiku	35	Tribeca Grill	24
Jean Georges	24	Tse Yang	28
JoJo	24	Turkish Kitchen	17
Josephina	25	21 Club	35
Kellari Taverna	25	Utsav	16
Kings' Carriage House	19	ViceVersa	24
Korea Palace	18	Vong	20
La Boîte en Bois	25	Water's Edge	35
La Mangeoire	17	Zarela	17

PT = pre-theater only; where two prices are listed, the first is pre-theater and the second for normal dinner hours.

Abboccato/PT	$38	Le Boeuf/Mode	39
Akdeniz	20	L'Ecole	40
Aki/PT	28	Le Madeleine	32
Alcala	40	Le Rivage	35
Alouette/PT	24	Le Singe Vert/PT	27
Anthos/PT	38	Levana	30
A.O.C. Bedford/PT	32	Luca	23
Artisanal	35	Madison Bistro	31
Atlantic Grill/PT	28	Mamlouk	40
Avra/PT	37	Maria Pia	22
Baldoria/PT	38	Marseille	29
Bay Leaf/PT	21	McCormick/Schmick's/PT	30
Becco	22	Métisse/PT	20
Bistro du Nord/PT	20	Metrazur	35
Bistro 61/PT	21	Mi Cocina/PT	30
Bombay Palace	24/30	Molyvos/PT	35
Brasserie Julien/PT	25	Montparnasse	23
Bryant Park Grill/PT	30	Ocean Grill/PT	28
B. Smith's	30	Odeon/PT	32
Cafe Centro	35	Osteria del Circo	35
Cafe Un Deux	29	Ouest/PT	33
Capsouto Frères	35	Pascalou/PT	19
Cascina/PT	25	Pasha/PT	24
Caviar Russe	30	Payard Bistro	35
Cebu/PT	21	Pigalle/PT	25
Chez Napoléon	30	p*ong	25
Chin Chin	35	Quercy	25
Cibo	30	Remi/PT	35
Compass	35	Russian Samovar	28
Del Frisco's/PT	40	San Domenico/PT	38
Demarchelier	25	Sharz Cafe/PT	20
Dervish Turkish/PT	24	Shula's Steak/PT	35
Duane Park Cafe	35	Sorrel	25
etcetera etcetera	35	Sugiyama/PT	32
Garden Cafe	32	Sushi Yasuda	21
Gascogne/PT	28	Table d'Hôte	23/27
Gavroche/PT	20	Tempo	25
Gigino	28	Thalia/PT	35
Hangawi	38	Todai	26
Henry's End/PT	23	Trata Estiatorio/PT	25
HQ/PT	25	Trattoria Dopo Teatro/PT	23
Indochine/PT	28	Turkish Cuisine	27
Jarnac	36	21 Club/PT	40
Jewel of India/PT	28	Utsav/PT	28
Kellari Taverna/PT	30	Vatan	24
Klee Brasserie/PT	30	ViceVersa	35
Koi/PT	39	Villa Berulia	35
La Baraka	25/37	Village	29
La Boîte en Bois/PT	36	Vincent's	30
La Mangeoire	25/32	Vivolo/PT	26
La Mediterranée/PT	25	Vong/PT	35
La Petite Auberge	27	Water Club/PT	40

RESTAURANT
DIRECTORY

| | FOOD | DECOR | SERVICE | COST |

Abboccato *Italian* — 22 | 19 | 21 | $62

W 50s | Blakely Hotel | 136 W. 55th St. (bet. 6th & 7th Aves.) | 212-265-4000 | www.abboccato.com

"Interesting", "refined" Italian fare and an "unbeatable location" across from City Center ensure this "sophisticated" Midtowner is a "hit" with the "pre-theater" crowd; "high-end" from the "dim", "retro-feeling" room and "attentive" service to the "costly" tab, it pleases all but a frugal few.

Abigael's *Pan-Asian* — 19 | 14 | 17 | $47

Garment District | 1407 Broadway (bet. 38th & 39th Sts.) | 212-575-1407 | www.abigaels.com

Kosher "pioneer"/"celebrity chef" Jeffrey Nathan is in the kitchen at this "solid" bi-level Garment Districter that pleases the observant with its Pan-Asian fare and sushi served at street level and steaks downstairs; now if only the "outdated" decor and "mediocre" service could get an "uplift."

Aburiya Kinnosuke *Japanese* — 24 | 18 | 21 | $45

E 40s | 213 E. 45th St. (bet. 2nd & 3rd Aves.) | 212-867-5454

You can travel "to Tokyo" without leaving East Midtown via this perpetually "packed", "upscale" Japanese grill that's prized for its "extremely flavorful" robata specialties and "charming" crew; check out the "chalkboard" specials, then "sit in the back to watch your food cook."

Acappella 🗷 *Italian* — 23 | 20 | 23 | $70

TriBeCa | 1 Hudson St. (Chambers St.) | 212-240-0163 | www.acappella-restaurant.com

"Dark" and "romantic", this "white-tablecloth" TriBeCa Northern Italian piles on the antipasti and other "delicious" "old-world" delights served "with flair" by "over-the-top" waiters; just "hold your breath when the bill comes" – and "decide the tip" before downing the gratis "housemade grappa."

NEW Accademia di Vino *Italian* — - | - | - | M

E 60s | 1081 Third Ave. (bet. 63rd & 64th Sts.) | 212-888-6333

The former Mainland space has been reworked into this new UES enoteca/trattoria, a grottolike affair with two wine bars and a long, meandering dining room; Italian small plates and mains can be paired with vino from its 500 bottle–strong cellar or rotating by-the-glass list.

Acqua *Italian* — 18 | 17 | 18 | $38

W 90s | 718 Amsterdam Ave. (bet. 94th & 95th Sts.) | 212-222-2752 | www.acquanyc.com

Every neighborhood could use a "solid", "casual" Italian like this "steady" Upper Westsider; although service can be "slow", at least its "cozy" space is "easier to navigate" than the always-packed "Gennaro's down the street."

Adä *Indian* — 23 | 21 | 21 | $53

E 50s | 208 E. 58th St. (bet. 2nd & 3rd Aves.) | 212-371-6060 | www.adanyc.com

"Towering above the usual", this "quiet" East Midtown "upmarket Indian" is where "incredible flavors and presentations" arrive via an "amiable, professional" staff; if dinner is slightly "pricey" for the genre, there's always the $14.95 prix fixe lunch.

Adrienne's Pizzabar ● Pizza
23 | 16 | 15 | $23

Financial District | 87 Pearl St. (bet. Broad St. & Hanover Sq.) | 212-248-3838

"Always packed", this Financial District Italian purveys "heavenly" thin-crust pizzas and other eats for little dough; the scene approaches "bedlam" (especially at lunch) and service "needs work", but to most it's "worth it" – especially if you nab a table out on "charming" Stone Street.

Aesop's Tables ⑤Ⓜ American/Mediterranean
▽ 21 | 18 | 20 | $42

Staten Island | 1233 Bay St. (Maryland Ave.) | 718-720-2005

Delivering "enjoyable meals and evenings" for years, this "cozy" Staten Island Med–New American remains a "friendly" refuge from Manhattan prices; even those who find it just "decent" "always return with the warm weather" when the "beautiful garden" is open.

Afghan Kebab House Afghan
19 | 10 | 17 | $23

E 70s | 1345 Second Ave. (bet. 70th & 71st Sts.) | 212-517-2776
W 50s | 764 Ninth Ave. (bet. 51st & 52nd Sts.) | 212-307-1612
Jackson Heights | 74-16 37th Ave. (bet. 74th & 75th Sts.) | Queens | 718-565-0471

"Smoky, juicy" kebabs "bursting with flavor" are the "highlight" at these "friendly" Afghan eateries that are "cheap, cheap" – especially when you factor in the BYO policy; ignore the "hole-in-the-wall" atmosphere and just focus on the "feast."

Agata & Valentina Ristorante Italian
18 | 18 | 17 | $44

E 70s | 1513 First Ave. (79th St.) | 212-452-0691 | www.agatavalentina.com

"*Delizioso*" Sicilian fare made with the "freshest ingredients" have this "low-key" UES Italian gaining status as a "strong neighborhood" entry; it gets the nod for its "soaring", recently "reconfigured" space, but service still "needs polishing."

Agave ● Southwestern
18 | 18 | 17 | $36

W Village | 140 Seventh Ave. S. (bet. Charles & W. 10th Sts.) | 212-989-2100 | www.agaveny.com

It feels like "Santa Fe" at this "noisy" Villager whose "clean, white" setting provides a "comfortable" backdrop for its "zippy margs" and "solid" Southwestern eats; "reasonable" prices and "sidewalk seating" perfect for "people-watching" make the "slooow" service easy to overlook.

Agnanti ● Greek
24 | 15 | 19 | $33

Bay Ridge | 7802 Fifth Ave. (78th St.) | Brooklyn | 718-833-7033
Astoria | 19-06 Ditmars Blvd. (19th St.) | Queens | 718-545-4554
www.agnantimeze.com

Meze-loving masses laud this Astoria–Bay Ridge taverna twosome for its "irresistible" Greek fare at "easy" rates; factor in "warm" service and "pleasant" sidewalk seats, and it's no wonder there are "killer waits on weekends."

Aix Brasserie French
20 | 21 | 19 | $59

W 80s | 2398 Broadway (88th St.) | 212-874-7400 | www.aixnyc.com

The menu, revamped last year, is "still creative" at this multilevel UWS French "neighborhood brasserie"; while the bar – which does a "delicious burger" – remains "buzzing", critics citing "mediocre" output say the overall experience "isn't worth" the tab.

Aja ❶ *Pan-Asian*

| | 20 | 22 | 19 | $44 |

E 50s | 1068 First Ave. (58th St.) | 212-888-8008

A "swanky", "cool place" for midpriced Pan-Asian fare, this "dimly lit" "surprise" near the Queensboro Bridge lures a "young", "energetic" crowd with its "exotic" setup "complete with giant Buddha" and "see-through floor"/koi pond; N.B. a Village offshoot is expected soon.

AJ Maxwell's Steakhouse ⑤ *Steak*

| | 22 | 19 | 22 | $67 |

W 40s | 57 W. 48th St. (bet. 5th & 6th Aves.) | 212-262-6200 | www.ajmaxwells.com

"Not bad for a new steakhouse", this "expense account"–oriented Rock Center arrival's setting is somewhat "sparse", save for a "beautiful mural" behind the bar; though the rib-eyes are "huge" and the service "personal", up till now the vibe has been on the "sedate" side.

Akdeniz ⑤ *Turkish*

| | 20 | 12 | 19 | $29 |

W 40s | 19 W. 46th St. (bet. 5th & 6th Aves.) | 212-575-2307 | www.akdenizturkishusa.com

"You can make a wonderful meal of the meze" alone at this "tiny", "reliable" Midtown Turk considered a "true find"; the "breads, spreads and grilled fish" come to the table "fast and fresh", transporting you to "Istanbul" at "bargain" rates – especially via the $19.95 dinner prix fixe.

Aki Ⓜ *Japanese*

| | 25 | 14 | 21 | $43 |

G Village | 181 W. Fourth St. (bet. Barrow & Jones Sts.) | 212-989-5440

Maybe it's not such a "secret anymore", but this "friendly" Village Japanese sliver is "still one of the best bargains" around given its "innovative", "exceptional" Caribbean-influenced sushi; groupies gush it's "Nobu at half the price" – and way less than half the space.

Aki Sushi *Japanese*

| | 19 | 12 | 18 | $31 |

E 70s | 1425 York Ave. (bet. 75th & 76th Sts.) | 212-628-8885
Garment District | 128 W. 36th St. (bet. B'way & 7th Ave.) | 212-868-8091
Gramercy | 121 E. 27th St. (bet. Lexington Ave. & Park Ave. S.) | 212-213-9888
W 50s | 366 W. 52nd St. (bet. 8th & 9th Aves.) | 212-262-2888

It's "nothing fancy" – just "good, cheap sushi" – which suits fine the many fans of this "reliable" Japanese mini-chain; still, some who note that there's "no decor at all" opt for "fast delivery."

NEW A La Turka ❶ *Turkish*

| | 18 | 12 | 16 | $35 |

E 70s | 1417 Second Ave. (74th St.) | 212-744-2424 | www.alaturkarestaurant.com

Generally considered a "good UES addition", this "casual", "inexpensive" Turk (from the team that ran Sultan) dishes up "reliable" meze and other classics; still, the less enthused say it has almost "no atmosphere" and a staff that tends toward "disorganized."

Al Bustan *Lebanese*

| | 19 | 13 | 18 | $42 |

E 50s | 827 Third Ave. (bet. 50th & 51st Sts.) | 212-759-5933 | www.albustanny.com

"Dependable" as ever, this longtime Lebanese remains a good bet for a "tasty" Midtown meal; however, given the "dog-eared" "'80s decor" and merely "acceptable" service, a few feel the experience "isn't worth the price tag."

Alcala *Spanish*   ∇ 20 | 16 | 21 | $48

E 40s | 342 E. 46th St. (bet. 1st & 2nd Aves.) | 212-370-1866 | www.alcalarestaurant.com

"Tucked away near the U.N.", this "intimate" Spanish-Basque bastion and its "charming" staff caters to a "traditional" crowd with "delicious" "real-deal" dishes; for best results, sit in the "lovely garden" and "forget you're in" Midtown.

NEW Alchemy M *American*   ∇ 18 | 21 | 17 | $36

Park Slope | 56 Fifth Ave. (bet. Bergen St. & St. Marks Pl.) | Brooklyn | 718-636-4385 | www.alchemybrooklyn.com

While this New American has practiced alchemy by turning an old Park Slope hardware shop into a Brit-style gastropub, it's "still working out some kinks"; most agree it's a "nice addition" to Fifth Avenue, but be prepared for "crowds" and "squished" seating at communal tables.

Z Al Di La *Italian*   26 | 18 | 22 | $45

Park Slope | 248 Fifth Ave. (Carroll St.) | Brooklyn | 718-783-4565 | www.aldilatrattoria.com

"Al-di-lightful", this "really special" Park Slope Venetian showcases Anna Klinger's "superlative" cuisine, served by a "caring" crew in a "cozy" "communal" dining room; the "no-reservations policy" leads to "painful waits", though, so "get your gondola there early" – or try their "wonderful" "around-the-corner" wine bar.

Alfama *Portuguese*   22 | 21 | 21 | $49

W Village | 551 Hudson St. (Perry St.) | 212-645-2500 | www.alfamarestaurant.com

Everything from the "Lisboa"-worthy fare to the "attentive" service and "lovely blue-and-white-tiled" decor makes it feel like "an evening in Portugal" at this slightly "pricey" Village "charmer"; for the ultimate "transporting" experience, come for Wednesday's live *fado* fest.

Al Forno Pizzeria *Pizza*   19 | 13 | 17 | $25

E 70s | 1484 Second Ave. (bet. 77th & 78th Sts.) | 212-249-5103

"Easygoing" and "affordable", this UES pie parlor is a hit with "families and groups" who come for the "delicious thin-crust" pizzas from a "real brick oven" and "mammoth salads"; better still, you avoid the waits at nearby rivals.

Alfredo of Rome *Italian*   19 | 18 | 18 | $46

W 40s | 4 W. 49th St. (bet. 5th & 6th Aves.) | 212-397-0100 | www.alfredos.com

"Reliably good" but "no surprises" is the word on this slightly "pricey" Rock Center Italian with branches in Rome and Las Vegas; maybe it's a bit "touristy" with staffers too focused on "turning over tables", but as for that namesake dish, it's "the best ever."

Algonquin Hotel Round Table *American*   16 | 23 | 19 | $52

W 40s | Algonquin Hotel | 59 W. 44th St. (bet. 5th & 6th Aves.) | 212-840-6800 | www.algonquinhotel.com

"History, location and atmosphere" highlight this Theater District former "literary hangout", but not the "overpriced", just "average"

	FOOD	DECOR	SERVICE	COST

Traditional American eats; ergo, most agree it's "best for drinks" in the "elegant" "wood-paneled" lobby or cabaret in the next-door Oak Room.

Alias *American*   23 | 15 | 20 | $36

LES | 76 Clinton St. (Rivington St.) | 212-505-5011 |
www.aliasrestaurant.com

Where "hipsters" head to "go off the diet", this "friendly" LES American spins "upscale twists on comfort food" using "fresh, seasonal ingredients"; "reasonable" prices and "spruced-up diner" digs make a "refreshing change" from the ordinary; P.S. the $25 Sunday dinner prix fixe is a "steal."

Ali Baba *Turkish*   23 | 14 | 17 | $29

Murray Hill | 212 E. 34th St. (bet. 2nd & 3rd Aves.) | 212-683-9206 |
www.alibabaturkishcuisine.com

"The Bosporus" meets Murray Hill at this Turkish house of "delicious" kebabs, "Middle Eastern–style" pizzas and "various dips" offered at "bargain" rates; devotees could "eat here for 1,001 nights", "slow" service and "cramped" quarters notwithstanding; P.S. "dine in the garden when it's open."

Alice's Tea Cup *Tearoom*   19 | 21 | 18 | $25

E 60s | 156 E. 64th St. (Lexington Ave.) | 212-486-9200
NEW **E 80s** | 220 E. 81st St. (bet. 2nd & 3rd Aves.) | 212-734-4832
W 70s | 102 W. 73rd St. (bet. Amsterdam & Columbus Aves.) |
212-799-3006
www.alicesteacup.com

"It's always tea time" at these "pastel" "wonderlands" of "decadent scones", finger sandwiches and other "dainty" treats that are a hit with "girls aged 8 to 80" (it's the culinary "equivalent of a chick flick"); just "beware the jabberwocky" – "long waits" and "spacey service."

Aliseo Osteria del Borgo Ⓜ *Italian*   ▽ 23 | 20 | 23 | $43

Prospect Heights | 665 Vanderbilt Ave. (bet. Park & Prospect Pls.) |
Brooklyn | 718-783-3400

"Delicious", "inventive" dishes inspired by the Marche region and built on "artisanal" ingredients make this "tiny" Prospect Heights Italian a local standout; "personal service" and decor with "grandma charm" add to the overall "relaxed" vibe.

Alma *Mexican*   20 | 21 | 18 | $32

Carroll Gardens | 187 Columbia St., 2nd fl. (Degraw St.) | Brooklyn |
718-643-5400 | www.almarestaurant.com

Score a "coveted rooftop table" to best enjoy this "offbeat" Carroll Gardens Mexican and its "spectacular" view of the harbor and "Manhattan skyline"; the "killer margaritas" and "fresh", affordable fare are also agreeable, as is the "downstairs bar" where you can while away the inevitable "wait."

NEW Almond Flower Bistro *American*   ▽ 23 | 22 | 24 | $32

Little Italy | 96 Bowery (bet. Grand & Hester Sts.) | 212-966-7162 |
www.almondflowerbistro.com

No, it's not another Chinese eatery along the Bowery – this new bistro is a "welcome surprise" with its "sensational" New American fare at "bargain prices"; "attentive" service and a downtown-stylish, yet "romantic", space are two other reasons early-goers call it a "hit."

	FOOD	DECOR	SERVICE	COST

NEW Aloe M *Eclectic* — | — | — | M

E Village | 406 E. Ninth St. (bet. Ave. A & 1st Ave.) | 212-358-8400
Its name is short for 'a little of everything', so it's no surprise that this tiny East Villager specializes in Eclectic eats, happily offered at affordable rates; its rustic space holds just three tables on the ground level, but there's more seating in a log cabin–like subterranean room.

Alouette ● *French* 20 | 17 | 18 | $44

W 90s | 2588 Broadway (bet. 97th & 98th Sts.) | 212-222-6808 | www.alouettenyc.com
Upper Westsiders say "*oui*" to this "warm" neighborhood bistro where the "traditional" French fare is "consistently" good and the overall mood "inviting"; relatively "reasonable checks" plus a $24 early-bird dinner prix fixe compensate for digs that are "a little tight."

Alta *Mediterranean* 23 | 21 | 19 | $45

G Village | 64 W. 10th St. (bet. 5th & 6th Aves.) | 212-505-7777 | www.altarestaurant.com
"Behind a hidden doorway" dwells this "cozy" "tavernlike" Villager serving up "inventive" Med small plates paired with a "terrific" wine list; its "warm fireplace" abets an atmosphere that's so "romantic", you don't notice how those bitty dishes "can add up" to an alta tab.

Z Alto Z *Italian* 26 | 25 | 25 | $81

E 50s | 11 E. 53rd St. (bet. 5th & Madison Aves.) | 212-308-1099 | www.altorestaurant.com
As chef Michael White picks up where Scott Conant left off, "power" patrons are watching to see how this "formal" East Side Italian evolves; known for its "fantastic", "intriguing" cuisine, "outstanding" wine list and "ultrachic", glass wine cellar–lined decor, all hope that everything stays the same, except maybe the "sky-high prices."

Ama *Italian* 22 | 19 | 19 | $52

SoHo | 48 MacDougal St. (bet. King & Prince Sts.) | 212-358-1707 | www.amanyc.com
"Creative approaches to pasta" and other Puglia-inspired foods "delight" fashionable followers of this "white-walled" SoHo Southern Italian; the "friendly owner" justifiably "takes pride" in the place, making for "pleasant" overall experiences despite service that can be "slow."

NEW Amalia *Mediterranean* ▽ 21 | 22 | 19 | $60

W 50s | 204 W. 55th St. (bet. B'way & 7th Ave.) | 212-245-1234 | www.amalia-nyc.com
Carved out of a "renovated carriage house", this bi-level newcomer adjacent to Midtown's Dream Hotel exudes downtown "cool" with its brick walls, black chandeliers and industrial-chic basement; surveyors are "pleasantly surprised" by the "pricey" coastal Med fare – if only it would work out the service "kinks."

Amaranth ● *Mediterranean* 20 | 17 | 19 | $57

E 60s | 21 E. 62nd St. (bet. 5th & Madison Aves.) | 212-980-6700 | www.amaranthrestaurant.com
It's "kiss, kiss, hug, hug" at this "noisy", pricey East Side Mediterranean bistro favored by a "very attractive" "Euro" crowd; despite "solid" fare, it's really more about the "scene" ("many women seem to be with

their uncles"), and, as for the service, it's either "lovely" or "arrogant" depending on who you know.

Amarone ● *Italian* — 19 | 13 | 19 | $37
W 40s | 686 Ninth Ave. (bet. 47th & 48th Sts.) | 212-245-6060 |
www.amaronenyc.com
"Dependable" Italian classics worthy of your "nonna", "solid service" and "accessible" prices make it easy to overlook the "cramped quarters" at this Hell's Kitchen trattoria; still, its main virtue may be its "pre-theater" "convenience."

NEW **Amazing 66** *Chinese* — ▽ 23 | 14 | 17 | $23
Chinatown | 66 Mott St. (bet. Bayard & Canal Sts.) | 212-334-0099
"Truly amazing" is the early word on this "fresh, delicious" C-town Cantonese newcomer that's "drawing crowds" with its extensive menu and astounding $4.95 lunch special; its menu features the usual suspects plus specialties like frog and conch for the more daring.

Amber ● *Pan-Asian* — 22 | 22 | 19 | $37
E 80s | 1406 Third Ave. (80th St.) | 212-249-5020
Upper Eastsiders pack this "jazzed-up" Pan-Asian, where the "hot staff" and "hip" decor lend a "downtown-comes-uptown" vibe; while the "noisy" bar scene may overshadow the "quality" sushi and other "fusion" fare, there's always the more "serene" back room.

American Girl Place Café *American* — 13 | 22 | 19 | $34
E 40s | 609 Fifth Ave. (49th St.) | 212-644-1145 | www.americangirlplace.com
A "mother-daughter" must-do, this "little girls' paradise" can "provide a laugh-a-minute experience, if you have doll guests at your table"; as ratings show, the American food is decent enough – with the afternoon tea party as the highlight.

American Grill *American* — 20 | 18 | 19 | $45
Staten Island | 1180 Victory Blvd. (Clove Rd.) | 718-442-4742 |
www.americangrillnyc.com
Following its move and ownership change a few years back, surveyors split over this still "solid" Staten Island American: depending on who you ask, the food "quality has gone up" or it's "not as good", while it's either "overpriced" or "worth every penny"; your call.

Amma *Indian* — 24 | 17 | 22 | $43
E 50s | 246 E. 51st St. (bet. 2nd & 3rd Aves.) | 212-644-8330 |
www.ammanyc.com
With food so "amazing" it's almost "unfair" to the rest of the city's tandoori houses, this Midtown Northern Indian provides a "gourmet experience" in "calm", if "cramped", quarters; "gracious" service rounds out the "refined" experience; P.S. the $85 tasting menu with wine pairings is "a must!"

Ammos *Greek* — 22 | 22 | 21 | $51
E 40s | 52 Vanderbilt Ave. (bet. 44th & 45th Sts.) | 212-922-9999
Astoria | 20-30 Steinway St. (bet. 20th Ave. & 20th Rd.) | Queens |
718-726-7900 ● Ⓜ
www.ammosnewyork.com
The "haute-classic" Greek fare is a "cut above" the norm at these "upmarket" Midtown-Astoria siblings known for their "impeccably fresh"

| | FOOD | DECOR | SERVICE | COST |

seafood; "transporting" "island" decor and "friendly" service complete the "pricey", but always "enjoyable", picture.

Amorina Ⓜ *Pizza* ▽ 23 | 14 | 18 | $22

Prospect Heights | 624 Vanderbilt Ave. (Prospect Pl.) | Brooklyn | 718-230-3030 | www.amorinapizza.com

It's not "your conventional slice" at this "reasonable" Prospect Heights pizzeria/trattoria where many of the "fantabulous" Roman-style pies are topped with "quirky" ingredients (think "figs and Gorgonzola"); fortunately for more traditional types, there are also pastas and other Italian "comfort" favorites.

Amy Ruth's *Soul Food* 22 | 11 | 17 | $24

Harlem | 113 W. 116th St. (bet. Lenox & 7th Aves.) | 212-280-8779 | www.amyruthsharlem.com

"For a few fabulous greasy minutes", you're "back in Dixie" as you tuck into an "artery-clogging feast" at this Harlem "soul-food classic"; regulars attest "you won't be disappointed" with the fried chicken, waffles and such – or the "cheap" prices; if you've been partying late, keep in mind that it's "open all night" on weekends; N.B. the departure of founder Carl Redding puts the above ratings in question.

Amy's Bread *Sandwiches* 23 | 11 | 16 | $13

Chelsea | Chelsea Mkt. | 75 Ninth Ave. (bet. 15th & 16th Sts.) | 212-462-4338
G Village | 250 Bleecker St. (bet. Carmine & Leroy Sts.) | 212-675-7802
W 40s | 672 Ninth Ave. (bet. 46th & 47th Sts.) | 212-977-2670
www.amysbread.com

"Magical ovens" must produce the "stellar" breads and other "addictive" treats at this "wholesome" bakery/sandwich shop trio; but "rushed" counter service and "always-crowded", "no-atmosphere" digs mean many feel they're best for "popping in" and out.

Angelica Kitchen ⊘ *Vegan/Vegetarian* 21 | 15 | 18 | $24

E Village | 300 E. 12th St. (bet. 1st & 2nd Aves.) | 212-228-2909 | www.angelicakitchen.com

A "vegan heaven" since 1976, this "bohemian" East Villager still has fans "lining up" for its "tasty" bargain organic eats, "communal tables" and "crunchy" staffers; you'll leave its "spartan" quarters in a "Zen state of mind" – just remember to "bring cash" (no credit cards).

Angelina's *Italian* ▽ 23 | 19 | 20 | $57

Staten Island | 26 Jefferson Blvd. (Annadale Rd.) | 718-227-7100 | www.angelinasristorante.com

Italian fare "excellent" enough to "rival Manhattan's best" makes this a "Staten Island staple", which also boasts "music, dancing" and a hostess who "makes meals memorable" with "jokes and magic tricks"; given all that, most don't mind much if prices are "a bit high."

Angelo & Maxie's ● *Steak* 21 | 18 | 19 | $55

Flatiron | 233 Park Ave. S. (19th St.) | 212-220-9200 | www.angelo-maxies.com

"Young corporate types" gravitate to this "high-energy" Flatiron meetery for its "big, juicy" steaks and bustling (à la "Joey from Long Island/hot divorcée") "bar scene"; sure, it's "crowded" and "loud", but relatively "reasonable prices" compensate; P.S. check out the "bargain" $21 lunch prix fixe.

| | FOOD | DECOR | SERVICE | COST |

Angelo's of Mulberry Street ●Ⓜ *Italian* — 23 | 16 | 20 | $44

Little Italy | 146 Mulberry St. (bet. Grand & Hester Sts.) | 212-966-1277 | www.angelomulberry.com

More than a century old and "still going strong", this "festive" Little Italy "landmark" gratifies "pasta and garlic lovers" with "quintessential" red-sauce dishes to make you "think you died and went to Naples"; it's one of the "best bets" on the strip, but remember "you go for the food, not the decor."

Angelo's Pizzeria *Pizza* — 20 | 12 | 15 | $24

E 50s | 1043 Second Ave. (55th St.) | 212-521-3600
W 50s | 117 W. 57th St. (bet. 6th & 7th Aves.) | 212-333-4333
W 50s | 1697 Broadway (bet. 53rd & 54th Sts.) | 212-245-8811
www.angelospizzany.com

Thin-crust pizzas with "just-right" sauce and "quality" toppings "are the thing" at these "casual" Midtown Italians; a boon to "lunching co-workers" and "families with kids", they offer "decent prices" that override "spotty" service and "uninspiring" settings.

Angus McIndoe ● *American* — 16 | 14 | 18 | $40

W 40s | 258 W. 44th St. (bet. B'way & 8th Ave.) | 212-221-9222 | www.angusmcindoe.com

"Basic" American fare with a heaping side of "B'way buzz" is the deal at this "raucous hangout" for "performers and their public" in the Theater District; just don't be surprised if the servers are more interested in being "your star" than "your waiter."

Annie's *American* — 18 | 14 | 16 | $29

E 70s | 1381 Third Ave. (bet. 78th & 79th Sts.) | 212-327-4853

"Get your brunch fix on" at this UES American whose "generously portioned" "comfort" food may be "a little too popular" (expect "hourlong waits"); "oblivious service" and a "no-stroller policy" "don't deter" the morning masses, but "dinners are good too" and "not crowded."

Z Annisa *American* — 27 | 22 | 26 | $73

G Village | 13 Barrow St. (bet. 7th Ave. S. & W. 4th St.) | 212-741-6699 | www.annisarestaurant.com

"Top-tier chef" Anita Lo's Village oasis woos patrons with "refined, beautiful" New American cuisine, "impeccable service" and "stylish" "white-curtained" decor that add up to "magical" meals; such "superior" experiences don't come cheap, but for a relative bargain "go for the tasting menu" at $88.

Anthony's *Italian* — ∇ 21 | 15 | 20 | $23

Park Slope | 426A Seventh Ave. (bet. 14th & 15th Sts.) | Brooklyn | 718-369-8315

"Hearty", "fresh" pastas and such plus "feather"-light "crispy-crust" pizzas are what keep Park Slopers coming back to this "homey", "friendly" "neighborhood" Southern Italian and its "garden in back"; fans sigh if only "it were bigger" and easier to "get into."

NEW Anthos Ⓢ *Greek* — ∇ 25 | 21 | 24 | $66

W 50s | 36 W. 52nd St. (bet. 5th & 6th Aves.) | 212-582-6900

The "amazing" "haute Greek cuisine" based on the "finest fresh ingredients" and "fabulous service" provide the wow factor at this Midtown

newcomer from Donatella Arpaia (davidburke & donatella) and rising
oque Michael Psilakis (Kefi); the space is "pleasant" but on the plain
side for such "top-of-the-line prices."

Antica Venezia *Italian*
▽ 23 | 23 | 25 | $52

W Village | 396 West St. (W. 10th St.) | 212-229-0606 | www.avnyc.com
West Villagers are "transported to Italy" via this "off-the-beaten-
track" "charmer" that romances diners with "mouthwatering" food,
"phenomenal sunset" views "over the Hudson" and "warm", "class-
act" service; in short, "grab a table while you can."

Antonucci *Italian*
20 | 16 | 18 | $51

E 80s | 170 E. 81st St. (bet. Lexington & 3rd Aves.) | 212-570-5100
"Spirited and enjoyable", this "welcoming" UES "storefront" Italian is
fast becoming a local standby for "solid" fare enjoyed in "friendly" (if
"noisy") environs; though not cheap, it's possible to have "a good
night out" here for less than at bigger-ticket destinations.

A.O.C. ● *French*
20 | 17 | 18 | $36

W Village | 314 Bleecker St. (Grove St.) | 212-675-9463 | www.aocnyc.com
Enjoying a "local" following for its "dependable" French classics, this
"solid" West Village bistro also offers a "comfortable" atmosphere at
competitive prices – not to mention a "pleasant" "garden out back";
the only complaint is service that "could be better."

A.O.C. Bedford *European*
23 | 20 | 21 | $49

G Village | 14 Bedford St. (bet. Downing & Houston Sts.) | 212-414-4764
"Teeny" and "inviting", this Greenwich Village Southern European has
established itself as a "neighborhood favorite", where "tight seating"
is easy to take given the "terrific" food and "classy" service; generally
"reasonable", it becomes a downright "bargain" when you factor in the
prix fixe deals and BYO nights.

ápizz' 🗷 *Italian*
24 | 21 | 20 | $45

LES | 217 Eldridge St. (bet. Rivington & Stanton Sts.) | 212-253-9199 |
www.apizz.com
A "nondescript facade" belies the "bright" "fresh, seasonal" menu at
this "relaxed, hip" LES Italian; specializing in pizzas and other rustic
"wood-oven" dishes, it has relatively "reasonable" prices that help
compensate for its "not-ideal" location.

applewood 🅼 *American*
25 | 20 | 22 | $48

Park Slope | 501 11th St. (bet. 7th & 8th Aves.) | Brooklyn | 718-768-2044 |
www.applewoodny.com
"Tapping into the zeitgeist" perfectly, this "unpretentious" Park Slope
New American bases its "excellent" menu on organic ingredients
"culled from local farms"; its dining room is "cozy and warm", its staff
"couldn't be nicer" and it's an area "top choice for brunch."

AQ Cafe 🗷 *Scandinavian*
▽ 20 | 16 | 12 | $19

Murray Hill | Scandinavia House | 58 Park Ave. (bet. 37th & 38th Sts.) |
212-847-9745 | www.aquavit.org
"How Swede it is" say those who get their "meatball and lingonberry
fixes" via Marcus Samuelsson's lunch-only Murray Hill Scandinavian
cafeteria that's like "Aquavit on a budget"; "spartan" digs, "surly" service
and frequent "long lines" are made up for by those "great-deal" prices.

	FOOD	DECOR	SERVICE	COST

☑ Aquagrill *Seafood*   26 | 19 | 23 | $58

SoHo | 210 Spring St. (6th Ave.) | 212-274-0505 | www.aquagrill.cor
Still a "winner" for "ocean-fresh" fare (don't miss the "fantastic rav
bar"), this ever-"popular" SoHo seafooder sparkles with "friendly, pol
ished service" and an overall "comfortable" vibe; if seating is a bi
"cramped", the "comparably reasonable prices" make up for a lot.

Aquamarine ● *Pan-Asian*   21 | 23 | 20 | $37

Murray Hill | 713 Second Ave. (bet. 38th & 39th Sts.) | 212-297-188
Decor touches like a "waterfall" and "tranquil birch forest" have local
calling this "trendy" Pan-Asian a "much-needed" addition to Murra
Hill; "better-than-average" cuisine (including sushi) and "caring ser
vice" round out the locals' endorsement.

☑ Aquavit *Scandinavian*   25 | 24 | 24 | $96

E 50s | 65 E. 55th St. (bet. Madison & Park Aves.) | 212-307-7311 |
www.aquavit.org
Chef Marcus Samuelsson's Midtown prix fixe–only Scandinavian is "
classic, and deservedly so" thanks to its near-"flawless" offering
(e.g. "life-changing" herring and aquavit), "serene", "modern" deco
and "first-rate" service; however, if you can't "find someone else to
pick up" the tab, consider trying the "more casual front cafe."

Arabelle *American/French*   21 | 26 | 22 | $78

E 60s | Plaza Athénée Hotel | 37 E. 64th St. (Madison Ave.) | 212-606-4647
www.arabellerestaurant.com
An "enchanting" "throwback" in the Plaza Athénée, this "formal", pri
fixe–only French-American boasts a "European-feeling" dining roon
and "old-world" pro service that unfortunately outshine the "pricey
cuisine; it's ideal for a "romantic dinner" (or "to take your mother")
but detractors detect a "snooty" attitude.

Areo ● Ⓜ *Italian*   25 | 19 | 20 | $50

Bay Ridge | 8424 Third Ave. (bet. 84th & 85th Sts.) | Brooklyn | 718-238-007
"Always delicious" and "always packed", this "boisterous" Bay Ridg
Italian is a perennial "hot spot"; given its "generous portions" of "tra
ditional" favorites, "friendly, flirtatious service" and "pleasant" (i
"noisy") air, it's no wonder that "getting a table" is a "challenge."

Arezzo Ⓢ *Italian*   ▽ 22 | 17 | 20 | $53

Flatiron | 46 W. 22nd St. (bet. 5th & 6th Aves.) | 212-206-0555 |
www.arezzo-nyc.com
This "wonderful" Flatiron Italian is relatively "undiscovered" despite th
fact that it produces "fantastic" Tuscan dishes from a "wood-burning
oven", whose "warmth" extends to the "attentive" service and "cozy"
"rustic" digs; with a "pretty back garden" and prices that are "reason
able" given the "upscale experience", more people should check it out

Arno Ⓢ *Italian*   ▽ 20 | 17 | 21 | $46

Garment District | 141 W. 38th St. (bet. B'way & 7th Ave.) | 212-944-7420
www.arnoristorante.com
A "busy, noisy" Italian with "old-school" "charm" to spare, this
Garmento Italiano turns out "consistently good" Tuscan standards a
a "fair" price; the decor may be "getting tired", but still there Arno ma
jor complaints – especially in this restaurant-challenged zone.

	FOOD	DECOR	SERVICE	COST

Aroma *Italian*
▽ 24 | 17 | 21 | $40

NoHo | 36 E. Fourth St. (bet. Bowery & Lafayette St.) | 212-375-0100 |
www.aromanyc.com

'Scrumptious, always fresh" seasonal Italian fare is the forte of this
"tiny", "homey" NoHo nook that also offers wine pairings from a list
boasting a few "rarities"; "warm" service and "affordable" checks cement its standing as a "true gem."

Arqua *Italian*
22 | 21 | 21 | $55

TriBeCa | 281 Church St. (White St.) | 212-334-1888 |
www.arquaristorante.com

Remaining a "solid standby" for over 20 years, this "sophisticated"
TriBeCa Northern Italian is a "trustworthy" source for "excellent"
cooking delivered by a "caring" staff; its "serene", "spacious" digs actually allow diners to "talk and hear" – i.e. here's an eatery "for adults."

Arté *Italian*
19 | 18 | 20 | $42

G Village | 21 E. Ninth St. (bet. 5th Ave. & University Pl.) | 212-473-0077
A "steady performer in the old-school model", this midpriced Village
Italian attracts a "mature crowd" with "tasty", "traditional" dishes and
"accommodating" service; its quarters are "a bit faded", but it's hard to
argue with "garden" seating in summer and "great fireplaces" in winter.

Arté Café *Italian*
18 | 17 | 17 | $34

W 70s | 106 W. 73rd St. (bet. Amsterdam & Columbus Aves.) |
212-501-7014 | www.artecafenyc.com

Ensconced in "newly renovated" digs with an "amazing back garden",
this Lincoln Center-area "standby" remains a "good bet" for "basic"
Italian eats pre-curtain; "dirt-cheap" prices mean that most diners
happily endure the "rushed" service.

Artie's *Seafood*
22 | 17 | 20 | $35

Bronx | 394 City Island Ave. (Ditmars St.) | 718-885-9885 |
www.artiesofcityisland.com

"Fresh" seafood and steaks at "prices that won't soak you" is the lure
at this "friendly" City Island vet; its "loyal", largely "local", clientele
doesn't mind the "lack of a water view" – or internal view for that matter since the "price is right."

Artie's Deli *Deli*
18 | 10 | 14 | $22

W 80s | 2290 Broadway (bet. 82nd & 83rd Sts.) | 212-579-5959 |
www.arties.com

At this "reincarnation" of the "old UWS Jewish deli" complete with
the "noise" and theatrically "crotchety waiters", you can skip the
"schlep" elsewhere for "overstuffed" sandwiches and "cure-all" matzo
ball soup; ignore the nothing-special Formica decor and "just keep
the dills coming."

☑ Artisanal *French*
23 | 20 | 20 | $52

Murray Hill | 2 Park Ave. (enter on 32nd St., bet. Madison & Park Aves.) |
212-725-8585 | www.artisanalbistro.com

It's a "cheese-lover's paradise" and French brasserie rolled into one at
Terrance Brennan's "consistently delicious", always "bustling" Murray
Hill place; you may have to "bring a megaphone" to be heard, then ask
your "friendly waiter" what's ripe "in the cave" today.

	FOOD	DECOR	SERVICE	COST

Arturo's Pizzeria ● *Italian*
| | 21 | 12 | 15 | $24 |

G Village | 106 W. Houston St. (Thompson St.) | 212-677-3820
Still "solid" after more than a half-century of peddling pizza, this
Village Italian supplies "consistently satisfying" crisp, coal-oven pie
to penny-wise patrons who relish the "old NY" atmosphere and "live
jazz piano", if not the "long" waits.

☑ Asia de Cuba *Asian/Cuban*
| | 23 | 24 | 20 | $58 |

Murray Hill | Morgans Hotel | 237 Madison Ave. (bet. 37th & 38th Sts.) |
212-726-7755 | www.chinagrillmgt.com
The "formula still works" at this eternally "glam" Murray Hill Cuban-
Asian known for its "fabulous fusion" flavors, "happening" vibe and
"stunning white-on-white" Philippe Starck–designed space; it all
comes accessorized with "NYC's finest hotties", blaring "noise levels", sometimes-"snobby" service and "pricey" tabs that allow you to
"pretend" you're in "South Beach."

NEW Asiakan *Japanese/Pan-Asian*
| | ∇ 19 | 18 | 20 | $32 |

W 90s | 710 Amsterdam Ave. (bet. 94th & 95th Sts.) | 212-280-8878
"A little more upscale" than the "plethora" of Pan-Asian sushi joints
that grace the UWS, this yearling is hailed by locals as a "welcome addition"; depending on whom you poll, the food is either "great" or "average", but all agree the service and prices are "quite nice."

☑ Asiate *French/Japanese*
| | 24 | 28 | 25 | $84 |

W 60s | Mandarin Oriental Hotel | 80 Columbus Circle, 35th fl. (60th St.
at B'way) | 212-805-8881 | www.mandarinoriental.com
Plan to be blown away by the "breathtaking views" "high above Central
Park" – as well as "beautiful" decor rated No. 1 in NYC – as you savor
"exciting" Japanese-French "fusion at its best" and enjoy "impeccable" service at chef Noriyuki Sugie's "posh" dining room at the Mandarin
Oriental Hotel; if the "sky-high" setting doesn't induce vertigo, the
towering tab may – though the $24 lunch prix fixe is a "bargain."

Aspen ● ☒ *American*
| | 20 | 24 | 17 | $49 |

Flatiron | 30 W. 22nd St. (bet. 5th & 6th Aves.) | 212-645-5040 |
www.aspen-nyc.com
If you "snag a seat by the fire", the "ski lodge" decor at this "cool" Flatiron
New American can transport you to "the slopes of Colorado"; the newfangled tapas may be "tasty", but you come for the "vibe" (this is where
"beautiful women flock" and "beer flows like wine"), not the food.

☑ Atlantic Grill ● *Seafood*
| | 22 | 19 | 20 | $51 |

E 70s | 1341 Third Ave. (bet. 76th & 77th Sts.) | 212-988-9200 |
www.brguestrestaurants.com
It's "smooth sailing" at Steve Hanson's "delicious fish haunt", which
UES locals "pack" "every night of the week" to dive into the "freshest"
seafood at "totally doable" prices; "after all these years", angling for a
reservation is still a challenge – "that says it all!"

August *European*
| | 23 | 21 | 20 | $45 |

W Village | 359 Bleecker St. (bet. Charles & W. 10th Sts.) | 212-929-4774 |
www.augustny.com
Pleased patrons "happily return" to this "rustic", "romantic"
Villager for its "robust" regional European cuisine ("anything out

of the wood-burning oven is awesome"); the "glassed-in patio" makes it all the more "great for a date", as does the fact that they now take reservations.

Au Mandarin Chinese
20 | 15 | 18 | $32

Financial District | World Financial Ctr. | 200-250 Vesey St. (West St.) | 212-385-0313 | www.aumandarin.com

Expect to find "much better than average" Chinese dishes "served with style" and "priced to match" at this restaurant inside the World Financial Center; just note that the "atrium" acoustics make you feel like "you're eating inside of a mall."

⦿ Aureole Ⓩ American
27 | 25 | 26 | $105

E 60s | 34 E. 61st St. (bet. Madison & Park Aves.) | 212-319-1660 | www.charliepalmer.com

Excelling "in all categories", Charlie Palmer's "flower-filled" East Side "celebratory dining spot" continues to delight with "outstanding" prix fixe-only New American fare and "phenomenal service" that add up to a "royal experience" surely "worth the cost"; N.B. à la carte dining is an option at lunch, when there's also a "bargain" $38 set menu.

Aurora Italian
26 | 22 | 20 | $43

NEW SoHo | 510 Broome St. (bet. Thompson St. & W. B'way) | 212-334-9020 | www.auroraristorante.com

Williamsburg | 70 Grand St. (Wythe Ave.) | Brooklyn | 718-388-5100 | www.aurorabk.com⊟

"Wonderful" and "constantly getting better" is the word on this "top-notch" Piedmontese duo where you'll swear the ingredients "were harvested yesterday"; the "rustic" decor of the Williamsburg original is echoed at the newer SoHo offshoot, while service is "warm" and prices simpatico at both; P.S. in Brooklyn, go for the "magical" garden in warmer months.

Austin's Steakhouse Steak
▽ 21 | 18 | 20 | $56

Bay Ridge | 8915 Fifth Ave. (90th St.) | Brooklyn | 718-439-5000 | www.austinssteakhouseny.com

"Steaks and sides" "done right" come with a helping of "chatty", "friendly" service at this "small" Bay Ridge chophouse; all in all, it's a pleasant place, but perhaps a "tad expensive" "for the area."

A Voce Italian
25 | 20 | 22 | $67

Gramercy | 41 Madison Ave. (26th St.) | 212-545-8555 | www.avocerestaurant.com

Chef Andrew Carmellini is a "true innovator" who's "giving a new voice" to Italian cuisine at this Madison Square Park "standout"; "efficient" pro service helps offset "pricey" tabs and a room that some find hard to warm up to given its "metallic" look and "deafening" acoustics - there's now outdoor seating as an alternative.

Avra ◑ Greek
24 | 21 | 21 | $55

E 40s | 141 E. 48th St. (bet. Lexington & 3rd Aves.) | 212-759-8550 | www.avrany.com

"Always bustling", this Greek bistro in East Midtown features some of the "freshest fish around", "prepared beautifully"; add "pleasant" surroundings and "attentive" service, and you have happy diners who forgive the "high decibels" and steep "by-the-pound" prices.

| | FOOD | DECOR | SERVICE | COST |

Awash *Ethiopian*
22 | 12 | 16 | $22

E Village | 338 E. Sixth St. (bet. 1st & 2nd Aves.) | 212-982-9589 ◐
W 100s | 947 Amsterdam Ave. (bet. 106th & 107th Sts.) | 212-961-1416
www.awashnyc.com

"Great platters" of "flavorful" Ethiopian fare and a steady supply o[f] "spongy bread" make this East Village–UWS pair "popular with students" and others who find it "fun" to eat with their hands; maybe the "slow" service and "drab" decor are "hard to digest", but "smashing good-deal" prices go down easy.

Azafran 🖂 Ⓜ *Spanish*
21 | 19 | 20 | $48

TriBeCa | 77 Warren St. (bet. Greenwich St. & W. B'way) | 212-284-0578 |
www.azafrannyc.com

Made for "group grazing", this "trendy" TriBeCa *taperia* tenders "delicious" Spanish tidbits from an "open kitchen"; those small plates "add up fast" and the "deafening" din makes the place "azafrantic at times."

Azul Bistro ◐ *Argentinean/Steak*
▽ 22 | 18 | 17 | $41

LES | 152 Stanton St. (Suffolk St.) | 646-602-2004 | www.azulnyc.com

"Red meat lovers" "devour" "tender, tasty" Argentine steaks and "wash everything down" with "affordable" wines at this "funky" Lower Eastsider with a "youthful" vibe and clientele; the only real complaint is about service "that could "be better."

Azuri Cafe 🚫 *Israeli*
▽ 25 | 3 | 8 | $14

W 50s | 465 W. 51st St. (bet. 9th & 10th Aves.) | 212-262-2920

Fans of "fantastic falafel and shimmering schwarma" brace themselves to "just eat and deal" at this West Side Israeli kosher "hole-in-the-wall"; "dingy" decor and a perpetually "grouchy" proprietor are part of the package, but "at these prices, who can kvetch?"

Ⓩ Babbo ◐ *Italian*
27 | 23 | 25 | $76

G Village | 110 Waverly Pl. (bet. MacDougal St. & 6th Ave.) | 212-777-0303 |
www.babbonyc.com

"When it's this good" "it's not hype" is still the consensus as Mario Batali and Joe Bastianich celebrate the 10th anniversary of their "fabulously popular" Village flagship that's voted NYC's No. 1 Italian; given its "mind-blowing" cuisine, "epic wine list", "superlative" service and "cozy" carriage house setting, you'd better "keep their reservation number on redial"; sure, it's "expensive", but it's "worth every *centesimo*."

NEW Babouche *French/Moroccan*
▽ 20 | 23 | 19 | $42

SoHo | 92 Prince St. (bet. B'way & Mercer St.) | 212-219-8155
Park Slope | 2 Lincoln Pl. (5th Ave.) | Brooklyn | 718-636-2100 ◐
www.babouchenyc.com

With "sumptuous interiors" straight out of Marrakech, this SoHo French-Moroccan (with a newer outpost in Park Slope) attracts a "hip crowd" that grooves on "great flavors" both "strong and subtle"; so go "lounge on pillows", eat and imagine you're in the casbah.

Baci & Abbracci ◐ *Italian*
▽ 20 | 18 | 20 | $33

Williamsburg | 204 Grand St. (bet. Bedford & Driggs Aves.) | Brooklyn |
718-599-6599 | www.baciabbracciny.com

Along with the "fantastic" brick-oven pizza, there are other "fresh", "homey" dishes made "with love" at this "laid-back" Williamsburg

	FOOD	DECOR	SERVICE	COST

Italian; its "beautiful garden" beats the "mod" dining room, but anywhere you dine, you'll be treated "wonderfully."

Baldoria *Italian*

| | 22 | 17 | 20 | $54 |

W 40s | 249 W. 49th St. (bet. B'way & 8th Ave.) | 212-582-0460 | www.baldoriamo.com

A spin-off of Rao's "but easier to get into", Frank Pellegrino Jr.'s "consistently good" Theater District Italian serves "red-sauce" favorites in "stepped-back-in-time" digs; it may be "noisy" and "a bit pricey", but hey, "you can't beat those meatballs" – or the "great jukebox."

ⓩ Balthazar ☽ *French*

| | 23 | 23 | 20 | $53 |

SoHo | 80 Spring St. (bet. B'way & Crosby St.) | 212-965-1414 | www.balthazarny.com

Still *"très bon"* "after all these years", Keith McNally's exuberantly "chaotic" SoHo brasserie delivers "wonderful" French food in an "amazingly authentic" "Parisian" setting; it successfully caters to everyone from sunglasses-sporting "celebs" and "socialites" to "tourists" and "B&T" types, all of whom pack in "elbow-to-elbow" for a taste of "big, brassy, fun."

Baluchi's *Indian*

| | 18 | 14 | 15 | $26 |

E 50s | 224 E. 53rd St. (bet. 2nd & 3rd Aves.) | 212-750-5515
E 80s | 1724 Second Ave. (bet. 89th & 90th Sts.) | 212-996-2600
E Village | 104 Second Ave. (6th St.) | 212-780-6000 ☽
Gramercy | 329 Third Ave. (bet. 24th & 25th Sts.) | 212-679-3434
G Village | 361 Sixth Ave. (Washington Pl.) | 212-929-2441
G Village | 90 W. Third St. (bet. Sullivan & Thompson Sts.) | 212-529-5353
SoHo | 193 Spring St. (bet. Sullivan & Thompson Sts.) | 212-226-2828
TriBeCa | 275 Greenwich St. (Warren St.) | 212-571-5343
W 50s | 240 W. 56th St. (bet. B'way & 8th Ave.) | 212-397-0707
Forest Hills | 113-30 Queens Blvd. (bet. 76th Ave. & 76th Rd.) | Queens | 718-520-8600
www.baluchis.com
Additional locations throughout the NY area

"Dependably tasty" if "not exciting" Indian eats make this "cheap" chain a "reliable" choice when "you want your chicken tikka"; the "50-percent-off lunch" is one of the "best deals in town", but at other times the "worn-out decor" and poky service make "delivery" the way to go.

Bamonte's *Italian*

| | 23 | 15 | 21 | $43 |

Williamsburg | 32 Withers St. (bet. Lorimer St. & Union Ave.) | Brooklyn | 718-384-8831

Dating to 1900, this Williamsburg "classic" serves "plentiful portions" of "quintessential" Italian fare to local "families" and "fauxhemians"; the "fabulous food" "makes up for" the "dated" decor, and you can expect good service from the "tuxedoed" waiters – some of whom look like they've been there "since day one."

Bandol Bistro *French*

| | 19 | 16 | 18 | $46 |

E 70s | 181 E. 78th St. (bet. Lexington & 3rd Aves.) | 212-744-1800 | www.bandolbistro.com

This "neighborhood refuge" on the UES serves a "limited" but "flavorful French" lineup and "great wines by the glass" in a "romantic, cozy" space; however, the fact that it recently came under "new management" puts the above ratings in question.

	FOOD	DECOR	SERVICE	COST

Banjara ◗ *Indian*
23 | 16 | 17 | $31

E Village | 97 First Ave. (6th St.) | 212-477-5956 |
www.banjarany.com

"Finer fare" distinguishes this "value"-oriented East Village Indian
considered a "step above" the Curry Row competition; it "may not be
the fanciest" place and service is "hit-or-miss", but all the same it's
voted "worth a detour."

Bann *Korean*
▽ 24 | 24 | 21 | $46

W 50s | Worldwide Plaza | 350 W. 50th St. (bet. 8th & 9th Aves.) |
212-582-4446 | www.bannrestaurant.com

At this "sceney", "innovative Korean", the drill is cook-it-yourself barbecue and "wonderful" "fresh" fusion fare in a "somewhat hidden"
Worldwide Plaza location; the "serene setting" and "unrushed service" make it all the more "worth" it to those in-the-know.

Bann Thai *Thai*
21 | 18 | 19 | $29

Forest Hills | 69-12 Austin St. (Yellowstone Blvd.) | Queens | 718-544-9999 |
www.bannthairestaurant.com

"Typical Thai" but "still delicious" is the feeling about this "steady"
Forest Hills standby, where the "small" quarters are "comfortable"
and the service "gracious"; still, a handful of sophisticates says "why
eat here" when there's real-deal Thai "minutes away"?

Bao Noodles *Vietnamese*
20 | 15 | 16 | $25

Gramercy | 391 Second Ave. (bet. 22nd & 23rd Sts.) | 212-725-7770
"Tiny", "funky" and "no-frills", this Gramercy joint specializes in
"pho-licious" Vietnamese soups and sandwiches that are "way better
than average"; sure, "service lacks", but given the "just-right prices",
it may offer the "best bang for the buck" in the area.

Bao 111 ◗ *Vietnamese*
21 | 19 | 17 | $38

E Village | 111 Ave. C (bet. 7th & 8th Sts.) | 212-254-7773 |
www.bao111.com

"Full of kick and life", this "hip", "more upscale" East Village
Vietnamese has a winning formula of "flavorful" food, "lethal drinks"
and "late-night" hours; with all the "noise", you almost forget any service flaws – and the extra cost "for the trendy setting."

☑ Bar Americain *American*
23 | 23 | 22 | $61

W 50s | 152 W. 52nd St. (bet. 6th & 7th Aves.) | 212-265-9700 |
www.baramericain.com

"Big flavors", "big space" and electric "energy" sums up Bobby Flay's
"spirited romp" that updates American comfort classics in one of those
Midtown "places to be seen" filled with "media execs on expense accounts"; factor in service that's "charming and efficient", and everyone "comes away happy."

Baraonda ◗ *Italian*
18 | 17 | 15 | $47

E 70s | 1439 Second Ave. (75th St.) | 212-288-8555 |
www.baraondany.com

At this UES "Euro-centric" Italian, the "upbeat" vibe "never goes out of
style" and the "hot crowd" outweighs "subpar service"; most rate the
kitchen's output "decent", but given the "colorful" scenery and wee-
hours "tabletop dancing", "who cares about food?"

	FOOD	DECOR	SERVICE	COST

arbès ◗ French/Moroccan
22 | 18 | 19 | $43

Murray Hill | 21 E. 36th St. (bet. 5th & Madison Aves.) | 212-684-0215

Murray Hill's own "Arabian dream", this "adorable" French-Moroccan an "unexpected find" for a "succulent" "taste of Fez" and "warm service" at "budget-minded" prices; the "intimate" space "gets very ght", but still it's the area's bès bet for "a change from the usual."

arbetta ◗ ⑤ Ⓜ Italian
20 | 23 | 21 | $59

W 40s | 321 W. 46th St. (bet. 8th & 9th Aves.) | 212-246-9171 | www.barbettarestaurant.com

Restaurant Row "monument" dating back "over 100 years", this brownstone Northern Italian is a redoubt of "rococo" "elegance" here "gracious" staffers serve "reliably fine food"; a few deem it dated", but it "continues to impress" and the "lovely" garden remains a real treat"; N.B. check out the private party rooms.

arbounia Mediterranean
20 | 22 | 18 | $52

Flatiron | 250 Park Ave. S. (20th St.) | 212-995-0242 | www.barbounia.com

his "refined" Flatiron Mediterranean attracts a "noisy", "trendy" crowd with its "eye-catching" but "comfy" space and "terrific" food; espite scattered criticism for "absent-minded" service, overall most gree it's "worthy" of the relatively "big" tab.

arbuto Italian
22 | 18 | 18 | $50

W Village | 775 Washington St. (bet. Jane & W. 12th Sts.) | 212-924-9700 | www.barbutonyc.com

"Freshness is key" to Jonathan Waxman's "innovative", "market-riven" menu at this West Village Italian in a "converted garage" with "hip" "industrial vibe"; the "lackadaisical" staff and "painful" acoustics detract, but you'll still "feel cool" even if it's hot.

ardolino ◗ Italian
18 | 15 | 18 | $34

70s | 1496 Second Ave. (78th St.) | 212-734-9050 | www.bardolinorestaurantnyc.com

reshly expanded, this UES "neighborhood Italian" now offers more oom to enjoy its "decent" "homestyle cooking" and "solid service"; he experience may be "ordinary", but considering the "relaxed" feel nd "reasonable prices" that's "all to the good."

⒩ⓔⓦ BarFry ◗ Eclectic/Japanese
- | - | - | M

Village | 50 Carmine St. (bet. Bedford & Bleecker Sts.) | 212-929-5050 | www.barfrynyc.com

rom chef Josh DeChellis (ex Sumile Sushi) comes this new Village empura bar where the mostly Japanese menu is tricked up with po' oys, beef beignets and a smartly parsed wine list; the casual, white-iled room dominated by a long bar seems designed with a young crowd in mind, ditto the low price point.

arking Dog American
15 | 13 | 14 | $24

70s | 1453 York Ave. (77th St.) | 212-861-3600

90s | 1678 Third Ave. (94th St.) | 212-831-1800 ⊟

Murray Hill | Affinia Dumont | 150 E. 34th St. (bet. Lexington & 3rd Aves.) | 212-871-3900 ◗

Chowhounds" can park with "Fido outside" this East Side trio, whose cutesy" "canine theme" and "low-cost" American "basics" get a "paws up" from the "stroller set"; then again, the menu needs "some new tricks" and you'll have to "sit up and beg" for service.

barmarché ◑ *American* ▽ 19 | 19 | 16 | $38

NoLita | 14 Spring St. (Elizabeth St.) | 212-219-2399 | www.barmarche.com
"Casual" and "cozy", this "cool" NoLita bistro gives its "hip" habitués an economical "place to unwind" over "fresh" "New American varia-tions" and "above-average cocktails"; it's a favored break from the "more trendy spots" in spite of service so "unhurried" it's "aloof."

NEW Bar Martignetti ◑ *American* ▽ 18 | 16 | 14 | $40

Little Italy | 406 Broome St. (bet. Centre & Lafayette Sts.) | 212-680-5600 | www.barmartignetti.com
Done up in "faux brasserie" fashion, this "loud", boisterous Little Italy newcomer is already overflowing with stylish types looking to fill up on "decent" New American fare before (or after) "partying" at nearby bars; tipplers who don't want to travel too far head for the "downstairs club."

Barney Greengrass Ⓜ⊅ *Deli* 23 | 8 | 14 | $26

W 80s | 541 Amsterdam Ave. (bet. 86th & 87th Sts.) | 212-724-4707 | www.barneygreengrass.com
"You haven't had Nova on a bagel" till you visit this Upper West Side "institution", which is once again voted NYC's No. 1 deli thanks to its "blissfully authentic" "Jewish breakfasts"; if the "tu-mult", "shabby" surroundings and servers' "shtick" elicit an "oy vey", "consider takeout."

Barolo *Italian* 18 | 21 | 17 | $52

SoHo | 398 W. Broadway (bet. Broome & Spring Sts.) | 212-226-1102 | www.nybarolo.com
It's "all about" the "enchanting" alfresco "escape" at this sprawling SoHo Italian whose "transporting" garden is "legendary"; the menu is "consistently good" too ("albeit not cheap"), but most look for "ro-mance" "in the atmosphere, not the food."

Bar Pitti ◑⊅ *Italian* 22 | 14 | 17 | $39

G Village | 268 Sixth Ave. (bet. Bleecker & Houston Sts.) | 212-982-3300
"Prime sidewalk" tables (not the bland interior) make this "hopping" Village Italian a "perennial place to be" for "robust" pastas with "a celeb or two" on the side; it's a "solid" "alternative to Da Silvano" with "decent prices", but "pitti the fool" at the rear of the line to get in.

NEW Bar Stuzzichini *Italian* - | - | - | M

Flatiron | 928 Broadway (bet. 21st & 22nd Sts.) | 212-780-5100 | www.barstuzzichini.com
Stuzzichini (small plates) are the focus at this new Flatiron Southern Italian where customers pick from three seating areas: a front wine bar, a marble antipasto bar or the dining room; perfect for the tapas-like lineup, its list of vinos includes lots of choices by the glass.

Bar Toto ◑ *Italian* 19 | 18 | 18 | $27

Park Slope | 411 11th St. (6th Ave.) | Brooklyn | 718-768-4698 | www.bartoto.com
"Lots of locals" turn up at this "friendly" Park Slope Italian to "kick back" and scarf "tasty" pastas, pizzas and panini "for cheap"; it's a

toto-ly "low-key" "joint" with "outdoor seating" and "few surprises" – and there's "nothing wrong with that."

Basilica ●Ⓜ *Italian*

FOOD	DECOR	SERVICE	COST
19	14	18	$31

W 40s | 676 Ninth Ave. (bet. 46th & 47th Sts.) | 212-489-0051
Devotees "squeeze" in to this "dark", "postage stamp-size" Hell's Kitchen "secret" for "fresh" Italian classics and "quick" service "pre-show"; as for prices, the $24 prix fixe including "a bottle of decent wine" ranks with "the best bargains in town."

NEW Basso56 ● *Italian*

▽ 23	18	22	$44

W 50s | 234 W. 56th St. (bet. B'way & 8th Ave.) | 212-265-2610 | www.basso56.com
Westsiders already feel "at home" at this "consummate" midpriced Italian following a "welcome move from Downtown" that left its "delicious" "homespun preparations" intact; the "sleek" space and "engaging" service has its new neighborhood calling it a "winner."

Basta Pasta *Italian*

21	16	19	$42

Flatiron | 37 W. 17th St. (bet. 5th & 6th Aves.) | 212-366-0888 | www.bastapastanyc.com
"The usual pastas" take some "curveballs" at this "informal" Flatiron Italian thanks to the "inventive" "merging" of "flavorful" "Japanese touches" from a "team of professionals" manning the "open kitchen"; it's "confusing at first", but "curious" converts concede "somehow it works."

Battery Gardens *American/Continental*

18	24	18	$51

Financial District | SW corner of Battery Park (State St.) | 212-809-5508 | www.batterygardens.com
For a "scenic" recharge in Battery Park, this American-Continental commands a "peerless" "harbor view" that's best admired from the "wonderful" patio; the menu is also "commendable", but the panorama is what makes going "out of the way" to get here "worthwhile."

Bay Leaf *Indian*

19	15	16	$37

W 50s | 49 W. 56th St. (bet. 5th & 6th Aves.) | 212-957-1818
"Very decent quality" with "no pretensions" sums up this white-tablecloth Indian near Carnegie Hall that's possibly most "noteworthy" for its $14.95 lunch buffet; dinner is also "satisfying" – though "at a price" – but critics say the service "needs to try harder."

Bayou *Cajun*

▽ 22	20	21	$33

Staten Island | 1072 Bay St. (bet. Chestnut & St. Mary's Aves.) | 718-273-4383 | www.bayoustatenisland.com
"Staten Island's version of the Big Easy", this ultra-"cozy" Cajun-Creole kitchen's "addictive" cooking and down-home decor conjure up a "genuine" "N'Awlins feel"; with a "friendly" crew that keeps the mood "relaxed", it's a "no-lose situation" for a Dixie fix.

Beacon *American*

22	21	21	$60

W 50s | 25 W. 56th St. (bet. 5th & 6th Aves.) | 212-332-0500 | www.beaconnyc.com
Waldy Malouf will "light your fire" at this Midtown New American, which produces "memorable" "wood-grilled" fare in an "impressive" "multilevel" space; it's a "mecca for corporate" types willing to drop "a lot of dollars", though the "prix fixe deals" are a beacon for all.

	FOOD	DECOR	SERVICE	COST

Beast *Mediterranean* ▽ 20 | 16 | 17 | $30

Prospect Heights | 638 Bergen St. (Vanderbilt Ave.) | Brooklyn |
718-399-6855

"Dependable" and "different", this "funky" "local" "hangout" in Prospect
Heights features a "reasonable" "eclectic" Med menu whose "savory"
small plates are a step up from "the typical" pub grub; the "dark", "totally
cozy" setting is "relaxing", and service is likewise "leisurely."

Z Becco ◑ *Italian* 22 | 18 | 21 | $43

W 40s | 355 W. 46th St. (bet. 8th & 9th Aves.) | 212-397-7597 |
www.becconyc.com

"Loosen" your belt for Joe Bastianich's "energetic" Restaurant Row
Italian, which "continues to amaze" with its $21.95 all-you-can-eat
"pasta-gasm" special and its "massive" cache of $20-and-under
wines; given pre-theater mobs more suited to "Grand Central", "instant", "no-attitude" service is also a big plus.

Beccofino *Italian* ▽ 22 | 19 | 19 | $32

Bronx | 5704 Mosholu Ave. (bet. Fieldston Rd. & Spencer Ave.) |
718-432-2604

Riverdale "finally" boasts a "neighborhood red-sauce" option courtesy
of this "welcoming" Italian and its "plentiful" portions of "simply fabulous" "comfort food"; it's "intimate" and "not too pricey", but you'll
have to "get there early" to "beat the crowds."

Bella Blu *Italian* 19 | 16 | 17 | $48

E 70s | 967 Lexington Ave. (bet. 70th & 71st Sts.) | 212-988-4624

To lose the blues, visit this Upper East Side Northern Italian, an "entertaining scene" serving "solid" pastas and wood-oven pizzas to a
"loud", "bubbly" crowd; meanwhile curmudgeons cite "expensive"
specials and a room that's due for an "extreme makeover."

Bella Via *Italian* ▽ 23 | 18 | 20 | $31

LIC | 47-46 Vernon Blvd. (48th Ave.) | Queens | 718-361-7510 |
www.bellaviarestaurant.com

With "terrific" "coal-oven" pizza and "authentic" pastas, this Long
Island City Italian "competes with the best" for "everyday" eating at a
"reasonable" cost; the pace is "relaxed", and the "outer-borough vibe"
has visitors saying they "feel right at home."

Bellavitae ◑ *Italian* 22 | 18 | 20 | $52

G Village | 24 Minetta Ln. (bet. MacDougal St. & 6th Ave.) | 212-473-5121 |
www.bellavitae.com

Aficionados of "rustic Italian" repasts "treasure" this Village enoteca
for the "delectable" small-plate offerings, "well-selected" wines and
"warm", "old-country" feel; though "a little haughty" and costing "a
hefty sum", it's "one to remember" when Babbo's backed up.

Belleville ⊘ *French* 18 | 19 | 16 | $35

Park Slope | 350 Fifth St. (5th Ave.) | Brooklyn | 718-832-9777 |
www.bellevillebistro.com

This "reasonable" Park Slope "replication" of a "Left Bank" bistro
offers "comforting" French "classics" in "très belle" environs; "low
key" "without attitude", it's a "neighborhood favorite" especially
for weekend brunch.

| | FOOD | DECOR | SERVICE | COST |

‌ello 🅉 *Italian*
20 | 16 | 20 | $46

W 50s | 863 Ninth Ave. (56th St.) | 212-246-6773 | www.bellorestaurant.com

"Convenience without too high prices" keeps "pre-theater" folks faithful to this Hell's Kitchen "oldie" and its "trustworthy" Italian fare; it's "spacious", "gracious" and offers "the plus of free parking" after ‌ PM – "what else can you want?"

‌ello Sguardo ● *Mediterranean*
19 | 16 | 18 | $37

W 70s | 410 Amsterdam Ave. (bet. 79th & 80th Sts.) | 212-873-6252

‌or a "fresh take on Mediterranean standards", check out this Upper ‌Westsider, where the "zesty" small plates "hit the spot" with fans who "feel like grazing" at a "moderate" cost; "attentive service" seals its ‌ppeal as a "comfortable" "neighborhood hangout."

‌en & Jack's Steak House *Steak*
23 | 17 | 22 | $66

‌ 40s | 219 E. 44th St. (bet. 2nd & 3rd Aves.) | 212-682-5678 | www.benandjackssteakhouse.com

‌ots of "suits" steer to this Grand Central–area steakhouse, which lives up to its "steakhouse pedigree" with "ample" portions of "top-‌ight" beef served by "professionals"; critics cite the "forgettable de-‌or" and "steep prices" as hard to swallow.

‌en Benson's *Steak*
24 | 18 | 22 | $65

W 50s | 123 W. 52nd St. (bet. 6th & 7th Aves.) | 212-581-8888 | www.benbensons.com

‌ "perennial favorite for the business" class, this "high-energy" Midtown ‌neatery "holds its own" in the "upper tier" with *Flintstones*-scale ‌teaks, "nearly fatal" martinis and service from "seasoned vets"; as for ‌he "din", "sparse" decor and "brusque" attitude, "it's a guy thing."

‌EW Benjamin Steak House *Steak*
▽ 23 | 21 | 23 | $60

‌ 40s | 52 E. 41st St. (bet. Madison & Park Aves.) | 212-297-9177 | www.benjaminsteakhouse.com

‌f you're a steak person", this latest "Peter Luger knockoff" "sets itself ‌part" in Midtown with fine meats and "gentrified" digs with "high ‌eilings" and a fireplace; "top-notch" service matches the "sophisti-‌ated" setup, and though "expensive" it's "worth" all those benjamins.

‌en's Kosher Deli *Deli*
17 | 10 | 14 | $23

‌arment District | 209 W. 38th St. (bet. 7th & 8th Aves.) | 212-398-2367
‌ayside | Bay Terrace | 211-37 26th Ave. (211th St.) | Queens |
‌18-229-2367
www.bensdeli.net

‌When "big mouths" "need to nosh", this low-budget Garment District-‌ayside kosher deli duo does a "speedy" job supplying "heaping" sand-‌wiches from a "broad" menu; service is "curt" and decor "dreary", but ‌hat comes with the territory – which also may require "Tums."

‌eppe 🅉 *Italian*
23 | 20 | 22 | $54

‌latiron | 45 E. 22nd St. (bet. B'way & Park Ave. S.) | 212-982-8422 | www.beppenyc.com

‌Go twice and you're a regular" at this "comfy yet classy" Flatiron ‌find" for "lusty Tuscan" fare served by a "warm, smart staff"; combin-‌ng "fresh" "culinary ideas" with a "homey feel", it maintains such high quality" that few fret if the tabs get "a bit pricey."

	FOOD	DECOR	SERVICE	COST

Bereket ⏱✏ *Turkish*
18 | 3 | 12 | $12

LES | 187 E. Houston St. (Orchard St.) | 212-475-7700

To "cure" the "post-clubbing munchies" there's always this 24/7 Lower Eastsider, a "late-night fixture" vending "heartwarming" "Turkish eats" at "bargain" rates; sure, the "lunch-counter" setup is "spartan", but all those "taxi drivers can't be wrong."

Beso *Nuevo Latino*
19 | 12 | 14 | $25

Park Slope | 210 Fifth Ave. (Union St.) | Brooklyn | 718-783-4902

"Bright and cheerful", this Park Sloper "fills you up" with its "creative yet accessible", "excellent-value" Nuevo Latino dishes; despite "random" service and "garagelike" digs, local amigos "line up" for the "amazing brunch", but strangely it's a "sleeper" at night.

Bette ⏱🗷 *European*
19 | 21 | 19 | $56

Chelsea | 461 W. 23rd St. (bet. 9th & 10th Aves.) | 212-366-0404 | www.betterestaurant.com

"Pretty" people "bet on" the "social atmosphere" at Amy Sacco's West Chelsea "hideaway", a mix of "mod" and "sexy" that's *très* trendy" "in a good way"; many appreciate the "creative" European cuisine, but critics complain it's "pricey" – and say the novelty is "waning."

Better Burger *Hamburgers*
15 | 10 | 13 | $14

Chelsea | 178 Eighth Ave. (19th St.) | 212-989-6688 ⏱
Murray Hill | 561 Third Ave. (37th St.) | 212-949-7528
W 40s | 587 Ninth Ave. (bet. 42nd & 43rd Sts.) | 212-629-6622
www.betterburgernyc.com

At this "alternative fast-food" mini-chain, the organic beef burgers, "veggie options" and "air-baked fries" let "health-conscious" sorts "indulge without the guilt"; "inventive" sauces "add a nice touch", but dissenters dub them "blander burgers" – "sometimes you need the grease."

Bettola ⏱ *Italian*
21 | 16 | 18 | $36

W 70s | 412 Amsterdam Ave. (bet. 79th & 80th Sts.) | 212-787-1660 | www.bettolanyc.com

There's "real Italian" "in the 'hood" thanks to this "quaint" Upper Westsider, where "amazing, crispy-thin" pizza leads a "solid" lineup of "rustic" fare; "sweet service", "alfresco" tables and "reasonable" tabs cement its rep as a "winning" bet.

Beyoglu ⏱ *Turkish*
21 | 17 | 17 | $33

E 80s | 1431 Third Ave. (81st St.) | 212-650-0850

Even those with "no idea how to pronounce it" call this "upbeat" Upper East Side Turk a "keeper", adding that the "delish" "shareable" mezes are "the way to go"; "fair prices" ensure it's "always packed", and "sidewalk dining" offers relief from the sorta "cheesy" interior.

BG *American*
▽ 20 | 23 | 20 | $48

W 50s | Bergdorf Goodman | 754 Fifth Ave., 7th fl. (bet. 57th & 58th Sts.) | 212-872-8977

"Well-coiffed shoppers" lunch in "high style" at this New American "tucked away" in Bergdorf's; it's "surprisingly good" culinarily and "even better" "aesthetically", so most don't let the "over-the-top" prices" distract from the "people-watching" and "lovely view" of Central Park.

	FOOD	DECOR	SERVICE	COST

Bianca ⊭ *Italian*
▽ 22 | 16 | 20 | $33

NoHo | 5 Bleecker St. (bet. Bowery & Elizabeth St.) | 212-260-4666
"Hearty" "housemade" specialties from the Emilia-Romagnia region make this "spirited little" NoHo Italian an "excellent" pick; those "who know" "true value" are typically "clamoring for entry", so expect "tight" seating and a "wait", despite the efforts of an "efficient staff."

Bice ● *Italian*
20 | 19 | 19 | $60

E 50s | 7 E. 54th St. (bet. 5th & Madison Aves.) | 212-688-1999 | www.bicenewyork.com
Known for nonstop "action" by "good-looking", "Euro"-centric sorts, this Midtown Northern Italian provides "quality" fare along with "loud" "networking" and a super sidewalk "show"; there's also "hospitable service" (if you're "a VIP"), but it's "no bargain" and the "attitude" can be a "bice."

Big Nick's Burger Joint ● *Hamburgers*
17 | 5 | 14 | $16

W 70s | 2175 Broadway (77th St.) | 212-362-9238
W 70s | 70 W. 71st St. (Columbus Ave.) | 212-799-4444
Westsiders "craving" "greasy goodness" frequent these separately owned "dive diners", where "burgers rule" the "novel"-length menus supplying "monstrous portions" at "bargain" rates; they're longtime "go-to spots" (with 24/7 service on Broadway) even if the "seedy" digs are widely nixed.

Big Wong ⊭ *Chinese*
22 | 5 | 11 | $13

Chinatown | 67 Mott St. (bet. Bayard & Canal Sts.) | 212-964-0540
For "filling" Chinese "cheap eats", you can't go wong with the "traditional" congees and "BBQ meats" at this "no-nonsense" "C-town staple"; despite "perfunctory" service, "elbow-to-elbow" seating, "nonexistent" decor and an "unfortunate name", it's "always crowded" 'cause the food "rocks."

Biricchino ⊠ *Italian*
20 | 13 | 18 | $38

Chelsea | 260 W. 29th St. (8th Ave.) | 212-695-6690 | www.biricchino.com
"Known for" its "must-have" homemade sausages, this "steady" Northern Italian near Madison Square Garden is an "unexpected" source of "solid" cooking at "reasonable" prices; though "not much to look at", it's "handy" in an area "devoid of many choices."

Bistro Cassis *French*
20 | 17 | 16 | $42

W 70s | 225 Columbus Ave. (bet. 70th & 71st Sts.) | 212-579-3966 | www.bistrocassisnyc.com
To feed your "French jones" try this "authentic" West Side bistro, a "quaint" "neighborhood haunt" offering "flavorful" "classic" fare; though it's "always crowded" and "service-challenged" in "true Parisian style", its "popularity" and no-reservations rule make "a wait" de rigueur.

Bistro Citron *French*
21 | 19 | 20 | $40

W 80s | 473 Columbus Ave. (bet. 82nd & 83rd Sts.) | 212-400-9401 | www.bistrocitronnyc.com
Upper Westsiders "welcome" the "lively" "French experience" at this "well-priced" yearling that feels like "you could be in Paris"; given its "hearty" bistro "hits", "atmospheric" surroundings, "warm" service and "outdoor seating", it's no wonder it has *beaucoup* backers.

	FOOD	DECOR	SERVICE	COST

Bistro du Nord *French* — 18 | 15 | 16 | $46

E 90s | 1312 Madison Ave. (93rd St.) | 212-289-0997

A "steady" haven for "the Carnegie Hill set", this petite bistro has a loyal "local" following for its "old-world French" cooking and "bargain" prix fixes; then again, "service is sketchy" and you may need a "shoehorn" to get into the "narrow duplex" space.

Bistro Les Amis ● *French* — 21 | 18 | 21 | $40

SoHo | 180 Spring St. (Thompson St.) | 212-226-8645 | www.bistrolesamis.com

Friends tend to "linger" at this "cozy" "little" SoHo bistro, where the "caring" service, French "comfort food" and moderate prices amount to the "perfect date"; it's "not too fancy", but admirers only "wish there were more of these."

Bistro Le Steak ● *French* — 17 | 14 | 17 | $45

E 70s | 1309 Third Ave. (75th St.) | 212-517-3800 | www.bistrolesteak.com

With "no surprises", this Upper East Side "neighborhood" French bistro–steakhouse recalls the "'burbs" with its "straightforward" bites and "reasonable" prices; as for allegations of "tired" looks and "variable" service, its regulars shrug "*c'est la vie.*"

Bistro 61 *French* — 20 | 15 | 19 | $37

E 60s | 1113 First Ave. (61st St.) | 212-223-6220 | www.bistro61.com

Amis "appreciate" the "authenticity" at this "compact" French bistro by the Queensboro Bridge, where the "caring" service and "ambitious" French fare "make one want to stay the night"; it claims a "loyal following", not least because "the price is right."

Bistro Ten 18 *American* — 20 | 19 | 20 | $36

W 100s | 1018 Amsterdam Ave. (110th St.) | 212-662-7600 | www.bistroten18.com

Morningside Heights goes "upscale" at this pleasingly priced New American bistro with "surprisingly good" food and "warm" service; the "romantic fireplace" and St. John the Divine views make it "a real asset" for visiting Columbia "parents."

NEW Bistro 33 *French/Japanese* — - | - | - | M
(fka Lil' Bistro 33)

Astoria | 19-33 Ditmars Blvd. (21st St.) | Queens | 718-721-1933 | www.bistro33nyc.com

Only the 'Lil' got lost in this Japanese-French bistro's recent move to roomier digs near Astoria Park; it has grown in other ways too, expanding its sushi menu and adding take-out service, a liquor license and sidewalk seating.

Black Duck *American/Seafood* — ▽ 20 | 19 | 20 | $46

Gramercy | Park South Hotel | 122 E. 28th St. (bet. Lexington Ave. & Park Ave. S.) | 212-448-0888 | www.blackduckny.com

It's easy to overlook, but this "intimate" New American in a Gramercy hotel is worth ducking into for its "lovingly prepared" seafood specialties served "without attitude"; feathering the nest are a "working fireplace" and live jazz.

	FOOD	DECOR	SERVICE	COST

NEW **Black Pearl** *Seafood* | 17 | 14 | 17 | $37

Chelsea | 37 W. 26th St. (bet. B'way & 6th Ave.) | 212-532-9900 |
www.blackpearlonline.com

Fans of "proper lobster rolls" and other "classic" "New England clam-
bake" fare "look no further" than this "laid-back" "fish shack" newly
moored in Chelsea; a few complain about "lackluster" atmospherics
and "ordinary" eating, but supporters shrug "no frills necessary."

Blair Perrone Steakhouse ⑤ *Steak* | 21 | 23 | 22 | $69

E 40s | 885 Second Ave. (bet. 47th & 48th Sts.) | 212-796-8000 |
www.blairperrone.com

A "refreshing" "change of pace", this "beautifully appointed"
Midtowner features "first-rate" steak and "attentive service" from an
ex-Peter Luger/Mark Joseph team; "many suits" salute the "indul-
gence", even if hedgers hint it "falls a bit short" for the "hefty pricing."

Blaue Gans ◑ *Austrian/German* | 20 | 18 | 19 | $46

TriBeCa | 139 Duane St. (bet. Church St. & W. B'way) | 212-571-8880 |
www.wallse.com

"*Wursthaus* meets TriBeCa" at this "casual" bistro from Wallsé's Kurt
Gutenbrunner offering "good old" Austro-German "staples" with "finesse"; maybe the "hip", spacious quarters are "not elegant", but "fair
pricing" and "unpretentious" staffers make it *gemütlich* all the same.

Blockheads Burritos *Mexican* | 17 | 10 | 15 | $18

E 50s | 954 Second Ave. (bet. 50th & 51st Sts.) | 212-750-2020
E 80s | 1563 Second Ave. (bet. 81st & 82nd Sts.) | 212-879-1999
Murray Hill | 499 Third Ave. (bet. 33rd & 34th Sts.) | 212-213-3332
W 50s | Worldwide Plaza | 322 W. 50th St. (bet. 8th & 9th Aves.) |
212-307-7029
www.blockheads.com

It's easy to satisfy "a big appetite" for a "little money" at this Mexican
mini-chain, where "zeppelin"-size burritos and "potent margaritas" are
the big "crowd-pleasers"; on the other hand, for many the "el blando"
surroundings make "fast delivery" "the way to go."

Blossom *Vegan/Vegetarian* | 21 | 19 | 21 | $38

Chelsea | 187 Ninth Ave. (bet. 21st & 22nd Sts.) | 212-627-1144 |
www.blossomnyc.com

"Fine vegan dining" that "doesn't scream 'bean curd'" is the forte of
this "cozy" Chelsea "haven" whose "wholesome" global fare is so "creative" it's "hard to believe it's good for you"; though it's a bit pricey "for
its type", the "organic wine list" alone makes it "worth considering."

NEW **BLT Burger** *Hamburgers* | 19 | 14 | 16 | $24

G Village | 470 Sixth Ave. (bet. 11th & 12th Sts.) | 212-243-8226 |
www.bltburger.com

For the "burger lover" in everyone, Laurent Tourondel's "casual" new
Villager does well with patties both "classic" and "postmodern"; all hail
the fair prices, if not the "confused service" and "unremarkable" decor.

BLT Fish ⑤ *Seafood* | 23 | 20 | 20 | $61

Flatiron | 21 W. 17th St. (bet. 5th & 6th Aves.) | 212-691-8888 |
www.bltfish.com

A "catch" "from top to bottom", Laurent Tourondel's Flatiron seafooder offers both a "classy" "skylit upstairs" room for "high-end" din-

ing and a "relaxed" "lively" downstairs beach bar for "casual" "surf fare"; wave off the "dent in your wallet" and you "can't go wrong."

NEW BLT Market *American* — | — | — | VE

W 50s | Ritz-Carlton | 1430 Sixth Ave. (CPS) | 212-521-6125 | www.bltmarket.com

Cross a farmer's market with the Ritz-Carlton and you get this pricey newcomer from Laurent Tourondel, where the focus is on seasonal, sometimes local ingredients that are the basis for its monthly changing menus and weekly specials; in the reconfigured former Atelier space, it's now done up in cheery agrarian chic, with big windows looking out onto the street and sidewalk seating in summer; N.B. there are even a few comestibles for sale up front.

BLT Prime *Steak* 24 | 22 | 22 | $72

Gramercy | 111 E. 22nd St. (bet. Lexington Ave. & Park Ave. S.) | 212-995-8500 | www.bltprime.com

A "snazzy" steakhouse with a New American "twist", Laurent Tourondel's Gramercy "bovine bonanza" matches "expertly prepared" meat with a "palette" of à la carte sauces and sides in a "vibrant, modern" setting; it's a "top choice" for carnivores with "contemporary" tastes – "just bring lots of moo-la."

BLT Steak ⑤ *Steak* 24 | 21 | 21 | $70

E 50s | 106 E. 57th St. (bet. Lexington & Park Aves.) | 212-752-7470 | www.bltsteak.com

As the progenitor of the "elite" BLT empire, this "dressed-up" East Midtown chophouse offers its "succulent" meats à la carte with "creative sides" and "VIP" service; it's "very 'in'" with "upscale", "high-decibel-level" "business" types who say it's "worth the premium" (if you can "get in the door").

bluechili ● *Pan-Asian* 19 | 16 | 17 | $37

W 50s | 251 W. 51st St. (bet. B'way & 8th Ave.) | 212-246-3330 | www.bluechilinyc.com

Something "different" for the Theater District, this Pan-Asian provides "lots of flavor for the buck" in "clublike", "futuristic" digs with "morphing" "mood lighting" and a "martini bar"; critics are chilly over "inattentive" service, but to most it's still "kinda cool."

Blue Fin ● *Seafood* 22 | 22 | 19 | $55

W 40s | W Times Sq. | 1567 Broadway (47th St.) | 212-918-1400 | www.brguestrestaurants.com

A Times Square "highlight", Steve Hanson's "splashy" seafooder is "jumping" with locals and sightseers lured by the "solid" "quality" fish and "upscale", bi-level space; despite the "din" and "erratic" service from "aspiring actors", "it works" for "the theatergoing masses" even "at those prices."

Blue Ginger *Japanese/Pan-Asian* ▽ 22 | 18 | 19 | $36

Chelsea | 106 Eighth Ave. (bet. 15th & 16th Sts.) | 212-352-0911

Chelsea-ites "welcome" this Pan-Asian sushi purveyor after a "hype-free" arrival, notably for its "creative" "specialty rolls", "traditional entrees" and "gracious service"; as the "neighborhood" vibe implies, it's "reliable" for "a low-key" night.

	FOOD	DECOR	SERVICE	COST

Ⓩ Blue Hill *American* | 26 | 22 | 25 | $73 |

G Village | 75 Washington Pl. (bet. MacDougal St. & 6th Ave.) |
212-539-1776 | www.bluehillnyc.com

"I found my thrill" declare disciples at Dan Barber's gastronomic "temple" near Washington Square, whose "delectable" yet "unfussy" New American cuisine lets "the freshest" "organic" ingredients "shine through"; served with "genuine care" in a "subtly elegant" setting with a "quaint garden", it's an "artful" experience "for grown-ups."

Blue 9 Burger ●♨ *Hamburgers* | 18 | 5 | 10 | $10 |

E Village | 92 Third Ave. (bet. 12th & 13th Sts.) | 212-979-0053

"Reminiscent of" California's "In-N-Out Burger", this "late-night" East Villager vends "sloppy" "bundles of joy" to "campus" refugees undergoing a "cash crunch"; "dingy digs and "apathetic" counterfolk aside, it's a "super" "hangover" remedy.

Ⓩ Blue Ribbon ● *American* | 25 | 19 | 22 | $50 |

SoHo | 97 Sullivan St. (bet. Prince & Spring Sts.) | 212-274-0404
Park Slope | 280 Fifth Ave. (bet. 1st St. & Garfield Pl.) | Brooklyn |
718-840-0404
www.blueribbonrestaurants.com

First "prize" destinations, these "welcoming" SoHo–Park Slope New Americans from the Bromberg brothers stay "energized" into the "after hours" with an "interesting", "attractive" crowd; the cost runs "high" and waits "long", but "there's a reason" so many "love these places" – "astounding" food.

Blue Ribbon Bakery ● *American* | 24 | 19 | 20 | $39 |

G Village | 33 Downing St. (Bedford St.) | 212-337-0404 |
www.blueribbonrestaurants.com

Famed for "incredible" "fresh bread", this Village "winner" from the Bromberg brothers "pleases diverse tastes" with its "delightful" New American menu and "smart wine list"; no wonder "low-key" fans "line up for" the "limited" space, especially during the "awesome brunch."

Ⓩ Blue Ribbon Sushi ● *Japanese* | 25 | 19 | 21 | $54 |

SoHo | 119 Sullivan St. (bet. Prince & Spring Sts.) | 212-343-0404
Park Slope | 278 Fifth Ave. (bet. 1st St. & Garfield Pl.) | Brooklyn |
718-840-0408
www.blueribbonrestaurants.com

Surmounting the "summits" for sushi "verging on sublime", this SoHo–Park Slope pair purveys "exquisite" cuts of "mind-blowing" fish so "fresh" they "apparently swim to the plate"; the "Zen" "grotto" surroundings, "pleasant" service and "excellent sakes" are "soothing" enough to offset "top-dollar" tabs, but "go early or late" to "avoid crowds."

Blue Smoke *BBQ* | 22 | 17 | 19 | $41 |

Gramercy | 116 E. 27th St. (bet. Lexington Ave. & Park Ave. S.) |
212-447-7733 | www.bluesmoke.com

To "scratch the itch" for "pit BBQ", scoot over to this saucy Gramercy smokehouse and "pig out" on "meaty", "melt-in-your-mouth" ribs and "must-have" sides; sticklers say the "city-esque" setup sends a "mixed message", but it "holds its own" at "legit prices"; P.S. "sweet jazz" "beckons" in the club downstairs.

	FOOD	DECOR	SERVICE	COST

Z Blue Water Grill ● *Seafood*   23 | 22 | 21 | $53

Union Sq | 31 Union Sq. W. (16th St.) | 212-675-9500 |
www.brguestrestaurants.com

A "felicitous" island of "city chic", Steve Hanson's "Union Square anchor" serves "top-shelf" seafood in a "glossy" marble-clad "converted bank" boasting a "great veranda" and "jazz combo" sets downstairs; thanks to its "social" atmosphere and "excellent brunch", it's one of NYC's most popular, and though "too friggin' loud", at least it's "never dull."

Boathouse *American*   16 | 25 | 16 | $52

E 70s | Central Park | Central Park Lake, enter on E. 72nd St. (Central Park Dr. N.) | 212-517-2233 |
www.thecentralparkboathouse.com

Like "dining in a postcard", Central Park's "enchanted" "pond-side" New American is "one of a kind" for "bucolic" tranquility and romance; the "marginal food" and "so-so service" stir sinking sensations at "this price point", but the "great escape" "is its own reward."

Bobby Van's Grill ● Z *Steak*   22 | 19 | 21 | $64

W 50s | 135 W. 50th St. (bet. 6th & 7th Aves.) | 212-957-5050

Bobby Van's Steakhouse *Steak*

E 40s | 230 Park Ave. (46th St.) | 212-867-5490 Z
E 50s | 131 E. 54th St. (bet. Lexington & Park Aves.) |
212-207-8050
Financial District | 25 Broad St. (Exchange Pl.) | 212-344-8463 Z
www.bobbyvans.com

"Meat-and-potatoes" mavens get "just what they want" from these "businessy" "standby" steakhouses, namely "quality cuts" and "solicitous service" in a "typical" "two-martini" milieu; they stay "up to par" with "no surprises" apart from the "intriguing" "bank vault" room at the Downtown outpost.

Boca Chica *Pan-Latin*   20 | 15 | 16 | $29

E Village | 13 First Ave. (1st St.) | 212-473-0108

A "*muy caliente*" draw for "younger" compadres, this "bohemian" East Villager serves "addictive" Pan-Latin "cheap eats" and "deadly" *bebidas*; if the "lines", "noise" and "tight squeeze" don't "drive you loco", it's a "fun" "experience."

Bocca Lupo ● M *Italian*   ▽ 21 | 20 | 19 | $31

Cobble Hill | 391 Henry St. (Warren St.) | Brooklyn | 718-243-2522

"Cool" but "neighborly", this Cobble Hill yearling "works big-time" for locals wolfing down "delicious" "tapas-style" Italian and "wonderful" vinos at "the right price"; its "smart" mix of "industrial" and "family" elements have proven predictably "popular" among Smith Street refugees.

Bocelli *Italian*   ▽ 25 | 23 | 23 | $48

Staten Island | 1250 Hylan Blvd. (bet. Clove & Old Town Rds.) |
718-420-6150 | www.bocellirest.com

Staten Islanders attest this Italian rises "above the usual" given the "high standards" of its cooking and staffers who see that "everyone is treated like family"; eye-catching Tuscan decor and weekend crooners also share the credit for making it "so satisfying."

	FOOD	DECOR	SERVICE	COST

Bogota Latin Bistro *Pan-Latin* — 21 | 19 | 18 | $28

Park Slope | 141 Fifth Ave. (bet. Lincoln & St. Johns Pls.) | Brooklyn | 718-230-3805 | www.bogotabistro.com

"Say *hola*" to the "friendly" "fiesta" feeling at this "winning" Park Slope Pan-Latin, which plies its "refreshing" fare and "delicious drinks" at a "budget-conscious" cost; the "buzzing" premises include a "year-round" patio, and "you never leave hungry or thirsty."

Bôi *Vietnamese* — 19 | 17 | 19 | $38

E 40s | 246 E. 44th St. (bet. 2nd & 3rd Aves.) | 212-681-6541

NEW **Bôi to Go** 🅢🍴 *Vietnamese*

E 40s | 800 Second Ave. (bet. 42nd & 43rd Sts.) | 212-681-1122 www.boi-restaurant.com

"Oh, bôi" enthuse aficionados of the "exotic flavors" at this "minimalist" Midtown Vietnamese, known for the "subtlety" of its "solid" specialties; it generally assembles "the U.N. crowd", and the new take-out venue vends "great sandwiches" that make for a "unique" lunch.

Bolo *Spanish* — 24 | 20 | 21 | $55

Flatiron | 23 E. 22nd St. (bet. B'way & Park Ave. S.) | 212-228-2200 | www.bolorestaurant.com

Fans cheer "*olé*" to Bobby Flay's "colorful" Flatiron Spaniard, which bowls 'em over "year after year" with "memorable" "nouvelle" Iberian cooking matched with well-chosen wines; "attentive staffers" help make it "worth the price tag", though contras contend it's starting to "show its age."

Bombay Palace *Indian* — 18 | 16 | 17 | $41

W 50s | 30 W. 52nd St. (bet. 5th & 6th Aves.) | 212-541-7777 | www.bombay-palace.com

For a "reliable" "fix" of "the Raj", this Midtown Indian "standby" furnishes all the subcontinental "classics" in a "spacious", "unpretentious" setting; evenings boast an "extensive menu", but the best time to go is for the $14.95 lunch buffet spread – "your whole office will be there."

Bombay Talkie *Indian* — 20 | 18 | 16 | $35

Chelsea | 189 Ninth Ave. (bet. 21st & 22nd Sts.) | 212-242-1900

Indian with a "hip" "twist" is the featured attraction at this "neat" Chelsea duplex, serving "imaginative riffs" on "street snacks" against a "Bollywood art" backdrop; while admirers talk up the "delicious" "concept", it bombs with critics who slam the "slackadaisical" staff.

Bond 45 ◗ *Italian* — 20 | 18 | 19 | $50

W 40s | 154 W. 45th St. (bet. 6th & 7th Aves.) | 212-869-4545 | www.bond45.com

"Once a clothing store", this "expansive" Times Square space is now an "accommodating" pseudo–19th century outlet for "plentiful" helpings of "traditional Italian" steak and seafood; although "really loud" and "not exactly the Armani" of its kind, it fits the area to a T.

Bondi Road *Australian* — ∇ 21 | 18 | 20 | $31

LES | 153 Rivington St. (bet. Clinton & Suffolk Sts.) | 212-253-5311 | www.bondiroad.com

You're bound to bond with "friendly" "Oz" expats at this "laid-back", "great-value" LES Australian, "known for fish 'n' chips" and

FOOD DECOR SERVICE COST

"solid" pub grub served in "kitschy" "beach getaway" digs; admirers of the "surfer cool" suggest that you "come for the fish and stay to booze."

Bond Street ◐ *Japanese*   25 | 22 | 19 | $60
NoHo | 6 Bond St. (bet. B'way & Lafayette St.) | 212-777-2500
Still a "hot spot" after recovering from a recent fire, this NoHo Japanese serves "fabulous designer sushi" in "sexy" environs complete with a "dark" downstairs lounge pouring "fancy drinks"; for better or worse, "hipper-than-thou" service and "expensive" tabs are just part of the "scene" that "never misses a beat."

Bonita ◑ *Mexican*   19 | 16 | 17 | $22
NEW **Fort Greene** | 243 DeKalb Ave. (Vanderbilt Ave.) | Brooklyn | 718-622-5300
Williamsburg | 338 Bedford Ave. (bet. S. 2nd & 3rd Sts.) | Brooklyn | 718-384-9500
www.bonitanyc.com
Peso-pinchers "never tire" of the "comforting" "homestyle Mexican" fare at this "down-to-earth" Williamsburg "staple" and its new Fort Greene sibling that's big with "hipster Pratt kids"; "cramped", "no-frills" digs and "so-so" service belie the name, but still the "crowds" keep coming.

Boqueria ◑ *Spanish*   23 | 18 | 19 | $46
Flatiron | 53 W. 19th St. (bet. 5th & 6th Aves.) | 212-255-4160 | www.boquerianyc.com
A "*fantastico*" take on Barcelona's tapas "tradition", this "energetic", "minimal"-size Flatiron fandango can get "crazy busy"; service "glitches" and tabs that tend to "creep up" on you do nothing to reduce the "ridiculous waits" that arise from its "no-reservations policy."

Borgo Antico ◑ *Italian*   19 | 17 | 20 | $41
G Village | 22 E. 13th St. (bet. 5th Ave. & University Pl.) | 212-807-1313 | www.borgoanticony.com
Don't expect fireworks at this Village Italian "sleeper", however, it's an "amenable" option with "serviceable" food, "comfortable" "rustic" surroundings and "capable service"; in sum, it "satisfies" at a "moderate" cost – "if you're in the neighborhood."

NEW Borough Food & Drink ◑ *American*   – | – | – | M
Flatiron | 12 E. 22nd St. (bet. B'way & Park Ave. S.) | 212-260-0103 | www.chinagrillmgt.com
A collaboration of Zak Pelaccio (Fatty Crab) and Jeffrey Chodorow (China Grill), this new Flatironer celebrates old NY via a nostalgic American menu covering everything from fried chicken to herring and sausage plates, all via local purveyors; the space resembles a rural country store, albeit one packed with noisy city slickers.

Bottega del Vino *Italian*   22 | 20 | 20 | $62
E 50s | 7 E. 59th St. (bet. 5th & Madison Aves.) | 212-223-3028 | www.bottegadelvinonyc.com
Known for its vino list running to "biblical" length, this Midtown Italian wine bar is a "very Euro" "hideaway" for "excellent" pastas served amid "Tirolean decor"; the "jet-set" vibe is worthy of its Veronese parent, as is the "platinum-card" pricing.

	FOOD	DECOR	SERVICE	COST

Bottino *Italian* — 19 | 18 | 17 | $44

Chelsea | 246 10th Ave. (bet. 24th & 25th Sts.) | 212-206-6766 |
www.bottinonyc.com

To take a "break from gallery-hopping", try this West Chelsea "art
world" "mainstay", serving "fine" Tuscan bites in a "modern" space
with a "fantastic back garden"; it's an area "best bet" even if some say
there's "too much attitude" on exhibit.

Bouchon Bakery *American/French* — 23 | 13 | 17 | $28

W 60s | Time Warner Ctr. | 10 Columbus Circle, 3rd fl. (60th St. at B'way) |
212-823-9366 | www.bouchonbakery.com

Thomas Keller's "magic touches" lend a New American accent to
French classics at this "elegant" cafe/patisserie specializing in "high-
end" sandwiches and "exquisite pastries"; despite the "hectic" "mall setting" and "lackluster service", the majority deems it a "legitimate treat."

Bouillabaisse 126 *French* — 22 | 16 | 17 | $40

Carroll Gardens | 126 Union St. (bet. Columbia & Hicks Sts.) | Brooklyn |
718-855-4405 | www.bouillabaisse126.com

The name and owners have changed, but the "rich" "signature dish"
remains a "must-try" at this Carroll Gardens joint, where "interesting"
West African influences now add to the French menu; a "homey" interior
and "charming garden" complement its "tastefully" "simple" style.

☑ Bouley ❿ *French* — 28 | 26 | 27 | $94

TriBeCa | 120 W. Broadway (Duane St.) | 212-964-2525 |
www.davidbouley.com

David Bouley's TriBeCa "mecca" "never ceases to amaze", carrying
"class" to an "exemplary level" with "stunning" New French cuisine
and "dazzling" but "unstuffy service"; the "opulent" space's "vaulted
ceilings" and "soothing" lighting impart a "sense of contentment" that
"memories are made of"; no, it's "not cheap"; N.B. watch for a 2008
move to gorgeous new digs down the block.

☑ Bouley, Upstairs *Eclectic* — 26 | 17 | 20 | $46

TriBeCa | Bouley Bakery & Mkt. | 130 W. Broadway, 2nd fl. (Duane St.) |
212-608-5829 | www.davidbouley.com

David Bouley lets "his hair down" at this "lively", "informal" TriBeCan
showcasing "impeccable" "open-kitchen" Eclectic "flights of fancy"
paired with "phenomenal sushi"; "it's a terrific deal" to boot, but given
the "tiny" space and "no-rez policy", the word is "come early or wait."

Brasserie ❿ *French* — 20 | 22 | 19 | $51

E 50s | 100 E. 53rd St. (bet. Lexington & Park Aves.) | 212-751-4840 |
www.rapatina.com

A "way cool" "futuristic" layout is the backdrop for this East Midtown
French brasserie that attracts the "business" set from breakfast
through late dinner; while "the 'wow' factor" and "hopping" bar scene
can "dazzle", there are "few surprises" by way of food or service.

Brasserie 8½ *French* — 22 | 24 | 22 | $56

W 50s | 9 W. 57th St. (bet. 5th & 6th Aves.) | 212-829-0812 |
www.brasserie812.com

The "sweeping staircase" into this "submerged" Midtown brasserie is
an "impressive" lead-in to "ambitious" French cooking that "lives up to

the promise" of the "spacious, chic" setting; "service is also first rate" rendering the "upscale experience" far more than half "inviting."

Brasserie Julien French

19	20	17	$44

E 80s | 1422 Third Ave. (bet. 80th & 81st Sts.) | 212-744-6327 | www.brasseriejulien.com

Yorkville denizens indulge "their inner Francophiles" at this "reliable" provider of "decent" French fare and a "funky art deco" mise-en-scène, with a "warm" vibe and "live jazz on weekends", it's ideal for a date.

Brasserie Ruhlmann French

17	21	18	$52

W 50s | 45 Rockefeller Plaza (enter on 50th St., bet. 5th & 6th Aves.) | 212-974-2020 | www.brasserieruhlmann.com

With a "striking" "deco interior", this "elegant" French brasserie offers "agreeable business" dining on "prime Rock Center" turf; though the "just fair" food and "spotty" service stir skepticism, fans feel it's "finding its way" since Laurent Tourondel took charge.

Bravo Gianni ● Italian

23	13	21	$63

E 60s | 230 E. 63rd St. (bet. 2nd & 3rd Aves.) | 212-752-7272

Ultra-"personable" chef-owner Gianni Garavelli leads a "capable staff" at this UES "mainstay", which still earns ovations for its "outstanding" Northern Italian food and "unpressured" vibe; the "dated decor" "needs work", but regulars might as well be "royalty here."

Bread Tribeca Italian

19	16	16	$38

TriBeCa | 301 Church St. (Walker St.) | 212-334-8282 | www.breadtribeca.com

Bread ● Sandwiches

NoLita | 20 Spring St. (bet. Elizabeth & Mott Sts.) | 212-334-1015

However you slice it, this "casual" TriBeCan is a "decent nosh stop" offering "fresh" "sandwich lunches" and "solid" "home-cooked" Italian fare for "reasonable" dough; "bustling" "young" clients keep the "minimalist" setting "crowded" and the staff often "overwhelmed"; N.B. there's a smaller, separately operated affiliate in NoLita.

Breeze French/Thai

▽ 20	15	16	$33

W 40s | 661 Ninth Ave. (bet. 45th & 46th Sts.) | 212-262-7777 | www.breezenyc.com

A "quick" crew dishes out the "tasty" Thai-French fusion fare at this modern Hell's Kitchen storefront; it can be "loud with music and videos" and looks "dinerlike", but for such "a good value" no one seems to mind.

Brennan & Carr ●⇄ Sandwiches

19	10	15	$17

Sheepshead Bay | 3432 Nostrand Ave. (Ave. U) | Brooklyn | 718-646-9559

This "long-lived institution" in Sheepshead Bay still "hits the spot" with au jus-"soaked" roast beef sandwiches that require "a ton of napkins" but not too many dollars; the "dingy" digs "haven't changed" in decades (ditto the servers), but you'll be too busy mopping up the "juice running down your chin" to notice.

NEW brgr Hamburgers

18	14	14	$16

Chelsea | 287 Seventh Ave. (bet. 26th & 27th Sts.) | 212-488-7500 | www.brgr.us

The idea is to "create your own" beef, turkey or veggie burger, or pick from a host of other "inventive combos" at this new David Rockwell-designed Chelsea patty palace; "great fries and shakes" round out the "McDonald's for grown-ups" menu, though surveyors say it's "slightly overpriced" and "disorganized."

Bricco *Italian*

19 | 17 | 18 | $44

W 50s | 304 W. 56th St. (bet. 8th & 9th Aves.) | 212-245-7160 | www.bricconyc.com

"Warm and inviting", this "reliable", "fair-priced" Hell's Kitchen Italian works equally well for "business lunches" or "romantic dinners"; while brick-oven pizza is the menu "standout", fans also tout the "attentive yet unobtrusive" service.

Brick Cafe *French/Italian*

20 | 21 | 18 | $31

Astoria | 30-95 33rd St. (31st Ave.) | Queens | 718-267-2735 | www.brickcafe.com

Patrons of this Astoria Franco-Italian bistro enthuse over its "cozy", "rustic" interior in the winter and "outdoor seating fabulous for people-watching" in summer; "quality" food for a "very fair price" and a "staff that works hard to please" make this a "local favorite."

Bridge Cafe *American*

22 | 18 | 21 | $44

Financial District | 279 Water St. (Dover St.) | 212-227-3344

For a "truly old NY" experience, "seek out" this circa-1794 brick-walled tavern "under the Brooklyn Bridge"; besides the "excellent" New American menu, the "warm" staff does its best to be sure "you'll leave happy."

Brio *Italian*

18 | 14 | 17 | $40

E 60s | 137 E. 61st St. (Lexington Ave.) | 212-980-2300 | www.brionyc.com

"Convenient to Bloomingdale's", this Italian is an "easy lunch" stop for shoppers seeking inexpensive, "delicious" pastas or thin-crust pizzas; however, "uncomfortable seating" and "too-modern" decor have regulars saying it was "better before" the last renovation.

Brioso *Italian*

▽ 25 | 20 | 23 | $45

Staten Island | 174 New Dorp Ln. (9th St.) | 718-667-1700 | www.briosoristorante.com

"Excellent food, excellent service" give the brio to the DiMaggio brothers' Italian ristorante on Staten Island; while the "elegant" space can get "crowded and noisy" at peak hours, it's a "wonderful" dining experience overall, particularly "for the money."

Brooklyn Diner USA ● *Diner*

17 | 15 | 16 | $31

NEW **W 40s** | 155 W. 43rd St. (bet. B'way & 6th Ave.) | 212-265-5400
W 50s | 212 W. 57th St. (bet. B'way & 7th Ave.) | 212-977-2280
www.brooklyndiner.com

Shelly Fireman's Midtown "re-creations of the city's diners of old" serve up "enormous portions" of American "comfort food" that are "worth a week of dieting"; they're also a "good value", which accounts for all of those "tourists" and "real NYers" who "crowd" in.

Brooklyn Fish Camp *Seafood*

23 | 14 | 19 | $40

Park Slope | 162 Fifth Ave. (Degraw St.) | Brooklyn | 718-783-3264 | www.brooklynfishcamp.com

Mary Redding's Park Slope seafooder reels 'em in with "wonderful, fresh fish dishes" (including a famously "fabulous lobster roll") and "attentive, friendly" service; less happy campers crab about slightly "pricey" tabs and "bland" decor – unless you "eat out in the lovely garden."

Brother Jimmy's BBQ *BBQ* `16` `10` `14` `$23`

E 40s | Grand Central | lower level (42nd St. & Vanderbilt Ave.) | 212-661-4022
E 70s | 1485 Second Ave. (bet. 77th & 78th Sts.) | 212-288-0999 ◗
E 90s | 1644 Third Ave. (92nd St.) | 212-426-2020 ◗
NEW **Garment District** | 416 Eighth Ave. (31st St.) | 212-967-7603 ◗
W 80s | 428 Amsterdam Ave. (bet. 80th & 81st Sts.) | 212-501-7515 ◗
www.brotherjimmys.com
Basically a "big frat party", this low-budget "Southern-themed" BBQ quintet draws recent "college grads" with "cheap drinks" and "good grub" served by "scantily clad coed" types; while "family-friendly in the early evening", these joints get "rowdy" fast – luckily there's "delivery."

Brown Café *American* ▽ `25` `19` `19` `$27`

LES | 61 Hester St. (bet. Essex & Ludlow Sts.) | 212-477-2427
The "simple, delicious" American menu crafted from "top-notch" ingredients plus a "stellar brunch" draw a "relaxed twenty- and thirtysomething" crowd to this "delightful" Lower Eastsider; the "homey" vibe and "modest cost" make it "worth the wait" for a seat in the "little" available space.

Bruckner Bar & Grill ◗ *American* ▽ `21` `18` `17` `$21`

Bronx | 1 Bruckner Blvd. (3rd Ave.) | 718-665-2001 | www.brucknerbar.com
This "gritty" Mott Haven "beer and a burger joint" plays host to SoBro "artists" chowing down on "surprisingly good", "bargain"-priced American eats; weekly poetry readings, live music and a billiards table are a plus in an area where there's "not much around" yet.

Bryant Park Grill/Cafe *American* `17` `21` `17` `$45`

W 40s | behind NY Public Library | 25 W. 40th St. (bet. 5th & 6th Aves.) | 212-840-6500 | www.arkrestaurants.com
It's all about the "great location" at this "Midtown oasis" where on "sunny days" most "go for drinks" after work at the alfresco Cafe, and in winter sit "by a window" in the Grill's "pretty" dining room; just keep in mind it's really the "lovely setting" that "you're paying for" – the "so-so" American fare's "forgettable."

B. Smith's Restaurant Row *Southern* `19` `19` `18` `$46`

W 40s | 320 W. 46th St. (bet. 8th & 9th Aves.) | 212-315-1100 | www.bsmith.com
Theatergoing diners and "tourists" alike appreciate TV personality Barbara Smith's "upscale take" on "down-home" Southern food, calling her "feel-good" fixture on Restaurant Row "uniformly fine"; still, the sentiment isn't unanimous – a few find it "gimmicky" and "not what it once was."

Bubba Gump Shrimp Co. ◗ *American/Seafood* `14` `16` `17` `$29`

W 40s | 1501 Broadway (bet. 43rd & 44th Sts.) | 212-391-7100 | www.bubbagump.com
"Sure, it's a tourist trap", but this Times Square theme joint can be "really fun" and offers "delicious shrimp" cooked every which way; no surprise, there's "lots of Forrest Gump memorabilia" around, but

	FOOD	DECOR	SERVICE	COST

Forrest's quote, 'life's like a box of chocolates, you never know what you are going to get', could easily apply here.

Bubby's *American* | 18 | 14 | 14 | $28 |

TriBeCa | 120 Hudson St. (N. Moore St.) | 212-219-0666
Dumbo | 1 Main St. (bet. Plymouth & Water Sts.) | Brooklyn | 718-222-0666 Ⓜ
www.bubbys.com

You'd better "bring an appetite" for the "huge portions" of American "down-home cooking" at these underdecorated TriBeCa and Dumbo neighborhood havens; they're best known for their "fantastic brunch", but beware – it's "popular" with the "stroller set", so expect "kids everywhere" along with "long lines" and a little "attitude."

☑ Buddakan ❶ *Asian Fusion* | 23 | 27 | 21 | $62 |

Chelsea | 75 Ninth Ave. (16th St.) | 212-989-6699 |
www.buddakannyc.com

Stephen Starr's "awe-inspiring" Chelsea "spectacle" "lives up to the hype" with a "bold, beautiful" space "like a movie set" and an equally appealing "young, chic" customer base, and the "feast for the eyes" is nearly matched by the "delicious", "pricey" Asian fusion fare; as "everyone" wants to "eat here" it gets "way crowded" and "loud", so "go early" if you want to avoid the "zoo."

☑ Buddha Bar ❶ *Asian Fusion* | 19 | 26 | 17 | $60 |

Meatpacking | 25 Little W. 12th St. (bet. 9th Ave. & Washington St.) | 212-647-7314 | www.buddhabarnyc.com

"Wow" – this "cavernous" Meatpacking "club du jour's" "Disney-like" interior is a "must-see", with "jaw-dropping" features like a "giant" 17-ft. Buddha, semi-private pagodas, koi ponds and "amazing" jelly-fish–filled aquariums; the Asian fusion fare is "surprisingly decent" – "if you ever get it" – but as the "everything big" approach includes the bill, it may be better "for a drink and a gander."

Buenos Aires ❶ *Argentinean* | 21 | 15 | 19 | $37 |

E Village | 513 E. Sixth St. (bet. Aves. A & B) | 212-228-2775

Operating in a "small, crowded" East Village space, this "down-to-earth" "taste of Argentina" purveys "delicious" steaks, empanadas and well-selected wines for "prices almost as affordable as Buenos Aires"; the atmosphere stays "lively" despite service on "Argentinean time."

Bukhara Grill *Indian* | 20 | 15 | 18 | $36 |

E 40s | 217 E. 49th St. (bet. 2nd & 3rd Aves.) | 212-888-2839 |
www.bukharany.com

Midtowners keep cumin to this "authentic" Indian serving "excellent tandoori" dishes and other well-priced, "dependable" fare, including a $13.95 lunch buffet; the "tranquil" atmosphere is abetted by a "charming" second-floor terrace and "pleasant" service.

Bull and Bear ❶ *Steak* | 19 | 20 | 19 | $58 |

E 40s | Waldorf-Astoria | 570 Lexington Ave. (49th St.) | 212-872-4900 |
www.waldorfastoria.com

"Clubby" and "masculine", this Waldorf-Astoria "throwback" evokes "old NY" and attracts "power-lunchers" with "hearty he-man steaks" and "excellent cocktails"; "attentive" service rounds out the experience, just "hope it's a bull market when paying the bill."

| | FOOD | DECOR | SERVICE | COST |

Bull Run *American*   18 | 16 | 17 | $45

Financial District | Club Quarters Hotel | 52 William St. (Pine St.) | 212-859-2200 | www.bullrunwallstreet.com

A "calm spot" in the Financial District, this New American is "full of suits" for lunch or after-market drinks; "ho-hum" decor and "reliable", if "unspectacular", fare at "Wall Street prices" mean it might not do such bullish business elsewhere.

Burger Heaven *Hamburgers*   16 | 8 | 14 | $18

E 40s | 20 E. 49th St. (bet. 5th & Madison Aves.) | 212-755-2166
E 40s | 291 Madison Ave. (bet. 40th & 41st Sts.) | 212-685-6250
E 50s | 536 Madison Ave. (bet. 54th & 55th Sts.) | 212-753-4214
E 50s | 9 E. 53rd St. (bet. 5th & Madison Aves.) | 212-752-0340
E 60s | 804 Lexington Ave. (62nd St.) | 212-838-3580
E 80s | 1534 Third Ave. (bet. 86th & 87th Sts.) | 212-722-8292
www.burgerheaven.com

When "busy NY" needs a "boigah" "in a hurry" there's this "reliable" "local" chain of "coffee shop–style" joints serving "juicy" patties and other "diner basics"; it's "not much in decor or service" but you get "great bang for your buck" and it's still "a cut above" most other fast-fooders.

burger joint at   24 | 9 | 11 | $14
Le Parker Meridien ●⊄ *Hamburgers*

W 50s | Le Parker Meridien | 119 W. 56th St. (bet. 6th & 7th Aves.) | 212-708-7414 | www.newyork.lemeridien.com

"Don't let the line scare you" off this "hole-in-the-wall" hamburger "heaven" "behind the curtain" in an "upscale hotel" lobby; many argue that the "amazing" grilled patties here are "among the best in NYC", but the waits for one of its "handful" of seats mean most Midtowners will never know.

Burritoville *Tex-Mex*   16 | 7 | 12 | $12

E 40s | 152 E. 43rd St. (bet. Lexington & 3rd Aves.) | 212-880-8300 🆉
E 50s | 866 Third Ave. (52nd St.) | 212-980-4111
E 70s | 1487 Second Ave. (bet. 77th & 78th Sts.) | 212-472-8800 ●
E Village | 141 Second Ave. (bet. 8th & 9th Aves.) | 212-260-3300 ●
Financial District | 80 Nassau St. (bet. Fulton & John Sts.) | 212-285-0070
Garment District | 352 W. 39th St. (9th Ave.) | 212-563-9088
TriBeCa | 116 Chambers St. (Church St.) | 212-566-2300
W 40s | 625 Ninth Ave. (44th St.) | 212-333-5352 ●
W 70s | 166 W. 72nd St. (bet. Amsterdam & Columbus Aves.) | 212-580-7700 ●
W Village | 298 Bleecker St. (7th Ave. S.) | 212-633-9249
www.burritoville.com
Additional locations throughout the NY area

"Huge burritos at a cheap price" draw the "super hungry" to this "addictive" Tex-Mex chain where "fresh ingredients" and "amazing vegetarian choices" mean you can actually eat "hearty" and "healthy" simultaneously; if you'd rather pass on the "no-frills" eat-in experience, they "deliver a second after you hang up the phone."

Butai *Japanese*   ▽ 22 | 21 | 18 | $44

Gramercy | 115 E. 18th St. (bet. Irving Pl. & Park Ave. S.) | 212-387-8885 | www.butai.us

Winning "kudos" for its midpriced Japanese robata dishes, this "Gramercy gem" is also praised for its "calming" "loungelike" space;

portions may be "small", but the "helpful, friendly staff keeps the plates coming", leaving fans wondering "why this place is often empty."

Butter ●🗷 American | 19 | 23 | 19 | $56 |

E Village | 415 Lafayette St. (bet. Astor Pl. & 4th St.) | 212-253-2828 | www.butterrestaurant.com

While the New American "food is pretty good" at this bi-level East Villager, it's the "stylish" "sexy" vibe that butters up its "hip, pretty" crowd; if the place slips up, most fault staff "attitude" and "high prices."

Cabana ● Nuevo Latino | 21 | 18 | 17 | $35 |

E 60s | 1022 Third Ave. (bet. 60th & 61st Sts.) | 212-980-5678
Seaport | Pier 17 | 89 South St. (Fulton St.) | 212-406-1155
Forest Hills | 107-10 70th Rd. (bet. Austin St. & Queens Blvd.) | Queens | 718-263-3600
www.cabanarestaurant.com

"Always a fiesta", these "hopping" Cuban "hot spots" host "upbeat" crowds downing "delicious mojitos" and "full-flavored" Nuevo Latino fare; "pleasant" but "slow" service and "long waits" are part of the deal; P.S. the Seaport location offers a lovely "view of the water."

Cacio e Pepe Italian | 22 | 17 | 21 | $40 |

E Village | 182 Second Ave. (bet. 11th & 12th Sts.) | 212-505-5931 | www.cacioepepe.com

Those "addicted" to the namesake dish and other "creative", "fresh" offerings at this East Village "taste of Rome" also tout the "warm, genuine" service and moderate "price point"; it gets even better "in warm weather" when the "enchanting garden" is an option.

NEW Cacio e Vino ● Italian | ▽ 21 | 18 | 20 | $33 |

E Village | 80 Second Ave. (bet. 4th & 5th Sts.) | 212-228-3269 | www.cacioevino.com

From the Cacio e Pepe folks, this convivial East Village Sicilian *spuntino* specializes in pizzas from a wood-fired oven; besides being inexpensive, the menu reflects an artisan's pride; N.B. it's currently BYO.

NEW Cafe & Wine Room, A 🎹 Caribbean/French | - | - | - | I |

W 100s | 973 Columbus Ave. (bet. 107th & 108th Sts.) | 212-222-2033

Formerly called 'A', this bite-size Morningside Heights French-Caribbean has changed its name and moved a block north to slightly roomier digs (28 seats); its tiny kitchen turns out the same hearty menu of affordable, organic dishes and the BYO policy remains, but plans are afoot to start selling wine as well.

Cafe Asean ⊞ SE Asian | 21 | 13 | 18 | $26 |

G Village | 117 W. 10th St. (bet. Greenwich & 6th Aves.) | 212-633-0348

A "panoply" of "perfectly spiced" Southeast Asian fare is served by "sweet" staffers at this "bargain" Villager; inside, the "funky" digs are "cute but cramped", but in season the "tranquil refuge" of a patio "adds charm" to the experience

Cafe Bar ● Greek/Mediterranean | ▽ 20 | 20 | 17 | $21 |

Astoria | 32-90 36th St. (34th Ave.) | Queens | 718-204-5273

Part "coffeehouse", part "bar/lounge", this Astoria Greek-Med is a "comfy" local "hangout" with "mismatched" "'60s and '70s" furniture, big-screen TVs and free WiFi; though "hipsters" hail the "simple" budget eats and "outdoor dining", for most it's about the "fun" scene.

Ⓩ Café Boulud French
27 | 23 | 26 | $79

E 70s | Surrey Hotel | 20 E. 76th St. (bet. 5th & Madison Aves.) | 212-772-2600 | www.danielnyc.com

Dining is "bliss" at "Daniel's Uptown sibling", where the "superb experiences" are "less formal" and less costly (if still "not cheap") than at the flagship; a "chic" UES clientele "savors each bite" of its "innovative" French fare served in "simple, elegant" environs by "pampering" pro staffers; P.S. lunch is a particularly "good buy."

Cafe Centro 🅂 Mediterranean
20 | 18 | 19 | $46

E 40s | MetLife Bldg. | 200 Park Ave. (45th St.) | 212-818-1222 | www.patinagroup.com

"Meeting a need" just "steps from Grand Central", this midpriced purveyor of "surprisingly good" Med fare makes a "smart choice for a business lunch" or bite before "catching the train"; "quick service" and a "prime" location mean it's always "jumping", though less so at dinner.

Cafecito 🍴 Cuban
21 | 14 | 17 | $24

E Village | 185 Ave. C (bet. 11th & 12th Sts.) | 212-253-9966

A slice of "Little Havana" on Avenue C, this "funky" East Village Cuban dishes up *muy bueno* eats plus mojitos that "rock"; on weekends there's "a hell of a line" and "tight seating" too, but amigos come for the "amazing value."

NEW Cafe Cluny ◗ American/French
19 | 18 | 18 | $50

W Village | 284 W. 12th St. (W. 4th St.) | 212-255-6900

West Villagers are "coming in droves" to this "adorable" newcomer done up in modern "country cottage" chic; "cheery service" and "delicious" (if "not adventurous") Franco-American fare are two reasons it's "so popular", though a puzzled few still wonder "what the hype's about."

Cafe Colonial Brazilian
▽ 20 | 15 | 14 | $27

NoLita | 276 Elizabeth St. (Houston St.) | 212-274-0044 | www.cafecolonialny.com

It's been a local "favorite for years", and this NoLita Brazilian still "keeps it interesting" with a "something-for-everyone" menu and "dilapidated-chic" aesthetic; it's particularly popular at "breakfast and brunch", when devotees "brave the lines" and iffy service for "tasty" "hangover cures."

Cafe Con Leche Cuban/Dominican
18 | 11 | 16 | $23

W 80s | 424 Amsterdam Ave. (bet. 80th & 81st Sts.) | 212-595-7000
W 90s | 726 Amsterdam Ave. (bet. 95th & 96th Sts.) | 212-678-7000

"Ample-size breakfasts for economy-size" budgets are the big draws at these "crowded" UWS Cuban-Dominicans known for the "eponymous beverage"; however, "don't-look" interiors and an "air of chaos" have many opting for "convenient takeout."

Café d'Alsace ◗ French
21 | 18 | 17 | $47

E 80s | 1695 Second Ave. (88th St.) | 212-722-5133 | www.cafedalsace.com

Upper Eastsiders "love" this "bustling" French brasserie's "you're-in-France" feel and "delicious, hearty" Alsace specialties supplemented by a 500-strong suds selection supervised by a "beer sommelier"; its "popularity" leads to "rushed" service and "crowded", "noisy" conditions – though you can escape to the "outdoor seats."

Café de Bruxelles ● *Belgian*

21 | 15 | 18 | $41

W Village | 118 Greenwich Ave. (13th St.) | 212-206-1830

"If you want to feel like a Villager, eat at the bar" of this "gracious" Belgian "standby" where the "fabulous" moules frites and trappist beers go down well in "old Europe"–like digs; if trendoids find the vibe "staid", loyalists insist it has "charm" aplenty.

⚡ Café des Artistes ● *French*

22 | 26 | 23 | $69

W 60s | 1 W. 67th St. (bet. Columbus Ave. & CPW) | 212-877-3500 | www.cafenyc.com

George and Jenifer Lang's "NY icon" near Lincoln Center is "still one of the most beautiful, romantic places to dine" thanks to a space resplendent with "fresh flowers" and Howard Chandler Christy's "magical" "murals of nubile nymphs"; add "outstanding" French fare and "gracious" service, and it's "a superb evening every time" – "perfect for 'marry me' or "I'm sorry!'"; N.B. dinner only, except for brunch on weekends.

Café du Soleil *French/Mediterranean*

19 | 17 | 14 | $38

W 100s | 2723 Broadway (104th St.) | 212-316-5000

"Cheerful" and "sunny" as its name, this French-Med is "always full" thanks to "solid" bistro eats, sidewalk seats, proximity to Columbia and "value" specials; "amateur-hour" service is the only real storm cloud.

Café Español ● *Spanish*

20 | 14 | 19 | $32

G Village | 172 Bleecker St. (bet. MacDougal & Sullivan Sts.) | 212-505-0657 | www.cafeespanol.com

G Village | 78 Carmine St. (bet. Bedford St. & 7th Ave. S.) | 212-675-3312

You "feel like you're in España", particularly after a few pitchers of sangria, at these separately owned Village Spaniards purveying "tasty tapas" and "terrific paella"; "affordable" prices (especially the Monday lobster deal), "friendly service" and outside seating keep locals loyal.

Café Evergreen *Chinese*

20 | 13 | 18 | $32

E 60s | 1288 First Ave. (bet. 69th & 70th Sts.) | 212-744-3266

Saving Eastsiders a "trek to Chinatown", this Cantonese "godsend" is most appreciated for its "super dim sum" and surprisingly "extensive wine list"; "attentive service" enhances the dining here, though its dining room does the opposite.

Cafe Fiorello ● *Italian*

20 | 16 | 18 | $48

W 60s | 1900 Broadway (bet. 63rd & 64th Sts.) | 212-595-5330 | www.cafefiorello.com

"Lincoln Center–goers" laud this across-the-street Italian for its "outstanding antipasto bar" and "thin-crust pizza"; it can be a "squeeze" pre-"curtain", but "pro waiters" will "get you to your performance on time"; P.S. the sidewalk seats are "the best in the house."

Café Frida *Mexican*

19 | 16 | 16 | $38

W 70s | 368 Columbus Ave. (bet. 77th & 78th Sts.) | 212-712-2929 | www.cafefrida.com

"Terrific guac" stars at this "lively" UWS "hacienda" whose "awesome margaritas" and "gourmet Mexican" go for not too many pesos; it gets "loud" and service is "lackluster", but casanovas claim its "sexy", "dark" digs make an ideal "place to close" a deal.

NEW Cafe Fuego ❶ *Pan-Latin*   ▽ 19 | 18 | 17 | $28

E Village | 9 St. Marks Pl. (bet. 2nd & 3rd Aves.) | 212-677-7300 | www.cafefuego.com

Providing a respite "from the hustle and bustle of St. Marks", this East Village yearling is perfect for a "chill night" given its "flavorful" Pan-Latin fare dished up in cozy, "well-lit" digs; there's also a speakeasy-esque bar/lounge area, plus patio seating in warmer months.

Cafe Gitane ❶⊄ *French/Moroccan*   20 | 17 | 16 | $25

NoLita | 242 Mott St. (Prince St.) | 212-334-9552

It's worth paying "just to people-watch" at this Morocco-meets-Paris NoLita "hipster", where the "sunglasses-sporting" "Euro" "eye candy" is just as "delicious" as the "cheap" eats; if you'd rather skip the "constantly hopping" "scene", hit the take-out window instead.

⧖ Café Gray *French*   25 | 24 | 24 | $82

W 60s | Time Warner Ctr. | 10 Columbus Circle, 3rd fl. (60th St. at B'way) | 212-823-6338 | www.cafegray.com

Gray Kunz's Asian-accented French brasserie in the Time Warner Center is voted an all-around "wonderful experience" from the "palate-pleasing" cuisine and "spectacular wine list" to the "smooth" service; debate continues over David Rockwell's "glitzy" decor and the decision to "place the kitchen between diners and the view", but then "who looks out the window" with such "gorgeous food" on your plate?; P.S. it's a shame they "stopped lunch service", because dinner tabs tip to the "high-end."

Café Habana ❶ *Cuban/Mexican*   22 | 13 | 15 | $24

NoLita | 17 Prince St. (Elizabeth St.) | 212-625-2001

NEW Habana Outpost ⊄ *Cuban/Mexican*

Fort Greene | 755-757 Fulton St. (S. Portland Ave.) | Brooklyn | 718-858-9500

www.ecoeatery.com

"It's easier to get into Cuba" than into this "tiny", "bursting-at-the-seams" NoLita "scenester", so you'd better "be willing to wait" for the "cheap", *"delicioso"* Cuban-Mexican dishes and drinks; if "ditsy" service and "cramped", "dingy" digs annoy, there's always the "next-door" take-out annex, not to mention the eco-conscious Fort Greene branch.

Cafe Joul *French*   18 | 13 | 17 | $44

E 50s | 1070 First Ave. (bet. 58th & 59th Sts.) | 212-759-3131

Just "what a bistro should be" say Sutton Place denizens of this "nothing-fancy" French "find"; the pricing gets mixed reactions ("affordable" vs. "expensive for what it is") but still most feel lucky to have such a "pleasant, reliable" neighbor.

Cafe Lalo ❶⊄ *Coffeehouse/Dessert*   19 | 19 | 13 | $20

W 80s | 201 W. 83rd St. (bet. Amsterdam Ave. & B'way) | 212-496-6031 | www.cafelalo.com

"Take a date" and try not to "drool" over the "sinful sweets" at this UWS "dessert staple"/"faux Parisian" cafe made famous (and "touristy") by *You've Got Mail*; there are "cheery lights in the trees outside", but once you're inside the "cramped" seating and "flaky" service aren't so charming.

Cafe Loup ● *French*

18 | 16 | 19 | $43

G Village | 105 W. 13th St. (bet. 6th Ave. & 7th Ave. S.) | 212-255-4746
Village folks "love" this "neighborhood staple" for its "hearty", "reasonable" French bistro fare, "no-rush" vibe and "convivial" service; though it's "showing signs of wear", "happy patrons" say its "cozy" room "feels like home."

Cafe Luluc ●⇼ *French*

20 | 16 | 16 | $27

Cobble Hill | 214 Smith St. (Baltic St.) | Brooklyn | 718-625-3815
"*Très bon*" "basic" French bistro fare for half what you'd pay "on the other side of the river" endears "locals" to this "hip" Cobble Hiller; despite "modest" decor and a "cash-only" policy, it's "popular" enough to make it "hard to get a table" – though at least there's a "lovely" garden in which to "wait."

Cafe Luxembourg ● *French*

20 | 18 | 19 | $50

W 70s | 200 W. 70th St. (bet. Amsterdam & West End Aves.) | 212-873-7411
"Still going strong" since 1982, this "timeless" UWS French bistro is always "jam-packed" with a "good-looking crowd" (including the occasional "celeb"); the "scene" gets "noisy", but *c'est la vie* – it's "perfect before or after Lincoln Center."

Cafe Mogador ● *Moroccan*

21 | 16 | 17 | $27

E Village | 101 St. Marks Pl. (bet. Ave. A & 1st Ave.) | 212-677-2226 | www.cafemogador.com
A "neighborhood favorite" for almost 25 years thanks to its "cheap", "delectable" Moroccan tagines and other classics, this East Villager has the locals "leaving full and happy"; despite "pretty lax" service, the overall "warm", "laid-back" vibe keeps it "packed."

Café Pierre *Continental/French*

23 | 25 | 24 | $69

E 60s | Pierre Hotel | 2 E. 61st St. (5th Ave.) | 212-940-8195
An "elegant" "retreat" from Midtown's "hustle and bustle", this Pierre Hotel "stalwart" offers "old-fashioned luxury" to "old-money" types with its "excellent" French-Continental cuisine that makes any meal, from breakfast to "special occasion" dinner; just make sure "Daddy Warbucks" is picking up the check, and remember jackets are required.

Cafe Ronda *Mediterranean/ S American*

18 | 16 | 16 | $33

W 70s | 249-251 Columbus Ave. (bet. 71st & 72nd Sts.) | 212-579-9929 | www.caferonda.com
An "eclectic mix" of folks frequents this "reasonable" UWS Med–South American for "creative" tapas nibbled in "lively", often "noisy" environs; it's also a "great bunch place", if you can snag an "outside" seat, though "slow" service and a "small space" mean you may do some "waiting."

Café Sabarsky/Café Fledermaus *Austrian*

22 | 24 | 19 | $40

E 80s | Neue Galerie | 1048 Fifth Ave. (86th St.) | 212-288-0665 | www.wallse.com
Kurt Gutenbrunner's "beautiful, old-world" Austrian cafe within the Neue Galerie makes a "charming" backdrop for "superb", "pricey" soups, sandwiches and "decadent desserts"; "long waits" are part of the deal, so if you're "in a hurry" try the "less-crowded Fledermaus."

	FOOD	DECOR	SERVICE	COST

Cafe Spice *Indian* | 18 | 14 | 15 | $27 |

E 40s | Grand Central | lower level (42nd St. & Vanderbilt Ave.) | 646-227-1300
G Village | 72 University Pl. (bet. 10th & 11th Sts.) | 212-253-6999
W 50s | 54 W. 55th St. (bet. 5th & 6th Aves.) | 212-489-7444
www.cafespice.com
"If you can't make it to Curry Hill", try this "bargain" Indian trio that "satisfies" with "nicely spiced" basics and "well-poured drinks"; the "mod" sit-down branches are "busy" despite "slow service", while the "quick" Grand Central takeout–only counter is a hit with the "commuter crowd."

Cafe Steinhof *Austrian* | 19 | 17 | 18 | $26 |

Park Slope | 422 Seventh Ave. (14th St.) | Brooklyn | 718-369-7776 | www.cafesteinhof.com
You'll be "full for days" after a "hearty" meal at this "funky" Park Slope "find" for simple "Austrian comfort food" at "value" rates; live music Wednesdays and film Sundays are draws, but "everybody seems to have fun" due to the "warm" service and "free-flowing beer."

Cafeteria ● *American* | 18 | 16 | 14 | $30 |

Chelsea | 119 Seventh Ave. (17th St.) | 212-414-1717
The "air-kiss" and "eye-candy quotient" remains "high" at this "modern", "24/7" Chelsea American; whether it's for "weekend brunch", lunch after "shopping Loehmann's" or "post-clubbing", the "cheap", "tasty" "comfort" fare ensures there's "always a wait"; if it's "not as trendy as it used to be", the servers still have "'tude" aplenty.

Cafe Un Deux Trois ● *French* | 16 | 14 | 16 | $41 |

W 40s | 123 W. 44th St. (bet. B'way & 6th Ave.) | 212-354-4148 | www.cafeundeuxtrois.biz
"Perfectly good" French bistro fare makes this "bustling" and "noisy" Times Square standby a "safe bet" for "midrange" "pre/post theater" eats; though it's "worn around the edges", it has a "family"-friendly atmosphere and "gets you in and out" in time for your show.

Caffe Bondi *Italian* | ▽ 22 | 18 | 18 | $38 |

Staten Island | 1816 Hylan Blvd. (Dongan Hills Ave.) | 718-668-0100
There's no need for Staten Islanders to cross the Verrazano for "Sicilian food with plenty of character" thanks to this "delicious" "Manhattan transplant" "without the Manhattan prices"; the "relaxed" atmosphere and courteous service keep it a mainstay.

Caffe Buon Gusto *Italian* | 18 | 14 | 17 | $32 |

E 70s | 236 E. 77th St. (bet. 2nd & 3rd Aves.) | 212-535-6884
Brooklyn Heights | 151 Montague St. (bet. Clinton & Henry Sts.) | Brooklyn | 718-624-3838
At these UES–Brooklyn Heights "mix-and-match" Italian "neighborhood favorites", the interiors are "homey" enough for a dinner "with friends" or other casual occasion; "solid" food and service and "inexpensive" tabs keep the regulars regular.

Caffe Cielo ● *Italian* | 19 | 16 | 19 | $45 |

W 50s | 881 Eighth Ave. (bet. 52nd & 53rd Sts.) | 212-246-9555
It's a Hell's Kitchen "staple" that "changes little", which suits its regulars who cite "reliable", "reasonable" Northern Italian classics,

"pleasant" quarters and "fast service" as reasons to "go back"; its theater-"convenient" location and $12.95 brunch are two more.

NEW Caffe Emilia ●♿ Italian

FOOD	DECOR	SERVICE	COST
-	-	-	I

E Village | 139 First Ave. (bet. 9th St. & St. Marks Pl.) | 212-388-1234
From the owners of Gnocco and Perbacco comes this new East Village Italian cafe providing espresso drinks and inexpensive artisanal sandwiches, salads and such; added virtues are a staff of beautiful Euro types and an informal, concrete-meets-art deco outdoor dining space.

Caffe Grazie Italian

FOOD	DECOR	SERVICE	COST
19	17	20	$48

E 80s | 26 E. 84th St. (bet. 5th & Madison Aves.) | 212-717-4407 | www.caffegrazie.com
"Lots of museum gift shop bags" tell the story of this UES Italian relied upon as a "convenient" choice "near the Met"; most tout its "tasty" fare, "relaxing" townhouse setting and "gracious" service, but a few find it a bit "ordinary" "for the price."

Caffe Linda ⊠ Italian

FOOD	DECOR	SERVICE	COST
18	12	17	$30

E 40s | 145 E. 49th St. (bet. Lexington & 3rd Aves.) | 646-497-1818
"Dependable pastas" and other Italiana lure Midtowners from their desks to this "unpretentious" trattoria; "friendly" (if "slow") service and "decent prices" add to the appeal, though it gets "loud" and "crowded at lunch."

Caffé on the Green ⊠ Italian

FOOD	DECOR	SERVICE	COST
21	22	21	$51

Bayside | 201-10 Cross Island Pkwy. (bet. Clearview Expwy. & Utopia Pkwy.) | Queens | 718-423-7272 | www.caffeonthegreen.com
Formerly home to Rudolph Valentino and Fiorello LaGuardia, this "charming" Bayside Italian's "lovely setting indoors and out" is "perfect for celebrating"; further justifying the "pricey" tabs are an "excellent" kitchen and service that's "so very nice."

Calle Ocho Nuevo Latino

FOOD	DECOR	SERVICE	COST
22	22	19	$46

W 80s | 446 Columbus Ave. (bet. 81st & 82nd Sts.) | 212-873-5025 | www.calleochonyc.com
Every bit as "boisterous" as its namesake street in Miami's Little Havana, this UWS Nuevo Latino entertains a "sexy", "young" crowd grazing on "pricey" but "creative" bites; factor in "spicy decor", "convivial" service and "exotic drinks", and you've got a "fun", high–"noise quotient" "night out."

CamaJe ● American/French

FOOD	DECOR	SERVICE	COST
▽ 23	15	19	$35

G Village | 85 MacDougal St. (bet. Bleecker & Houston Sts.) | 212-673-8184 | www.camaje.com
With the air of a "secret" find on an "out-of-the-way Paris street", this "terrific little" Village bistro's French-American fare comes via a "sweet" staff; it can be a "squeeze", but it's "romantic" for dining à deux; P.S. "try the cooking classes" or don a blindfold for one of their 'dark dining' events.

NEW Caminito ⊠ Argentinean/Steak

FOOD	DECOR	SERVICE	COST
-	-	-	M

Harlem | 1664 Park Ave. (bet. 117th & 118th Sts.) | 212-289-1343
Just about everything's grilled at this tiny, reasonable East Harlem hacienda serving up typical Argentinean steakhouse fare with wines from the motherland; although it's not a place to see and be seen, its

brick-lined interior and exterior Spanish tiles bring a welcome dash of charm to the area.

Campagnola ● *Italian*   23 | 17 | 21 | $66

E 70s | 1382 First Ave. (bet. 73rd & 74th Sts.) | 212-861-1102

At this East Side "old-school" Italian "scene", a "well-heeled clientele" (including a sprinkling of "celebrities") samples "simple" fare that's "delicious from start to finish"; "it pays to be a regular" when it comes to service, and as for the notable bill, it's "worth every penny" for the "people-watching" alone.

Canaletto *Italian*   ▽ 21 | 15 | 22 | $50

E 60s | 208 E. 60th St. (bet. 2nd & 3rd Aves.) | 212-317-9192

"Attentive" service and "delicious" "traditional" Northern Italian "chow" at "fair prices" have earned this Eastsider "standby" status; maybe there's "no wow factor" here, but to most it's just the kind of "relaxing" place a "neighborhood" eatery "should be."

Candle Cafe *Vegan/Vegetarian*   23 | 17 | 21 | $36

E 70s | 1307 Third Ave. (bet. 74th & 75th Sts.) | 212-472-0970

Candle 79 *Vegan/Vegetarian*

E 70s | 154 E. 79th St. (bet. Lexington & 3rd Aves.) | 212-537-7179
www.candlecafe.com

"Makes you proud to be veg" rave regulars of these "friendly" Upper Eastsiders purveying the "tastiest vegetarian/vegan food in the city"; they're places to "bring meat-eater friends without apologizing" – especially the Candle 79 location, whose "better decor" comes at only "slightly higher" rates.

Canyon Road *Southwestern*   19 | 16 | 16 | $36

E 70s | 1470 First Ave. (bet. 76th & 77th Sts.) | 212-734-1600 | www.arkrestaurants.com

Getting "happy" is the name of the game at this UES Southwestern "fiesta" filled with "young" partakers of "dynamite" margaritas that "do the trick" and "above-average" Tex-Mex; though often "crowded", its candlelit, O'Keeffe-worthy decor and "friendly" vibe make it an "excellent date" place.

Capital Grille *Steak*   23 | 22 | 23 | $63

E 40s | 155 E. 42nd St. (bet. Lexington & 3rd Aves.) | 212-953-2000 | www.thecapitalgrille.com

"Midtown business" types "power lunch" over "massive", "well-prepared" steaks at this chop chain link manned by staffers so "friendly", they "must be imported from the Atlanta home office"; quartered in "Philip Johnson's beautiful pyramid space" in the Chrysler Center, the "impressive" setting comes with matching prices.

Capsouto Frères *French*   24 | 23 | 24 | $55

TriBeCa | 451 Washington St. (Watts St.) | 212-966-4900 | www.capsoutofreres.com

"Visit Provence for a few hours" via this "out-of-the-way" TriBeCa "oasis" that "delights" with "nothing-flashy" French bistro classics "expertly done" (the soufflés are a must), "wonderful wines" and service to "make you feel like family"; its "lovely", "high-ceilinged" room works equally well for a "romantic" tête-à-tête or "brunch with friends."

	FOOD	DECOR	SERVICE	COST

Caracas Arepa Bar *Venezuelan* — 26 | 13 | 15 | $17
E Village | 93½ E. Seventh St. (bet. Ave. A & 1st Ave.) | 212-529-2314
Caracas to Go *Venezuelan*
E Village | 91 E. Seventh St. (1st Ave.) | 212-228-5062
www.caracasarepabar.com

This East Villager offers "something different", i.e. "wildly satisfying" Venezuelan street food, notably "dreamy", "addictive" stuffed arepas; eminently "affordable" prices ensure "the line never ceases" to get into its "closet-size" space – "thank goodness" there's "takeout."

Cara Mia *Italian* — 20 | 15 | 19 | $35
W 40s | 654 Ninth Ave. (bet. 45th & 46th Sts.) | 212-262-6767 | www.nycrg.com

Excelling at "fresh pastas" and other "reasonable" "basics", this "charming" Hell's Kitchen Italian can be a "tight fit", but "simpatico" staff and "value" pricing make it a "favorite" of locals and "pre-theater" eaters.

Caravan of Dreams *Vegan/Vegetarian* — ▽ 24 | 18 | 19 | $26
E Village | 405 E. Sixth St. (1st Ave.) | 212-254-1613 | www.caravanofdreams.net

"Healthy food" that's the stuff of dreams leaves even "meat eaters" "feeling satisfied" at this "hip" East Village kosher vegan, especially when washed down with "organic wine and beer"; the mood is "post-hippie earthy" (they even offer yoga classes), abetted by a "young, sincere" staff and prices as "wholesome" as the cooking.

Carl's Steaks *Cheese Steaks* — 22 | 6 | 13 | $11
Murray Hill | 507 Third Ave. (34th St.) | 212-696-5336 ◐
TriBeCa | 79 Chambers St. (bet. B'way & Church St.) | 212-566-2828
www.carlssteaks.com

"Forget the two-hour drive" – even City of Brotherly Love "natives" concede the "sublime cheese steaks" at these "cheap" Murray Hill-TriBeCa twins are just about "as good as the real" "South Philly" deal; "cramped" digs with "limited seating" and wadda ya want service have many getting it "to go."

Z Carlyle Restaurant *French* — 21 | 26 | 24 | $77
E 70s | Carlyle Hotel | 35 E. 76th St. (Madison Ave.) | 212-744-1600 | www.thecarlyle.com

Impossibly "luxurious", this "elegant" UES hotel dining room has "dignified" diners "feeling pampered" thanks to "service of the first order" and "decadent" New French fare; the "tranquil", "handsome" space is ideal for "special occasions", so long as you wear a jacket (required at dinner) and come prepared to pay like "royalty"; N.B. your best buy is breakfast, brunch or afternoon tea.

Z Carmine's *Italian* — 19 | 15 | 18 | $38
W 40s | 200 W. 44th St. (bet. B'way & 8th Ave.) | 212-221-3800 ◐
W 90s | 2450 Broadway (bet. 90th & 91st Sts.) | 212-362-2200
www.carminesnyc.com

"Bring your appetite" and "all your friends" to "*mangia*" "a lotta food" at these "glutton's delights" dishing up family-style Southern Italian "red sauce" at "bargain" rates; they're "overcrowded" and there's "always a wait", but "tourists" and "locals" alike consider that part of the "bustling", "party" vibe.

	FOOD	DECOR	SERVICE	COST

Z .Carnegie Deli ◐✿ *Deli* — 21 | 9 | 13 | $27

W 50s | 854 Seventh Ave. (55th St.) | 212-757-2245 | www.carnegiedeli.com
One sandwich could "feed an army" and the "classic" cheesecake "is the standard by which all others should be judged" at this Midtown "granddaddy of delis"; "true NYers" and "tourists" sit "shoulder-to-shoulder" in its "dumpy" quarters presided over by "fast", "surly servers" who've been on the job "since the beginning of time" – may this "quintessential NY" experience "never change."

NEW Carniceria *Steak* — - | - | - | M

Cobble Hill | 241 Smith St. (Douglass St.) | Brooklyn | 718-237-9100
Aside from the moose-antler lighting fixtures, little remains of Cobble Hill's short-lived Porchetta, whose owners have redone it as this low-key Latin American steakhouse; locals appreciate that its grass-fed beef (from chef Alex Garcia of Calle Ocho fame) comes for not a lot of green.

Carol's Cafe ⓈⓂ *Eclectic* — ▽ 26 | 18 | 21 | $56

Staten Island | 1571 Richmond Rd. (bet. Four Corners Rd. & Seaview Ave.) | 718-979-5600 | www.carolscafe.com
"'Delightful' best describes" chef Carol Frazzetta and her "ever-changing menu" of "imaginative" Eclectic dishes "served with TLC" in a "well-appointed" space; ardent admires insist "it's worth a trip" to SI, though the "Manhattan quality" comes complete with Midtown prices.

Casa Ⓢ *Brazilian* — ▽ 22 | 18 | 20 | $40

W Village | 72 Bedford St. (Commerce St.) | 212-366-9410 | www.casarestaurant.com
Having mastered the art of "well-done simplicity", this "unassuming" Village Brazilian boasts a "cozy, casual" ambiance and "helpful", "charming" staff; however, it's the "strong caipirinhas", "terrific" "homestyle" dishes and moderate tabs that "make you want to eat here" again and again.

Casa Mono ◐ *Spanish* — 25 | 18 | 20 | $50

Gramercy | 52 Irving Pl. (17th St.) | 212-253-2773
"*Muy delicioso*" small plates and "superb wines" star at Mario Batali's "better-than-Barcelona" Gramercy Spaniard; whether you "sit at the bar and watch the chefs work" or squeeze into the "sardine can"–size dining area, "be prepared to wait" for a seat and bring plenty of pesos because those "flavorful" bites "add up."

Cascina ◐ *Italian* — 18 | 15 | 17 | $41

W 40s | 647 Ninth Ave. (bet. 45th & 46th Sts.) | 212-245-4422 | www.cascina.com
They sure "know how to cook" at this "reliable" Hell's Kitchen Italian, a "great pre-theater choice" for "moderately priced" pizza and pasta paired with "fine wines" from its own vineyard in The Boot; the "cozy", "rustic" space can get "crowded", but no matter what they'll "get you to the show on time."

Casimir ◐ *French* — 19 | 18 | 15 | $36

E Village | 103-105 Ave. B (bet. 6th & 7th Sts.) | 212-358-9683 | www.casimirrestaurant.com
A great "first-date place", this "straight-out-of-Paris" Alphabet City bistro "sets the mood" with "dark", "romantic" atmosphere and a

"lovely garden"; the "wonderful" French fare comes with "attitude" as an unwanted "garnish", but "bargain prices" compensate.

NEW Catch 22 *Argentinean/Italian* — | — | — | M

Williamsburg | 312 Graham Ave. (Ainslie St.) | Brooklyn | 718-782-3199 | www.gocatch22.com

Catering to both the Neapolitan and Latin communities that straddle Williamsburg's Grand Street, chef Alex Garcia (Calle Ocho) crafts a beef-heavy Argentinean-Italian fusion menu at this newcomer; its old-fashioned decor isn't aimed at the area's younger crowd, but the varied sangrias hold multigenerational appeal.

Caviar Russe *American* 24 | 22 | 23 | $87

E 50s | 538 Madison Ave., 2nd fl. (bet. 54th & 55th Sts.) | 212-980-5908 | www.caviarrusse.com

To dine "like a Romanov", you only need to go one flight up at this Midtown "heaven for caviar lovers", where those "amazing" eggs and "outstanding sushi" are served in a "jewel-box" setting by "attentive" pros; while it's priced for "royals", even an "average Joe can afford" the prix fixe deals, and it's always a good bet for "special celebrations."

Z Cávo ● *Greek* 21 | 26 | 19 | $42

Astoria | 42-18 31st Ave. (bet. 42nd & 43rd Sts.) | Queens | 718-721-1001 | www.cavocafelounge.com

An Astoria "surprise", this "modern Greek" scores points with its "sexy", "high-ceilinged" space, three-story waterfall and "beautiful" garden that "feels like Europe"; maybe the service "could be better", but the food is right up there with the "after-hours" "bar scene."

Cebu ● *Continental* ▽ 21 | 17 | 18 | $37

Bay Ridge | 8801 Third Ave. (88th St.) | Brooklyn | 718-492-5095

The Bay Ridge "after-hours crowd" frequents this "quaint" Continental "hideaway" for its solid "late-night" eats (open till 3 AM); the setup includes a bar area perfect for "people-watching" and an "intimate back room with fireplace"; P.S. it's also "worth a visit" for weekend brunch.

Celeste ⊅ *Italian* 24 | 11 | 16 | $33

W 80s | 502 Amsterdam Ave. (bet. 84th & 85th Sts.) | 212-874-4559

"Look for the crowd outside" to spot this "tiny" UWS Neapolitan famed for its "cheap" yet celestial fare; despite "no reservations", "long waits", "elbow-to-elbow tables" and "rushed" service, most surveyors "love it" all the same.

Cellini ☒ *Italian* 21 | 18 | 22 | $56

E 50s | 65 E. 54th St. (bet. Madison & Park Aves.) | 212-751-1555 | www.cellinirestaurant.com

Dealmakers "leave happy" from this "old faithful" for Midtown "business lunches", where "reliable", "old-school" Northern Italian fare is ferried by a "welcoming" staff; the decor's "dated" but "soothing", and "quiet" dinner hours can even be romantic – at least until the bill comes.

Cendrillon ☒ *Asian/Filipino* ▽ 20 | 17 | 20 | $40

SoHo | 45 Mercer St. (bet. Broome & Grand Sts.) | 212-343-9012 | www.cendrillon.com

"Intriguing", "flavorful" Filipino-Asian dishes "prepared with care" keep fans "coming back" to this SoHo "gem"; a "comfy", "low-key" setting and service that "makes you feel like family" have followers wondering why it's among the area's "best-kept secrets."

Centolire *Italian* | 20 | 22 | 19 | $59 |

E 80s | 1167 Madison Ave. (bet. 85th & 86th Sts.) | 212-734-7711 | www.centolire.ypguides.net

Eastsiders get "dressed up" for "special-occasion" visits to Pino Luongo's "cut-above" Italian set in an "elegant townhouse"; the "upscale" Tuscan fare, "formal" service and glass elevator ride to the "lovely" upstairs dining room can run up, but the $24.50 "prix fixe lunch is a bargain."

Centovini *Italian* | ▽ 21 | 22 | 20 | $55 |

SoHo | 25 W. Houston St. (bet. Greene & Mercer Sts.) | 212-219-2113 | www.centovininyc.com

From the owners of I Trulli and the design gallery Moss comes this SoHo enoteca where "cool", "aggressively modern" decor meets first-class casual Italian fare paired with a "winning wine list"; it's "expensive", but from the "cordial service" to the "trendy" vibe, it's "right on the money."

Centrico *Mexican* | 20 | 18 | 19 | $46 |

TriBeCa | 211 W. Broadway (Franklin St.) | 212-431-0700 | www.myriadrestaurantgroup.com

"Satisfy your Mexican craving" at Drew Nieporent's "much-needed" TriBeCan, where chef Aarón Sanchez's "vibrant", *"nuevo"* dishes are chased with "killer" margaritas; service is mostly "accommodating", and for those who find the interior "a little sterile", in summer there's always the outside seating.

NEW Centro Vinoteca ● *Italian* | - | - | - | M |

W Village | 74 Seventh Ave. S. (Barrow St.) | 212-367-7470 | www.centrovinoteca.com

New to the bustling Seventh Avenue strip, this midpriced West Village Italian is luring a chic crowd with its small plates (called *piccolini*), as well as heartier pastas and such, via a former Felidia chef; the white-tiled space is warmed by vintage chandeliers and a curved wooden bar, and there's also a window-lined second-floor dining room.

'Cesca *Italian* | 23 | 21 | 21 | $58 |

W 70s | 164 W. 75th St. (Amsterdam Ave.) | 212-787-6300 | www.cescanyc.com

At this "pricey" but "wildly popular" Westsider, "sumptuous", "hearty rustic" Southern Italian fare "warms the soul", as does the "inviting", "grown-up" interior (it's "roomy" enough to "actually have a private conversation") and "gracious" service; in a word, "bravo!"; N.B. Tom Valenti is no longer involved.

Chadwick's *American* | 22 | 19 | 22 | $42 |

Bay Ridge | 8822 Third Ave. (89th St.) | Brooklyn | 718-833-9855 | www.chadwicksny.com

This "friendly" Bay Ridge American remains a neighborhood "favorite" for superior steaks and seafood enjoyed amid "homey", "publike" environs; it "caters to an older crowd" with specials like the $20.95 early-bird, but there's also a "decent bar scene" with an appealing "everyone-knows-everyone" vibe.

	FOOD	DECOR	SERVICE	COST

Chance *Pan-Asian* ▽ 21 | 18 | 20 | $32

Boerum Hill | 223 Smith St. (Butler St.) | Brooklyn | 718-242-1515 |
www.chancecuisine.com

At this "affordable" Boerum Hill Pan-Asian, "well-done" dishes are
served in a "cool", modern space starring a "hypnotic waterfall behind
the bar"; most find the service and back garden "lovely", but are particularly drawn to the $6.00 lunch deal.

🔒 Chanterelle *French* 27 | 26 | 27 | $119

TriBeCa | 2 Harrison St. (Hudson St.) | 212-966-6960 |
www.chanterellenyc.com

"Damn near perfect", David and Karen Waltuck's TriBeCa French
"benchmark" keeps "getting better with age", providing a "regal dining
experience" across "all categories"; "every bite of every course is
heavenly", while the "elegant", "understated" interior is perfect for
"special occasions" with "spot-on", "balletic" service to match; it's
"oh so pricey", but "worth every dollar" to most; N.B. dinner is prix fixe
only, but ordering à la carte is an option at Thursday-Saturday lunch.

Chanto *Japanese* ▽ 22 | 21 | 22 | $65

G Village | 133 Seventh Ave. S. (bet. Charles & W. 10th Sts.) | 212-463-8686 |
www.chantonyc.com

Making a strong "first impression" with its "contemporary" space
spanning four "dramatic" levels, this Greenwich Village "haute"
Japanese is the first stateside foray of an Osaka-based chain; its "flair"
extends to the "refreshing" "fusion" fare and "helpful" service, and
is priced accordingly.

Charles' Southern-Style Kitchen *Southern* ▽ 24 | 4 | 14 | $18

Harlem | 2839 Frederick Douglass Blvd. (151st St.) |
212-926-4313 Ⓜ

NEW **Harlem** | 308 Lenox Ave. (bet. 125th & 126th Sts.) |
212-722-7727 ❶⇄

"Skip a meal before" hitting this pair of "genuine" Harlem soul fooders
in order to take best advantage of the "amazing" "bargain" all-you-
can-eat buffet; the staff shows "Southern hospitality", but since the
decor's "not much to look at" "takeout" might be the route to go.

Chat 'n Chew ❶ *American* 16 | 13 | 14 | $22

Union Sq | 10 E. 16th St. (bet. 5th Ave. & Union Sq. W.) | 212-243-1616 |
www.chatnchewnyc.com

As a fallback for "stick-to-your-ribs" "comfort" classics in "huge portions", this "funky", "family-friendly" Union Square American may be
worth considering; the "staff isn't making a career" in service and the
"hokey" decor is of the "knickknack-filled basement" variety, but it
definitely "won't break the bank."

NEW Chat Noir *French* 18 | 16 | 19 | $52

E 60s | 22 E. 66th St. (bet. 5th & Madison Aves.) | 212-794-2428 |
www.bistrochatnoir.com

Off to a "promising start", this UES French 'gastro-bistro' is drawing
"great-looking people" to its "hidden" townhouse lair manned by a
"welcoming staff"; as a result, despite prices that "reflect the high-
rent locale", most consider themselves lucky to cross its path and
nab a seat.

	FOOD	DECOR	SERVICE	COST

Chef Ho's Peking Duck Grill *Chinese* — 22 | 14 | 19 | $29

E 80s | 1720 Second Ave. (bet. 89th & 90th Sts.) | 212-348-9444
Upper Eastsiders wonder "why go Downtown" when you can get "real deal" Chinese for "reasonable" rates at this "local favorite" where the namesake dish is a "must-get"; its "quiet dining room", though a bit "drab", is "nice enough for an evening out" and the service is "pro" - hey, "it's packed for a reason."

NEW Chennai *Indian/Vegetarian* — - | - | - | !

E 80s | 1663 First Ave. (bet. 86th & 87th Sts.) | 212-831-1114
From the owners of Yorkville's Dakshin comes this unassuming white tablecloth kosher vegetarian Indian; its low-cost menu is varied enough that diners shouldn't miss the meat as they dine in pleasant exposed-brick environs.

Chennai Garden 🅼 *Indian/Vegetarian* — 21 | 10 | 14 | $21

Gramercy | 129 E. 27th St. (bet. Lexington Ave. & Park Ave. S.) | 212-689-1999
Diners "don't miss the meat" at this "solid" Curry Hill vegetarian kosher "must-try" for "South Indian classics"; though "service varies" and the decor is "nothing special", you get "great bang for your buck", particularly the $6.95 all-you-can-eat lunch buffet.

NEW Cheryl's Global Soul 🅼 *Soul Food* ▽ 22 | 21 | 20 | $28

Prospect Heights | 236 Underhill Ave. (bet. Prospect Pl. & St. Marks Ave.) | Brooklyn | 347-529-2855
For soul food that "rocks your soul", plus "delicious baked goods", try TV personality Cheryl Smith's "excellent" Prospect Heights newcomer; "innovative", modern decor, "welcoming" service and praiseworthy prices make it an ideal "addition to the 'hood."

Chestnut 🅼 *American* — 23 | 17 | 21 | $40

Carroll Gardens | 271 Smith St. (bet. Degraw & Sackett Sts.) | Brooklyn | 718-243-0049 | www.chestnutonsmith.com
"Original", "well-prepared" seasonal dishes and "accommodating", "knowledgeable" service make this Carroll Gardens New American "stand out"; locals "feel right at home" in its "modern", "unpretentious" digs and "pretty garden", and the "deal" of a Tuesday–Wednesday prix fixe keeps 'em coming back.

Chez Jacqueline *French* — 18 | 16 | 19 | $43

G Village | 72 MacDougal St. (bet. Bleecker & Houston Sts.) | 212-505-0727
"Like a trip to" the "French country", this "sweet little" Gallic Villager offers bistro classics "done well" for a "fair price"; the "gracious" staff and "cozy", "relaxing" atmosphere ensure it remains a "neighborhood anchor."

Chez Josephine ●🅼 *French* — 20 | 21 | 21 | $50

W 40s | 414 W. 42nd St. (bet. 9th & 10th Aves.) | 212-594-1925 | www.chezjosephine.com
You can "make a night of theater last two hours longer" at this "homage" to Josephine Baker overseen by her adopted son, "host-with-the-most" Jean-Claude; the decor is "bordello-romantic" meets "gay Paree" (*avec* "dynamite piano player"), the French bistro fare is "solid" and, *meilleur de tous*, you'll likely "leave with a story."

NEW Chez Lola French | - | - | - | M |

Clinton Hill | 387 Myrtle Ave. (bet. Clermont & Vanderbilt Aves.) | Brooklyn | 718-858-1484

The younger sibling of Fort Greene's Chez Oskar, this new French bistro is helping gentrify Clinton Hill's infamous 'Murder Avenue'; locals can't refuse the moderately priced eclectic menu served in sexy, art deco-ish digs, and there's a sizable heated garden to boot.

Chez Napoléon 🗷 French | 20 | 13 | 20 | $45 |

W 50s | 365 W. 50th St. (bet. 8th & 9th Aves.) | 212-265-6980 | www.cheznapoleon.com

"Old-fashioned" "Left Bank" charm evokes "times past" for the many longtime customers of this petite Theater District "classic"; its "well-prepared" French cooking, "warm" service, "old-school prices" and even its "dated" decor reinforce that feeling – loyalists laud "long may it last."

Chez Oskar ◑ French | ▽ 19 | 18 | 17 | $29 |

Fort Greene | 211 DeKalb Ave. (Adelphi St.) | Brooklyn | 718-852-6250 | www.chezoskar.com

This "reliable" Fort Greene French bistro has become a local "favorite" thanks to its "tasty" classics ("amazing brunch"), "hip vibe" and low tabs; service can be overly "mellow", but that affords time to enjoy the "cozy" interior and "outdoor sidewalk seats."

Chiam Chinese Cuisine Chinese | 23 | 19 | 22 | $44 |

E 40s | 160 E. 48th St. (bet. Lexington & 3rd Aves.) | 212-371-2323

It's no wonder that this "high-end" Midtown Chinese "has held up over the years" given its "marvelous" food, "excellent" wine list, "superior" service" and "lovely space"; favored by "corporate" types, it's especially "bustling" at lunch.

Chianti 🖩 Italian | 21 | 17 | 19 | $39 |

Bay Ridge | 8530 Third Ave. (86th St.) | Brooklyn | 718-921-6300 | www.chianti86.com

"Fantastic family-style fare like mama used to cook" makes this "boisterous" midpriced Bay Ridge Italian "great for group" dining; the "casual" atmosphere and "delightful staff" keep "locals" "coming back for more" and more.

Chickpea ◑ Mideastern | 19 | 8 | 13 | $10 |

E Village | 210 E. 14th St. (bet. 2nd & 3rd Aves.) | 212-228-3445
E Village | 23 Third Ave. (bet. 9th St. & St. Marks Pl.) | 212-254-1187

"Tasty" Middle Eastern "temptations" are the draw at this "quick, cheap" East Village duo; "pita fresh from the oven" and "really good falafel" particularly "hit the spot" "late-night", but just "don't expect much" decorwise – most maintain it's "better for takeout."

ChikaLicious 🖩 Dessert | 24 | 17 | 23 | $22 |

E Village | 203 E. 10th St. (bet. 1st & 2nd Aves.) | 212-995-9511 | www.chikalicious.com

To reach "sweet-tooth heaven", chick out this "exquisite" East Village dessert specialist where "edible art" takes the form of "oh-so-'licious" three-course, fixed-price lineups with optional wine pairings, served by a "stellar" staff; there's often a "line out the door", but "addicts" assure it's "worth the wait."

	FOOD	DECOR	SERVICE	COST

NEW Chiles & Chocolate
Oaxacan Kitchen *Mexican* ▽ 18 | 13 | 15 | $28

Park Slope | 54 Seventh Ave. (bet. Lincoln & St. John's Pls.) | Brooklyn | 718-230-7700

It's "just what Park Slope needed" enthuse eaters at this "delightful" Mexican arrival where the "authentic Oaxacan" menu is centered on the namesake ingredients (think "outrageous mole"); it manages to be both "delicious and inexpensive" – and complaints about its "minute space" have been answered with the post-Survey addition of an all-weather patio.

Chimichurri Grill ● *Argentinean/Steak* 21 | 14 | 20 | $46

W 40s | 606 Ninth Ave. (bet. 43rd & 44th Sts.) | 212-586-8655 | www.chimichurrigrill.com

You "can't beat the beef" at this Hell's Kitchen Argentinean where "big" steaks bathed in the "wonderful" eponymous sauce come in "cramped" quarters; still, "charming service" and not-too-bad tabs have most calling it an "excellent pre-theater" choice.

China Chalet *Chinese* 19 | 14 | 19 | $27

Financial District | 47 Broadway (bet. Exchange Pl. & Morris St.) | 212-943-4380
Financial District | 90 Broad St. (Stone St.) | 212-747-9099 ☒
Staten Island | 4326 Amboy Rd. (Armstrong Ave.) | 718-984-8044 ●
www.chinachalet.com

For three decades the "go-to Chinese lunch spots" for "Wall Street workers", these affordable Financial District "survivors" (with a Staten Island outpost) "never fail to satisfy"; service is "pleasant" too, but given decor that's "a bit faded", many go the "takeout" or "fast delivery" route.

NEW China de Puebla *Mexican* - | - | - | M

Harlem | 3143 Broadway (LaSalle St.) | 212-222-8666 | www.chinadepuebla.com

As the name suggests, this Harlem newcomer offers Asian-accented Mexican cuisine, with a decor palette that pays homage to its native country with white walls, red cushions and a green-accented oak bar; moderate prices and artfully prepared cocktails abet the festive vibe.

China Fun ● *Chinese* 16 | 10 | 13 | $23

E 60s | 1221 Second Ave. (64th St.) | 212-752-0810
W 70s | 246 Columbus Ave. (bet. 71st & 72nd Sts.) | 212-580-1516

Maybe these "no-frills" crosstown Chinese have been slipping, but they remain "quick and cheap", if "not exactly gourmet", and they also serve sushi; "they know how to turn the tables", so they're good for a "quick pre-movie or weeknight meal."

China Grill *Asian* 22 | 20 | 18 | $55

W 50s | 60 W. 53rd St. (bet. 5th & 6th Aves.) | 212-333-7788 | www.chinagrillmgt.com

This "great big" Midtown "staple" for Asian fare "hasn't lost its luster", attracting a "steady parade" of "corporate" types for "pricey" "power" meals, plus a smattering of "tourists"; the lure is "sophisticated" food and drink that's "perfect for groups" and enjoyed in "lively", "noisy" environs.

Chinatown Brasserie ● *Chinese*

| | 21 | 23 | 19 | $49 |

NoHo | 380 Lafayette St. (Great Jones St.) | 212-533-7000 |
www.chinatownbrasserie.com

At this "trendy" NoHo Chinese, the "upscale" menu runs the gamut
from "excellent" renditions of standards like Peking duck and BBQ ribs
to all-day dim sum; true, it comes at "double the price of Chinatown",
but if you factor in the "grandiose", "Shanghai-glam" interior, it's probably "worth the premium."

Chin Chin ● *Chinese*

| | 22 | 18 | 21 | $48 |

E 40s | 216 E. 49th St. (bet. 2nd & 3rd Aves.) | 212-888-4555 |
www.chinchinny.com

For "gourmet Chinese" in Midtown, you can't do much better than this
veteran whose fare is "excellent no matter what the dish", and served in
"stylish", "calm" digs; maybe it's "pricey", but most are "happy to pay."

Chino's *Asian*

| | ▽ 22 | 15 | 19 | $30 |

Gramercy | 173 Third Ave. (bet. 16th & 17th Sts.) | 212-598-1200 |
www.chinosnyc.com

It's "fun to share" at this "delicious" Gramercy Asian specializing in
"interesting" small plates and "creative" cocktails; "friendly" service
and "value" pricing (e.g. the "bargain $12 lunch special") make the
"tiny", "cramped" setting easy to overlook.

Chipotle *Mexican*

| | 18 | 10 | 14 | $12 |

E 40s | 150 E. 44th St. (bet. Lexington & 3rd Aves.) | 212-682-9860
E 50s | 150 E. 52nd St. (bet. Lexington & 3rd Aves.) | 212-755-9754
E Village | 19 St. Marks Pl. (bet. 2nd & 3rd Aves.) | 212-529-4502
Financial District | 2 Broadway (Whitehall St.) | 212-344-0941
Flatiron | 680 Sixth Ave. (bet. 21st & 22nd Sts.) | 212-206-3781
Garment District | 304 W. 34th St. (8th Ave.) | 212-268-4197
G Village | 55 E. Eighth St. (bet. B'way & University Pl.) | 212-982-3081
SoHo | 200 Varick St. (bet. Houston & King Sts.) | 646-336-6264
W 40s | 9 W. 42nd St. (bet. 5th & 6th Aves.) | 212-354-6760
Brooklyn Heights | 185 Montague St. (Court St.) | Brooklyn | 718-243-9109
www.chipotle.com

It "used to be owned by McDonald's", but this "assembly-line Mexican"
chain is "not your typical fast-fooder" given its "comparatively
healthy" "choose-your-own" ingredients; at lunch it's "bustling with
business folks" in need of a "burrito fix", so expect "lines out the door."

ChipShop *British*

| | 18 | 13 | 16 | $20 |

Brooklyn Heights | 129 Atlantic Ave. (bet. Clinton & Henry Sts.) |
Brooklyn | 718-855-7775
Park Slope | 383 Fifth Ave. (bet. 6th & 7th Sts.) | Brooklyn | 718-832-7701 ⊅
www.chipshopnyc.com

British expats "hankering for" a taste of home hit these "friendly" Park
Slope–Brooklyn Heights chippies, where the "artery-clogging" fare (from
"fish 'n' chips" to "deep-fried Twinkies") goes well with "imported" suds;
it's as "authentic as you can get", but "just don't tell your internist."

Chiyono ●Ⓜ *Japanese*

| | ▽ 23 | 15 | 19 | $32 |

E Village | 328 E. Sixth St. (bet. 1st & 2nd Aves.) | 212-673-3984 |
www.chiyono.com

Chef-owner Chiyono Mirano's "Japanese home cooking" sans sushi
"dazzles" at her "unique" East Village namesake; the "friendly com-

munal" setup and "hospitable service" lend "charm" to a "small" space, ditto the low prices.

Chocolate Room, The 🎵 Dessert | 25 | 19 | 20 | $17 |

Park Slope | 86 Fifth Ave. (bet. St. Marks Pl. & Warren St.) | Brooklyn | 718-783-2900 | www.thechocolateroombrooklyn.com

"Talk about dying and going to heaven" – this Park Slope dessert destination presents a "chocoholic's dream" menu of "cocoas" and "sweets", plus "wines to drink with them"; its "boîtelike" interior is ideal for "cozying up with a date."

Cho Dang Gol Korean | ▽ 21 | 15 | 16 | $28 |

Garment District | 55 W. 35th St. (bet. 5th & 6th Aves.) | 212-695-8222 | www.chodanggolny.com

So dang "good" is what satisfied samplers say about the "fresh" "housemade" tofu at this Garment District Korean, where the "authentic" specialties can be "tough to decipher" without help from the "pleasant" staff; low prices seal the deal.

Chola Indian | 23 | 17 | 20 | $37 |

E 50s | 232 E. 58th St. (bet. 2nd & 3rd Aves.) | 212-688-4619 | www.fineindiandining.com

The "flavorful" Indian fare will bring you "closer to Nirvana" according to acolytes of this "authentic" Eastsider; "couldn't-be-nicer" service plus a "popular" $13.95 lunch "buffet bargain" are two more reasons it's a "favorite."

Chop't Creative Salad American | 20 | 9 | 14 | $13 |

E 50s | 165 E. 52nd St. (bet. Lexington & 3rd Aves.) | 212-421-2300 ⑤
E 50s | 60 E. 56th St. (bet. Madison & Park Aves.) | 212-750-2467 ⑤
Union Sq | 24 E. 17th St. (bet. B'way & 5th Ave.) | 646-336-5523 www.choptsalad.com

You can "invent your own" leafy creation at these "quick" salad shops boasting lots of "fresh ingredients" and "tasty dressings" "chopped to perfection"; though some suggest "prices should be chop't too", the fact that it's "mobbed at lunch" speaks for itself.

Chow Bar Asian Fusion | 21 | 17 | 18 | $40 |

W Village | 230 W. Fourth St. (W. 10th St.) | 212-633-2212

Thanks to its "ingenious" Asian Fusion menu and "creative" cocktails, this West Villager "still feels fresh"; the "vibrant" atmosphere, central "location" and moderate prices draw "young" types who go both for "group" get-togethers and "dates."

Christos Steak House ⦿ Steak | 22 | 17 | 21 | $57 |

Astoria | 41-08 23rd Ave. (41st St.) | Queens | 718-777-8400 | www.christossteakhouse.com

The "melt-in-your-mouth meat" plus appetizers and sides "with a Greek twist" at this Astoria surf 'n' turfer stand up to the Manhattan competition; though it may be "pricey", most maintain "you get what you pay for."

Churrascaria Plataforma ⦿ Brazilian | 23 | 19 | 21 | $67 |

W 40s | 316 W. 49th St. (bet. 8th & 9th Aves.) | 212-245-0505 | www.churrascariaplataforma.com

(continued)

Churrascaria TriBeCa ◐ *Brazilian*

TriBeCa | 221 W. Broadway (bet. Franklin & White Sts.) | 212-925-6969 | www.churrascariatribeca.com

"Go hungry" and "wear loose pants" to these "all-you-can-eat", prix fixe-only Brazilian meatfests where "sword"-happy staffers serve "skewer after skewer" of "superb" cuts to a "rapacious clientele"; the "bustling" milieu is most "fun for groups", and though the bill can run up, your "food coma" keeps you from caring.

Cibo *American/Italian*

20 | 18 | 20 | $45

E 40s | 767 Second Ave. (41st St.) | 212-681-1616

"Well-prepared" Tuscan–New American fare and a "cheery staff" have made a "neighborhood classic" of this East Midtowner; for "business lunches" or "pleasant" dinners, its "comfortable" space and "bargain prix fixe" deals produce reliably "satisfying" experiences.

Cilantro ◐ *Southwestern*

17 | 14 | 17 | $28

E 70s | 1321 First Ave. (71st St.) | 212-537-4040
E 80s | 1712 Second Ave. (bet. 88th & 89th Sts.) | 212-722-4242
www.cilantronyc.com

"Crunchy chips", "spicy salsa" and "marvelous margaritas" make these UES family-style Southwesterners a good bet (especially given their big portions and fair prices); Monday's $10 fajita special – "Holy frijoles, Batman!" – keeps the neighbors coming.

Cipriani Dolci ◐ *Italian*

18 | 20 | 16 | $49

E 40s | Grand Central | West Balcony (42nd St. & Vanderbilt Ave.) | 212-973-0999 | www.cipriani.com

The "impressive view" overlooking Grand Central Station makes this "sophisticated" balcony Italian a no-brainer for "drinks" or a "convenient" meal "en route to a train"; though it's a "little pricey", its "elegant setting" is worth visiting at least once, especially with "visitors" in tow.

Cipriani Downtown ◐ *Italian*

20 | 19 | 18 | $67

SoHo | 376 W. Broadway (bet. Broome & Spring Sts.) | 212-343-0999 | www.cipriani.com

"It's all about" the "models, moguls" and other "famous faces" at this super-glam SoHo Italian where "beautiful" types come to sip "Bellinis to die for" and "play, not eat" (though the fare is "delish"); maybe it's "more show than substance", with prices to match, but as a place to "see and be seen" it's hard to beat.

Circus *Brazilian*

20 | 19 | 20 | $54

E 60s | 132 E. 61st St. (bet. Lexington & Park Aves.) | 212-223-2965 | www.circusrestaurante.com

A "departure from the same-old", this "upbeat" East Side Brazilian plies "imaginative" dishes and "must-have caipirinhas" in "cheerful" circus-like digs; with "accommodating" service and tabs "reasonable" for the zip code, "well-heeled" regulars wonder why it's not better known.

Citrus Bar & Grill *Asian/Nuevo Latino*

20 | 19 | 17 | $39

W 70s | 320 Amsterdam Ave. (75th St.) | 212-595-0500 | www.citrusnyc.com

"Young" things who pack this "upbeat" UWS Asian–Nuevo Latino say it's "awesome" to find "margaritas and sushi" in one "cool" place; the

| | FOOD | DECOR | SERVICE | COST |

edibles, service and setting are "decent" enough, but most come for
the "party" powered by "potent" cocktails and "outdoor" seating.

City Bakery Bakery
21 | 13 | 13 | $19

Flatiron | 3 W. 18th St. (bet. 5th & 6th Aves.) | 212-366-1414 |
www.thecitybakery.com

Its buffet/salad bar is a "knockout", but for most it's "all about" th
"decadent" desserts at Maury Rubin's Flatiron "winner"; it would a
be "divine" but for the "overcrowded", underdecorated bi-leve
"cafeteria-style" setting and "sticker shock at the register."

City Crab & Seafood Co. Seafood
17 | 14 | 16 | $42

Flatiron | 235 Park Ave. S. (19th St.) | 212-529-3800 | www.citycrabnyc.com
Though crabby critics feel it's "faded", this "lively" Flatiron "seafood
joint" seems to do swimmingly thanks to its "ample portions" of
"fresh" fin fare; "modest prices" for the genre ensure it remains
"busy" "port of call."

City Hall ⑤ Seafood/Steak
21 | 21 | 20 | $54

TriBeCa | 131 Duane St. (bet. Church St. & W. B'way) |
212-227-7777 | www.cityhallnyc.com

"Bankers, brokers and barristers" blatantly broach "business" at Henry
Meer's "masculine" TriBeCa surf 'n' turf "classic"; sure, it's costly to b
part of "power at play", but the place is "quality" top-to-bottom, an
the "soaring space" exudes "old NY."

City Lobster & Crab Co. Seafood
18 | 15 | 16 | $49

W 40s | 121 W. 49th St. (bet. 6th & 7th Aves.) | 212-354-1717 |
www.citylobster.com

A "well-situated" standby for "business lunches" or "pre-theater", th
"decent" Radio City–area seafooder serves up "fresh" shore fare a
"reasonable" prices; though service is just "ok" and the feel a b
"cookie cutter", it fills the bill for a "decent" "Midtown bite."

Clinton St. Baking Co. American
24 | 14 | 18 | $25

LES | 4 Clinton St. (bet. Houston & Stanton Sts.) | 646-602-6263 |
www.greatbiscuits.com

It feels like "the whole city" lines up for brunch at this "homey" LE
bakery/cafe, where "pancakes to die for" and other "comfort staples
keep wait times "crazy" on weekends; service is "friendly" despite th
"mob", but for the "crowd"-averse there's always less-busy dinner.

Coals ⑤ Pizza
▽ 22 | 17 | 19 | $19

Bronx | 1888 Eastchester Rd. (Morris Park Ave.) | 718-823-7002 |
www.coalspizza.com

"Every pizza-lover should know about" this "unique", "friendly" Bronx
joint, which "breaks the mold" with "grilled" pies (sounds strange, but
"it works") served "quick"; the "limited" but "delicious" menu also in
cludes soups, panini and such, washed down with "first-rate" brews.

Coco Pazzo Italian
22 | 20 | 21 | $66

E 70s | 23 E. 74th St. (bet. 5th & Madison Aves.) | 212-794-0205 |
www.cocopazzonewyork.ypguides.net

"Refined" and "very UES", this Northern Italian "perennial favorite
draws a "mature" mix of "locals" and "celebs" for a taste of "old N
glamour" and Mark Strausman's "elegant" cooking; its "pleasant

| | FOOD | DECOR | SERVICE | COST |

...ace is manned by a surprisingly "unstuffy" staff, and though it's
...ricey", the regulars couldn't care less.

...ocotte ☑ *American/French* ▽ 20 | 18 | 18 | $36

...ark Slope | 337 Fifth Ave. (4th St.) | Brooklyn | 718-832-6848 |
...ww.cocotterestaurant.com

...onsidered one of Park Slope's "gems" among those in-the-know, this
...cozy" French–New American remains a "best-kept secret" despite its
...ne fare and service; "reasonable prices" (especially on "bargain"
...wo-for-one Thursdays") are the crowning touch.

...offee Shop ● *American/Brazilian* 15 | 12 | 11 | $29

...nion Sq | 29 Union Sq. W. (16th St.) | 212-243-7969

...his "bustling" Union Square "institution" is best known for its "reli-
...ble" Brazilian-American grub, "campy" "diner-style" decor and
...snooty", "model"-turned-waitress staff; maybe it's not quite the
...scene" it used to be, but it stays "packed" into "the wee hours."

...olors ☑ *Eclectic* 19 | 19 | 21 | $49

...Village | 417 Lafayette St. (bet. Astor Pl. & 4th St.) | 212-777-8443 |
...www.colors-nyc.com

...he idea behind this East Villager was to establish a "cooperative
...wned by the staff" (many of them "former Windows on the World"
...orkers"), and their "investment shows" in the thoughtful "global"
...enu and "sincere service"; a "warm" deco space and Public Theater-
...andy location make it doubly "worth a visit."

...olumbus Bakery *Bakery* 18 | 11 | 10 | $17

...√ 80s | 474 Columbus Ave. (bet. 82nd & 83rd Sts.) | 212-724-6880 |
...ww.arkrestaurants.com

..Terrific" baked goods and "healthy" lunch options ensure this
...Vestside bakery/cafe is usually "packed"; despite "bumper-to-
...umper strollers", a "confusing ordering system" and "service without
..smile", there's no shortage of fans.

...omfort Diner *Diner* 16 | 12 | 15 | $21

...40s | 214 E. 45th St. (bet. 2nd & 3rd Aves.) | 212-867-4555
...latiron | 25 W. 23rd St. (bet. 5th & 6th Aves.) | 212-741-1010
...ww.comfortdiner.com

..Truly comforting", this "time-capsule" twosome dishes up a "slice of
..americana" via its "large" menu of low-priced "home-cooking" clas-
..ics and "kitschy" "'50s "decor"; enough enjoy the "nostalgia" trip that
..'s "terribly busy on weekends."

...d Compass *American* 22 | 22 | 22 | $58

...√ 70s | 208 W. 70th St. (bet. Amsterdam & West End Aves.) |
...12-875-8600 | www.compassrestaurant.com

..Pointed in the right direction" under a "talented" new chef, this "attrac-
..ive", "modern" UWS New American turns out "creative", "delicious"
..are at "reasonable" prices "for the quality"; the "gracious" service also
..doesn't disappoint", ditto the convenience to Lincoln Center.

...ongee ● *Chinese* 21 | 14 | 14 | $20

...hinatown | 98 Bowery (bet. Grand & Hester Sts.) | 212-965-5028 |
...ww.congeeinc98.com

(continued)

(continued)

Congee Bowery ❶ Chinese
LES | 207 Bowery (bet. Delancey & Rivington Sts.) | 212-766-2828

Congee Village ❶ Chinese
LES | 100 Allen St. (bet. Broome & Delancey Sts.) | 212-941-1818

The "secret's out" about the "amazing" namesake rice porridge a
these separately owned LES-Chinatown Cantonese whose committe
converts consider "crazy lines" and "noisy, crowded" conditions we
"worth" it given the "high quality" at "tremendous-value" prices; P.S. th
"ridiculously kitschy" Congee Village branch is fun "for a party."

Convivium Osteria Mediterranean
25 | 23 | 21 | $48

Park Slope | 68 Fifth Ave. (bet. Bergen St. & St. Marks Ave.) | Brooklyn
718-857-1833 | www.convivium-osteria.com

Groupies gladly "travel to eat" at this Park Slope Med "hideaway" tha
remains "excellent all around", from the "simple, delicious" food an
wine to the "transporting" "rustic" environs and "charming" servic
the only rub is the "price"; P.S. "don't miss" the "romantic" garden.

Cookshop ❶ American
23 | 19 | 21 | $51

Chelsea | 156 10th Ave. (20th St.) | 212-924-4440 | www.cookshopny.con
"Fresh", "locally grown" "ingredients are king" at this "hip" Wes
Chelsea American serving "well-executed" seasonal dishes; th
"always-changing menu", "lovely staff" and "smart", "modern" spac
make a "winning combo", so it's no wonder tables are "hard to get."

Coppola's ❶ Italian
19 | 15 | 17 | $35

Gramercy | 378 Third Ave. (bet. 27th & 28th Sts.) | 212-679-0070
W 70s | 206 W. 79th St. (bet. Amsterdam Ave. & B'way) | 212-877-3840
www.coppolas-nyc.com

These "neighborhood joints" offering "huge portions" of "traditiona
Italian "basics done well" offer "solid" value; the service is "a little u
even" and the "homey" spaces can get "tight", but there's alway
the "delivery option."

Cornelia Street Cafe ❶ American/French
19 | 15 | 17 | $32

G Village | 29 Cornelia St. (bet. Bleecker & W. 4th Sts.) | 212-989-9319
www.corneliastreetcafe.com

With "reliable" French-American fare, "cheerful" service and "fre
quent events" in the "downstairs performance space", this "darling
"vintage Village" "favorite" keeps it "lively"; it's particularly popula
for brunch, though the $21 prix fixe dinner is an "excellent value" too

Corner Bistro ❶ Hamburgers
22 | 9 | 12 | $16

W Village | 331 W. Fourth St. (Jane St.) | 212-242-9502

Despite the notoriously "long waits", some of the "best burgers i
town" and $2.50 "pints of McSorley's" keep this ancient "Village tavern
hopping; you eat on "paper plates with plastic forks" and service ca
be "surly", but it's the "juicy", "cheap" patties that keep 'em coming

Cortina Italian
∇ 18 | 15 | 17 | $35

E 70s | 1448 Second Ave. (bet. 75th & 76th Sts.) | 212-517-2066 |
www.ristorantecortina.com

Eastsiders "save their carbs" for this "friendly neighborhood stop
serving "basic, dependable" Northern Italian favorites; the "low-l

om" is "pleasant" enough and allows for "quiet conversation", while
modest prices" mean "locals" can stay within their budgets.

osette *French* — 21 | 14 | 20 | $39

urray Hill | 163 E. 33rd St. (bet. Lexington & 3rd Aves.) | 212-889-5489
hough "a little frayed", this "tiny", "Left Bank"-like Murray Hill
ench bistro is a "wonderful find" for "buttery" classic fare and ser-
ce "warm" enough to "make you feel like a long-lost" relative; "af-
rdable" tabs further boost the "charm" factor.

osi *Sandwiches* — 16 | 10 | 11 | $14

50s | 60 E. 56th St. (bet. Madison & Park Aves.) | 212-588-1225
nancial District | World Financial Ctr. | 200 Vesey St. (West St.) |
.2-571-2001
atiron | 700 Sixth Ave. (bet. 22nd & 23rd Sts.) | 212-645-0223
arment District | 498 Seventh Ave. (bet. 36th & 37th Sts.) | 212-947-1005
Village | 504 Sixth Ave. (13th St.) | 212-462-4188 ●
EW G **Village** | 53 E. Eighth St. (bet. Greene & Mercer Sts.) |
.2-260-1507
Village | 841 Broadway (13th St.) | 212-614-8544 ●
40s | 11 W. 42nd St. (bet. 5th & 6th Aves.) | 212-398-6662
50s | Paramount Plaza | 1633 Broadway (51st St.) | 212-397-9838
70s | 2160 Broadway (76th St.) | 212-595-5616
ww.getcosi.com
dditional locations throughout the NY area

antabulous" "fresh" flatbread and "flavorful" fillings find favor at
is "solid" sandwich chain; decor and service quality "depend on the
cation", but "slow-moving lines" are a constant during "jam-packed"
nch hours – and "good luck finding a seat."

ounter ● *Vegan/Vegetarian* — 22 | 21 | 22 | $38

Village | 105 First Ave. (bet. 6th & 7th Sts.) | 212-982-5870 |
ww.counternyc.com
Common ground" for "devoted carnivores" and "vegans" alike, this
pscale" East Village vegetarian serves up its "flavorful" fare in "chic",
ontemporary" quarters; "attentive", "unpretentious service" and rea-
▸nable rates are other reasons eaters of all stripes consider it "cool."

ountry ☒ *American* — 23 | 23 | 21 | $127

ramercy | Carlton Hotel | 90 Madison Ave., 2nd fl. (29th St.) |
12-889-7100

afé at Country ● *American*

ramercy | Carlton Hotel | 90 Madison Ave. (29th St.) | 212-889-7100
ww.countryinnewyork.com
here's "certainly nothing rural" about Geoffrey Zakarian's "sophisti-
▸ted" "winner" in the "revamped Carlton Hotel" – it "wows" with
▸umptuous" prix fixe-only New American fare, an "elegant" dining
oom and "formal service" that together "make it feel like a special oc-
asion"; "bargain"-seekers tout the "more casual" downstairs Café at
ountry, where you can get a "delicious" meal minus the "high-end" tab.

owgirl *Southwestern* — 16 | 17 | 16 | $27

Village | 519 Hudson St. (W. 10th St.) | 212-633-1133 |
ww.cowgirlnyc.com
ou'd better "check your diet at the door" of this "kitschy", "fes-
▸ve" (read: "noisy") "Western-themed" Villager whose "hearty"

Southwestern "comfort food" comes via staffers with a "sense of hmor"; "fun" for "kiddie cowpokes" by day, later on it morphs int"singles scene" fueled by "knock-your-socks-off" margaritas.

Cozy Soup & Burger ❶ *Hamburgers/Soup*
| 18 | 8 | 14 | $17 |

G Village | 739 Broadway (Astor Pl.) | 212-477-5566

"Huge burgers", "legendary split-pea soup" and other "classic dinstaples make this 24/7 Villager a "godsend to the NYU students" w"pack" in for "midnight snacks"; sure, it's a "dive", but service"quick" enough to satisfy the 3 AM "urge to nosh."

Ⓩ Craft *American*
| 25 | 23 | 24 | $74 |

Flatiron | 43 E. 19th St. (bet. B'way & Park Ave. S.) | 212-780-0880
www.craftrestaurant.com

"Simple food perfectly prepared" and a "mix-and-match" orderiroutine are keys to the success of Tom Colicchio's "original" FlatirNew American "masterpiece", where diners "love" the "chic" ("nstuffy") setting and "attentive but not intrusive" service; just remember to bring your "platinum card."

Craftbar *American*
| 22 | 18 | 19 | $49 |

Flatiron | 900 Broadway (bet. 19th & 20th Sts.) | 212-461-4300 |
www.craftrestaurant.com

Craft's "delightful", "more casual" Flatiron sibling offers "simpler fabut with comparable" quality to its namesake's – perfect if you waTom Colicchio's New American cooking "on a [relative] budget"; "upbeat staff" abets the overall "exciting", "unpretentious" feel.

Craftsteak *Steak*
| 22 | 23 | 22 | $79 |

Chelsea | 85 10th Ave. (bet. 15th & 16th Sts.) | 212-400-6699 |
www.craftsteaknyc.com

At Tom Colicchio's Chelsea steakhouse, a "knowledgeable staf"guides" guests through the "mouthwatering" selection of stea(grass-fed, corn-fed, Wagyu) and "scrumptious" sides; the "sophiscated", "soaring space" wins wows, but a "disappointed" contingefinds that overall it "lacks finesse", especially given the "over-thtop" price point.

NEW Crave Ceviche Bar *Pan-Latin*
| - | - | - | M |

E 50s | 946 Second Ave. (bet. 50th & 51st Sts.) | 212-355-6565 |
www.craveceviche.com

Serving up an innovative, midpriced menu focused on fish anmeat 'cooked' Latin American–style in citrus juices, this tinEclectic East 50s boîte creates a decidedly downtown vibe with clean, white decor; N.B. until late-night, the seats at the bar are fdiners, not winers.

Crema Ⓜ *Mexican*
| 21 | 18 | 17 | $44 |

Chelsea | 111 W. 17th St. (bet. 6th & 7th Aves.) | 212-691-4477 |
www.cremarestaurante.com

Just about the "crema the crop" for "upscale" Nuevo Mexican, chJulieta Ballesteros' Chelsea "favorite" is rated a "taste sensatiothanks to its "creative" cuisine and "dynamite" drinks; the "brightcolored", "narrow" dining area is "welcoming", but some say the stacould be "a bit more" so.

	FOOD	DECOR	SERVICE	COST

rispo ● *Italian* — 23 | 19 | 19 | $45

Village | 240 W. 14th St. (bet. 7th Ave. S. & 8th Ave.) | 212-229-1818 | ww.crisporestaurant.com

Once a neighborhood secret", this Village Northern Italian is now wnright "bustling" thanks to "delicious" cuisine, "warm" service d "comfortable", "rustic" space that includes a "year-round gar-en"; though not cheap, it probably "could charge twice what it does."

Cru ☒ *European* — 26 | 23 | 26 | $108

Village | 24 Fifth Ave. (9th St.) | 212-529-1700 | www.cru-nyc.com

s the "right place for wine lovers", but don't let this Villager's ible"-length list of *vins* overshadow the "equally impressive" odern European cuisine; yes, its prix fixe–only menus start at $78, t to most they're "worth the expense" considering the "five-star ser-ce" and "charming", "special occasion"–worthy decor; N.B. the ca-al no-reserving front room is à la carte.

uba *Cuban* — 21 | 19 | 17 | $36

Village | 222 Thompson St. (bet. Bleecker & W. 3rd Sts.) | 212-420-7878 | ww.cubanyc.com

ns "can't say enough" about this "boisterous" Village Cuban, a nojito heaven" where "inexpensive" "flavorful food", live jazz and ree, hand-rolled cigars" make it feel like "you've landed in Havana"; s no wonder the "tiny space" often gets "crowded" and "noisy."

uba Cafe *Cuban* — 18 | 16 | 18 | $31

nelsea | 200 Eighth Ave. (bet. 20th & 21st Sts.) | 212-633-1570 | ww.chelseadining.com

'ith a "lively" "Latin flair", this Chelsea Cuban "staple" serves "heaps" "fresh" fare and "tasty mojitos" amid "festive" island-themed decor; affable staff and "fair" prices add to the overall "good vibe."

ubana Café ●≠ *Cuban* — 20 | 16 | 16 | $21

Village | 110 Thompson St. (bet. Prince & Spring Sts.) | 212-966-5366
arroll Gardens | 272 Smith St. (bet. Degraw & Sackett Sts.) | Brooklyn | 18-858-3980
ww.cubanacafeelchulo.com

nese "laid-back" Carroll Gardens-Village "slices of Havana" boast riendly" staffers serving up *muy bueno* Cuban "cheap eats"; "tables e so close" that their "colorful" quarters almost feel "crowded when npty", but "fantastic" cocktails "make the squeeze" quite "bearable."

ube 63 ● *Japanese* — 21 | 15 | 17 | $34

ES | 63 Clinton St. (bet. Rivington & Stanton Sts.) | 212-228-6751 Ⓜ
obble Hill | 234 Court St. (bet. Baltic & Warren Sts.) | Brooklyn | 18-243-2208
ww.cube63.com

ou'll "save big bucks" at this LES–Cobble Hill Japanese duo that slices value sushi" and has a "BYO policy" to keep the bill down; it's a "favor-e" for "fresh fish", so be prepared to "get there super-early" or "wait."

ucina di Pesce ● *Italian* — 17 | 14 | 17 | $28

Village | 87 E. Fourth St. (bet. Bowery & 2nd Ave.) | 212-260-6800 | ww.cucinadipesce.com

his "reliable" East Village Italian "does the trick" for "tasty" "basics" iat leave diners feeling "well fed" for "a bargain" – especially "before

6:30 PM", when the "unbeatable" $11.95 early-bird is an option,
"fine garden" and "cheerful" service further explain why it's such a h|

Curry Leaf *Indian* `20` `10` `16` `$25`

Gramercy | 99 Lexington Ave. (27th St.) | 212-725-5558 |
www.curryleafnyc.com

"The spice is right" – and so is the price – at Kalustyan's "traditior
Indian" in Gramercy, where "big servings" of "mouthwatering" dish
place it "a step up" from its neighbors; though the decor is strictly "n|
frills", "polite" service compensates.

Da Andrea *Italian* `24` `16` `22` `$36`

W Village | 557 Hudson St. (bet. Perry & W. 11th Sts.) | 212-367-197*
www.biassanot.com

At this "local legend", West Village "regulars" swear by the "excep
tional", "authentic" Emilian dishes; add "delightful" staffers,
"quaint" "tiny" space and unpretentious prices, and most agree i*
"worth" the inevitable "killer wait."

Da Ciro *Italian/Pizza* `21` `16` `20` `$43`

Murray Hill | 229 Lexington Ave. (bet. 33rd & 34th Sts.) | 212-532-1636 |
www.daciro.com

Brick-oven "gourmet pizzas" to "make you weak at the knees" pl|
other "fine" Italian standards have earned this "low-key" Murray Hil|
"local favorite" status; it can get "noisy" and "a little pricey", but "r|
peat customers" find it more than "worthwhile."

Dae Dong ● *Korean* `18` `12` `15` `$29`

Garment District | 17 W. 32nd St. (bet. B'way & 5th Ave.) | 212-967-190(
Bayside | 220-15 Northern Blvd. (220th St.) | Queens | 718-631-71(
BBQ that's "tasty", "plentiful" and "inexpensive" is the deal a
this Bayside–Garment District Korean-Japanese pair; tabletop coo|
ing makes for a "fun" time "with friends" (even if you come awa|
"smelling like your meal") – as for the service and setting, the ratinç
speak for themselves.

Da Filippo *Italian* `19` `15` `19` `$53`

E 60s | 1315 Second Ave. (bet. 69th & 70th Sts.) | 212-472-6688 |
www.dafilipporestaurant.com

"Colorful" owner Carlo Meconi and his "friendly" staff "know the
regulars by name" at this "high-end" East Side Northern Italian th|
collects a "neighborhood crowd" for "solid" "basics" in "generous po|
tions"; though some bemoan "rising prices", for most it's a "favorit|
all the same.

☑ Daisy May's BBQ USA *BBQ* `24` `6` `13` `$22`

W 40s | 623 11th Ave. (46th St.) | 212-977-1500 | www.daisymaysbbq.co|
"BBQ heaven" dwells in Hell's Kitchen at this "budget-friendly" "pit" st|
whose "smoky, delicious" meats include "the best ribs north of th|
Mason-Dixon", joined by "addictive" "Southern sides"; if the "picni
table" seating isn't your thing, check out their squadron of street carts

Dakshin Indian Bistro *Indian* ▽ `20` `10` `19` `$25`

E 80s | 1713 First Ave. (bet. 88th & 89th Sts.) | 212-987-9839
"Better-than-average" Indian delivered by staffers who "make you fe|
like a family member" explains why this UES "hole-in-the-wall" is a l|

	FOOD	DECOR	SERVICE	COST

l "favorite"; even those put off by the "cramped", "no-decor" digs
d the $7.95 lunch buffet hard to pass up.

allas BBQ ● *BBQ*

| | | 15 | 9 | 14 | $21 |

helsea | 261 Eighth Ave. (23rd St.) | 212-462-0001
70s | 1265 Third Ave. (bet. 72nd & 73rd Sts.) | 212-772-9393
Village | 132 Second Ave. (St. Marks Pl.) | 212-777-5574
ashington Heights | 3956 Broadway (166th St.) | 212-568-3700
40s | 241 W. 42nd St. (bet. 7th & 8th Aves.) | 212-221-9000
70s | 27 W. 72nd St. (bet. Columbus Ave. & CPW) | 212-873-2004
owntown | 180 Livingston St. (bet. Hoyt & Smith Sts.) | Brooklyn |
8-643-5700
www.dallasbbq.com

ou don't leave hungry" from this "no-frills" chain known for its "hu-
ongous portions" of "decent" BBQ washed down with "jumbo"
inks; the "loud", "cafeterialike" digs may have you feeling like one of
e herd, but hey, it's "super-fast" and "cheap."

anal *French/Mediterranean*

| | | 22 | 21 | 20 | $37 |

Village | 90 E. 10th St. (bet. 3rd & 4th Aves.) | 212-982-6930
diosyncratic and charming" as ever, this affordable East Village
ideaway" presents a "limited" but "delicious" French-Med lineup;
e "funky" "thrift store–chic" aesthetic appeals to locals, as do the
asual but attentive" servers and "lovely back garden."

ani 🗷 *Italian*

| | | ▽ 20 | 20 | 19 | $50 |

oHo | 333 Hudson St. (Charlton St.) | 212-633-9333 |
www.danirestaurant.com

Creative Sicilian" fare draws fans to Don Pintabona's "wonderful"
alian in way West SoHo; a "pleasant" crew, "inviting" room and side-
alk seating seal the deal; N.B. it's now open for weekday lunch only.

a Nico *Italian*

| | | 21 | 17 | 19 | $37 |

ttle Italy | 164 Mulberry St. (bet. Broome & Grand Sts.) | 212-343-1212 |
www.danicoristorante.com

n a "warm summer night", a table in the "wonderful" garden of this
alian eatery is truly "Little Italy at its finest"; the modestly priced
od is "fresh", portions "solid" and service "attentive."

Daniel 🗷 *French*

| | | 28 | 28 | 28 | $132 |

60s | 60 E. 65th St. (bet. Madison & Park Aves.) | 212-288-0033 |
www.danielnyc.com

n "unparalleled dining experience" awaits at Daniel Boulud's "im-
eccable" UES namesake, the "standard" for "luxe" prix fixe–only New
ench fare and rated NYC's No. 1 for Food; add an "amazing" wine
st, "breathtaking" decor and "flawless", "white-glove service" and
's easy to see why this is at the "top of the NY dining food chain"; of
ourse, the tab is equal to a "mortgage payment", but "if you're going
 splurge", splurge on "perfection"; N.B. you can order à la carte in
e lounge; jackets required.

a Noi *Italian*

| | | 24 | 20 | 22 | $44 |

IEW Staten Island | 138 Fingerboard Rd. (Tompkins Ave.) | 718-720-1650
taten Island | 4358 Victory Blvd. (Westshore Expwy.) | 718-982-5040
nsiders gladly "travel to eat" at this "top-rate" SI Northern Italian
now with a new "happening" Fingerboard Road location), which

cooks up "some of the best food on the Island"; service is "friend
and the rates "reasonable", so, no surprise, it's "popular" enough
draw "crowds" and "long waits."

🅩 Danube ●🅩 Austrian

26 | 27 | 26 | $8(

TriBeCa | 30 Hudson St. (bet. Duane & Reade Sts.) | 212-791-3771
www.davidbouley.com

At David Bouley's "transporting" "TriBeCa gem", the "Klimt"-inspir
dining room (among the "most beautiful in NYC") takes you back to
more elegant time", while "sensational" French-accented Viennese fa
an "outstanding wine list" and "seamless", "pampering" service co
plete the "magical" experience; as one would expect, tabs also are "op
lent"; P.S. for a "very special" private party, check out the downsta

Darbar Indian

▽ 20 | 15 | 18 | $34

E 40s | 152 E. 46th St. (bet. Lexington & 3rd Aves.) | 212-681-4500
www.darbarny.com

It's "dependably delicious" as well as "affordable", so it's no wond
that this East Midtown Indian "packs in the crowds", particularly
the $10.95 lunch buffet; its "understated" space is "pleasant" (esp
cially upstairs) and service "friendly" – what more could you ask?

Da Silvano ● Italian

20 | 15 | 17 | $62

G Village | 260 Sixth Ave. (bet. Bleecker & Houston Sts.) | 212-982-2343
www.dasilvano.com

At Silvano Marchetto's Tuscan "scene" in the Village, "A-listers"
the "air-kiss count" at "charming", "hard-to-get" sidewalk table
though to many the "real star is the cooking" here; opinions are sp
on service ("snooty" vs. "down to earth"), and prices ("stratospher
vs. less than you'd pay to see your fellow diners on stage).

Da Tommaso ● Italian

20 | 14 | 19 | $45

W 50s | 903 Eighth Ave. (bet. 53rd & 54th Sts.) | 212-265-1890

It plies "tasty" Northern Italian "standards" and gets you "in and ou
with "minimal fuss", so it's no wonder show-goers "depend" on th
"convenient" Theater District vet; the decor "could use updating", b
regulars just "don't look at anything but the food."

Da Umberto 🅩 Italian

25 | 18 | 23 | $60

Chelsea | 107 W. 17th St. (bet. 6th & 7th Aves.) | 212-989-0303

Seekers of "old-fashioned Italian dining at its best" collect at th
"dignified" Chelsea "institution" where the "superb" Tuscan fa
comes via "solicitous" "pro" waiters; most agree it "still has it" after
these years, though there are a few complaints about "tired" dec
and "formidable" tabs.

🅩 davidburke & donatella American

25 | 23 | 23 | $75

E 60s | 133 E. 61st St. (bet. Lexington & Park Aves.) | 212-813-2121
www.dbdrestaurant.com

Chef David Burke's East Side New American never fails to "impres
with its "innovative", "whimsical" cuisine "served impeccably" wi
oh-so-"chic" co-owner Donatella Arpaia's oversight; the "funk
townhouse setting and "flamboyant" extras like a limo for smoke
parked out front mean meals here are just plain "fun", except possib
the prices – but then there's always the $24 prix fixe lunch "bargain

	FOOD	DECOR	SERVICE	COST

avid Burke at Bloomingdale's American — 18 | 13 | 14 | $30

50s | Bloomingdale's | 159 E. 59th St. (bet. Lexington & 3rd Aves.) |
.2-705-3800 | www.burkeinthebox.com

wo favorite things" – "shopping and eating" – merge in "delicious"
shion at chef David Burke's "affordable" New American pit stop in-
de Bloomie's, featuring a cafe and adjacent "self-serve" "gourmet
st-food" shop; downsides are "discombobulated" service and an
wkward", "cramped" setting.

awat Indian — 23 | 18 | 21 | $46

50s | 210 E. 58th St. (bet. 2nd & 3rd Aves.) | 212-355-7555

urry queen" Madhur Jaffrey's East Midtowner reigns as a "favorite"
r "first-rate" Indian ferried by an "attentive" staff; maybe the prices
e a bit "high" and the setting could use a little "sprucing up", but
ost subjects say it's "still one of the best in town."

db Bistro Moderne French — 25 | 21 | 22 | $63

40s | City Club Hotel | 55 W. 44th St. (bet. 5th & 6th Aves.) |
.2-391-2400 | www.danielnyc.com

r the "ultimate" in Theater District dining, patrons pick Daniel
oulud's "snazzy French bistro" where the "top-notch" fare (including
at "legendary" $32 hamburger) tastes even better thanks to
harming" staffers who are "prompt" "without being pushy"; sure,
rices are steep", but then again the $45 dinner prix fixe is a "bargain
r a Boulud place."

eborah Ⓜ American — 21 | 14 | 20 | $36

Village | 43 Carmine St. (bet. Bedford & Bleecker Sts.) | 212-242-2606 |
ww.deborahlifelovefood.com

:omfort food" embodying an "interesting mix" of "haute and homey"
the deal at Deborah Stanton's "lovely little" Village New American;
air prices" compensate for the "narrow" space's slightly "claustro-
iobic" feel, and in summer there's always the "secret back garden."

ee's Brick Oven Pizza Ⓜ Mediterranean/Pizza — 22 | 17 | 18 | $27

•rest Hills | 107-23 Metropolitan Ave. (74th Ave.) | Queens |
l8-793-7553 | www.deesnyc.com

)ee-licious pizza" and a "plethora" of "tasty", "affordable" Med
shes make this "festive" (read: "noisy") Forest Hills eatery a favorite
"families with young kids"; despite "constant crowds", there's al-
ays "room to breathe" in its "comfy, casual" space.

eGrezia Ⓢ Italian — 22 | 20 | 22 | $60

50s | 231 E. 50th St. (bet. 2nd & 3rd Aves.) | 212-750-5353 |
ww.degreziaristorante.com

\ delightful surprise" hidden "partially underground", this Eastsider's
lelicious" Italian "classics" come on the high side via an "attentive"
o staff; perhaps trendsters find it "slightly stuffy", but mature "reg-
ars" "love" the "wonderful" "old-world" vibe.

egustation Ⓢ French/Spanish — 26 | 21 | 25 | $56

Village | 239 E. Fifth St. (bet. 2nd & 3rd Aves.) | 212-979-1012

oodies "yearning to try something new" hit Jack and Grace Lamb's
5-seat, "no-reservations" East Village tasting bar to "watch the in-
entive chef" prepare "stellar" French-Spanish small plates full of

"clean, bold flavors"; it's exciting culinary "theater" with "luxurio service" to boot, leaving just "one problem" – "long waits."

☑ Del Frisco's ● Steak 　　　25 | 22 | 22 | $70
W 40s | 1221 Sixth Ave. (48th St.) | 212-575-5129 | www.delfriscos.cc
"Boisterous" after-work types collect at this "snazzy", "hangar"-si Midtown "he-man's" steakhouse for "generous" pours and "giganti "first-rank" cuts via a "good-looking" crew; the "Texas"-scale tabs do faze "deep-pocketed" "movers and shakers", but wallet-watche stick to the $39.95 prix fixe; N.B. there are several luxe party rooms

Delmonico's ☒ Steak 　　　22 | 22 | 21 | $61
Financial District | 56 Beaver St. (S. William St.) | 212-509-1144 | www.delmonicosny.com
A Financial District "landmark" (circa 1827), this rehabbed stea house draws "Wall Street carnivores and cashivores" for "migh slabs" and "classic" sides tendered by an "unflappable" staff; its se ting of "sumptuous simplicity" continues to serve the 21st century versions of Diamond Jim Brady or John D.

☑ Del Posto Italian 　　　25 | 26 | 24 | $88
Chelsea | 85 10th Ave. (16th St.) | 212-497-8090 | www.delposto.con
"Dazzled" disciples of the "dress-up dining" at this Batali-Bastiani "instant classic" in Chelsea "come out reeling" after savoring its "su lime", "authentic" Italian cuisine, "phenomenal wine list" and servi as polished as the "beautiful marble floors" and dark-wood paneling its grand main dining room; yes, tabs here can "suck expense accoun dry", but there's always the "less-formal", "less-expensive" enoteca

Delta Grill ● Cajun/Creole 　　　19 | 15 | 17 | $32
W 40s | 700 Ninth Ave. (48th St.) | 212-956-0934 | www.thedeltagrill.co
"Wickedly good" Cajun-Creole eats keep patrons "marching in" to th Hell's Kitchen "dive" for "mammoth", "spicy", "stick-to-your-ribs" r pasts; service seems "uninterested", but the "cheap" rates and li music on weekends create a "down-home" New Orleans mood.

Demarchelier French 　　　17 | 15 | 15 | $47
E 80s | 50 E. 86th St. (bet. Madison & Park Aves.) | 212-249-6300 | www.demarchelierrestaurant.com
"Still drawing a crowd" after all these years, this "bustling" UES Fren balances "reliable" fare, a "lively bar" and "people-watching" galo against "sardine seating", "worn" decor and "haughty" service; in "food-challenged" area, it easily qualifies as a "neighborhood favorite.

Demetris ● Greek 　　　▽ 21 | 15 | 19 | $34
Astoria | 32-11 Broadway (bet. 32nd & 33rd Sts.) | Queens | 718-278-1877
It's "nothing fancy", but for "huge portions" of "fresh", "simple", "de ish" fish and other "conventional Greek" favorites, put this Astor seafood house on your list to try; "cheery, bright" decor, a "friendly "family"-oriented vibe and "good prices" round out the endorsemen

Denino's Pizzeria ⊘ Pizza 　　　25 | 10 | 18 | $19
Staten Island | 524 Port Richmond Ave. (bet. Hooker Pl. & Walker St.) | 718-442-9401
Maybe "it's not much to look at", but that "all melts away" when th "been-there-forever" Staten Island pie purveyor presents its "f

<table><thead><tr><th></th><th>FOOD</th><th>DECOR</th><th>SERVICE</th><th>COST</th></tr></thead></table>

ous", "delicious" pizzas and "pitchers of cold beer" at "low, low ices"; bring your bowling team and a "huge appetite."

ᴇᴡ Dennis Foy 🗷 American ▽ 24 22 24 $64
BeCa | 313 Church St. (bet. Lispenard & Walker Sts.) | 212-625-1007 | ww.dennisfoynyc.com

"understated addition" to the TriBeCa dining scene, this "inviting" ew American from Dennis Foy (Mondrian, EQ) has outgrown any start-
 "kinks" and is winning "wows" with its "wonderful" cuisine, "lovely" rvice and "serene", "modern interior" hung with "the chef's own intings"; tabs are a "comparative bargain" for a "foodie restaurant."

ervish Turkish ◗ Turkish 19 15 19 $35
40s | 146 W. 47th St. (bet. 6th & 7th Aves.) | 212-997-0070 | ww.dervishrestaurant.com

Theater District "change of pace", this Turkish "delight" dispenses "delectable array" of dishes via waiters who'd willingly "whirl around get you out on time"; it's "low on ambiance" but "the price is right", pecially the $23 early-bird prix fixe.

ᴇᴡ DeStefano's Steakhouse 🅼 Steak – – – E
illiamsburg | 89 Conselyea St. (Leonard St.) | Brooklyn | 718-384-2836 like most of Williamsburg's youthfully oriented newcomers, this eakhouse honors its deep-rooted Italian community with old-style stas and chops; the *Moonstruck* and *Saturday Night Fever* posters tside add some kitsch, but the snug interior keeps it simple with od wainscoting and family photos.

estino ◗ Italian 18 18 16 $56
50s | 891 First Ave. (50th St.) | 212-751-0700 | www.destinony.com e "jet set" rubs elbows with "quieter" Sutton Place denizens at this mping" "upscale" Italian where the "best meatballs" lead an other-se "hit-or-miss" "red-sauce" lineup; the fact that Justin Timberlake is backer adds "glitz", but "steep" prices and "bored" staffers don't.

eux Amis French 19 16 20 $50
50s | 356 E. 51st St. (bet. 1st & 2nd Aves.) | 212-230-1117 "welcoming" owner adds a "convivial" feel to this "unpretentious" st Midtown favorite; "don't expect fireworks", just "appealing", bundant" French bistro fare in a "low-key" setting, and maybe the nid-summer night" bonus of "sidewalk seating."

evin Tavern American 18 22 19 $53
BeCa | 363 Greenwich St. (bet. Franklin & Harrison Sts.) | 212-334-7337 | vw.devintavern.com

ere's "space for all" in this "big", "gorgeous" TriBeCa New American nose "modern ski-chalet"–like space is augmented with a "warm" d "clubby" downstairs lounge; surveyors split on the "pricey", leasantly varied" offerings ("amazing" vs. "passable"), but a post-rvey chef change should help.

ᴇᴡ Dieci ◗🗷 Italian ▽ 23 20 26 $39
Village | 228 E. 10th St. (bet. 1st & 2nd Aves.) | 212-387-9545 | ww.dieciny.com

e chef, owners, architect and "outstanding" staff may all be panese, but this "tiny" new sub-sidewalk East Villager trades in

| | FOOD | DECOR | SERVICE | COST |

"wonderful", well-priced Italian small plates; its sleek, "low-ke
space reflects the designer's minimalist Asian aesthetic.

☑ Di Fara ⌿ Pizza
27 | 4 | 7 | $1:

Midwood | 1424 Ave. J (bet. 14th & 15th Sts.) | Brooklyn | 718-258-13
It "looks like hell" and waits can be "timed with a calendar", but Domi
De Marco's "legendary" circa-1963 Midwood "mecca of pizza" crea
pies that are pure "heaven"; in sum, they're "all they're cracked up
be" – i.e. No. 1 in NYC.

Dim Sum Go Go Chinese
20 | 11 | 14 | $2:

Chinatown | 5 E. Broadway (Chatham Sq.) | 212-732-0797
"Made-to-order" "delicate, flavorful" dim sum comes "fresh out of t
kitchen" at this "white-tablecloth" Chinatown "standout"; it's "che:
and, despite "abrupt" service, more "peaceful" than the "hust
bustle" trolly type, even if some say "no pushcarts mean no fun."

Diner ◑ Diner
22 | 18 | 17 | $3:

Williamsburg | 85 Broadway (Berry St.) | Brooklyn | 718-486-3077
www.dinernyc.com
The "place that defined cool" in Williamsburg, this "lovingly renovat
diner" draws "arty" locals for "creative", "elevated" (yet affordab
New American grub dished up by a "relaxed" "hipster" staff; just kn
"it's a jungle on weekends" when "waits can be grueling", especia
for the "incredible brunch."

Dinosaur Bar-B-Que Ⓜ BBQ
22 | 16 | 17 | $2!

Harlem | 646 W. 131st St. (12th Ave.) | 212-694-1777 |
www.dinosaurbarbque.com
"Lip-smacking", "dino-size" BBQ and "good fixin's" washed down w
"amazing" microbrews make it "worth the hike" to this "cavernoι
West Harlem "faux" "roadhouse"; prices are "cheap to boot", so no wι
der it's often "crowded bedlam" here and a reservation is essential

Dirty Bird to-go American
17 | 5 | 12 | $1!

W Village | 204 W. 14th St. (bet. 7th Ave. S. & 8th Ave.) | 212-620-4836
www.dirtybirdtogo.com
A "welcome break from" the norm, this Village take-out joint serv
"succulent" free-range chicken, fried and rotisserie, plus "fresh" sid
still, critics squawk about "small portions" and seriously basic digs

Dishes Sandwiches
22 | 13 | 12 | $1:

E 40s | 6 E. 45th St. (bet. 5th & Madison Aves.) | 212-687-5511
E 40s | Grand Central | lower level (42nd St. & Vanderbilt Ave.) |
212-808-5511
E 50s | Citigroup Ctr. | 399 Park Ave. (54th St.) | 212-421-5511 ⑤
"Killer lines" form at lunchtime for this Midtown trio's "unbelievable
lection" of "terrific sandwiches", "can't-go-wrong" soups and "gourm
salads rated "way above the competitors'"; the answer to anyone w
claims "it's on the pricey side" is that "you're paying for quality."

District American
20 | 19 | 20 | $5:

W 40s | Muse Hotel | 130 W. 46th St. (bet. 6th & 7th Aves.) | 212-485-299
www.districtnyc.com
At this New American pre-curtain "favorite" within the Muse Hot
David Rockwell's "clever" "theater"-esque decor creates a "calm ·

	FOOD	DECOR	SERVICE	COST

is" amid the Times Square "frenzy"; "satisfying", "imaginative" fare, "personal service" and a "get-your-money's-worth" prix fixe should put it center stage.

Ditch Plains ● Seafood
17 | 16 | 17 | $37

G Village | 29 Bedford St. (Downing St.) | 212-633-0202 | www.ditch-plains.com

"Named after a Montauk surf break", Marc Murphy's "sceney" Village seafooder offers "interesting" "twists on traditional" shore favorites; it exudes a "mellow" vibe that makes it a "lovely place to loiter", though a few shrug "solid" but "forgettable."

Divino Italian
18 | 15 | 19 | $41

E 80s | 1556 Second Ave. (bet. 80th & 81st Sts.) | 212-861-1096 | www.divinoristorante.net

A "gracious host" sets the tone at this "relaxed" UES Northern Italian whose "reliable" cuisine holds "no surprises" but has you leaving "full and happy"; the "cute", candlelit setting may need "fixing up", but "attentive" staffers and "weekend music" keep locals "loyal" all the same.

Diwan Indian
▽ 21 | 17 | 18 | $33

E 40s | Helmsley Middletowne | 148 E. 48th St. (bet. Lexington & 3rd Aves.) | 212-593-5425

"Delicious, aromatic" Indian cuisine at modest prices makes this an East Midtown mainstay; it's particularly "busy" at lunch time, when business types pile in for the $13.95 "top-of-the-line buffet."

Django ☒ French/Mediterranean
20 | 23 | 20 | $52

E 40s | 480 Lexington Ave. (46th St.) | 212-871-6600 | www.djangorestaurant.com

"Drinks after work" have special "allure" in the "sea-of-suits" downstairs lounge at this "exotic" Midtowner, while "inventive", "tasty" French-Med cuisine holds sway in the "relatively tranquil" upstairs; all that jangles is "the price."

Docks Oyster Bar Seafood
19 | 16 | 17 | $47

E 40s | 633 Third Ave. (40th St.) | 212-986-8080
W 80s | 2427 Broadway (bet. 89th & 90th Sts.) | 212-724-5588
www.docksoysterbar.com

"Briny-fresh" fish, a "terrific raw bar" and "quality martinis" lure "oyster heads" and others to this "big, loud", "no-frills" pair of midpriced seafood "standbys"; admirers advise "for best results, keep it simple" – and remember that service is "catch as catch can."

Do Hwa Korean
21 | 19 | 17 | $38

G Village | 55 Carmine St. (bet. Bedford St. & 7th Ave. S.) | 212-414-1224 | www.dohwanyc.com

K-town" comes to Greenwich Village via this "cool", "minimalist" Korean specializing in "high-quality" BBQ meats; it's "a bit of a scene", where even "hit-or-miss service" doesn't dampen the "nightclub" vibe, abetted by "original cocktails" from a "sleek" bar, all at a modest cost.

Dok Suni's ●⌖ Korean
▽ 21 | 14 | 17 | $29

E Village | 119 First Ave. (bet. 7th St. & St. Marks Pl.) | 212-477-9506

"Calling all spicy-food lovers": this "dimly lit" East Village Korean attracts a "youngish crowd" with "consistently fine" eats, "potent martinis", "sweet", if distracted, service and a "funky vibe"; overall, it's "comfy" place for a date, as well as a "cash-only" "bargain."

Dominick's ⊘ *Italian*   22 | 9 | 16 | $35

Bronx | 2335 Arthur Ave. (bet. Crescent Ave. & E. 187th St.) | 718-733-2807.
"Go with friends" to best enjoy the "delicious" "red-sauce" Italia served "rough and tumble" at the elbow-to-elbow communal tables c this "quirky" Bronx "time warp"; there are no reservations, no men ("let the waiter order") and no bill (they "make up a price" and you pa in cash) – i.e. it's "a real NY experience"; N.B. a recent redo isn't re flected in the above Decor score.

Don Giovanni ● *Italian*   17 | 12 | 15 | $26

Chelsea | 214 10th Ave. (bet. 22nd & 23rd Sts.) | 212-242-9054
W 40s | 358 W. 44th St. (bet. 8th & 9th Aves.) | 212-581-4939
www.dongiovanni-ny.com
"Out-of-control" portions ensure "you won't walk out hungry" fro these "hopping" West Side Italian "carbfests" that locals "depend" o for "pleasing" pastas and brick-oven pizzas; service is "lackluster" an the decor a bit "tired", but sidewalk seating is redeeming in season.

Donguri Ⓜ *Japanese*   ▽ 27 | 15 | 24 | $62

E 80s | 309 E. 83rd St. (bet. 1st & 2nd Aves.) | 212-737-5656 |
www.dongurinyc.com
Now specializing in soba and udon noodle dishes, this UES Japanes "jewel" gets high ratings for the "artistic quality and precision" of i cooking (which excludes sushi); the staff presiding over its "Toky apartment"–size space is "beyond excellent", and while tabs are "e pensive", they're "not exorbitant" for such a "treat."

Don Pedro's *Caribbean/S American*   23 | 17 | 19 | $35

E 90s | 1865 Second Ave. (96th St.) | 212-996-3274 | www.donpedros.net
This "slightly upscale" UES Caribbean–South American brings "artis tic flair" to its "excellent", "savory" dishes, while "amiable service keeps the atmosphere "warm" – as do the "wonderful cocktails"; all i all, it's counted as a "gem" in an underserved neighborhood.

Don Peppe Ⓜ⊘ *Italian*   25 | 10 | 18 | $44

Ozone Park | 135-58 Lefferts Blvd. (149th Ave.) | Queens |
718-845-7587
"Noisy, celebratory" dining is the style at this "old-fashioned" cash-only Ozone Park Italian "icon" dishing up "outstanding "garlic"-laden classics on "huge" "family-style platters" plus "hous wine in unmarked bottles"; just "don't expect white-glove service" a "fancy setting."

Dos Caminos *Mexican*   20 | 20 | 18 | $43

E 50s | 825 Third Ave. (50th St.) | 212-336-5400
Gramercy | 373 Park Ave. S. (bet. 26th & 27th Sts.) | 212-294-1000
SoHo | 475 W. Broadway (Houston St.) | 212-277-4300
www.brguestrestaurants.com
There's "never a dull moment" at Steve Hanson's "energetic" trio "dressed-up" midpriced Mexicans; starting with the "made-at-you table guacamole", the menu still "dazzles", while "knockout marg take the edge off of "so-so" service and the "noise" kicked up by a those "singles and yuppies."

| | FOOD | DECOR | SERVICE | COST |

owntown Atlantic ⓜ *American*   19 | 16 | 19 | $32

erum Hill | 364 Atlantic Ave. (bet. Bond & Hoyt Sts.) | Brooklyn |
8-852-9945 | www.downtownatlantic.com

this "friendly" Boerum Hill New American, there's "straight-ahead"
e plus "out-of-this-world" desserts from a "cute little front bakery";
:tor in "cozy" digs and tabs "easy on the pocketbook", and you've
t the "perfect neighborhood restaurant."

oyers Vietnamese *Vietnamese*   20 | 6 | 13 | $16

inatown | 11-13 Doyers St., downstairs (Chatham Sq.) | 212-513-1521

a "subterranean" "secret den" on a "movie set–like" Chinatown
eet there's this "dirt-cheap" producer of "fresh", "terrific" Vietnamese
shes; given the "value", those "in-the-know" shrug "who cares"
out "erratic" service or "tacky", "dungeon"-like digs?

ressler *American*   24 | 25 | 23 | $47

illiamsburg | 149 Broadway (bet. Bedford & Driggs Aves.) | Brooklyn |
8-384-6343 | www.dresslernyc.com

Iaking a hell of an entrance", Williamsburg's "upscale but not up-
ht" New American "new kid on the block" is voted "fabulous" all
ound, mixing a "gorgeous" space (full of "handcrafted" "decorative
tails") with "spot-on" service and "stylish", "well-executed" cuisine
u'd "pay double for in Manhattan"; advice: go "while you still can."

uane Park Cafe *American*   24 | 19 | 23 | $52

BeCa | 157 Duane St. (bet. Hudson St. & W. B'way) | 212-732-5555 |
vw.duaneparkcafe.com

legant" New American food "perfectly served" is the forte of this
anquil" TriBeCa "find"; maybe it's "dwarfed by the big boys" nearby,
t "aficionados" report that it "never fails to please."

ue ◑ *Italian*   22 | 17 | 21 | $45

70s | 1396 Third Ave. (bet. 79th & 80th Sts.) | 212-772-3331

very neighborhood should be so lucky" gloat groupies of this "con-
nial" UES "staple" serving "solid" Northern Italian at "decent prices"
the area; it's a "kitchen away from home" for an "older crowd"
eking "low-key" meals that are "always on the mark."

uke's *Southern*   16 | 13 | 14 | $24

amercy | 99 E. 19th St. (Park Ave. S.) | 212-260-2922
EW Murray Hill | 560 Third Ave. (37th St.) | 212-949-5400
vw.dukesnyc.com

Iouthwatering pulled pork" and "juicy burgers" are among the
uthern-style "cheap eats" that come with "strong drinks" at these
owdy" "frat parties"; most like the "damn fine trashy food" and "hot"
itresses, but others suggest you "tie your arteries closed" first.

uMont *American*   23 | 17 | 17 | $27

illiamsburg | 432 Union Ave. (bet. Devoe St. & Metropolitan Ave.) |
ooklyn | 718-486-7717 | www.dumontrestaurant.com

uMont Burger ◑ *American*

illiamsburg | 314 Bedford Ave. (bet. S. 1st & 2nd Sts.) | Brooklyn |
8-384-6127

dgy and hipster-laden", this "cozy" Williamsburg New American
acks 'em in" with its "appealing" "comfort" fare, which tastes better

with some elbow room out in the "wonderful garden"; "insane
good" burgers and sandwiches are served until the wee hours at t
Bedford Avenue offshoot.

Dumpling Man ● Chinese | | | | 19 | 7 | 13 | $11

E Village | 100 St. Marks Pl. (bet. Ave. A & 1st Ave.) | 212-505-2121 |
www.dumplingman.com

"Marvelous", "chubby dumplings" in "exciting flavors" are made "hy‍
notically" before your eyes at this East Village Chinese; its "bar‍
bones" space is "teeny", meaning for most it's "strictly takeaway", a‍
happily "not many pennies are needed" for a "fast fix."

Dylan Prime Steak | | | 24 | 23 | 22 | $64

TriBeCa | 62 Laight St. (Greenwich St.) | 212-334-4783 |
www.dylanprime.com

"Not your grandpa's steakhouse", this "suave" TriBeCa version go‍
well beyond red meat as it attracts "suits" and "young singles" with
first-class fare, "solicitous" service and a next-door "bar scene tha‍
a blast"; no wonder it's a "bit expensive."

NEW Earthen Oven Indian | | | 21 | 12 | 19 | $34

W 70s | 53 W. 72nd St. (Columbus Ave.) | 212-579-8888

"Terrifically tasty" dishes (via ex Tamarind chefs) come out of the ta‍
door at this "friendly", "high-end" Indian newcomer near Linc‍
Center that has already won a loyal following; despite a lacklust‍
"long, narrow" space that has seen "quite a lot of turnover" over t‍
years, this one seems to be here to stay.

East Buffet Eclectic | | | 20 | 14 | 12 | $27

Flushing | 42-07 Main St. (Maple Ave.) | Queens | 718-353-6333 |
www.eastusa.com

The "elaborate" "all-you-can-eat" buffet boasting every taste "you c‍
imagine" (200-plus dishes) is the thing at this "enormous" Asia‍
Eclectic Flushing "palace", though you can go à la carte too; expec‍
"madhouse on weekends", when "value"-seekers come to "chow dow‍

East Manor Chinese | | | ▽ 19 | 14 | 13 | $24

Flushing | 46-45 Kissena Blvd. (Laburnum Ave.) | Queens | 718-888-899‍
"Sunday morning dim sum" is the ticket at this big, "busy" Flushi‍
Chinese, but it also offers the same wide "variety" of "deliciou‍
"cheap", "cart"-borne tidbits daily at lunch; it's "crowded" and has su‍
par service, so think of it as an "adventure" and "be prepared to wai‍

East of Eighth ● Eclectic | | | 16 | 15 | 18 | $31

Chelsea | 254 W. 23rd St. (bet. 7th & 8th Aves.) | 212-352-0075 |
www.eastofeighth.com

"Hot scene downstairs, quieter dining upstairs" and a "relaxing o‍
door garden" are the highlights of this "low-budget" Chelsea Eclec‍
cafe; for "best value" join the neighbors at the "$18 early-bird specia‍
and don't forget brunch."

NEW East Village Yacht Club ⊠ American | | | - | - | - | M

E Village | 42 E. First St. (bet. 1st & 2nd Aves.) | 212-777-5617 |
www.evyc.com

This new East Village duplex replicates an upper-crust country club‍
its ample use of nautical memorabilia; the Cape Cod-esque dow‍

| | FOOD | DECOR | SERVICE | COST |

stairs dining room features suitably Waspy American fare (think Cobb salad, spinach dip, icebox cake) priced to please parsimonious preppies.

E.A.T. *American*
| 19 | 11 | 14 | $39 |

E 80s | 1064 Madison Ave. (bet. 80th & 81st Sts.) | 212-772-0022 | www.elizabar.com

"Handy" as a "shopping" or museum-hopping "reenergizer", Eli Zabar's beloved "chaotic" UES "emporium" is renowned for "fabulous sandwiches" and other "stylish" choices; it draws a "chic" local crowd that doesn't blink at "iffy service", "zero" decor and record-breaking rates – at this point it's a "NY fixture."

Eatery ◐ *American*
| 19 | 16 | 16 | $32 |

W 50s | 798 Ninth Ave. (53rd St.) | 212-765-7080 | www.eaterynyc.com
The look is *"Mad Max* minimalist" at this Hell's Kitchen New American, where a "cool", "elbow-to-elbow" crowd creates "quite the scene" while munching "inventive home cooking" (e.g. "slammin'" mac 'n' jack); service is overly "relaxed", but at least the prices are too.

Ecco ☒ *Italian*
| 21 | 17 | 20 | $52 |

TriBeCa | 124 Chambers St. (bet. Church St. & W. B'way) | 212-227-7074
"Traditional" is the word for this "reliable" TriBeCa Italian offering "well-prepared" favorites in an "old-school", "Sinatra"-worthy setting; most agree it's "pricey" but "worth it", especially when the "weekend piano bar" is in session and the mood gets "romantic."

Edgar's Cafe ◐⇏ *Coffeehouse*
| 18 | 18 | 15 | $20 |

W 80s | 255 W. 84th St. (bet. B'way & West End Ave.) | 212-496-6126
A raven couldn't find a more "dizzying array of desserts" than at this "bohemian" UWS coffeehouse-cum-Edgar Allan Poe homage; it's a "pleasant hangout" and good for an affordable "late-night nosh", but given the "not-so-special" service, "don't be in a rush."

Edison Cafe ⇏ *Coffee Shop*
| 15 | 8 | 13 | $21 |

W 40s | Edison Hotel | 228 W. 47th St. (bet. B'way & 8th Ave.) | 212-840-5000
Widely known as "the Polish Tea Room" or the Shubert Cafeteria, this "kitschy", "cheap" Theater District coffee shop has become a "legend" thanks to its Broadway "celebrity-sighting" and "old-fashioned Jewish" staples like matzo ball soup and blintzes; maybe it's in line for a "rehab", but most feel "they should landmark the interior."

NEW Ed's Lobster Bar Ⓜ *Seafood*
| ▽ 23 | 15 | 16 | $42 |

NoLita | 222 Lafayette St. (bet. Kenmare & Spring Sts.) | 212-343-3236 | www.lobsterbarnyc.com

"Sensational" "lobster roll fixes" can now be had in NoLita thanks to this "excellent" "New England–style" seafood arrival from an ex–Pearl Oyster Bar sous-chef; despite "amateurish service" and other "newness" "kinks", its counter seats and handful of tables are already a squeeze.

Edward's ◐ *American*
| 16 | 14 | 17 | $29 |

TriBeCa | 136 W. Broadway (bet. Duane & Thomas Sts.) | 212-233-6436 | www.edwardsnyc.com

"Part diner, part bistro", this "welcoming", well-priced TriBeCa American is where "locals gather" to "unwind" over "reliable" comfort fare, including "fantastic breakfasts"; by day there are "tons of kids", but nighttime brings a "swinging" "bar scene" and even "an occasional celeb" sighting.

	FOOD	DECOR	SERVICE	COST

Eight Mile Creek ● *Australian* ▽ 20 | 15 | 19 | $40

Little Italy | 240 Mulberry St. (bet. Prince & Spring Sts.) | 212-431-4635
www.eightmilecreek.com

"G'day, mate" – at this Little Italy taste of "Down Under", the "mid-priced" Aussie grub includes some "exotic" choices like kangaroo; it's "overrun with expats" so expect appealing "Oz attitude" and "energy", whether upstairs, in the casual downstairs pub or in the "cool garden."

EJ's Luncheonette ⊟ *American* 15 | 9 | 14 | $22

E 70s | 1271 Third Ave. (73rd St.) | 212-472-0600
W 80s | 447 Amsterdam Ave. (bet. 81st & 82nd Sts.) | 212-873-3444
"Darn-good breakfasts" star at these crosstown "retro-'50s" diners that proffer a "giant menu" of "homespun" affordable Americana, they're "havens" for the "mommy brigade" and "mobbed on week-ends", despite "dumpy digs" and "get 'em in, get 'em out" service.

Elaine's ● *American/Italian* 13 | 14 | 13 | $54

E 80s | 1703 Second Ave. (bet. 88th & 89th Sts.) | 212-534-8103
Among "the last of the old NY haunts with old NYers still haunting it", Elaine Kaufman's "playground" hosts an UES crowd of "characters" and "literary folk" who don't mind that the Italian-American fare is "mediocre", the service "surly" and the "tavern" digs in need of an "update"; Page Six mentions notwithstanding, ordinary joes wonder "what's all the fuss about?"

El Centro ● *Mexican* 18 | 17 | 18 | $27

W 50s | 824 Ninth Ave. (54th St.) | 646-763-6585 |
www.elcentro-nyc.com
A "cut above" "your usual Mexican", this "happening" Hell's Kitchen cantina plies a "young" crowd with "cheap eats" delivered by a "chirpy" staff; its "kitschy", "cramped" space gets "loud", but patrons "chugging the house margaritas" don't seem to mind.

El Charro Español *Spanish* 22 | 15 | 22 | $40

G Village | 4 Charles St. (bet. Greenwich Ave. & 7th Ave. S.) | 212-242-9547 |
www.el-charro-espanol.com
Offering a "hospitable bit of old Spain" since 1925, this "off-the-beaten-path" Villager turns out "surprisingly good" "Spanish classics" ferried by "genuine, kind" staffers; as for the "cozy" subterranean space, you'll feel you took "a time machine to an earlier era."

El Cid ⧆Ⓜ *Spanish* 21 | 13 | 19 | $35

Chelsea | 322 W. 15th St. (bet. 8th & 9th Aves.) | 212-929-9332
"Wonderful tapas" "pile up fast and furious" at this "unassuming" Chelsea Spaniard serving "all the old reliables" plus "knockout san-gria" in the "smallest piece of real estate" around; just "ignore the silly outdated" decor and "elbow your way to a table."

Elephant, The ● *French/Thai* ▽ 21 | 16 | 15 | $36

E Village | 58 E. First St. (bet. 1st & 2nd Aves.) | 212-505-7739 |
www.elephantrestaurant.com
You couldn't even think about "fitting an elephant" into the "tiny" quar-ters of this "funky", "raucous" Thai-French East Villager; still, "crowds "squeeze in" for "knock-your-socks-off" Thai-French fare and "fancy cocktails", never mind the "lackluster service" and "noisy" acoustics.

lephant & Castle ● *Pub Food*

17 | 14 | 17 | $26

Village | 68 Greenwich Ave. (bet. Perry St. & 7th Ave. S.) | 212-243-1400 | ww.elephantandcastle.com

Dependable" for "comforting" American "pub grub" and an "exceptional brunch", this "lively" Villager has been a "neighborhood hangut" going way back; space is "tight", but the "sweet" (if sometimes razzled") staff and "moderate prices" compensate.

EW eleven B. ● *Italian/Pizza*

– | ⟋ | – | I

Village | 174 Ave. B (11th St.) | 212-388-9811 | www.11Bexpress.com

ld-school with a 21st-century edge, this new East Village Italian oasts rustic tables and an antique fireplace, plus plasma TVs; its hin-crust" pizzas and other affordable standards are served by a personable" crew, and are available to-go at the next-door annex.

Eleven Madison Park *French*

26 | 26 | 26 | $104

ramercy | 11 Madison Ave. (24th St.) | 212-889-0905 | ww.elevenmadisonpark.com

ow with a "brilliant" New French menu from executive chef Daniel umm, Danny Meyer's "magical" Madison Square Park "triumph" is better than ever"; "it's posh", with "polished service" in a "huge", gorgeous" "vaulted room", and although the prix fixe "price tags qual" its "high culinary" standard and a few mutter about "midget ortions", most "blather on" about "blissdom."

Faro ● Ⓜ *Spanish*

23 | 11 | 18 | $38

Ⅴ Village | 823 Greenwich St. (Horatio St.) | 212-929-8210 | ww.elfaronyc.com

Age does no harm" to this "convivial" Village Spaniard and the "fantastic paella" and other "delicious", "garlicky" standards it's been erving for 80 years; its "shoebox" digs are beyond "faded" and even he "old-time" waiters "seem the same" from decade to decade, but at's all "part of the charm."

liá Ⓜ *Greek*

▽ 25 | 19 | 23 | $46

ay Ridge | 8611 Third Ave. (bet. 86th & 87th Sts.) | Brooklyn | 18-748-9891 | www.eliarestaurant.com

abulous" "fresh seafood" "prepared with a light touch" is the forte of is "charming", "no-fuss" Bay Ridge Hellenic; the "wonderful" staff reats you like family", while the whitewashed walls and flower-filled eck have you imagining "you're in Greece."

lias Corner ● 🕏 *Greek/Seafood*

22 | 8 | 13 | $36

storia | 24-02 31st St. (24th Ave.) | Queens | 718-932-1510

 say it's "nothing fancy" is an understatement, but this affordable storia Greek "dive" is nevertheless a source for first-rate grilled fish d other "remarkable" Hellenic classics; service is "brusque", "napns are paper" and it's cash-only, but go once, you'll go again.

lio's ● *Italian*

23 | 16 | 19 | $59

80s | 1621 Second Ave. (bet. 84th & 85th Sts.) | 212-772-2242

Getting a table is always a challenge" at this "chic" UES Italian known s much for its clientele of "famous faces" and "'in' crowd" types as for s "consistently delicious" fare; service is "professional" enough, but ou may "feel a little left out" if "you're not a regular."

	FOOD	DECOR	SERVICE	COST

El Malecon *Dominican* — 21 | 8 | 14 | $17

Washington Heights | 4141 Broadway (175th St.) | 212-927-3812 ●
W 90s | 764 Amsterdam Ave. (bet. 97th & 98th Sts.) | 212-864-564▮
Bronx | 5592 Broadway (231st St.) | 718-432-5155 ◑
www.maleconrestaurants.com

"Hearty", "honest" eats ("heavenly" rotisserie chicken) at minim▮
cost have kept these "lively", "friendly" Uptown Dominicans perpet▮
ally "packed"; decor is strictly "bare-bones", but "lightning-fast deli▮
ery" is the way to avoid it.

elmo ◑ *American* — 15 | 17 | 15 | $32

Chelsea | 156 Seventh Ave. (bet. 19th & 20th Sts.) | 212-337-8000
www.elmorestaurant.com

"Chelsea boys" "show off their muscles" amid a nonstop "party"▮
this "retro"-"trendy" New American "upscale diner"; some say it
"better for the drinks than the grub" (though brunch is a standout▮
but "hot waiters" and "decent prices" keep it humming.

El Parador Cafe *Mexican* — 20 | 16 | 21 | $42

Murray Hill | 325 E. 34th St. (bet. 1st & 2nd Aves.) | 212-679-6812
www.elparadorcafe.com

"Still flying under the radar", this Murray Hill Mexican standby make▮
a "delightful break from the nuevo invasion" with its "surprising▮
decent" dishes and a "hospitable" staff; digs are so "dated" it▮
"soothing" – ditto the "fabulous sangria" and margaritas.

El Paso ◑ *Mexican/Spanish* — - | - | - | M

G Village | 134 W. Houston St. (bet. MacDougal & Sullivan Sts.) |
212-673-0828 | www.elpasonyc.com

Modest prices and generous portions keep the trade brisk at this ve▮
erable Villager offering a large array of Spanish-Mexican dishes in▮
small setting; it's a quiet refuge from the trendier neighbors nearb▮
drawing in loyal supporters and curious passersbys.

El Paso Taqueria *Mexican* — 22 | 11 | 17 | $23

E 100s | 1642 Lexington Ave. (104th St.) | 212-831-9831 ◑
E 90s | 64 E. 97th St. (Park Ave.) | 212-996-1739
NEW **Harlem** | 237 E. 116th St. (bet. Lexington & 3rd Aves.) |
212-860-4875 ◑
www.elpasotaqueria.com

"Gringos are made to feel welcome" at this "terrific" "far UES" tr▮
serving "super-good", "real-deal" Mexican "prepared with heart"; th▮
"homey" surroundings are "not much to look at" and "slow service is▮
downside" but "bargain" rates trump all.

El Pote ⧖ *Spanish* — 21 | 14 | 21 | $41

Murray Hill | 718 Second Ave. (bet. 38th & 39th Sts.) | 212-889-668▮
Don't judge this "gracious" Murray Hill Spaniard by its facade, b▮
cause "waiting within" is a "lively clientele" partaking of "pleasi▮
paella" and other *bueno* "down-to-earth" dishes; maybe it could u▮
a "face-lift", but most just "focus on the food."

El Quijote ◑ *Spanish* — 19 | 14 | 17 | $39

Chelsea | 226 W. 23rd St. (bet. 7th & 8th Aves.) | 212-929-1855
You half expect "Ricky Ricardo will walk in" to this "cheerful" Chelse▮
"golden oldie" (circa 1930) famed for its "classic" "lobster-drive▮

FOOD	DECOR	SERVICE	COST

panish cooking and "strong sangria"; portions are "ample" and prices
air", so most "look past" "siesta-paced service" and "campy" decor.

mbers *Steak*

| 22 | 13 | 17 | $44 |

ay Ridge | 9519 Third Ave. (bet. 95th & 96th Sts.) | Brooklyn | 718-745-3700
Nothing beats the T-bone for two" at this "casual" Bay Ridge steak-
ouse claim carnivores who don't let "long waits" or "crowded", "run-
own" digs dampen the fire; further fanning the ardor are "valet
arking" and prices that "won't break the bank."

mpanada Mama ● *S American*

| 20 | 10 | 14 | $15 |

W 50s | 763 Ninth Ave. (bet. 51st & 52nd Sts.) | 212-698-9008
Myriad" "cheap" empanadas with "assorted fillings" (even dessert
ptions) are the draw at this "funky" Hell's Kitchen South American
torefront; it's a "tiny place" where "cooked-to-order" means "slow
ervice", so "bring your patience."

mpire Diner ● *Diner*

| 15 | 15 | 14 | $24 |

helsea | 210 10th Ave. (22nd St.) | 212-243-2736
Possibly the hippest diner on earth", this Chelsea vet is "still going
trong", dishing up "reliable comfort food" 24/7; its "black-and-chrome"
art deco" digs (circa 1929), long hours and sidewalk seating are long-
tanding lures that become irresistible to club-goers after 2 AM.

mpire Szechuan ● *Chinese*

| 15 | 9 | 14 | $22 |

Village | 15 Greenwich Ave. (bet. Christopher & W. 10th Sts.) |
12-691-1535 | www.empiretogo.com
Village | 173 Seventh Ave. S. (bet. Perry & W. 11th Sts.) |
12-243-6046
Washington Heights | 4041 Broadway (bet. 170th & 171st Sts.) |
12-568-1600
W 60s | 193 Columbus Ave. (bet. 68th & 69th Sts.) | 212-496-8778
W 100s | 2642 Broadway (100th St.) | 212-662-9404 | www.empiretogo.com
round "just about every corner", this "Empire of cheap Chinese"
ooking can be "counted on" for its "huge menu" that drifts over to
ushi at times; the food is "pretty good" but "the decor isn't appetiz-
g", leading many to consider it more of a "delivery standby."

mployees Only ● *European*

| 18 | 21 | 18 | $42 |

W Village | 510 Hudson St. (bet. Christopher & W. 10th Sts.) |
12-242-3021 | www.employeesonlynyc.com
Outstanding mixology" and a "gorgeous faux-speakeasy" setting
nake for "fantastic bar" action at this "cocktail-centric" West Villager;
hough secondary to the "scene", its "surprisingly good" European
ood is served until "late night" and out in an "adorable garden."

nergy Kitchen *Health Food*

| 18 | 6 | 14 | $13 |

helsea | 307 W. 17th St. (bet. 8th & 9th Aves.) | 212-645-5200
E 40s | 300 E. 41st. St. (2nd Ave.) | 212-687-1200
E 50s | 1089 Second Ave. (bet. 57th & 58th Sts.) | 212-888-9300
W 40s | 417 W. 47th St. (bet. 9th & 10th Aves.) | 212-333-3500
W Village | 82 Christopher St. (bet. Bleecker St. & 7th Ave. S.) |
12-414-8880
ww.energykitchen.com
Who knew healthy could taste so good?" pant partakers of the bison
urgers, "creative wraps" and other "nutritious" "fast food" dispensed

te at zagat.com

| | FOOD | DECOR | SERVICE | COST |

by this "quick" quintet; costs are "low", but given the "sterile environ-
ment", "post-gym" types may opt "for takeout" or energetic delivery

EN Japanese Brasserie *Japanese*
22 | 25 | 20 | $56

W Village | 435 Hudson St. (Leroy St.) | 212-647-9196 | www.enjb.com
The "high-design", "large, open" quarters at this "chic" West Village
threaten to "outshine" the "delicious" Japanese small plates (including "outstanding housemade tofu"); it gets bonus points for a "helpful"
staff and a "sake lover's dream" bar, if not its high-EN tabs.

Ennio & Michael *Italian*
21 | 16 | 21 | $42

G Village | 539 La Guardia Pl. (bet. Bleecker & W. 3rd Sts.) | 212-677-8577
www.ennioandmichael.com
Loyal locals rely on this "comforting" Village Italian for its "peaceful"
ambiance" and "warm hospitality", not to mention "wholesome"
"classic" cuisine; maybe the decor's "a little plain-Jane", but in summer there's dining on the "nicest" terrace.

Enzo's *Italian*
23 | 14 | 20 | $35

Bronx | 1998 Williamsbridge Rd. (Neill Ave.) | 718-409-3828 Ⓜ
Bronx | 2339 Arthur Ave. (bet. Crescent Ave. & E. 186th St.) | 718-733-4455
These Bronx "crowd-pleasers" prepare "standard Italian to perfection"
and "don't mess it up" with newfangled ideas; everything comes via
"warm", "hustling" staff at "more than fair" prices, but beware – "no
reserving" equals "long waits", and once inside, the decor is "blah."

Epices du Traiteur *Mediterranean/Tunisian*
21 | 16 | 20 | $42

W 70s | 103 W. 70th St. (Columbus Ave.) | 212-579-5904
"Vive la différence!" declare diners "enjoying" the "interesting", "delicious" Med-Tunisian fare at this "popular" (i.e. sometimes "overcrowded") Lincoln Center-area "find"; "competent service" is a plus,
as are "affordable" rates and the garden when open.

Erawan *Thai*
22 | 20 | 19 | $37

Bayside | 213-41 39th Ave. (Bell Blvd.) | Queens | 718-229-1620
Bayside | 42-31 Bell Blvd. (bet. 43rd Ave. & Northern Blvd.) | Queens |
718-428-2112
www.erawan-seafoodandsteak.com
"Getting more popular all the time" (i.e. more "crowded"), thes
good-buy Bayside Thais offer "top-notch" dishes running "from
traditional to exotic", with the 39th Avenue branch specializing i
Siamese takes on steak and seafood; service with a "smile" overcome
any "language problems."

Erminia 🛢 *Italian*
25 | 24 | 25 | $63

E 80s | 250 E. 83rd St. (bet. 2nd & 3rd Aves.) | 212-879-4284
Romance practically "seeps from the walls" at this UES Italian "hideaway", where an "attentive staff" dispenses *delizioso* Roman dishe
in a "small, well-appointed" candlelit room; it "sets the stage" for "lovers" "to get engaged", but even old married couples suggest celebrating "happy anything" here.

Esca ◐ *Italian/Seafood*
25 | 20 | 21 | $67

W 40s | 402 W. 43rd St. (9th Ave.) | 212-564-7272 | www.esca-nyc.com
A Batali-Bastianich-Pasternak production, this "airy" Theater Distric
Italian seafooder has "true foodies swooning" over its "piscator

excellence" – and "the pastas are no slouch either"; add a "solicitous" staff and a "splurge"-size tab seems quite reasonable.

Esperanto ● Nuevo Latino
20 | 17 | 18 | $29

E Village | 145 Ave. C (9th St.) | 212-505-6559 | www.esperantony.com

"Food as hot as the patrons" plus "powerful drinks" and low prices mean this "perky" East Village Nuevo Latino speaks the language of "young, vibrant" types who pack in for a "sultry meal" and a "good time"; service may be "lackadaisical", but not the "lively" music.

ESPN Zone American
12 | 19 | 14 | $29

W 40s | 1472 Broadway (42nd St.) | 212-921-3776 | www.espnzone.com

You can be certain "your game will be on" and the "kids will have a blast" at this "oversized" Times Square American that's the "ultimate in sports bars"; it's "crazy loud" and "you don't go for the food" or the "spotty" service, but "real fans" and "tourists" give it a rousing "rah rah" nonetheless. ●

Ess-a-Bagel Deli
23 | 6 | 13 | $10

E 50s | 831 Third Ave. (bet. 50th & 51st Sts.) | 212-980-1010
Gramercy | 359 First Ave. (21st St.) | 212-260-2252
www.ess-a-bagel.com

"Not for carbophobes", these "rushed" East Side delis proffer "fresh, hot, chewy" "doughy" bagels "bigger than your head", crowned with "every topping known to man"; service is "crusty", decor "not pretty" and lines "long", but the price is right.

Essex ● M American
20 | 17 | 15 | $29

LES | 120 Essex St. (Rivington St.) | 212-533-9616 | www.essexnyc.com

This "funky" LES New American is "packed on weekends" when "young" locals and "Uptown tourists" mingle for the "killer" "liquid brunch", and nobody notices "patchy" service; cognoscenti say the affordable Jewish-Latin–accented eats are "even better for dinner."

NEW Estancia 460 Argentinean/Italian
▽ 21 | 18 | 20 | $41
(fka Sosa Borella)

TriBeCa | 460 Greenwich St. (bet. Desbrosses & Watts Sts.) | 212-431-5093 | www.estancia460.com

Despite its new moniker, this TriBeCa Italian-Argentinean still feels like the same "laid-back", "homey" place that chic "neighborhood regulars" have been coming to for years; a "winning" menu of "consistent" fare, decent prices and "friendly" service are the reasons why.

Etats-Unis American
25 | 16 | 22 | $57

E 80s | 242 E. 81st St. (bet. 2nd & 3rd Aves.) | 212-517-8826

A "relaxed" UES "charmer", this "pint-size" New American offers "consistently interesting", sometimes "inspired" dishes delivered by "pleasant" staffers in "minimalist" digs; those seeking "the same great food at lower prices" cross the street to its "tiny", "happening" wine bar.

etcetera etcetera ● M Italian
20 | 19 | 20 | $48

W 40s | 352 W. 44th St. (bet. 8th & 9th Aves.) | 212-399-4141 | www.etcrestaurant.com

Personable" waiters preside over the "stylish" setting of this "nifty" Theater District Italian offering "inventive", "beautifully presented" dishes, including many available in "half portions"; if the "harsh acoustics" are irksome, keep in mind "upstairs is much quieter than down" at this "worthy spin-off of ViceVersa."

	FOOD	DECOR	SERVICE	COST

Ethiopian Restaurant *Ethiopian* — 17 | 12 | 17 | $26

E 80s | 1582 York Ave. (bet. 83rd & 84th Sts.) | 212-717-7311
"Basic decor and basic service" accompany the "authentic Ethiopian eats" at this "informal" UES "cubbyhole"; the "vegetarian-friendly" (and wallet-friendly) fare may be an "acquired taste", but "who doesn't love eating with their hands?"

Ethos ● *Greek* — 22 | 16 | 19 | $37

Murray Hill | 495 Third Ave. (bet. 33rd & 34th Sts.) | 212-252-1972 | www.ethosnyc.com
NEW Astoria | 33-04 Broadway (bet. 33rd & 34th Sts.) | Queens | 718-278-1001
"Fantastic" fish is "grilled to perfection" at this "busy" Murray Hill Greek, where the "traditional cooking" has surveyors shouting "*opa!*" and the prices have them "dancing in the aisles" – never mind the "uninspiring" decor and "slow" service; N.B. the Astoria location opened post-Survey.

NEW E.U., The ● *European* — ▽ 20 | 23 | 19 | $43
(aka European Union)

E Village | 235 E. Fourth St. (bet. Aves. A & B) | 212-254-2900 | www.theeunyc.com
"Bringing sophistication to the gastropub model", this "ambitious", "good-looking" European done up in "signature AvroKO" style turns out an "eclectic" range of "buzzworthy" "morsels"; its "low-key" vibe suits its "young" "Alphabet City crowd", leaving "sporadic" service as its only demerit.

Euzkadi *Spanish* — ▽ 21 | 19 | 17 | $37

E Village | 108 E. Fourth St. (bet. 1st & 2nd Aves.) | 212-982-9788 | www.euzkadirestaurant.com
"Unpronounceable" though it may be, admirers aver the name of this "fun" East Village Basque "should be on everyone's lips" given its "wonderful tapas"; an "artistic setting" and "friendly prices" attract "young" types, who add Tuesday flamenco as "another reason to come."

Evergreen Shanghai *Chinese* — 19 | 12 | 16 | $23

Murray Hill | 10 E. 38th St. (bet. 5th & Madison Aves.) | 212-448-1199
The "genuine" "Shanghainese cuisine" at this Murray Hill Chinese includes dishes "rarely found on menus in English", as well as "marvelous dim sum" and "soup dumplings", all "priced right"; there's almost "no atmosphere" but service is "super fast" – a good thing because it's often "nuts at lunchtime."

Excellent Dumpling House ⊅ *Chinese* — 21 | 5 | 11 | $15

Chinatown | 111 Lafayette St. (bet. Canal & Walker Sts.) | 212-219-0212
"True to its name", this usually "mobbed" Chinatowner turns out "transcendent dumplings" as well as Shanghai-style "staples" like "delicious" noodle dishes; its prices are so "low", most happily "forget" the "eat-and-run" pace, "awful decor" and "cafeteria seating" next to "strangers on jury duty."

	FOOD	DECOR	SERVICE	COST

Extra Virgin *Mediterranean* — 21 | 17 | 18 | $40

W Village | 259 W. Fourth St. (bet. Charles & Perry Sts.) | 212-691-9359 | www.extravirginrestaurant.com

"Pretty people" populate this "loud" West Villager serving "tempting" midpriced Med fare and a "sumptuous Sunday brunch"; those who "survive the wait" to get in find sometimes "scatterbrained" staffers and tables in "close proximity", though "sidewalk seating" is an "enjoyable" warm weather option.

NEW Fabio Piccolo Fiore *Italian* — - | - | - | M

E 40s | 230 E. 44th St. (bet. 2nd & 3rd Aves.) | 212-922-0581

The underserved area around Grand Central gets a boost with the arrival of this "cheery" new Italian, a "grown-up" enclave that's surprisingly upscale given the down-to-earth pricing; the twist here is that the chef is willing to go beyond the menu to "prepare special requests."

Fairway Cafe *American* — 18 | 8 | 11 | $28

W 70s | 2127 Broadway, 2nd fl. (74th St.) | 212-595-1888
Red Hook | 480-500 Van Brunt St. (Reed St.) | Brooklyn | 718-694-6868 | www.fairwaymarket.com

"A haven" from the "hubbub" of the supermarkets they're part of, these budget-friendly "pit stops" deliver "surprisingly good" "simple" American fare, plus steaks at dinnertime in the UWS original; service is "crazy confusion" in digs "low on ambiance", though the Red Hook site boasts "priceless views" of the "harbor and Miss Liberty."

Falai Ⓜ *Italian* — 25 | 19 | 21 | $53

LES | 68 Clinton St. (bet. Rivington & Stanton Sts.) | 212-253-1960 | www.falainyc.com
Falai Panetteria *Italian*
LES | 79 Clinton St. (Rivington St.) | 212-777-8956
NEW Caffe Falai ⊕ *Italian*
SoHo | 265 Lafayette St. (Prince St.) | 917-338-6207 | www.falainyc.com

"Outstanding" "modern" Italian fare from chef Iacopo Falai is the hallmark of this "hip", "sophisticated", minimalist" Lower Eastsider; its nearby Panetteria offshoot affords a casual alternative, while the latest progeny in SoHo, Caffe Falai, proffers "divine pastries and bread" (both serve breakast and lunch).

F & B *Hot Dogs* — 18 | 9 | 13 | $11

Chelsea | 269 W. 23rd St. (bet. 7th & 8th Aves.) | 646-486-4441
E 50s | 150 E. 52nd St. (bet. Lexington & 3rd Aves.) | 212-421-8600 Ⓢ
www.gudtfood.com

"Combos for every taste" grace the lineup of "cheap" "designer franks" and "enticing toppings" proffered by this "no-guilt dog" duo, as do frites, beignets and other "interesting" Euro-style "street food"; they're certainly "nothing fancy" (champagne splits notwithstanding), so most get it "to go."

F & J Pine Restaurant ⊕ *Italian* — 20 | 19 | 19 | $34

Bronx | 1913 Bronxdale Ave. (bet. Morris Park Ave. & White Plains Rd.) | 718-792-5956

"Baseball fans" and others seeking "extra inning-size portions" of "red-sauce" Italian fare in the "Boogie Down" hit this "big and bustling" "Yankee hangout"; it's something of a "mob scene" with "long waits" on weekends and game days, despite scattered quibbles about "quantity over quality."

Farm on Adderley *American* 23 | 19 | 20 | $36

Ditmas Park | 1108 Cortelyou Rd. (bet. Stratford & Westminster Rds.) | ⱡ Brooklyn | 718-287-3101 | www.thefarmonadderley.com

Greeted as a "godsend" to Ditmas Park, this "gracious" New American yearling "fills up quickly" with diners out to harvest "smart", "satisfying" fare cooked with "fresh, seasonal ingredients"; "cheerful" staffers, "comfortable" digs (including a back patio) and "1990 prices" brand it an oasis in a "restaurant desert."

Fatty Crab ● *Malaysian* 21 | 12 | 15 | $39

W Village | 643 Hudson St. (bet. Gansevoort & Horatio Sts.) | 212-352-3590 | www.fattycrab.com

"Bold", "no-holds-barred" Malaysian "street food" that "rocks" is the reason to "fight the crowds" at Zak Pelaccio's "hugely loud" West Village "shoebox"; service is on the "hipster-doofus" side, plus "there's the wait", but it's the "best 2 AM snack ever" – and a good buy at any time.

☒ Felidia *Italian* 25 | 21 | 23 | $73

E 50s | 243 E. 58th St. (bet. 2nd & 3rd Aves.) | 212-758-1479 | www.lidiasitaly.com

Lidia Bastianich's "class act" is even "better than on TV" at her East Side "heavenly haute Italian", where the "exquisite" cuisine is "anything but predictable"; a "spectacular" wine list, "beautiful townhouse" setting and "stellar" staff contribute to the "memorable evenings" out, and though "you really pay", it's "worth every penny."

Félix ● *French* 16 | 17 | 15 | $41

SoHo | 340 W. Broadway (Grand St.) | 212-431-0021 | www.felixnyc.com

A "playground" for the "beautiful", "international" set, this "loud, lively", "very SoHo" French bistro delivers "decent" eats in "airy" digs with "two walls of open doors"; "brunch is a highlight", but the "rowdy patrons and inevitable dancing" always steal the show.

Ferrara ● *Bakery* 22 | 16 | 16 | $20

Little Italy | 195 Grand St. (bet. Mott & Mulberry Sts.) | 212-226-6150 | www.ferraracafe.com

With its *delizioso* pastries and espresso, this "charming", modestly priced Little Italy "landmark" has been a "heavenly dessert" haven since 1892; service may be "brassy" and the "out-of-control crowd" "touristy", but "lines move quickly", making it "a must" – "calories be damned!"

NEW Fette Sau *BBQ* ▽ 19 | 19 | 11 | $25

Williamsburg | 354 Metropolitan Ave. (bet. Havemeyer & Roebling Sts.) | Brooklyn | 718-963-3404

At this new Williamsburg "roadhouse" from the owners of Spuyten Duyvil, you order your BBQ "by the pound", choose from an "impressive" list of whiskeys and beers on tap, and park it at a "communal" picnic table; just "get there early" because the food really does "run out."

	FOOD	DECOR	SERVICE	COST

Fiamma Osteria *Italian* — 25 | 23 | 23 | $66

SoHo | 206 Spring St. (bet. 6th Ave. & Sullivan St.) | 212-653-0100 |
www.brguestrestaurants.com

"Excellent from start to finish", Steve Hanson's "gorgeous", "pricey"
SoHo triplex blends "sublime" Italian cuisine and "smooth", "pampering service" to produce an atmosphere of "simple sophistication"
that's "wonderfully romantic"; N.B. a recent renovation and a new
chef put the above ratings in question.

NEW **15 East** 🛭 *Japanese* — ▽ 26 | 22 | 23 | $73

Union Sq | 15 E. 15th St. (bet. 5th Ave. & Union Sq. W.) | 212-647-0015 |
www.15eastrestaurant.com

They've "done it again" swoon sushiphiles of this "exceptional" Union
Square arrival from the owners of Tocqueville; the modern Japanese
fare (via ex-Jewel Bako chef Masato Shimizu) has early fans calling it
"comparable to" the genre's top players, while "fab" service and a "relaxing" vibe help diners forget how much it all costs.

57 *American* — 22 | 24 | 23 | $74

50s | Four Seasons Hotel | 57 E. 57th St. (Madison Ave.) | 212-829-3859 |
www.fourseasons.com

"Easy for business meetings", this "three-meal" New American dining
room off the Four Seasons' soaring I.M. Pei–designed lobby makes a
low-key "alternative" to the hotel's main eatery, L'Atelier de Joël
Robuchon; most consider it a "comfortable" choice, except when it
comes to paying.

Fig & Olive *Mediterranean* — 20 | 20 | 18 | $44

60s | 808 Lexington Ave. (bet. 62nd & 63rd Sts.) | 212-207-4555
NEW **Fig & Olive Downtown** ● *Mediterranean*

Meatpacking | 420 W. 13th St. (bet. 9th Ave. & Washington St.) |
212-924-1200
www.figandolive.com

"Olive oil–infused everything" is the signature of this "lively"
Mediterranean duo offering "fresh, flavorful" "little plates" as well as
"oils, tapenades" and such to buy; the newer Meatpacking District
branch "is bigger and prettier", but both suffer from "erratic service."

Filli Ponte 🛭 *Italian* — 21 | 20 | 21 | $63

TriBeCa | 39 Desbrosses St. (West St.) | 212-226-4621 |
www.filliponte.com

The "traditional Italian" fare is a tremendous, theatrical "treat" at this
way West TriBeCan, where the vibe is "old-school" (think "Brooklyn in
Manhattan"), the pace "slow" and the "wiseguys-and-wannabes"
crowd isn't the kind you joke about; the "mighty-fine view of the Hudson"
is good enough to trump "expensive" tabs, especially at sunset.

Fino 🛭 *Italian* — ▽ 20 | 17 | 21 | $47

Financial District | 1 Wall Street Ct. (Pearl St.) | 212-825-1924 |
www.finony.com

Murray Hill | 4 E. 36th St. (bet. 5th & Madison Aves.) | 212-689-8040
"Old-style" Italian "with service to match" can be found at this "consistent" twosome offering "well-prepared" standards in a "soothing,
quiet atmosphere" conducive to "business lunches or dinners"; the
Murray Hill original loses points for digs that are not so fino anymore.

	FOOD	DECOR	SERVICE	COST

Fiorentino's *Italian*

19 | 13 | 18 | $32

Gravesend | 311 Ave. U (bet. McDonald Ave. & West St.) | Brooklyn | 718-372-1445

"Large portions" of "zesty", "homey", "authentic Brooklyn" Neapolitan fare and "generous, cheap" pours keep this Gravesend "favorite" "mobbed" and "noisy"; maybe the "1974 decor" "needs a facelift", but the "family atmosphere" and big "bang for your buck" justify "long waits" on weekends.

NEW Fiorini 🛇 *Italian*

- | - | - | M

E 50s | 209 E. 56th St. (bet. 2nd & 3rd Aves.) | 212-308-0830 | www.fiorinirestaurant.com

Longtime restaurateur Lello Arpaia returns to East Midtown with this elegant, moderately priced (for the neighborhood) arrival serving up old-school Italian favorites and wines from The Boot; its cream-colored quarters clad with cherry-red booths are presided over by accommodating, *Italiano*-speaking servers.

FireBird 🅼 *Russian*

18 | 25 | 20 | $62

W 40s | 365 W. 46th St. (bet. 8th & 9th Aves.) | 212-586-0244 | www.firebirdrestaurant.com

You'll "feel like Russian royalty" at this "lush", "atmospheric" Restaurant Row duplex "full of artwork" "from the czarist era"; "solid standbys like blini with caviar" and "honey-infused vodka" served by "attentive" "tunic-clad" staffers keep up the illusion, but "boy, you pay for it."

Firenze ⏺ *Italian*

21 | 20 | 22 | $44

E 80s | 1594 Second Ave. (bet. 82nd & 83rd Sts.) | 212-861-9368

Though "barely bigger than a breadbox", this "tempting" Tuscan trattoria on the UES is a favorite for "romance", turning out "super" Tuscan dishes via a "friendly" staff; "she'll be smiling through the candlelight", especially after the "free grappa" that rounds out the "memorable experience."

NEW Fireside *Eclectic*

▽ 21 | 19 | 18 | $57

E 50s | Omni Berkshire Place Hotel | 19 E. 52nd St. (bet. 5th & Madison Aves.) | 212-754-5011 | www.fireside-nyc.com

At this "trendy" Midtown newcomer in the Omni Berkshire Place, a dramatic floor-to-ceiling hearth is the focal point, and the crowd a mix of tourists and nearby business types; the draw is the "pricey" but "remarkably good" lineup of Eclectic small plates that chef Sam DeMarco (ex First) terms 'cocktail cuisine.'

Fish *Seafood*

20 | 14 | 18 | $39

G Village | 280 Bleecker St. (Jones St.) | 212-727-2879

A "fishmonger on the premises" hints at the "quality" at this "laid-back" yet "energetic" faux "New England fish shack" in the Village; the chef's "wizardry with seafood" far outweighs the "sketchy service" and "cool hovel" digs, while "fair prices" are the catch of the day.

Five Front *American*

21 | 19 | 19 | $39

Dumbo | 5 Front St. (Old Fulton St.) | Brooklyn | 718-625-5559 | www.fivefrontrestaurant.com

Something of a "hidden gem", this "unpretentious" Dumbo "neighborhood bistro" turns out "serious" New American fare in "pretty" quarters; for a "magical evening", "grab a seat" in the "gorgeous" bamboo garden with the "Brooklyn Bridge yawning above" – occasional "slow" service is the "only flaw", but moderate prices compensate.

NEW Five Guys *Hamburgers* | - | - | - | I |

Brooklyn Heights | 138 Montague St. (bet. Clinton & Henry Sts.) | Brooklyn | 718-797-9380
College Point | 132-01 14th Ave. (132nd St.) | Queens | 718-767-6500
www.fiveguys.com

The first NYC links of a chain voted one of the most popular in our DC Survey, these outer-borough burger joints are set to be joined soon by three Manhattan locations; the service is strictly assembly-line and the ketchup-red digs geared mostly for takeout, but low prices encourage return visits.

5 Ninth ● *Eclectic* | 19 | 21 | 18 | $53 |

Meatpacking | 5 Ninth Ave. (bet. Gansevoort & Little W. 12th Sts.) | 212-929-9460 | www.5ninth.com

Though its founding chef has left, this "hip" Meatpacking District townhouse carries on with "bold" Eclectic fare served to a "pretty" crowd; the "sweet back garden" wins raves, but a few say it doesn't make up for the "uneven service" and "expensive" tabs.

Five Points ● *American/Mediterranean* | 22 | 21 | 20 | $47 |

NoHo | 31 Great Jones St. (bet. Bowery & Lafayette St.) | 212-253-5700 | www.fivepointsrestaurant.com

A "stream running through" the room to "a skylit nook" in back brings a touch of "soothing" "Zen" to this otherwise "thunderous" NoHo Med-New American; "hordes" gather for its "talented cooking", including a "spectacular" brunch, served by a "cheerful" staff.

NEW Flatbush Farm *American* | ▽ 19 | 19 | 18 | $37 |

Park Slope | 76 St. Marks Ave. (bet. Flatbush & 6th Aves.) | Brooklyn | 718-622-3276 | www.flatbushfarm.com

The mood is always "easygoing" at this "friendly" Park Slope yearling whose New American fare comes in "minimalist" quarters done up with "rustic farm implements"; though some cite "inconsistency" as a problem, all agree they're "trying hard" and a new chef post-Survey shows promise.

Flea Market Cafe ● *French* | 19 | 17 | 16 | $28 |

E Village | 131 Ave. A (bet. 9th St. & St. Marks Pl.) | 212-358-9282

Apart from its "transporting" "Tompkins Square Park view", this "cheery" East Village bistro has a real "Parisian feel", with "cheap", "simple French food", "funky" decor ("everything's for sale") and generally "no-attitude" service; given all that, most "put up with dense seating" and high decibels.

Fleur de Sel *French* | 25 | 21 | 23 | $91 |

Flatiron | 5 E. 20th St. (bet. B'way & 5th Ave.) | 212-460-9100 | www.fleurdeselnyc.com

"Petite and charming", Cyril Renaud's "transcendent" prix fixe-only Flatiron French blooms with "extraordinary" Breton dishes that are "creative without being outlandish"; a "splendid" if "high-end" "wine selection" and "unobtrusive" service make dinner a "special occasion", albeit a "stiffly priced" one, while the $29 prix fixe lunch is "a swell deal."

	FOOD	DECOR	SERVICE	COST

Flor de Mayo ◐ *Chinese/Peruvian*
| | 20 | 9 | 16 | $21 |

W 80s | 484 Amsterdam Ave. (bet. 83rd & 84th Sts.) | 212-787-3388
W 100s | 2651 Broadway (101st St.) | 212-663-5520

Diners "come out raving" about the "celestial" rotisserie chicken at these "busy" UWS Chinese-Peruvians; despite "run-down" digs, they're favorites with those on "a shoestring budget", so there's "almost always a wait."

Flor de Sol ⊠ *Spanish*
| | 20 | 20 | 19 | $42 |

TriBeCa | 361 Greenwich St. (bet. Franklin & Harrison Sts.) | 212-366-1640 | www.flordesolnyc.com

"Tops for tapas", this "flirty" TriBeCa Spaniard's "seductive", candlelit ambiance also makes it a perfect "date" place, "noisy" acoustics notwithstanding; the midweek "flamenco music" livens things up, as does the "killer sangria" and "hot" staff.

Florent ◐ *French*
| | 20 | 14 | 16 | $31 |

Meatpacking | 69 Gansevoort St. (bet. Greenwich & Washington Sts.) | 212-989-5779 | www.restaurantflorent.com

"Good, honest" French bistro fare "shines" 24/7 at this Meatpacking District "original"; it's the "come-as-you-are eclectic" clientele, "kitschy" diner digs and "entertainingly snippy staff" that make it "a hoot in the middle of the night" – though it's "one cool hang" at any time, and a bargain too.

Flor's Kitchen *Venezuelan*
| | ∇ 16 | 13 | 18 | $28 |

G Village | 170 Waverly Pl. (Christopher St.) | 212-229-9926 | www.florskitchen.com

Greenwich Villagers flock to this "cute", "tiny" Venezuelan for "satisfying arepas" and such; the "simple" eats are a rare "easy-on-the-wallet" option in these parts, while the "lovely" staff contributes to its "warm, neighborhood" feel.

Food Bar ◐ *American*
| | 16 | 15 | 16 | $31 |

Chelsea | 149 Eighth Ave. (bet. 17th & 18th Sts.) | 212-243-2020

"Cool, hip, trendy, cute – but enough about the waiters" at this "festive", "*très gay*" Chelsea New American; "no one comes for the food", but happily "hanging with friends" while taking in the "eye candy" comes at "reasonable" rates.

Fornino *Pizza*
| | 22 | 14 | 17 | $22 |

Williamsburg | 187 Bedford Ave. (N. 7th St.) | Brooklyn | 718-384-6004

"Subtle flavors" from the "freshest ingredients" (including herbs from the back garden) make the "fancy" brick-oven pizza at this Williamsburg emporium just about "as good as it gets"; the decor is "not as inspired", though, so "delivery and takeout" should be kept in mind.

44 & X Hell's Kitchen ◐ *American*
| | 21 | 18 | 19 | $45 |

W 40s | 622 10th Ave. (44th St.) | 212-977-1170 | www.44andX.com

"Delicious" "spins" on comfort classics (e.g. "kickin' mac 'n' cheese"), "sassy" "model/waiters" and "fresh, bright" digs make this Hell's Kitchen American "stand out"; "extra-loud" acoustics and a "gas station" view don't stop the "crowds" from coming.

	FOOD	DECOR	SERVICE	COST

☑ Four Seasons ⑤ *Continental* | 25 | 27 | 26 | $91 |

E 50s | 99 E. 52nd St. (bet. Lexington & Park Aves.) | 212-754-9494 | www.fourseasonsrestaurant.com

Still a "stunner" after nearly 50 years, this "timeless" Midtown "classic" (led by suave host-owners Alex von Bidder and Julian Niccolini) delivers "first-class" Continental cuisine to an "oh-so-urbane crowd" that's practically a "who's who of the city", while service is "superior" and the "NY landmark" surroundings famously "sleek and sumptuous"; regulars tout lunching among "power players" in the Grill room or in the "serene" Pool Room at night, allowing that, yes, it's "expensive", but "if it's awesome you want, this is the place"; N.B. jackets required.

Fragole *Italian* | 23 | 17 | 20 | $29 |

Carroll Gardens | 394 Court St. (bet. Carroll St. & 1st Pl.) | Brooklyn | 718-522-7133 | www.fragoleny.com

"Simple", "flavorful" Italian dishes that stand out in the "red-sauce neighborhood" of Carroll Gardens make this "unassuming little hole-in-the-wall" one "popular" place; the "long list of blackboard specials", "warm" service and "gentle prices" are other reasons it's a "winner."

Francisco's Centro Vasco *Spanish* | 22 | 13 | 18 | $45 |

Chelsea | 159 W. 23rd St. (bet. 6th & 7th Aves.) | 212-645-6224

"It's all about" the "succulent, gargantuan lobsters" at this "festive" (read: "noisy") Chelsea Spanish "old-timer", so "strap on a bib" and make allowances for "servers doing their best" in digs that "could use sprucing up"; after all, the "deals" are almost as "mouthwatering" as the crustaceans.

Frank ●⌷ *Italian* | 24 | 14 | 16 | $33 |

E Village | 88 Second Ave. (bet. 5th & 6th Sts.) | 212-420-0202 | www.frankrestaurant.com

"They ain't lining up outside all night for nothin'" say fans of this "homey" East Village Italian and its "cheap", "robust, bristling-with-flavor" eats; frankly, service is "rushed, even brusque", and space "unbelievably tight" – "it should be annoying, but instead it's wonderful."

Frankie & Johnnie's Steakhouse ⑤ *Steak* | 21 | 14 | 19 | $59 |

Garment District | 32 W. 37th St. (bet. 5th & 6th Aves.) | 212-947-8940
W 40s | 269 W. 45th St. (bet. B'way & 8th Ave.) | 212-997-9494 ●
www.frankieandjohnnies.com

"Hungry carnivores" get their fixes at these "old-fashioned" chophouses where super steaks are "prepared with care" and served by "pro" staffers; the "tired" Times Square mezzanine original shows its 1926 "speakeasy beginnings", while the newer Garment District spin-off in John Barrymore's onetime townhouse has "charm."

Frankies Spuntino *Italian* | 24 | 19 | 19 | $33 |

LES | 17 Clinton St. (bet. Houston & Stanton Sts.) | 212-253-2303 ●
Carroll Gardens | 457 Court St. (bet. 4th Pl. & Luquer St.) | Brooklyn | 718-403-0033 ⌷
www.frankiesspuntino.com

"Rustic Italian" small plates with "robust flavors" and "sophisticated twists" come out of "teeny kitchens" at this "low-key" duo; it lacks the wonderful garden" of the Carroll Gardens original, but the newer LES "walk-in closet" is still "charming", and both boast "gentle prices."

	FOOD	DECOR	SERVICE	COST

Frank's *Italian/Steak*

19 | 13 | 17 | $52

Chelsea | 410 W. 16th St. (bet. 9th & 10th Aves.) | 212-243-1349
A real "guy's place", this "casual", "old-style" Italian steakhouse proffers aged beef and "great beers" within a "sparsely decorated" Chelsea Market space behind the family-run butcher shop; service is "friendly", if "slow", so most just sit back and enjoy the "camaraderie."

Franny's ⓜ *Pizza*

23 | 17 | 19 | $34

Prospect Heights | 295 Flatbush Ave. (bet. Prospect Pl. & St. Marks Ave.) | Brooklyn | 718-230-0221 | www.frannysbrooklyn.com
The "sophisticated", "crispy-crust" pies come with "local, seasonal", "housemade" credentials at this "upscale" Prospect Heights pizza place that also does "divine" apps, pastas and "innovative cocktails"; "pleasant" service and a "date"-worthy backyard hit a high note, but some feel the prices are relatively "steep" "for what you get."

Fratelli *Italian*

▽ 21 | 17 | 20 | $34

Bronx | 2507 Eastchester Rd. (Mace Ave.) | 718-547-2489
Turning out "typical" standards but "delicious" specials, this "quaint, romantic" white-tablecloth Bronx Italian earns its status as a "popular neighborhood place"; service is "good", prices "affordable" and it's "quiet" enough to "have a conversation", so really "you can't go wrong."

Fraunces Tavern ⓩ *American*

15 | 21 | 18 | $43

Financial District | 54 Pearl St. (Broad St.) | 212-968-1776 | www.frauncestavern.com
You "dine with the ghosts of the Colonial army" at this "charming" "landmark" tavern dating back to 1762; the Traditional American fare is "only so-so" (hopefully "George Washington had better luck"), so most consider it good for a drink when in the Financial District but otherwise "strictly for history buffs" and "out-of-towners."

NEW Frederick's

19 | 16 | 17 | $58

Downtown ❶ *French/Mediterranean*
W Village | 637 Hudson St. (Horatio St.) | 212-488-4200
Frederick's Madison *French/Mediterranean*
E 60s | 768 Madison Ave. (bet. 65th & 66th Sts.) | 212-737-7300
www.fredericksnyc.com
The French-Med fare is "good" at these "trendy" "magnets" for "Gucci and Prada"–clad "Euros", but they're mostly about the "fun scene"; sidewalk seats are a plus at the UES branch, while the new Villager is "working out kinks" – if they're "expensive", that's the price of "chic."

Fred's at Barneys NY *American/Italian*

20 | 18 | 17 | $46

E 60s | Barneys NY | 660 Madison Ave., 9th fl. (60th St.) | 212-833-2200
"Fashionistas" "rest from the rigors of shopping" at this "frenetic" Midtown Tuscan–New American serving "solid", predictably "expensive" fare; "hearty" portions "can feed two people (or four models)", and though service is merely "middling", at dinner there's "less turmoil."

Freemans ❶ *American*

21 | 23 | 19 | $42

LES | Freeman Alley (off Rivington St., bet. Bowery & Chrystie St.) | 212-420-0012 | www.freemansrestaurant.com
"Hidden" down a "narrow alley", this "eccentric" LES New American earns its "high hipness quotient" with a blend of "amazing" "comfort

	FOOD	DECOR	SERVICE	COST

food" and "lodgelike", "taxidermy-chic" looks; a recent expansion has shortened waits, but the "friendly" staff still can get "overwhelmed" by the "beautiful" "throngs."

French Roast ● *French* | 14 | 14 | 13 | $27 |

G Village | 78 W. 11th St. (6th Ave.) | 212-533-2233
W 80s | 2340 Broadway (85th St.) | 212-799-1533
www.frenchroastny.com

Stick with "something simple" and this "pseudo-French" pair providing "passable" eats will suffice; hey, they're "cheap" and "open 24/7", so even with "somnambulant service" and "squished" "fake bistro" digs, they're "a godsend when you need a midnight snack."

Fresco by Scotto **Ⓢ** *Italian* | 23 | 19 | 21 | $61 |

E 50s | 34 E. 52nd St. (bet. Madison & Park Aves.) | 212-935-3434
Fresco on the Go **Ⓢ** *Italian*
E 50s | 40 E. 52nd St. (bet. Madison & Park Aves.) | 212-754-2700
www.frescobyscotto.com

"Local news and TV celebs" show up at the "hospitable" Scotto family's Midtown Tuscan "powerhouse", a "lively, bright" setting for "fabulous" food and "attentive service"; for less of a "wallet buster", the take-out annex offers "Fresco food at deli prices" – "what's not to like?"

fresh *Seafood* | 24 | 20 | 22 | $60 |

TriBeCa | 105 Reade St. (bet. Church St. & W. B'way) | 212-406-1900 | www.freshrestaurantnyc.com

A "seafood lover's" "paradise", this "out-of-the-way" "upscale" TriBeCan "doesn't get enough attention" declare devotees of its "superbly fresh" fin fare; a "lovely staff" presides over its "spacious" "serene room", so its "loud" acoustics at prime times and high prices all the time are the only downsides.

Friend of a Farmer *American* | 17 | 18 | 16 | $29 |

Gramercy | 77 Irving Pl. (bet. 18th & 19th Sts.) | 212-477-2188

"Escape the city" at this "cheerful" "little country inn" transplanted to Gramercy, complete with "exposed beams", "comfy fireplace" and "tasty", modestly priced homespun American fare; the "snail's-pace" service doesn't help the "huge lines" that form at weekend brunch, but for most it's "worth the wait."

🆕 FR.OG **Ⓢ** *Eclectic/French* | ▽ 21 | 16 | 15 | $59 |

SoHo | 71 Spring St. (bet. Crosby & Lafayette Sts.) | 212-966-5050 | www.frognyc.com

Its name stands for 'France Origine', the thread uniting all of chef Didier Virot's "excellent" global dishes, which dart from Morocco to Vietnam and are served in a "stark-white" SoHo duplex accented with "over-the-top" splashes of color; exotic libations from bars both upstairs and down fuel the scene.

Fuleen Seafood ● *Chinese/Seafood* | ▽ 24 | 9 | 16 | $26 |

Chinatown | 11 Division St. (bet. Bowery & E. B'way) | 212-941-6888

"Truly singular tastes" swim your way at this "excellent" Chinatown seafooder where fish "directly from the tanks" is "masterfully prepared" "Hong Kong–style" way into the wee hours; "dull" decor and "language-related confusion" are swept away by the prices – "what a deal!"

	FOOD	DECOR	SERVICE	COST

Fushimi *Japanese*
▽ 26 | 24 | 22 | $48

Staten Island | 2110 Richmond Rd. (Lincoln Ave.) | 718-980-5300
An "evening of pleasure" awaits at this Staten Island Japanese "standout" known for its "wonderful array" of "consistently excellent" sushi as well as for its "hectic", "trendy" "Manhattan"-esque ambiance; even its "city prices" don't slow the "happening bar scene."

Gabriela's *Mexican*
17 | 17 | 16 | $32

W 90s | 688 Columbus Ave. (bet. 93rd & 94th Sts.) | 212-961-0574 | www.gabrielas.com
"Spacious" and "cheery", this UWS "everyday Mexican" is usually "filled to overflowing" – just like the "big" plates of "tasty" eats; nostalgists claim it's "not the same" since moving to more "upscale" digs last year, but no one complains about the "fab patio" or "amazing margaritas."

Gabriel's ⑤ *Italian*
22 | 19 | 22 | $60

W 60s | 11 W. 60th St. (bet. B'way & Columbus Ave.) | 212-956-4600 | www.gabrielsbarandrest.com
Gabriel Aiello's "gracious touch" is in evidence at his "delightful", "understated" Tuscan "stalwart" near Lincoln Center, where an always "interesting crowd" convenes for "terrific" fare ferried by a "cordial" staff "choreographed to curtain-time"; an "impressive, reasonably priced wine list" caps it all off.

Gahm Mi Oak ● *Korean*
▽ 22 | 13 | 16 | $21

Garment District | 43 W. 32nd St. (bet. B'way & 5th Ave.) | 212-695-4113
"Magnificent" "Korean soul food" fixes can be found 24/7 at this "inexpensive", "dependable" Garment Districter beloved for its "famed hangover cure", "heavenly *sollongtang*" soup; as for the "spartan" digs, "after a long night of partying" most hardly notice.

Gallagher's Steak House ● *Steak*
20 | 17 | 18 | $62

W 50s | 228 W. 52nd St. (bet. B'way & 8th Ave.) | 212-245-5336 | www.gallaghersnysteakhouse.com
"Classic NY" from its "top-quality", top-dollar steaks to its "ornery waiters", this "honest-to-goodness, old-time chophouse" has been a Theater District "mainstay" since 1927; yes, it's "a little run-down" but the "gritty", sports-memorabilia-and-checkered-tablecloth atmosphere is part of its "manly" charm.

❷ Garden Cafe ⑤Ⓜ *American*
27 | 20 | 25 | $50

Prospect Heights | 620 Vanderbilt Ave. (Prospect Pl.) | Brooklyn | 718-857-8863
There must be "magic" in the "postage-stamp kitchen" at John and Camille Policastro's "petite" Prospect Heights New American for it to conjure food this "fabulous"; a "convivial", "romantic" vibe, "personal attention" and all-around "understated class" ensure that customers "dress nicely" and "keep coming back" "for those special nights" here.

Gargiulo's *Italian*
21 | 18 | 21 | $43

Coney Island | 2911 W. 15th St. (bet. Mermaid & Surf Aves.) | Brooklyn | 718-266-4891 | www.gargiulos.com
"Take your nonny" and "your appetite" to this "cavernous" circa-1907 Coney Island Southern Italian "landmark" for "satisfying" fare straight

| | FOOD | DECOR | SERVICE | COST |

outta the "heyday of cuisine in Brooklyn", delivered by "outstanding", "old-time" waiters; the "fun part" is "rolling the dice" after dinner – "if you get lucky" the meal's free.

☑ Gari *Japanese*   26 | 14 | 20 | $73
W 70s | 370 Columbus Ave. (bet. 77th & 78th Sts.) | 212-362-4816
☑ Sushi of Gari Ⓜ *Japanese*
E 70s | 402 E. 78th St. (bet. 1st & York Aves.) | 212-517-5340
☑ NEW Sushi of Gari 46 Ⓜ *Japanese*
W 40s | 347 W. 46th St. (bet. 8th & 9th Aves.) | 212-957-0046
Gari Sugio's Japanese empire continues to grow, with a new Restaurant Row outpost joining his "wonderful" UES and UWS locations; no matter where you taste it, his "right-out-of-the-ocean" sushi is "exquisite" and "totally unique", and the omakase option an opportunity for "multiple novel treats" – though a "trip to Japan may be less expensive."

Gascogne *French*   22 | 19 | 21 | $49
Chelsea | 158 Eighth Ave. (bet. 17th & 18th Sts.) | 212-675-6564 | www.gascognenyc.com
Its "warm farmhouse feel" "transports you to SW France", while this Chelsea "sleeper's" "terrific cassoulet" and other "solid" bistro classics "warm" the soul; a few claustrophobes chafe in the "cramped space", but all agree "for a sure thing, take a date" to the *très romantique* back garden.

NEW Gaucho Steak Co. *Argentinean/Steak*   – | – | – | M
W 50s | 752 10th Ave. (bet. 51st & 52nd Sts.) | 212-957-1727 | www.gauchosteakco.com
On a rapidly gentrifying Hell's Kitchen strip, chef Alex Garcia (Calle Ocho) has opened this gaucho-themed, wood and leather-adorned Argentinean steakhouse; it dishes up good-value offerings – none of the sizable cuts of grass-fed Uruguayan beef top $20 – that can be washed down with sangria or South American wines.

Gavroche *French*   19 | 16 | 19 | $42
W Village | 212 W. 14th St. (bet. 7th Ave. S. & 8th Ave.) | 212-647-8553 | www.gavroche-ny.com
A "beautiful garden" makes this West Village French bistro an "oasis" on a busy street; its "no-nonsense" offerings – including a "high-value" $20 early-bird – are served "without pretense" under the supervision of a "friendly, attentive" owner; in short, it's an overall "comfortable" choice.

Geisha ⓩ *Japanese*   23 | 21 | 20 | $61
E 60s | 33 E. 61st St. (bet. Madison & Park Aves.) | 212-813-1112 | www.geisharestaurant.com
"Innovative", "jewel-bright" French-influenced Japanese cuisine comes "with a side of beautiful people" at this East 60s duplex; the David Rockwell–designed space is "hip" yet "lovely", though tight tables and "nouvelle portions" at "nouvelle prices" may be problems.

NEW Gemma ◖ *Italian*   – | – | – | E
E Village | Bowery Hotel | 335 Bowery (E. 3rd St.) | 212-505-9100 | www.theboweryhotel.com
In the chic new Bowery Hotel comes this buzzy Italian with an open kitchen, wood-fired pizza oven and a serious chef behind the burners;

the warm room resembles a rustic farmhouse, with windowed doors that open to the street in warm weather – something unthinkable in these parts just a few years back.

Gennaro ⊄ Italian
25 | 14 | 17 | $38

W 90s | 665 Amsterdam Ave. (bet. 92nd & 93rd Sts.) | 212-665-5348 | www.gennarorestaurant.com

Upper Westsiders gennar-ally gush over this "unassuming" cash-only Italian "gem", citing "sophisticated" preparations at "bargain" prices; to cope with "awful lines", "crapshoot" service and a room "packed tighter than a box of pasta", go at off-hours.

NEW Georgia's Eastside BBQ M⊄ BBQ
_ | _ | _ | I

LES | 192 Orchard St. (bet. Houston & Stanton Sts.) | 212-253-6280

Mounds of barbecued ribs on the cheap, beer-steamed before grilling, Georgia-style, are the deal at this rib-thin LES roadhouse; it has but a modicum of kitsch and even fewer tables – but if you can't find a seat there's always takeout as an option.

Ghenet Ethiopian
▽ 22 | 14 | 16 | $31

NoLita | 284 Mulberry St. (bet. Houston & Prince Sts.) | 212-343-1888 | www.ghenet.com

At this "low-key" NoLita Ethiopian, the "terrific combinations" of "spicy", family-style Ethiopian eats are "scooped and blended" with traditional injera bread rather than fork and spoon; "somewhat slow" service is outweighed by very "fair" rates for the chance to "amaze your taste buds."

Giambelli ● Italian
21 | 17 | 22 | $59

E 50s | 46 E. 50th St. (bet. Madison & Park Aves.) | 212-688-2760 | www.giambelli50th.com

For "a trip down memory lane" *amici* meander over to this 50-year-old Midtown ristorante, where "civilized" staffers who've "been there for-ever" serve up "delicious" Italian standards; never mind if trendier types rate the experience "tired" and "overpriced."

Gigino at Wagner Park Italian
20 | 19 | 19 | $42

Financial District | 20 Battery Pl. (West St.) | 212-528-2228 | www.gigino-wagnerpark.com

Gigino Trattoria Italian

TriBeCa | 323 Greenwich St. (bet. Duane & Reade Sts.) | 212-431-1112 | www.gigino-trattoria.com

TriBeCa families flock to this "rough-hewn", midpriced "Roman trat-toria" for "solid", "casual" favorites like "thin and crispy pizzas"; its sleeker, smaller Battery Park sibling – whose "marvelous" patio offers "breathtaking" views of Lady Liberty and the harbor – not surprisingly draws a more "touristy" crowd.

Gilt ⑤ M American
▽ 25 | 26 | 25 | $109

E 50s | NY Palace Hotel | 455 Madison Ave. (bet. 50th & 51st Sts.) | 212-891-8100 | www.giltnewyork.com

"Living up to its name", this "elegant" Midtown showplace is a "sub-lime" foil for new chef Christopher Lee's "divine" yet "user-friendly" New American cuisine offered via a $78 (and up) prix fixe–only menu; its "stunning" "mural and statue"-adorned space meets the gold stan-dard, as do its 1,500-strong wine list and "impeccable" service, adding up to undeniably "decadent" experiences that leave luxury-loving loyalists "feeling no guilt."

Ginger Chinese
▽ 21 | 19 | 18 | $29

Harlem | 1400 Fifth Ave. (116th St.) | 212-423-1111 |
www.gingerexpress.com

Specializing in heart-healthy Chinese-style dishes, this East Harlem standout makes its "neighborhood crowd" "happier and happier"; the room's "loungelike" look also elevates it above the average Sino spot; N.B. a recent chef change may outdate the above Food score.

Gin Lane ● Continental
17 | 24 | 19 | $54

Chelsea | 355 W. 14th St. (bet. 8th & 9th Aves.) | 212-691-0555 |
www.ginlanenyc.com

"Cool", "classy" quarters crowned with a "huge", "unexpected" skylight give this Chelsea Continental yearling a "dramatic" look; many find its "standard" eats "underwhelming" and "overpriced", but "divine" specialty cocktails made by "cute, savvy" mixologists help compensate.

Gino ⌀ Italian
21 | 13 | 20 | $48

E 60s | 780 Lexington Ave. (bet. 60th & 61st Sts.) | 212-758-4466

From the "hearty" Southern Italian "home cooking" to the "funky zebra" wallpaper and "gentlemanly" "career waiters", this "institution" near Bloomingdale's is a "throwback to the '50s"; critics call it "cramped" and "shabby", but amici who adore its "utter lack of pretension" assert "some things should never change."

Giorgione Italian
23 | 19 | 20 | $49

SoHo | 307 Spring St. (bet. Greenwich & Hudson Sts.) | 212-352-2269
Giorgione 508 Italian
SoHo | 508 Greenwich St. (bet. Canal & Spring Sts.) | 212-219-2444

Touting "top-notch ingredients" from owner and eminent grocer Giorgio DeLuca, this "hip" West SoHo trattoria is a "fun place" to savor "delicious" Italian fare and vino while "taking in the scene"; servers are "charming but harried" amid the "bustle", so some opt for the nearby cafe/mini-market 508 instead.

Giorgio's of Gramercy American
22 | 17 | 21 | $47

Flatiron | 27 E. 21st St. (bet. B'way & Park Ave. S.) | 212-477-0007 |
www.giorgiosofgramercy.com

"Cozy" and "intimate", this Flatiron "hidden treasure" offers terrific, "something-for-everyone" New American cuisine delivered by a staff that "knows its food and wine"; it may not be cheap, but its "hefty portions" make for "great value."

Giovanni Venticinque Italian
▽ 22 | 19 | 22 | $61

E 80s | 25 E. 83rd St. (bet. 5th & Madison Aves.) | 212-988-7300

"Just a hop-step away from the Met", this UES Italian refreshes "weary museumgoers" with its "excellent", albeit "expensive", Tuscan fare ferried by "efficient" staffers; its "quiet", candlelit quarters allow diners to "actually converse", making it a fallback for many a mature local.

Girasole ● Italian
20 | 15 | 20 | $56

E 80s | 151 E. 82nd St. (bet. Lexington & 3rd Aves.) | 212-772-6690

It's "not exactly trendy", but this "reliable" UES ristorante still draws crowds of "wealthy over-50" types with its "satisfying", "inventive" *cucina* and "professional" service; at dinnertime the "understated" environs are "full of life" (read: "noisy").

Gnocco Caffe ● *Italian* ▽ 21 | 16 | 18 | $37

E Village | 337 E. 10th St. (bet. Aves. A & B) | 212-677-1913 | www.gnocco.com

The namesake fried-dough appetizer "will gnocc your socks off" and the pizzas are "delicious" too at this "quaint" East Villager; the "lovely" garden and low prices have locals calling it a "major sleeper."

Gobo *Vegan/Vegetarian* 22 | 18 | 18 | $32

E 80s | 1426 Third Ave. (81st St.) | 212-288-5099
G Village | 401 Sixth Ave. (bet. 8th St. & Waverly Pl.) | 212-255-3242 ●
www.goborestaurant.com

"For the sophisticated vegan" and curious carnivore alike, this "upscale" Village-UES pair delivers "creative", Asian-accented vegetarian fare via a "chef with imagination"; other appeals are "calming" settings that are somehow "both bustling and Zen" and "budget"-friendly rates.

Golden Unicorn *Chinese* 20 | 12 | 13 | $24

Chinatown | 18 E. Broadway, 2nd fl. (Catherine St.) | 212-941-0911

A "dim sum bonanza" awaits at this "big, loud" Chinatown vet where "locals and visitors alike" "eat themselves silly" on "sumptuous, lip-smacking" morsels from "swift" rolling carts; the weekend scene gets "wild and crazy", but "get there before noon and the wait's minimal."

NEW Gold St. ● *Eclectic* ▽ 15 | 17 | 18 | $26

Financial District | 2 Gold St. (bet. Maiden Ln. & Platt St.) | 212-747-0797 | www.goldstnyc.com

"Finally a 24-hour joint in the Financial District" cheer customers of this "diner"-inspired newcomer whose "huge variety" of affordable Eclectic fare spans everything from sushi to Kobe sliders to breakfast classics served round the clock; its sprawling setup includes a full bar and outdoor seating, with "accommodating" service to ice the cake.

Gonzo *Italian/Pizza* 21 | 17 | 18 | $45

G Village | 140 W. 13th St. (bet. 6th Ave. & 7th Ave. S.) | 212-645-4606

"Delicious grilled pizzas" with "razor-thin" crusts and "toppings that change seasonally" are the trademark of this "friendly" Village Italian; the "lovely" back dining room with its high "painted-wood ceiling" "gets pretty noisy", but "easy-on-the-pocketbook" prices compensate.

good *American* 20 | 16 | 18 | $33

W Village | 89 Greenwich Ave. (bet. Bank & W. 12th Sts.) | 212-691-8080 | www.goodrestaurantnyc.com

The "epitome of a neighborhood eatery", this "friendly, down-to-earth" West Village New American "lives up to its name" with "superior baked goods" and other "comfort" dishes "prepared with care"; it's known especially as a "brunch-lover's heaven", so "get there early" or face "lines."

goodburger *Hamburgers* 18 | 8 | 12 | $13

E 40s | 800 Second Ave. (43rd St.) | 212-922-1700
NEW E 50s | 636 Lexington Ave. (54th St.) | 212-838-6000
www.goodburgerny.com

Its name represents "truth in advertising" declare devotees of this "funky" East Midtown duo's "juicy", "made-to-order" patties; "when

	FOOD	DECOR	SERVICE	COST

ou want the grease", its "tiny" burgers – along with "crispy" fries and
diet-blowing" shakes – "hit the spot", though a budget-minded few
ite prices a bit "high" for "fast food."

Good Enough to Eat *American*
20 | 15 | 16 | $25

V 80s | 483 Amsterdam Ave. (bet. 83rd & 84th Sts.) | 212-496-0163 |
www.goodenoughtoeat.com

t slings "down-home", "affordable" Americana "like you wish you had
he energy to cook", so this Upper Westsider's "cramped", "country-
itsch" digs and "distracted" service are easy to ignore; its brunch
draws "outrageous" lines, but to regulars it's "good enough to wait."

☑ Good Fork Ⓜ *Eclectic*
26 | 20 | 22 | $40

Red Hook | 391 Van Brunt St. (bet. Coffey & Van Dyke Sts.) | Brooklyn |
718-643-6636 | www.goodfork.com

A "bright star" in Red Hook, this "cozy", "pocket-size" yearling is "always
packed" with fans of its "innovative" Eclectic eats with "inspired Korean
touches" and "sophisticated" drinks; run by an "adorable husband-and-
wife team", it's developing a reputation for "trying hard to please."

Goodies *Chinese*
20 | 7 | 14 | $17

Chinatown | 1 E. Broadway (bet. Catherine & Oliver Sts.) | 212-577-2922

"Addictive", "dirt-cheap" soup dumplings plus "tasty housemade noodles" draw aficionados to this no-frills Shanghainese standby; its "off-
the-strip" location for many is a "relief from" Chinatown "madness."

☑ NEW Gordon Ramsay *French*
25 | 24 | 25 | $126

W 50s | The London NYC | 151 W. 54th St. (bet. 6th & 7th Aves.) |
212-468-8888 | www.gordonramsay.com

"Crusty" TV chef Gordon Ramsay "leaves the terror in the kitchen" at
his "sublime" New French arrival in Midtown's London NYC hotel, his
first U.S. foray, which "lives up to the hype" with "meticulously prepared", prix fixe-only cuisine full of "complex and layered" flavors;
service is "flawless without being stuffy", though the "modern", neu-
ral-toned decor gets mixed reviews ("elegant" and "refined" vs.
"bland" and "sterile"); naturally, all of this "understated" "excellence"
is "not for the faint of pocketbook"; N.B. jackets required.

☑ Gotham Bar & Grill *American*
27 | 25 | 26 | $72

G Village | 12 E. 12th St. (bet. 5th Ave. & University Pl.) | 212-620-4020 |
www.gothambarandgrill.com

At this Village culinary "temple", "grand master" Alfred Portale continues to "excite" enthusiasts with his "soigné" "skyscrapers" of
spectacular" New American fare, while staffers "grant your wishes
before you even know what to ask for" in a room that's "urbane" but
"never pretentious"; to a few it "feels dated", but the majority declares
this "quintessential NYC" experience still "vibrant after all these years."

Grace's Trattoria *Italian*
18 | 16 | 18 | $43

E 70s | 201 E. 71st St. (bet. 2nd & 3rd Aves.) | 212-452-2323 |
www.gracestrattoria.com

An adjunct to the "famous grocery store next door", this "cozy", "ca-
ual" Italian "standby" is "always crowded" with UES local "regulars"
illing up on "fresh, simple" Pugliese specialties; though "nothing
pectacular", it's "reliable for a quiet lunch or dinner."

	FOOD	DECOR	SERVICE	COST

Gradisca *Italian*
▽ 21 | 17 | 17 | $47

G Village | 126 W. 13th St. (bet. 6th Ave. & 7th Ave. S.) | 212-691-4886
www.gradiscanyc.com

"Amazing housemade pastas" and other "hearty" Italian classics earn this "cozy" Villager local "favorite" status; its grottolike digs are doubly "inviting on a cold night", though critics find them "too dark" and "noisy", also citing "folksy", "inattentive" service.

☑ Gramercy Tavern *American*
27 | 25 | 27 | $92

Flatiron | 42 E. 20th St. (bet. B'way & Park Ave. S.) | 212-477-0777 | www.gramercytavern.com

Supporters of this "superb-in-all-respects" Flatiron New American hail the new chef – Michael Anthony, formerly of Blue Hill at Stone Barns – and salute his "spellbinding" market-centric cuisine, matched with an "extraordinary wine list"; the flower-filled, "rustic-yet-refined" main room "puts diners at ease", as does the "quicksilver" staff that's "on top of everything without being on top of you"; prix fixe–only tabs are "costly" and reservations "tough" ("getting into Harvard is easier"), but there's always the "lower-priced", "drop-in" front tavern.

Grand Café ● *Eclectic*
▽ 17 | 22 | 16 | $23

Astoria | 37-01 30th Ave. (37th St.) | Queens | 718-545-1494

"Athens meets South Beach" at this "glitzy", "energetic" Astorian, a "weekend hot spot" in a "prime location" for "chatting and people-watching over brunch"; the Eclectic eats are "light" and "reasonable", but be ready to "hang out" for a while, since service can be "slow."

Grand Sichuan *Chinese*
22 | 7 | 12 | $23

Chelsea | 229 Ninth Ave. (24th St.) | 212-620-5200 ●
Chinatown | 125 Canal St. (Chrystie St.) | 212-625-9212 ⊘
E 50s | 1049 Second Ave. (bet. 55th & 56th Sts.) | 212-355-5855
E Village | 19-23 St. Marks Pl. (bet. 2nd & 3rd Aves.) | 212-529-4800
Murray Hill | 227 Lexington Ave. (bet. 33rd & 34th Sts.) | 212-679-9770
Rego Park | 98-108 Queens Blvd. (bet. 66th & 67th Aves.) | Queens | 718-268-8833
www.thegrandsichuan.com

"Spices that'll kick you all the way to China" are in liberal use at this "genuine-article" Szechuan mini-chain where even the less "assertive" dishes have "loads of flavor"; it's "low on decor" and "service could be warmer", but no one seems to mind much.

Grand Tier Restaurant ☒ *American/Continental*
19 | 24 | 22 | $77

W 60s | Metropolitan Opera House | Lincoln Center Plaza, 2nd fl. (bet. 63rd & 65th Sts.) | 212-799-3400 | www.patinagroup.com

When attending "that special opera" or any Lincoln Center performance, ticket-holders can dine at this "beautiful" Met venue; its "luxury" and "convenience" are the main attraction, as the American-Continental fare is "predictable" – and you "may hit high C" when you "see the bill."

Gray's Papaya ●⊘ *Hot Dogs*
20 | 4 | 12 | $5

Garment District | 539 Eighth Ave. (37th St.) | 212-904-1588
G Village | 402 Sixth Ave. (8th St.) | 212-260-3532
W 70s | 2090 Broadway (72nd St.) | 212-799-0243

"These puppies hit the spot" howl lovers of the "snappy", "juicy", "dirt cheap" links washed down with "refreshing" tropical juice drinks at

| | FOOD | DECOR | SERVICE | COST |

this 24/7 trio of "stand-up" "hot dog heavens"; "loved" by everyone from "bankers" to eaters "on a pauper's pension", it should be registered as a "NY landmark."

NEW Grayz *Eclectic*

- | - | - | E

W 50s | 13-15 W. 54th St. (bet. 5th & 6th Aves.) | 212-262-4600 | www.grayz.net

Cocktails and hors d'oeuvres get the Gray Kunz treatment at this new Midtown Eclectic set to open in the Rockefeller townhouse that was formerly home to Aquavit; the meandering space (a series of cozy chambers leading to a transporting atrium) will offer a full lunch menu, and after dark, haute drinks and snacks; it's also available for private parties.

Great Jones Cafe ◑ *Cajun*

19 | 12 | 16 | $27

NoHo | 54 Great Jones St. (bet. Bowery & Lafayette St.) | 212-674-9304 | www.greatjones.com

Revelers recover from "long nights out" over "amazing Bloody Mary"–fueled "killer brunch" at this "cheap" NoHo Cajun "dive", a "down-to-earth" scene with "friendly" staffers and "zydeco on the jukebox"; "be prepared to wait for a table", though, 'cause the space is "infinitesimal."

Great NY Noodle Town ◑⊄ *Noodle Shop*

22 | 5 | 12 | $16

Chinatown | 28½ Bowery (Bayard St.) | 212-349-0923

This "basic" C-towner churns out "fantastic" salt-baked seafood and noodle dishes into the wee hours for those willing to sit "elbow to elbow with strangers"; ignore the "nonexistent" decor and "gruff" service and focus on the "cheap" tabs.

Greek Kitchen *Greek*

19 | 13 | 17 | $28

W 50s | 889 10th Ave. (58th St.) | 212-581-4300 | www.greekkitchennyc.com

Cheap and "authentic" enough to draw droves of "native Greeks", this decidedly "unpretentious" Hellenic in way West Hell's Kitchen proffers "delicious" meze and other "fresh", "simple" fare; a "friendly" vibe makes it a "pleasant" change of pace before or after Lincoln Center.

Green Field Churrascaria *Brazilian*

19 | 14 | 19 | $36

Corona | 108-01 Northern Blvd. (108th St.) | Queens | 718-672-5202

It's "gluttony gone wild" at this "noisy" all-you-can-eat Corona "palace" where the "meat, meat and more meat" "keeps coming" via "skewer"-wielding waiters – and the salad bar "ain't no joke either"; the fact that this football field–size Brazilian rodizio is "run by Koreans" just typifies "Queens in all its ethnic glory."

Greenhouse Café *American*

19 | 18 | 19 | $34

Bay Ridge | 7717 Third Ave. (bet. 77th & 78th Sts.) | Brooklyn | 718-833-8200 | www.greenhousecafe.com

Turning out "tasty", "affordable" eats, this "family-oriented" Bay Ridge New American remains a "staple" for its "pretty" glass-clad back room, 40-ft. mahogany bar and live entertainment on Saturday nights; "friendly" service further boosts the "wonderful" vibe.

Grifone ☒ *Italian*

23 | 18 | 24 | $59

E 40s | 244 E. 46th St. (bet. 2nd & 3rd Aves.) | 212-490-7275 | www.grifonenyc.com

"Old-world charm and class abound" at this "intimate" U.N.-area ristorante where "wealthier locals" and "diplomats" "savor the flavors"

	FOOD	DECOR	SERVICE	COST

of "terrific" Northern Italian classics; staffers "treat you like family" and the "kitchen is happy to accommodate", but just be sure to budget for the "pricey" tabs.

☑ Grimaldi's ⊅ Pizza
25 | 10 | 14 | $20

Dumbo | 19 Old Fulton St. (bet. Front & Water Sts.) | Brooklyn | 718-858-4300 | www.grimaldis.com

"Thin, crispy crusts" and "perfect sauce" make the "sublime" coal-oven pizzas at this cash-only Dumbo "landmark" "craveable" enough to inspire interborough "pilgrimages"; plan on "lines", crowds and "brusque" service, but then "you're not there for the ambiance."

☑ Grocery, The ☒ American
26 | 16 | 24 | $60

Carroll Gardens | 288 Smith St. (bet. Sackett & Union Sts.) | Brooklyn | 718-596-3335

"Success hasn't spoiled" this "brilliant" "mom-and-pop" Carroll Gardens New American, whose "haute cuisine with humility" lets its "supremely fresh" seasonal ingredients "shine through"; given the "teeny" confines (augmented in summer with a "lovely garden") and the staff's "personal attention", an evening here feels a bit "like being at a friend's for dinner", i.e. a friend who's a great cook.

Grotta Azzurra ❶ Italian
18 | 16 | 17 | $41

Little Italy | 177 Mulberry St. (Broome St.) | 212-925-8775 | www.grottaazzurrany.com

"The fish aren't the only ones wearing sharkskin" at this Little Italy eatery, a reincarnation of the 1908 original; *amici* applaud "honest" Southern Italian fare and "bargain prix fixe menus", but nostalgists who deem this redux a "shadow of its former self" come away feeling blue.

NEW Guadalupe Mexican
∇ 19 | 19 | 16 | $29

Inwood | 597 W. 207th St. (bet. B'way & Vermilyea Ave.) | 212-304-1083 | www.guadaluperestaurant.com

At this new Inwood Mexican, "approachable" south-of-the-border specialties and "marvelous margaritas" materialize in a "loftlike" space that "feels like an old-world church"; service "needs work", but neighbors "happy to have this new choice" nearby are "really rooting" for it.

Guantanamera ❶ Cuban
∇ 22 | 15 | 19 | $36

(fka Azucar)

W 50s | 939 Eighth Ave. (bet. 55th & 56th Sts.) | 212-262-5354 | www.guantanameranyc.com

"Delicious", "lively Latin" dishes and "sugarcane spear"-adorned mojitos ensure everyone's "Havana great meal" at this affordable West Midtown Cuban; other pluses are an "entertaining cigar roller" and nightly live music – though all that "fun" can get "loud."

NEW Gus' Place ❶ Greek/Mediterranean
20 | 16 | 20 | $37

G Village | 192 Bleecker St. (bet. MacDougal St. & 6th Ave.) | 212-777-1660

"New location, same warm welcome" report Village Gus-tomers "thrilled" by the return (after two years) of this longtime source for "savory" Greek-Med fare; boosting the "charm" factor of its "tiny", "rustic" digs is a small sidewalk patio, not to mention the presence of the "genial" owner and namesake.

	FOOD	DECOR	SERVICE	COST

Gusto *Italian*
22 **21** **19** **$53**

Village | 60 Greenwich Ave. (Perry St.) | 212-924-8000 |
www.gustonyc.com

New chef Amanda Freitag is "coming into her own" at this "hip" but
friendly" Greenwich Village Italian, turning out "skillful" *cucina* full of
bright, distinctive" flavors; its "snazzy" black-and-white "*La Dolce
Vita*" decor has a "glamorous" feel, as does the "buzzy, beautiful",
high-energy" crowd.

Gyu-Kaku *Japanese*
21 **20** **20** **$43**

NEW E 40s | 805 Third Ave., 2nd fl. (50th St.) | 212-702-8816
Village | 34 Cooper Sq. (bet. Astor Pl. & 4th St.) | 212-475-2989
www.gyu-kaku.com

NYC lounge meets Asian BBQ" at these "chic" East Village–Midtown
nks of a Japanese chain where diners grill "high-quality" marinated
neats, seafood and veggies on their own charcoal braziers; it's great
or groups, though the "costs can add up" and a few wonder "why pay"
o "do all the work"?

Hacienda de Argentina ● *Argentinean/Steak*
21 **21** **19** **$51**

70s | 339 E. 75th St. (bet. 1st & 2nd Aves.) | 212-472-5300 |
www.haciendadeargentina.com

Carnivores have a cow over the "tender" grass-fed beef at this "very
Buenos Aires" UES steakhouse that's cheap for the genre; "polite"
taffers and "dark", "hacienda"-style environs with glowing candles
and date-worthy "romantic" overtones.

Hakata Grill *Japanese*
20 **15** **18** **$35**

W 40s | 230 W. 48th St. (bet. B'way & 8th Ave.) | 212-245-1020

how-goers "squeeze in a bite of sushi" pre-curtain at this Theater
District Japanese "secret", appreciated for its "tasty", "fresh" fish;
ure, seating is "elbow-to-elbow" and the pace often "hurried", but
ew fret much given the "inexpensive" tabs.

Hale & Hearty Soups ⊄ *Sandwiches/Soup*
19 **7** **12** **$11**

Chelsea | Chelsea Mkt. | 75 Ninth Ave. (bet. 15th & 16th Sts.) |
212-255-2400
40s | 685 Third Ave. (43rd St.) | 212-681-6460 🛢
40s | Grand Central | lower level (42nd St. & Vanderbilt Ave.) |
212-983-2845
60s | 849 Lexington Ave. (bet. 64th & 65th Sts.) | 212-517-7600
Financial District | 55 Broad St. (Beaver St.) | 212-509-4100 🛢
Garment District | 462 Seventh Ave. (35th St.) | 212-971-0605 🛢
W 40s | Rockefeller Plaza | 30 Rockefeller Plaza (49th St.) | 212-265-2117 🛢
W 40s | 49 W. 42nd St. (bet. 5th & 6th Aves.) | 212-575-9090 🛢
W 50s | 55 W. 56th St. (bet. 5th & 6th Aves.) | 212-245-9200 🛢
Brooklyn Heights | 32 Court St. (Remsen St.) | Brooklyn |
718-596-5600 🛢
www.haleandhearty.com
additional locations throughout the NY area

Given its "bewildering" "variety" of "hit-the-spot" potages, this ubiq-
uitous "cafeteria-style" chain is like the "Baskin-Robbins of soup"; it
ets "hectic" during "prime lunch hours" and "inattentive" staffers can
e "as cold as the gazpacho", but at least the "pace is quick" and the
price is right.

	FOOD	DECOR	SERVICE	COST

Hallo Berlin *German*

17 | 8 | 12 | $21

W 40s | 626 10th Ave. (bet. 44th & 45th Sts.) | 212-977-1944

Cheap, "hearty" Teutonic "peasant food" and "good German beers on tap" are what this West Hell's Kitchen "bratwurst central" is all about; frank fans figure the "sausages and brew are worth" enduring "nonexistent ambiance" and "surly", "painfully slow" service.

Hampton Chutney Co. *Indian*

20 | 10 | 15 | $15

SoHo | 68 Prince St. (bet. Crosby & Lafayette Sts.) | 212-226-9996
W 80s | 464 Amsterdam Ave. (bet. 82nd & 83rd Sts.) | 212-362-5050
www.hamptonchutney.com

So "huge" they're "shareable", the bargain "nouvelle dosas" at these "casual" storefront siblings "light up your mouth" with "refreshing Indian fusion flavors"; though the SoHo "hipster" magnet is short on seats, its roomier UWS offshoot is "paradise for mothers with strollers."

Hangawi *Korean*

23 | 24 | 21 | $46

Murray Hill | 12 E. 32nd St. (bet. 5th & Madison Aves.) | 212-213-0077
www.hangawirestaurant.com

"Exit a busy street" in Murray Hill and enter a "temple of tranquility" at this vegetarian Korean where the "intriguing", "high-end" fare "goes way beyond kimchi" and the staff is "lovely" and "attentive"; just be sure to "wear nice socks" because you have to "check your shoes at the door."

Hard Rock Cafe ● *American*

13 | 20 | 14 | $30

W 40s | 1501 Broadway (43rd St.) | 212-343-3355 | www.hardrock.com
"Tourists, teens" and types who "really like being surrounded by gold records and guitars" groove on this "loud", "hectic", "kitschy" Times Square "rock mall"; admittedly, "you come for the show", not the "so-so" American grub, but "you'll be safe with a burger and a shake."

Harrison, The *American*

24 | 21 | 23 | $61

TriBeCa | 355 Greenwich St. (Harrison St.) | 212-274-9310 |
www.theharrison.com

"Sophisticated" but "not stuffy", this "welcoming" TriBeCan turns out "bold" New American fare paired with "excellent wines" to "young CEO types" and other "grown-ups"; "mellow" "pro" staffers "serve with class", ensuring that, despite the "high" tab, "you can't go wrong here."

Harry Cipriani ● *Italian*

- | - | - | VE

E 50s | Sherry Netherland | 781 Fifth Ave. (bet. 59th & 60th Sts.) |
212-753-5566 | www.cipriani.com

Serving pasta and Bellinis again after a lengthy face-lift, this haute Venetian in the Sherry Netherland with a polished new look is still attracting enough Euro jet-setters and society types to make it a people-watching paradise; comically high pricing doesn't mean a thing to this crowd since it's all about the scene here.

Harry's Cafe ●⊠ *Eclectic*

22 | 21 | 22 | $52

Financial District | 1 Hanover Sq. (bet. Pearl & Stone Sts.)

Harry's Steak ⊠ *Steak*

Financial District | 97 Pearl St. (bet. Broad St. & Hanover Sq.)
212-785-9200 | www.harrysnyc.com

This Financial District twofer within the "beautiful", "historic" 1870s India House ministers "attentively" to area bulls and bears; the "un-

| | FOOD | DECOR | SERVICE | COST |

pretentious" upstairs Eclectic cafe features a "great, friendly bar", while the steakhouse proffers "excellent" beef and wines in a setting so "clubby" you may "forget you're in a basement."

Haru *Japanese*
21 | 17 | 17 | $40

E 40s | 280 Park Ave. (48th St.) | 212-490-9680
E 70s | 1327 Third Ave. (76th St.) | 212-452-1028 ◑
E 70s | 1329 Third Ave. (76th St.) | 212-452-2230 ◑
Flatiron | 220 Park Ave. S. (18th St.) | 646-428-0989 ◑
W 40s | 205 W. 43rd St. (bet. B'way & 8th Ave.) | 212-398-9810 ◑
W 80s | 433 Amsterdam Ave. (bet. 80th & 81st Sts.) | 212-579-5655 ◑
www.harusushi.com

"Haray" cheer fans of this "lively" Japanese chain that reels in "young" types who "crave a scene" with their modestly priced, "whale-size sushi"; it's "reliable" for a "quick" bite, but don't plan on "settling in for a chat", as the staff "works to turn over tables" and noise can be "haruble."

Hasaki ◑ *Japanese*
23 | 14 | 18 | $41

E Village | 210 E. Ninth St. (bet. 2nd & 3rd Aves.) | 212-473-3327

"Excellent" classic Japanese fare, including "quality" sushi, gives "value" at this East Village "gem"; there's little "elbow room", but sentimental sorts claim "cozy" confines and a "jazzy soundtrack" render it "improbably romantic", that is if you "arrive early" to avoid the "legendary" lines.

Hatsuhana ⊠ *Japanese*
24 | 15 | 20 | $50

E 40s | 17 E. 48th St. (bet. 5th & Madison Aves.) | 212-355-3345
E 40s | 237 Park Ave. (46th St.) | 212-661-3400
www.hatsuhana.com

For "power lunches" or "after-work dinners", Midtowners count on these longtime sushi siblings likened to "Toyotas that never break down"; maybe the ambiance is "austere" and "pedestrian concoctions outweigh creative ones", but for "consistently fresh" (if "expensive") fish, most consider them "toro-tastic."

Havana Alma de Cuba *Cuban*
21 | 17 | 19 | $34

W Village | 94 Christopher St. (bet. Bedford & Bleecker Sts.) | 212-242-3800 | www.havanavillagenyc.com

With its "amazing" mojitos, "authentic" Cuban food and "cheerful" service, not to mention "wonderful live music", this "welcoming", well-priced West Villager has "first-date place" written all over it; the "tiny" digs are often "crowded", but the "outside garden is a plus."

Havana Central *Cuban*
17 | 15 | 16 | $30

Union Sq | 22 E. 17th St. (bet. B'way & 5th Ave.) | 212-414-2298
W 40s | 151 W. 46th St. (bet. 6th & 7th Aves.) | 212-398-7440 ◑
NEW **W 100s** | 2911 Broadway (bet. 113th & 114th Sts.) | 212-662-8830
www.havanacentral.com

These three amigos boast "decent" "nuevo" Cuban basics in "festive" quarters; "under-par" service can detract, but it's made up for by the lively bar scene and "affordable" tabs; there's "often live music" at the UWS branch on Broadway, housed in the former West End bar.

Haveli ◑ *Indian*
23 | 16 | 20 | $32

E Village | 100 Second Ave. (bet. 5th & 6th Sts.) | 212-982-0533

"Fabulous spicing without the grease" ensures this East Village Indian "stalwart" remains a "league above" its Curry Row neighbors; its rela-

| | FOOD | DECOR | SERVICE | COST |

tively "upscale" (yet still affordable) approach costs "a little more", but it's "reliable", with "attentive" service and "no disco lights."

NEW Hawaiian Tropic Zone ◗ American   ▽ 16 | 18 | 15 | $43

W 40s | 729 Seventh Ave. (49th St.) | 212-626-7312 |
www.hawaiiantropiczone.com

"*Baywatch* meets Manhattan" at this "eye-popping" new Theater District themer, a three-level, 16,000-sq.-ft. party where "cute" waitresses "not wearing much" steal the show from David Burke's just-"good" New American fare; critics put off by the "frat-house-for-suits" vibe dismiss it as "Hooter's goes to the beach."

Hearth American/Italian   25 | 21 | 24 | $63

E Village | 403 E. 12th St. (1st Ave.) | 646-602-1300 |
www.restauranthearth.com

Chef Marco Canora's "informal" but culinarily "serious" Tuscan-accented East Village New American features "no trendy cooking", just "exquisite", "imaginative" dishes from an open kitchen; it also boasts a "well-chosen" wine list and "top-notch service", ensuring it's a "hit on every level", "big prices" aside.

Heartland Brewery Pub Food   14 | 13 | 15 | $28

Garment District | Empire State Bldg. | 350 Fifth Ave. (34th St.) |
212-563-3433
Seaport | South Street Seaport | 93 South St. (Fulton St.) | 646-572-2337
Union Sq | 35 Union Sq. W. (bet. 16th & 17th Sts.) | 212-645-3400
W 40s | 127 W. 43rd St. (bet. B'way & 6th Ave.) | 646-366-0235 ◗
W 50s | 1285 Sixth Ave. (51st St.) | 212-582-8244
www.heartlandbrewery.com

With five locations around Manhattan, this microbrewery chain "not unexpectedly produces good beer", but also offers "surprisingly" "tasty" and "inexpensive" pub fare; accordingly, it's usually packed after work with a "young crowd", though critics pan its "generic" eats and say it feels "remarkably like a corporate restaurant in a suburban mall."

Heidelberg German   17 | 16 | 16 | $34

E 80s | 1648 Second Ave. (bet. 85th & 86th Sts.) | 212-628-2332 |
www.heidelbergrestaurant.com

A "throwback" to the heyday of Yorkville's Germantown, this "everything-Deutsch" "charmer" produces hard-to-find classics served by a lederhosen-clad staff; some find the "biergarten" setting "cheesy", but most embrace the "festive" spirit and low prices.

Hell's Kitchen Mexican   23 | 16 | 19 | $43

W 40s | 679 Ninth Ave. (bet. 46th & 47th Sts.) | 212-977-1588 |
www.hellskitchen-nyc.com

Look for "inventive", "spicy" dishes washed down with "delightfully toxic" margaritas at this "small", "friendly" Hell's Kitchen Mexican; maybe its "stark" interior "needs flavor", but the prices are "gentle" and it "works well for pre-theater."

Henry's End American   25 | 14 | 23 | $45

Brooklyn Heights | 44 Henry St. (Cranberry St.) | Brooklyn | 718-834-1776 |
www.henrysend.com

"If game is your thing", the hunt ends at this "hearty" Brooklyn Heights New American beloved for its "creative dishes" and "varied" wine list, as

	FOOD	DECOR	SERVICE	COST

well as for its modest prices and "pleasant" staff; the "tight quarters" have "zero ambiance", but otherwise it's a "first-rate" experience.

Highline ❶ *Thai* | 19 | 22 | 17 | $36 |

Meatpacking | 835 Washington St. (Little W. 12th St.) | 212-243-3339 | www.nychighline.com

A "funky", "manageable alternative" to more "flashy" Meatpacking District neighbors, this sprawling, tri-level source for solid, "affordable" Thai fare is lots of "fun"; the soundtrack "can be loud" and the service variable, but its "very cool" "modern" space trumps all.

NEW Hill Country *BBQ* | - | - | - | M |

Chelsea | 30 W. 26th St. (bet. B'way & 6th Ave.) | 212-255-4544 | www.hillcountryny.com

Taking you to Texas Hill Country by way of Chelsea, this big, boisterous, bi-level newcomer features three in-house smokers manned by a seasoned pit master (Robbie Richter) and decor right out of a back country roadhouse; the meats and sides are ordered from a counter, then carried on trays to long communal tables, and the result is a place that tastes, looks and smells as good as anything in the Lone Star state.

Hispaniola ❶ *Dominican* | ▽ 21 | 21 | 17 | $42 |

Washington Heights | 839 W. 181st St. (bet. Cabrini Blvd. & Pinehurst St.) | 212-740-5222 | www.hispaniolarestaurant.com

"Breathtaking views of the GW Bridge" are the thing at this "upscale" Washington Heights Dominican, though the "delicious" Asian-inflected fare is also a draw; it's a "must-try" for an Uptown adventure.

HK ❶ *American* | ▽ 16 | 16 | 15 | $29 |

Garment District | 523 Ninth Ave. (39th St.) | 212-947-4208

Despite its "dreary location" behind the Port Authority, this "reliable" Garment District American serves "decent", comforting "diner fare" in starkly modern digs; service is "spotty" and the "decibels" "loud", but it's a "terrific bargain", and in warmer weather, you can escape to the patio.

Holy Basil ❶ *Thai* | 22 | 19 | 19 | $31 |

E Village | 149 Second Ave., 2nd fl. (bet. 9th & 10th Sts.) | 212-460-5557 | www.holybasilrestaurant.com

"Dark", "atmospheric" digs boost the "romance" factor at this East Village "upstairs hideaway" that's popular for "inexpensive" but high-rated Thai dishes; "gracious" service and prime "people-watching" from the balcony round out the endorsement.

Home *American* | 20 | 15 | 19 | $40 |

G Village | 20 Cornelia St. (bet. Bleecker & W. 4th Sts.) | 212-243-9579 | www.recipesfromhome.com

Who knew "home cooking" could be "gourmet", but the "expertly prepared" "inventive spins" on comfort classics at this "welcoming", "true Village joint" keep folks coming back; its "quaint", "narrow" space gets "crowded", but the garden gives diners needed "elbow room."

Hope & Anchor *Diner* | 18 | 15 | 18 | $20 |

Red Hook | 347 Van Brunt St. (Wolcott St.) | Brooklyn | 718-237-0276 | www.hopeandanchordiner.com

The staff and owners of this "funky", "laid-back" Red Hook diner make patrons "feel at home", as does the kitchen's "satisfying", low-budget output; between the "excellent" brunch and "drag queen"-hosted karaoke nights, it's no wonder this "remote outpost" keeps the locals coming.

	FOOD	DECOR	SERVICE	COST

NEW House, The ◑ *Mediterranean* ▽ 22 | 27 | 21 | $52

Gramercy | 121 E. 17th St. (bet. Irving Pl. & Park Ave. S.) | 212-353-2121 | www.thehousenyc.com

Set in an "exquisite" 1850s Gramercy Park carriage house, this "elegant", pricey Med "hideaway" strikes a "romantic" chord with its dark woods, fireplace and flickering candles; the menu of "mostly small plates" veers toward Italy and is calibrated to a "fabulous" list of vinos.

Houston's *American* 20 | 18 | 19 | $36

E 50s | Citigroup Ctr. | 153 E. 53rd St. (enter at 3rd Ave. & 54th St.) | 212-888-3828
Gramercy | NY Life Bldg. | 378 Park Ave. S. (27th St.) | 212-689-1090
www.hillstone.com

"In a sea of upscale bar grub", this "dependable" American chain stands out with "surprisingly good" food, service and prices; not surprisingly, "killer waits" are common, but "slammin' drinks", a "huge happy-hour scene" and that "to-die-for spinach dip" are your reward.

HQ *American* ▽ 19 | 18 | 18 | $42

SoHo | 90 Thompson St. (bet. Prince & Spring Sts.) | 212-966-2755

A "refreshing change" from the usual "SoHo scene", this "unpretentious", relatively inexpensive New American offers "tasty" bistro fare via an "attentive", "witty" staff; its "cozy, warm" HQ features a frontage of French doors ideal for "people-watching."

HSF ⇪ *Chinese* 20 | 9 | 12 | $23

Chinatown | 46 Bowery (bet. Bayard & Canal Sts.) | 212-374-1319

"Carts galore" brimming with "delicious", reasonably priced dim sum explain the everlasting popularity of this Chinatown Cantonese "institution"; it's "a zoo, plain and simple", with "off-putting" service and decidedly downscale digs, but get there early to avoid the "maddening crowds."

Hudson Cafeteria ◑ *American/Eclectic* 19 | 22 | 18 | $47

W 50s | Hudson Hotel | 356 W. 58th St. (bet. 8th & 9th Aves.) | 212-554-6000 | www.chinagrillmgt.com

"Hearty", "stylish" comfort fare served in "pseudo" college dining hall digs ("high ceilings", "Gothic" lighting, "wooden communal tables") is the drill at this hotel American-Eclectic; most agree it's "not trendy anymore", but it's still a good bet before or after "Lincoln Center" or if you get a room upstairs.

NEW Hudson River Café ◑ *American/Seafood* – | – | – | M

Harlem | 697 W. 133rd St. (12th Ave.) | 212-491-9111 | www.hudsonrivercafe.com

Under the steel trusses just north of Harlem's Fairway Market, a former mechanic's shop has been transformed into this airy New American seafooder with a California-winery look; inside wrought-iron gates there's bi-level patio seating and an outdoor bar pouring until the wee hours.

	FOOD	DECOR	SERVICE	COST

Hummus Place ● *Israeli/Vegetarian* — 23 | 11 | 17 | $14

E Village | 109 St. Marks Pl. (bet. Ave. A & 1st Ave.) | 212-529-9198
G Village | 99 MacDougal St. (bet. Bleecker & W. 3rd Sts.) | 212-533-3089
NEW W 70s | 305 Amsterdam Ave. (bet. 74th & 75th Sts.) |
212-799-3335
www.hummusplace.com

As the name suggests, this Israeli trio is a "one-note Johnny" – but oh,
"what a note" sing "addicts" of its "out-of-this-world hummus" and other
"amazing", "cheap" vegetarian snacks; the setups are "small and
cramped", but "pleasant" (if "uncoordinated") service compensates.

NEW Hurapan Kitchen *Thai* — ∇ 20 | 19 | 20 | $43

G Village | 29 Seventh Ave. S. (bet. Bedford & Morton Sts.) |
212-727-2678

"Inventive", "delicious" spins on Thai standards are the specialty of this
Village newcomer, whose "attentive" crew presides over a "pretty",
somewhat "upscale" room; it's a little "expensive" for the genre, but
after an "innovative sake cocktail" or two, most hardly notice.

Ichimura 🗷 *Japanese* — ∇ 24 | 11 | 17 | $84

E 50s | 1026 Second Ave. (bet. 54th & 55th Sts.) | 212-355-3557

Sushi-seekers retreat from the hustle of Midtown at this "undiscovered"
Japanese where the monastic decor allows diners to focus on the fresh
fish; yes, it all comes at a "high-end" price – it would be a challenge not
to exceed the $30 minimum – but enthusiasts aren't deterred.

Ichiro ● *Japanese* — 20 | 12 | 18 | $32

E 80s | 1694 Second Ave. (bet. 87th & 88th Sts.) | 212-369-6300 |
www.ichi-ro.com

"Ample", "consistently fresh" sushi that "couldn't be much cheaper",
doled out by an "able" staff, keeps this UES "neighborhood" Japanese
"crowded"; most everyone agrees it's a "solid" bet for everything but
the "plain" setting.

Ici 🗷 *American/French* — 22 | 19 | 19 | $39

Fort Greene | 246 DeKalb Ave. (bet. Clermont & Vanderbilt Aves.) |
Brooklyn | 718-789-2778 | www.icirestaurant.com

With Franco-American "seasonal dishes that always shine" and appealing decor and pricing, this Fort Greene spot has Brooklynites wondering "why go into Manhattan?"; there are a few gripes about
"uneven" service, but all agree that the garden is "lovely."

I Coppi *Italian* — 23 | 20 | 20 | $43

E Village | 432 E. Ninth St. (bet. Ave. A & 1st Ave.) | 212-254-2263 |
www.icoppinyc.com

"Happiness" is the "spectacular" year-round back garden of this "rustic" East Village Tuscan "standout"; there's "no attitude here", just
"excellent" "classic" pastas and "wood-fired" entrees perfect for pair-
ing with its "fabulous" Tuscan wines.

Ideya *Caribbean* — ∇ 20 | 15 | 17 | $36

SoHo | 349 W. Broadway (bet. Broome & Grand Sts.) | 212-625-1441 |
www.ideya.net

A "welcome escape" from the usual SoHo hot spots, this "casual",
"welcoming" Caribbean dishes up "flavorful" fare and "killer" mojitos

at surprisingly "affordable" prices given the zip code; the mood is "festive" (read: "loud") and the staff "friendly" if sometimes "harried."

Il Bagatto ●Ⓜ *Italian* | 23 | 16 | 16 | $36 |

E Village | 192 E. Second St. (bet. Aves. A & B) | 212-228-0977

"Loyal regulars" frequent this "small", "down-to-earth" East Village Italian for its "high-quality" classic cuisine and wines offered at "reasonable" rates; despite "Christmas-light" decor, "curt" service and occasional "waits", "you don't mind once you taste the food."

Il Bastardo ● *Italian/Steak* | 19 | 18 | 18 | $40 |

Chelsea | 191 Seventh Ave. (bet. 21st & 22nd Sts.) | 212-675-5980 | www.ilbastardonyc.com

The "sensuous" room at this Chelsea Tuscan steakhouse has a "lounge feel" left over from its nightclub days, complete with "loud" acoustics and a "happening" "after-work" scene; most find the "basic" fare to be "well prepared", and the $15 prix fixe lunch to be a deal.

NEW Il Brigante *Italian* | ▽ 21 | 17 | 17 | $29 |

Seaport | 214 Front St. (bet. Beekman St. & Peck Slip) | 212-285-0222

Set in the historic South Street Seaport, this new Italian trattoria has made itself welcome with a rustic space warmed by a wood-burning oven churning wonderful pizzas and "fresh" pastas at budget-friendly prices; service and decor are more debatable.

Il Buco ● *Italian/Mediterranean* | 25 | 23 | 22 | $59 |

NoHo | 47 Bond St. (bet. Bowery & Lafayette St.) | 212-533-1932 | www.ilbuco.com

"Sublime", "seasonal" Italian-Med cuisine as "utterly fabulous" as the "*molto bello*" clientele is the hallmark of this NoHo "hipster"; its "tight" but "charming", "antiques"-adorned digs and "big prices" can be a "squeeze", but overall, you'll be glad you went.

Il Cantinori *Italian* | 22 | 20 | 21 | $59 |

G Village | 32 E. 10th St. (bet. B'way & University Pl.) | 212-673-6044 | www.ilcantinori.com

Adorned with "over-the-top flowers" and the "occasional celeb", this Village "standby" manages to combine "sophisticated" aesthetics with an "unpretentious" vibe, while the "classic" Northern Italian fare is "terrific"; in sum, "when money doesn't matter", it's "superb."

Il Corallo Trattoria *Italian* | 22 | 12 | 19 | $27 |

SoHo | 176 Prince St. (bet. Sullivan & Thompson Sts.) | 212-941-7119

The menu's "endless" choices "make it difficult to decide" among the many "well-prepared" pastas this "friendly", usually "packed" SoHo Italian is known for; most overlook the bland setting because "you can't find a better deal."

Il Cortile ● *Italian* | 23 | 20 | 20 | $50 |

Little Italy | 125 Mulberry St. (bet. Canal & Hester Sts.) | 212-226-6060 | www.ilcortile.com

Made for those who "love garlic" and "phenomenal red sauce", this "old-world" Little Italy vet's "delicious" edibles are delivered by "personable" waiters; sure, it's a bit "pricey", but the atmosphere is "lively" and there's an "elegant" back "garden room" perfect for "romance."

	FOOD	DECOR	SERVICE	COST

Fornaio *Italian*
21 | 14 | 18 | $34

ttle Italy | 132A Mulberry St. (bet. Grand & Hester Sts.) | 212-226-8306

a neighborhood full of "touristy" spots, this "dependable", "reason-
ˈbly priced" Little Italy "favorite" is deemed an "island of authentic-
ˈy"; "to-die-for" meatballs, "al dente" pasta and, of course, "fresh"
ˈd sauce are its forte – "don't look for frills, just bring an appetite."

Gattopardo ● *Italian*
23 | 18 | 23 | $61

𝙒 50s | 33 W. 54th St. (bet. 5th & 6th Aves.) | 212-246-0412 |
ˈww.ilgattopardonyc.com

ˈoasting an "ideal" Midtown location, this "unheralded" "gem" also
ˈoffers "sublime" Neapolitan dishes and "outstanding" service; it's
ˈpricey" and the decor gets mixed reactions ("minimalist and chic" vs.
ˈmply "stark"), but for the area, it's a "blessing."

Il Giglio 🛂 *Italian*
26 | 18 | 24 | $76

ˈiBeCa | 81 Warren St. (bet. Greenwich St. & W. B'way) | 212-571-5555 |
ˈww.ilgigliorestaurant.com

ˈon't "fill up on the freebie appetizers" lest you miss out on the full
ˈirst-rate", "explosion-of-flavors" experience at this "old-world", "up-
ˈcale" TriBeCa Tuscan, presided over by a staff that "couldn't be bet-
ˈr"; though you may "need a loan" to settle the check, most surveyors
ˈay it's "worth every penny."

Mattone 🛂 *Italian/Pizza*
▽ 21 | 13 | 17 | $30

ˈriBeCa | 413 Greenwich St. (Hubert St.) | 212-343-0030

ˈTerrific" brick-oven pizzas have those in-the-know calling this "rea-
ˈnable" TriBeCa Italian "joint" a solid "staple" in a "neighborhood
ˈat needs it"; still, it flies somewhat under the radar, perhaps because
ˈf its "small quarters" and nonexistent decor.

Menestrello 🛂 *Italian*
▽ 22 | 18 | 22 | $60

𝙒 50s | 50 E. 50th St. (bet. Madison & Park Aves.) | 212-421-7588

ˈs "new location is a winner" declare "business-lunch" regulars and
ˈe other necessarily well-heeled devotees of this "old-world" East
ˈlidtown Italian; maybe the "cozy" setting is only "so-so", but it's
ˈot the same "wonderful" food and "friendly" pro service as ever –
ˈlad they're back."

Il Mulino 🛂 *Italian*
27 | 18 | 24 | $83

Village | 86 W. Third St. (bet. Sullivan & Thompson Sts.) | 212-673-3783 |
ˈww.ilmulinonewyork.com

ˈge has not diminished" the "one-of-a-kind" experience at this "out-
ˈanding", "crowded" Village Italian "classic", where nearly "every
ˈish is a masterpiece", and the "white-glove" service has patrons feel-
ˈg "like royalty"; while some insist "it's the best meal you'll ever
ˈave", it's also among "the hardest to book and the hardest to pay
ˈr" – to improve your chances in both respects, go for lunch.

Nido 🛂 *Italian*
23 | 18 | 22 | $66

𝙒 50s | 251 E. 53rd St. (bet. 2nd & 3rd Aves.) | 212-753-8450 |
ˈww.ilnidonyc.com

ˈhe "fantastic", "traditional" Northern Italian cuisine and "first-rate"
ˈervice at this "old-school" Midtown "standby" "still pass muster",
ˈut the setting "reminiscent of a bygone era" is getting "as tired as

Paris Hilton on a Monday morning"; still, for most the "well-spaced ta
bles allowing for conversation" alone justify the "pricey" tabs.

Il Palazzo *Italian*　　　　▽ 23 | 19 | 21 | $46

Little Italy | 151 Mulberry St. (bet. Grand & Hester Sts.) | 212-343-7700
The seafood dishes are "particularly recommended" at this "festive"
Little Italy stalwart, but of course "you can get some fantastic pasta
here too; its "friendly" service and "pleasant" glass-enclosed garden
place it "a cut above" most others on Mulberry Street.

Il Postino ● *Italian*　　　　22 | 19 | 20 | $62

E 40s | 337 E. 49th St. (bet. 1st & 2nd Aves.) | 212-688-0033 |
www.ilpostinorestaurant.com
A staff of "theatrical" waiters who recite a lengthy "specials list" are
the "corporate" crowd's "guide" to this "understated" Midtown
Italian's "terrific", "traditional" fare; just "be careful to ask for prices
lest your tab "creep up."

Il Riccio ● *Italian*　　　　21 | 15 | 19 | $54

E 70s | 152 E. 79th St. (bet. Lexington & 3rd Aves.) | 212-639-9111
"Tiny and crowded" it may be, but given its "delicious" Southern
Italian fare, UES "locals" don't mind sitting "elbow to elbow" at this
"unpretentious" trattoria; besides, there's a "welcoming" staff, relatively "reasonable" rates for a "high-priced neighborhood" and the
chance to spy the occasional "celeb."

☑ Il Tinello ⑤ *Italian*　　　　26 | 21 | 26 | $66

W 50s | 16 W. 56th St. (bet. 5th & 6th Aves.) | 212-245-4388
"Tuxedoed waiters" serve the "sumptuous" Northern Italian dishes
with "courtesy" and "elegance" at this "serene" "white-tablecloth"
Midtown "classic"; it "caters to an older crowd" that "loves its old-
fashioned feel" and doesn't blink at the up-to-date prices.

Il Vagabondo *Italian*　　　　19 | 15 | 18 | $43

E 60s | 351 E. 62nd St. (bet. 1st & 2nd Aves.) | 212-832-9221 |
www.ilvagabondo.com
It "says a lot" that this "reliable" East Side Italian is praised for "never
changing" after 50 years – and given its "terrific" pastas and other
"bargain"-priced "standards", thank goodness it hasn't; it even boasts
a "bocce ball court" for killing time "between courses."

Inagiku *Japanese*　　　　23 | 19 | 22 | $60

E 40s | Waldorf-Astoria | 111 E. 49th St. (bet. Lexington & Park Aves.) |
212-355-0440 | www.inagiku.com
"Meticulous", "kimono-clad" staffers lend a "refined" air to this
"quiet" Midtown sushi specialist that offers "top-of-the-line" rolls at
similar prices; some find the atmosphere a bit "lacking", but the "tran-
sient" "business" crowd doesn't seem to notice.

Indochine ● *French/Vietnamese*　　　　20 | 19 | 18 | $50

E Village | 430 Lafayette St. (bet. Astor Pl. & 4th St.) | 212-505-5111 |
www.indochinenyc.com
"Convenient" before a show at the Public, this "hopping" East Village
French-Vietnamese standby features "delicious" cuisine ferried by
"modelicious waitresses"; it's an overall "sexy" scene, though been-
there-done-that types assert the "colonial"-themed decor is "dated."

	FOOD	DECOR	SERVICE	COST

Industria Argentina ● *Argentinean/Steak* | ▽ 20 | 19 | 19 | $47

TriBeCa | 329 Greenwich St. (bet. Duane & Jay Sts.) | 212-965-8560 | www.iatribeca.com

"Beautiful people" boost the "buzz" at this "sophisticated" TriBeCa Argentinean steakhouse; it can get "a bit expensive", but then again, considering the "swish" surroundings and zip code, most feel it delivers "decent value."

Indus Valley *Indian* | 23 | 16 | 20 | $31

W 100s | 2636 Broadway (100th St.) | 212-222-9222

Upper Westsiders are all aglow about the "fascinating spicing" at this "top-shelf" Indian, where the "fresh" dishes are "cooked to your palate"; the "charming" staff and "modest prices" more than compensate for its "small", "crowded" space; P.S. the $12.95 lunch prix fixe is "unbeatable."

NEW Inn LW12 ● *American* | ▽ 19 | 24 | 18 | $48

Meatpacking | 7 Ninth Ave. (Little W. 12th St.) | 212-206-0300

This attractive, "ski lodge"-esque new Meatpacking District triple-decker showcases a "pricey" American gastropub menu that's "actually very good"; definitely "a scene", it's still "working out the kinks", but it gets points for "originality" – and for serving till 3 AM.

'ino ● *Italian* | 24 | 15 | 19 | $27

G Village | 21 Bedford St. (bet. Downing St. & 6th Ave.) | 212-989-5769 | www.cafeino.com

Diners are "cramped" enough to "feel like pressed panini" themselves at this "teeny" Village Italian wine bar, but its "cheap", "hauntingly" "marvelous" sandwiches make up for the "squeeze" – as well as the "waits"; for "small bites", "nobody does it better."

'inoteca ● *Italian* | 23 | 18 | 19 | $37

LES | 98 Rivington St. (Ludlow St.) | 212-614-0473 | www.inotecanyc.com

Like its smaller sibling, 'ino, this "vibrant", "friendly" LES Italian is a "grazer's paradise" of *fantastico* salumi, cheeses and panini paired with "terrific" wines; those "tidbits" can "easily rack up a big bill", but after sampling them, "you'll know why you waited so long" for a seat.

NEW Insieme *Italian* | ▽ 26 | 20 | 24 | $72

W 50s | The Michelangelo Hotel | 777 Seventh Ave. (bet. 50th & 51st Sts.) | 212-582-1310 | www.restaurantinsieme.com

Marco Canora (Hearth) "has outdone himself" at this new Midtown "winner" where half of the "terrific" Italian dishes are "traditional" and the other half "modern", and all are high-priced; service is "relaxed", but the contemporary room draws mixed reactions ("classy" vs. "ice palace").

Intermezzo ● *Italian* | 18 | 16 | 17 | $32

Chelsea | 202 Eighth Ave. (bet. 20th & 21st Sts.) | 212-929-3433 | www.intermezzony.com

"Wedged in among the local trendies", this "reasonable" Chelsea Italian offers "no surprises", just an "attentive" staff doling out "large portions" of "reliable" pastas with "zesty sauces"; the "live DJ" music is "loud", but that suits the "young, lively crowd."

	FOOD	DECOR	SERVICE	COST

Iron Sushi *Japanese*

19 | 13 | 18 | $28

E 70s | 355 E. 78th St. (bet. 1st & 2nd Aves.) | 212-772-7680
Murray Hill | 440 Third Ave. (bet. 30th & 31st Sts.) | 212-447-5822

"Huge slabs" of "fresh" fish grace the "larger-than-life", "creative" rolls at this "no-frills" East Side sushi duo deemed a "superb value"; the "attentive staff" makes the "mundane surroundings" easy to overlook, but there's also "speedy delivery" as an option.

Isabella's ● *American/Mediterranean*

20 | 19 | 18 | $42

W 70s | 359 Columbus Ave. (77th St.) | 212-724-2100 | www.brguestrestaurants.com

"They have the formula down pat" at this "deservedly popular" longtime Med–New American, an UWS "oasis" for "unrushed", "delicious" meals overseen by "pleasant" staffers; outdoor seating and prime "people-watching" make it "hard to beat", especially at Sunday brunch.

NEW Isabella's Oven ●⊄ *Pizza*

- | - | - | M

LES | 365 Grand St. (Essex St.) | 212-529-5206 | www.isabellasoven.com

This new LES Italian turns out simple salads, pastas and sandwiches, but the real stars are its brick-oven pizzas cooked to slightly charred perfection; the storefront space seats about 10, but there's a big patio in back where locals linger over beer and wine and take in occasional live jazz.

Ise *Japanese*

22 | 12 | 18 | $38

E 40s | 151 E. 49th St. (bet. Lexington & 3rd Aves.) | 212-319-6876
Financial District | 56 Pine St. (bet. Pearl & William Sts.) | 212-785-1600 ⊠
W 50s | 58 W. 56th St. (bet. 5th & 6th Aves.) | 212-707-8702

It's a good sign that this "reliable" *izakaya* trio is "filled" at lunch "with Japanese businessmen" who come for "excellent", "affordable" katsu, sushi and sashimi; the "fluorescent-lit" setups are "forgettable", but "you can't go wrong with anything on the menu."

NEW Island *Mediterranean*

∇ 18 | 21 | 18 | $32

Astoria | 35-15 36th St. (bet. 35th & 36th Aves.) | Queens | 718-433-0690 | www.islandcafebar.com

At this easily affordable, Euro-chic oasis set in a sea of Astoria warehouses, the specialty is Med small plates; it's easy to get lost in its "huge" clublike space, which includes two levels of dining areas, canopied lounges with settees, several bars and a fully decked-out DJ suite.

Island Burgers & Shakes ⊄ *Hamburgers*

22 | 8 | 14 | $16

W 50s | 766 Ninth Ave. (bet. 51st & 52nd Sts.) | 212-307-7934

"Divine" shakes and "hearty burgers" with a "mind-boggling variety" of toppings set this "cheap", "surf"-themed Hell's Kitchen "shack" apart from the pack; most don't care about its "hole-in-the-wall" setup, but the "no-fries" situation is an "Achilles heel."

Ithaka ● *Greek/Seafood*

20 | 16 | 19 | $43

E 80s | 308 E. 86th St. (bet. 1st & 2nd Aves.) | 212-628-9100 | www.ithakarestaurant.com

If you're in a "Greek isles mood", travel to this Yorkville "favorite" proffering "flavorful" seafood in "traditional" taverna environs enhanced by "lovely" live guitar music; "warm" service and "reasonable" prices are two more reasons it "deserves to be more popular."

	FOOD	DECOR	SERVICE	COST

Tre Merli *Italian* | 18 | 18 | 17 | $43 |

SoHo | 463 W. Broadway (bet. Houston & Prince Sts.) | 212-254-8699
W. Village | 183 W. 10th St. (W. 4th St.) | 212-929-2221
www.itremerli.com

Oozing "Italian chic" and "trendy" bar "action", this "breezy", mid-priced SoHo trattoria has a "smaller" Village "brother" that's more on the "cute and romantic" side; at both, the food's "good", if "not memorable", and the servers, though not so good, are memorable.

Trulli *Italian* | 22 | 20 | 20 | $56 |

Gramercy | 122 E. 27th St. (bet. Lexington Ave. & Park Ave. S.) |
212-481-7372 | www.itrulli.com

Whether you sit "inside by the fire or out on the patio", this "classy" Gramercy Italian's "earthy" Pugliese cuisine is "trulli" *delizioso*; some say it's "overpriced", but the "inviting" staff and an "incredible wine list" (also poured at the "attached enoteca") have most saying this "well-orchestrated act" is "worth it."

Tzocan *Mexican* | 23 | 12 | 18 | $33 |

E 100s | 1575 Lexington Ave. (101st St.) | 212-423-0255
E. Village | 438 E. Ninth St. (bet. Ave. A & 1st Ave.) | 212-677-5856 ●

French-influenced "Mexican haute cuisine" is the specialty of the UES branch of this "friendly", "reasonable" pair, while the East Village original offers straightforward south-of-the-border cooking; the "tight" digs "aren't much to look at", but given the "jazzy" tastes and low prices, "who cares?"

Tvo & Lulu *Caribbean/French* | ▽ 22 | 13 | 18 | $27 |

SoHo | 558 Broome St. (bet. 6th Ave. & Varick St.) | 212-226-4399

"Wonderful", "organic" French-Caribbean fare at "out-of-this-world-inexpensive" prices (abetted by a BYO policy) keeps this "charming", "cash-only" West SoHo "shoebox" "packed"; it changed hands recently, but early reports say it's as "friendly" as ever.

EW Izakaya Ten ● *Japanese* | ▽ 19 | 20 | 18 | $40 |

Chelsea | 207 10th Ave. (bet. 22nd & 23rd Sts.) | 212-627-7777

This slim Chelsea space was first D'or Ahn, then briefly, Anzu, and now it's been remade again as this less-expensive "publike" Japanese *izakaya* specializing "tasty little plates"; a wild exterior paint job and wide sake selection distinguishes what's otherwise basically a neighborhood joint.

Jack Bistro ● *French* | 17 | 16 | 18 | $36 |

G. Village | 80 University Pl. (11th St.) | 212-620-5544

"Pleasant" and "unpretentious", this "well-rounded" Villager makes a "dependable" local "hangout" for a "casual" French bistro bite "that won't break the bank"; it's "nothing earth-shattering", but the overall "relaxing dining experience" "fills a void" in the area.

Jack's Luxury Oyster Bar ●图 *Continental/French* | ▽ 24 | 17 | 21 | $63 |

E. Village | 101 Second Ave. (bet. 5th & 6th Sts.) | 212-979-1012

The "luxurious" French-Continental fare remains "out-of-this-world" and the service pleasingly "low-key" at this recently relocated East Villager; nonetheless, nostalgists noting its new "postage-stamp

space" lament the loss of its "original townhouse" digs that were "s
much a part" of its "romantic" charm.

Jackson Diner ⌘ Indian | 22 | 10 | 14 | $22

Jackson Heights | 37-47 74th St. (bet. Roosevelt & 37th Aves.) | Queens |
718-672-1232

Maybe it "looks like a canteen", but this Indian vet is a "reigning rajah"
Jackson Heights thanks to its "stupendously delicious" dishes; yes, i
high quality and low prices can lead to total "bedlam", but the $8.9
buffet brunch is "a steal" that leaves everyone "stuffed and happy."

Jackson Hole American | 17 | 9 | 14 | $20

E 60s | 232 E. 64th St. (bet. 2nd & 3rd Aves.) | 212-371-7187 ◗
E 80s | 1611 Second Ave. (bet. 83rd & 84th Sts.) | 212-737-8788 ◖
E 90s | 1270 Madison Ave. (91st St.) | 212-427-2820
Murray Hill | 521 Third Ave. (35th St.) | 212-679-3264 ◗
W 80s | 517 Columbus Ave. (85th St.) | 212-362-5177
Bayside | 35-01 Bell Blvd. (35th Ave.) | Queens | 718-281-0330 ◗
Jackson Heights | 69-35 Astoria Blvd. (70th St.) | Queens | 718-204-7070 ◖
www.jacksonholeburgers.com

"Don't plan on running a marathon" after consuming one of the "co
lossal" burgers this "cheap", "child-friendly" "diner-style" chain is f
mous for; "you can smell the grease" in its "often-crowded" quarter
and the "desultory waiters" aren't much help, but you won't find
better "hangover" cure.

Jack the Horse Tavern American | 20 | 20 | 19 | $38

Brooklyn Heights | 66 Hicks St. (Cranberry St.) | Brooklyn | 718-852-5084
www.jackthehorse.com

The "creative" New American cooking at this "charming" Brookly
Heights "tavern" is gaining a "solid fan base", despite "smallish po
tions" and tabs "slightly pricey" for the genre; still, most surveyors a
won over by the "chic" ambiance and "responsive" staff.

Jacques French | 18 | 17 | 17 | $42

E 80s | 206 E. 85th St. (bet. 2nd & 3rd Aves.) | 212-327-2272
NoLita | 20 Prince St. (bet. Elizabeth & Mott Sts.) | 212-966-8886
www.jacquesnyc.com

"Must-try" moules frites are the star at these "pleasant", "very Frencl
brasseries that also offer a menu of "decent" Gallic "standards" (with
slight North African "flair" at the NoLita branch); the prices are "rea
sonable" enough so that most don't mind the "spotty" service.

Jacques-Imo's NYC Cajun/Creole | 17 | 14 | 16 | $32

W 70s | 366 Columbus Ave. (77th St.) | 212-799-0150 |
www.jacquesimosnyc.com

"It's not Mardi Gras", but this "funky", low-budget UWS "N'Awlins
transplant offers plenty of "fun", not to mention "darn good" Cajur
Creole fare (try the "kickin'" fried chicken); the setting is "strippe
down" and service "can be slow", but you may "end up dancing o
your chair" anyway.

Jaiya Thai Thai | 22 | 10 | 13 | $27

Gramercy | 396 Third Ave. (28th St.) | 212-889-1330 | www.jaiya.co
"Not for the faint of heart", the "fiery hot" dishes at this "authentic
Gramercy Thai are so "stunningly delicious" and their price tags s

"gentle", the "bossy" service and "lacking" decor are beside the point; "just be careful", because "hot means inferno."

Jake's Steakhouse *Steak* 24 | 19 | 21 | $49

Bronx | 6031 Broadway (242nd St.) | 718-581-0182 | www.jakessteakhouse.com

Somewhat "unexpected" for the zip code, this "friendly", "special-occasion" Riverdale steakhouse owned by meat wholesalers "rivals the best in Manhattan" but is "considerably cheaper"; the "second-floor view of Van Cortlandt Park" makes for "fond memories."

Jane ● *American* 21 | 18 | 19 | $41

G Village | 100 W. Houston St. (bet. La Guardia Pl. & Thompson St.) | 212-254-7000 | www.janerestaurant.com

"Satisfying all around", this "casual" Village New American is "deservedly packed", especially during its "top-notch brunch"; "everyone can find something to like" on its midpriced menu, delivered by "pro" servers in "large, open" quarters.

Japonais Ⓑ *Japanese* 20 | 23 | 18 | $58

Gramercy | 111 E. 18th St. (bet. Irving Pl. & Park Ave. S.) | 212-260-2020 | www.japonaisnewyork.com

Maybe "it's all about the scene" at this "crowded", "cavernous" Gramercy Japanese fusion specialist, but they "do pay attention to" the "tasty" fare too; its "beautiful", "other-worldly", red-lacquered space (complete with two "hip" lounges) helps justify "pricey" tabs, if not occasionally "snobby" service.

Japonica *Japanese* 22 | 14 | 20 | $45

G Village | 100 University Pl. (12th St.) | 212-243-7752 | www.japonicanyc.com

The "crowds confirm the quality" at this "tried-and-true" Village Japanese "institution", where devotees swear by the "huge" pieces of "fresh" (practically "still flapping") sushi served by "attentive" staffers; just try not to notice the "cramped", "lackluster" setup.

Jarnac Ⓜ *Mediterranean* 22 | 19 | 23 | $52

W Village | 328 W. 12th St. (Greenwich St.) | 212-924-3413 | www.jarnacny.com

"Charming" waiters tend to a "restaurant full of regulars" at this "cozy" West Village "hideaway", where the Med menu boasts a "fabulous cassoulet" and the "very visible" owner ensures even "first-timers aren't neglected"; it's a "definite find" and "great for a date", slightly "pricey" tabs notwithstanding.

Jasmine *Thai* 19 | 15 | 16 | $25

E 80s | 1619 Second Ave. (84th St.) | 212-517-8854

"For your Thai cravings on the Upper East Side", this vet "hits the mark" with "quick fixes" of "solid" "standards"; it "can get loud" and "crowded", but those "inexpensive" prices ensure that, for most locals, it's the "perfect standby."

Jean Claude ⊄ *French* ▽ 22 | 16 | 20 | $43

SoHo | 137 Sullivan St. (bet. Houston & Prince Sts.) | 212-475-9232

"If you can't live in Paris", there's this "charming" SoHo French bistro whose "intimate", "candlelit" quarters make a "romantic" backdrop for

| | FOOD | DECOR | SERVICE | COST |

"expertly prepared" "classic" offerings; it's a "perennial date place fo the young and budget-conscious" – just remember it's "cash only."

☑ Jean Georges ☒ French — 28 | 26 | 27 | $120

W 60s | Trump Int'l Hotel | 1 Central Park W. (bet. 60th & 61st Sts.) | 212-299-3900 | www.jean-georges.com

"From start to finish", expect "profound dining experiences" a Jean-Georges Vongerichten's "stunning", jackets-required Ne French "temple to gastronomy" at Columbus Circle, where the regular changing, prix fixe–only menus based on fresh seasonal ingredients a probably the "most creative" in town; add "flawless" formal servic (supervised by the chef's brother, Philippe), "elegant", recently redor rooms overlooking Central Park and alfresco seating, and it's no wonde it's voted one of the city's most popular places; P.S. for "NYC's be bargain", the Nougatine Room offers "ethereal" $24 prix fixe lunche

Jewel Bako ●☒ Japanese — 25 | 22 | 22 | $74

E Village | 239 E. Fifth St. (bet. 2nd & 3rd Aves.) | 212-979-1012

A "jewel indeed", this "tiny", dinner-only East Village Japanese cut "perfect" sushi (including "exotic" choices "flown in from all over th world") presented in "the coolest" bamboo-lined space abetted b "delightful" service overseen by "amazing" hosts Jack and Grac Lamb; however, wallet-watchers beware: "someone has to foc that FedEx bill."

Jewel of India Indian — 20 | 18 | 19 | $37

W 40s | 15 W. 44th St. (bet. 5th & 6th Aves.) | 212-869-5544 | www.jewelofindiarestaurant.com

"It's all about the $15.95 lunch buffet" at this "friendly" Midtow Indian standby dishing up "authentic" eats to "continuous" crowd of "bargain"-hunters and business types; although it's quite com fortable, critics contend that the decor has become "dull" an could use "a little zip."

J.G. Melon ●⊄ Pub Food — 21 | 12 | 15 | $25

E 70s | 1291 Third Ave. (74th St.) | 212-744-0585

An UES crowd "heavy on Lillys and Lacostes" counts on this "dar noisy" "burger champ" for "cheap" pub grub; "rude" staffers, "jam packed", "worn" digs and a "cash-only" policy are all "part of th experience" – and all "worth it" for those "unmatchable" pattie and cottage fries.

Jing Fong Chinese — 19 | 13 | 13 | $21

Chinatown | 20 Elizabeth St. (bet. Bayard & Canal Sts.) | 212-964-525€

"Chase after those carts" cry devotees of this "gigantic" Chinatow dim sum emporium evoking the floor of the "NYSE" (lots of "noise lots of "pointing"); "shared tables", "long waits" and "not-so charming" service make for a "zoo"-like vibe, but hey, "take a risk – it only cost a few yuan."

JJ's Asian Fusion Ⓜ Asian Fusion — ▽ 25 | 15 | 20 | $28

Astoria | 37-05 31st Ave. (bet. 37th & 38th Sts.) | Queens | 718-626-8888 www.myjjs.com

"Delicious, stylish fusion" fare and "solid", "fresh" sushi at incredib "reasonable prices" make this "friendly" Astorian a contender for th

| | FOOD | DECOR | SERVICE | COST |

best Asian food in Queens award"; the space is "nothing spectacu-
r", but there's always "super-fast delivery"; P.S. the "edamame pot-
ickers are a must."

oe Allen ● *American* | 17 | 15 | 18 | $42

W 40s | 326 W. 46th St. (bet. 8th & 9th Aves.) | 212-581-6464 |
www.joeallenrestaurant.com

or a "boffo" pre- or post-show "experience", hit this "longtime"
heater District "tradition" for "unpretentious" American "comfort"
are at "reasonable" rates; for most, the likelihood of "rubbing elbows
with Broadway stars" outweighs the "sketchy" service and "pub"-like
gs that "need a face-lift."

oe & Pat's *Italian/Pizza* | ∇ 22 | 13 | 18 | $20

taten Island | 1758 Victory Blvd. (Manor Rd.) | 718-981-0887
Now you're talking pizza" cry surveyors smitten with this "old-style"
taten Islander's "excellent thin-crust" pies; it also proffers "typical"
ed-sauce "staples" in dinerlike digs – i.e. it's a "basic Italian" joint like
ey were "way back when."

oe's Pizza *Pizza* | 23 | 5 | 11 | $8

Village | 7 Carmine St. (bet. Bleecker St. & 6th Ave.) | 212-255-3946 ●
EW Midwood | 1621 Kings Hwy. (Ocean Ave.) | Brooklyn |
18-339-4525
ark Slope | 137 Seventh Ave. (bet. Carroll St. & Garfield Pl.) | Brooklyn |
18-398-9198

Locals and tourists alike" line up for "fabulous slices of "cheap"
classic NY pizza" with the "perfect balance of cheese and crispiness" at
hese separately owned, "standing-room-only" Village-Brooklyn joints;
fast delivery" is one way to avoid "the wait."

oe's Shànghai *Chinese* | 22 | 9 | 13 | $23

hinatown | 9 Pell St. (bet. Bowery & Mott St.) | 212-233-8888
W 50s | 24 W. 56th St. (bet. 5th & 6th Aves.) | 212-333-3868
lushing | 136-21 37th Ave. (bet. Main & Union Sts.) | Queens |
18-539-3838
www.joeshanghairestaurants.com

Ethereal soup dumplings" are the claim to fame of this "no-frills"
hanghainese trio; getting in requires "waiting (and waiting)", "shar-
g tables with strangers" and enduring "erratic service", but those
off-the-charts good" morsels make it all "worthwhile."

EW Johnny Utah's ● *BBQ/Southwestern* | – | – | – | M

W 50s | 25 W. 51st St., downstairs (bet. 5th & 6th Aves.) | 212-265-8824 |
www.johnnyutahs.com

YC now has a mechanical bull to call its own thanks to this upscale
aloon that just rode into Rock Center; its rib-sticking, midpriced
outhwestern fare, backed by impressive tequilas and whiskeys
oured at a lengthy bar, can be savored in banquettes with views of the
ng, or in private dining rooms.

ohn's of 12th Street *Italian* | 19 | 14 | 18 | $34

Village | 302 E. 12th St. (2nd Ave.) | 212-475-9531
Fuhgeddaboutit" – for "huge portions" of "cheap" Italian fare "oozing
heese and red sauce", East Villagers hit this 100-year-old "staple"
here "friendly" staffers make "everyone feel like a regular"; its dark,

| | FOOD | DECOR | SERVICE | COST |

"dripping candles"-adorned space is great for "first dates", while disguising the fact that it "needs a face-lift."

John's Pizzeria ☻ *Pizza* | 22 | 12 | 15 | $22

E 60s | 408 E. 64th St. (bet. 1st & York Aves.) | 212-935-2895
G Village | 278 Bleecker St. (bet. 6th Ave. & 7th Ave. S.) | 212-243-1680 ⊽
W 40s | 260 W. 44th St. (bet. B'way & 8th Ave.) | 212-391-7560
www.johnspizzerianyc.com

"I'll be eating here as long as I have teeth" vow die-hard fans of this "coal-oven" pizzeria trio turning out "fantastic" "crispy, thin-crust pies - "no slices!" - that leave you "wondering how you ate it all"; most prefer the circa-1929 Village original, but prepare for "long lines" at all three locations.

JoJo *French* | 24 | 22 | 22 | $67

E 60s | 160 E. 64th St. (bet. Lexington & 3rd Aves.) | 212-223-5656 |
www.jean-georges.com

"Sample a great chef's wizardry" in "romantic" townhouse quarters at Jean-Georges Vongerichten's "elegant" East Side French bistro, presided over by a "warm", "polished" staff; surveyors split allegiances between upstairs and downstairs, but no matter where you sit it's "consistently excellent"; P.S. the $24 prix fixe lunch is "a steal."

Jolie *French* | 20 | 20 | 20 | $38

Boerum Hill | 320 Atlantic Ave. (bet. Hoyt & Smith Sts.) | Brooklyn |
718-488-0777 | www.jolierestaurant.com

A "delightful" Boerum Hill "surprise", this "smooth" French "boîte" enjoys a loyal local following for its "authentic", "beautifully prepared" dishes delivered by an "unrushed" staff; it's "lovely for a romantic night out", especially when you can "sit out in the garden."

Josephina ☻ *American* | 18 | 16 | 18 | $47

W 60s | 1900 Broadway (bet. 63rd & 64th Sts.) | 212-799-1000 |
www.josephinanyc.com

"The waiters know how to use a watch" at this "huge", "hectic" New American across from Lincoln Center, where the staff "handles theater and music audiences" "seamlessly", i.e. "in plenty of time for the curtain"; the menu's "not exciting", but it's "satisfying" and "decently priced" too.

Joseph's Restaurant ⑤ *Italian* | ▽ 21 | 17 | 22 | $52

Financial District | 3 Hanover Sq. (Pearl St.) | 212-747-1300
To uncover this "old-world" Hanover Square Italian, descend "below street level" where you'll find a "pricey" "treasure" that's become a "staple in the financial community" for its "authentic" fare, "pro" service and "clubby" vibe; "dated" decor notwithstanding, most would bank on it as a "no-fail choice."

Josie's *Eclectic* | 19 | 15 | 16 | $33

Murray Hill | 565 Third Ave. (37th St.) | 212-490-1558
W 70s | 300 Amsterdam Ave. (74th St.) | 212-769-1212
🆕 **Josie's Kitchen** *Eclectic*
E 80s | 1614 Second Ave. (84th St.) | 212-734-6644
www.josiesnyc.com

The "wholesome", "budget"-friendly New American fare is "health conscious" enough to appease "granola-and-veggie" types at this

| | FOOD | DECOR | SERVICE | COST |

lectic trio, and fortunately it has the "flavor" to satisfy "taste-seekers"
o; given the prices, most don't mind that the decor and service are
ninspiring", but a few wonder "where are the guys?"

ya 🌱 Thai
23 | 17 | 18 | $22

obble Hill | 215 Court St. (bet. Warren & Wycoff Sts.) | Brooklyn |
8-222-3484

uper-cheap", "out-of-this-world" fare is the reason that this
riendly" Cobble Hill Thai is "perpetually packed"; its "rock 'n' roll at-
osphere" complete with "LaGuardia"-worthy "noise" levels is "not
eat for conversation", but the "lovely garden" is a quieter option.

ibilee French
22 | 15 | 18 | $48

50s | 347 E. 54th St. (bet. 1st & 2nd Aves.) | 212-888-3569 |
ww.jubileeny.com

Mmm-ussels" headline the "perfect bistro" menu at this relatively
easonable" Sutton Place "favorite" that's as "French as French gets";
espite uneven service and dated decor, it's still good enough and
zy enough to stay "crowded" with "knowing locals."

les ◐ French
19 | 19 | 17 | $37

Village | 65 St. Marks Pl. (bet. 1st & 2nd Aves.) | 212-477-5560 |
ww.julesbistro.com

ive jazz is what makes it special" say surveyors of this "charming"
ast Village French bistro, where the "reliable" fare plays second fiddle
the "fun scene"; "nothing will blow you over" here – including the
easonable" check – but to most it's a "neighborhood asset."

inior's Diner
18 | 11 | 15 | $23

40s | Grand Central | lower level (42nd St. & Vanderbilt Ave.) |
2-983-5257

40s | Shubert Alley | 1515 Broadway (enter on 45th St., bet. B'way &
h Ave.) | 212-302-2000 ◐

owntown | 386 Flatbush Ave. Ext. (DeKalb Ave.) | Brooklyn |
8-852-5257 ◐

ww.juniorscheesecake.com

t's the cheesecake, stupid" – beyond the "heavenly" signature dessert
this Downtown Brooklyn "institution", the "classic" NY deli eats are
eemed "just ok" and the "nostalgic" decor "cheesy"; the Manhattan
anches are "good bets" when you "need to make a train" or a curtain.

ai 🄯🄼 Japanese
▽ 25 | 23 | 24 | $74

60s | Ito En | 822 Madison Ave., 2nd fl. (bet. 68th & 69th Sts.) |
2-988-7277 | www.itoen.com

Delicious", "meticulously prepared" Japanese kaiseki is the hallmark
this "refined" "secret" above the tea boutique Ito En; its "serene"
tting is a "respite from the frenzy" of UES shopping, but just remem-
er "peace" can be "pricey."

EW Kaijou Japanese
– | – | – | M

nancial District | 21 South End Ave. (W. Thames St.) | 212-786-9888 |
ww.kaijounewyork.com

e main attraction at this new Battery Park City eatery is its idyllic
aterfront location, but well-priced Japanese classics also make it a
elcome find; its Hudson River views with the Statue of Liberty in the
stance can be enjoyed from inside or out on the spacious patio.

	FOOD	DECOR	SERVICE	COST

NEW Kampuchea *Cambodian* ▽ 20 | 18 | 19 | $28
LES | 78 Rivington St. (Allen St.) | 212-529-3901 |
www.kampucheanyc.com

NYC "could use more Cambodian places", and this "funky" LES arriv
is filling the void with noodle dishes, sandwiches and other "flavorfu
Khmer "street food" at the "right" price; "loud" music, "hip crowd
and "communal tables" make for a "lively" scene.

Kang Suh ● *Korean* ▽ 20 | 12 | 16 | $34
Garment District | 1250 Broadway (32nd St.) | 212-564-6845

"Always tasty (and always open)", this big, budget-friendly 24/
Korean BBQ "fixture" in the Garment District allows you to "cook yo
own" "meltingly tender beef" or order from a menu that includ
sushi; just "eat fast" because "they rush you out the door."

Z Kanoyama ● *Japanese* 27 | 16 | 19 | $51
E Village | 175 Second Ave. (11th St.) | 212-777-5266 | www.kanoyama.co

A "seat at the sushi bar is a beautiful thing" at this "friendly", "mode
ately priced" East Village Japanese where you can watch "pristin
fish that "you've never heard of" get "lovingly" sliced and rolled; "wo
is getting out", though, so "go early before the place fills up."

Kati Roll Co. *Indian* 20 | 5 | 11 | $12
G Village | 99 MacDougal St. (bet. Bleecker & W. 3rd Sts.) | 212-420-6517 ●
W 40s | 140 W. 46th St. (bet. 6th & 7th Aves.) | 212-730-4280

This Delhi duo is always "packed to bursting", and so are its "chea
delicious" "Indian burritos" (aka kati rolls); Midtown office types se
it out for "quick lunches", while in the Village "college kids" hit
"post-partying", but "hole-in-the-wall" setups and "poor" servi
mean many tout it "to go."

Katsu-Hama *Japanese* 20 | 9 | 15 | $24
E 40s | 11 E. 47th St. (bet. 5th & Madison Aves.) | 212-758-5909 |
www.katsuhama.com

"Sushi isn't the only Japanese food" note fans of the "light, crisp
fried pork cutlets that are the mainstay of this Midtown katsu speci
ist; the decor "isn't fancy" by any means and service is "slightly u
even", but it's a "reliable" "bargain" that's "filling" and "flavorful."

Katz's Delicatessen *Deli* 23 | 9 | 11 | $21
LES | 205 E. Houston St. (Ludlow St.) | 212-254-2246 | www.katzdeli.com

As "quintessential NY" as the "yellow taxi", this "last-of-its-kind" L
deli is famed for its "orgasmic" (see *When Harry Met Sally*) corn
beef and pastrami sandwiches dispensed in "fluorescent-an
linoleum" digs worthy of a "prison mess hall"; it's "intimidating t
first time you go" given the "loud" crowds and "gruff" countermen, b
that's "all part of the charm"; N.B. this may well be the best museu
of American history in the country.

Keens Steakhouse *Steak* 24 | 22 | 22 | $62
Garment District | 72 W. 36th St. (bet. 5th & 6th Aves.) | 212-947-3636 |
www.keens.com

The ultimate "old-school boy's club" is this circa-1885 Garment Distri
steakhouse where the "unique and heavenly mutton chops" and oth
"fantastic meats" come via an "attentive" crew; its "ancient" cl

ipe-adorned quarters (complete with "elegant" private rooms) "reek of history and show business", but prices are strictly up-to-date.

NEW Kefi ☢ Greek
23 | 16 | 17 | $36

W 70s | 222 W. 79th St. (bet. Amsterdam Ave. & B'way) | 212-873-0200

Formerly Onera, this "lively" UWS nook from Michael Psilakis scores well for "delicious, inventive" Greek food and wines at "value" prices; less popular are its "cramped" digs, "long waits", "rushed service", no-rez and "cash-only" policies, but the fact that most "keep coming back" speaks volumes.

Kellari Taverna ● Greek
23 | 23 | 21 | $48

W 40s | 19 W. 44th St. (bet. 5th & 6th Aves.) | 212-221-0144 | www.kellari.us

The "fantastically simple" whole grilled fish is "a must" at this "upscale" Theater District Greek, where "fabulously prepared" cuisine comes in "lush", "airy" quarters via a "pleasant" crew; it's a bit on the "expensive" side, but "bargain" prix fixe deals ensure it's usually affordable.

Kelley & Ping Pan-Asian
16 | 13 | 12 | $24

E Village | 325 Bowery (2nd St.) | 212-475-8600
SoHo | 127 Greene St. (bet. Houston & Prince Sts.) | 212-228-1212
www.eatrice.com

"Reliable" for "quick, tasty" Pan-Asian "comfort food", this East Village-SoHo noodle duo is self-serve "cafeteria by day", "candlelit" restaurant by night; the service "could use some work", ditto the "hard seats" in "crowded, noisy" quarters, but "cheap" prices keep 'em "bustling."

Killmeyer's Old Bavaria Inn German
▽ 21 | 21 | 21 | $32

Staten Island | 4254 Arthur Kill Rd. (Sharrotts Rd.) | 718-984-1202 | www.killmeyers.com

You can "linger in the old world" for a while at this "gemütlich" SI German, where "substantial", well-priced classics plus brews from a "phone book-size menu" are "best when the biergarten is open"; quite simply, it's "worth the trip."

Kings' Carriage House American
21 | 26 | 22 | $60

E 80s | 251 E. 82nd St. (bet. 2nd & 3rd Aves.) | 212-734-5490 | www.kingscarriagehouse.com

Located in an "intimate" "English manor"-like house, this UES New American draws "special-occasion" diners and "ladies who lunch" with its "ravishing" decor and "graciously served", prix fixe-only fare; it's favored for "elegant" afternoon tea, but just "prepare to shell out" for all that "très romantique" charm.

King Yum Chinese
▽ 17 | 15 | 19 | $25

Fresh Meadows | 181-08 Union Tpke. (181st St.) | Queens | 718-380-1918 | www.kingyumrestaurant.com

Since the '50s", this "kitschy" Fresh Meadows veteran has dished up "quality" Cantonese-Polynesian fare with a heaping side of "nostalgia"; sure, "tacky lives" on in its "tiki" trappings, "drinks with umbrellas" and karaoke nights, but "for cheap Chinese food as you remember it, it's the king."

	FOOD	DECOR	SERVICE	COST

Kin Khao *Thai*

22 | 17 | 18 | $37

SoHo | 171 Spring St. (bet. Thompson St. & W. B'way) | 212-966-3939 | www.eatrice.com

"Still sexy and tasty after all these years", this "funky" SoHo Thai plies its "trendy", youthful crowd with "phenomenal cocktails" and "solid" "affordable" fare; it's a good pick for dates and groups, but since it takes no reservations, expect to "wait."

NEW Ki Sushi *Japanese*

▽ 25 | 22 | 23 | $33

Boerum Hill | 122 Smith St. (bet. Dean & Pacific Sts.) | Brooklyn | 718-935-0575

Some say the "fresh, creative" sushi at this "tranquil" new Boerum Hill Japanese is some of the "best in Brooklyn"; insiders advise "sit at the bar", where the "skilled", "gracious chefs" "know just what to recommend"; P.S. the "lunch specials are a steal."

Kitchen Club *French/Japanese*

▽ 22 | 18 | 22 | $47

NoLita | 30 Prince St. (Mott St.) | 212-274-0025 | www.thekitchenclub.com

"You'll make fast friends" with the "warm" owner and her "precious pooch" at this "quaint" NoLita French-Japanese, where "eager-to-please" staffers dispense "divine dumplings" and other "high-quality" fare; it's "not particularly inexpensive", but regulars don't mind given the "unpretentious" vibe and handy "adjoining sake bar."

Kitchenette *Southern*

19 | 15 | 15 | $22

TriBeCa | 156 Chambers St. (bet. Greenwich St. & W. B'way) | 212-267-6740
W 100s | 1272 Amsterdam Ave. (bet. 122nd & 123rd Sts.) | 212-531-7600

You'd better "loosen your belt" before taking on the cheap comfort dishes doled out at these "no-frills, retro" Southerners; "strollers and poseurs" alike crowd the "shabby-chic" digs, though "ungodly waits" and "harried service" are often the norm, especially at the "zoolike" brunch.

Z Kittichai *Thai*

23 | 27 | 20 | $59

SoHo | 60 Thompson Hotel | 60 Thompson St. (bet. Broome & Spring Sts.) | 212-219-2000 | www.kittichairestaurant.com

"Sleek and sexy", this SoHo Thai dishes up "divine", "innovative" cuisine in a Zen-like, "drop-dead gorgeous" setting; sure, "it's a scene" and the "high impress-a-date factor" comes steep, but then "what did you expect?"

NEW Klee Brasserie *American/European*

21 | 19 | 19 | $52

Chelsea | 200 Ninth Ave. (bet. 22nd & 23rd Sts.) | 212-633-8033 | www.kleebrasserie.com

There's a "buzz around" this Chelsea yearling that was "just what the neighborhood needed", with "terrific" Euro-American fare, "low-key classy" environs and "friendly service"; downsides include "lots of noise", "close seating" and upmarket tabs.

Klong ● *Thai*

19 | 18 | 16 | $25

E Village | 7 St. Marks Pl. (bet. 2nd & 3rd Aves.) | 212-505-9955 | www.klongnyc.com

Despite looking expensive, this "trendy" East Village Thai's "street food" makes for "good cheap eating"; however, "on busy nights" you may feel "rushed", and the noise can rise to "club scene" levels.

	FOOD	DECOR	SERVICE	COST

nickerbocker Bar & Grill ◑ *American* 20 | 18 | 19 | $46

Village | 33 University Pl. (9th St.) | 212-228-8490 |
ww.knickerbockerbarandgrill.com

st known for its "solid" New American steakhouse fare in "hefty
rtions", this "friendly" "Village staple" also provides "live jazz on
eekends"; it gets "noisy", and the "'70s decor" borders on "tired",
t there's a reason it's been a local "fixture" for three decades.

nife + Fork Ⓜ *European* ▽ 23 | 18 | 21 | $52

Village | 108 E. Fourth St. (bet. 1st & 2nd Aves.) | 212-228-4885 |
ww.knife-fork-nyc.com

xceptionally well-prepared", "innovative" modern European fare
d first-rate "personal service" are earning this "tiny", "quaint" year-
g a rep as an "East Village foodie heaven"; it's "pricey à la carte", so
siders recommend the $45 six-course tasting menu and booking
ead since "getting a table is a chore."

EW Kobe Club ◑Ⓩ *Steak* 20 | 22 | 18 | $146

50s | 68 W. 58th St. (bet. 5th & 6th Aves.) | 212-644-5623 |
ww.kobeclubny.com

"mind-blowing" variety of Wagyu beef (domestic, Australian and Jap-
ese) "like butter" is the thing at this slick new Midtowner from restau-
teur Jeffrey Chodorow; "happening" types gladly "risk their lives"
neath a ceiling hung with 2,000 "samurai swords" in its "cool", moody
ace, but the real danger may be the "out-of-this-world" tabs.

odama ◑ *Japanese* 19 | 9 | 16 | $30

40s | 301 W. 45th St. (bet. 8th & 9th Aves.) | 212-582-8065

ecializing in "delicious", moderately priced sushi at a pace that'll
t you "in and out in time" for your show, this Theater District
panese "stalwart" is usually "busy"; it doesn't matter that the "min-
alist" digs definitely "aren't fancy."

oi *Japanese* 23 | 23 | 19 | $62

40s | Bryant Park Hotel | 40 W. 40th St. (bet. 5th & 6th Aves.) |
2-921-3330 | www.koirestaurant.com

"very swank" sister to the LA eatery of the same name, this Midtown
panese "hot spot" attracts "young 'in'" types with its "brilliant" sash-
i, sushi and cooked fare; "variable" service and "scary prices" are eas-
overlooked since the "achingly hip" vibe "makes you feel like a star."

orea Palace Ⓩ *Korean* 18 | 14 | 16 | $33

50s | 127 E. 54th St. (bet. Lexington & Park Aves.) | 212-832-2350 |
ww.koreapalace.com

s a "typical Korean BBQ house", but this bright neon Midtowner does
shi too, and comes as a "pleasant surprise" with its "courteous" ser-
ce and "tasty" chow nearly "as good as you'll find in K-town"; expect
inerlike" decor and modest prices, especially at the $17.95 lunch.

o Sushi *Japanese* 19 | 14 | 19 | $31

70s | 1329 Second Ave. (70th St.) | 212-439-1678
80s | 1619 York Ave. (85th St.) | 212-772-8838 |
ww.newkosushi.com

ough separately owned, both of these "neighborly" UES sushi
tandbys" offer an "incredible variety" of "fresh fish" and "innova-

tive" rolls at "value prices"; they're "nothing fancy", but the "hospit￫
ble staff" and "tasty" offerings ensure they're "always crowded."

Kuma Inn ◨⧏ *Filipino/Thai* ▽ 24 | 15 | 19 | $34

LES | 113 Ludlow St., 2nd fl. (bet. Delancey & Rivington Sts.) | 212-353-8866
www.kumainn.com

"Foodies-in-the-know" flock to this LES Filipino-Thai "hole-in-th￫
wall" to sample its "delectable" and eminently "affordable" Asia￫
inspired tapas and bask in the warmth of its "gracious hosts"; t￫
"secret upstairs location" and "tiny" size make it "good for a tryst"
that is, "if you can find it."

Kum Gang San ● *Korean* 21 | 14 | 16 | $32

Garment District | 49 W. 32nd St. (bet. B'way & 5th Ave.) |
212-967-0909

Flushing | 138-28 Northern Blvd. (bet. Bowne & Union Sts.) | Queens￫
718-461-0909

The Korean "equivalent of the Greek diner", down to its 24/7 hou￫
and "diverse menu", this Garment District–Flushing duo dishes o￫
"delicious BBQ" and plenty more; despite "spotty" service, "elbow-t￫
elbow crowds" and "awesomely cheesy" decor, they're "terrific fun."

Kuruma Zushi ⓢ *Japanese* ▽ 28 | 15 | 21 | $138

E 40s | 7 E. 47th St., 2nd fl. (bet. 5th & Madison Aves.) |
212-317-2802

Sushi "as elegant as raw fish can get" is the province of this mezzani￫
Midtown Japanese that caters to the connoisseur with "divine" sas￫
imi, "very formal" service and an "extraordinary omakase"; the "spa￫
tan" setup is easily outweighed by the "heavenly" cuisine, althoug￫
"Tokyo prices" will surely "bring you back to earth."

Kyma *Greek* 18 | 15 | 18 | $41

W 40s | 300 W. 46th St. (8th Ave.) | 212-957-8830

A "welcome surprise" in the Theater District, this "reliable" Gre￫
proffers the "usual standards done with finesse", including "simp￫
grilled fish", all at "reasonable" rates; the interior strikes some ￫
"a little too bright", but never mind – "fast service" means y￫
"make your curtain."

NEW Kyotofu ●◨ *Dessert* ▽ 23 | 21 | 21 | $26

W 40s | 705 Ninth Ave. (bet. 48th & 49th Sts.) | 212-974-6012 |
www.kyotofu-nyc.com

"You'll never look at tofu the same way" after visiting this "small￫
"sleek" Midtown Japanese dessert specialist where "sublime", most￫
soy-based creations "take sweet nothings to a higher level"; inside￫
suggest "skip the savory" options and "go straight to dessert" with t￫
advice of the "knowledgeable staff."

La Baraka *French* 21 | 17 | 23 | $41

Little Neck | 255-09 Northern Blvd. (2 blocks e. of Little Neck Pkwy.￫
Queens | 718-428-1461 | www.labarakarest.com

"Family-owned" for nearly 30 years, this Little Neck "treasure" ￫
as renowned for its "caring proprietors" (and hostess "Lucette￫
kisses") as for its "bargain"-priced "country French" menu; som￫
find it a bit "dated", but ultimately the proprietor's "charm" obliterat￫
any possible complaint.

| | FOOD | DECOR | SERVICE | COST |

La Bergamote *Bakery/French*
24 | 15 | 15 | $14

Chelsea | 169 Ninth Ave. (20th St.) | 212-627-9010

For "glorious pastries" and other "fabulous" Gallic goods, this "small" Chelsea bakery/cafe is a natural for breakfast or lunch; "surly service" makes it feel all the more "like being in Paris", though that doesn't make it any less "tempting."

La Boîte en Bois *French*
21 | 15 | 20 | $50

W 60s | 75 W. 68th St. (bet. Columbus Ave. & CPW) | 212-874-2705 | www.laboitenyc.com

This "sweet little" Lincoln Center-area bistro features a "wonderful" French menu "unspoiled by modernity", backed up by "attentive service" and an "excellent" $36 early-bird prix fixe; show-goers say its "close quarters prepare one for the theater seats" to come.

La Bonne Soupe *French*
18 | 13 | 15 | $28

W 50s | 48 W. 55th St. (bet. 5th & 6th Aves.) | 212-586-7650 | www.labonnesoupe.com

You'll cross the "final fondue frontier" at this "old-fashioned" Midtown bistro where "delicious onion soup" and other "hearty" Gallic offerings prove there's still some "truth in advertising"; though service can be "indifferent" and the quarters "a bit too cozy", its "budget-friendly" prix fixes are always appreciated.

La Bottega ● *Italian/Pizza*
18 | 21 | 15 | $42

Chelsea | Maritime Hotel | 88 Ninth Ave. (17th St.) | 212-243-8400 | www.themaritimehotel.com

Thanks to a "popular" outdoor terrace and the "glam crowd" it attracts, this "festive" Chelsea Italian is a "scene with a capital S" come summertime; few seem to mind the "lackluster" service since most of the young diners are principally here to cruise.

L'Absinthe *French*
22 | 22 | 20 | $65

E 60s | 227 E. 67th St. (bet. 2nd & 3rd Aves.) | 212-794-4950 | www.labsinthe.com

Done up like a "Parisian brasserie in all its art nouveau glory", this "sophisticated" Eastsider serves first-rate French fare to a "clientele that's as haute as the food"; "heart-stopping" prices may be a downside, but most feel the place is worth every euro.

La Cantina Toscana *Italian*
▽ 24 | 14 | 21 | $50

E 60s | 1109 First Ave. (bet. 60th & 61st Sts.) | 212-754-5454

A "sleeper" for "wonderful" Tuscan cooking, this "authentic" East Side Italian offers "excellent homemade pastas" and "superb wild game" paired with a "first-rate wine list"; "tiny" digs and somewhat "pricey" tabs are fully offset by "helpful" service and "old-world charm."

Lady Mendl's Ⓜ *American*
22 | 26 | 24 | $43

Gramercy | Inn at Irving Pl. | 56 Irving Pl. (bet. 17th & 18th Sts.) | 212-533-4466 | www.ladymendls.com

"Edith Wharton is alive" and well at this "dignified" Gramercy tea salon where the "lovely service", Victorian atmosphere and tasty finger sandwiches make you "feel like royalty"; for best results, "bring your mother" and don't fret over the prices – "it's really all about the experience."

	FOOD	DECOR	SERVICE	COST

La Esquina ● *Mexican*   21 | 21 | 16 | $39

Little Italy | 106 Kenmare St. (bet. Cleveland Pl. & Lafayette St.) |
646-613-7100 | www.esquinanyc.com

There are three dining options at this "ultracool" Little Italy Mexican:
a 24-hour taqueria, a "funky" sit-down cafe and a subterranean, semi-
secret "grotto"; catering to the "über-trendy", the latter's "infuriating"
reservation policy and "Stalin-era bouncers" make normal folks stay
upstairs where there's "less fuss."

La Flor Bakery & Cafe ⊟ *Bakery*   ▽ 24 | 16 | 19 | $24

Woodside | 53-02 Roosevelt Ave. (53rd St.) | Queens | 718-426-8023
"*Muy delicioso*" Mexican-Eclectic sweet and savory items prove the
kitchen really "knows its stuff" at this Woodside bakery/cafe; "don't
be fooled by the exterior" or the sometimes "spotty service" – what it
"lacks in looks", it "makes up for in taste" and "value."

La Focaccia ● *Italian*   ▽ 20 | 18 | 18 | $37

W Village | 51 Bank St. (W. 4th St.) | 212-675-3754
"Romantic at night and friendly all day", this "old-style" Village Italian
"charmer" offers "tasty, fresh" pasta plus "affordable" meat and fish
"grilled to perfection"; service is "attentive", but the "small" space
means you're apt to share the experience with whoever sits next to you.

La Giara *Italian*   19 | 16 | 18 | $35

Murray Hill | 501 Third Ave. (bet. 33rd & 34th Sts.) | 212-726-9855 |
www.lagiara.com
"Pleasant" and "reliable", this Murray Hill Italian is known for its
"wholesome" "homemade pastas" and "bargain" $19.95 early-bird;
"simple" decor, sidewalk seats and "friendly service" make for "solid
but not extraordinary" dining.

La Gioconda *Italian*   20 | 13 | 19 | $41

E 50s | 226 E. 53rd St. (bet. 2nd & 3rd Aves.) | 212-371-3536 |
www.lagiocondany.com
"Smiling" staffers serve "homey" Italian vittles at this Turtle Bay
"sleeper" that's well regarded for its "fair" prices, a "rare thing in
Manhattan"; sure, the "exposed-brick" decor is "dull" and the
"postage-stamp" dimensions "too small for comfort", but regulars report it's "like going home."

La Goulue ● *French*   20 | 19 | 18 | $62

E 60s | 746 Madison Ave. (bet. 64th & 65th Sts.) | 212-988-8169 |
www.lagouluerestaurant.com
"Fashionable" Euros and other "10021 fixtures" tout the "above-
average" French fare (at way above-average cost) and "chic Parisian
feel" at this UES bistro that's known for its "lively" "kissy-kissy scene";
service may be "sporadic", but there's no denying that "zing in the air."

⊠ La Grenouille ⊠ *French*   27 | 28 | 27 | $120

E 50s | 3 E. 52nd St. (bet. 5th & Madison Aves.) | 212-752-1495 |
www.la-grenouille.com
NY's "last great haute French" restaurant, the Masson family's "timeless" Midtowner is "superlative" in every way, boasting "done-to-
perfection" cuisine, "impeccable service" and an "enchanting" room
filled with "flowers galore" (even the "diners exude class"); yes, you

| | FOOD | DECOR | SERVICE | COST |

may need to "raid your piggy bank" to foot the prix fixe-only bill at this *magnifique* grande dame", but all concur it's "worth the splash"; N.B. jackets required.

La Grolla *Italian*
20 | 13 | 19 | $42

W 70s | 413 Amsterdam Ave. (bet. 79th & 80th Sts.) | 212-496-0890 | www.lagrolla.us

"Authentic" dishes from Italy's Val d'Aosta region fill out the "relatively inexpensive" menu of this "solid" UWS trattoria where the "welcoming" staffers have "real accents"; it may be "cramped" and "lacking lighting", but at least the "food is beautiful."

Lake Club *Continental/Seafood*
∇ 21 | 24 | 21 | $46

Staten Island | 1150 Clove Rd. (Victory Blvd.) | 718-442-3600 | www.lake-club.com

A "gorgeous venue" for a "classy evening" out, this Staten Island Continental seafooder overlooking "pretty" Clove Lake is all about "fine dining" and "courteous" service; it's "a little pricey", but bargain-hunters tout "Sunday brunch" as a more affordable alternative.

La Lanterna di Vittorio ● *Italian*
20 | 23 | 18 | $28

G Village | 129 MacDougal St. (bet. W. 3rd & 4th Sts.) | 212-529-5945 | www.lalanternacaffe.com

"Nothing beats the ambiance" of this "romantic" Village Italian, a "paradise on rainy nights" thanks to its "roaring fireplaces", "live jazz" and "covered garden"; the "limited menu" leans toward pizzas and "heavenly" desserts, but most are too busy "snuggling" to notice the food.

La Locanda dei Vini *Italian*
∇ 21 | 14 | 20 | $44

W 40s | 737 Ninth Ave. (bet. 49th & 50th Sts.) | 212-258-2900 | www.lalocandadeivinirestaurant.com

Ok, maybe the "modest" storefront exterior suggests that this mid-priced Hell's Kitchen Italian is just another "local haunt", but proponents praise its "hearty, well-prepared" food, "charming" service and "amiable" vibe; it's also a "good bet pre-theater."

La Lunchonette *French*
22 | 14 | 19 | $41

Chelsea | 130 10th Ave. (18th St.) | 212-675-0342

A "welcome relief from Chelsea trendiness", this "slice of beatnik France" is a "foie-gras-and-cassoulet kind of place" with "delicious" Gallic grub; though the digs "could use a face-lift", its "diverse" clientele couldn't care less as it all comes without a bank-breaking bill.

La Mangeoire *French*
19 | 19 | 19 | $47

50s | 1008 Second Ave. (bet. 53rd & 54th Sts.) | 212-759-7086 | www.lamangeoire.com

"Like an old friend", this East Midtown bistro is a "steady standby" for classic French fare, "fine house wines" and "gracious service"; throw in a "romantic", "Provençal setting" with "gorgeous flowers", and "you might be dining in France" – though "without the Paris prices."

La Masseria ● *Italian*
22 | 19 | 21 | $53

W 40s | 235 W. 48th St. (bet. B'way & 8th Ave.) | 212-582-2111 | www.lamasserianyc.com

With a "perfect location" for pre-show dining, this "upscale" Theater District Southern Italian "gets you in and out on time" with "high-quality

| | FOOD | DECOR | SERVICE | COST |

cooking" served in a "spacious", "farmhouse"-esque setting; though it's "expensive", "the secret's out", so be ready for "noise" and "crowds."

La Mediterranée French
19 | 17 | 19 | $48

E 50s | 947 Second Ave. (bet. 50th & 51st Sts.) | 212-755-4155 | www.lamediterraneeny.com

"Good old-style French food", "gracious service" and a nightly pianist have made this "casual" Midtown bistro a local "fixture"; it's a "favorite among "mature" folks who like the fair prices and "time-warp" decor.

La Mela ● Italian
18 | 12 | 17 | $35

Little Italy | 167 Mulberry St. (bet. Broome & Grand Sts.) | 212-431-9493 | www.lamelarestaurant.com

Expect "minimal decision making" at this "shut-up-and-eat" Little Italy Italian where five-course, "family-style" meals can be had for a flat $32 price; it's especially "fun with a group" that doesn't mind "touristy" neighbors and an emphasis on "quantity over quality."

La Mirabelle French
22 | 18 | 23 | $48

W 80s | 102 W. 86th St. (bet. Amsterdam & Columbus Aves.) | 212-496-045
There's "nothing trendy or gimmicky" going on at this "old-fashioned" UWS French bistro where a "delectable" menu is served by a "treat you-like-family" staff; maybe the decor hovers between "homey" and "fusty", but that's how its "mature following" likes it.

Lan ● Japanese
▽ 25 | 18 | 20 | $47

E Village | 56 Third Ave. (bet. 10th & 11th Sts.) | 212-254-1959 | www.lan-nyc.com

"Not your typical sushi/sashimi place", this "attractive" East Village Japanese also offers "awesome cooked food" like shabu-shabu paired with an "extensive sake list"; though a bit "expensive" and "dark" inside, it's "still going strong" after a decade in business.

Land Thai
23 | 16 | 18 | $25

NEW **E 80s** | 1565 Second Ave. (bet. 81st & 82nd Sts.) | 212-439-184
W 80s | 450 Amsterdam Ave. (bet. 81st & 82nd Sts.) | 212-501-812
www.landthaikitchen.com

"When they say spicy they mean it" at this crosstown duo where the "authentic" Thai dishes "seem a lot more upscale than they cost"; the tiny digs are "chic" in a "downtown" way, but service seems "rushed."

L & B Spumoni Gardens Dessert/Pizza
22 | 10 | 14 | $21

Bensonhurst | 2725 86th St. (bet. 10th & 11th Sts.) | Brooklyn | 718-449-6921 | www.spumonigardens.com

This Bensonhurst Italian "tradition" serves what could be the "best Sicilian squares in the universe" along with "luscious" spumoni; there's "no decor to speak of" and frequent "long waits", but it's got "tons of character" and picnic tables for alfresco dining.

Landmarc ● French
23 | 19 | 21 | $49

TriBeCa | 179 W. Broadway (bet. Leonard & Worth Sts.) | 212-343-3883
NEW **W 60s** | Time Warner Ctr. | 10 Columbus Circle, 3rd fl. (60th St at B'way) | 212-823-6123
www.landmarc-restaurant.com

Marc Murphy's "informal" bistros serve "spot-on" French fare but are best known for their wine lists with "gentle markups"; the more rusti-

TriBeCa original is smaller than its sprawling Time Warner Center sibling, but the "no-reservations" policy spells a "rush for tables" at both.

Landmark Tavern *American/Irish* | 18 | 20 | 20 | $38 |

W 40s | 626 11th Ave. (46th St.) | 212-247-2562 |
www.thelandmarktavern.org

A "landmark indeed", this circa-1868 Hell's Kitchen tavern is complete with "ghosts of dock workers at the bar"; its Irish-American "upscale pub grub" may be "generic", but it's worth a visit for the "history" alone.

La Paella *Spanish* | 20 | 18 | 17 | $34 |

E Village | 214 E. Ninth St. (bet. 2nd & 3rd Aves.) | 212-598-4321 |
www.lapaellanyc.com

"Delicious" tapas and "potent" sangria at "great prices" make for "satisfying" repasts at this "atmospheric" East Village Spaniard that draws a "hip" "hodgepodge" of a crowd; though service is only "adequate" and the room sometimes "loud", it still enjoys a "romantic" reputation.

La Palapa ❷ *Mexican* | 20 | 17 | 18 | $34 |

E Village | 77 St. Marks Pl. (bet. 1st & 2nd Aves.) | 212-777-2537
G Village | 359 Sixth Ave. (bet. Washington Pl. & W. 4th St.) | 212-243-6870
www.lapalapa.com

Celebrated for "dressed-up" but priced-down Mexicana, this "festive" cross-Village duo's "multiflavored margs" can keep anyone happy; their daytime "laid-back" vibe turns *mucho sexy* after dark, when the "loud and frenetic" pace can transform them into "a bit of a madhouse."

La Petite Auberge *French* | 20 | 15 | 21 | $45 |

Gramercy | 116 Lexington Ave. (bet. 27th & 28th Sts.) | 212-689-5003 |
www.lapetiteaubergeny.com

It "hasn't changed in 30 years", but this "welcoming" Gramercy bistro "keeps chugging along" on the strength of its "solid" French fare, "old-school" staffers and "inexpensive" price point; "nouvelle it's not", but the "dated" setting has a pleasing "Paris-in-the-'50s" feel.

La Pizza Fresca Ristorante *Italian* | 22 | 17 | 17 | $38 |

Flatiron | 31 E. 20th St. (bet. B'way & Park Ave. S.) | 212-598-0141 |
www.lapizzafrescaristorante.com

Behind an "unassuming facade", this "simple yet sophisticated" Flatiron Italian dishes out "delicious" brick-oven Neapolitan pizza and pastas accompanied by an "outstanding wine list"; just "bring a lot of lira" and some patience, as the service can be "leisurely."

La Ripaille *French* | ▽ 23 | 20 | 21 | $48 |

W Village | 605 Hudson St. (bet. Bethune & W. 12th Sts.) | 212-255-4406 |
www.laripailleny.com

"For a true taste of small-town French cuisine", this venerable Villager features "perfectly done" traditional dishes in an "old-school" setting complete with sidewalk seating; it's best known for an "ever-present owner" who sees to it that "everyone leaves with a smile."

La Rivista ❷🗷 *Italian* | 18 | 15 | 19 | $46 |

W 40s | 313 W. 46th St. (bet. 8th & 9th Aves.) | 212-245-1707 |
www.larivistanyc.com

"Definitely convenient" if "not terribly original", this midpriced Restaurant Row Italian offers "plentiful" portions of "better-than-average" grub in "pleasant" albeit "simple" environs; bonuses include a nightly pianist and the "real money saver" of "discounted parking."

Las Ramblas ● Spanish ▽ 23 | 17 | 22 | $36

G Village | 170 W. Fourth St. (bet. Cornelia & Jones Sts.) | 646-415-7924 | www.lasramblasnyc.com

Thankfully still "under the radar", this "charming" Village Spaniard combines "modern tapas", "super sangria" and "enthusiastic" service in one "tiny" space at one modest price; fans say it's the "closest you'll get to Barcelona in NY" given food "so good, it's hard to stop ordering."

La Taqueria Mexican 19 | 11 | 14 | $15

Park Slope | 74 Seventh Ave. (bet. Berkeley & Lincoln Pls.) | Brooklyn | 718-398-4300

Rachel's Taqueria ⊄ Mexican

Park Slope | 408 Fifth Ave. (bet. 7th & 8th Sts.) | Brooklyn | 718-788-1137 www.rachelstaqueria.com

"Colossal burritos" and other Mexican standards fill out the menu of these "down-to-earth" Park Slope taqueria twins; though "schlumpy" decor makes them "better for takeout", they're "quick and inexpensive" enough to be local "staples."

La Taza de Oro 🗷⊄ Diner 18 | 6 | 16 | $14

Chelsea | 96 Eighth Ave. (bet. 14th & 15th Sts.) | 212-243-9946

The "lunch counter lives on" at this Chelsea Puerto Rican that "gives greasy spoons a good name" with its "authentic" renditions of "old-school rice and beans"; sure, it's "funky" and has "been around for a million years", but those "cheapo" tabs can't be beat.

☒ L'Atelier de Joël Robuchon French 27 | 24 | 26 | $131

E 50s | Four Seasons Hotel | 57 E. 57th St. (bet. Madison & Park Aves.) | 212-350-6658 | www.fourseasons.com

From the "brilliant" Robuchon comes this "off-the-charts" "consolidation of French technique and Japanese style", where "decadent" dishes in "tapas-style" portions come with a "perfectly designed wine list" and "impeccable service"; although there are comfortable tables, "counter seating is the way to go" in the "minimalist", "casually elegant" space, as the "theater of the open kitchen" is almost as "memorable" as the "eye-popping prices."

Lattanzi ●☒ Italian 22 | 18 | 21 | $53

W 40s | 361 W. 46th St. (bet. 8th & 9th Aves.) | 212-315-0980 | www.lattanzinyc.com

Although "always a winner pre-theater", this Restaurant Row Italian is best "after 8 PM" when there's more time to savor the menu's Roman-Jewish specialties (e.g. the "superb fried artichokes"); a "lovely back garden" and "welcoming service" add to the "romantic", if "expensive", experience.

Lavagna Italian 24 | 18 | 20 | $43

E Village | 545 E. Fifth St. (bet. Aves. A & B) | 212-979-1005 | www.lavagnanyc.com

This little Alphabet City "neighborhood favorite" "hits all the right notes" with an "inventive" Italian menu, "friendly service" and a "reasonable price-to-quality ratio"; the "cozy" space is often "crowded", but still "sophisticated" enough to be a "great date restaurant."

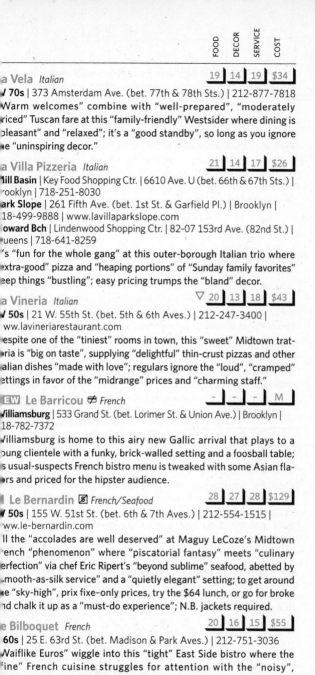

	FOOD	DECOR	SERVICE	COST

a Vela *Italian* | 19 | 14 | 19 | $34

W 70s | 373 Amsterdam Ave. (bet. 77th & 78th Sts.) | 212-877-7818

"Warm welcomes" combine with "well-prepared", "moderately priced" Tuscan fare at this "family-friendly" Westsider where dining is pleasant" and "relaxed"; it's a "good standby", so long as you ignore the "uninspiring decor."

a Villa Pizzeria *Italian* | 21 | 14 | 17 | $26

Mill Basin | Key Food Shopping Ctr. | 6610 Ave. U (bet. 66th & 67th Sts.) | Brooklyn | 718-251-8030

Park Slope | 261 Fifth Ave. (bet. 1st St. & Garfield Pl.) | Brooklyn | 718-499-9888 | www.lavillaparkslope.com

Howard Bch | Lindenwood Shopping Ctr. | 82-07 153rd Ave. (82nd St.) | Queens | 718-641-8259

It's "fun for the whole gang" at this outer-borough Italian trio where "extra-good" pizza and "heaping portions" of "Sunday family favorites" keep things "bustling"; easy pricing trumps the "bland" decor.

a Vineria *Italian* | ▽ 20 | 13 | 18 | $43

W 50s | 21 W. 55th St. (bet. 5th & 6th Aves.) | 212-247-3400 | www.lavineriarestaurant.com

Despite one of the "tiniest" rooms in town, this "sweet" Midtown trattoria is "big on taste", supplying "delightful" thin-crust pizzas and other Italian dishes "made with love"; regulars ignore the "loud", "cramped" settings in favor of the "midrange" prices and "charming staff."

NEW Le Barricou ⊘ *French* | – | – | – | M

Williamsburg | 533 Grand St. (bet. Lorimer St. & Union Ave.) | Brooklyn | 718-782-7372

Williamsburg is home to this airy new Gallic arrival that plays to a young clientele with a funky, brick-walled setting and a foosball table; its usual-suspects French bistro menu is tweaked with some Asian flavors and priced for the hipster audience.

Le Bernardin ☒ *French/Seafood* | 28 | 27 | 28 | $129

W 50s | 155 W. 51st St. (bet. 6th & 7th Aves.) | 212-554-1515 | www.le-bernardin.com

All the "accolades are well deserved" at Maguy LeCoze's Midtown French "phenomenon" where "piscatorial fantasy" meets "culinary perfection" via chef Eric Ripert's "beyond sublime" seafood, abetted by "smooth-as-silk service" and a "quietly elegant" setting; to get around the "sky-high", prix fixe–only prices, try the $64 lunch, or go for broke and chalk it up as a "must-do experience"; N.B. jackets required.

e Bilboquet *French* | 20 | 16 | 15 | $55

60s | 25 E. 63rd St. (bet. Madison & Park Aves.) | 212-751-3036

"Waiflike Euros" wiggle into this "tight" East Side bistro where the "fine" French cuisine struggles for attention with the "noisy", "buzzy" scene; on the downside, "if you don't know the staff, don't expect great service."

e Boeuf à la Mode *French* | 21 | 19 | 21 | $54

80s | 539 E. 81st St. (bet. East End & York Aves.) | 212-249-1473

There's "no rush" at this Yorkville "golden oldie" that's been serving "reliable" French bistro standards for 45-plus years; "seasoned wait-

ers" and a "circa-1953 Paris" setting appeal to its "mature" crowd, ne
the "inflated" tabs or "worn-around-the-edges" decor.

Le Cirque ⊠ *French* 23 | 25 | 23 | $94

E 50s | One Beacon Court | 151 E. 58th St. (bet. Lexington & 3rd Aves.)
212-644-0202 | www.lecirque.com

Midtown's third incarnation of Sirio Maccioni's literally "movable ci
cus" is as "haute as ever", from the "sumptuous" French cuisine, "co
mopolitan" crowd and "fabulous" service to its "smashing moder
look"; despite "arm-and-a-leg" pricing, it "can be hard to book", s
"reserve in advance" and dress appropriately ("Chanel" suggested fo
ladies, jackets required for men); N.B. the less formal front cafe is be
ing turned into a wine lounge with a small-plates menu.

L'Ecole ⊠ *French* 23 | 19 | 22 | $52

SoHo | French Culinary Institute | 462 Broadway (Grand St.) | 212-219-3300
www.frenchculinary.com

"Student chefs" cook for "extra credit" at the French Culinary Institute
SoHo lab/eatery that offers an "ever-changing menu" of Gallic stan
dards at a "haute bargain" $39.95 tab; "consistency may not be 10
percent", but service is "sweet" and it's "all in the name of education

Le Colonial *French/Vietnamese* 20 | 22 | 19 | $51

E 50s | 149 E. 57th St. (bet. Lexington & 3rd Aves.) | 212-752-0808
www.lecolonialnyc.com

Think "colonial-era" Saigon to get the gist of this "sexy" Eastsider whe
"delicious" French-Vietnamese dishes are served in a cross between
"tiki lounge" and a "Far East movie set"; except for the "spotty" servic
and distinctly "Manhattan prices", most feel "positively transported

Leela Lounge *Indian* ▽ 22 | 18 | 16 | $33

G Village | 1 W. Third St. (bet. B'way & Mercer St.) | 212-529-2059
www.leelalounge.com

Putting a "modern spin on traditional" dishes, this "chic" Villag
Indian employs "no butter or heavy cream" for more "healthy" re
pasts; though the "eager" service sometimes wobbles, "pittance
prices and a "relaxed" ambiance compensate.

Le Gamin *French* 19 | 16 | 15 | $25

E Village | 536 E. Fifth St. (bet. Aves. A & B) | 212-254-8409 ●
G Village | 132 W. Houston St. (bet. MacDougal & Sullivan Sts.) |
212-475-1543 ⊅
W Village | 522 Hudson St. (bet. Charles & W. 10th Sts.) | 212-807-7357 ●
Prospect Heights | 556 Vanderbilt Ave. (bet. Bergen & Dean Sts.) |
Brooklyn | 718-789-5171
www.legamin.com

"Inexpensive" Gallic grub graces the menus of these "laid-back" bi
tros where many report "brunch is the standout" meal; they're s
"markedly French" that you'll need the "patience of a saint" to de
with the "absentminded" service.

Le Gigot Ⓜ *French* 24 | 19 | 23 | $53

G Village | 18 Cornelia St. (bet. Bleecker & W. 4th Sts.) | 212-627-3737
www.legigotrestaurant.com

"When homesick for Paris", expats head for this "miniature" Villag
bistro specializing in "delicious" Provençal cooking served by a "wo

derful" crew; there's agreement on the "expensive" tabs, but debate over the dimensions: "cozy" vs. "cramped."

Le Grainne Cafe ❶ *French* ▽ 19 | 15 | 13 | $23

Chelsea | 183 Ninth Ave. (21st St.) | 646-486-3000 | www.legrainnecafe.com

Chelsea's "literati and artisti" tout this "pleasant" French cafe for its "fantastic" lattes and crêpes, not to mention the low cost; allow yourself "plenty of time", however, and "make sure you like your dinner guest": service can be "slooow."

Le Jardin Bistro *French* 18 | 17 | 18 | $42

NoLita | 25 Cleveland Pl. (bet. Kenmare & Spring Sts.) | 212-343-9599 | www.lejardinbistro.com

"Lingering is welcome" at this affordable NoLita French bistro where "awesome alfresco" dining is embellished by a "romantic" grapevine-covered trellis; admirers avow it's "great year-round", citing "tasty" vittles and "pleasant" (if "slow") service.

Le Madeleine *French* 20 | 18 | 19 | $46

W 40s | 403 W. 43rd St. (bet. 9th & 10th Aves.) | 212-246-2993 | www.lemadeleine.com

Beloved for its "charming", glass-enclosed garden room, this long-running Hell's Kitchen French bistro is also known for "reliable" cooking that "won't break the bank"; it's currently "battling to keep its space", so regulars suggest "visit while you still can."

Le Marais *French/Steak* 20 | 15 | 16 | $51

W 40s | 150 W. 46th St. (bet. 6th & 7th Aves.) | 212-869-0900 | www.lemarais.net

Giving glatt kosher a "French spin", this Theater District steakhouse features "excellent quality meats" either on the plate or from its "in-house butcher shop up front"; even though it's "pricey", "loud" and underserviced, it still "packs 'em in" nightly.

Le Miu ❶ *Japanese* ▽ 25 | 16 | 19 | $55

E Village | 107 Ave. A (bet. 6th & 7th Sts.) | 212-473-3100 | www.lemiusushi.com

"Classing up" Alphabet City, this "not-what-you'd-expect" Japanese offers both "superb sushi" and "sophisticated" cooked dishes; though "pricey for the location", wags tag it "Nobu for less", citing a five-course, $55 prix fixe that's actually a "good value."

Le Monde ❶ *French* 17 | 18 | 14 | $32

W 100s | 2885 Broadway (bet. 112th & 113th Sts.) | 212-531-3939 | www.lemondenyc.com

"Decent French-flavored cuisine" and a chance to "relax" and "actually enjoy reading" have Columbia students touting this Morningside Heights bistro; the $24 lunch prix fixe is another reason it's a neighborhood "favorite", though the principal downside is "mediocre" service.

Lemongrass Grill *Thai* 17 | 13 | 15 | $23

Financial District | 84 William St. (Maiden Ln.) | 212-809-8038
G Village | 9 E. 13th St. (bet. 5th Ave. & University Pl.) | 646-486-7313
Murray Hill | 138 E. 34th St. (bet. Lexington & 3rd Aves.) | 212-213-3317
W 90s | 2534 Broadway (bet. 94th & 95th Sts.) | 212-666-0888

(continued)

(continued)

Lemongrass Grill

Cobble Hill | 156 Court St. (bet. Dean & Pacific Sts.) | Brooklyn | 718-522-9728

Park Slope | 61A Seventh Ave. (bet. Berkeley & Lincoln Pls.) | Brooklyn | 718-399-7100

For a "quick fix", try out this "budget-friendly", "Thai-for-beginners" chain, even if the food's strictly "by the numbers"; since the settings tend to "lack atmosphere", aesthetes opt for their "lightning-fast delivery."

Lenny's *Sandwiches*   19 | 9 | 15 | $13

E 50s | 1024 Second Ave. (54th St.) | 212-355-5700

NEW **E 60s** | 1269 First Ave. (68th St.) | 212-288-0852

E 70s | 1481 Second Ave. (77th St.) | 212-288-5288

Financial District | 108 John St. (bet. Cliff & Pearl Sts.) | 212-385-2828

Flatiron | 16 W. 23rd St. (5th Ave.) | 212-462-4433

NEW **G Village** | 418 Sixth Ave. (9th St.) | 212-353-0300

W 40s | 60 W. 48th St. (bet. 5th & 6th Aves.) | 212-871-6677

NEW **W 40s** | 613 Ninth Ave. (43rd St.) | 212-957-7800

W 70s | 302 Columbus Ave. (74th St.) | 212-580-8300

W 80s | 489 Columbus Ave. (84th St.) | 212-787-9368

www.lennysnyc.com

"Well-oiled machines", this "proliferating" low-budget chain vends "substantial" sandwiches via an "assembly-line" staff that gets you "in and out in minutes"; even so, the "school cafeteria vibe" leads some to opt for "no-hassle delivery."

L'Entrecote ⓩ *French*   ▽ 19 | 14 | 21 | $49

E 50s | 1057 First Ave. (bet. 57th & 58th Sts.) | 212-755-0080

Harking back to "pre-nouvelle cuisine" days, this Sutton Place "time-tripper" is a "very French" source for Gallic classics; the "pocket-size" space is "inviting" thanks to owners who "take hospitality seriously."

Leo's Latticini Ⓜ *Deli/Italian*   ▽ 28 | 10 | 25 | $12

(aka Mama's of Corona)

Corona | 46-02 104th St. (46th Ave.) | Queens | 718-898-6069

A longtime Corona "cornerstone", this 1920-vintage Italian deli is renowned as a "great workingman's lunch spot" with "excellent sandwiches" and "fab fresh mozzarella"; it may be "nothing fancy", but "smiling" staffers and bargain prices "take you back to the old country."

Le Pain Quotidien *Bakery/Belgian*   19 | 15 | 14 | $21

E 60s | 833 Lexington Ave. (bet. 63rd & 64th Sts.) | 212-755-5810

E 70s | 252 E. 77th St. (bet. 2nd & 3rd Aves.) | 212-249-8600

E 80s | 1131 Madison Ave. (bet. 84th & 85th Sts.) | 212-327-4900

Flatiron | ABC Carpet & Home | 38 E. 19th St. (bet. B'way & Park Ave. S.) | 212-673-7900

G Village | 10 Fifth Ave. (8th St.) | 212-253-2324

NEW **G Village** | 801 Broadway (11th St.) | 212-677-5277

SoHo | 100 Grand St. (bet. Greene & Mercer Sts.) | 212-625-9009

W 50s | 922 Seventh Ave. (58th St.) | 212-757-0775

W 60s | 60 W. 65th St. (bet. B'way & CPW) | 212-721-4001

W 70s | 50 W. 72nd St. (bet. Columbus Ave. & CPW) | 212-712-9700

www.painquotidien.com

Additional locations throughout the NY area

This "informal" Belgian bakery/cafe chain is noted for its "scrumptious" breads, sandwiches and other light, "mostly organic" fare; the "pleasant formula" features "communal tables" and "farmhouse-cool" settings, marred only by "unpredictable" service at prime times.

Le Perigord *French*
24 | 20 | 24 | $76

E 50s | 405 E. 52nd St. (bet. FDR Dr. & 1st Ave.) | 212-755-6244 | www.leperigord.com

"One of the last of the classics", this "old-line" Sutton Place "bastion of France" exudes "elegance" with its "superb" "cordon bleu cuisine" and "seamless", "tuxedoed" service overseen by owner Georges Briguet; *mais oui*, you'll pay for this "step back in time", but its "well-heeled" following agrees it's "worth every franc", especially once former chef Antoine Bouterin returns to the kitchen.

NEW Le Petit Bistro ● *French*
- | - | - | I

Chelsea | 258 W. 15th St. (bet. 7th & 8th Aves.) | 212-929-3270

Despite new owners and a new name, little has changed at this former Chelsea branch of Le Gamin, where traditional French bistro items are served in casual, petite quarters; laid-back service and tabs that don't add up to more than a few euros contribute to the sanguine vibe.

NEW Le Petit Marché *French*
∇ 22 | 20 | 21 | $44

Brooklyn Heights | 46 Henry St. (bet. Cranberry & Middagh Sts.) | Brooklyn | 718-858-9605

Bringing some Gallic flair to Brooklyn Heights, this new French bistro is already "bustling" thanks to a "solid" kitchen, "warm", exposed-brick decor and "welcoming" service; though tables are "packed together", the pricing is *bon marché*.

Le Refuge *French*
21 | 20 | 20 | $54

E 80s | 166 E. 82nd St. (bet. Lexington & 3rd Aves.) | 212-861-4505 | www.lerefugenyc.com

There's "no pretension" at this "quiet" UES "fixture" that's been "popular for years" given its French *campagne* cooking, "country inn" feel and "great little garden"; though "a touch pricey", to most it's "well worth it."

Le Refuge Inn Ɱᗒ *French*
∇ 24 | 26 | 24 | $58

Bronx | Le Refuge Inn | 586 City Island Ave. (bet. Beach & Cross Sts.) | 718-885-2478 | www.lerefugeinn.com

Set in a landmark Bronx waterfront inn, this "lovely" French "oasis" offers "outstanding" cuisine along with "warm service" in a "white-tablecloth" Victorian setting; sure, this "unique experience" comes at a price, but "romantic" folk spring for a "room for the night" after dinner.

Le Rivage *French*
19 | 16 | 20 | $43

W 40s | 340 W. 46th St. (bet. 8th & 9th Aves.) | 212-765-7374 | www.lerivagenyc.com

"Raising predictability to an art form", this venerable Restaurant Row "staple" is still as "convenient" as it is "tasty"; though the room may be a bit "tired", the "well-prepared" French dishes are "reasonably priced", especially the "terrific" $35 post-theater prix fixe.

Les Enfants Terribles ● *African/French*
∇ 19 | 18 | 16 | $34

LES | 37 Canal St. (Ludlow St.) | 212-777-7518 | www.lesenfantsterriblesnyc.com

An "out-of-the-way" *boîte* in a "turning-trendy" neighborhood, this "lively", low-cost Lower Eastsider fields a "flavorful" French-African

menu served by a staff that's "happy" if "too relaxed"; naughty night owl
come for the "cool bar scene", complete with DJs and "exotic cocktails."

Les Halles ● *French*

20 | 17 | 16 | $44

Financial District | 15 John St. (bet. B'way & Nassau St.) | 212-285-858!
Gramercy | 411 Park Ave. S. (bet. 28th & 29th Sts.) | 212-679-4111
www.leshalles.net

Even if "rock star chef" Anthony Bourdain is "nowhere in sight", hi
"hearty" hallmarks (steaks "like butta", "stellar fries") keep these
"energetic" French bistros "jammed" with fans; in spite of "off
handed service" and an "earsplitting din", they still "hit the spot
for "affordable" grazing.

Le Singe Vert ● *French*

19 | 16 | 16 | $40

Chelsea | 160 Seventh Ave. (bet. 19th & 20th Sts.) | 212-366-4100 |
www.lesingevert.com

"Hip locals" dig this "very French" Chelsea bistro where "straight
ahead", midpriced Gallic fare is served by an "inconsistent" crew in a
"cramped", "backstreets-of-Paris" setting; sidewalk tables are just th
ticket during warm weather, but there's lots of "noise in all seasons."

Le Tableau *French*

24 | 16 | 20 | $45

E Village | 511 E. Fifth St. (bet. Aves. A & B) | 212-260-1333 |
www.letableaunyc.com

"Off the beaten path in the trendy East Village", this top-of-the-lin
French bistro is celebrated for its "imaginative" kitchen, "jolly" servic
and tabs that "don't break the bank"; no surprise, the "tiny dimen
sions" can "translate into long waits" and "crowds."

Levana *Mediterranean*

▽ 20 | 16 | 18 | $65

W 60s | 141 W. 69th St. (bet. B'way & Columbus Ave.) | 212-877-8457
www.levana.com

To go "upscale" and "still have it kosher", try this "unusual"
Mediterranean near Lincoln Center, where the "reliable" glatt men
features "less traditional" choices like venison; despite "looking an
feeling its age", it's "well worth" the "pricey" outlay.

Le Veau d'Or 🖾 *French*

▽ 17 | 14 | 19 | $53

E 60s | 129 E. 60th St. (bet. Lexington & Park Aves.) | 212-838-8133
"Time-warp" aficionados say that visiting this 1937-vintage East Sid
bistro is "like coming home to grandma's" since it "keeps chuggin
along" with a "no-surprises" "French comfort food" menu; the date
decor is something that grandpa would have liked.

Lever House 🖾 *American*

22 | 22 | 21 | $73

E 50s | 390 Park Ave. (enter on 53rd St., bet. Madison & Park Aves.) |
212-888-2700 | www.leverhouse.com

An ever-"buzzing" magnet for the "corporate-card" crowd, this mo
Midtowner owes its success to Dan Silverman's "enticing" New
American menu; its "striking", "futuristic" setting can be "rathe
noisy", though it's still suitable for "business entertaining."

L'Express ● *French*

17 | 14 | 14 | $30

Flatiron | 249 Park Ave. S. (20th St.) | 212-254-5858 | www.lexpressnyc.com
One of NYC's "few" all-nighters, this 24/7 Flatiron bistro can get "ri
diculously busy" serving "simple" French fare for "reasonable" sums

| | FOOD | DECOR | SERVICE | COST |

a few express doubts about the "tight" tables and "indifferent" staff, but "where else can clubbers get a decent meal at 4 AM?"

Le Zie 2000 ● *Italian* — 21 | 14 | 19 | $39

Chelsea | 172 Seventh Ave. (bet. 20th & 21st Sts.) | 212-206-8686 | www.lezie.com

"Always buzzing", this "tightly packed" Chelsea trattoria does "unusual" Venetian-style food at "affordable" rates (though they "knock up the prices for the specials"); the rear dining room and bar are "quieter" if you "don't like to chew and shout at the same time."

Liebman's *Deli* — 19 | 9 | 15 | $20

Bronx | 552 W. 235th St. (Johnson Ave.) | 718-548-4534 | www.liebmansdeli.com

A "real throwback", this easily affordable Bronx Jewish deli is an "old-time temple" to all the "traditional" kosher "standards", from "authentic" knishes to big fat sandwiches; noodges note there's "no ambiance", apparently not realizing that's the way delis are supposed to look.

Lil' Frankie's Pizza ●⑄ *Pizza* — 22 | 17 | 18 | $25

E Village | 19-21 First Ave. (bet. 1st & 2nd Sts.) | 212-420-4900 | www.lilfrankies.com

Frank's "funkier offshoot" is a "haven" for "young" East Villagers who make it a "go-to" for cheap, "casual" Italian eats, notably its thin-crust pizza and "homemade pastas"; it's a "cozy" lil' space with "piped-in tunes", but the "hip" hordes can be a "hassle."

Lili's Noodle Shop & Grill *Noodle Shop* — 16 | 12 | 15 | $22

E 80s | 1500 Third Ave. (bet. 84th & 85th Sts.) | 212-639-1313
Financial District | Embassy Suites | 102 North End Ave. (Vesey St.) | 212-786-1300 | www.lilisnoodle.com
W 50s | 200 W. 57th St. (enter on 7th Ave., bet. 56th & 57th Sts.) | 212-586-5333 | www.lilis57.com

Comments range from "the best Chinese in the area" to "waste of a good space", but the majority feels this noodle-shop trio is a "good bet" if "you're expecting a cheap, fast meal" that's "well prepared and fresh."

Lima's Taste ● *Peruvian* — ▽ 21 | 14 | 15 | $34

W Village | 122 Christopher St. (Bedford St.) | 212-242-0010 | www.limastaste.com

You'll get a taste of the Andes at this "authentic" West Villager where the "real Peruvian" menu (led by "primo" ceviche) is a bona fide "winner"; given its "homey" looks, regulars focus on the "potent drinks" and "reasonable tabs" instead.

☒ L'Impero ☒ *Italian* — 26 | 23 | 24 | $74

E 40s | 45 Tudor City Pl. (42nd St.) | 212-599-5045 | www.limpero.com
New chef Michael White faces high expectations at this Tudor City "jewel" where "well-heeled" diners feel "cosseted" by the "superior" Italian fare, "calming" milieu and "polished" service; comparatively "reasonable prix fixe" deals help allay the "upper-echelon" cost.

Lisca *Italian* — 20 | 16 | 20 | $42

W 90s | 660 Amsterdam Ave. (bet. 92nd & 93rd Sts.) | 212-799-3987
A "homey neighborhood spot" "without a scene or attitude", this "family-run" UWS Tuscan is "better than most" at providing "reliable"

good food along with "engaging service"; it's especially "welcome" given its "decent" prices and "quiet" acoustics.

Little D Eatery ⓜ *American/Eclectic* ▽ 20 | 15 | 18 | $39

Park Slope | 434 Seventh Ave. (bet. 14th & 15th Sts.) | Brooklyn | 718-369-3144 | www.littled-eatery.com

"Mix and match" is the philosophy at this Park Slope Eclectic–New American where the "seasonal selection" of small plates presents an "array of appealing choices" delivered by an "attentive staff"; the format's a little "unexpected", but it's a "solid local" that price-sensitive "Slopers swear by."

Little Giant *American* 22 | 18 | 20 | $42

LES | 85 Orchard St. (Broome St.) | 212-226-5047 | www.littlegiantnyc.com

This Lower East Side "charmer" "works wonders" with New Americana thanks to the "creative flair" of its "tiny open kitchen"; the "unpretentious" style and "reasonable"-for-the-quality prices ensure that this "little place with a big heart" is "packed regularly."

Little Owl *American/Mediterranean* 24 | 18 | 22 | $50

W Village | 90 Bedford St. (Grove St.) | 212-741-4695 | www.thelittleowlnyc.com

Despite "matchbox" dimensions, this "ambitious" West Villager "delivers big" with "flawless execution" of Med–New American dishes backed up by "smart" service; all agree it's "something special", in fact enough so that it's "nearly impossible to get a table."

Lobster Box ❶ *Seafood* 17 | 15 | 16 | $41

Bronx | 34 City Island Ave. (bet. Belden & Rochelle Sts.) | 718-885-1952 | www.lobsterbox.com

Buoyed by "water views" of the Sound, this City Island seafood "perennial" is a "bountiful" endeavor famed for "lobster done every which way"; it's a no-brainer on "summer weekends", but given the "clichéd decor" and "indifferent service", some think it may be "coasting."

Locanda Vini & Olii ⓜ *Italian* ▽ 26 | 24 | 24 | $47

Clinton Hill | 129 Gates Ave. (bet. Cambridge Pl. & Garden Ave.) | Brooklyn | 718-622-9202 | www.locandany.com

A "lovely" former Clinton Hill pharmacy is the backdrop for this mid-priced Tuscan's "mouthwatering" "rustic" offerings and "hands-on" service; indeed, the "care and effort" on display have the locals so "pleased" that they "feel guilty telling" about it.

Lodge ❶ *American* ▽ 16 | 20 | 17 | $29

Williamsburg | 318 Grand St. (Havemeyer St.) | Brooklyn | 718-486-9400 | www.lodgenyc.com

Whether "ironic" or "genuinely cool", the "hunting lodge" theme is the "big draw" at this Williamsburg American; "heavily tattooed" staffers serving "simple" eats and drinks in "Mason jars" keep the "local hipsters" content, especially at brunch time.

Loft ❶ *French/Italian* 17 | 20 | 14 | $42

W 80s | 505 Columbus Ave. (bet. 84th & 85th Sts.) | 212-362-6440 | www.loftnyc.net

The Upper West Side tries for "trendy" at this "loungey" venue, offering "overdue" refuge for "well-kept" types who hail the "flavorful"

Franco-Italian menu and "lively bar scene"; "rude" service and "too much hype" are the downsides.

Lombardi's ⊕ *Pizza*

24 | 13 | 16 | $22

NoLita | 32 Spring St. (bet. Mott & Mulberry Sts.) | 212-941-7994 | www.firstpizza.com

For a "pie with few rivals", this NoLita "mainstay" lives up to its billing for "top-class" coal-fired pizza with a "distinct smoky taste", "ultrathin crust" and "zesty" toppings; given all this, be prepared for "crazy lines."

Londel's Supper Club Ⓜ *Southern*

▽ 22 | 17 | 19 | $31

Harlem | 2620 Frederick Douglass Blvd. (bet. 139th & 140th Sts.) | 212-234-6114 | www.londelsrestaurant.com

Proprietor Londel Davis "makes you feel welcome" at his Harlem Southerner, home to "soulfully solid" spreads in "plentiful" portions; extras include live jazz on weekend evenings and a "wonderful" Sunday buffet for those ready to "brunch it up."

London Lennie's *Seafood*

21 | 17 | 18 | $41

Rego Park | 63-88 Woodhaven Blvd. (bet. Fleet Ct. & Penelope Ave.) | Queens | 718-894-8084 | www.londonlennies.com

Ever "dependable" for fish lovers, this "longtime favorite" in Rego Park serves the "freshest seafood" in roomy digs; though the setup's "a little stodgy" and the acoustics "loud", it remains "wildly popular", with "waits for seating" the norm.

Long Tan ◑ *Thai*

19 | 18 | 18 | $28

Park Slope | 196 Fifth Ave. (bet. Berkeley Pl. & Union St.) | Brooklyn | 718-622-8444 | www.long-tan.com

This "out-of-the-ordinary" Park Slope Thai earns "popularity" with its "inventive" cooking and "good value"; the "sleek" design and pleasant garden add points for "cool", while "excellent" drinks create "a bit of a scene" with the "loyal" bar crowd.

Loreley *German*

▽ 18 | 15 | 16 | $26

LES | 7 Rivington St. (Bowery St.) | 212-253-7077 | www.loreleynyc.com

"Younger" folk gather on "bench seating" at this "boisterous", low-budget LES brauhaus to wash down "hearty" German "comfort" grub with an "outstanding" selection of brews; revelers report the "good times" get "even better" in the biergarten out back.

NEW Los Dados *Mexican*

- | - | - | M

Meatpacking | 73 Gansevoort St. (Washington St.) | 646-810-7290 | www.losdadosmexican.com

Mexican regional home cooking comes to the Meatpacking District via this new cantina that's the brainchild of chef Sue Torres (Sueños) and nightlife maven David Rabin (Lotus); the cozy space, fka Meet, features a communal table, kitschy religious shrines and a festive feel fueled by moderate tabs and free-flowing tequila.

Los Dos Molinos Ⓢ Ⓜ *Southwestern*

21 | 17 | 16 | $32

Gramercy | 119 E. 18th St. (bet. Irving Pl. & Park Ave. S.) | 212-505-1574

At this "upbeat" Gramercy Southwesterner, the "fairly priced" vittles deliver a fiery "kick" best quenched with "fishbowl margaritas"; "peak hours" typically draw "noisy" crowds undeterred by the "cheesy decor" and sometime service.

165

	FOOD	DECOR	SERVICE	COST

Loulou *French*

Fort Greene | 222 DeKalb Ave. (bet. Adelphi St. & Clermont Ave.) | Brooklyn | 718-246-0633 | www.louloubrooklyn.com

▽ 22 | 20 | 20 | $35

The French countryside comes to Fort Greene via this budget-friendly bistro, serving "consistently top-notch" Gallic "standbys" in a "warm" milieu complete with a "lovely" garden; the "cozy" room can be a "squeeze", but flirts observe that's all the more *romantique*."

Luca *Italian*

20 | 15 | 19 | $39

E 80s | 1712 First Ave. (bet. 88th & 89th Sts.) | 212-987-9260 | www.lucatogo.com

Known for chef-owner Luca Marcato's "personal touch", this "inviting" Yorkville Italian "hits the spot" with its "addictive" "rustic" cooking and "family atmosphere"; *certo*, the room's "not fancy", but "satisfying" eats at a "reasonable price" make it a local "staple."

NEW Lucali ⊘ *Pizza*

▽ 27 | 21 | 20 | $18

Carroll Gardens | 575 Henry St. (bet. Carroll St. & 1st Pl.) | Brooklyn | 718-858-4086

"Old-school styling" yields "pizza perfection" at this new Carroll Gardens "neighborhood joint", an "instant classic" for "transcendent" brick-oven pies served in "charming" digs that recall "Brooklyn gone by"; manned by a chef-owner who's "committed to the art", it attracts "long lines" "for a good reason."

Lucien ● *French*

21 | 18 | 19 | $41

E Village | 14 First Ave. (1st St.) | 212-260-6481 | www.luciennyc.com

"Oh-so-Gallic", this "intimate" East Village "hideaway" "transports you to Paris" with its French bistro "classics" and "convivial" setting overseen by "beloved" owner Lucien Bahaj; for "relaxed" regulars, the "tight" space and "slow service" are just part of the deal.

Lucky Strike ● *French*

17 | 15 | 16 | $33

SoHo | 59 Grand St. (bet. W. B'way & Wooster St.) | 212-941-0772 | www.luckystrikeny.com

You "don't dress up" for the "easygoing" "Left Bank experience" at this SoHo "stalwart" from Keith McNally; despite seeming "passé" to trendoids, it's a "standby" for "basic" French bistro fare and classic cocktails, loaded with locals in the mood to "unwind."

Lucy *Pan-Latin*

19 | 20 | 18 | $46

Flatiron | ABC Carpet & Home | 35 E. 18th St. (bet. B'way & Park Ave. S.) | 212-475-5829 | www.lucylatinkitchen.com

"Dark and hip", this Flatiron Pan-Latino in ABC Carpet & Home allows patrons the chance to nibble on "intriguing" vittles, then "do some shopping" afterward; though service skews toward "slow", at least they "don't rush you out."

Lumi ● *Italian*

19 | 18 | 19 | $52

E 70s | 963 Lexington Ave. (70th St.) | 212-570-2335 | www.lumirestaurant.com

"Steady" as they come, this "attractive" UES Italian supplies "satisfying" food and "old-world" service in fireplace-equipped quarters abetted by an "alfresco" cafe; most maintain it's a "solid" local alternative, though some surmise "you can do better for the money."

	FOOD	DECOR	SERVICE	COST

NEW Lunetta Ⓜ Italian
▽ 20 | 17 | 18 | $35

Boerum Hill | 116 Smith St. (bet. Dean & Pacific Sts.) | Brooklyn | 718-488-6269 | www.lunetta-ny.com

Moonstruck admirers claim the Italian cooking "can be a revelation" at this "cheerful" Smith Street newcomer where a "skilled" chef turns out "innovative" seasonal fare; customers also reflect warmly on the "casual" interior, backyard garden and "reasonable" cost.

Ⓩ Lupa ● Italian
25 | 18 | 21 | $50

G Village | 170 Thompson St. (bet. Bleecker & Houston Sts.) | 212-982-5089 | www.luparestaurant.com

The Batali-Bastianich-Denton "magic" will "blow you away" at this "down-to-earth" Village Italian with "dynamite" Roman cuisine served by an "enthusiastic" staff at less than their usual prices; the "hectic" atmosphere and "cheek-by-jowl" seating are "part of the charm", but "eternal" waits remain a "hassle."

Lure Fishbar Seafood
23 | 24 | 23 | $58

SoHo | 142 Mercer St., downstairs (Prince St.) | 212-431-7676 | www.lurefishbar.com

Making a "shipshape" "comeback" following a fire, this SoHo seafooder wins kudos for its "super-fresh fish" and sushi, "first-rate" service and elegant, "yachtlike" space; despite the "high price tag", its "attitude-less" allure keeps the "upscale" clientele "all on board."

Lusardi's Italian
24 | 18 | 22 | $59

E 70s | 1494 Second Ave. (bet. 77th & 78th Sts.) | 212-249-2020 | www.lusardis.com

A "longtime" UES "favorite", this "clublike" enclave "never loses its touch" for "top-flight" Northern Italian food and "professional" service; sure, it's "pricey" and "a little stuffy", but "well-heeled" locals attest it's "worth every penny."

Luz Nuevo Latino
▽ 24 | 20 | 20 | $31

Fort Greene | 177 Vanderbilt Ave. (bet. Myrtle Ave. & Willoughby St.) | Brooklyn | 718-246-4000 | www.luzrestaurant.com

Enlightened diners make this "cool" Fort Greene Nuevo Latino a "destination" for an "inventive menu" supplemented by "fruity drinks"; it's still "little known", but the "low-key" style and big "bang for your buck" promise a bright future.

Macelleria ● Italian/Steak
21 | 18 | 19 | $50

Meatpacking | 48 Gansevoort St. (bet. Greenwich & Washington Sts.) | 212-741-2555 | www.macelleriarestaurant.com

Honoring the Meatpacking District's roots, this "old-school" Italian steakhouse offers "high quality" and "big portions" in "cozy" digs with "meat-fridge" fixtures and a "top-notch" wine cellar; the "simple" style is "refreshing" in this "bandwagon" neighborhood, though skeptics synopsize it as a "second-tier" experience.

Madison Bistro French
18 | 15 | 17 | $45

Murray Hill | 238 Madison Ave. (bet. 37th & 38th Sts.) | 212-447-1919 | www.madisonbistro.com

"Quaint" and "unpretentious", this "snug" Murray Hill bistro does a "super" job accommodating its *réguliers* with "old-time" French comfort food and "obliging" service; notwithstanding "tightly placed tables" and "pricey" propensities, it's "popular and appropriately so."

Madison's *Italian* — 20 | 17 | 19 | $40

Bronx | 5686 Riverdale Ave. (259th St.) | 718-543-3850

With a "quite decent" stab at "stylish" atmospherics, this midpriced "neighborhood" Italian ranks with "Riverdale's best" for "tasty food in comfortable surroundings"; its "upscale Manhattan" feel is a "treat" for the "core group of locals" who madly "love it."

Magnolia *American* — 19 | 17 | 17 | $30

Park Slope | 486 Sixth Ave. (12th St.) | Brooklyn | 718-369-4814 | www.magnoliabrooklyn.com

Defining a "great local", this "cute" New American stirs up "neighborhood hype" in Park Slope with "damn good food", "tasteful" decor and "friendly service"; even those who deem it "ordinary" concede it's "convenient."

NEW Mai House ●Ⓩ *Vietnamese* — 21 | 21 | 20 | $54

TriBeCa | 186 Franklin St. (bet. Greenwich & Hudson Sts.) | 212-431-0606 | www.myriadrestaurantgroup.com

"Pretty" people and power spice cadets make themselves at home at this TriBeCa newcomer that produces "spot-on" "nouveau Vietnamese" cooking and flaunts "exciting plays on the traditional" (as does the "spacious", minimally "chic" setting); paupers pout it's "expensive", but the "flair" will mai-ghtily "impress a date."

Maison ● *French* — 17 | 16 | 16 | $35

W 50s | 1700 Broadway (enter on 7th Ave., bet. 53rd & 54th Sts.) | 212-757-2233 | www.maisonnyc.com

"Low-maintenance types" claim this "handy" Midtown brasserie delivers the goods, supplying "reasonably priced" "basic French" fare 24/7 in a "casual" milieu; it's best known for its vast outdoor seating, leading cynics to suggest "maybe the tourists are right about this one."

Malagueta Ⓜ *Brazilian* — ▽ 26 | 12 | 22 | $30

Astoria | 25-35 36th Ave. (28th St.) | Queens | 718-937-4821

A "taste of Rio" in Astoria, this "tranquil" Brazilian "hideaway" is a "joy" for "incredible" "home-cooked food" and "warm service" at a pleasing price; too bad they "forgot about the decor", but its rep as a "diamond in the rough" is beginning to reach beyond the borough.

Malatesta Trattoria ●⊄ *Italian* — 21 | 17 | 18 | $32

W Village | 649 Washington St. (Christopher St.) | 212-741-1207

For "all-authentic" Northern Italiana, this way West Villager passes the test with its "tasty", "no-nonsense" cooking and "hot Euro" staffers; the "chill" sidewalk tables and "great value" are similarly "worth the trek."

Maloney & Porcelli *Steak* — 22 | 19 | 21 | $64

E 50s | 37 E. 50th St. (bet. Madison & Park Aves.) | 212-750-2233 | www.maloneyandporcelli.com

"Suits drinking brown liquor" wolf down "man-size" slabs of "prime meat" (including that "famous" crackling pork shank) at this handsome Midtown chop shop; it's a "formulaic" but "consistently solid"

| | FOOD | DECOR | SERVICE | COST |

spread, and they'll always "treat you right", even if it's best savored "on someone else's tab."

Mamá Mexico ◑ *Mexican*
`20` `17` `17` `$36`

E 40s | 214 E. 49th St. (bet. 2nd & 3rd Aves.) | 212-935-1316
W 100s | 2672 Broadway (102nd St.) | 212-864-2323
www.mamamexico.com

There's always a "hopping" scene going on at this affordable Mexican duo where the "mariachi action", "flowing tequila" and "gaudy" backdrops can lead to "too much fun"; "fantastic" food (including "fresh guacamole made at your table") helps make the "really noisy" acoustics more bearable.

Mama's Food Shop 🛐🥡 *American*
`20` `11` `15` `$15`

E Village | 200 E. Third St. (bet. Aves. A & B) | 212-777-4425 |
www.mamasfoodshop.com

When "stomach and pocketbook are both close to empty", the "punky" cafeteria staff at this East Village "hole-in-the-wall" "piles your plate" with "classic" American "home cookin'" for "cheap"; regulars with a "serious addiction" shrug "simple is best."

Mamlouk ◑Ⓜ *Mideastern*
▽ `23` `18` `18` `$48`

E Village | 211 E. Fourth St. (bet. Aves. A & B) | 212-529-3477

"Pace yourself" at this East Village Middle Easterner where the "wonderful" eats "keep coming and coming" via a $40 prix fixe "feast" that spans six courses; what with the "rich" food, "cool" Arabian interior and weekend "belly dancers", it's a "totally different experience."

Mancora ◑ *Peruvian*
▽ `21` `15` `20` `$26`

E Village | 99 First Ave. (6th St.) | 212-253-1011

"One of the best values" around, this "authentic" East Village Peruvian plies "hearty servings" of "delectable" rotisserie chicken and other "mouthwatering discoveries" at a cost comparable to "eating at home"; maybe the decor "could be better", but otherwise surveyors say they're "impressed."

Mandarin Court *Chinese*
`20` `8` `13` `$20`

Chinatown | 61 Mott St. (bet. Bayard & Canal Sts.) | 212-608-3838

"Excellent dim sum" for just a "small sum" is the verdict on this Chinatown "old-timer" that rolls out a "wide variety" of "hot, fresh treats"; despite "zero ambiance", chow that's this "hard to resist" keeps business "bustling."

Mandoo Bar *Korean*
`20` `12` `16` `$20`

Garment District | 2 W. 32nd St. (bet. B'way & 5th Ave.) | 212-279-3075

The "superlative dumplings" at this "no-fuss" Garment District Korean are just the ticket for a "quick bite"; don't mind the "spartan" setup – the can-do staffers and bargain prices will keep you "happy."

Manducatis *Italian*
`22` `13` `19` `$45`

LIC | 13-27 Jackson Ave. (47th Ave.) | Queens | 718-729-4602 |
www.manducatis.com

As a "last redoubt for mama's cooking", this "true family" Italian in Long Island City seems "lost in time" with its "soulful" "homestyle" dishes, "wonderful wines" and "old-world" hospitality; the aging digs "may need a makeover", but otherwise it has an "amazing reputation."

	FOOD	DECOR	SERVICE	COST

Manetta's 🔲 *Italian* ∇ 22 17 20 $38

LIC | 10-76 Jackson Ave. (49th Ave.) | Queens | 718-786-6171

This "family-run" LIC Italian "neighborhood favorite" does wonders with its "wood-fired pizzas" and "homemade pastas"; the "accommodating" service and "affordable" cost translate into "lots of repeat business."

Mangia 🔲 *Mediterranean* 20 12 13 $21

E 40s | 16 E. 48th St. (bet. 5th & Madison Aves.) | 212-754-7600
Financial District | Trump Bldg. | 40 Wall St. (bet. Nassau & William Sts.) | 212-425-4040
Flatiron | 22 W. 23rd St. (bet. 5th & 6th Aves.) | 212-647-0200
W 50s | 50 W. 57th St. (bet. 5th & 6th Aves.) | 212-582-5554
www.mangiatogo.com

"Corporate" types count on this Med foursome for classy "take-out lunches" featuring "lots of choices" from a "fancy salad bar" to the "imaginative" sandwich board; ok, the "cost adds up" and service is "spotty", but it sure it's "quick" and "easy."

NEW Mantra 986 *American/Pan-Asian* - - - M

E 50s | 986 Second Ave. (bet. 52nd & 53rd Sts.) | 212-813-1595 | www.mantra986.com

A nightclub-ish setting is the backdrop for this new split-level East Midtowner that appeals to a young crowd with a midpriced mix of New American and Pan-Asian dishes; an upstairs lounge (with a balcony overlooking Second Avenue) handles the overflow and can be reserved for private parties.

Mara's Homemade *Cajun/Creole* 19 10 19 $31

E Village | 342 E. Sixth St. (bet. 1st & 2nd Aves.) | 212-598-1110 | www.marashomemade.com

At this East Village "hole-in-the-wall", you'll find "awesome" Cajun-Creole cookin' and "authentic N'Awlins style"; true, it's on the "funky" side, but "festive drinks" and the chance to "eat crawfish like a pro" make for real "fun on the bayou."

Marco Polo Ristorante *Italian* ∇ 20 17 20 $46

Carroll Gardens | 345 Court St. (Union St.) | Brooklyn | 718-852-5015 | www.marcopoloristorante.com

"Old favorites" save the day at this Carroll Gardens Italian turning out *molto bene* standards in a kitschy but "comfortable" setting enhanced by "snappy" service; holdouts hedge it's a bit "pricey" and "stuffy", but "Tony and Carmela could eat here happily."

Maremma ● *Italian*  21 19 20 $51

W Village | 228 W. 10th St. (bet. Bleecker & Hudson Sts.) | 212-645-0200 | www.maremmanyc.com

Overseen by Cesare Casella and his "solicitous staff", this bi-level West Villager augments its "impressive" Tuscan menu with "inventive surprises" without losing "that comfort-food feeling"; an "inviting" haven of "eclectic" rusticana, it has finally "found its groove."

Maria Pia *Italian* 19 15 18 $36

W 50s | 319 W. 51st St. (bet. 8th & 9th Aves.) | 212-765-6463 | www.mariapianyc.com

The "genuine article", this "cordial" Theater District Italian serves "flavorful red-sauce" fare with "no noses" in the air and, better still, for "moderate" sums (the $21.95 dinner "prix fixe is so worth it"); since the "nondescript" room can get "cramped" during the "pre-theater rush", the "garden is a must."

Marina Cafe *Seafood*

| 18 | 22 | 18 | $42 |

Staten Island | 154 Mansion Ave. (Hillside Terr.) | 718-967-3077 | www.marinacafegrand.com

A "grand view" of Great Kills Harbor and "fine fresh seafood" are the main "attractions" at this Staten Island cafe, though the "updated decor" also helps justify the "Park Avenue prices"; merrymakers maintain "summer evenings" on the tiki bar deck are "not to be missed."

Marinella *Italian*

| ▽ 23 | 17 | 22 | $40 |

G Village | 49 Carmine St. (Bedford St.) | 212-807-7472

Hailed as a "quintessential local joint", this Village "blackboard-menu" Italian is a "superior" source of "old-school" cuisine and service so "super-friendly" it's "like coming home"; the "peaceful" vibe and modest prices prove it's "not trendy at all."

Mario's 🅜 *Italian*

| 22 | 16 | 21 | $40 |

Bronx | 2342 Arthur Ave. (bet. 184th & 186th Sts.) | 718-584-1188

"Retro in the best of ways", this "family-run" 1919-vintage "charmer" remains an Arthur Avenue "favorite" for "generations of red-sauce lovers" who understand that the combo of classic Southern Italiana and great thin-crust pizza "refreshes the soul"; equally stirring is the "attentiveness" of its "staff of old-timers."

MarkJoseph Steakhouse 🅩 *Steak*

| 24 | 18 | 21 | $69 |

Financial District | 261 Water St. (off Peck Slip) | 212-277-0020 | www.markjosephsteakhouse.com

"They mean business" at this "manly" Financial District chop shop that "wows Wall Street types" with "big", "succulent steaks" "seared to perfection" and dispatched by "slick" servers; cash-endowed carnivores overlook the "stark" backdrop as well as the typically pricey steakhouse tabs.

Markt *Belgian*

| 19 | 18 | 16 | $42 |

Flatiron | 676 Sixth Ave. (21st St.) | 212-727-3314 | www.marktrestaurant.com

Expect the "same look and feel" on a "smaller" scale at this "trendy Belgian brasserie" that's traded its Meatpacking District address for new Flatiron digs; it remains a "no-brainer" for those in the markt for "premier moules frites" blessed by Belgian brews.

Maroons *Jamaican*

| 22 | 15 | 18 | $35 |

Chelsea | 244 W. 16th St. (bet. 7th & 8th Aves.) | 212-206-8640 | www.maroonsnyc.com

The "heavy-duty home cooking" and light-duty tabs leave 'em "fat and happy" at this Chelsea Jamaican-Southerner whose "soulful" specialties deliver a "spicy kick"; indeed, the grub's so "satisfying", it's easy to overlook being packed in "tight" and marooned by "hit-or-miss" service.

Marseille ● *French/Mediterranean*

| 20 | 19 | 19 | $47 |

W 40s | 630 Ninth Ave. (44th St.) | 212-333-3410 | www.marseillenyc.com

Beaucoup "brasserie character" (including "upbeat din") marks this Hell's Kitchen French-Med where the "tempting" menu surprises with "refreshing twists"; add "congenial" servers who "get you out fast" and you have an "obvious pre-theater choice."

Maruzzella ● *Italian*

	FOOD	DECOR	SERVICE	COST
	22	16	22	$40

E 70s | 1483 First Ave. (bet. 77th & 78th Sts.) | 212-988-8877 | www.maruzzellanyc.com

A "local favorite" that's even "more inviting since an expansion", this "reliable" UES Italian is a "go-to" for "delightful traditional" eats for fairly "favorable" fares; given the "super" service, locals "wish there were more like it."

Mary Ann's *Tex-Mex*

	FOOD	DECOR	SERVICE	COST
	15	11	14	$25

Chelsea | 116 Eighth Ave. (16th St.) | 212-633-0877 ⊅
E Village | 80 Second Ave. (5th St.) | 212-475-5939 ⊅
TriBeCa | 107 W. Broadway (bet. Chambers & Reade Sts.) | 212-766-0911 | www.maryannsmexican.com
W 90s | 2452 Broadway (bet. 90th & 91st Sts.) | 212-877-0132

"Why go to Cabo" when there's this "high-volume" Tex-Mex mini-chain made for "gorging on staples" chased with "mean margaritas"; contras condemn the "predictable" chow, "tacky" looks and "sloppy" service, but admit they do the job while staying "totally affordable."

Mary's Fish Camp Ⓢ *Seafood*

	FOOD	DECOR	SERVICE	COST
	25	13	18	$41

W Village | 64 Charles St. (W. 4th St.) | 646-486-2185 | www.marysfishcamp.com

Camp followers dream of the "transcendent lobster roll" and other "fresher-than-fresh seafood" at this "upbeat little" Village "fish shack"; the "beachy", ultra-"informal" space is "always jammed", but drift by once and you'll be "hooked."

Mas Ⓢ *American*

	FOOD	DECOR	SERVICE	COST
	25	24	25	$74

G Village | 39 Downing St. (bet. Bedford & Varick Sts.) | 212-255-1790 | www.masfarmhouse.com

"Go with someone special" to this "intimate" Village New American, a paradigm of "relaxed sophistication" where chef Galen Zamarra's "exceptional", "market-fresh" menu wins mas-sive support; its "impressive wine list", "classic service" and "stylish rustic" setting are likewise "well worth" the "grown-up" cost.

Ⓩ Masa Ⓢ *Japanese*

	FOOD	DECOR	SERVICE	COST
	27	24	26	$485

W 60s | Time Warner Ctr. | 10 Columbus Circle, 4th fl. (60th St. at B'way)
Ⓩ Bar Masa ●Ⓢ *Japanese*
W 60s | Time Warner Ctr. | 10 Columbus Circle, 4th fl. (60th St. at B'way)
212-823-9800 | www.masanyc.com

At this Zen-like Time Warner Center Japanese, you can enjoy star chef Masayoshi Takayama's "exquisite" omakase – an "unforgettable" "parade of perfection" for an "astronomical" $400 prix fixe that some consider a deal when compared to the cost of floor seats for the Knicks; the more "unassuming" Bar Masa next door is "not cheap", but still a "bargain compared to its big brother."

Ⓩ Matsuri ● *Japanese*

	FOOD	DECOR	SERVICE	COST
	23	26	20	$59

Chelsea | Maritime Hotel | 369 W. 16th St., downstairs (9th Ave.) | 212-243-6400 | www.themaritimehotel.com

This "top-of-the-line", bottom-of-the-building Chelsea Japanese earns "wows" for its spectacular subterranean setting, not to mention

hef Tadashi Ono's "brilliant sushi", a "knockout sake list" and "hospi-
ble" service; the "happening scene" is populated by "trendy" folk
quipped with "deep pockets", while its adjacent nightclub/party
ace is a great venue to celebrate with your 175 dearest friends.

Maurizio Trattoria *Italian* ▽ 21 17 21 $50

Village | 35 W. 13th St. (bet. 5th & 6th Aves.) | 212-206-6474 |
www.mauriziotrattoria.com

's something of a "neighborhood secret", but cognoscenti count on
is "delightful little" Village Tuscan for "well-executed" "classic"
shes and "gracious personal service"; a location "across from the
uad Cinema" makes it a natural, if pricey, post-flick pick.

Max *Italian* 23 15 17 $27

Village | 51 Ave. B (bet. 3rd & 4th Sts.) | 212-539-0111 ●⊄
NEW **TriBeCa** | 181 Duane St. (bet. Greenwich & Hudson Sts.) |
12-966-5939
www.max-ny.com

Max SoHa ●⊄ *Italian*

W 100s | 1274 Amsterdam Ave. (123rd St.) | 212-531-2221 |
www.maxsoha.com

Earthy" meals that "linger in your mind" make this "quaint" East
illager (with a "collegiate" outpost near Columbia and a new TriBeCa
bling) a "favorite" for "homestyle Italian" cooking; "shockingly low"
rices keep them packed.

Max Brenner *Dessert* 17 19 14 $24

NEW **E Village** | 141 Second Ave. (9th St.) | 212-388-0030
nion Sq | 841 Broadway (bet. 13th & 14th Sts.) | 212-388-0030
www.maxbrenner.com

Go right to dessert" at this "Wonka-esque" global chocolatier whose
sweet feasts" easily outperform its "average" French fare; apart from
eing off-limits for weight-watchers, the main problem here is
flighty" servers suffering from "sugar shock."

Maya *Mexican* 23 19 19 $51

60s | 1191 First Ave. (bet. 64th & 65th Sts.) | 212-585-1818 |
www.modernmexican.com

Haute Mexican" cooking gets an "imaginative spin" at this "stylish"
astsider that "outshines" its rivals with "superior" cuisine and
prompt" service; "wickedly good" margaritas fuel the fiestalike fun,
ut bring *mucho dinero* to settle the bill.

NEW Maze *French* 23 21 20 $71

W 50s | The London NYC | 151 W. 54th St. (bet. 6th & 7th Aves.) |
12-468-8889 | www.thelondonnyc.com

If you can't get in to Gordon Ramsay", this Midtown hotel's "more re-
axed" bar/eatery offers the "same quality" from the same chef via an
exquisite" lineup of New French small plates; the "refined" feel and
spot-on" service score well too, but the cost of a meal here can "add up."

Maz Mezcal *Mexican* 20 17 18 $36

80s | 316 E. 86th St. (bet. 1st & 2nd Aves.) | 212-472-1599 |
www.mazmezcal.com

ong a "best bet" for a "true Mexican fix", this "lively" UES eatery
atches "top-notch" menu "classics" with "deadly" tequilas and sim-

| | FOOD | DECOR | SERVICE | COST |

patico service; it's "lotsa fun" for "reasonable" sums, but "go early
since it's often "jammed" with compadres.

McCormick & Schmick's *Seafood*

20 | 18 | 20 | $50

W 50s | 1285 Sixth Ave. (enter on 52nd St., bet. 6th & 7th Aves.) |
212-459-1222 | www.mccormickandschmicks.com

Linkage to a "big fish" chain makes this Midtowner a "safe" harbor fc
a "mind-boggling selection" of "solid basic seafood"; aye, the eatin
and "Anywhere, USA" vibe show "little imagination", but overall th
"mainstream" shtick is "better than you'd expect."

Mediterraneo ◐ *Italian/Pizza*

19 | 15 | 15 | $39

E 60s | 1260 Second Ave. (66th St.) | 212-734-7407 |
www.mediterraneonyc.com

Young "Euros" ensure this "causal", affordable East Side Italian is "a
ways filled" as they sample a "tasty array of pastas" and "thin-crus
pizzas" served by expats "right off the boat"; those parked on th
"coveted" sidewalk seats suggest it's "more about the scene."

Mee Noodle Shop *Noodle Shop*

18 | 4 | 12 | $15

E 40s | 922 Second Ave. (49th St.) | 212-888-0027
Murray Hill | 547 Second Ave. (bet. 30th & 31st Sts.) |
212-779-1596
W 50s | 795 Ninth Ave. (53rd St.) | 212-765-2929

Meting out "fresh", "stewlike soups" at "unbeatable" prices, this "no
fuss" Chinese noodle trio is hard to beat for a "satisfying quick feed"
"slapdash" service and "dumpy" digs cause many to opt for the
"lightning"-fast delivery.

☑ Megu *Japanese*

24 | 26 | 22 | $94

TriBeCa | 62 Thomas St. (bet. Church St. & W. B'way)
☑ Megu Midtown *Japanese*
E 40s | Trump World Tower | 845 United Nations Plaza (1st Ave. & 47th St.)
212-964-7777 | www.megunyc.com

For a "dining event" that "makes a mega-impression", this "glitzy
Japanese duo flaunts "lavish surroundings" (built around an "ic
Buddha"), "brilliant" "work-of-art" food and "bend-over-backward
service"; if the Eastsider is "less awe-inspiring" than the "soaring
TriBeCa original, they're equally "hyper-priced."

Meltemi *Greek/Seafood*

18 | 13 | 18 | $46

E 50s | 905 First Ave. (51st St.) | 212-355-4040

"No froufrou" distracts from the "standard Greek fare" at this Eas
Midtown "warhorse", a "hospitable" retreat for "nicely done" seafooo
some sniff "unmemorable", but for "U.N. types" and area "ancients"
it's like a "trip to the old country."

Menchanko-tei *Noodle Shop*

20 | 10 | 15 | $22

E 40s | 131 E. 45th St. (bet. Lexington & 3rd Aves.) |
212-986-6805 ◐
W 50s | 43-45 W. 55th St. (bet. 5th & 6th Aves.) | 212-247-1585
www.menchankotei.com

"Budget-minded salarymen" declare that these inexpensive Midtow
ramen shops are the "real deal" for "heaping bowls" of "awesom
Japanese soul food"; skeptics menchan the barely "utilitarian" setup
but note you'll be "in and out" in a flash.

Mercadito *Mexican* | 22 | 16 | 16 | $38 |

E Village | 179 Ave. B (bet. 11th & 12th Sts.) | 212-529-6490
W Village | 100 Seventh Ave. S. (bet. Bleecker & Grove Sts.) | 212-647-0830
www.mercaditony.com

You "can't get a better fish taco" than at these "creative" cross-Village Mexicans with "eminently shareable" small plates and "potent" potables; party-poopers protest "skimpy" portions that can "run up a tab."

NEW Mercat ● ☒ *Spanish* | - | - | - | E |

NoHo | 45 Bond St. (bet. Bowery & Lafayette St.) | 212-529-8600 |
www.mercatnyc.com

Bustling from day one, this hip NoHo arrival is Barcelona native Jaime Reixach's attempt to re-create the tapas bars of his hometown; the white-tiled space, with open kitchen, separate jamon and cheese station and a downstairs lounge, can be echo-y, so brush up on your lip-reading.

Mercer Kitchen ● *American/French* | 22 | 23 | 19 | $56 |

SoHo | Mercer Hotel | 99 Prince St. (Mercer St.) | 212-966-5454 |
www.jean-georges.com

The "cool factor" is intact at Jean-Georges Vongerichten's SoHo French–New American, whose subterranean "chicness" and "pricey", "well-crafted menu" make everyone from "glitterati" to "out-of-towners" feel "special"; the crowd sure "looks good" in the "dark" setting, though the "staff could use some attitude sprucing."

Mermaid Inn *Seafood* | 23 | 17 | 20 | $43 |

E Village | 96 Second Ave. (bet. 5th & 6th Sts.) | 212-674-5870 |
www.themermaidnyc.com

Seemingly shipped from "somewhere in Maine", this "unpretentious" East Village seafooder "hits the mark" with "high-quality" cooking that appeals to "serious" afishionados; the "cheery staff", "quaint nautical decor" and "garden area" help make it an inn spot.

☒ Mesa Grill *Southwestern* | 24 | 20 | 21 | $55 |

Flatiron | 102 Fifth Ave. (bet. 15th & 16th Sts.) | 212-807-7400 |
www.mesagrill.com

Showcasing "Southwestern with snazz", this seriously tabbed Flatiron standby is home plate for TV super-chef Bobby Flay, whose "bold riffs" on regional cuisine "pack a big taste wallop" (brunch is sure to "wake you up"); "enthusiastic" service bolsters the "loud", "upbeat" vibe in a room that's lately been looking a little "long in the tooth."

Meskerem *Ethiopian* | 20 | 8 | 13 | $23 |

G Village | 124 MacDougal St. (bet. Bleecker & W. 3rd Sts.) | 212-777-8111
W 40s | 468 W. 47th St. (bet. 9th & 10th Aves.) | 212-664-0520 ●

To "break out of your normal routine", try the "hands-on" experience at this Ethiopian duo where "hearty", "perfectly spiced" stews served "sans utensils" are scooped up with "tangy" injera bread; "amazing value" helps offset the "low-frills" feel and "haphazard service."

Métisse *French* | 19 | 16 | 19 | $40 |

W 100s | 239 W. 105th St. (bet. Amsterdam Ave. & B'way) | 212-666-8825 |
www.metisserestaurant.com

A "tried-and-true respite" for "Columbia profs" and other clued-in locals, this "nifty" Upper Westsider supplies "well-executed", well-priced French classics in a "quiet", "cozy" milieu; if the "staff lacks finesse, it makes up for it in charm."

Metrazur 🗷 *American*　　　　　20 | 21 | 18 | $49

E 40s | Grand Central | East Balcony (42nd St. & Park Ave.) | 212-687-4600 | www.charliepalmer.com

"Exciting" views of Grand Central's Concourse and "solid" New American cuisine set Charlie Palmer's balcony "bastion" apart from the pack; it's "expensive" and the "commuters scurrying" around below may be "faster than the waiters", but there's more than enough incentive here to take another train.

NEW Metro Marché *French*　　　　19 | 15 | 19 | $36

W 40s | Port Authority | 625 Eighth Ave. (41st St.) | 212-239-1010 | www.metromarche.com

Granted, it's the "last place you'd look" for a French brasserie, but this Port Authority newcomer is a "pleasant surprise" for "reasonably priced" Gallic grub and "quick" service; though "somewhat impersonal", it's a "convenient oasis" before a show or "hopping a Greyhound."

Mexicana Mama 🎵🗷 *Mexican*　　　23 | 13 | 18 | $35

G Village | 47 E. 12th St. (bet. B'way & University Pl.) | 212-253-7594
W Village | 525 Hudson St. (bet. Charles & W. 10th Sts.) | 212-924-4119

At the "high end of Mexican", this taqueria twosome turns out "mouthwatering" dishes with "nuevo twists" that most "can't get enough of"; those opposed to "cramped seating and killer waits" should forgo the "teeny" West Village original for its "larger" eastern offshoot.

Mexican Radio ☽ *Mexican*　　　　18 | 13 | 15 | $32

NoLita | 19 Cleveland Pl. (bet. Kenmare & Spring Sts.) | 212-343-0140 | www.mexrad.com

Twentysomethings "tune in" to this "casual", low-budget NoLita joint for its "yummy" if "unadventurous" Mexican eats and "kitschy-cool" setting; service may be "on siesta", but after a few "deadly" margaritas "not too much of the meal matters."

Mezzaluna ☽ *Italian*　　　　　19 | 15 | 17 | $44

E 70s | 1295 Third Ave. (bet. 74th & 75th Sts.) | 212-535-9600 | www.mezzalunany.com

Regulars who make this UES Italian vet their "local canteen" crowd in for "fine" "fresh" pastas and "wood-oven" pizzas; though the "close quarters" and upscale prices detract, it's "worth bumping elbows" for a meal that you "can always count on."

Mezzogiorno ☽ *Italian*　　　　20 | 17 | 18 | $42

SoHo | 195 Spring St. (Sullivan St.) | 212-334-2112 | www.mezzogiorno.com

For a "SoHo shopping break" and a conversation without shouting, there's always this "comfortable" Tuscan "old reliable" with its "strong" renditions of pizza and pasta "staples"; "passable" service and spendy tabs are balanced by "sidewalk dining" that's perfect on a "summer day."

Mezzo Mezzo ☽ *Greek*　　　　▽ 18 | 17 | 18 | $33

Astoria | 31-29 Ditmars Blvd. (bet. 32nd & 33rd Sts.) | Queens | 718-278-0444 | www.mezzomezzony.com

This "homey" Astorian is a "casually accommodating" place with "enjoyable" Greek grub, an "outdoor cafe" and Saturday night "belly dancing";

ough "un-mythical" on the whole, it works as an affordable "alternative" to "waiting on line at Taverna Kyclades up the block."

Michael Jordan's
The Steak House NYC Steak
20 | 21 | 19 | $62

40s | Grand Central | West Balcony (42nd St. & Vanderbilt Ave.) | 212-655-2300 | www.theglaziergroup.com

To "eat like Mike", try this "competitive" mezzanine meatery "overlooking the rush" of Grand Central Concourse, scoring well for its "generous" cuts of "quality" beef; some blow the whistle on "expense-account" pricing and "delayed" service, but the $24 prix fixe lunch is a winner and overall it scores "more often than the Knicks."

Michael's Ⓢ Californian
21 | 21 | 21 | $66

W 50s | 24 W. 55th St. (bet. 5th & 6th Aves.) | 212-767-0555 | www.michaelsnewyork.com

You can eavesdrop on the "next big media merger" while enjoying "classy" Californian cuisine and "professional service" at this "attractive", airy Midtown "power spot"; the "unparalleled people-watching" and "contemporary art" displays help distract from the "Beverly Hills" pricing.

Mi Cocina Mexican
22 | 18 | 19 | $41

W Village | 57 Jane St. (Hudson St.) | 212-627-8273

They know "what Mexican cuisine is all about" at this "cozy" West Village stalwart that "avoids the typical" with its "consistently excellent" cooking; given the "sunny" service and "absolute treat" of a tequila selection, amigos ignore the "steep"-for-the-genre prices.

Mill Basin Kosher Deli Deli
21 | 15 | 17 | $22

Mill Basin | 5823 Ave. T (59th St.) | Brooklyn | 718-241-4910 | www.millbasindeli.com

At this kosher Jewish deli-cum-"art gallery", "all the classic dishes" (i.e. "pastrami supreme") are offered alongside classic Erté and Lichtenstein "eye candy" on the walls; service is "genial" if "maybe too fast", and some say the "overstuffed" sandwiches are "overpriced", but that probably comes from being in Mill Basin.

Mill Korean Korean
19 | 13 | 16 | $20

W 100s | 2895 Broadway (bet. 112th & 113th Sts.) | 212-666-7653

With its "magnum-size portions" of Seoul food, this "inexpensive" UWS "neighborhood staple" helps Columbia students "soothe a craving" "without heading to Koreatown"; too bad the "cramped digs" and "thinly spread" service can make the scene "a little chaotic."

Milos, Estiatorio ◐ Greek/Seafood
26 | 23 | 22 | $73

W 50s | 125 W. 55th St. (bet. 6th & 7th Aves.) | 212-245-7400 | www.milos.ca

"Zeus couldn't eat better" than mere mortals do at this all-white, high-ceilinged Midtown Greek known for "pristine" seafood "grilled to perfection" (the "only way to get it fresher is to stick your head in the fish tank"); "smooth service" and "resortlike" decor add to the "quality" experience, but "bring the platinum card" to deal with the Olympic prices – or stick to its less expensive, but equally delicious, appetizers.

	FOOD	DECOR	SERVICE	COST

Minetta Tavern ● *Italian*
| 18 | 18 | 18 | $42 |

G Village | 113 MacDougal St. (bet. Bleecker & W. 3rd Sts.) | 212-475-385

For a "trip down memory lane", visit this 1937-vintage Village "hide away" where "old-fashioned" waiters bring out "huge portions" (Northern Italian fare; except for the prices, "they haven't changed th menu in decades", and if it's looking "a little worn", at least it's "reliable

Mingala Burmese *Burmese*
| 20 | 10 | 17 | $23 |

E 70s | 1393B Second Ave. (bet. 72nd & 73rd Sts.) | 212-744-8008
E Village | 21-23 E. Seventh St. (bet. 2nd & 3rd Aves.) |
212-529-3656

"Good for vegetarians", these Burmese twins offer a "different" cuisin that's a "gentler" combination of Indian, Chinese and Thai tastes; the de cor's either "folksy" or "drab", but there's no debating the "low prices

Mint *Indian*
| ▽ 19 | 19 | 15 | $44 |

E 50s | San Carlos Hotel | 150 E. 50th St. (bet. Lexington & 3rd Aves.)
212-644-8888 | www.mintny.com

"Solid" subcontinental specialties that "don't cost a mint" satisfy survey ors at this "upscale" East Midtown Indian; the "sleek" interior may see "a bit unsettling" as does service that "leaves a lot to be desired."

Miracle Grill *Southwestern*
| 18 | 14 | 17 | $31 |

W Village | 415 Bleecker St. (bet. Bank & W. 11th Sts.) | 212-924-1900
Park Slope | 222 Seventh Ave. (4th St.) | Brooklyn | 718-369-4541

"Tasty" Southwestern vittles make for "worthy" brunches at this "laid back", low-priced duo in the Village and Park Slope; the settings ar "comfortable" – Brooklyn's "wonderful" deck actually "manages to fee private" – though some report "spotty service" from Miracle worker

Miriam *Israeli/Mediterranean*
| 21 | 18 | 19 | $32 |

NEW **Cobble Hill** | 229 Court St. (bet. Baltic & Warren Sts.) | Brooklyn
718-522-2220
Park Slope | 79 Fifth Ave. (Prospect Pl.) | Brooklyn | 718-622-2250
www.miriamrestaurant.com

With their "zesty", "inventive" Israeli/Med eats, this pleasingly price Park Sloper and its new Cobble Hill spin-off are "keepers" with espe cially "busy" weekend brunches; "romantic" settings with mosaic and lanterns make them "feel exotic and homey at the same time."

Mishima *Japanese*
| 23 | 12 | 20 | $36 |

Murray Hill | 164 Lexington Ave. (bet. 30th & 31st Sts.) | 212-532-9596
www.mishimany.com

Murray Hillers bow to this split-level Japanese's "melt-on-your tongue fresh" sushi as well as "perfectly executed" cooked item "bargain" pricing and "accommodating" service add to the "peaceful "pleasant" vibe; P.S. "definitely eat upstairs."

Miss Mamie's *Southern*
| ▽ 21 | 12 | 18 | $26 |

Harlem | 366 W. 110th St. (bet. Columbus & Manhattan Aves.) |
212-865-6744

Miss Maude's *Southern*
Harlem | 547 Lenox Ave. (bet. 137th & 138th Sts.) | 212-690-3100
www.spoonbreadinc.com

The "chicken's always crispy" at this "deeelicious" Harlem soul foo duo where "happiness is short ribs, collards and beer"; ok, they're nc

uch on looks, but when you're hankering for small-town North
arolina, this is the fastest way to get there.

Mizu Sushi ☒ Japanese | 22 | 14 | 17 | $36

latiron | 29 E. 20th St. (bet. B'way & Park Ave. S.) | 212-505-6688
"Creative rolls with fresh ingredients" at "affordable" prices are
ne forte of this Flatiron Japanese where rustic, exposed-brick
ecor and a "loud" hip-hop soundtrack lure the young and "rambunc-
ous"; it's "extremely popular" on weekends, so brace yourself
or "intolerable lines."

Mo-Bay ◐ Caribbean/Soul Food | 21 | 18 | 15 | $29

Harlem | 17 W. 125th St. (bet. 5th & Lenox Aves.) | 212-876-9300 |
ww.mobayrestaurant.com
"Caribbean–soul food fusion" is the thing at this "laid-back" Harlem
int where the food and the tabs are as "good" as the service is
slow"; there's also "great" live jazz for music aficionados, though the
sound of the band can be overwhelming."

Moda Italian/Mediterranean | – | – | – | E

W 50s | Flatotel | 135 W. 52nd St. (bet. 6th & 7th Aves.) | 212-887-9880 |
ww.flatotel.com
ustic Mediterranean/Italian dishes are served in the sleek dining
oom of this Midtown hotel that's perhaps better known for its out-
oor patio bar, a popular after-work destination set in an atrium
reezeway; although the food's on the pricey side, it does offer a
argain $24.07 lunch.

☐ Modern, The ☒ American/French | 26 | 26 | 24 | $110

W 50s | Museum of Modern Art | 9 W. 53rd St. (bet. 5th & 6th Aves.) |
12-333-1220 | www.themodernnyc.com
et in a "coolly elegant" room overlooking MoMA's sculpture garden,
anny Meyer's "splendid" French–New American is helmed by chef
iabriel Kreuther who "balances tradition with innovation" for prix fixe
eals that are "as sophisticated as any Picasso" (and almost as ex-
ensive); a "thoroughly professional" staff adds to the "formal" scene,
hough the "livelier" adjacent bar offers a "more flexible" small-plates
enu at a "more reasonable" price; N.B. jackets required at dinner.

NEW Moim Ⓜ Korean | – | – | – | M

ark Slope | 206 Garfield Pl. (bet. 7th & 8th Aves.) | Brooklyn | 718-499-8092 |
ww.moimrestaurant.com
ark Slope goes Korean with the arrival of this slick newcomer just off
eventh Avenue featuring modern, moderately priced dishes served in
leek, black brick-lined environs; an appealing back patio is just the
cket for warm-weather dining.

Molyvos ◐ Greek | 22 | 19 | 20 | $53

W 50s | 871 Seventh Ave. (bet. 55th & 56th Sts.) | 212-582-7500 |
ww.molyvos.com
A "reliable favorite" for "delectable" Greek eats, this warm, "welcom-
ng" Midtown taverna is also admired for its "dedicated" servers and
spacious" setting; it works as both an "ideal lunch venue" or dinner
estination "before Carnegie Hall", and though "pricey", the $36 pre-
heater prix fixe is enough of "a steal" to keep the place packed.

	FOOD	DECOR	SERVICE	COST

NEW Momento *Italian* | – | – | – | E |

Astoria | 29-35 Newton Ave. (bet. 28th & 30th Sts.) | Queens | 718-267-2771 | www.momentobistro.com

Rustic French doors lining the facade of this new Astoria Italian sug gest a sleepy little country bistro, but inside are several dining areas a well as two bars; a sizable wine list and occasional live entertainmen keep the energy level high.

Momofuku Noodle Bar *Noodle Shop* | 24 | 13 | 16 | $27 |

E Village | 163 First Ave. (bet. 10th & 11th Sts.) | 212-475-7899 | www.eatmomofuku.com

David Chang's "addictive" noodle soups and pork buns keep th "hordes" coming to this "affordable" Japanese-inspired East Village a "necessary foodie experience" with waits "no matter when you go" sure, it's "absurdly small" and service can be "harried", but "it couldn be more delicious."

Momofuku Ssäm Bar ◑ *American/Korean* | 24 | 16 | 18 | $33 |

E Village | 207 Second Ave. (13th St.) | 212-254-3500 | www.eatmomofuku.com

Think "haute cuisine in blue jeans" to get the gist of David Chang's Nev American–Korean yearling, a "simple" East Villager with "more space than his Noodle Bar but the same "amazing blend of flavors"; "real deal" burritolike *ssäms* are offered for lunch and "gutsy" seasonal con coctions for dinner, but either way, you can expect "crushing crowds.

Momoya *Japanese* | 24 | 20 | 18 | $41 |

Chelsea | 185 Seventh Ave. (21st St.) | 212-989-4466

"Skillful" sushi chefs whip up "wonderfully inventive" maki paired wit "great sake" at this "refined" Chelsea Japanese; while the "minimalist decor lies somewhere between "cool" and "cold", the warm reactiol from locals is translating into "increasing waits."

Monkey Bar 🅱 *American* | – | – | – | E |

E 50s | Elysée Hotel | 60 E. 54th St. (bet. Madison & Park Aves.) | 212-838-2600 | www.theglaziergroup.com

Reinvented yet again, this longtime fixture in Midtown's Elysée Hote is now helmed by chef Patricia Yeo, who's fashioned a New Americar menu inflected with subtle Asian touches; the stylish room, reminis cent of a plush 1940s supper club, oozes enough retro charm to dis tract from the very up-to-the-minute pricing, while the adjacent ba continues to host all kinds of youthful monkey business.

Mon Petit Cafe *French* | 18 | 14 | 18 | $36 |

E 60s | 801 Lexington Ave. (62nd St.) | 212-355-2233 | www.monpetitcafe.com

"Convenient to Bloomie's" and "perfect for ladies of a certain age" this "lace-curtain" UES bistro "serves the neighborhood well" wit "tasty", "reasonably priced" French fare; popular for lunch, it' "calmer" at dinner.

Monster Sushi *Japanese* | 18 | 10 | 15 | $31 |

Chelsea | 158 W. 23rd St. (bet. 6th & 7th Aves.) | 212-620-9131 ◑

W 40s | 22 W. 46th St. (bet. 5th & 6th Aves.) | 212-398-7707

(continued)

Monster Sushi

W Village | 535 Hudson St. (Charles St.) | 646-336-1833 |
www.monstersushi.com

The "name says it all" at this Japanese threesome where the "ridiculously large" rolls and "mounds" of sashimi are "monstrous" enough to be "borderline silly"; "Morimoto it's not", but tabs are "moderate" enough to blunt the "so-so" service and "stark" settings.

Montparnasse ◑ French

19 | 18 | 18 | $45

50s | The Pod Hotel | 230 E. 51st St. (bet. 2nd & 3rd Aves.) | 212-758-6633 | www.montparnasseny.com

A "steady standby", this "traditional" Midtown French gratifies with "excellent coq au vin" and a "well-priced" $22.95 pre-theater deal; its "mature" clientele appreciates the "deferential" service and tables spaced "far enough apart" to allow "intimate conversation."

NEW Morandi ◑ Italian

19 | 18 | 19 | $54

W Village | 211 Waverly Pl. (Charles St.) | 212-627-7575 |
www.morandiny.com

Über-restaurateur Keith McNally does Italian for the first time at this "buzzy" new Village trattoria featuring his usual transporting atmospherics – in this case, "Tuscan farmhouse" chic; behind the stoves, Jody Williams (ex Gusto) turns out an "inventive" seasonal menu that would be "secondary to the scene" only here.

Moran's Chelsea American

18 | 19 | 19 | $42

Chelsea | 146 10th Ave. (19th St.) | 212-627-3030 |
www.moranschelsea.com

"Old-fashioned in every way", this Chelsea "trip back in time" purveys "hearty" Americana in a "Waterford-and-wood-burning-fireplace" setting; add in "accommodating" staffers who "pour a great Guinness" and the "whole is definitely equal to more than the sum of its parts."

Morgan, The Ⓜ American

20 | 23 | 21 | $41

Murray Hill | The Morgan Library & Museum | 225 Madison Ave. (bet. 36th & 37th Sts.) | 212-683-2130

Murray Hill's revamped Morgan Library offers two lunchtime venues: "charming" atrium cafe or J.P. Morgan's "clubbier" former dining room; both feature a moderately priced New American menu that "blends old NY and modern influences."

◪ Morimoto Japanese

24 | 26 | 22 | $82

Chelsea | 88 10th Ave. (bet. 15th & 16th Sts.) | 212-989-8883 |
www.morimotonyc.com

"It's showtime" at this "flashy" West Chelsea Japanese where Iron Chef Masaharu Morimoto's "mouthwatering delicacies" "vie for attention" with Tadao Ando's "spectacular", "ultramodern" interiors and the "futuristic loos"; even though it "costs a bundle", many urge you to "splurge for omakase."

Morrell Wine Bar & Cafe American

19 | 16 | 19 | $45

W 40s | 1 Rockefeller Plaza (49th St., bet. 5th & 6th Aves.) | 212-262-7700 | www.morrellwinebar.com

Situated in the "heart of Rockefeller Plaza", this petite, "packed" cafe provides a full-on "view of the Christmas tree" during the holidays and "great people-watching" all year round, particularly from its sidewalk seats; look for an "incredible international wine list" paired with "dependable" albeit "pricey" Americana.

Morton's, The Steakhouse *Steak* | 24 | 20 | 22 | $69 |

E 40s | 551 Fifth Ave. (45th St.) | 212-972-3315 |
www.mortons.com

This costly Midtown chophouse caters to captains of commerce content to pay "primo prices for prime meat" in a dark wood-paneled, oldboy setting; though many "could do without" the "Saran-wrapped show-and-tell presentation – "I know what steak looks like" – at least the waiters are "friendly" about it.

Moustache ●⌿ *Mideastern* | 21 | 11 | 14 | $23 |

E Village | 265 E. 10th St. (bet. Ave. A & 1st Ave.) | 212-228-2022
W Village | 90 Bedford St. (bet. Barrow & Grove Sts.) | 212-229-2220
"Smooth-as-silk hummus" and other "deliciously seasoned" Middle Eastern eats are the draw at these crosstown Village siblings; "cheap tabs make them always "crowded", and though both are "tiny", the East Side branch spreads out with a bonus "back garden."

Moutarde *French* | 18 | 19 | 16 | $36 |

Park Slope | 239 Fifth Ave. (Carroll St.) | Brooklyn | 718-623-3600
"Young, carefree Park Slope" types say this "surprisingly durable" Gallic bistro offers a "well-executed" menu of *cuisine de maman* in a "French Disneyland" setting; "indifferent service" and "tight quarters" detract, though for most it's an easily affordable "Plan B."

Mr. Chow ● *Chinese* | 20 | 19 | 18 | $74 |

E 50s | 324 E. 57th St. (bet. 1st & 2nd Aves.) | 212-751-9030
Mr. Chow Tribeca ● *Chinese*
TriBeCa | 121 Hudson St. (N. Moore St.) | 212-965-9500 |
www.mrchow.com
Michael Chow's "perennial see-and-be-seen" Midtown Chinese continues after 29 years to feed "zingy" Sino specialties and "flowing lychee martinis" to a "dressy", often celeb-studded, crowd; trouble is the waiters may insist on "ordering for you", resulting in "three times what you can eat at four times what you should pay"; N.B. the year-old TriBeCa spin-off has yet to win a following.

☑ Mr. K's *Chinese* | 23 | 24 | 23 | $57 |

E 50s | 570 Lexington Ave. (51st St.) | 212-583-1668 |
www.mrks.com
"Not Chinatown" by a long shot, this "glam" Midtown Chinese is known for "retro", "refined" dishes served by a "top-shelf" staff in a "Pepto-Bismol pink" deco setting; its "wannabe-emperor-and-empress" crowd shrugs off the "pricey"-for-the-genre tabs.

Mr. Tang *Chinese* | 19 | 13 | 15 | $27 |

Chinatown | 50 Mott St. (Bayard St.) | 212-233-8898
Brighton Beach | 2650 Coney Island Ave. (Ave. X) | Brooklyn |
718-769-9444 ⌿
"Reliable sources" of "fresh seafood" and other "traditional" Chinese cookery, this Brighton Beach/C-town duo is "trying to be gourmet, but isn't quite there yet"; modest pricing makes the "rude" service and crude decor easier to overlook.

	FOOD	DECOR	SERVICE	COST

Mughlai ● Indian
W 70s | 320 Columbus Ave. (75th St.) | 212-724-6363

19 | 13 | 17 | $32

Having "stood the test of time", this "solid" UWS Indian continues to serve "satisfying", "spiced-just-right" standards for "affordable" tabs; the staff may be "underseasoned" and decor "no-frills", but you "can't beat the location."

My Moon Mediterranean
Williamsburg | 184 N. 10th St. (bet. Bedford & Driggs Aves.) | Brooklyn | 718-599-7007 | www.mymoonnyc.com

▽ 19 | 28 | 20 | $34

Perhaps Williamsburg's "best place for a first date", this "romantic" Mediterranean boasts an "amazing outdoor garden" as well as a "Gothic" "converted-warehouse" interior; while the modestly priced menu is quite "good", many wish it "matched the ambiance."

Nam Vietnamese
TriBeCa | 110 Reade St. (W. B'way) | 212-267-1777 | www.namnyc.com

22 | 18 | 20 | $39

"Highly satisfying" food with "beguiling flavor combinations" draws "great-looking" folk to this "civilized" Vietnamese parked in an "out-of-the-way" TriBeCa address; "pleasant" servers and "chic" digs make it "feel a lot more expensive than it is."

Nana ✍ Asian Fusion
Park Slope | 155 Fifth Ave. (bet. Lincoln & St. Johns Pls.) | Brooklyn | 718-230-3749 | www.nana-parkslope.com

21 | 18 | 19 | $28

"You can make a meal of the appetizers alone" at this "consistent", cash-only Park Slope Asian fusion specialist where the extensive offerings are all "easy on the wallet"; it "would be even better without the DJ", but the "spectacular" garden is a respite from the "loud" interior.

Nanni ⓩ Italian
E 40s | 146 E. 46th St. (bet. Lexington & 3rd Aves.) | 212-697-4161 | www.nannirestaurant.com

24 | 15 | 22 | $54

"As delicious today as it was decades ago", this "old-world" vet just east of Grand Central vends rather "pricey" Northern Italiana via old-school waiters "full of personality"; it feels like "home away from home" to fans, in part due to the "elbow-to-elbow" seating and "land-that-time-forgot" decor.

Naples 45 ⓩ Italian
E 40s | MetLife Bldg. | 200 Park Ave. (45th St.) | 212-972-7001 | www.patinagroup.com

17 | 14 | 16 | $34

Brick-oven pizza is "the thing to order" at this "large", inexpensive Italian that's almost as "loud" as the adjacent Grand Central Terminal; it's "convenient" for commuters and "informal business lunches", so just ignore the "harried" staff and "Pottery Barn" decor; closed weekends.

Native Eclectic
Harlem | 161 Lenox Ave. (118th St.) | 212-665-2525

▽ 19 | 16 | 15 | $32

Happy habitués hail this "hip" Harlem haunt for its "unusual" Eclectic menu that "stretches across the continents" yet still supplies some serious "soul-food flair"; fair pricing and "outdoor seating" (a rarity in this "gentrifying neighborhood") offset the "small" setting and any lack of service.

	FOOD	DECOR	SERVICE	COST

NEW Natsumi ◗ *Italian/Japanese* — | — | — | E

W 50s | Amsterdam Court Hotel | 226 W. 50th St. (bet. B'way & 8th Ave.) |
212-258-2988

From the team behind Haru comes this original new Theater Distric
Italo-Japanese fusion practitioner whose menu includes the likes o
green tea ravioli; the two-part setting features a sushi bar/dining room
separated by a hotel lobby from the lounge/raw bar.

Neary's ◗ *Pub Food* 15 | 11 | 17 | $42

E 50s | 358 E. 57th St. (1st Ave.) | 212-751-1434

The nearest NYC comes to having a real leprechaun, host-owne
Jimmy Neary "seems to know everyone on the East Side" and feed
them all at this "classic" Midtown pub where the "filling", "old
fashioned" Irish grub comes with a side of "nostalgia"; its "crew o
characters – employees included" – is worth the price of admission.

Negril ◗ *Caribbean/Jamaican* 20 | 17 | 16 | $34

Chelsea | 362 W. 23rd St. (bet. 8th & 9th Aves.) | 212-807-6411
G Village | 70 W. Third St. (bet. La Guardia Pl. & Thompson St.) |
212-477-2804 Ⓜ

"Fiery jerk" and other "scrumptious" spicy specialties transport
Manhattanites to Jamaica at these "lively" tropical twins where "ur-
ban cool and Caribbean heat" collide; while the Village outpost is
larger and more upscale, both share "slow" island service.

Nello ◗ *Italian* 19 | 17 | 16 | $79

E 60s | 696 Madison Ave. (bet. 62nd & 63rd Sts.) | 212-980-9099

It helps to "be a celebrity to be seated and served well" at this Madison
Avenue Northern Italian; while the food's "refined", the crowd "Euro'
and the mood "buzzy", mega-"attitude" and "wild overpricing" make
the experience a hell no to average Joes.

NEW Nelson Blue ◗ *New Zealand* — | — | — | M

Seaport | 233 Front St. (Peck Slip) | 212-346-9090 |
www.nelsonblue.com

Docked on burgeoning Front Street, this New Zealand gastropub is
adding to what may become the Seaport's new Restaurant Row; expect
Kiwi dishes at publike prices paired with antipodean suds served in
airy digs adorned with handcrafted tribal objects like a Maori war canoe

Nëo Sushi ◗ *Japanese* 22 | 17 | 19 | $54

W 80s | 2298 Broadway (83rd St.) | 212-769-1003 |
www.neosushi.com

"Creative, not-so-traditional" sushi graces the menu of this UWS
Japanese, a "Nobu wannabe" whose "adventurous" approach and
"pretty-to-look-at" plates amaze maki mavens; a few find it "overly nëo"
and "exorbitantly priced", but it's "wonderful for a special splurge."

Neptune Room *Seafood* 22 | 19 | 21 | $49

W 80s | 511 Amsterdam Ave. (bet. 84th & 85th Sts.) | 212-496-4100 |
www.theneptuneroom.com

"Fresh-off-the-boat", "still-wriggling" seafood is the catch of the day
at this UWS seafooder also equipped with a "basic raw bar"; though
"a little expensive for the quality", compensations include "friendly
service", "cool loos" and a "great brunch – without a line."

	FOOD	DECOR	SERVICE	COST

ero ● *Italian* — 20 | 18 | 17 | $42

eatpacking | 46 Gansevoort St. (Greenwich St.) | 212-675-5224 |
ww.neronyc.com

omething real" in the "overhyped Meatpacking District", this "un-
rrated" Italian serves "solid" food for "decent" dough without the
ttitude" or "glitz" of its nearby rivals; a high-ceilinged, brick-lined
tting and "dim lighting" make it "romantic", despite "no-
rsonality" service.

ew Bo-Ky ⇱ *Noodle Shop* — ▽ 22 | 5 | 12 | $12

inatown | 80 Bayard St. (bet. Mott & Mulberry Sts.) | 212-406-2292
doesn't get cheaper or more authentic" than this C-town noodle
op where Chinese and Vietnamese super soups make "jury duty"
ore palatable; though "decor and service are nonexistent", it's "al-
ays crowded" given its "best-value" tabs and tastes.

ew Green Bo ●⇱ *Chinese* — 22 | 5 | 12 | $18

inatown | 66 Bayard St. (bet. Elizabeth & Mott Sts.) | 212-625-2359
ublime" soup dumplings and other "heavenly" Shanghainese spe-
alties spur the "lines" at this Chinatown "hole-in-the-wall"; "shock-
gly low" tabs make up for "no atmosphere whatsoever", "indifferent
rvice" and "sharing tables with strangers."

ew Leaf Cafe Ⓜ *American* — 20 | 23 | 17 | $40

ashington Heights | Fort Tryon Park | 1 Margaret Corbin Dr. (190th St.) |
2-568-5323 | www.nyrp.org
ou won't believe you're in Manhattan" at this "picturesque" New
nerican in Fort Tryon Park, a "little vacation from the city" with "sur-
isingly good" food and a "magical terrace"; having the talented Scott
mpbell (@SQC) signed on as executive chef is a good omen.

ew York Burger Co. *Hamburgers* — 18 | 8 | 11 | $13

atiron | 303 Park Ave. S. (bet. 23rd & 24th Sts.) | 212-254-2727
atiron | 678 Sixth Ave. (bet. 21st & 22nd Sts.) | 212-229-1404
ww.newyorkburgerco.com
reshly prepared" patties that "don't skimp" on the meat backed up by
and-cut fries" and "thick shakes" make these Flatiron "burger facto-
es" a "not-bad backup" when Shake Shack is backed up; too bad the
cor and service "don't match the food quality."

ha Trang *Vietnamese* — 21 | 7 | 15 | $16

inatown | 148 Centre St. (bet. Walker & White Sts.) | 212-941-9292
inatown | 87 Baxter St. (bet. Bayard & Canal Sts.) | 212-233-5948
ese "no-nonsense" Chinatown Vietnamese offer "delectable" spe-
alties "sautéed with just the right amount of piquancy" and sold for
ock-bottom" dough; even though the decor's "questionable", "hus-
ng" servers "will have you in and out so quickly it won't matter."

ice Matin ● *French/Mediterranean* — 20 | 18 | 17 | $45

70s | 201 W. 79th St. (Amsterdam Ave.) | 212-873-6423 |
ww.nicematinnyc.com
"touch of the Riviera on 79th Street", this "breezy" French-Med
stro is a "popular" stop for "*très UWS*" types seeking "satisfying",
idpriced repasts; the "cheery" vibe and "faux brasserie gestalt"
ercome a staff with "turnover higher than *The Apprentice*."

	FOOD	DECOR	SERVICE	COST

Nick & Stef's Steakhouse ⓧ *Steak*
`22` `18` `21` `$60`

Garment District | 9 Penn Plaza (enter on 33rd St., bet. 7th & 8th Aves.) | 212-563-4444 | www.patinagroup.com

"Convenient" to both Penn Station and MSG (with a "private entrance to the arena no less), this Midtown carnivorium serves "juicy" steaks a "mostly male" audience; maybe it "could use more spark", but it's "better than you'd expect" with "fast service" to get you to the game on tim

Nick and Toni's Cafe *Mediterranean*
`18` `14` `17` `$49`

W 60s | 100 W. 67th St. (bet. B'way & Columbus Ave.) | 212-496-4000 | www.nickandtoniscafe.com

East Hampton meets the UWS at this "dependable" yet "pricey" Me a "cozy" spin-off that's "not as glitzy or trendy" as the Long Island ori inal; a "wood-burning oven" lends flavor to "everything from pizza fish", though the service could stand some fire under it.

Nick's *Pizza*
`24` `13` `17` `$23`

E 90s | 1814 Second Ave. (94th St.) | 212-987-5700 ◗
Forest Hills | 108-26 Ascan Ave. (bet. Austin & Burns Sts.) | Queens 718-263-1126 ⊟

"Superlative" thin-crust pizzas with "charred, crispy crusts" an "primo" toppings "make the world a better place" at this pizzeria pai sure, the ambiance is "very basic" and staffers "seem trained to avo smiling", but "who cares" with pies and prices this "heavenly"?

Nicky's Vietnamese Sandwiches ⊟ *Sandwiches*
`21` `5` `15` `$9`

E Village | 150 E. Second St. (Ave. A) | 212-388-1088
Boerum Hill | 311 Atlantic Ave. (bet. Hoyt & Smith Sts.) | Brooklyn | 718-855-8838 Ⓜ

"Tiny" is putting it mildly at these "no-frills" Vietnamese storefron cranking out "exceptional" *banh mi* sandwiches and "homemade len onade" to a "mostly take-out" crowd; granted, they're "nothing fancy but the "dirt-cheap" tabs make them just right for a "quick bite."

Nicola's ◗ *Italian*
`22` `16` `21` `$58`

E 80s | 146 E. 84th St. (bet. Lexington & 3rd Aves.) | 212-249-9850

A "neighborhood joint" in the "richest zip code in the country", th UES Italian draws "Dalton and Spence parents" with its "elevated cooking and "skilled" service; still, it's "on the expensive side", an "best if they know you" – otherwise you may be "ignored."

99 Miles to Philly ◗⊟ *Cheese Steaks*
`18` `6` `14` `$11`

E Village | 94 Third Ave. (bet. 12th & 13th Sts.) | 212-253-2700 | www.99milestophilly.net

South Philly "seems closer than 99 miles" away at this East Village where "decent replicas" of the city's trademark gooey, "drippy" chees steak sandwich keep the "faithful" coming; given its "cheap prices", n one cares about the "slow" service and authentically absent decor.

Ninja *Japanese*
▽ `19` `25` `21` `$68`

TriBeCa | 25 Hudson St. (bet. Duane & Reade Sts.) | 212-274-8500 | www.ninjanewyork.com

"More theme park than restaurant", this "entertaining" TriBeC Japanese looks like a mountainside "Ninja village" where "better tha xpected" food is served by a "funny" staff performing "bonus" magic icks; it's "delightfully tacky" if "unbelievably pricey", and works best ith "kids" in tow.

	FOOD	DECOR	SERVICE	COST

'ino's ❶ *Italian* — 21 | 18 | 21 | $55

70s | 1354 First Ave. (bet. 72nd & 73rd Sts.) | 212-988-0002 | ww.ninosnyc.com

NEW Nino's Bellissima Pizza *Italian*

40s | 890 Second Ave. (bet. 47th & 48th Sts.) | 212-355-5540

Nino's Positano *Italian*

40s | 890 Second Ave. (bet. 47th & 48th Sts.) | 212-355-5540 | ww.ninospositano.com

Nino's Tuscany *Italian*

W 50s | 117 W. 58th St. (bet. 6th & 7th Aves.) | 212-757-8630 | ww.ninostuscany.com

ans of this Italian mini-chain single out the UES original for "celebrity ghtings" and "snazzy jazz", "cozy" Tuscany for "beautiful murals" nd "excellent piano", and the "comfortable" Positano for "quiet con-ersation" (plus brick-oven pizza from new offshoot Bellissima); all lo-ations share "classic" cooking, "seamless service" and serious tabs.

Nippon ☒ *Japanese* ▽ 22 | 17 | 20 | $49

50s | 155 E. 52nd St. (bet. Lexington & 3rd Aves.) | 212-758-0226 | ww.restaurantnippon.com

ne of NYC's first sushi restaurants, this "old-style" East Midtowner as been serving "traditional" Japanese fare since 1963; it's just as reliable" (and "pricey") today, though the "classic", cypress-lined igs are either "dated" or "aging gracefully", depending on who's talking.

NEW Noble Food & Wine ☒ *American* – | – | – | M

NoLita | 7 Spring St. (bet. Bowery & Elizabeth St.) | 212-777-0877

t this new NoLita wine bar/eatery you'll find locally sourced New mericana either at a granite-topped bar or in a low-lit, wood-paneled ack room; a state-of-the-art wine preservation system allows oeno-hiles to enjoy by-the-glass samplings of high-end vintages.

� Nobu *Japanese* 27 | 23 | 23 | $82

riBeCa | 105 Hudson St. (Franklin St.) | 212-219-0500

ヨ Nobu, Next Door ❶ *Japanese*

riBeCa | 105 Hudson St. (bet. Franklin & N. Moore Sts.) | 12-334-4445

ww.myriadrestaurantgroup.com

Exquisite", "palate-awakening" Japanese-Peruvian delicacies gratify ourmets at this ever-"buzzing" TriBeCan that hosts a "who's who" rowd right out of an "episode of *Entourage*"; constants include "infor-native" service and "one big bill" at meal's end, but "getting a table is problem – unless you're Cameron Diaz"; its more "casual" Next Door ibling is "less expensive" and "every bit as delicious", "without the eservation fuss" since it only takes walk-ins.

ヨ Nobu 57 ❶ *Japanese* 26 | 24 | 22 | $82

W 50s | 40 W. 57th St. (bet. 5th & 6th Aves.) | 212-757-3000 | ww.myriadrestaurantgroup.com

Differentiated from its Downtown sire by its "bigger" dimensions, David Rockwell's "stunning" design and somewhat "easier" reservations, this "glam" Midtowner serves the same "provocative" Japanese-Peruvian fusion fare for the same "spendy" tabs; but even this "hedge-fund cafeteria" lacks the original's "intimacy", the "hip folk, "tourists" and "movie stars" in attendance don't seem to mind.

Nocello *Italian* | 21 | 16 | 21 | $49 |

W 50s | 257 W. 55th St. (bet. B'way & 8th Ave.) | 212-713-0224 | www.nocello.net

"Carnegie Hall convenience" is the main selling point of this Midtow Tuscan where the midpriced food is "well prepared" and the "genial service "fast paced"; maybe the "old-world" decor could stand a re furb, but it's still plenty "popular."

Noche Mexicana *Mexican* | ▽ 22 | 9 | 16 | $18 |

W 100s | 852 Amsterdam Ave. (bet. 101st & 102nd Sts.) | 212-662-6900 | www.noche-mexicana.com

For "addictive", "real-deal" Mexicana, the "college crowd" join Columbia-area locals at this "tiny hole-in-the-wall" where prices ar such a "bargain" that nobody minds the strictly "no-frills" digs and oftentimes "slow" service.

NoHo Star ● *American* | 18 | 15 | 16 | $31 |

NoHo | 330 Lafayette St. (Bleecker St.) | 212-925-0070 | www.nohostar.cor Still twinkling "after all these years", this low-cost NoHo "stalwart dishes up "solid", "dependable" New American grub "morning, noo and night" while adding a "Chinese slant" come suppertime; locals lik its "homey" feel and overlook the "din" and "below-average" service.

Nomad *African* | ▽ 22 | 19 | 21 | $33 |

E Village | 78 Second Ave. (4th St.) | 212-253-5410 | www.nomadny.com Wanderers seeking "authentic" North African fare report that thi East Village yearling turns out "savory" tagines and other "aromatic" dishes in "cramped but stylish" digs; better yet, it's "value priced" and staffed by a "well-intentioned" crew.

NEW NoNO Kitchen *Cajun/Creole* | ▽ 19 | 16 | 19 | $31 |

Park Slope | 293 Seventh Ave. (bet. 7th & 8th Sts.) | Brooklyn | 718-369-8348 Bringing "Bourbon Street to Brooklyn", this "change-of-pace" Park Slope newcomer dispenses "satisfying" Cajun-Creole eats way north of New Orleans; though it's still "ironing out some kinks", "helpful service and "down-home value" suggest it's "a comer."

Noodle Pudding ⓂΞ *Italian* | 24 | 17 | 21 | $36 |

Brooklyn Heights | 38 Henry St. (bet. Cranberry & Middagh Sts.) | Brooklyn | 718-625-3737

A "cast of regulars" forms "lines out the door" for the "delectable" "affordable" home cooking at this "loud" and "crowded" Brooklyn Heights Italian; "above-and-beyond service" embellishes its glow, tarnished only by the "bummer" no-reservations policy.

Nook ●Ξ *Eclectic* | 22 | 12 | 17 | $30 |

W 50s | 746 Ninth Ave. (bet. 50th & 51st Sts.) | 212-247-5500 | www.nynook.com

Though "just as tiny as the name suggests", this Hell's Kitchen Eclectic delivers "big tastes" with a "short but fabulous menu"; the BYO policy compensates for the "cramped" quarters and staff "attitude."

	FOOD	DECOR	SERVICE	COST

rma's *American* — 25 | 19 | 21 | $36

50s | Le Parker Meridien | 118 W. 57th St. (bet. 6th & 7th Aves.) | 2-708-7460 | www.parkermeridien.com

y, wake up! – "astounding" breakfasts and brunches are served at s "swanky" Midtown New American where the "good-humored ff" keeps its "power-player" crowd happy; sure, it "costs" and can : "crowded as the dickens", but "where else can you get oatmeal lée" – or a $1,000 caviar omelet?

rth Square *American* — 22 | 18 | 21 | $45

illage | Washington Square Hotel | 103 Waverly Pl. (MacDougal St.) | 2-254-1200 | www.northsquareny.com

"under-the-radar" subterranean "surprise", this "grown-up" New erican may be the "best unhip place in the Village"; given the "styl-" cooking, "courteous" service and "gentle prices", it's no wonder s plead "don't tell anyone."

otaro *Italian* — 20 | 16 | 21 | $36

rray Hill | 635 Second Ave. (bet. 34th & 35th Sts.) | 212-686-3400 | ww.notaroristorante.com

en it comes to "reliable finds", this Murray Hill Tuscan "sleeper" is preciated for its "well-prepared standards", "solicitous service" and argain" tabs (especially that $19.95 early-bird); regulars say the mily atmosphere" is perfect for "relaxing and lingering."

ovecento ● *Argentinean/Steak* — ▽ 22 | 17 | 17 | $41

Ho | 343 W. Broadway (bet. Broome & Grand Sts.) | 212-925-4706 | vw.novecentogroup.com

ve for its "fantastic" Argentine steaks, this SoHo "standby" is the pposite of a standard steakhouse" – "no suits, no porterhouse and big bills", just "flavorful" fare, "laid-back service" and a "very wntown scene" that only "gets loud when there's soccer on TV."

ovitá *Italian* — 24 | 19 | 22 | $53

amercy | 102 E. 22nd St. (bet. Lexington Ave. & Park Ave. S.) | 2-677-2222 | www.novitanyc.com

ramercy's secret winner", this "elegant-casual" Northern Italian st keeps getting better" with "high-quality" cooking, "gracious ser- e" and an "intimate" air; since it's "across from a major modeling ency", keep your eye out for random mannequins drifting in.

urnberger Bierhaus *German* — ▽ 21 | 16 | 20 | $35

aten Island | 817 Castleton Ave. (Davis Ave.) | 718-816-7461 | vw.nurnbergerbierhaus.com

lks with "Teutonic appetites" say this "old-world" German pub on aten Island's North Shore doles out "tremendous portions" of "au- entic" grub washed down with "great" beer; though on the "small" de, it's home to a "boisterous" bar scene.

yonya ●⍧ *Malaysian* — 22 | 12 | 13 | $21

tle Italy | 194 Grand St. (bet. Mott & Mulberry Sts.) | 212-334-3669 **nset Park** | 5323 Eighth Ave. (54th St.) | Brooklyn | 718-633-0808 ww.penangusa.com

nusual spices" make for "fantastic" Malaysian meals at this "de- rvedly popular" Little Italy/Sunset Park pair that's "not for the timid

palate" ("be brave and enjoy"); fans ignore the "spotty servic
and "no-credit-card" policy since the price point is "almost t
cheap to believe."

Oceana ☒ *American/Seafood*   26 | 23 | 24 | $93

E 50s | 55 E. 54th St. (bet. Madison & Park Aves.) | 212-759-5941 |
www.oceanarestaurant.com

Dining's "still shipshape" at this pricey Midtown New American, t
"kingfish" of seafood with "delectable" fresh fare heading the "s
perb", $78 prix fixe–only menu; "doting service" and a "soothing na
tical setting" ("portholes and all") make for an experience that's
transporting you can almost feel the salt spray.

Ocean Grill ◐ *Seafood*   23 | 20 | 20 | $51

W 70s | 384 Columbus Ave. (bet. 78th & 79th Sts.) | 212-579-230(
www.brguestrestaurants.com

"Fail-safe seafood" so fresh it's "still flapping" is the signature of Ste
Hanson's "ocean-liner"-like UWS poisson palace where a "hap
vibe" and an "accommodating" crew have fans angling for reserv
tions; it can be "noisy", but the "bargain" $24.07 lunch prix fixe a
"lovely brunch" are a "catch."

Odeon ◐ *American/French*   19 | 18 | 18 | $44

TriBeCa | 145 W. Broadway (bet. Duane & Thomas Sts.) | 212-233-0507
www.theodeonrestaurant.com

Ever the "late-night" dining "landmark", this TriBeCa "trailblazer" pr
sents "well-prepared" Franco-American bistro fare "without prete
sion"; it's still "a bit of a scene" with a smattering of "celebs" pos
against an "art deco" backdrop, though regulars say the "later you g
the better it is."

O.G. ◐ *Pan-Asian*   ▽ 23 | 15 | 23 | $35

E Village | 507 E. Sixth St. (bet. Aves. A & B) | 212-477-4649

"Throw away your old ideas" about Pan-Asian fare: the "innovativ
menu at this "creative little" East Village "gem" trumps the "tigh
seating and "simple" decor; "terrific service" and "good value" ha
made it a "solid neighborhood favorite."

Old Homestead *Steak*   23 | 17 | 20 | $67

Meatpacking | 56 Ninth Ave. (bet. 14th & 15th Sts.) | 212-242-904(
www.theoldhomesteadsteakhouse.com

This circa-1868 Meatpacking District chop shop earned its spurs te
dering "flawless", "William Howard Taft–size" portions of beef th
are "worth the weighty price"; its "old-school character" extends
both decor and service, but there's modernization afoot via a ne
sidewalk cafe dubbed Prime Burger, vending gourmet patties.

Olea *Mediterranean*   ▽ 20 | 20 | 19 | $33

Fort Greene | 171 Lafayette Ave. (Adelphi St.) | Brooklyn | 718-643-7003
www.oleabrooklyn.com

It's "hard to go wrong" ordering from the "ambitious" menu of "cla
sic" Mediterranean tapas and main courses at this "friendly" Fo
Greene spot; abetted by a "well-chosen" wine list, the "low-key, lo
lit" room can turn "surprisingly romantic" after dark – fortunately t
bill won't disrupt that mood.

| | FOOD | DECOR | SERVICE | COST |

liva ● *Spanish* — ▽ 20 | 14 | 17 | $34

S | 161 E. Houston St. (Allen St.) | 212-228-4143 | www.olivanyc.com

r "tapas galore" tempered with some "good sangria", try this LES
asque where the modest pricing, "great bartenders" and overall "fun
mosphere" make for "lively" dining; more sedate types caution the
ood is good if you can take the noise."

lives *Mediterranean* — 22 | 21 | 20 | $57

nion Sq | W Union Sq. | 201 Park Ave. S. (17th St.) | 212-353-8345 |
ww.toddenglish.com

"champion" at putting together "well-crafted" meals, chef Todd
nglish "knows how to do it right" at his "modern" Med in the W Union
quare Hotel; though a few find it "not as fantastic as the prices would
ggest", the "busy bar scene" puts plenty of "electricity in the air."

llie's *Chinese* — 16 | 9 | 13 | $21

EW **W 40s** | Manhattan Plaza | 411 W. 42nd St. (bet. 9th & 10th Aves.) |
2-868-6588

60s | 1991 Broadway (bet. 67th & 68th Sts.) | 212-595-8181 ●
80s | 2315 Broadway (84th St.) | 212-362-3111 ●
100s | 2957 Broadway (116th St.) | 212-932-3300 ●

renetic and crowded", this "cheap 'n' cheerful" West Side foursome
famed for "decent" Chinese food served so fast "you arrive at 7 and
e out by 6:45"; those opposed to "dingy" digs, "wham-bam" vibes
d "grumpy" service advise "order in."

mai *Vietnamese* — 23 | 17 | 18 | $39

helsea | 158 Ninth Ave. (bet. 19th & 20th Sts.) | 212-633-0550 |
ww.omainyc.com

lidden" behind a "nondescript" Chelsea storefront, this "tiny"
etnamese offers "upscale" fare that's "so good they don't need a
gn on the door"; the "simple" setting may be "cramped", but a "nice"
aff and tabs that "won't break the bank" supply the "oh-my" factor.

men ● *Japanese* — ▽ 25 | 19 | 20 | $54

Ho | 113 Thompson St. (bet. Prince & Spring Sts.) | 212-925-8923

elicate", Kyoto-style dishes that "reflect the nuances of Japanese
isine" are the hallmark of this sushi-free SoHo "retreat"; yes, it's "a
t pricey", but where else are patrons so "in awe of the food" they may
· "sitting next to Richard Gere and not even realize it"?

EW **Omido** ● *Japanese* — - | - | - | E

50s | 1695 Broadway (bet. 53rd & 54th Sts.) | 212-247-8110 |
ww.omidonyc.com

tterman groupies now have an upscale option in this small Midtown
panese next to the Ed Sullivan Theater that's been stylishly designed
the AvroKO team; the standard offerings include sushi, sashimi and
oked staples that can be paired with a selection of beer and sake.

monia Cafe ● *Greek* — 19 | 14 | 15 | $20

y Ridge | 7612-14 Third Ave. (bet. 76th & 77th Sts.) | Brooklyn |
8-491-1435

storia | 32-20 Broadway (33rd St.) | Queens | 718-274-6650

veet tooths "forget counting calories" and "indulge" in "scrump-
us" Greek desserts at this Hellenic coffeehouse twosome; the

"relaxing European atmosphere" comes by way of "open-air seating", "good strong coffee" and "unrushed" service that will make you fe you're in Athens.

Once Upon a Tart . . . *Coffeehouse*

22 | 13 | 14 | $15

SoHo | 135 Sullivan St. (bet. Houston & Prince Sts.) | 212-387-8869
www.onceuponatart.com

"Aromatic tarts" are the specialty at this "quaint" SoHo cafe also o fering "wholesome salads", "tasty sandwiches" and other "deliciou goodies"; "mishmash decor", a "cramped" setting and "sourpuss" se vice suggest it may be better to "sit outside."

One *American*

18 | 21 | 17 | $52

Meatpacking | 1 Little W. 12th St. (9th Ave.) | 212-255-9717 |
www.onelw12.com

It's "all about the scene" at this "dark" Meatpacking District resto lounge where "pretty people party", pausing to put away "prett good", pretty pricey New American small plates washed down wit "interesting cocktails"; since it's "more club than restaurant", sit ou side to "hear and be heard."

O'Neals' ◑ *American*

17 | 16 | 19 | $45

W 60s | 49 W. 64th St. (bet. B'way & CPW) | 212-787-4663 |
www.onealsny.com

Located "in the shadow of Lincoln Center", this warm, atmospher "neighborhood tavern" with "tons of tables" and a "hopping bar" turn out "down-to-earth" American "square meals" for fairly "reasonable sums; the staff "gets you out fast for your concert", though word is it best "after the theater crowd leaves."

One 83 *Italian*

21 | 22 | 23 | $48

E 80s | 1608 First Ave. (bet. 83rd & 84th Sts.) | 212-327-4700 |
www.one83restaurant.com

"Adults" seeking "quiet", "civilized" dining head for this midprice UES Northern Italian "sleeper", an "all-around fine" place with "co sistently good food", well-spaced tables and an "eager-to-pleas staff; another plus: a "covered garden that's a treat" in warm weathe

☑ One if by Land, Two if by Sea *American*

23 | 26 | 24 | $89

G Village | 17 Barrow St. (bet. 7th Ave. S. & W. 4th St.) | 212-228-0822
www.oneifbyland.com

"As romantic as they say", this "genteel" Village New American set "Aaron Burr's old carriage house" is made for "proposing in style blending a "beautiful", flower-filled room and "soft piano-playin, with an "elegant" $75 prix fixe menu and "superior service"; "so wh if it costs a bundle", you'll reap the rewards when you get home.

101 *American/Italian*

19 | 19 | 18 | $41

Bay Ridge | 10018 Fourth Ave. (bet. 100th & 101st Sts.) | Brooklyn 718-833-1313 ◑
Staten Island | 3900 Richmond Ave. (Amboy Rd.) |
718-227-3286 ☒

Known best for its "boisterous" "bar scene", this Bay Ridge Italia New American (with a SI offshoot) still delivers "consistently decer fare; there's "people-watching" aplenty via a crowd that ranges fro "yuppies" to *Saturday Night Fever* wannabes.

.07 West *Cajun/Tex-Mex* | 18 | 13 | 17 | $28 |

Washington Heights | 811 W. 187th St. (bet. Ft. Washington & Pinehurst Aves.) | 212-923-3311
W 100s | 2787 Broadway (bet. 107th & 108th Sts.) | 212-864-1555
www.107west.com

Two West Side Cajun-Tex-Mex "standbys" that can be counted on for "large portions" of "tasty" "comfort" fare at "fair prices"; no surprise, they attract lots of "families" and other locals who consider them a "solid" bet despite "tired" decor and "slow" (if "congenial") service.

Ono *Japanese* | 21 | 24 | 19 | $63 |

Meatpacking | Gansevoort Hotel | 18 Ninth Ave. (enter on 13th St., bet. Hudson St. & 9th Ave.) | 212-660-6766 | www.chinagrillmgt.com

Jeffrey Chodorow's "cool" Meatpacking District Japanese is the "gorgeous" backdrop for "super" sushi and robata grill items served either in the "sleek" interior or "tented garden"; it can be "expensive" and a "tad too trendy", but the crowd's "great-looking" and the drinks "stiff."

NEW Open the Sesame ⊅ *Thai* | – | – | – | I |

LES | 198A Orchard St. (bet. Houston & Stanton Sts.) | 212-777-7009

Exotic SE Asian street food is the focus at this unassuming LES Thai whose menu also includes more standard noodle and rice dishes; a nondescript facade and a meditative mood within make it a low-budget alternative to the neighborhood's typically trendy scenes.

Orchard, The ☒ *American* | 24 | 22 | 21 | $51 |

LES | 162 Orchard St. (bet. Rivington & Stanton Sts.) | 212-353-3570 | www.theorchardny.com

"Proving how far the LES has come", this "sophisticated" New American "winner" ("ápizz's sister restaurant") serves "delicious", "Mediterranean-inspired" cuisine in a "calm", "minimalist" room "bathed in an amber glow"; strong points include the "phenomenal flatbreads", "thoughtful service" and "well-spaced tables."

Oriental Garden *Chinese/Seafood* | 24 | 12 | 16 | $30 |

Chinatown | 14 Elizabeth St. (bet. Bayard & Canal Sts.) | 212-619-0085

Setting the "standard for fresh-from-the-tank" seafood, this "dynamite" Chinatown Cantonese also rolls out "limitless dim sum varieties"; the "right price" makes the perpetual "noise", "inattention to decor" and "hurried but hilarious" service more palatable.

Orsay ● *French* | 18 | 20 | 17 | $54 |

70s | 1057 Lexington Ave. (75th St.) | 212-517-6400 | www.orsayrestaurant.com

"Snob appeal" makes the "straightforward" bistro fare all the tastier at this "very UES" French brasserie with an "elegant art nouveau" ambiance; though some are put off by the "high prices" and "attitude français", the "ladies who lunch" trill it "hits just the right note."

Orso ● *Italian* | 23 | 17 | 20 | $54 |

W 40s | 322 W. 46th St. (bet. 8th & 9th Aves.) | 212-489-7212 | www.orsorestaurant.com

There's a "showbiz feeling" in the air at this Restaurant Row Northern Italian where the "wonderful" cooking and "welcoming atmosphere" make it a pre-show "favorite" and an "après-theater" "hangout for the stars"; to get in, go at "off hours" (i.e. lunch), otherwise this can be one of the "toughest tickets" on Broadway.

Osaka *Japanese*

▽ 21 | 16 | 18 | $32

Cobble Hill | 272 Court St. (bet. Degraw & Kane Sts.) | Brooklyn | 718-643-0044 | www.osakany.com

If you like your sushi "huge" and your rolls "monster-size", this "reasonably priced" Cobble Hill Japanese sets the standard for "hip Brooklyn dining"; maybe the decor "needs updating", but the "peaceful" back garden is "wonderful for eating under the stars."

Osso Buco *Italian*

17 | 14 | 17 | $34

E 90s | 1662 Third Ave. (93rd St.) | 212-426-5422
G Village | 88 University Pl. (bet. 11th & 12th Sts.) | 212-645-4525
www.ossobuco2go.com

"Solid, hearty" and "huge" sum up the "reliable" repasts at these "ebullient", "family-style" Italians (think "Carmine's without the fanfare") where "large groups" have "fun sharing"; "cheap enough" tabs defuse the "no-frills" settings and any service deficits.

Osteria al Doge ◑ *Italian*

20 | 17 | 19 | $48

W 40s | 142 W. 44th St. (bet. B'way & 6th Ave.) | 212-944-3643 | www.osteria-doge.com

The "well-managed" staff is "mindful of curtain times" at this "charming" if "high-decibel" "pre-theater standby" off Times Square; its audience applauds the "upscale" Italian cuisine with a "Venetian disposition" and the "balcony seating option" when the "close quarters" get "too lively."

Osteria del Circo ◑ *Italian*

22 | 23 | 21 | $60

W 50s | 120 W. 55th St. (bet. 6th & 7th Aves.) | 212-265-3636 | www.osteriadelcirco.com

"Deluxe" dishes served by a "pro staff" in a "colorful", "circuslike setting" make for "showy" dining at the Maccioni family's "festive" Northern Italian "near Carnegie Hall and City Center"; though a "high price tag" is part of the package, the $25 "prix fixe lunch is a bargain."

Osteria del Sole ◑ *Italian*

21 | 17 | 17 | $43

W Village | 267 W. Fourth St. (Perry St.) | 212-620-6840

"*Authentico*" Sardinian cuisine paired with a winning wine list make this moderately priced Village Italian a "local treasure"; granted, one man's "cozy" is another's "cramped", but there's agreement on the "pleasant" vibe and "accommodating service" by "real Italians."

Osteria Gelsi ◑ *Italian*

24 | 17 | 19 | $45

Garment District | 507 Ninth Ave. (38th St.) | 212-244-0088 | www.gelsiny.com

Despite an "iffy" Garment District location behind Port Authority, this "real-deal" Italian is "worth the journey" for "novel Puglian food that's "cooked with loving care"; "family-run" and "reasonably priced", it's a "delightful change in a changing neighborhood."

Osteria Laguna ◑ *Italian*

21 | 18 | 19 | $43

E 40s | 209 E. 42nd St. (bet. 2nd & 3rd Aves.) | 212-557-0001 | www.osteria-laguna.com

"Above-average" Italian cooking draws "business-lunchers" to this "sunny" Midtowner near the U.N., an "airy" retreat with French doors

at open to the street; a "reasonably priced" wine list plus "courte-
us" service add to the all-around "pleasant" experience, even when
he "noise level" rises.

Ota-Ya Japanese
20 | 15 | 19 | $32

80s | 1572 Second Ave. (bet. 81st & 82nd Sts.) | 212-988-1188 |
www.ota-ya.com

"Everything's fresh and delicious" at this "surprisingly quiet" UES
Japanese "sleeper", a "local sushi joint" that's developing a "loyal following" with its "creative rolls", "inexpensive pricing" and "spot-on
service"; too bad the "bland atmosphere" has some yawning "boring."

Otto ❶ Pizza
22 | 19 | 19 | $38

Village | 1 Fifth Ave. (enter on 8th St., bet. 5th Ave. & University Pl.) |
212-995-9559 | www.ottopizzeria.com

"Top-notch gourmet" pizzas, "lick-the-plate" pastas and a "powerhouse Italian wine list" arrive in a faux "train station" setting at this
"bustling" Batali-Bastianich Village enoteca/pizzeria that's "as good
as Lupa – at half the price and twice the noise"; no surprise, it draws
lots of "kids", "parties" and "rambunctious" types.

d Ouest American
25 | 21 | 22 | $61

V 80s | 2315 Broadway (bet. 83rd & 84th Sts.) | 212-580-8700 |
www.ouestny.com

Upper Westsiders rave about this "polished" New American destination where Tom Valenti's "exceptional" "comfort food with a spark" is
served by a crew of "polite" staffers in a "smart", "1940s-inspired"
setting; it's "not cheap" but "reservations are hard to come by",
because once you settle into one of those "commodious banquettes",
you'll feel "celebratory."

ur Place Chinese
20 | 15 | 19 | $34

50s | 141 E. 55th St. (bet. Lexington & 3rd Aves.) | 212-753-3900 |
www.ourplace-teagarden.com
80s | 1444 Third Ave. (82nd St.) | 212-288-4888 |
www.ourplaceuptown.com

The "always delish", "high-end" Shanghai cuisine at these "white-
tablecloth" Eastsiders may cost "a bit more" but is worth a bit more;
"relaxed" settings and "efficient" service make the "super-fast delivery" beside the point.

utback Steakhouse Steak
14 | 12 | 15 | $32

50s | 919 Third Ave. (enter on 56th St., bet. 2nd & 3rd Aves.) |
212-935-6400
atiron | 60 W. 23rd St. (bet. 5th & 6th Aves.) | 212-989-3122
yker Heights | 1475 86th St. (15th Ave.) | Brooklyn |
718-837-7200
ayside | Bay Terrace | 23-48 Bell Blvd. (26th Ave.) | Queens |
718-819-0908
mhurst | Queens Pl. | 88-01 Queens Blvd. (56th Ave.) | Queens |
718-760-7200
www.outback.com

You'll get a "cookie-cutter" "fill up" at this "faux Australian" steakhouse chain where the "average" chow suffers from "sodium overload"; sure, "you might as well be in Toledo", but "kids love it" so long
as you "order what they do best" – that bloomin' onion.

	FOOD	DECOR	SERVICE	COST

NEW Ovelia *Greek*   ▽ 21 | 21 | 16 | $32

Astoria | 34-01 30th Ave. (bet. 34th & 35th Sts.) | Queens | 718-721-7217
www.ovelia-ny.com

Expect "simple, traditional" food at this "palatable" new Astoria Gree▮
where the vibe's decidedly more "trendy" than the status quo, wi▮
"modern" decor, club music and a fiber optic–embedded bartop; "sau▮
sages ground on the premises" bump up the "authenticity" factor a▮
do those low outer-borough prices.

Oyster Bar ⧆ *Seafood*   21 | 17 | 16 | $46

E 40s | Grand Central | lower level (42nd St. & Vanderbilt Ave.) |
212-490-6650 | www.oysterbarny.com

Though Grand Central's "classic" seafooder has "been there forever▮
it's still "required eating" for anyone hooked on "marvelous, unadu▮
terated fish", "legendary pan roasts", "unsurpassed oysters" and ▮
spectacular white wine list; the "cavernous" underground space an▮
"vaulted tile ceiling" make for a "louder-than-a-train-whistle" exper
ence that's "totally Manhattan."

NEW Pacificana *Chinese*   ▽ 24 | 21 | 22 | $29

Sunset Park | 813 55th St., 2nd fl. (8th Ave.) | Brooklyn |
718-871-2880

More "high class" now than during its last life as Ocean Palace, th▮
Sunset Park address now houses a new Cantonese rolling out some ▮
"NY's best dim sum" in a "lovely", "high-ceilinged" space; "unusu▮
variety" and fair pricing blot out any "minor language problems."

Paladar ◑ *Nuevo Latino*   ▽ 18 | 14 | 17 | $34

LES | 161 Ludlow St. (bet. Houston & Stanton Sts.) | 212-473-3535
www.paladarrestaurant.com

There's "lots of spice for the buck" at this "hip" LES Nuevo Latino,
"festive" venue for chef Aarón Sanchez's "inventive" eats washe▮
down with "*muy bonito*" mojitos; "crazy wait times" on weekends pa▮
quickly enough at the "fun" bar.

Z Palm *Steak*   24 | 17 | 21 | $66

E 40s | 837 Second Ave. (bet. 44th & 45th Sts.) | 212-687-2953 ⧆
E 40s | 840 Second Ave. (bet. 44th & 45th Sts.) | 212-697-5198
W 50s | 250 W. 50th St. (bet. B'way & 8th Ave.) |
212-333-7256 ◑
www.thepalm.com

"Masculine eating" is alive and well at these "boisterous" crosstow▮
chophouses where a "gruff" crew dishes out "gargantuan steaks" an▮
"colossal lobsters" in "macho" surroundings; purists prefer the orig▮
nal, circa-1926 west-side-of-Second-Avenue location, but wherev▮
you wind up, you'd better "have plenty of money in your palm."

Paloma ◑Ⓜ *American*   ▽ 19 | 18 | 19 | $27

Greenpoint | 60 Greenpoint Ave. (bet. Franklin & West Sts.) | Brooklyn
718-349-2400 | www.palomanyc.com

A *Top Chef* contestant crafts an "original" New American menu at th▮
Greenpoint "hipster" joint where the "video projections on the wall"
everything from "Bollywood to Bardot" – are either "brilliant" or "di▮
tracting"; many wonder "is it a club or a restaurant?", but all agree i▮
a great value.

	FOOD	DECOR	SERVICE	COST

NEW Palo Santo *Pan-Latin* ▽ 25 | 23 | 20 | $39

Park Slope | 652 Union St. (bet. 4th & 5th Aves.) | Brooklyn | 718-636-6311 | www.palosanto.us

Adventurous types are "well rewarded" at this "welcome" Park Slope newcomer purveying a "tapas-style" array of "superb" Pan-Latin vittles; "friendly" service, "reasonable rates" and a "gorgeous brownstone" setting complete with a "tropical garden" make this one a "must go."

Pampano *Mexican/Seafood* 25 | 22 | 21 | $54

E 40s | 209 E. 49th St. (bet. 2nd & 3rd Aves.) | 212-751-4545 | www.modernmexican.com

Taking a "quantum leap above your everyday Mexican", this "luscious" Midtowner from chef Richard Sandoval and tenor Plácido Domingo specializes in "complex", "original" seafood that's "beautiful to behold"; add a "bright", split-level setting and "prompt, helpful" staff, and most patrons just "want to sing."

NEW Pamplona ● *Spanish* – | – | – | M

Gramercy | 37 E. 28th St. (bet. Madison Ave. & Park Ave. S.) | 212-213-2328

A reworking of the former fine-dining room Ureña, this new Gramercy Spaniard from chef Alex Ureña is a casual take on its predecessor offering a foam-free, tapas-heavy Basque bistro menu in all-beige, cozy-chic environs; enhancing the pleasant vibe is the decidedly relaxed price point.

Pam Real Thai Food ⊅ *Thai* 22 | 8 | 15 | $22

W 40s | 402 W. 47th St. (bet. 9th & 10th Aves.) | 212-315-4441 ●Ⓜ
W 40s | 404 W. 49th St. (bet. 9th & 10th Aves.) | 212-333-7500
www.pamrealthai.com

At this Hell's Kitchen duo, the "authentically seasoned", truly "tasty" Thai and tempting tabs easily trump the "no-credit-cards" policy, '80s airline terminal" look and service that's "a tad abrupt"; order takeout, and pam!, it's there.

Panino'teca 275 Ⓜ *Italian* ▽ 18 | 16 | 17 | $23

Carroll Gardens | 275 Smith St. (bet. Degraw & Sackett Sts.) | Brooklyn | 718-237-2728 | www.paninoteca275.com

Carroll Gardens locals looking to "lounge with some wine and antipasti" like this "family-friendly" Italian dispensing "inventive panini" as well as "flavorful" entrees; "totally affordable" tabs and a "relaxing" back garden cancel out the "cramped" interior and "spotty" service.

Paola's *Italian* 23 | 19 | 22 | $52

E 80s | 245 E. 84th St. (bet. 2nd & 3rd Aves.) | 212-794-1890 | www.paolasrestaurant.com

Paola Bottero's "warm" greeting sets the tone at this "homey" UES Italian standby known for its "good all-around menu" of traditional classics"; the flower-bedecked room exudes "charm", while sidewalk eating on a "leafy block" is a big bonus.

Papaya King *Hot Dogs* 20 | 4 | 12 | $7

E 80s | 179 E. 86th St. (3rd Ave.) | 212-369-0648 ●⊅
Harlem | 121 W. 125th St. (bet. Lenox & 7th Aves.) | 212-678-4268 ⊅

(continued)

(continued)

Papaya King

W Village | 200 W. 14th St. (7th Ave. S.) | 212-367-8090 ◗
www.papayaking.com

"Tube steak" connoisseurs commend the "juicy" grilled franks paired
with "frothy" potables at these "stand-up", low-down "snack shacks";
forget the "yelling" staff and "gross" decor – it's "hard to say no" when
you're paying "almost nothing" for an "only-in-NY experience."

Pappardella ◗ *Italian*

19	16	18	$36

W 70s | 316 Columbus Ave. (75th St.) | 212-595-7996

Upper Westsiders in need of "comforting Italian" food head to this
perennially "pleasing" pasta palace where the "hearty" portions are
"ample enough for leftovers"; prices are "affordable", the staff
"cordial" and there's "bonus" sidewalk seating when it gets too "loud"
and "close" inside.

Paradou ◗ *French*

19	17	18	$44

Meatpacking | 8 Little W. 12th St. (bet. Greenwich & Washington Sts.) |
212-463-8345 | www.paradounyc.com

Approximating "Marseille in Manhattan", this "intimate" French "oasis" in the Meatpacking District offers well-priced Provençal fare in an
"unpretentious" setting; occasionally "rude" service is forgotten once
you're seated in its "delightful" if "unfancy" all-seasons garden.

Paris Commune *French*

18	18	17	$41

W Village | 99 Bank St. (Greenwich St.) | 212-929-0509 |
www.pariscommune.net

"Everyone looks pretty" at this "charming" Village bistro offering "affordable", "down-to-earth" French food and a "perfect brunch"; some say it's
"gone downhill" after moving from its "old space", yet it's usually
"packed" – go figure; P.S. there's a "sexy, secluded wine bar" downstairs.

Park, The ◗ *Mediterranean*

15	23	14	$41

Chelsea | 118 10th Ave. (bet. 17th & 18th Sts.) | 212-352-3313 |
www.theparknyc.com

Folks flaunting "sunglasses at night" like this "sexy" West Chelsea
"scene" for its "stone fireplaces", hot tubs and a "lovely garden" (the
"main draw"); critics say it's "losing its steam", citing a "mundane"
Med menu and a staff apparently off "auditioning for something" else.

NEW Park Avenue . . . *American*

-	-	-	E

E 60s | 100 E. 63rd St. (bet. Lexington & Park Aves.) | 212-644-1900 |
www.parkavenyc.com

The former Park Avenue Cafe space has morphed into this homage to
the four seasons, where the hip AvroKO-designed decor totally changes
quarterly; the inventive New American cooking is similarly seasonal
and priced to match its tony East Side address.

Park Place *Continental*

∇ 20	15	19	$37

Bronx | 5816 Mosholu Ave. (B'way) | 718-548-0977

"One of Riverdale's better neighborhood restaurants", this "excellent
value" Continental "churns out great specials" that are big enough to
be "shareable"; "pleasant" service keeps longtimers repeating, but
even they concede the "need for a face-lift."

ark Side ● *Italian* 24 | 19 | 21 | $44

orona | 107-01 Corona Ave. (51st Ave.) | Queens | 718-271-9321

"Tuxedo-clad" waiters present "excellent" Italian "classics" at this "old-world" Corona "institution" that's always "mobbed" with a "dolled-up", "pinky-ringed" crowd; "long waits" are the norm, but you an pass the time watching "old men play bocce" across the street.

ark Terrace Bistro *French/Moroccan* ∇ 22 | 20 | 20 | $34

nwood | 4959 Broadway (bet. Isham & 207th Sts.) | 212-567-2828 | www.parkterracebistro.com

"flavorful", "aromatic" fare and a "shadowy", "romantic" ambiance ombine to make this "breath-of-fresh-air" French-Moroccan a "great ate" place in underserved Inwood; "enthusiastic" staffers, "reason-ble" prices and a "downtown ambiance" ice the cake.

arma ● *Italian* 22 | 14 | 20 | $55

70s | 1404 Third Ave. (bet. 79th & 80th Sts.) | 212-535-3520

"f you're a regular, you're family" at this "old-fashioned" Northern alian turning out "pricey", "high-quality" food ferried by "kind wait-rs"; although the storefront setting "could use some updating", its ell-heeled UES crowd likes it as is.

ars Grill House & Bar *Persian* ∇ 21 | 14 | 18 | $32

helsea | 249 W. 26th St. (bet. 7th & 8th Aves.) | 212-929-9860

"good addition to the Chelsea dining scene", this "sweet little" ersian proffers "surprisingly good" kebabs and such for "affordable" bs in a "cafe"-style space; it's "never crowded, but it deserves to be."

ascalou *French* 22 | 14 | 18 | $42

90s | 1308 Madison Ave. (bet. 92nd & 93rd Sts.) | 212-534-7522

"tretch your legs" before squeezing into this Carnegie Hill boîte, a miniature" setting for "terrific French fare" at "fair prices"; service re-ects the "congenial" vibe within, though diners bigger than a "size vo" may want to "snag an outside table."

asha *Turkish* 21 | 18 | 19 | $40

70s | 70 W. 71st St. (bet. Columbus Ave. & CPW) | 212-579-8751 | www.pashanewyork.com

stanbul, here we come": this Lincoln Center–area Turk purveys "well-iced" meals in an "exotic" setting so "dark" you'll need "night vision ggles to read the menu"; "gracious service" seals the deal.

asquale's Rigoletto *Italian* 23 | 17 | 20 | $41

onx | 2311 Arthur Ave. (Crescent Ave.) | 718-365-6644

cals "have a blast" at this "popular" Arthur Avenue "throwback" own for its "generous helpings" of "no-fuss, no-muss" Italian stan-rds; "plenty of hospitality" and pleasing pricing make this "festive" arn of a place" ideal for "family gatherings."

asticcio *Italian* · 19 | 18 | 19 | $38

urray Hill | 447 Third Ave. (bet. 30th & 31st Sts.) | 212-679-2551
EW Glendale | Shops at Atlas Park | 80-00 Cooper Ave. (80th St.) | ueens | 718-417-1544
www.pasticcionyc.com

na favorita" in Murray Hill, this longtime Italian is "full of friendly eople" noshing on "traditional" eats or sampling sparkling vino at

Proseccheria, its wine bar; early visitors to the new Glendale offshoot in the Shops at Atlas Park say it's a "nice choice in the mall."

⊠ Pastis ❶ French   21 | 20 | 17 | $46

Meatpacking | 9 Ninth Ave. (Little W. 12th St.) | 212-929-4844 | www.pastisny.com

Keith McNally produces "French bistro to perfection" at this very "cosmopolitan" Meatpacking District "pioneer", a "baby" Balthazar that "packed to the gills" with "fashionistas", "tourists" and the "am-famous-yet?" set; although the staff is more "preoccupied with crowd control", it serves "genuinely worthwhile food" here; P.S. "it's tamer at breakfast" – and just as "glam."

Pastrami Queen Deli   19 | 5 | 13 | $22

E 70s | 1125 Lexington Ave. (bet. 78th & 79th Sts.) | 212-734-1500 www.pastramiqueen.com

"Kosher's last frontier" on the UES, this relocated (and "newly shrunken") deli supplies "incredible cholesterol" via its "fabulous overstuffed sandwiches; drawbacks include "no ambiance" and the fact that "you'll leave larger than when you entered"; N.B. don't forget to bring your Lipitor.

Patois Ⓜ French   21 | 19 | 19 | $37

Carroll Gardens | 255 Smith St. (bet. Degraw & Douglass Sts.) | Brooklyn | 718-855-1535

The "first of the chic Smith Street" destinations, this Carroll Garden "labor of love" features "never-fail" French bistro eats served in "well-tailored" interior or rear "garden getaway"; oddly enough, what was once a "special-occasion place" is now "one of the more reasonable spots on the strip."

Patricia's ❶ Italian   22 | 12 | 19 | $26

Bronx | 1080 Morris Park Ave. (bet. Haight & Lurting Aves.) | 718-409-906
Bronx | 3764 E. Tremont Ave. (bet. Randall & Roosevelt Aves.) | 718-918-1800

"Inexpensive", "family-oriented" Bronx Italians serving "flavorful" pizza and pastas in "loud, crowded" digs with "not much room to relax"; "storefront" decor complete with "TV sets" doesn't appeal, "get it to go"

Patroon ⊠ American/Steak   21 | 20 | 21 | $63

E 40s | 160 E. 46th St. (bet. Lexington & 3rd Aves.) | 212-883-7373 www.patroonrestaurant.com

"Masters of the universe" dig the smooth 1930s-NY vibe at Ken Aretsky's "clubby" Midtown New American, where "excellent" steak "pro" service and "expense-account" pricing make it a prime player for "power dining"; bonuses include a swinging rooftop bar and a variety of "handsome" private rooms; open weekdays only.

Patsy's Italian   21 | 16 | 20 | $51

W 50s | 236 W. 56th St. (bet. B'way & 8th Ave.) | 212-247-3491 | www.patsys.com

"Sinatra's ghost still haunts" this "retro" Southern Italian near Carnegie Hall that's a "throwback" in many ways other than its pricing; "crusty waiters", "celebrity pix on the walls" and a crowd that looks like a "casting call for the *Sopranos*" add up to a "so NY" experience or a so-so experience depending whom you ask.

Patsy's Pizzeria *Pizza*

20 | 12 | 15 | $24

Chelsea | 318 W. 23rd St. (bet. 8th & 9th Aves.) | 646-486-7400
E 60s | 1312 Second Ave. (69th St.) | 212-639-1000
E 60s | 206 E. 60th St. (bet. 2nd & 3rd Aves.) | 212-688-9707
G Village | 67 University Pl. (bet. 10th & 11th Sts.) | 212-533-3500
Harlem | 2287-91 First Ave. (bet. 117th & 118th Sts.) | 212-534-9783
Murray Hill | 509 Third Ave. (bet. 34th & 35th Sts.) | 212-689-7500
W 70s | 61 W. 74th St. (bet. Columbus Ave. & CPW) | 212-579-3000
www.patsyspizzeriany.com

"Perfectly charred" brick-oven pizzas with "zesty sauce" and "delicious thin crusts" overcome the "lackluster service" and "nonexistent" decor at this all-over-town chainlet; piezanos praise East Harlem's "venerable" independent original as "still the best", and "worth the trek."

Paul & Jimmy's *Italian*

19 | 16 | 20 | $44

Gramercy | 123 E. 18th St. (bet. Irving Pl. & Park Ave. S.) | 212-475-9540 | www.paulandjimmys.com

"Always quiet" and "comfortable", this "reliable" third-generation Gramercy Italian is "growing old gracefully" (if "not adventurously"); the midpriced, "traditional red-sauce" menu holds "no surprises", but "loyal" adherents stick by its "old-time" ways.

Payard Bistro ⏹ *Dessert/French*

24 | 21 | 20 | $53

E 70s | 1032 Lexington Ave. (bet. 73rd & 74th Sts.) | 212-717-5252 | www.payard.com

"Sinful desserts" are "virtually mandatory" at François Payard's stylish UES patisserie/French bistro that also works for breakfast, "fancy" lunches, "elegant afternoon tea" or "*magnifique*" dinners; somewhat "snooty" staffers set back the "civilized" if "pricey" experience.

Peanut Butter & Co. *Sandwiches*

20 | 12 | 16 | $13

G Village | 240 Sullivan St. (bet. Bleecker & W. 3rd Sts.) | 212-677-3995 | www.ilovepeanutbutter.com

"If peanut butter's your idea of heaven", then this Village cafe is the "pearly gates", serving "lip-smacking" sandwiches including the infamous 'Elvis' (PB&J, banana and bacon – "yum"); "overpricing" is overlooked for the "novelty" of "eating like a kid" again.

⏹ Pearl Oyster Bar ⏹ *Seafood*

26 | 15 | 19 | $43

G Village | 18 Cornelia St. (bet. Bleecker & W. 4th Sts.) | 212-691-8211 | www.pearloysterbar.com

"Neptune would be proud" of the "legendary" lobster rolls and "sublime" New England–style fish served at Rebecca Charles' "no-frills" Village seafood shack; it's "cheaper than driving to Maine", though it may take as long given the "endless waits" to get in.

Pearl Room *Seafood*

23 | 21 | 22 | $47

Bay Ridge | 8201 Third Ave. (82nd St.) | Brooklyn | 718-833-6666 | www.thepearlroom.com

"Excellent" cooking, "personable service" and a "cool", "modern" atmosphere make this "upscale" Bay Ridge seafooder a "classy" destination, though a few carp at the "Manhattan prices"; the "top-shelf" bar does a "brisk business" too, sometimes "three deep" with amenable "young singles."

	FOOD	DECOR	SERVICE	COST

Peasant ⓜ Italian
24 | 23 | 20 | $54

NoLita | 194 Elizabeth St. (bet. Prince & Spring Sts.) | 212-965-9511 | www.peasantnyc.com

"Unconventional" cuisine served from an "opera set of an open kitchen" is the draw at this "candlelit" NoLita Italian that's "fit for a king" – and priced accordingly – though needing a "waiter to decipher" the foreign-language menu strikes some as "a bit much"; romeos rhapsodize over its more "casual" subterranean wine bar.

Peep ◑ Thai
19 | 20 | 17 | $31

SoHo | 177 Prince St. (bet. Sullivan & Thompson Sts.) | 212-254-7337 | www.peepsoho.net

"Crazy crowds" of the "young" and "trendy" meet cute at this "affordable" SoHo Thai where the "pink neon", "Hello Kitty" decor matches the "zingy" chow; the real "peep show" comes via "novelty bathrooms" whose one-way mirrors allow you to contemplate the scene "from your throne" – and pray that they're really one-way.

Peking Duck House Chinese
22 | 15 | 18 | $36

Chinatown | 28 Mott St. (bet. Mosco & Pell Sts.) | 212-227-1810
E 50s | 236 E. 53rd St. (bet. 2nd & 3rd Aves.) | 212-759-8260
www.pekingduckhousenyc.com

"Carved tableside", the "luscious" namesake specialty is "as good as it gets" at this Chinese pair, though some say the rest of the menu isn't "all it's quacked up to be"; decor varies from the "spare-as-a-bone" Midtown location to the "fancy-for-Chinatown" Downtown sibling.

Pellegrino's Italian
22 | 18 | 21 | $40

Little Italy | 138 Mulberry St. (bet. Grand & Hester Sts.) | 212-226-3177

Just the way "out-of-towners picture Little Italy", this "bustling", modestly priced trattoria offers *delizioso* basics served by "bantering waiters" "straight out of the old country"; dining options include the "comfy" if "plain" interior or alfresco "curbside tables" with "people watching" on the side.

Penelope ⊄ American
21 | 17 | 18 | $23

Murray Hill | 159 Lexington Ave. (30th St.) | 212-481-3800 | www.penelopenyc.com

"Tantalizing" "down-home cooking" and "country cottage" decor make this "girlie" Murray Hill American feel like "grandma's kitchen"; downsides include "long waits for brunch" and a "cash-only policy", but you "can't complain with such reasonable prices."

Pepe Giallo To Go Italian
21 | 10 | 15 | $24

Chelsea | 253 10th Ave. (bet. 24th & 25th Sts.) | 212-242-6055
Pepe Rosso Italian
E Village | 127 Ave. C (8th St.) | 212-529-7747
Pepe Rosso Caffe Italian
E 40s | Grand Central | lower level (42nd St. & Vanderbilt Ave.) | 212-867-6054
NEW Pepe Rosso Osteria ⑤ Italian
W 50s | 346 W. 52nd St. (bet. 8th & 9th Aves.) | 212-245-4585
Pepe Rosso To Go Italian
SoHo | 149 Sullivan St. (bet. Houston & Prince Sts.) | 212-677-4555

(continued)

Pepe Verde To Go 🏷 *Italian*

W Village | 559 Hudson St. (bet. Perry & W. 11th Sts.) | 212-255-2221
www.peperossotogo.com
"Simple pastas" "in a hurry" sum up the scene at these "Italian pit stops" where the "cheap" chow is served in "food-court" settings; they're fine "for the eat-and-run crowd", though best for "takeout."

Pepolino *Italian* | 24 | 17 | 22 | $50

TriBeCa | 281 W. Broadway (bet. Canal & Lispenard Sts.) | 212-966-9983 |
www.pepolino.com
For "upscale Northern Italian with downtown coolness", it's "worth the schlep" to this TriBeCa "diamond in the rough" where "original" dishes and "amiable service" distract from the "expensive" tabs and "cramped" digs; for more breathing room, "ask for an upstairs table."

NEW Pera 🅂 *Mediterranean/Turkish* | 22 | 23 | 19 | $54

40s | 303 Madison Ave. (bet. 41st & 42nd Sts.) | 212-878-6301 |
www.peranyc.com
A "breath of fresh air" near Grand Central, this "upscale" Med new-comer provides "delicious" offerings with a Turkish bent in "elegant yet not stuffy" digs; the high "suit ratio" reflects the immoderate prices, so "make sure you're able to expense" this one.

Perbacco ●🏷 *Italian* | 24 | 16 | 20 | $40

E Village | 234 E. Fourth St. (bet. Aves. A & B) | 212-253-2038
"Mouthwatering" Italian "small bites" paired with "sensational wines" keep regulars "enthralled" at this "cute little East Villager; ok, it's "crowded", a bit "rushed" and "cash only", but a staff that was apparently "in Rome until yesterday" lays on the "charm."

NEW Peri Ela 🏷 *Turkish* | ▽ 19 | 17 | 20 | $40

90s | 1361 Lexington Ave. (bet. 90th & 91st Sts.) | 212-410-4300 |
www.periela.com
Already a "popular" choice in "barren" Carnegie Hill, this young Turk is "refreshingly different", offering "authentic" eats served by a staff that's "shyly friendly if a tad unskilled"; the space is "small" yet "pleasant", the BYO policy a definite "plus" and the "cash-only" rule a drag.

NEW Perilla *American* | - | - | - | E

G Village | 9 Jones St. (bet. Bleecker & W. 4th Sts.) | 212-929-6868 |
www.perillanyc.com
Last year's *Top Chef* winner, Harold Dieterle, strikes out on his own at this Glim Village newcomer (fka Inside) offering New Americana with an Eastern bent that's been drawing crowds from day one; the understated verging on spare interior is in sharp contrast to the emphatic pricing.

Periyali *Greek* | 23 | 20 | 22 | $55

Flatiron | 35 W. 20th St. (bet. 5th & 6th Aves.) | 212-463-7890 |
www.periyali.com
"Lovely renovated decor" is receiving almost as many kudos as the "inspired" "haute Greek" cooking at this perennial Flatiron "grande dame"; while the "subdued" atmosphere and "truly gracious" staff please longtime regulars, younger types say "unexciting" – at least until they see the check.

	FOOD	DECOR	SERVICE	COST

Per Lei ● *Italian*
20 | 17 | 17 | $50

E 70s | 1347 Second Ave. (71st St.) | 212-439-9200 | www.perleinyc.com
Spun off from nearby Baraonda, this similarly "Euro-trendy" Upper Eastsider delivers "surprisingly good" Italian food in a "striking" room or at sidewalk seats perfect for "people-watching"; on the downside critics claim it's "not a place to have a conversation" and has "more style than substance."

Perry Street ● *American*
24 | 24 | 23 | $71

W Village | 176 Perry St. (West St.) | 212-352-1900 | www.jean-georges.com
Jean-Georges Vongerichten's "sophisticated" Way West Village New American is the "restaurant equivalent of haute couture", with a "sleek minimalist" room setting the stage for "exquisite" cookery; add "subtle" service, a "sexy", "Gucci-sunglasses" crowd and a "bargain" $24 prix fixe lunch to offset the otherwise "steep prices", and you've got a "must-try" destination.

☑ Per Se *American/French*
28 | 28 | 28 | $301

W 60s | Time Warner Ctr. | 10 Columbus Circle, 4th fl. (60th St. at B'way) | 212-823-9335 | www.perseny.com
Like a "four-hour stroll through culinary paradise", Thomas Keller's French–New American offers "epic dining" in a "Zen-like space" featuring "drop-dead views" of Central Park and Columbus Circle; "telepathic service" (voted No. 1 in this Survey) adds to the overall "magic" so even if the reservations process can be "grueling" and the prix fixe only tariffs "stratospheric", this "once-in-a-blue-moon treat" is "everything it's cracked up to be" – "Per-Fect!"; N.B. jackets required.

Persepolis *Persian*
19 | 15 | 18 | $37

E 70s | 1407 Second Ave. (bet. 73th & 74th Sts.) | 212-535-1100 | www.persepolisnyc.com
There's no visa required to "visit Persia on the UES" at this "exotic" spot offering "fragrant", "savory" food (especially the "unique" signature dish, sour cherry rice); its new digs are "peppered with Iranian expats" who relish the "relaxed" pace and "modest" tabs.

Pershing Square *American/French*
15 | 16 | 16 | $37

E 40s | 90 E. 42nd St. (Park Ave.) | 212-286-9600 | www.pershingsquare.com
Just south of Grand Central, this "expansive" Franco-American brasserie is a good place to meet for breakfast, lunch or a drink before heading back to Stamford; despite its "great pancakes" and Midtown convenience, critics consider it "chainlike" and "way too noisy" at prime times.

Pescatore ● *Italian/Seafood*
18 | 15 | 18 | $39

E 50s | 955 Second Ave. (bet. 50th & 51st Sts.) | 212-752-7151 | www.pescatorerestaurant.com
Ever the "crowd-pleaser", this "mid-tier" Midtown "neighborhood trattoria delivers "well-executed" Italian seafood and pasta; perhaps "service could be better", but it's a real "price performer" with a striking "second-floor balcony" overlooking Second Avenue.

Petaluma *Italian*
18 | 16 | 18 | $44

E 70s | 1356 First Ave. (73rd St.) | 212-772-8800 | www.petalumanyc.com
"Solid as a rock", this longtime Yorkville Italian dispenses "pleasant" "no-fuss" food for "reasonable" costs in a "spacious", "white-linen"

setting; its client base ranges from the "stroller set" to "business-lunchers" to "Sotheby's dealers" who would auction off anything other than their table here.

☑ Peter Luger Steak House ⌘ *Steak*   28 | 14 | 20 | $71

Williamsburg | 178 Broadway (Driggs Ave.) | Brooklyn | 718-387-7400 | www.peterluger.com

The "holy grail of steakhouses", this Williamsburg "landmark" (NYC's No. 1 chop shop for the 24th year running) makes carnivores "salivate just hearing the name" that's synonymous with the "ultimate" in "succulent" beef, particularly those "buttery, perfectly marbled porterhouses"; "don't look for coddling" from the "brutally efficient" staff – just "consider them an amusement", like the "old-world" *brauhaus* atmospherics and that "outdated cash-only" policy.

Pete's Downtown Ⓜ *Italian*   ▽ 18 | 16 | 19 | $35

Dumbo | 2 Water St. (Old Fulton St.) | Brooklyn | 718-858-3510 | www.petesdowntown.com

Perhaps the "greatest view in the entire world" – Manhattan's Financial District across the river – is the draw at this Dumbo Italian where "an appetite and a camera" are the only requisites for entry; maybe the "old-style" grub is only "adequate", but living up to its nickname – the "poor man's River Café" – it's "reasonably priced."

Pete's Tavern ❶ *Pub Food*   14 | 16 | 16 | $30

Gramercy | 129 E. 18th St. (Irving Pl.) | 212-473-7676 | www.petestavern.com
It's "all about the ambiance" at this "boisterous" 1864-vintage Gramercy pub that "reeks of old NY", from the "warped wooden floors" to the "O.-Henry-ate-here memorabilia"; regulars stick to the "decent burgers" and try to avoid the "drunken frat boys" on game days.

Petite Abeille *Belgian*   19 | 14 | 16 | $28

Flatiron | 44 W. 17th St. (bet. 5th & 6th Aves.) | 212-604-9350
Gramercy | 401 E. 20th St. (1st Ave.) | 212-727-1505
TriBeCa | 134 W. Broadway (Duane St.) | 212-791-1360
W Village | 466 Hudson St. (Barrow St.) | 212-741-6479 ⌘
www.petiteabeille.com

"Easy dining" with "European flair" draws "all age groups" to these "bright" Belgian bistros for a moules frites fix washed down with imported brews; service may be "wonky", but "the price is right" and they sure "perk up the neighborhood."

NEW Petite Crevette ☒⌘ *Seafood*   ▽ 24 | 14 | 17 | $28

Carroll Gardens | 144 Union St. (enter on Hicks St.) | Brooklyn | 718-855-2632
"Delicious", "just-reeled-in fish" is the hook at this "sorta French" Carroll Gardens seafooder where "BYO" keeps prices low; "spotty service" and "hole-in-the-wall" looks are the catches, and "they're not kidding when they say petite."

Petrossian ❶ *Continental/French*   24 | 24 | 23 | $73

W 50s | 182 W. 58th St. (7th Ave.) | 212-245-2214 | www.petrossian.com
"Life is good" at this "sedate" French-Continental near Carnegie Hall, where the "first-class" fare, "gorgeous deco-inspired room" and "pitch-perfect service" make for a "czar's experience" (it also does the job for a "champagne and caviar fix"); if the "fancy prices" tend to "spoil the celebration", opt for a prix fixe menu or the "equally good cafe."

	FOOD	DECOR	SERVICE	COST

Philip Marie ●Ⓜ *American* | 20 | 18 | 21 | $40

W Village | 569 Hudson St. (W. 11th St.) | 212-242-6200 |
www.philipmarie.com

New Americana with "updated twists" lies in store at this "delightful
little" boîte with "reasonable" pricing, "wonderful" service and sidewalk
seating that's ideal for "Village people–watching"; the "private room
for two in the wine cellar" is just the ticket for "secretive romantics."

Philippe ● *Chinese* | 23 | 20 | 20 | $65

E 60s | 33 E. 60th St. (bet. Madison & Park Aves.) | 212-644-8885 |
www.philippechow.com

The "scene" is the thing at this Midtown Chinese yearling that strikes
some as a "Mr. Chow's clone" given its "adventurous chef", "sleek"
setting, dim lighting and "pounding music"; similarly, the "extraordinary" pricing doesn't faze "all the beautiful people" in attendance.

Pho Bang ⊄ *Vietnamese* | 21 | 6 | 13 | $13

Chinatown | 3 Pike St. (bet. Division St. & E. B'way) | 212-233-3947
Little Italy | 157 Mott St. (bet. Broome & Grand Sts.) | 212-966-3797
Elmhurst | 82-90 Broadway (Elmhurst Ave.) | Queens | 718-205-1500
Flushing | 41-07 Kissena Blvd. (Main St.) | Queens | 718-939-5520

Phans of "fab pho" report these "plain" Vietnamese noodle shops dish
up "surprisingly tasty" eats for excellent "bang pho the buck"; thus,
the "run-down" digs and "what-service?" service aren't so troubling
since "they're practically giving it away."

Phoenix Garden ⊄ *Chinese* | 24 | 8 | 13 | $27

E 40s | 242 E. 40th St. (bet. 2nd & 3rd Aves.) | 212-983-6666

"Chinatown comes Uptown" via this Tudor City–area Cantonese
where the "magnificent cooking" struggles against "ungracious service", "not-much-to-look-at" decor and a "cash-only" rule; redeeming
factors include "budget" pricing and a "BYO policy."

Pho Pasteur *Vietnamese* | ▽ 21 | 6 | 14 | $17

Chinatown | 85 Baxter St. (bet. Bayard & Canal Sts.) |
212-608-3656

"You can't go wrong with a bowl of pho" or other "filling" Vietnamese
"comfort food" served at this "refuge" from bustling C-town; "casual"
puts it politely, but "best-deal" tabs and a location "right behind the
courthouses" draw in-the-know jurors.

Pho Viet Huong *Vietnamese* | ▽ 23 | 10 | 14 | $17

Chinatown | 73 Mulberry St. (bet. Bayard & Canal Sts.) |
212-233-8988

"Pho-nominal" "homestyle Vietnamese" cooking makes for "happy
campers" at this Chinatown "cheapskates' paradise"; despite "sparse
decor" and "no service", this "real deal" helps "take the sting out
of jury duty."

Piadina ●⊄ *Italian* | ▽ 20 | 17 | 17 | $34

G Village | 57 W. 10th St. (bet. 5th & 6th Aves.) | 212-460-8017

Whether it's the "first date or the 10th", this "grottolike" Village
Italian is a "romantic" lair luring young "collegiate" types with "delicious" dishes, a "welcoming" vibe and, naturally, "good prices"; the
sole drawback is its "cash-only" status.

	FOOD	DECOR	SERVICE	COST

Piano Due ⊠ Italian
25 | 25 | 24 | $73

W 50s | Equitable Center Arcade | 151 W. 51st St., 2nd fl. (bet. 6th & 7th Aves.) | 212-399-9400 | www.pianoduenyc.net

"Still a secret", Michael Cetrulo's "tucked-away" Midtown Italian is "fabulous from soup to nuts", with a "flavorful, beautifully presented" menu served by an "exceptional" crew in a "plush", second-floor setting; downstairs, the "colorful" Palio bar is a suitable warm-up decorated with that "stunning" fresco of the "Siena horse race."

Piccola Venezia Italian
25 | 17 | 23 | $52

Astoria | 42-01 28th Ave. (42nd St.) | Queens | 718-721-8470 | www.piccola-venezia.com

"Don't let the neighborhood look deceive you": this "old-fashioned, red-velvet" Astoria Italian has long been a "destination" for "outstanding" red-sauce fare with "continental flair"; an "extensive wine cellar" and "terrific" service are additional pluses, so even though "expensive" for Queens, it's "cheaper" than what it would cost in Manhattan.

Piccolo Angolo Ⓜ Italian
25 | 13 | 21 | $38

W Village | 621 Hudson St. (Jane St.) | 212-229-9177 | www.piccoloangolo.com

"Colorful" owner Renato Migliorini makes you "feel like family" at his ultra-"cozy" Village Italian serving "gutsy", "homestyle cooking" for "moderate" sums; an "effusive" staff doles out portions big enough for "leftovers for a week" – no wonder there's "never an empty seat."

⊠ Picholine French/Mediterranean
27 | 24 | 25 | $87

W 60s | 35 W. 64th St. (bet. B'way & CPW) | 212-724-8585 | www.picholinenyc.com

"Celebrate", "pamper yourself" or just "swoon" at Terry Brennan's "better-than-ever" UWS French-Med where the "revamped" $65 prix fixe menu is "always excellent" and the "siren call of the cheese trolley" can be heard above the "raves" resounding through the "understatedly elegant" room; "dignified" service enhances the "formal atmosphere", while "top-notch" private party rooms seal the deal.

PicNic Market & Café Deli/French
20 | 14 | 18 | $38

W 100s | 2665 Broadway (101st St.) | 212-222-8222 | www.picnicmarket.com

Doing double duty as deli and cafe, this "gentrification personified" Upper Westsider purveys "no-pretensions" French fare "made with care" and served by an "earnest" staff; though a few feel it's a bit "pricey for the modest setting", that doesn't seem to be deterring anyone.

Pietrasanta Italian
19 | 13 | 17 | $36

W 40s | 683 Ninth Ave. (47th St.) | 212-265-9471

"Stick to the pasta" to savor the "simple", "homemade" victuals that this "popular" Hell's Kitchen Italian does best; the "cramped" space may be a tad "tattered" and service occasionally "chaotic", yet pretheater-goers endure both in exchange for inexpensive tabs.

Pietro's ⊠ Italian/Steak
23 | 14 | 21 | $60

E 40s | 232 E. 43rd St. (bet. 2nd & 3rd Aves.) | 212-682-9760

For "civilized" dining near Grand Central, check out this "step-back-in-time" Italian steakhouse that may "lack buzz" but still furnishes "first-

rate" meals and an "old-school" staff (including an "amazing coat
check woman"); like many of its "dedicated older followers", it "could
use a face-lift", though pricing is distinctly up to date.

Pigalle ◑ French
18 | 17 | 17 | $36

W 40s | Hilton Garden Inn Times Sq. | 790 Eighth Ave. (48th St.) |
212-489-2233 | www.pigallenyc.com

Sure, it's "usually mobbed", since this "convenient" Hell's Kitchen
"way station en route to the theater" churns out "reliable" French
brasserie eats at "survival prices"; even though the staff can be "overwhelmed", it still works well for a "quickie" before the show.

Pig Heaven ◑ Chinese
19 | 14 | 18 | $34

E 80s | 1540 Second Ave. (bet. 80th & 81st Sts.) | 212-744-4333

No surprise, "pork abounds" on the menu of this UES Chinese where
the "above-average" cooking is "so naughty but so good"; "gracious
hostess" Nancy Lee "remembers your favorites" and distracts from
the "kitschy", "porcine"-themed decor and that "turn-off" of a name.

Ping's Seafood ◑ Chinese/Seafood
22 | 12 | 13 | $26

Chinatown | 22 Mott St. (bet. Bayard & Pell Sts.) | 212-602-9988
Elmhurst | 83-02 Queens Blvd. (Goldsmith St.) | Queens | 718-396-1238

"Tasty morsels" of "classic Hong Kong seafood" and an "extensive selection" of "delicious dim sum" are dispensed by this "bustling"
Chinatown-Elmhurst pair where tabs are "reasonable" enough to
overcome the "shabby" setups and "annoyed" staff.

Pink Tea Cup ◑⊟ Soul Food/Southern
20 | 10 | 16 | $23

W Village | 42 Grove St. (bet. Bedford & Bleecker Sts.) | 212-807-6755 |
www.thepinkteacup.com

Despite the name, there's "nothing dainty" about this venerable
Villager specializing in "stick-to-your-hips" Southern cooking; both the
decor and service need "sprucing up", but those seeking a wallet
friendly "cholesterol splurge" are willing to brave the "lines" out the door.

Pinocchio Ⓜ Italian
21 | 16 | 23 | $45

E 90s | 1748 First Ave. (bet. 90th & 91st Sts.) | 212-828-5810

"Everyone knows everyone" at this "obscure" Yorkville "hideaway"
that's a neighborhood "asset" for locals; "wonderful" Italian classics
and a "couldn't-be-friendlier" owner are further advantages, though it
would be nice to have "a bit more space" in the "tight", "narrow" room.

Pintaile's Pizza Pizza
20 | 6 | 12 | $15

E 80s | 1573 York Ave. (bet. 83rd & 84th Sts.) | 212-396-3479
E 90s | 26 E. 91st St. (bet. 5th & Madison Aves.) | 212-722-1967

"Super-thin" whole-wheat crusts and "brilliant" toppings in "crazy
combinations" distinguish these "yuppie" Yorkville pizzerias that draw
everyone from the "lactose intolerant" to "vegans and full-fledged carnivores"; since decor is "limited", they're best for "takeout" or delivery.

Pio Pio Peruvian
23 | 13 | 16 | $22

E 90s | 1746 First Ave. (bet. 90th & 91st Sts.) | 212-426-5800
NEW **W 90s** | 702 Amsterdam Ave. (94th St.) | 212-665-3000
Bronx | 264 Cypress Ave. (bet. 138th & 139th Sts.) | 718-401-3300
Jackson Heights | 84-13 Northern Blvd. (bet. 84th & 85th Sts.) | Queens |
718-426-1010

| | FOOD | DECOR | SERVICE | COST |

(continued)

Pio Pio

Rego Park | 62-30 Woodhaven Blvd. (63rd Ave.) | Queens |
718-458-0606 ☞

"So much food for so little money" could be the motto of this Peruvian
mini-chain famed for "fabulous rotisserie chickens" slathered with
"addictive" sauces; "sardine" seating, "so-so service" and "raucous"
atmospherics come with the territory.

Pipa *Spanish*

21 | **23** | **17** | **$42**

Flatiron | ABC Carpet & Home | 38 E. 19th St. (bet. B'way & Park Ave. S.) |
212-677-2233 | www.abchome.com

"Young hotties" and "tinkling chandeliers" collide at this "shabby-
chic" Flatiron Spaniard that's "full of beautiful things to look at" while
you consume "tasty" tapas and "psychedelic sangria"; too bad the
staff "couldn't care less" and tabs may be "pricier than you'd like."

Pisticci *Italian*

23 | **19** | **20** | **$32**

W 100s | 125 La Salle St. (B'way) | 212-932-3500 |
www.pisticcinyc.com

Now that "word's out", this "charming" Columbia-area "hideaway" is
packed with "college students" tucking into "terrific" Italian repasts
and grooving to weekly "live jazz"; service is "friendly", the decor a
take on "nouveau-SoHo" rusticity and the price "just right."

Pizza 33 ◐ *Pizza*

21 | **7** | **12** | **$11**

Chelsea | 171 W. 23rd St. (bet. 6th & 7th Aves.) | 212-337-3661
Chelsea | 268 W. 23rd St. (8th Ave.) | 212-206-0999
NEW **G Village** | 527 Sixth Ave. (14th St.) | 212-255-6333
Murray Hill | 489 Third Ave. (33rd St.) | 212-545-9191
www.pizza33.net

"Godsends when the bars close", these brick-oven pizzerias are celebrated for both their "late-night" hours and "crispy, chewy crusts";
what with the "cramped" settings, they're best enjoyed "on the run."

P.J. Clarke's ◑ *Pub Food*

17 | **16** | **16** | **$33**

E 50s | 915 Third Ave. (55th St.) | 212-317-1616
NEW **P.J. Clarke's at Lincoln Square** ◑ *Pub Food*
W 60s | 44 W. 63rd St. (Columbus Ave.) | 212-957-9700
P.J. Clarke's on the Hudson *Pub Food*
Financial District | 4 World Financial Ctr. (Vesey St.) | 212-285-1500
www.pjclarkes.com

"Amazing burgers", "properly poured" brews and vintage decor are
the draws at this "pub-grub paradise" set in a circa-1884 Midtown sa-
loon; the newer satellites in the Financial District and opposite Lincoln
Center may be "Disney versions", but are popular nonetheless.

Place, The *American/Mediterranean*

21 | **21** | **22** | **$46**

W Village | 310 W. Fourth St. (bet. Bank & 12th Sts.) | 212-924-2711 |
www.theplaceny.com

"Dark" surroundings and a "delicious" Med-New American menu
make for a highly "romantic rendezvous" at this "candlelit" West
Villager; a "warm" staff and acoustics that allow you to "carry on a
conversation" add to the seductive feel; N.B. the short-lived 10th
Street satellite has shuttered.

	FOOD	DECOR	SERVICE	COST

Planet Thailand ◑ *Japanese/Thai* | 19 | 19 | 15 | $26 |

Williamsburg | 133 N. Seventh St. (bet. Bedford Ave. & Berry St.) | Brooklyn |
718-599-5758

Planethailand 212 ◑ *Thai*

Flatiron | 30 W. 24th St. (bet. 5th & 6th Aves.) | 212-727-7026 |
www.pt212.com

"Cheap and cheery", the "hip" Williamsburg branch of this Thai-
Japanese duo churns out "tasty" chow in a "cavernous", "dance
club"-like setting, while its smaller Flatiron sibling offers a more
limited menu and "Thai theme park" decor; "hit-or-miss" service is
available at both.

Pó *Italian* | 25 | 16 | 21 | $49 |

G Village | 31 Cornelia St. (bet. Bleecker & W. 4th Sts.) | 212-645-2189
NEW **Carroll Gardens** | 276 Smith St. (bet. Degraw & Sackett Sts.) |
Brooklyn | 718-875-1980
www.porestaurant.com

"True foodies" say this "still-going-strong" Village Italian turns out
"perfectly prepared" fare backed up by "smooth" service and a "no-
problem" price point; now if they could only do something about the
"tight" setting that makes "sitting on your neighbor's lap" part of the
package; N.B. the Carroll Gardens outPóst opened post-Survey.

Z Poke ⊠⊅ *Japanese* | 26 | 15 | 18 | $38 |

E 80s | 343 E. 85th St. (bet. 1st & 2nd Aves.) | 212-249-0569

"Super-fresh fish" meets "creative cutters" to become "sublime sushi"
at this "no-reservations" UES Japanese where the "BYO bonus" keeps
"prices cheap"; despite an "echo chamber" of a setting and "kind of
snarly" service, there are "long waits if you don't get there early."

Pomodoro Rosso *Italian* | 21 | 15 | 20 | $40 |

W 70s | 229 Columbus Ave. (bet. 70th & 71st Sts.) | 212-721-3009

An "easy walk from Lincoln Center", this "quintessential neighborhood Italian" packs 'em in with "dependable" "traditional" cooking at
"value" tabs; an "efficient" staff abets the "pleasant" vibe, even
though it's famed as the "Seinfeld break-up restaurant."

NEW p*ong ◑Ⓜ *Dessert* | ▽ 21 | 20 | 23 | $49 |

G Village | 150 W. 10th St. (bet. Greenwich Ave. & Waverly Pl.) |
212-929-0898 | www.p-ong.com

The latest of NY's high-concept dessert bars, this "heavenly" haute
Villager from sweets master Pichet Ong offers Asian-influenced
sweet-and-savory American small plates from a menu that includes expansive (and "expensive") tasting options; the "modern"
design is well-suited to its adventurous approach, including those
"sublime handcrafted cocktails."

Pongal *Indian/Vegetarian* | 21 | 13 | 15 | $24 |

E 60s | 1154 First Ave. (bet. 63rd & 64th Sts.) | 212-355-4600
Gramercy | 110 Lexington Ave. (bet. 27th & 28th Sts.) |
212-696-9458

"Dosas are the real winners" on the "flavorful" Southern Indian menu
of this kosher vegetarian duo where the food's "not too spicy, nor too
bland"; "devoted regulars" say the "bargain" rates trump the "nonexistent decor" and "clueless" service.

	FOOD	DECOR	SERVICE	COST

Pongsri Thai *Thai* — 20 | 11 | 17 | $24

Chelsea | 165 W. 23rd St. (bet. 6th & 7th Aves.) | 212-645-8808
Chinatown | 106 Bayard St. (Baxter St.) | 212-349-3132
Gramercy | 311 Second Ave. (18th St.) | 212-477-2727
W 40s | 244 W. 48th St. (bet. B'way & 8th Ave.) | 212-582-3392 ◐

"Quality" Thai "done right" with "subtle flavorings" keeps the "crowds" coming to this "popular" chainlet; "gentle prices" make up for the "advanced thrift shop" decor and "polite" but "conveyor belt"-style service.

Ponticello *Italian* — ▽ 23 | 18 | 21 | $48

Astoria | 46-11 Broadway (bet. 46th & 47th Sts.) | Queens | 718-278-4514 | www.ponticelloristorante.com

A "stroll down memory lane", this "old-school" Astoria Italian offers "first-rate" fare from a kitchen that's "willing to cook anything you want", "even if it's not on the menu"; service is "friendly", tabs are "pricey for Queens" and the crowd is right off of the *Godfather* set."

Pop Burger ◑ *American* — 19 | 14 | 12 | $19

Meatpacking | 58-60 Ninth Ave. (bet. 14th & 15th Sts.) | 212-414-8686 | www.popburger.com

"Addictive" mini-burgers channeling "White Castle" are the bait at this low-budget Meatpacking District New American, though it's the "awesome lounge scene" in back that keeps the crowd "buzzing late into the night"; many wonder "is the service supposed to be that bad?"

Popover Cafe *American* — 18 | 14 | 16 | $26

W 80s | 551 Amsterdam Ave. (bet. 86th & 87th Sts.) | 212-595-5555 | www.popovercafe.com

It's "all about the popovers" at this "favorite" UWS American whose well-priced, "tasty comfort food" plays second fiddle to its "warm, flaky" namesake; expect weekend "waits", "sweet but inefficient" service and a "cute", "gingham-tablecloth-and-teddy-bear"-laden setting.

Porcão Churrascaria *Brazilian/Steak* — 21 | 20 | 21 | $66

Gramercy | 360 Park Ave. S. (26th St.) | 212-252-7080 | www.porcaous.com

"Avoid the decoy food" at the "salad bar utopia" and save yourself for the "onslaught" of "exceptional" rodizio-style meats at this Gramercy Brazilian steakhouse; though the "price tag is a bit hefty", you do get an "astonishing amount of food" from a staff that "pays attention."

Porter House New York *Steak* — 22 | 25 | 22 | $76

W 60s | Time Warner Ctr. | 10 Columbus Circle, 4th fl. (60th St. at B'way) | 212-823-9500 | www.porterhousenewyork.com

A "stylish", wood-paneled room with Central Park views sets the stage for Michael Lomonaco's "21st-century steakhouse" on the fourth floor of the Time Warner Center, where the meat's "perfectly prepared" and the "sides live up to the main event"; factor in "attentive" service "without airs" for a "great experience" that "justifies the cost."

Portofino Grille *Italian* — 19 | 20 | 20 | $45

E 60s | 1162 First Ave. (bet. 63rd & 64th Sts.) | 212-832-4141 | www.portofinogrille.com

"Famous for its twinkling stars on the ceiling", this "reliable", up-market East Side "charmer" offers "tasty" Italian cuisine delivered by a "caring" staff; though a few find the "over-the-top" setting more "cheesy" than "cozy", the operative word here is "grown-up."

Portofino's *Italian/Seafood* ▽ 19 | 19 | 20 | $45

Bronx | 555 City Island Ave. (Cross St.) | 718-885-1220 | www.portofinocityisland.com

"Manhattan-style" dining comes to City Island at this "upscale" Italian known for its "surprisingly good" seafood and "old-fashioned service"; despite the "romantic" appeal (a fireplace in winter, an outdoor deck in summer), critics say it's "a bit pricey" and getting "tired."

Positano ● *Italian* ▽ 21 | 16 | 19 | $41

Little Italy | 122 Mulberry St. (bet. Canal & Hester Sts.) | 212-334-9808 | www.positanolittleitaly.com

"Quaint" and "relaxed", this "friendly" Little Italy standby turns out "home-cooked" Southern Italian food for moderate sums; regulars recommend a sidewalk table for its view of the "best show in town."

Post House *Steak* 23 | 20 | 22 | $72

E 60s | Lowell Hotel | 28 E. 63rd St. (bet. Madison & Park Aves.) | 212-935-2888 | www.theposthouse.com

A "gentleman's steakhouse" that "even women like", this "solid" Eastsider is "less cramped" and "more serene" than the competition; "top-flight" beef, "to-die-for" sides and "classy" service draw "upscale" eaters willing to pay – or "expense" – those "expected high prices."

Posto *Pizza* 23 | 15 | 18 | $24

Gramercy | 310 Second Ave. (18th St.) | 212-716-1200

"Crispy", "gossamer-thin" crusts accessorized with a "tremendous assortment of toppings" make for "heaven on a plate" at this "hip" Gramercy pizza purveyor; sure, the quarters are "tight" and the sidewalk seats overlook "blah Second Avenue", but at least the pricing is "kind."

Prem-on Thai ● *Thai* ▽ 21 | 20 | 18 | $33

G Village | 138 W. Houston St. (bet. MacDougal & Sullivan Sts.) | 212-353-2338 | www.prem-on.com

"Not your typical Thai", this "high-end", "high-fashion" Siamese on the Village/SoHo border offers "clever", "well-presented" dishes prepared just as "spicy as you want"; "stylish" modern decor, modest tabs and an overall cool vibe draw a "young-ish NYU crowd."

Press 195 *Sandwiches* 20 | 12 | 15 | $18

Park Slope | 195 Fifth Ave. (bet. Sackett & Union Sts.) | Brooklyn | 718-857-1950 ⊉

Bayside | 40-11 Bell Blvd. (bet. 40th & 41st Aves.) | Queens | 718-281-1950 | www.press195.com

"Superb ingredients" in "creative combinations" done "your way" make for "perfectly pressed" panini at this "casual" Brooklyn/Queens pair; "hip" ambiance and "delightful" backyard gardens im-press fans, but "be prepared to wait" since the "sandwiches take forever" to be made.

Primavera ● *Italian* 22 | 22 | 23 | $71

E 80s | 1578 First Ave. (82nd St.) | 212-861-8608 | www.primaveranyc.com

That "old-world elegance" "never fails to impress" at this UES standby where "well-heeled", well-coiffed regulars savor "outstanding Northern Italian cuisine served by a "first-class" crew (chef-owner

Nicola Civetta is as "smooth as a vintage Amarone"); P.S. it's "expensive", "not that anyone here cares."

Prime Grill *Steak*

FOOD	DECOR	SERVICE	COST
22	19	18	$65

E 40s | 60 E. 49th St. (bet. Madison & Park Aves.) | 212-692-9292 | www.theprimegrill.com

"You'd never know it's kosher", but this Midtown steakhouse "holds the dairy" while dishing out "high-quality" meats and "tasty sushi" in "traditional" digs; despite subprime service, "ambitious pricing" and "chaotic" decibel levels, the observant still "line up to get in."

Primola *Italian*

23	15	20	$60

E 60s | 1226 Second Ave. (bet. 64th & 65th Sts.) | 212-758-1775

"It pays to be a regular" at this "clubby" East Side Italian where "the better they know you, the better it is"; expect "delicious" cooking, "steep prices", "not much decor" and "every head turning to see who you are when you walk in the door."

NEW Provence ● *French*

▽ 21	20	20	$57

SoHo | 38 MacDougal St. (Prince St.) | 212-475-7500 | www.provencenyc.com

SoHo Francophiles "feel the Mistral blowing" at this "charming" bistro "newly reopened" by the team behind Cookshop and Five Points; the "fine food", "attractive" setting and all-weather garden room seem "better the second time around", even if it's a "little pricier" now too.

Provence en Boite *Bakery/French*

▽ 20	15	19	$34

Carroll Gardens | 263 Smith St. (Degraw St.) | Brooklyn | 718-797-0707 | www.provenceenboite.com

A "pleasant addition" to Carroll Gardens, this "mom-and-pop" French bistro supplies "basic fare" and "*superbe*" baked goods as well as "cheerful" owners; if the setting is too "casual", at least the "gorgeous" desserts and croissants count as "art."

Prune *American*

24	16	21	$48

E Village | 54 E. First St. (bet. 1st & 2nd Aves.) | 212-677-6221 | www.prunerestaurant.com

"Stretch your palate" at this "tiny" East Village "treasure" where chef Gabrielle Hamilton serves "hearty, heartfelt" and "never dull" New Americana; "everyone knows" about the "innovative" brunch, so "expect to wait" for a table and plan to be "crunched."

NEW PT ●⊅ *Italian*

▽ 24	18	21	$37

Williamsburg | 331 Bedford Ave. (bet. S. 2nd & 3rd Sts.) | Brooklyn | 718-388-7438

Just a few steps below street level, this "interesting" new Williamsburg enoteca (an offshoot of nearby D.O.C. Wine Bar) exudes "rusticity" with exposed-brick walls and diffused candlelight; the "reasonably priced" seasonal Italian menu is matched by "fabulous" wines from around The Boot.

Public *Eclectic*

23	26	21	$53

NoLita | 210 Elizabeth St. (bet. Prince & Spring Sts.) | 212-343-7011 | www.public-nyc.com

This "high-concept", high-noise-level NoLita Eclectic looks like a cross between a "library" and a "nightclub", and the "exotic" menu with "nouvelle Australian" accents is equally "adventurous"; though "not as insanely trendy as it used to be", it's still "hip", "hopping" and "not for the masses."

NEW Public House *Pub Food*

— | — | — | M

E 40s | 140 E. 41st St. (bet. Lexington & 3rd Aves.) | 212-682-3710 | www.publichousenyc.com

NYC gets its own link of the national franchise with the arrival of this new modestly priced Midtown megapub that's one block south of Grand Central; since the atmosphere could be Anywhere U.S.A., it's appropriately convenient for commuters.

Pump Energy Food *Health Food*

19 | 5 | 13 | $14

E 50s | Crystal Pavilion | 805 Third Ave. (50th St.) | 212-421-3055 Ⓢ
Flatiron | 31 E. 21st St. (bet. B'way & Park Ave. S.) | 212-253-7676
Garment District | 112 W. 38th St. (bet. B'way & 6th Ave.) | 212-764-2100
Murray Hill | 113 E. 31st St. (bet. Lexington Ave. & Park Ave. S.) | 212-213-5733
W 50s | 40 W. 55th St. (bet. 5th & 6th Aves.) | 212-246-6844
www.thepumpenergyfood.com

The "low-fat", "high-protein" offerings at this "dependable" health food mini-chain make its "gym-obsessed crowd" feel "virtuous", as does the "reasonable" pricing; what with the "eyesore" decor and servers tougher than your trainer, aesthetes advise "have it delivered."

Punch *Eclectic*

19 | 16 | 18 | $38

Flatiron | 913 Broadway (bet. 20th & 21st Sts.) | 212-673-6333 | www.punchrestaurant.com

Although this "unpretentious" Flatiron Eclectic boasts an "updated look", a new chef and a "tweaked" menu, it still remains "off the radar" for many; fans praise the "delightful" cooking, "unrushed" service and "value" pricing – adding that Wined Up, the upstairs lounge, may be "even better."

Pure Food and Wine *Vegan/Vegetarian*

22 | 22 | 21 | $55

Gramercy | 54 Irving Pl. (bet. 17th & 18th Sts.) | 212-477-1010 | www.purefoodandwine.com

"Stove-free" cooking is the hook at this "ingenious" Gramercy purveyor of "mind-changing" vegan fare that makes for "invigorating" raw dining; while a "lovely" garden adds to the "sensual" experience, some find it "a bit pricey" considering how "tough it is to get full" here.

Puttanesca *Italian*

18 | 16 | 17 | $37

W 50s | 859 Ninth Ave. (56th St.) | 212-581-4177 | www.puttanesca.com

"Good bang for the buck" keeps this "reliable" Hell's Kitchen Italian packed "before showtime", given its proximity to the Theater District and Lincoln Center; the food's "decent if generic", the service "hit-or-miss" and the acoustics reminiscent of an "airport runway."

Pylos ● *Greek*

25 | 22 | 21 | $42

E Village | 128 E. Seventh St. (bet. Ave. A & 1st Ave.) | 212-473-0220 | www.pylosrestaurant.com

At this "sexy" Greek "gem" in "funky Alphabet City", the "heavenly" offerings "taste like home cooking but better" and are enhanced by a "first-rate", all-Hellenic wine list; add in "attentive" service and "fantastic" decor and it's "worthy of a place on Mount Olympus."

	FOOD	DECOR	SERVICE	COST

Q Thai Bistro *Thai*
21 | 19 | 20 | $35

Forest Hills | 108-25 Ascan Ave. (bet. Austin & Burns Sts.) | Queens | 718-261-6599 | www.qbistrony.com
This Thai "neighborhood favorite" brings some "sophistication" to Forest Hills with its "French-influenced" "nouvelle" menu; in keeping with its "upscale" aspirations, the ambiance is "chic", the service "friendly" and the tabs tolerable, this being Queens.

Quaint *American*
▽ 20 | 19 | 19 | $30

Sunnyside | 46-10 Skillman Ave. (bet. 46th & 47th Sts.) | Queens | 917-779-9220 | www.quaintnyc.com
A "small, seasonal" New American menu brings Sunnysiders to this "charming" bistro with a "sweet little back garden"; despite the name, it's "far from old-fashioned" with the "open kitchen" producing "ambitious" comfort food that's aiming to be "SoHo" hip, but "not quite there" yet.

Quality Meats ● *American/Steak*
24 | 24 | 23 | $71

W 50s | 57 W. 58th St. (bet. 5th & 6th Aves.) | 212-371-7777 | www.qualitymeatsnyc.com
Midtowners who "feel like steak but want a hipper scene" than normal head for this New American chophouse set in a "butcher shop–chic" space, where a "dead-on" staff, "delectable" meats and "prime prices" are also part of the package; make sure not to miss the "tableside steak sauces" and "homemade ice cream."

Quatorze Bis *French*
21 | 18 | 20 | $56

E 70s | 323 E. 79th St. (bet. 1st & 2nd Aves.) | 212-535-1414
"When you can't get to Paris", there's always this *"charmant"* French bistro in the UES' "79th *arrondissement"* offering "above-average" "Gallic comfort cuisine" for rather "pricey" tabs; the "buzzy", "vibrant" scene keeps its "air-kissing" crowd content.

Quattro Gatti *Italian*
20 | 16 | 19 | $45

E 80s | 205 E. 81st St. (bet. 2nd & 3rd Aves.) | 212-570-1073
For "traditional red-sauce" cooking and "great service" ("if you can understand the waiters' accents"), try this UES Italian "standby"; while the "old-school" atmosphere is "soothing", some say it's "time to update the interior" or backdate the prices.

Queen *Italian*
24 | 14 | 19 | $41

Brooklyn Heights | 84 Court St. (bet. Livingston & Schermerhorn Sts.) | Brooklyn | 718-596-5955 | www.queenrestaurant.com
"Keepin' it real" in Brooklyn Heights, this 50-year-old "neighborhood secret" serves "totally delicious" Italian fare highlighted by the "best bread basket" and "amazing fresh mozzarella"; there's "nothing cutting-edge about it, and it's all the better for it", so just ignore the "chintzy" decor and "slow service."

Queen's Hideaway *American*
▽ 20 | 12 | 14 | $34

Greenpoint | 222 Franklin St. (bet. Green & Huron Sts.) | Brooklyn | 718-383-2355 | www.thequeenshideaway.com
A "hideaway indeed", this "tiny", low-budget Greenpoint "hole-in-the-wall" with "soul" features a "quirky" New American menu strong on "local, seasonal" ingredients; a back garden compensates for the

| | FOOD | DECOR | SERVICE | COST |

"disorganized service" and decor that "won't be in *Architectural Digest*" anytime soon.

Quercy *French*
▽ 20 | 14 | 18 | $37

Cobble Hill | 242 Court St. (bet. Baltic & Kane Sts.) | Brooklyn | 718-243-2151
Like its sibling, La Lunchonette, this Cobble Hill bistro dispenses "simple French fare" that's "authentic" and "dependable", "not ooh-la-la", in a "sweet neighborhood" setting; given the "friendly staff", affordable tabs and occasional live jazz, boosters feel it "should do better business."

Rachel's American Bistro ◑ *American*
17 | 13 | 17 | $36

W 40s | 608 Ninth Ave. (bet. 43rd & 44th Sts.) | 212-957-9050 | www.rachelsnyc.com
"Flavorful", modestly priced New Americana is yours at this "busy" Hell's Kitchen bistro that's particularly "convenient to the 42nd Street theater district"; it's "nothing fancy" – some say "nothing special" – but don't forget to "bring a shoehorn" to squeeze into the "tight quarters."

Rack & Soul *BBQ/Southern*
20 | 9 | 15 | $25

W 100s | 2818 Broadway (109th St.) | 212-222-4800 | www.rackandsoul.com
This "real-deal" UWS chicken 'n' ribs purveyor "goes whole hog" bringing "messy" BBQ and "down-home" Southern eats to the cost-conscious "Columbia crowd"; service may be only "adequate" and the decor a "step above a school cafeteria", but fans flock in for "finger-licking" rather than "frills."

Rain *Pan-Asian*
21 | 21 | 19 | $42

W 80s | 100 W. 82nd St. (bet. Amsterdam & Columbus Aves.) | 212-501-0776 | www.rainrestaurant.com
An "Upper West Side treasure", this "winning" Pan-Asian pioneer stays "crowded" thanks to "interestingly spiced" fusion fare that's "not too harmful on the wallet"; "noisy" conditions distract from the otherwise "transporting" "rain forest-like setting."

☑ Rainbow Room Ⓜ *Italian*
19 | 27 | 21 | VE

W 40s | GE Bldg. | 30 Rockefeller Plaza, 65th fl. (enter on 49th St., bet. 5th & 6th Aves.)

Rainbow Grill *Italian*
W 40s | GE Bldg. | 30 Rockefeller Plaza, 65th fl. (enter on 49th St., bet. 5th & 6th Aves.)
212-632-5100 | www.rainbowroom.com
"There's no place like" this 65th-floor Rock Center "destination" where the views are "worth a million bucks" and reflected in the "skyscraper prices"; the Northern Italian cuisine is "decent", but "you don't go for the food" – it's the "art deco splendor" and "revolving dance floor" that make for "enchanted evenings" here; it's open to the public select Fridays and Saturdays for prix fixe–only dinner ($200) and Sundays for brunch ($80); the adjacent Rainbow Grill offers a less pricey à la carte menu.

Rai Rai Ken ◑⇸ *Noodle Shop*
▽ 22 | 12 | 17 | $13

E Village | 214 E. 10th St. (bet. 1st & 2nd Aves.) | 212-477-7030
"As authentic as it comes", this "tiny", "counter-seating-only" East Village ramen shop has the requisite "long wooden bar" and "crowded Tokyo conditions"; the noodles are "seriously delicious", "incredibly satisfying" and "very affordable" – so start "praying for a seat."

| | | FOOD | DECOR | SERVICE | COST |

NEW Ramen Setagaya ✏ *Noodle Shop* — | — | — | I

E Village | 141 First Ave. (bet. 9th St. & St. Marks Pl.) | 212-529-2740

This East Village outpost of the Tokyo-based noodle chain is a ramen-only specialist where the inexpensive offerings are made from 90 per-cent Japanese ingredients; already challenging Momofuku Noodle Bar for authenticity, it claims that its secret weapon lies in the broth.

Z Rao's ⊠✏ *Italian* 22 | 16 | 21 | $61

Harlem | 455 E. 114th St. (Pleasant Ave.) | 212-722-6709 | www.raos.com

"Still the toughest reservation in town", Frank Pellegrino's "mystique"-laden East Harlem Southern Italian requires knowing a "friend with a table" for the chance to dine on "amazing" "old-world" dishes while rubbing elbows with the famous and the infamous; alternatives in-clude doing it yourself with a jar of their "supermarket sauce" or "fly-ing to Vegas to try the new one in Caesars Palace."

Raoul's ● *French* 24 | 20 | 21 | $55

SoHo | 180 Prince St. (bet. Sullivan & Thompson Sts.) | 212-966-3518 | www.raouls.com

Expect "ambiance à la Paris" at this "long-standing" (since 1975) dark French bistro that "never goes out of style"; it was "cool before SoHo was cool" thanks to its "excellent" steak au poivre, "charming" service and "romantic back garden", and if it's a little "expensive", "what a scene" you get in return.

Rare Bar & Grill *Hamburgers* 21 | 15 | 16 | $30

G Village | 228 Bleecker St. (bet. Carmine St. & 6th Ave.) | 212-691-7273

Murray Hill | Shelburne Murray Hill Hotel | 303 Lexington Ave. (37th St.) | 212-481-1999

www.rarebarandgrill.com

A "noisy" "young" crowd slips into "heavenly food comas" at these "high-end" burger joints where the "brilliant" beef can be customized "with all the fixin's"; maybe the decor and service are "nothing spe-cial", but neither is the tab and the "french fry sampler is unforgettable."

NEW Rayuela *Pan-Latin* — | — | — | M

LES | 165 Allen St. (bet. Rivington & Stanton Sts.) | 212-253-8840 | www.rayuelanyc.com

The name of this big new Lower Eastsider translates as 'hopscotch' and its Pan-Latin menu jumps around Latin America and Spain; built around a live olive tree, the stylish, split-level space exudes big-city rusticity.

Real Madrid *Spanish* ▽ 21 | 14 | 20 | $38

Staten Island | 2075 Forest Ave. (Union Ave.) | 718-447-7885 | www.realmadrid-restaurant.com

Serving "dependable" Spanish cuisine for over 20 years, this "authen-tic" Staten Island standby sure knows its seafood and sangria; its "rea-sonable" prices and "gracious" service work equally well for everyday dining or "special occasions."

Red Cat *American/Mediterranean* 24 | 20 | 22 | $53

Chelsea | 227 10th Ave. (bet. 23rd & 24th Sts.) | 212-242-1122 | www.theredcat.com

Chef-owner Jimmy Bradley's "Chelsea charmer" is "still purring along", luring "avid" regulars and other "adult diners" with its "smartly chosen" New American–Med offerings, "smiling waiters" and "buzzing atmosphere"; the only catch is, it's "so damn popular" that it can be "hard to snag a table."

Redeye Grill ◑ *American/Seafood*   20 | 19 | 19 | $53

W 50s | 890 Seventh Ave. (56th St.) | 212-541-9000 | www.redeyegrill.com
Shelly Fireman's "big", bustling New American attracts business-lunchers, show-goers and "tourists" with its across-the-street-from-"Carnegie-Hall convenience"; as befits the self-proclaimed "home of the dancing shrimp", you can expect "delish fish" and an "invigorating" atmosphere, though it's a bit "on the pricey side."

NEW Régate *French*   – | – | – | M

LES | 198 Orchard St. (bet. Houston & Stanton Sts.) | 212-228-8555 | www.regate-bistro.com
Young, easygoing Euros helm this new LES Gallic bistro, a tiny spot specializing in the casual cooking found at the French resort of Ile de Ré; affordable prices, amiable service and soccer broadcasts on the TV behind the bar reflect its modest intentions.

Regency *American*   ▽ 18 | 22 | 20 | $61

E 60s | Regency Hotel | 540 Park Ave. (61st St.) | 212-339-4050 | www.loewshotels.com
NY's "elite" types rise and shine with the "consummate power breakfast" at this East Side New American where big deals go down with the bacon and eggs and it's easy to play who's who; after dark, the space moonlights as Feinstein's, a "favorite" cabaret for top-line talent.

Regional *Italian*   17 | 15 | 15 | $35

W 90s | 2607 Broadway (bet. 98th & 99th Sts.) | 212-666-1915
This "undiscovered" Upper Westsider's "unusual" menu covers 20 "different regions of Italy", but despite "great potential", the cooking falls somewhere between "fairly good" and "average"; "spotty" service and a "sterile" setting don't help, though "at this price, who cares?"

Regional Thai *Thai*   18 | 12 | 15 | $28

Chelsea | 208 Seventh Ave. (22nd St.) | 212-807-9872
E 70s | 1479 First Ave. (77th St.) | 212-744-6374
Bringing "Thailand's greatest hits" to Chelsea and the UES, this "decent" duo draws "constant crowds" with its "reliable" kitchen and "value" pricing; regarding the "tired" decor and "spaced-out service", regulars have "two words" of advice: "take out."

Relish ◑ *American*   ▽ 22 | 21 | 19 | $28

Williamsburg | 225 Wythe Ave. (bet. Metropolitan Ave. & N. 3rd St.) | Brooklyn | 718-963-4546 | www.relish.com
A restored "stainless-steel dining car" is the setting for this Williamsburg New American serving a "satisfying" array of affordable comfort chow; "tragically hip" types stand in for the usual truck drivers, and instead of a parking lot, there's a "super-duper" garden.

Remi *Italian*   22 | 21 | 20 | $58

W 50s | 145 W. 53rd St. (bet. 6th & 7th Aves.) | 212-581-4242 | www.remi-ny.com
"Quality dining" is alive and well at this "memorable" Midtown Italian whose "well-balanced" menu skews Venetian; "graceful" service and

	FOOD	DECOR	SERVICE	COST

a "huge fresco" of the Grand Canal add to its allure, and though the pricing's decidedly "upscale", prix fixe deals are available.

René Pujol ⓜ French
| | 22 | 19 | 22 | $55 |

W 50s | 321 W. 51st St. (bet. 8th & 9th Aves.) | 212-246-3023 | www.renepujol.com

There's "nothing nouveau" going on at this "tried-and-true" Theater District "grande dame" serving "solid" French fare and a "quality" dinner prix fixe; the decor "could use some freshening", but "efficient" "pro" service means you'll make the curtain on time.

Republic Pan-Asian
| | 18 | 13 | 15 | $21 |

Union Sq | 37 Union Sq. W. (bet. 16th & 17th Sts.) | 212-627-7172 | www.thinknoodles.com

For "cheap eats", it's hard to beat this Union Square noodle shop where the Pan-Asian food's "delicious" and the service "militant" but "superquick"; downsides include "wood bench" "picnic table"–style seating and "ear-clanging" acoustics – so "don't go to discuss life with a friend."

Re Sette Italian
| | ▽ 23 | 19 | 21 | $53 |

W 40s | 7 W. 45th St. (bet. 5th & 6th Aves.) | 212-221-7530 | www.resette.com

Regional Barese dishes are "beautifully prepared" at this "relaxed" Midtown Italian that's "away from the crowds" yet "close to the theaters"; book a private party at the King's Table upstairs for "extraspecial" service and "eat like", well, you know . . .

NEW Resto ⓞⓜ Belgian
| | – | – | – | M |

Gramercy | 111 E. 29th St. (bet. Lexington Ave. & Park Ave. S.) | 212-685-5585 | www.restonyc.com

An instant scene, this casual new Gramercy Belgian is drawing young folks with a pleasing menu washed down with a long list of brews; prices are moderate, reservations aren't taken and the noise level is thunderous given its tile floor, tin ceiling, marble-topped bar and enthusiastic crowd.

NEW Revel ⓞ Eclectic
| | – | – | – | E |

Meatpacking | 10 Little W. 12th St. (bet. 9th Ave. & Washington St.) | 212-645-5369

The funky bar/eatery that's operated without a name for several years now has one, along with an expanded Eclectic menu that includes dishes cooked on volcanic stones; still, the big draw is its spectacular back garden that's a sanctuary from the Meatpacking District revelry.

Revival American/French
| | ▽ 19 | 16 | 15 | $31 |

Harlem | 2367 Frederick Douglass Blvd. (127th St.) | 212-222-8338 | www.harlemrevival.com

Still rather "unknown", this Harlem spot "tries interesting things" with varying degrees of success" by adding Caribbean, Creole and soul touches to its Franco-American menu; verdicts range from "amazing" to "disappointing", but it's still a "value" and certainly "welcome" in an underserved area.

Ribot ⑤ Mediterranean
| | ▽ 19 | 20 | 18 | $49 |

40s | 780 Third Ave. (48th St.) | 212-355-3700 | www.ribotnyc.com

Named for an Italian racehorse, this "elegant", "high-ceilinged" Midtowner trots out a Mediterranean menu that's "more than decent"

| | FOOD | DECOR | SERVICE | COST |

and "getting better"; naysayers whinny over "hovering" service and regret being the "only ones there without implants."

Rice ✿ *Eclectic*
19 | 14 | 17 | $20

Gramercy | 115 Lexington Ave. (28th St.) | 212-686-5400
NoHo | 292 Elizabeth St. (bet. Bleecker & Houston Sts.) | 212-226-5775 ●
Dumbo | 81 Washington St. (bet. Front & York Sts.) | Brooklyn | 718-222-9880
Fort Greene | 166 DeKalb Ave. (Cumberland St.) | Brooklyn | 718-858-2700
www.riceny.com

It's "rice every which way" at this "modest" Eclectic quartet where a "cornucopia" of "exotic" starch options lets you "have it your way" (especially if you're "vegetarian friendly"); maybe the end result is "uneven", but at least "very little money" is involved.

Rice 'n' Beans *Brazilian*
▽ 19 | 8 | 16 | $25

W 50s | 744 Ninth Ave. (bet. 50th & 51st Sts.) | 212-265-4444 | www.ricenbeansrestaurant.com

"Straight off a Rio side street", this Hell's Kitchen "sleeper" serves "transporting", "stick-to-your ribs" Brazilian grub for "dirt-cheap" tabs; the trade-offs are "nonattentive" (albeit "good-natured") service and digs the dimensions of a "coat closet."

Rickshaw Dumpling Bar *Chinese*
18 | 9 | 13 | $13

Flatiron | 61 W. 23rd St. (bet. 5th & 6th Aves.) | 212-924-9220
NEW **G Village** | 53 E. Eighth St. (bet. B'way & University Pl.) | 212-461-1750
www.rickshawdumplings.com

At this "fast food"–style Flatiron Chinese, exec chef Anita Lo vends "addictive dumplings" that can be "cleverly mixed and matched" with soup or salad for a "filling meal"; "confusing" menus and a "sterile", "cramped" setting are ultimately trumped by the super-"cheap" pricing; N.B. the Village branch opened post-Survey.

Riingo *American/Japanese*
19 | 19 | 19 | $57

E 40s | Alex Hotel | 205 E. 45th St. (bet. 2nd & 3rd Aves.) | 212-867-4200 | www.riingo.com

For "stylish" Midtown dining, Marcus Samuelsson's New American-Japanese fusionfest provides "tasty" dishes that are "pricey" but "less expensive" than his better-known Aquavit; the "skinny" setting and sometimes somnolent service are redeemed by "amazing" cocktails and "all-day-long" hours.

Risotteria *Italian*
21 | 10 | 16 | $23

G Village | 270 Bleecker St. (Morton St.) | 212-924-6664 | www.risotteria.com
Thanks to a "clever menu" in which "everything is gluten-free", this Village Italian "fulfills an important function" for folks with "dietary restrictions" (vegetarians included); its specialty risottos are "cheap and gratifying", even if the "phone booth–size" space is "not much to look at."

☑ River Café *American*
26 | 28 | 26 | $111

Dumbo | 1 Water St. (bet. Furman & Old Fulton Sts.) | Brooklyn | 718-522-5200 | www.rivercafe.com

"Sheer bliss from start to finish", Dumbo's "classic stunner" under the Brooklyn Bridge "wows visitors" with "top-notch" New American fare, a "flower-laden" interior and "glorious" river/skyline views (it's "the place to propose - no matter what the proposition"); just remember t "dress sharp" (jackets required) and prepare for a "wallet busting" ($95 prix fixe–only dinner); N.B. they do spectacular parties.

Riverdale Garden *American* | 24 | 19 | 18 | $46 |

Bronx | 4576 Manhattan College Pkwy. (242nd St.) | 718-884-5232 | www.riverdalegarden.com

The "Bronx is blessed" to have this "Manhattan-caliber" New American, whose "unassuming" setting belies its "consistently classy", "farm-fresh" preparations; though it's a bit "pricey" and service can be "idiosyncratic", a "beautiful" back garden and "valet parking" more than compensate.

River Room Ⓜ *Southern* | ▽ 19 | 24 | 15 | $42 |

Harlem | Riverbank State Park | W. 145th St. (Riverside Dr.) | 212-491-1500 | www.theriverroomofharlem.com

Set in Harlem's "secret" Riverbank State Park, this "upscale" yet mid-priced Southerner claims "priceless" views of the Hudson, Palisades and GW Bridge through its plate-glass windows; "pleasant" live weekend jazz jives with the "sophisticated" mood, not the "disappearing" staff.

⦿ Roberto ⑤ *Italian* | 27 | 18 | 21 | $49 |

Bronx | 603 Crescent Ave. (Hughes Ave.) | 718-733-9503 | www.robertobronx.com

At this "neighborhood treasure" in the Bronx's version of Little Italy, Roberto Paciullo sends diners on "life-changing" tours of his native Salerno ("forget the menu", he'll "take good care of you"); still, that no-reservations policy makes for "looong" waits.

Roberto Passon ● *Italian* | 22 | 16 | 20 | $44 |

W 50s | 741 Ninth Ave. (50th St.) | 212-582-5599 | www.robertopasson.com

"More than just a neighborhood trattoria", this "popular" Hell's Kitchen Italian draws both locals and the Broadway-bound with "straightforward" cooking plus "interesting flourishes"; though prices are generally "reasonable", "beware the cost of the specials."

Roc ● *Italian* | 21 | 20 | 21 | $52 |

TriBeCa | 190A Duane St. (Greenwich St.) | 212-625-3333 | www.rocrestaurant.com

This "consistent performer" in TriBeCa has the "quality" thing down pat, with "delicious" Italian food, "chic" digs and "charming" service; sure, you'll pay "above-average prices", but that doesn't faze its "rich and beautiful" following.

Rocco Ⓜ *Italian* | ▽ 20 | 13 | 19 | $38 |

G Village | 181 Thompson St. (bet. Bleecker & Houston Sts.) | 212-677-0590 | www.roccorestaurant.com

Serving "affordable", "well-prepared" Southern Italiana in the same Village spot since 1922, this "old-line", "elbows-on-the-table kind of place" is "like going home for a visit"; the decor is straight out of a "1940s movie version of what an Italian restaurant should be."

Rock Center Café *American* | 19 | 22 | 19 | $45 |

W 50s | Rockefeller Ctr. | 20 W. 50th St. (bet. 5th & 6th Aves.) | 212-332-7620 | www.patinarestaurantgroup.com

An all-seasons "people-watching" paradise, this midpriced Rock Center "tourist favorite" features an American menu that's "better than you'd expect"; still, it's the "skating rink" views in the winter and "alfresco summer dining" that make it a bona fide "NYC experience."

Rocking Horse Cafe *Mexican*
20 | 16 | 17 | $36

Chelsea | 182 Eighth Ave. (bet. 19th & 20th Sts.) | 212-463-9511 | www.rockinghorsecafe.com

"Festive" Chelsea "haute Mex" that draws "young", "cacophonous" crowds with "nouveau" cuisine washed down with "devastating margaritas"; despite some "inconsistent" moments (i.e. "slow service"), it's still a "scene" after 20 years in business.

Roebling Tea Room ◑ *American*
▽ 21 | 20 | 16 | $22

Williamsburg | 143 Roebling St. (Metropolitan Ave.) | Brooklyn | 718-963-0760 | www.roeblingtearoom.com

The "eclectic" array of affordable "small plates and sandwiches" at this Williamsburg tearoom is accompanied by a "huge selection" of leaves, plus "ample couches" and "high funk" decor; it draws a "cool crowd", which may explain the "glacial" service.

Rolf's *German*
17 | 20 | 16 | $39

Gramercy | 281 Third Ave. (22nd St.) | 212-477-4750

"Oof" goes the schnitzel at this long-running Gramercy Park German where the "authentic" fare comes with a side of "storybook" "spectacle" during the holidays via a "dizzying" display of Christmas lights; it's "from another world and time", starting with those "enormous portions."

Roll-n-Roaster ◑ *Sandwiches*
19 | 8 | 11 | $14

Sheepshead Bay | 2901 Emmons Ave. (bet. E. 29th St. & Nostrand Ave.) | Brooklyn | 718-769-5831 | www.rollnroaster.com

You can "have cheez on anything you pleez" at this Sheepshead Bay "institution" that's been rolling out "excellent roast beef sandwiches" and fries since 1970; regulars know it's a "quick bite" at a "good price", but when it comes to "decor, fuhgeddaboudit."

Room Service *Thai*
19 | 19 | 17 | $27

Chelsea | 166 Eighth Ave. (bet. 18th & 19th Sts.) | 212-691-0299

"Trendy to a fault", this Chelsea Thai looks like a chic hotel lobby with "techno-hallucinatory" decor, a "skinny" client base and an "energetic", "club music" soundtrack; "gimmicky" though it may be, the "imaginative" fusion fare comes at "unbelievably affordable" rates.

Roppongi *Japanese*
19 | 14 | 17 | $36

W 80s | 434 Amsterdam Ave. (81st St.) | 212-362-8182 | www.ropponginyc.net

"In the shadow of Haru" (its across-the-street rival), this UWS Japanese "secret" delivers "pleasant" repasts in "minimalist", "not as crowded" surroundings; the sushi is "fresh", the cooked dishes "creative" and, best of all, tabs are "reasonable for the neighborhood."

☑ Rosa Mexicano ◑ *Mexican*
22 | 21 | 20 | $47

E 50s | 1063 First Ave. (58th St.) | 212-753-7407
Flatiron | 9 E. 18th St. (bet. B'way & 5th Ave.) | 212-533-3350
W 60s | 61 Columbus Ave. (62nd St.) | 212-977-7700
www.rosamexicano.com

"Lively" folks in "celebratory" mode pack this "hip 'n' hopping" threesome for their "designer Mexican" settings and menus, led by "world-

| | FOOD | DECOR | SERVICE | COST |

lass" guacamole made tableside ("to kill for") and washed down with "deliciously deadly" pomegranate margaritas; though everything's "muy bien", they're "best experienced on someone else's dime."

NEW Rosanjin ⊠ Japanese ▽ 25 | 21 | 23 | $155

TriBeCa | 141 Duane St. (bet. Church St. & W. B'way) | 212-346-7991 | www.rosanjintribeca.com

"Beautiful in every way", this pocket-size new TriBeCa Japanese with museumlike hush is set in subtly sleek digs and purveys "authentic" "Kyoto-style" kaiseki dinners at "Per Se prices" ($150 prix fixe only); expect a traditional parade of "precious", artfully presented morsels.

Rose Water American 25 | 18 | 22 | $42

Park Slope | 787 Union St. (6th Ave.) | Brooklyn | 718-783-3800 | www.rosewaterrestaurant.com

"Green" is the watchword at this Park Slope New American whose "fresh-from-the-farmer's-market" menu "constantly evolves" with the chef's choice of both "lowly and lofty ingredients"; the "big flavors" may contrast with the "tiny room", but not with the overall "attention to detail" and "outstanding service."

Rossini's Italian 23 | 19 | 25 | $59

Murray Hill | 108 E. 38th St. (bet. Lexington & Park Aves.) | 212-683-0135 | www.rossinisrestaurant.com

Think "very old world" to get the gist of this Murray Hill Northern Italian vet known for its "delicious" food, "professional service" and live opera Saturday night; if the "decor's getting a little tired", the prices will keep you "wide awake."

Rothmann's Steak 22 | 20 | 22 | $65

E 50s | 3 E. 54th St. (bet. 5th & Madison Aves.) | 212-319-5500 | www.rothmannssteakhouse.com

This East Midtowner "may not get its due" among the city's steakhouse stars, but fans say it's a "serious contender" citing "fantastic" chops, "attentive" service and handsome "wood-and-linen" digs; given the strong "business" following, "corporate credit cards" absorb the "excessive" tabs.

Roth's Westside Steakhouse Steak 19 | 16 | 18 | $49

W 90s | 680 Columbus Ave. (93rd St.) | 212-280-4103 | www.rothswestsidesteakhouse.com

"Much needed on the UWS", this "dependable" chop shop embellishes its "solid" menu and "friendly" service with nightly "light jazz"; tabs are "not bad" for the genre, so most agree "you have to give it credit."

Rouge French 20 | 17 | 18 | $39

Forest Hills | 107-02 70th Rd. (Austin St.) | Queens | 718-793-5514

"Raising the bar in Forest Hills", this "inviting" bistro "fills a niche", dishing out "classic" French fare in a Left Bank setting; maybe it's "not exciting", but things pick up in the summer when "you can dine alfresco."

Royal Siam Thai 19 | 12 | 17 | $27

Chelsea | 240 Eighth Ave. (bet. 22nd & 23rd Sts.) | 212-741-1732

Typical "Thai value" keeps locals loyal to this "never-too-crowded" Chelsea "mainstay"; sure, the setting's "so-so" and there's "nothing unusual" on the plate, but what's there is "always good."

	FOOD	DECOR	SERVICE	COST

Roy's New York *Hawaiian*
25 | 19 | 22 | $54

Financial District | Marriott Financial Ctr. | 130 Washington St.
(bet. Albany & Carlisle Sts.) | 212-266-6262 | www.roysnewyork.com
Fans of Roy Yamaguchi say *"mahalo"* to this Financial District outpos
of the chef's Hawaiian empire, where "delicate, delicious" fusion far
can be savored "without the sunburn"; despite "high prices" and deco
that "transports you to a mall in the Midwest", many say it "doesn
get the recognition it deserves."

RUB BBQ *BBQ*
20 | 9 | 15 | $28

Chelsea | 208 W. 23rd St. (bet. 7th & 8th Aves.) | 212-524-4300 |
www.rubbbq.net
"No-nonsense" "Kansas City"-style barbecue is yours at this "rowdy
Chelsea pit stop that will "cure any urges" for "messy", hickory
smoked meat; ok, the setting and service are "not so special" and the
seem to "run out of some good stuff every night", but overall it's
"solid contender in NYC's BBQ wars."

Ruby Foo's ◗ *Pan-Asian*
19 | 21 | 17 | $42

W 40s | 1626 Broadway (49th St.) | 212-489-5600
W 70s | 2182 Broadway (77th St.) | 212-724-6700
www.brguestrestaurants.com
"Definitely not Chinatown", these "big, brash", party-centric Pan-Asian
serve a variety of "tasty" dishes in "flashy", "kitschy", "lacquered" set
tings that seem "turned up to 11"; they're "frenzied" "fun for the kids
and "tourists", so regulars advise "go at off times – if there are any."

Rue 57 ◗ *French*
19 | 18 | 17 | $45

W 50s | 60 W. 57th St. (6th Ave.) | 212-307-5656 | www.rue57.com
"Everyone gets what they like" at this "bustling" Midtowner that mir
gles midpriced French brasserie plates with sushi – a "strange" bu
"convenient" combo; "on-and-off service" and "acoustic trauma" de
tract, but it is "strategically located" for lunch or "after Carnegie Hall

Rughetta 🗟 *Italian*
22 | 16 | 21 | $44

E 80s | 347 E. 85th St. (bet. 1st & 2nd Aves.) | 212-517-3118 |
www.rughetta.com
"Known only to locals", this versatile UES Italian works well for eithe
a "romantic evening" or a "casual night out"; the "authentic Roman
cuisine is "excellent" and quite "reasonable", but the "narrow space
can get "crowded" – "pity it's not bigger."

Russian Samovar ◗ *Continental*
19 | 18 | 18 | $49

W 50s | 256 W. 52nd St. (bet. B'way & 8th Ave.) | 212-757-0168 |
www.russiansamovar.com
Caviar and "habit-forming flavored vodkas" collide at this Theate
District Continental that's straight out of "Mother Russia" with "sovie
service" and "KGB agent" look-alikes in attendance; the live piano mu
sic evokes "Moscow nights", albeit at "New York prices."

NEW Russian Tea Room *Continental/Russian*
19 | 25 | 19 | $69

W 50s | 150 W. 57th St. (bet. 6th & 7th Aves.) | 212-581-7100 |
www.russiantearoomnyc.com
Back after a four-year hiatus, this Midtown "icon" just "slightly to th
left of Carnegie Hall" offers modern takes on Continental and Russia

| | | FOOD | DECOR | SERVICE | COST |

classics at prices "fit for a czar"; even though it's "not what it once was", the "cheerfully gaudy" decor is little changed from Warner LeRoy's 1999 renovation, and if some sense an "identity crisis", it's "still an experience."

Ruth's Chris Steak House *Steak*　　　23 | 19 | 22 | $66

W 50s | 148 W. 51st St. (bet. 6th & 7th Aves.) | 212-245-9600 | www.ruthschris.com

Yes, this Theater District link of the New Orleans–based steakhouse chain is ever "dependable" for "succulent" slabs of beef "dripping with butter" that are "just as delicious as they are expensive"; while service is "gracious", some find the ambiance more "Omaha" than "New York."

Sabor ● *Nuevo Latino*　　　▽ 19 | 16 | 16 | $34

E 80s | 1725 Second Ave. (89th St.) | 212-369-9373

Back with an "eclectic" Nuevo Latino menu (and under nuevo ownership), this "welcoming", low-budget Yorkville "neighborhood" spot mixes "tasty", "ample-portioned tapas" with "strong sangria"; too bad the "crowded space" and "inattentive" service are "nothing special."

Sachiko's on Clinton ● Ⓜ *Japanese*　　　▽ 25 | 17 | 21 | $56

LES | 25 Clinton St. (bet. Houston & Stanton Sts.) | 212-253-2900 | www.sachikosonclinton.com

Sushi and sashimi are "artfully presented" and "impeccably fresh" at this "low-profile" LES Japanese; "knowledgeable" staffers help navigate the "subtly inventive" plates and "comprehensive sake menu", though to some eyes the "calm" interior reads as "bland."

Sacred Chow *Vegan/Vegetarian*　　　▽ 23 | 13 | 21 | $20

G Village | 227 Sullivan St. (bet. Bleecker & W. 3rd Sts.) | 212-337-0863 | www.sacredchow.com

For inexpensive kosher health food, try this Greenwich Village "secret" with its vegan "food from the gods" (there are "gluten-free" options too); adding to the authenticity, the "incredibly edible" offerings are dished out by servers "who look the part."

Sac's Place *Pizza*　　　▽ 21 | 13 | 17 | $24

Astoria | 25-41 Broadway (29th St.) | Queens | 718-204-5002

"Worth-the-trip" coal-fired pizza comes out of the brick oven of this "unassuming", "family-run" Astoria Italian where "they sell it by the slice" too; maybe the other offerings fall short, but the "addictive" pies are "neighborhood favorites."

🆕 Safran *French/Vietnamese*　　　▽ 20 | 20 | 18 | $37

Chelsea | 88 Seventh Ave. (bet. 15th & 16th Sts.) | 212-929-1778 | www.safran88.com

"Unique" French-Vietnamese fusion fare lands on an "otherwise drab strip" of Chelsea at this coolly "fashionable", yet eminently affordable, spot; locals agree it's a "great addition to the neighborhood."

S'Agapo ● *Greek*　　　▽ 20 | 11 | 18 | $35

Astoria | 34-21 34th Ave. (35th St.) | Queens | 718-626-0303

It's "easy to become a regular" at this "sweet", modestly priced Astoria Greek where service is "friendly" and the "no-frills" classics come "mom approved"; given that there's "nothing on the decor side" going on, the "outdoor seating" is a "saving grace."

	FOOD	DECOR	SERVICE	COST

Sahara ● *Turkish*

20 | 15 | 16 | $27

Gravesend | 2337 Coney Island Ave. (bet. Aves. T & U) | Brooklyn | 718-376-8594 | www.saharapalace.com

Setting the "standard for Turkish" in Gravesend, this "vast bazaar" purveys "authentic" dishes "by the truckload" at "fabulous" prices; despite "erratic" service and "not breathtaking" decor ("dim the lights, please"), it's "hard to stop eating" here.

Saigon Grill ● *Vietnamese*

22 | 12 | 15 | $24

G Village | 91-93 University Pl. (bet. 11th & 12th Sts.) | 212-982-3691
W 90s | 620 Amsterdam Ave. (90th St.) | 212-875-9072
www.saigongrill.com

"Phenomenal" eats, "budget" pricing and "chaotic" conditions say it all about these Vietnamese "mainstays"; despite "recent labor conflicts" that have suspended delivery, on-site your "food arrives immediately."

Sakagura *Japanese*

24 | 21 | 22 | $47

E 40s | 211 E. 43rd St., downstairs (bet. 2nd & 3rd Aves.) | 212-953-7253 | www.sakagura.com

Hidden in the "basement of a random office building" near Grand Central, this "eccentric" Japanese *izakaya* is praised for its "wide sake selection" as well as its "deft" small plates; perhaps dinnertime tabs can "add up", but "it's a bargain for lunch."

Sala *Spanish*

22 | 19 | 18 | $38

Flatiron | 35 W. 19th St. (bet. 5th & 6th Aves.) | 212-229-2300
NoHo | 344 Bowery (Great Jones St.) | 212-979-6606
www.salanyc.com

Full of "twentysomething tapas lovers", these "noisy", "date-worthy" Spaniards boast "on-point sangria" and "tempting" plates for "decent" dough; despite "long waits" to get in and "slow service", the "intimate" ambiance appeals to "romantic" types.

Salaam Bombay *Indian*

20 | 16 | 18 | $34

TriBeCa | 317 Greenwich St. (bet. Duane & Reade Sts.) | 212-226-9400 | www.salaambombay.com

An "extensive" lunch buffet at the "bargain" price of $13.95 lures "office gangs" to this TriBeCa Indian that's "several cuts above the rest"; too bad the à la carte dinner menu is a bit more "hit-or-miss" and the interior "has seen better days."

Sal Anthony's Lanza *Italian*

19 | 17 | 18 | $41

E Village | 168 First Ave. (bet. 10th & 11th Sts.) | 212-674-7014
Sal Anthony's S.P.Q.R. *Italian*
Little Italy | 133 Mulberry St. (bet. Grand & Hester Sts.) | 212-925-3120
www.salanthonys.com

This East Village–Little Italy pair is "fine" for "consistent" if "generic" Southern Italian dining; "generous portions" plus a "great prix fixe" draw an "older" following, and even if the decor is a bit "faded", some times "old school" is "what you want."

Sala Thai ● *Thai*

21 | 13 | 17 | $27

E 80s | 1718 Second Ave. (bet. 89th & 90th Sts.) | 212-410-5557

There's "tasty" Thai at this "grown-up" UES neighborhood "sleeper" that's "been there forever"; "pleasant", "well-presented" standards nd low prices compensate for "shabby surroundings" and service hat's just "adequate"; P.S. "delivery arrives in a flash."

alt ⓈＺ *American* | 21 | 18 | 20 | $41 |

oHo | 58 MacDougal St. (bet. Houston & Prince Sts.) | 212-674-4968
alt Bar ●ＺＭ⇄ *American*

ES | 29A Clinton St. (bet. Houston & Stanton Sts.) | 212-979-8471
www.saltnyc.com

nown for its "homey", "robust" cooking, this SoHo New American is taffed by a "gracious" crew who manages to make the "tight", communal table"-strewn space feel "cozy"; its LES offshoot is more f a "classy" drinks-and-nibbles joint, without a full-blown menu.

alute! *Italian/Mediterranean* | 19 | 20 | 18 | $47 |

Aurray Hill | 270 Madison Ave. (39th St.) | 212-213-3440 |
www.salutenyc.com

Aurray Hill "suits" tuck into "savory power lunches" and eavesdrop on great stock tips" at this "chic", midpriced Med-Italian; an "extensive" nenu and "decent" wine list suggest they're "trying hard to please", erratic" service and "expense-account prices" to the contrary.

amba-Lé ●⇄ *Brazilian* | ▽ 19 | 21 | 19 | $42 |

Village | 23 Ave. A (bet. Houston & 2nd Sts.) | 212-529-2919

Brazilian tapas washed down with cool caipirinhas keep this "original" ast Villager full; given the "live samba music" on weekends and noisy" ambiance, some see more scene than cuisine here.

ambuca *Italian* | 18 | 16 | 18 | $38 |

V 70s | 20 W. 72nd St. (bet. Columbus Ave. & CPW) | 212-787-5656 |
www.sambucanyc.com

Come hungry" to this "budget" UWS Italian that dishes out family-ize platters so "ginormous" that you can "bring six people and order or one"; the nondescript setting is "less chaotic than Carmine's", vhile a separate sans-gluten menu lets everyone "eat freely."

ammy's Roumanian *Jewish* | 19 | 9 | 17 | $49 |

ES | 157 Chrystie St. (Delancey St.) | 212-673-0330

Oy gevalt", this Lower East Side "cardiologist's nightmare" may be the last of its breed", what with its "heartburn"-inducing menu of Jewish tandards that are "to die for (and from)"; expect a "*meshuggah*" cene out of a "'50s bar mitzvah" complete with a pianist providing nother kind of "schmaltz."

an Domenico *Italian* | 23 | 21 | 22 | $75 |

V 50s | 240 Central Park S. (bet. B'way & 7th Ave.) | 212-265-5959 |
www.sandomeniconewyork.com

o "civilized" that "jackets are still required", this "timeless" CPS talian now in its 20th year is the "calm", "elegant" home to chef Odette Fada's "refined" cuisine and a "caring staff" overseen by owner ony May; granted, the "bill is as sophisticated as the food", but what lse would you expect from such a "special-occasion treat"?

IEW Sandro's ●Ｚ *Italian* | - | - | - | M |

80s | 306 E. 81st St. (bet. 1st & 2nd Aves.) | 212-288-7374

n a quiet UES block, chef Sandro Fioriti has revived his 1980s trat-oria in a modern, white brick–walled space; it serves as an attractive

Backdrop for midpriced Roman-style meals that go down nicely with house-infused grappa.

San Luigi *Italian*
16 | 13 | 14 | $34

W 70s | 311 Amsterdam Ave. (bet. 74th & 75th Sts.) | 212-362-882
This UWS Italian "new kid on the block" provides "hefty portions" bu rather "average" flavors in a setting that's a bit too "suburban" fc many ("TVs everywhere are a turnoff"); "affordable" tabs and "lov wine markups" help explain the "overwhelmed" service.

San Pietro 🗷 *Italian*
24 | 19 | 23 | $73

E 50s | 18 E. 54th St. (bet. 5th & Madison Aves.) | 212-753-9015 | www.sanpietro.net
"Business titans" rule at this "traditional" Midtown Italian that's hom to an "elite" crowd of lunchtime "regulars" (after dark, theatergoer supplant the "power hungry"); living up to its "high-end" standards the cooking is "fabulous", the service "polished" and the pricing "i the hedge fund manager's realm."

Sant Ambroeus *Italian*
22 | 19 | 19 | $57

E 70s | 1000 Madison Ave. (bet. 77th & 78th Sts.) | 212-570-2211
W Village | 259 W. Fourth St. (Perry St.) | 212-604-9254
www.santambroeus.com
"Fashionistas pretend to eat" their salads at this "super-soigné" du where the "excellent" Milanese fare lures in everyone from "art dealers to "society" dames to matinee idols; no kidding, the "people-watching is primo, ditto the "expensive-but-you're-worth-it-darling" prices.

Sapa *French/Vietnamese*
22 | 25 | 20 | $55

Flatiron | 43 W. 24th St. (bet. B'way & 6th Ave.) | 212-929-1800 | www.sapanyc.com
Maybe the "oh-so-cool" setting (and "theatrical" loo) is the "most im pressive aspect" of this Flatiron "experience", however, the "adventu ous" French-Vietnamese fusion fare more than holds its own; jus beware, "when the bar is in full holler", it can be a tad too "sceney N.B. the departure of chef Patricia Yeo puts its Food rating in questior

Sapori D'Ischia 🅼 *Italian*
25 | 17 | 21 | $46

Woodside | 55-15 37th Ave. (56th St.) | Queens | 718-446-1500
Obscured "amid Woodside warehouses", this daytime specialty foo shop morphs into a "gourmet restaurant" at night serving some prett "fabulous" Italian food – so long as you don't mind "salami hanging ov your head"; P.S. on Thursdays, live opera singers are the "big draw."

Sapphire Indian *Indian*
20 | 18 | 19 | $41

W 60s | 1845 Broadway (bet. 60th & 61st Sts.) | 212-245-4444 | www.sapphireny.com
For "convenience to Lincoln Center", this Indian gem off Columbu Circle is geographically desirable with "better-than-average" fare tha packs more "flavor" than the "bland" room; it may be "a little pricey for the genre, but the $12.95 lunch buffet is a bona fide "bargain."

Sapporo East ◗ *Japanese*
▽ 21 | 9 | 16 | $26

E Village | 164 First Ave. (10th St.) | 212-260-1330
"So-fresh" sushi and other "belly-filling" Japanese dishes promp "long lines" at this "no-frills" East Village "greasy spoon"; luckily, "e

icient" servers keep things "quick", and the "bargain" prices compensate for being "packed in like the 4 train at rush hour."

Sarabeth's American | 20 | 17 | 17 | $33 |

Chelsea | Chelsea Mkt. | 75 Ninth Ave. (bet. 15th & 16th Sts.) |
212-989-2424 | www.sarabeth.com

E 70s | Whitney Museum | 945 Madison Ave. (75th St.) | 212-570-3670 |
www.sarabeth.com **M**

E 90s | 1295 Madison Ave. (bet. 92nd & 93rd Sts.) | 212-410-7335 |
www.sarabeth.com

W 50s | 40 Central Park S. (bet. 5th & 6th Aves.) | 212-826-5959 |
www.sarabethscps.com

W 80s | 423 Amsterdam Ave. (bet. 80th & 81st Sts.) | 212-496-6280 |
www.sarabeth.com

These "genteel", "preppy" Americans boast "loyal followings" of ladies thanks to their "brunch for the ages" served in settings that lie somewhere between "Laura Ashley" and "Martha Stewart"; "crazy lines" and "inattentive service" can be avoided by showing up during "off hours."

Saravanaas Indian | ∇ 23 | 11 | 14 | $21 |

Gramercy | 81 Lexington Ave. (26th St.) | 212-679-0204 |
www.saravanaas.com

The "excellent" meatless menu at this "authentic" Gramercy South Indian opens the gates to "dosa heaven"; though service is "not too helpful" and the sari decor is "nothing to speak of", the "ridiculously cheap" tabs at this "veggie paradise" "make up for everything."

Sardi's **M** Continental | 16 | 21 | 19 | $52 |

W 40s | 234 W. 44th St. (bet. B'way & 8th Ave.) | 212-221-8440 |
www.sardis.com

"It is what it is" – a "Theaterland tradition" since 1921 with "prosaic" Continental cuisine that's eclipsed by the "caricatures of celebrities" on the walls; though the "glory days" may be long gone, it's still a "timeless" piece of "old NY" with waiters to match.

Sarge's Deli ● Deli | 19 | 7 | 14 | $23 |

Murray Hill | 548 Third Ave. (bet. 36th & 37th Sts.) | 212-679-0442 |
www.sargesdeli.com

"Matzo ball soup at midnight" is "no problem" at this "real-deal" 24/7 Murray Hill deli, a "been-there-forever" "time machine" serving "humongous" sandwiches made with meats pickled in-house; "depressing" decor and "crusty" service are part of the shtick.

NEW Sasabune **Z** Japanese | ∇ 26 | 10 | 20 | $83 |

E 70s | 401 E. 73rd St. (bet. 1st & York Aves.) | 212-249-8583

It's "omakase or the highway" at this UES "sushi boot camp" where chef Kenji Takahashi will "direct what and how you should eat"; there are "no rolls" and "no menus", just the "freshest fish money can buy" at correspondingly "high prices."

NEW Saucy ● Eclectic | - | - | - | M |

E 70s | 1409 York Ave. (75th St.) | 212-249-3700 | www.saucyny.com

The gimmick at this midpriced Yorkville Eclectic is a menu that lets diners choose from 50 different sauces to be paired with chicken, beef or pasta; the decor is equally quirky, featuring large spice-filled burlap bags hung from a mirrored ceiling.

	FOOD	DECOR	SERVICE	COST

Z Saul *American* | 27 | 19 | 24 | $57

Boerum Hill | 140 Smith St. (bet. Bergen & Dean Sts.) | Brooklyn |
718-935-9844 | www.saulrestaurant.com

Helmed by chef-owner Saul Bolton, this Boerum Hill New American
"deserves all the raves" for its "sophisticated" yet "unpretentious"
seasonal menu; a "remarkably helpful" staff, "civilized" setting and
fair pricing add up to a "top-flight" experience.

Savann *French/Mediterranean* | 19 | 14 | 18 | $40

W 70s | 414 Amsterdam Ave. (bet. 79th & 80th Sts.) | 212-580-0202 |
www.savann.com

This UWS "neighborhood standby" is a "pleasant" stop for "competent", "low-priced" French-Med dishes and also offers a "calm" atmosphere for conversation "without screaming"; its "underrated" status
may explain why it's "not more crowded."

Savoia *Pizza* | 21 | 16 | 18 | $29

Carroll Gardens | 277 Smith St. (bet. Degraw & Sackett Sts.) |
Brooklyn | 718-797-2727

"Fabulous" Neapolitan-style pizza from a wood-fired oven is the forte
of this "casual" Carroll Gardens Italian, but there's also a "short list"
of "hearty", equally "flavorful" main dishes; the "warm" albeit "unso-
phisticated" setting is particularly "good for families with kids."

NEW savorNY *Eclectic* | – | – | – | M

LES | 63 Clinton St. (bet. Rivington & Stanton Sts.) | 212-358-7125 |
www.savornyrestaurant.com

Snug is the word for this tiny LES newcomer serving affordable, globe-
trotting small plates off a menu split into three playful categories -
'forks, fingers and finales'; the wine list is sorted by tasting notes
rather than the usual red/white divide.

Savoy *American/Mediterranean* | 24 | 20 | 22 | $54

SoHo | 70 Prince St. (Crosby St.) | 212-219-8570 |
www.savoynyc.com

Peter Hoffman's SoHo "treasure" uses the "products of area farmers"
in "imaginative" ways as part of his Med–New American cooking; upstairs is more formal than the "convivial" first floor, but despite "romantic" fireplaces on both levels, some say a renovation several years
back "killed the charm."

Scaletta *Italian* | 21 | 18 | 22 | $51

W 70s | 50 W. 77th St. (bet. Columbus Ave. & CPW) | 212-769-9191 |
www.scalettaristorante.com

A "welcome respite" for the UWS, this "sedate" Northern Italian
draws "mature" types with "refined" cooking and "accommodating"
service; the "civilized" setting is conducive to "lingering conversa-
tions", even if younger folks feel out of place and outpriced.

Scalinatella ☻ *Italian* | 25 | 16 | 21 | $74

E 60s | 201 E. 61st St. (3rd Ave.) | 212-207-8280

"Sensational" *molto Italiano* classics come "from Capri with love" at
this UES rock-walled cellar; the genial mood and "courteous" staff
help blunt the considerable "sticker shock" – particularly the "prices
of the specials", which are "conveniently not mentioned."

	FOOD	DECOR	SERVICE	COST

Scalini Fedeli 🗷 *Italian* | 26 | 25 | 25 | $83 |

TriBeCa | 165 Duane St. (bet. Greenwich & Hudson Sts.) | 212-528-0400 | www.scalinifedeli.com

...om the "secluded cobblestone street" out front to the "serene" ...ood inside, this TriBeCa "delight" (the original Bouley) has got "spe-...al occasion" written all over it; chef Michael Cetrulo's "superb" ...orthern Italian cuisine and the staff's "impeccable" service justify ...sts that are definitely worth the $65 per head dinner prix fixe.

Scarlatto ◐ *Italian* | 21 | 18 | 19 | $43 |

W 40s | 250 W. 47th St. (bet. B'way & 8th Ave.) | 212-730-4535 | www.scarlattonyc.com

"...lowups from *Roman Holiday*" serve as decor at this Theater District ...orthern Italian set in the former digs of the much "missed" Pierre au ...nnel (the "show must go on"); it's already "very popular" due to its ...mple formula: "big portions" at "extremely reasonable prices."

Schiller's ◐ *Eclectic* | 18 | 19 | 16 | $36 |

LES | 131 Rivington St. (Norfolk St.) | 212-260-4555 | www.schillersny.com

...ink "Balthazar for emerging adults" to get the gist of this "high-...olume" LES Eclectic from Keith McNally that lures the "youthful" with ...uirky cocktails and "straightforward" bistro grub; though it may be ...oo sceney" for oldsters (i.e. anyone over 40), the "unisex bath-...oms" have universal appeal.

Scottadito Osteria Toscana *Italian* | ▽ 19 | 20 | 19 | $37 |

Park Slope | 788A Union St. (bet. 6th & 7th Aves.) | Brooklyn | ...8-636-4800 | www.scottadito.com

"...obust" Tuscan cuisine based on "fresh, organic" ingredients is yours at ...is Park Slope Italian that looks like a "rustic farmhouse"; the amorous ...dore the "fireplace" and "romantic wine cellar", while pragmatists ...e glad that they don't charge too much and "now take credit cards."

SEA *Thai* | 20 | 21 | 16 | $25 |

E Village | 75 Second Ave. (bet. 4th & 5th Sts.) | 212-228-5505
Williamsburg | 114 N. Sixth St. (Berry St.) | Brooklyn | 718-384-8850 ◐ | www.spicenyc.net

...he Williamsburg branch of this "trendy" Thai twosome is an "eye-...opping" thing with a "party central" vibe, "boom-box" acoustics and ...s own "pond and Buddha", while its plain-Jane East Village sibling ...akes tight seating to new levels"; either way, the vittles are tasty, ...heap and filling."

Sea Grill 🗷 *Seafood* | 24 | 24 | 22 | $65 |

W 40s | Rockefeller Ctr. | 19 W. 49th St. (bet. 5th & 6th Aves.) | ...12-332-7610 | www.theseagrillnyc.com

"...o what if it's touristy", the "sublime seafood" still shines at this ...ock Center favorite" where "window seats are a must" in the winter ... catch the "views of the Christmas tree" and ice skating rink; sure, ...ices are "prime", but worth it for "stylish", "special-occasion" dining.

EW Sea Salt ◐🗷 *Seafood* | - | - | - | M |

E Village | 99 Second Ave. (bet. 5th & 6th Sts.) | 212-979-5400

...display of seafood on ice anchors this East Village Med where chef ...rhan Yegen grills the day's catch, serving it either priced by the pound or as part of an à la carte menu; the airy, tile-lined space has fresh modern feel that's unusual for lower Second Avenue.

NEW Sense ●Ⓜ *Japanese*   – | – | – | M

Williamsburg | 106 N. Sixth St. (bet. Berry St. & Wythe Ave.) | Brooklyn 718-218-8666

Hyper-stylized but approachable, this new Williamsburg sensation welcomes diners with tricky lighting and a red-and-black color scheme that recalls a nightclub; the Japanese offerings – heavy on the sushi – seem almost incidental to the scene.

Serafina ● *Italian*   18 | 15 | 15 | $41

E 50s | 38 E. 58th St. (bet. Madison & Park Aves.) | 212-832-8888 Ⓢ
E 60s | 29 E. 61st St. (bet. Madison & Park Aves.) | 212-702-9898
E 70s | 1022 Madison Ave., 2nd fl. (79th St.) | 212-734-2676
NoHo | 393 Lafayette St. (4th St.) | 212-995-9595
W 50s | Dream Hotel | 210 W. 55th St. (B'way) | 212-315-1700
www.serafinarestaurant.com

Though each location of this "chic" Italian quintet "has a different feel", they all share "delicious thin-crust pizzas and salads" that attract an "energized", "Euro" following; critics note that "service could be improved – if there was any."

Serendipity 3 ● *Dessert*   18 | 19 | 14 | $29

E 60s | 225 E. 60th St. (bet. 2nd & 3rd Aves.) | 212-838-3531 | www.serendipity3.com

"Whimsy" is on the menu at this "kitschy" East Side dessert parlor cum-toy shop that looks like a "cross between grandma's attic and Alice's tea party"; while it's renowned for its "unforgettable" frozen hot chocolate that draws kids of all ages, less sweet are the "rude" staff and "tiresome", "touristy" lines.

Sette ● *Italian*   18 | 15 | 17 | $38

Chelsea | 191 Seventh Ave. (bet. 21st & 22nd Sts.) | 212-675-5935 www.settenyc.com

Maybe it "won't knock your socks off", but this "basic" Chelsea Italian is still a "good fallback" for "consistent", "midpriced" dining; a "neighborhood crowd" mixes with "see-and-be-seen types" and tries to forget the "loud" acoustics and "absentminded service."

Sette Enoteca e Cucina *Italian*   19 | 15 | 17 | $38

Park Slope | 207 Seventh Ave. (3rd St.) | Brooklyn | 718-499-7767 | www.setteparkslope.com

"Creative variations on Italian staples" abetted by an "affordable wine list" ("20 bottles for $20" apiece) are highlights of this Park Slope; service veers from "helpful" to "amateurish", while the former patio, now an enclosed "year-round" atrium, draws only middling response.

Sette Mezzo ●⊟ *Italian*   23 | 14 | 18 | $65

E 70s | 969 Lexington Ave. (bet. 70th & 71st Sts.) | 212-472-0400

Some dub it a "private club passing as a restaurant", and it certainly "helps if they know your face" at this UES "CEO" Italian serving "*bellissimo*" food "prepared with love"; "service can be rushed" and the "cash-only" pricing is as "uppity" as the scene, but the "rich and famous like it" and that's all that counts.

even ●🗷 American
18 | 18 | 17 | $41

Chelsea | 350 Seventh Ave. (bet. 29th & 30th Sts.) | 212-967-1919 | www.sevenbarandgrill.com

A "nice surprise" near MSG and Penn Station, this New American "oasis" works for pre- or post-event dining as well as "business lunches"; it's more a "white tablecloth" place than a pub, yet the bar is always "bustling" here.

'18 French
21 | 21 | 20 | $39

Astoria | 35-01 Ditmars Blvd. (35th St.) | Queens | 718-204-5553 | www.718restaurant.com

"Inventive" French cooking with a slight "Spanish flair" and "chic" loungelike quarters manned by a "sexy staff" ensure this Astorian shines as one of the neighborhood's "bright spots"; even those put off by the "limited menu" gravitate to the "sidewalk seating" for a "cocktail or two."

evilla ● Spanish
23 | 14 | 20 | $38

W Village | 62 Charles St. (W. 4th St.) | 212-929-3189 | www.sevillarestaurantandbar.com

After 67 years, "only the prices have changed" at this "garlicky" Village Spaniard that's a "sentimental favorite" for "addictive" paella and sangria "on the cheap"; the "well-seasoned waiters" and "run-down" decor provide "plenty of character."

Sezz Medi' Mediterranean/Pizza
21 | 16 | 18 | $32

W 100s | 1260 Amsterdam Ave. (123rd St.) | 212-932-2901 | www.sezzmedi.com

"Superb brick-oven pizza" backed up by "consistently tasty" Med mains mark this UWS "oasis" that lends some "sophistication to a strip of generic restaurants" in Morningside Heights; "uneven service" and undistinguished decor seem to be its only shortcomings.

foglia 🗷 Italian
23 | 19 | 20 | $56

90s | 1402 Lexington Ave. (92nd St.) | 212-831-1402 | www.sfogliarestaurant.com

Carnegie Hill dwellers are delighted to have a "destination restaurant in the neighborhood", this "seriously good", seriously "tiny" Northern Italian that's "all the rage" and thus "impossible to get into" ("if it were any smaller, it would be a phone booth"); thus, "reserve ahead" – way ahead.

Shabu-Shabu 70 Japanese
20 | 13 | 22 | $37

E 70s | 314 E. 70th St. (bet. 1st & 2nd Aves.) | 212-861-5635

"Super-super" say fans of the cook-it-yourself "signature dish" at this affordable UES Japanese that also vends "expertly prepared sushi"; "friendly" service that "feels like home" makes up for decor in need of an "extreme makeover."

Shabu-Tatsu Japanese
▽ 20 | 11 | 16 | $34

E Village | 216 E. 10th St. (bet. 1st & 2nd Aves.) | 212-477-2972

"Attentive" staffers are ready to "explain the ins and outs" of cooking your meal at this low-budget East Village Japanese that specializes in shabu-shabu and sukiyaki; "drab" surroundings to the contrary, it's "great for a group" in the mood for something "tasty and different."

	FOOD	DECOR	SERVICE	COST

Shaffer City Oyster Bar & Grill 🗷 *Seafood*   `21` `15` `20` `$48`
Flatiron | 5 W. 21st St. (bet. 5th & 6th Aves.) | 212-255-9827 |
www.shaffercity.com

"Fresh is the word" for this "unpretentious" Flatiron seafooder run b
the "entertaining" Jay Shaffer; the "huge assortment" of "first-class
oysters and fish may not be cheap, but the "suburban mall" decor is

Shake Shack *Hamburgers*   `23` `13` `12` `$14`
Flatiron | Madison Square Park | 23rd St. | 212-889-6600 |
www.shakeshack.com

Danny Meyer's alfresco "destination" in Madison Square Park venc
"craveable" burgers, hot dogs and "mind-freezingly thick" shakes; give
the high quality and modest prices, expect "legendary" lines, but
least it's now open year-round, with hours varying seasonally.

Shanghai Cuisine 🍽 *Chinese*   ▽ `21` `12` `14` `$22`
Chinatown | 89 Bayard St. (Mulberry St.) | 212-732-8988

"Perfectly cooked, very affordable" soup dumplings are the signatur
dish at this Chinatown "definition of a hole-in-the-wall" that also o
fers "tasty" Shanghainese "staples"; downsides include a "cash-only
policy and chop-chop "fast" service.

Shanghai Pavilion *Chinese*   `21` `19` `20` `$36`
E 70s | 1378 Third Ave. (bet. 78th & 79th Sts.) | 212-585-3388

"Impressively authentic" Shanghai dishes and a "polished staff" mak
this atypically "fancy" UES Chinese a "clear favorite in the neighbo
hood"; even better, it "feels like it should be expensive", but isn't.

Sharz Cafe & Wine Bar *Mediterranean*   `21` `15` `21` `$38`
E 80s | 435 E. 86th St. (bet. 1st & York Aves.) | 212-876-7282

"Much needed on the far East Side", this Med bistro "mainstay" sup
plies "fresh, satisfying" food for "bargain" tabs; the "intimate" dig
can get "crowded", but "knowledgeable" servers and a "wonderfu
wine selection make for a "good night out."

🆕 Sheep Station ●🍽 *Australian*   ▽ `19` `17` `18` `$24`
Park Slope | 149 Fourth Ave. (Douglass St.) | Brooklyn | 718-857-4337
www.sheepstation.net

"Aussie comfort food" lands in Park Slope at this "laid-back" new
comer where expats, "singles" and "artist types" dig the "Down Unde
vibe" and prices; although the "pioneering" eats "fall flat" for a few, a
"interesting selection of beer and wine" draws universal huzzahs.

Shelly's Trattoria *Italian*   `20` `17` `19` `$57`
W 50s | 41 W. 57th St. (bet. 5th & 6th Aves.) | 212-245-2422 |
www.shellysnewyork.com

Shelly Fireman's ever-evolving Midtowner has now added Italia
items to its former chops–and–raw bar lineup to mixed response (
"winner" vs. a "step down"); fortunately, it still boasts "City Center
convenience, "prompt" service and solid value.

Shula's Steak House *Steak*   `20` `19` `19` `$65`
W 40s | Westin NY Times Sq. | 270 W. 43rd St. (bet. B'way & 8th Ave.)
212-201-2776 | www.donshula.com

Coach Don Shula's Times Square chophouse is a shrine to "all thing
football", starting with its "pigskin menus"; while the Angus beef

| | FOOD | DECOR | SERVICE | COST |

eliable" enough, it's not in the same league as NYC's top steak-
₁uses, so critics blow the whistle on the "formulaic" digs and "prices
₁at'll send you to a heart doctor before the cholesterol does."

₁un Lee Cafe ◑ *Chinese* | 21 | 16 | 17 | $40 |

60s | 43 W. 65th St. (bet. Columbus Ave. & CPW) | 212-769-3888 |
ww.shunleewest.com

₁m sum carts "in constant motion" are the draw at this Lincoln Center-
₁ea Chinese that's "more casual" than its "big sister next door" (and
₁ore "reasonably priced"); though the "black-and-white checkerboard"
₁cor may "need a face-lift", the new sushi options are a "plus."

₁un Lee Palace ◑ *Chinese* | 24 | 20 | 22 | $55 |

₁0s | 155 E. 55th St. (bet. Lexington & 3rd Aves.) | 212-371-8844 |
ww.shunleepalace.com

₁e "emperor would be proud" of Michael Tong's "opulent" Midtown
₁inese that makes a "lavish impression" with its "fusion-free",
₁useum-quality meals" and "second-to-none" service; if you "like to
₁ess up" and are prepared to pay "premium prices", this "oldie but
₁odie" is certainly "worth the splurge."

₁un Lee West ◑ *Chinese* | 23 | 21 | 21 | $53 |

60s | 43 W. 65th St. (bet. Columbus Ave. & CPW) | 212-595-8895 |
ww.shunleewest.com

₁eservedly an institution", this "gourmet" Chinese near Lincoln Center
₁fers "interesting", "refined" dishes delivered by a "swift" staff in a
₁ow"-inducing black-and-white room; though diners like the dragons
₁ the lacquered walls, they're ambivalent about the "high prices."

₁am Square Ⓜ *Thai* | ▽ 24 | 19 | 21 | $28 |

₁onx | 564 Kappock St. (Henry Hudson Pkwy.) | 718-432-8200 |
ww.siamsq.com

"real find in Riverdale", this "quiet" Thai offers modestly priced,
₁usion-style" specials and "solid" standards "made with ingredients
₁u can clearly identify"; "courteous" servers add to the "warm" vibe.

₁EW Silent H *Vietnamese* | – | – | – | I |

₁illiamsburg | 79 Berry St. (N. 9th St.) | Brooklyn | 718-218-7063 |
ww.silenthbrooklyn.com

₁ling a Vietnamese niche in Williamsburg, this long, airy cafe is a nat-
₁al fit for its funky neighborhood with wooden benches and tall win-
₁ws overlooking the street; the menu is similarly area-appropriate
₁ven its low prices and BYO policy.

₁p Sak *Turkish* | 20 | 13 | 15 | $28 |

₁40s | 928 Second Ave. (bet. 49th & 50th Sts.) | 212-583-1900 |
ww.sip-sak.com

₁lavor abounds" at this "boisterous" U.N.-area Turk that's best known
₁r its "eccentric" chef-owner who provides "lots of drama"; the list of
₁expensive", "freshly prepared" dishes "goes on forever", but regu-
₁rs suggest making a meal from a "sampler of meze."

₁stina ◑ *Italian* | 24 | 18 | 20 | $67 |

₁80s | 1555 Second Ave. (bet. 80th & 81st Sts.) | 212-861-7660
₁rst-rate, "sophisticated" Italian cooking comes with a "big dollop of
₁genuity" at this "civilized" UES vet that draws a smart neighbor-

	FOOD	DECOR	SERVICE	COST

hood crowd; "attentive" service and a "terrific wine list" tru
the "expensive" tab.

NEW 67 Burger M *Hamburgers* ▽ 21 | 14 | 16 | $1
Fort Greene | 67 Lafayette Ave. (Fulton St.) | Brooklyn | 718-797-715
www.67burger.com

"Tasty burgers" meet "quirky atmosphere" at this "relaxed" BA
convenient Fort Greener where one "big", "tasty" patty and so
"scrumptious fries" are nearly "enough to feed a family"; thanks to
"special brews" on tap, the "slow" service is easier to overlook.

S'mac *American* 19 | 9 | 14 | $1
E Village | 345 E. 12th St. (bet. 1st & 2nd Aves.) | 212-358-7912 |
www.smacnyc.com

"Blow your low-carb diet" at this "funky" East Village American
"one-trick pony" serving only mac 'n' cheese in "sizzling skillets" (
ther "pre-designed concoctions" or "make-your-own combos");
portions are "large", the space "tiny" and the prices a "bargain."

Smith & Wollensky *Steak* 23 | 18 | 20 | $6
E 40s | 797 Third Ave. (49th St.) | 212-753-1530 |
www.smithandwollensky.com

This "macho" Midtown steakhouse is a "classic", "clubby" spot whe
"the boys go" to exercise their "expense accounts" on "big slabs of be
and fine wines; those seeking to "tone it down a little" hit Wollensk
Grill next door, with super burgers, lower prices and later hours.

NEW Smoke Joint *BBQ* 23 | 13 | 18 | $1
Fort Greene | 87 S. Elliot Pl. (Lafayette Ave.) | Brooklyn | 718-797-101
www.thesmokejoint.com

Small on space but big on flavor, this "no-frills" Fort Greene newcom
near BAM "hits the spot" for "darn good BBQ" smoked on-site ove
variety of woods; a "kooky" but "friendly" staff and "reasonal
prices" make it all the more "addictive."

Smorgas Chef *Scandinavian* 19 | 14 | 18 | $3
E 40s | 924 Second Ave. (49th St.) | 212-486-1411 ☾
Financial District | 53 Stone St. (William St.) | 212-422-3500
W Village | 283 W. 12th St. (4th St.) | 212-243-7073 ☾
www.smorgaschef.com

A "welcome change from the usual", these "inexpensive", "almost a
thentic" Scandinavians specialize in traditional items like meatba
gravlax and lingonberries; decor skews "shabby", except for t
"charming" Financial District satellite.

Snack *Greek* ▽ 24 | 11 | 17 | $2
SoHo | 105 Thompson St. (bet. Prince & Spring Sts.) | 212-925-104
Appropriately "snack-size", this SoHo Greek "matchbox" is a "have
for "high-class" Hellenica at "unbeatable prices" ("best food I've e
had in a closet"); plan on "getting to know your neighbo
intimately" – "if you can get a table", that is.

Snack Taverna *Greek* 22 | 16 | 18 | $4
W Village | 63 Bedford St. (Morton St.) | 212-929-3499
Hellenic dishes arrive with a "serious gourmet twist" at Snack's bigg
pricier Village sibling that recruits regulars with an "upscale yet dow

| | FOOD | DECOR | SERVICE | COST |

wn" vibe; the wine list is "well chosen", service "informal but infor-
ative" and the Greek coffee "stronger than Hercules."

oba Nippon *Japanese*
▽ 22 | 16 | 19 | $34

W 50s | 19 W. 52nd St. (bet. 5th & 6th Aves.) | 212-489-2525

Lunchtime is busy", but this affordable Japanese soba shop still sup-
lies a semblance of "serenity" in the "frenzy of Midtown" with its
bamboo walls" and "attentive" staff; "soba connoisseurs" report that
he "delicious namesake noodles" are made "fresh from their
wn buckwheat farm."

oba-ya *Japanese*
24 | 17 | 20 | $29

Village | 229 E. Ninth St. (bet. 2nd & 3rd Aves.) | 212-533-6966 |
ww.sobaya-nyc.com

or a "perfect slurp", check out this "buzzy" East Village Japanese
where a "rich variety of soba" are "handmade on-site"; since the staff
s as "sweet" as the tabs, it's naturally "very popular", so "just ignore
he packs of NYU students – they're harmless."

NEW Socialista *Cuban*
– | – | – | E

W Village | 505 West St. (bet. Horatio & Jane Sts.) | 212-929-4303 |
ww.socialista.us

he latest challenger for the 'it' restaurant crown is this new Cuban in
he far West Village, set in a faux-distressed space channeling
Hemingway's Havana; in contrast to the name, getting in is strictly
apitalista thanks to a secret reservations phone number.

oda Shop ⊠ *American/Dessert*
▽ 19 | 23 | 17 | $19

riBeCa | Cosmopolitan Hotel | 125 Chambers St. (bet. Church St. &
W. B'way) | 212-571-1100 | www.sodashopnewyork.com

Kids of all ages" dig the "old-fashioned" American comfort chow at
his "mom-and-pop shop" in TriBeCa outfitted in "retro" soda fountain
tyle; serving "mostly desserts" (plus "candy you haven't seen since
hildhood"), it's a "super-nostalgic" trip that's particularly "good for
amilies" with kids.

ofrito ● *Puerto Rican*
22 | 20 | 18 | $39

50s | 400 E. 57th St. (bet. 1st Ave. & Sutton Pl.) | 212-754-5999 |
ww.sofritony.com

immy Rodriguez's latest "hot, hot, hot" spot supplies "upscale" Puerto
Rican specialties that are "surprisingly inexpensive" given the "ritzy"
utton Place address; too bad about the "spotty" service, but few no-
ice, distracted by the "loud acoustics" and "big-time singles scene."

NEW Solace *American*
– | – | – | M

60s | 406 E. 64th St. (bet. 1st & York Aves.) | 212-750-0434

ituated in a converted UES townhouse, this inviting new arrival headed
y chef-owner David Regueiro (ex Aureole) serves seasonal New
Americana in a white-tablecloth setting; while its polished interior is
velcomingly warm, the spacious back patio may be the real star here.

olera ⊠ *Spanish*
22 | 19 | 21 | $55

50s | 216 E. 53rd St. (bet. 2nd & 3rd Aves.) | 212-644-1166 |
vww.solerany.com

here's "superb Spanish food" and "fine takes on classic tapas" at this
ast Midtown brownstone duplex; "attentive service" and "quiet",

| | FOOD | DECOR | SERVICE | COST |

"pleasant" environs make it especially appealing even if it's on the pricey side.

Solo *Mediterranean*
▽ 22 | 23 | 19 | $71

E 50s | Sony Plaza Atrium | 550 Madison Ave. (bet. 55th & 56th Sts.) | 212-833-7800 | www.solonyc.com

"Kosher chic" is alive and well at this "high-class" Midtown Med that's a "serious power scene for the Jewish community" – credit its "elegant" ambiance and "wonderful" glatt cuisine, not the fluctuating service and "overly expensive" pricing.

Sol y Sombra ● *Spanish*
▽ 19 | 15 | 18 | $37

W 80s | 462 Amsterdam Ave. (bet. 82nd & 83rd Sts.) | 212-400-401

"Relaxed" and "underappreciated", this UWS Spaniard is a "perfect light-bite" locus for "quality" tapas washed down with "*excelente*" sangria; still, both decor and service "need polishing" and "it can get expensive if you order enough to get really full."

Son Cubano ⊠ *Cuban*
21 | 21 | 19 | $47

Meatpacking | 405 W. 14th St. (bet. 9th Ave. & Washington St.) | 212-366-1640 | www.soncubanonyc.com

"Meaningful conversation is unlikely" at this "clubbish" Meatpacking District Cuban where "thunderous" live music and "*fantastico*" drinks fuel the "celebratory mood"; though the midpriced "food is better than it has to be", it's beside the point once the "sangria starts flowing."

Song ⊅ *Thai*
24 | 17 | 19 | $21

Park Slope | 295 Fifth Ave. (bet. 1st & 2nd Sts.) | Brooklyn | 718-965-1108

"Cheaper than eating at home", this "McDonald's priced" Park Slope Thai puts out "delicious" dishes that are "served quick"; but like its sibling, Joya, the "deafeningly loud" acoustics and industrial "concrete bunker" design "drown out any chance at conversation."

Sorrel Ⓜ ⊅ *American*
▽ 23 | 18 | 20 | $39

Prospect Heights | 605 Carlton Ave. (St. Marks Ave.) | Brooklyn | 718-622-1190

Hidden "on a quiet residential block" in Prospect Heights, this "little known", "cash-only" New American purveys an "excellent" seasonal menu that "changes daily"; despite the high "quality-to-cost ratio", it remains undiscovered.

Sosa Borella ● *Argentinean/Italian*
21 | 16 | 19 | $38

W 50s | 832 Eighth Ave. (50th St.) | 212-262-7774 | www.sosaborella.com

The Italian-Argentinean fusion at this Theater District "find" is "not so crazy", yielding an "interesting" menu that covers both countries' cuisines; thanks to its "casual vibe", "efficient" service and moderate tabs, it's winning a strong local following.

NEW Soto ● ⊠ *Japanese*
– | – | – | E

G Village | 357 Sixth Ave. (bet. Washington Pl. & W. 4th St.) | 212-414-3088

Atlanta sushi master Sotohiro Kosugi makes his NYC debut with this new high-end entry set in an unassuming Village storefront; look for unusual sushi and sashimi airlifted from Japan and Alaska, but remember such quality can't come cheap.

238

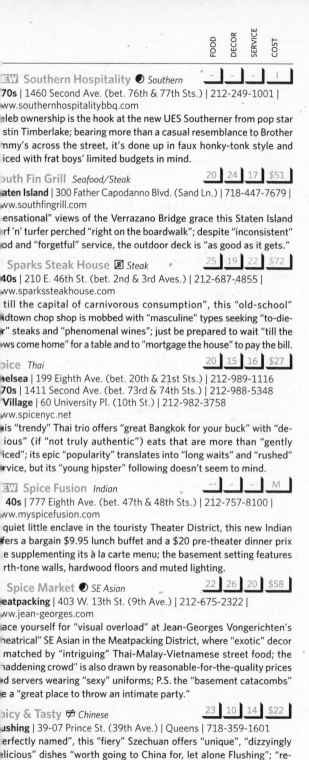

∃W Southern Hospitality ● *Southern* — — — I

70s | 1460 Second Ave. (bet. 76th & 77th Sts.) | 212-249-1001 |
ww.southernhospitalitybbq.com

:leb ownership is the hook at the new UES Southerner from pop star
stin Timberlake; bearing more than a casual resemblance to Brother
mmy's across the street, it's done up in faux honky-tonk style and
iced with frat boys' limited budgets in mind.

uth Fin Grill *Seafood/Steak* 20 | 24 | 17 | $51

aten Island | 300 Father Capodanno Blvd. (Sand Ln.) | 718-447-7679 |
ww.southfingrill.com

ensational" views of the Verrazano Bridge grace this Staten Island
rf 'n' turfer perched "right on the boardwalk"; despite "inconsistent"
od and "forgetful" service, the outdoor deck is "as good as it gets."

Sparks Steak House Ⓩ *Steak* 25 | 19 | 22 | $72

40s | 210 E. 46th St. (bet. 2nd & 3rd Aves.) | 212-687-4855 |
ww.sparkssteakhouse.com

till the capital of carnivorous consumption", this "old-school"
idtown chop shop is mobbed with "masculine" types seeking "to-die-
r" steaks and "phenomenal wines"; just be prepared to wait "till the
ws come home" for a table and to "mortgage the house" to pay the bill.

ice *Thai* 20 | 15 | 16 | $27

elsea | 199 Eighth Ave. (bet. 20th & 21st Sts.) | 212-989-1116
70s | 1411 Second Ave. (bet. 73rd & 74th Sts.) | 212-988-5348
Village | 60 University Pl. (10th St.) | 212-982-3758
ww.spicenyc.net

is "trendy" Thai trio offers "great Bangkok for your buck" with "de-
ious" (if "not truly authentic") eats that are more than "gently
iced"; its epic "popularity" translates into "long waits" and "rushed"
rvice, but its "young hipster" following doesn't seem to mind.

∃W Spice Fusion *Indian* — — — M

40s | 777 Eighth Ave. (bet. 47th & 48th Sts.) | 212-757-8100 |
ww.myspicefusion.com

quiet little enclave in the touristy Theater District, this new Indian
fers a bargain $9.95 lunch buffet and a $20 pre-theater dinner prix
e supplementing its à la carte menu; the basement setting features
rth-tone walls, hardwood floors and muted lighting.

Spice Market ● *SE Asian* 22 | 26 | 20 | $58

eatpacking | 403 W. 13th St. (9th Ave.) | 212-675-2322 |
ww.jean-georges.com

ace yourself for "visual overload" at Jean-Georges Vongerichten's
heatrical" SE Asian in the Meatpacking District, where "exotic" decor
matched by "intriguing" Thai-Malay-Vietnamese street food; the
naddening crowd" is also drawn by reasonable-for-the-quality prices
d servers wearing "sexy" uniforms; P.S. the "basement catacombs"
e a "great place to throw an intimate party."

icy & Tasty ⵌ *Chinese* 23 | 10 | 14 | $22

ushing | 39-07 Prince St. (39th Ave.) | Queens | 718-359-1601
erfectly named", this "fiery" Szechuan offers "unique", "dizzyingly
licious" dishes "worth going to China for, let alone Flushing"; "re-

markably low costs'" trump the "rough-and-tumble" decor and th
staff's "limited English."

Spiga *Italian*   21 | 17 | 17 | $48
W 80s | 200 W. 84th St. (bet. Amsterdam Ave. & B'way) | 212-362-5506
www.spiganyc.com
Featuring midpriced, "creative" Italian cooking, this "intimate" Upp‹
Westsider "hits the mark most of the time"; the "approachable wine lis
and "dark", "romantic" setting distract from the "indifferent" servic‹

Spigolo *Italian*   25 | 16 | 22 | $57
E 80s | 1561 Second Ave. (81st St.) | 212-744-1100
"Grand food" in a "miniature space" sums up this UES "gem" that
"much more than a neighborhood Italian"; owners Scott and Heath‹
Fratangelo "really care about their customers" and their "hard wo
shows" – no wonder this "success story" has turned into such a "tou‹
reservation", "even for regulars", high prices notwithstanding.

NEW Spirito Ⓜ *Italian*   – | – | – | M
Park Slope | 287 Ninth St. (bet. 4th & 5th Aves.) | Brooklyn | 718-832-008
The Vespa scooter hanging above the door signals that this new Pa
Slope arrival isn't your typical local trattoria, and the menu follov
through with both modern and classic takes on Italian dishes; a sizab
bar area and roof deck are inducements to linger here.

NEW Spitzer's Corner ◐ *American*   – | – | – | M
LES | 101 Rivington St. (Ludlow St.) | 212-228-0027
Creative New Americana accompanied by a vast list of craft beers
drawing hordes of hipsters to this new LES gastropub parked on
prime Rivington Street corner; communal picnic tables and walls lin‹
with reclaimed wood add to its casually rustic vibe.

NEW Spoon ◐ *Japanese/Pan-Asian*   – | – | – | M
E Village | 141 First Ave. (bet. 9th St. & St. Marks Pl.) | 212-529-27‹
Tucked behind the East Village's Ramen Setagaya noodle bar is th
new Pan-Asian with a loungelike vibe; the midpriced menu featur
Japanese small plates and sushi as well as Malaysian and Thai dishe
and there's a nifty back garden to boot.

NEW Spotlight Live ◐ *American*   – | – | – | E
W 40s | 1604 Broadway (bet. 48th & 49th Sts.) | 212-246-2693 |
www.spotlightlive.com
Think karaoke den meets *American Idol* to get the gist of this ne
Times Square dinner theater where wannabe warblers perform wi
pro backup singers (an outside JumboTron allows sidewalk critics
look too); needless to say, the glitzy, nightclubbish decor a‹
American menu take a back seat to the action onstage.

Spotted Pig ◐ *British*   22 | 17 | 16 | $43
W Village | 314 W. 11th St. (Greenwich St.) | 212-620-0393 |
www.thespottedpig.com
It's perpetually "SRO" at this "overly hip" British gastropub in the We
Village, where both "celebs" and the "teeming masses" turn up to "‹
out" on chef April Bloomfield's "amazing" "un-pub grub"; while h
gnudi may "send you to heaven", the "staff attitude" and "epic wait
for entry are not as celestial.

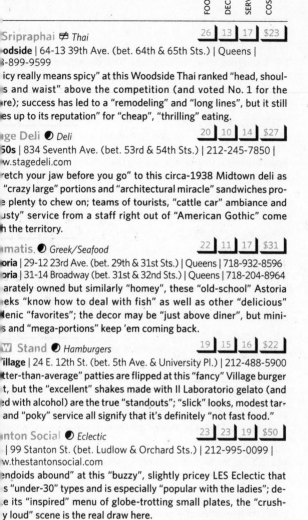

Sripraphai 🕎 *Thai* | 26 | 13 | 17 | $23 |

odside | 64-13 39th Ave. (bet. 64th & 65th Sts.) | Queens |
·-899-9599

"icy really means spicy" at this Woodside Thai ranked "head, shoul-
·s and waist" above the competition (and voted No. 1 for the
·re); success has led to a "remodeling" and "long lines", but it still
·es up to its reputation" for "cheap", "thrilling" eating.

ge Deli ◐ *Deli* | 20 | 10 | 14 | $27 |

50s | 834 Seventh Ave. (bet. 53rd & 54th Sts.) | 212-245-7850 |
·w.stagedeli.com

"etch your jaw before you go" to this circa-1938 Midtown deli as
· "crazy large" portions and "architectural miracle" sandwiches pro-
·e plenty to chew on; teams of tourists, "cattle car" ambiance and
·usty" service from a staff right out of "American Gothic" come
·h the territory.

matis. ◐ *Greek/Seafood* | 22 | 11 | 17 | $31 |

·oria | 29-12 23rd Ave. (bet. 29th & 31st Sts.) | Queens | 718-932-8596
·oria | 31-14 Broadway (bet. 31st & 32nd Sts.) | Queens | 718-204-8964

·arately owned but similarly "homey", these "old-school" Astoria
·eks "know how to deal with fish" as well as other "delicious"
·lenic "favorites"; the decor may be "just above diner", but mini-
·s and "mega-portions" keep 'em coming back.

W Stand ◐ *Hamburgers* | 19 | 15 | 16 | $22 |

·illage | 24 E. 12th St. (bet. 5th Ave. & University Pl.) | 212-488-5900

·tter-than-average" patties are flipped at this "fancy" Village burger
·t, but the "excellent" shakes made with Il Laboratorio gelato (and
·ed with alcohol) are the true "standouts"; "slick" looks, modest tar-
· and "poky" service all signify that it's definitely "not fast food."

·nton Social ◐ *Eclectic* | 23 | 23 | 19 | $50 |

| 99 Stanton St. (bet. Ludlow & Orchard Sts.) | 212-995-0099 |
·w.thestantonsocial.com

·ndoids abound" at this "buzzy", slightly pricey LES Eclectic that
·s "under-30" types and is especially "popular with the ladies"; de-
·e its "inspired" menu of globe-trotting small plates, the "crush-
·y loud" scene is the real draw here.

·ak Frites ◐ *French* | 18 | 16 | 16 | $42 |

·on Sq | 9 E. 16th St. (bet. 5th Ave. & Union Sq. W.) | 212-463-7101 |
·w.steakfritesnyc.com

· "eponymous dish" is the way to go at this "approachable" Union
·are French bistro; while the "Americanized" "midpriced" menu is
·re than adequate, "worn" decor and "inconsistent" service suggest
· place is "past its prime."

W Stella Maris *European* | - | - | - | M |

·port | 213 Front St. (bet. Beekman St. & Peck Slip) |
·-233-2417

·name means 'star of the sea', and not surprisingly, fresh-caught
· and a first-rate raw bar headline the moderately priced modern
·opean menu of this new Seaport bistro; a bakery/sandwich shop
·cent to its sleek dining room is open all day.

	FOOD	DECOR	SERVICE	COST

NEW Sticky Rice *Thai* ▽ 19 | 18 | 17 | $2

LES | 85 Orchard St. (bet. Broome & Grand Sts.) | 212-274-8208
For "interesting takes" on traditional Thai dishes and barbecue, **t**
"little" LES newcomer is fast becoming a "favorite"; the "relax**e**
mood makes it feel "undiscovered", but some say they need to work
improving service and fixing a few "bland" offerings.

NEW STK ❶ *Steak* 20 | 23 | 19 | $6

Meatpacking | 26 Little W. 12th St. (bet. 9th Ave. & Washington St
646-624-2444 | www.stkhouse.com
Appropriately set in the Meatpacking District, this "sceney", serio**u**
priced new steakhouse tweaks the genre with a "chic", "lady"-frien**d**
vibe; the "sleek" digs mirror its "trendy" location, replete wit**h**
"nightclub"-like setting and a "young" crowd, "bouncing from tabl**e**
table between courses."

Stone Park Café *American* 24 | 20 | 21 | $4

Park Slope | 324 Fifth Ave. (3rd St.) | Brooklyn | 718-369-0082 |
www.stoneparkcafe.com
"Taking a good local place to the next level", this Park Slope N
American draws "food-smart" folks with a "thoughtful" menu, "ha**n**
some" setting and "attractive" staff; in sum, it's a less expens
Brooklyn version of "Manhattan sophistication" and "always packe

Strip House ❶ *Steak* 25 | 22 | 21 | $7

G Village | 13 E. 12th St. (bet. 5th Ave. & University Pl.) | 212-328-00**0**
www.theglaziergroup.com
"Gypsy Rose Lee" would appreciate this "burlesque-themed" Vill
steakhouse for its "dimly lit" red interior festooned with vintage "pin
photos" (think "Smith & Wollensky meets Scores"); in addition to d
ble entendres, it also grinds out some of the city's best beef backe**d**
with "amazing" sides at "thank-God-for-expense-accounts" prices

Suba ❶ *Spanish* 21 | 26 | 19 | $!

LES | 109 Ludlow St. (bet. Delancey & Rivington Sts.) | 212-982-57**1**
www.subanyc.com
An "incredible redesign" has made this "super-sexy", high-end
Spaniard even more "alluring" with its ever-"romantic" grotto room
moat; the food is "much improved" thanks to a new chef and the c**o**
tails are "fantastic", but the "wow"-worthy scene "surpasses" the **r**

Sueños Ⓜ *Mexican* 23 | 19 | 20 | $4

Chelsea | 311 W. 17th St. (bet. 8th & 9th Aves.) | 212-243-1333 |
www.suenosnyc.com
"Way beyond the usual", Sue Torres' "upscale" Chelsea Mexica
known for its "authentic" eats jazzed up with "creative" flourishes
"congenial" service; it's "hidden in an alley" and "a little pricey" for
genre, but well "worth it."

Ⓩ Sugiyama ❶ⓈⓂ *Japanese* 27 | 20 | 26 | $!

W 50s | 251 W. 55th St. (bet. B'way & 8th Ave.) | 212-956-0670 |
www.sugiyama-nyc.com
It's all about "attention to detail" at Nao Sugiyama's "outstandi
Midtown Japanese known for its marvelous "modern kaiseki" m**e**
that are "as much about presentation as taste"; just "let them t

are of you", and the "soothing" "ceremonial" atmosphere will help
lunt the "heart attack"–inducing bill.

uperfine 🅼 *Mediterranean* ▽ 18 | 19 | 18 | $29

umbo | 126 Front St. (bet. Jay & Pearl Sts.) | Brooklyn | 718-243-9005
umbo's "hipster paradise", this "funky", low-budget Med is set in a
avernous former warehouse where "tasty" food, "vintage cocktails"
nd a "pool table" turn up the volume; service "needs to be quicker",
ut Sunday's "bluegrass brunch" is not to be missed.

upper ✒ *Italian* 24 | 19 | 19 | $35

Village | 156 E. Second St. (bet. Aves. A & B) | 212-477-7600 |
www.supperrestaurant.com
Delicious", well-priced Northern Italian cuisine, especially "amazing
astas", are dished out in "rustic", candlelit digs at this "truly unique"
ast Villager; "they don't take reservations" (or plastic), but the "long
aits" are made bearable by the "wine bar next door."

urya *Indian* ▽ 24 | 18 | 21 | $34

V Village | 302 Bleecker St. (bet. Grove St. & 7th Ave. S.) | 212-807-7770 |
www.suryany.com
Nice and spicy" food from "different regions of India" arrives in a
stark" setting at this Village "jewel in the crown"; service is "efficient"
nd the prices modest, but what's "really special" is the "cute garden."

ushi Ann 🆉 *Japanese* ▽ 23 | 16 | 20 | $60

50s | 38 E. 51st St. (bet. Madison & Park Aves.) | 212-755-1780 |
ww.sushiann.com
More "steady" than "trendy", this "traditional" Midtown Japanese is
ousy for lunch but more accessible at dinner", with "attentive" ser-
ice and a "somewhat formal" (verging on "sterile") setting; though
ne sushi is sublimely "delicate", the prices aren't.

ushiden *Japanese* 25 | 16 | 21 | $59

40s | 19 E. 49th St. (bet. 5th & Madison Aves.) | 212-758-2700
V 40s | 123 W. 49th St. (bet. 6th & 7th Aves.) | 212-398-2800 🆉
ww.sushiden.com
hese crosstown Midtown Japanese are popular with expats and
ousiness" types thanks to their "extraordinarily fresh fish" and "po-
te", "kimono-clad" servers; despite "austere decor", they are worth
exing the "expense account" for sushi that's the "genuine article."

ushi Hana ◗ *Japanese* 21 | 17 | 18 | $37

70s | 1501 Second Ave. (78th St.) | 212-327-0582
V 80s | 466 Amsterdam Ave. (bet. 82nd & 83rd Sts.) | 212-874-0369
or "civilized sushi", try these "above-average" crosstown Japanese
eighborhood places where the fish is "fresh, tasty" and "not overly
xpensive"; the UES outpost has the edge over its sibling thanks to
enovated" decor and a sake bar adjunct around the corner.

ushiSamba ◗ *Brazilian/Japanese* 22 | 20 | 17 | $48

latiron | 245 Park Ave. S. (bet. 19th & 20th Sts.) | 212-475-9377
V Village | 87 Seventh Ave. S. (Barrow St.) | 212-691-7885
www.sushisamba.com
olid sushi gets a "Latin spin" at these midpriced fusion specialists
here the "main attraction" is the "party-while-eating" vibe and

where you "don't expect to see your waiter that often"; the "nigh clubbish" scene crests at the Village outlet's "amazing" refurbishe roof deck and the Flatiron's "banging" adjacent lounge.

☑ Sushi Seki ●☒ *Japanese* 27 | 13 | 21 | $66

E 60s | 1143 First Ave. (bet. 62nd & 63rd Sts.) | 212-371-0238

"Put your trust in chef Seki" and he'll lead the way to "omakas heaven" at this "cult-ish" UES Japanese where the "faultless" sush easily out-"sparkles" the dull decor; even better, you can "keep it com ing" (while "spending a small fortune") until 3 AM.

Sushi Sen-nin *Japanese* 25 | 17 | 21 | $54

E 80s | 1420 Third Ave. (bet. 80th & 81st Sts.) | 212-249-4992 ☒
Murray Hill | 30 E. 33rd St. (bet. Madison Ave. & Park Ave. S.) |
212-889-2208
www.sushisennin.com

The "fish is as fresh as ever" at this Japanese twosome where sush seekers swear the "special rolls" look like "works of art" and are ap propriately priced; Murray Hill's "dramatic" new decor ratchets u the "wow" factor.

Sushiya *Japanese* ▽ 20 | 13 | 18 | $34

W 50s | 28 W. 56th St. (bet. 5th & 6th Aves.) | 212-247-5760 |
www.sushiya56.com

"Good if unspectacular sushi" is sliced for "moderate" sums at th Midtown Japanese with a "loyal following" at lunchtime; the "plain "unremarkable" setting is counterbalanced by "generally good se vice" and "not too crowded" conditions.

☑ Sushi Yasuda ☒ *Japanese* 28 | 22 | 24 | $78

E 40s | 204 E. 43rd St. (bet. 2nd & 3rd Aves.) | 212-972-1001 |
www.sushiyasuda.com

Sushi verges on the "spiritual" at this Grand Central–area "pinnacle once again voted NYC's No. 1 Japanese, where chef Naomichi Yasud provides raw fish "bliss" via "celestial" morsels that "span the seve seas" ("bring a snorkel if you want it fresher"); service is "knowledge able", the decor "simple" but elegant and the overall vibe "calm" – least until the bill arrives.

Sushi Zen ☒ *Japanese* 25 | 20 | 22 | $58

W 40s | 108 W. 44th St. (bet. B'way & 6th Ave.) | 212-302-0707 |
www.sushizen-ny.com

This "refined" Japanese, a "standard-bearer" for "high-quality sushi in the Theater District, gets "inventive" with "interestin combinations" as well as more traditional items; everything fine here, except perhaps for that "ka-ching" sound you hear whe paying the bill.

NEW Suteishi *Japanese* ▽ 25 | 20 | 23 | $44

Seaport | 24 Peck Slip (Front St.) | 212-766-2344 |
www.suteishi.com

A "pearl hidden in the Seaport" area, this new Japanese is a refuge f "delightful", moderately priced sushi sliced by one of th "friendliest chefs" around; the industrial-chic setting (think retrac able garage doors) on burgeoning Front Street features bonus views the Brooklyn Bridge.

	FOOD	DECOR	SERVICE	COST

Swagat Indian Cuisine Indian
| 19 | 11 | 18 | $27 |

W 70s | 411A Amsterdam Ave. (bet. 79th & 80th Sts.) | 212-362-1400
"Affordable" and "tasty" are the watchwords at this UWS Indian where the "vest-pocket" dimensions can result in "bumping elbows with your neighbor"; since the decor is strictly "hole-in-the-wall" and service "just ok", insiders tout "takeout" as the way to go; N.B. the Swagats and the Zagats are not related.

Sweet Melissa Dessert/Sandwiches
| 21 | 16 | 15 | $16 |

Cobble Hill | 276 Court St. (bet. Butler & Douglass Sts.) | Brooklyn | 718-855-3410
Park Slope | 175 Seventh Ave. (bet. 1st & 2nd Sts.) | Brooklyn | 718-502-9153
www.sweetmelissapatisserie.com
These "calorie rich" Brooklyn patisserie/sandwich shops (aka "Mommy & Me Central") offer "delicate" desserts that sate "sweet tooth cravings"; despite the "afternoon tea" and "wonderful" gardens, the "pricey" tabs and "disorganized" service may leave a sour taste.

Sweet-n-Tart Cafe ●🏱 Chinese
| 20 | 11 | 15 | $17 |

Flushing | 136-11 38th Ave. (Main St.) | Queens | 718-661-3380 | www.sweetntart.com
"Bring an adventurous spirit" to this cash-only Flushing Chinese featuring a "snack-heavy" menu of dim sum and "authentic Cantonese" items; despite "dated" decor, it's "quick, tasty" and, best of all, "cheap."

Sweetwater ●🏱 American/French
| ▽ 21 | 20 | 18 | $31 |

Williamsburg | 105 N. Sixth St. (bet. Berry St. & Wythe Ave.) | Brooklyn | 718-963-0608 | www.sweetwaterny.com
What started out as a Williamsburg "working class bar" is now a "trendy bistro" that has kept its cash-only, pre-gentrified prices; regulars report "surprisingly good" Franco-American food served by a "hipster" crew in an "inviting", "publike" space, plus a "beautiful garden."

Swifty's ● American
| 18 | 18 | 18 | $59 |

E 70s | 1007 Lexington Ave. (bet. 72nd & 73rd Sts.) | 212-535-6000 | www.swiftysny.com
"Blue bloods and blue hairs" populate this "Waspy" UES "club" where the "above-average" American grub plays second fiddle to "who sits where"; while it's not true that there's a "two-face-lift minimum" for entry, it does sport "more strands of pearls per square foot than any place in town."

Sylvia's Soul Food
| 19 | 13 | 16 | $29 |

Harlem | 328 Lenox Ave. (bet. 126th & 127th Sts.) | 212-996-0660 | www.sylviassoulfood.com
Whether it's "soul food heaven" or just "living on its reputation", this venerable Harlem "legend" still draws everyone from "Al Sharpton" to "Asian tour groups" with its "piping hot, stick-to-your-ribs" eats; "hit-or-miss" service and "not-so-nice" decor are beside the point during its entertaining jazz and gospel brunches.

Symposium Greek
| 20 | 15 | 20 | $25 |

W 100s | 544 W. 113th St. (bet. Amsterdam Ave. & B'way) | 212-865-1011
"Around since the days of Socrates" (actually 1969), this Columbia-area "godsend" offers "hearty" Greek dishes in "interesting" digs fes-

tooned "floor-to-ceiling" with "surreal murals"; "modest" prices and "warm" hospitality make it a "college student" perennial.

⧖ Tabla American
25 | 25 | 25 | $79

Gramercy | 11 Madison Ave. (25th St.) | 212-889-0667 | www.tablany.com

"Exotic and exquisite", this Madison Square Park "original" showcases chef Floyd Cardoz's New American dishes, inflected with "sensitive" Indian spicing and as "beautiful to look at as they are to eat"; "top-of-the-line" service and decor add to the overall "luscious" package, and though it "doesn't come cheap" ($64 and up prix fixe-only dinner), the Bread Bar downstairs offers equally "fantastic food for a fraction of the price."

Table d'Hôte French
21 | 16 | 19 | $46

E 90s | 44 E. 92nd St. (bet. Madison & Park Aves.) | 212-348-8125

"Delicious", midpriced French fare turns up at this "longtime favorite" UES bistro that also boasts "excellent prix fixes" and "convenience to the 92nd Street Y"; maybe it's "too small" for comfort, but at least you have the chance to "overhear a good conversation."

Taboon Mediterranean/Mideastern
24 | 20 | 20 | $50

W 50s | 773 10th Ave. (52nd St.) | 212-713-0271

Forget the "desolate location": this Med–Middle Eastern "treasure" parked "way out west on 10th Avenue" is "worth the trek" for "to-die-for bread" fresh from its taboon oven; "pleasant" service and a "relaxed" setting ice the cake.

NEW Tailor ◐ Ⓜ Dessert
– | – | – | E

SoHo | 525 Broome St. (bet. Sullivan & Thompson Sts.) | 212-334-5182 | www.tailornyc.com

Young, tattooed wd-50 disciple Sam Mason weaves the avant-garde techniques of molecular gastronomy with the vintage apothecary aesthetic peculiar to Downtown at this sepia-toned SoHo newcomer showcasing small plates of sweet and salty creations (half desserts, half savories – all pricey); a sizable downstairs bar/lounge shakes things up with similarly unconventional cocktails.

Takahachi Japanese
24 | 16 | 21 | $38

E Village | 85 Ave. A (bet. 5th & 6th Sts.) | 212-505-6524 ◐
TriBeCa | 145 Duane St. (bet. Church St. & W. B'way) | 212-571-1830
www.takahachi.net

Though it "flies under the radar", this "modest" Japanese duo offer "first-rate" sushi and "creative" hot dishes that are much "easier on the wallet" than its "flashier Downtown rivals"; all right, the atmosphere ain't about to achieve any awards, but the "superior service" just may.

Taksim Turkish
20 | 11 | 17 | $25

E 50s | 1030 Second Ave. (bet. 54th & 55th Sts.) | 212-421-3004 | www.taksim.us

The "cult following" of this East Midtown Turk thinks it's "all about the appetizers" and touts making a meal of the "tasty little snacks" ("if I knew it was this good, I wouldn't have redone my kitchen"); "dirt-cheap" tabs and a "cheerful" staff help distract from the "cramped" setup.

subscribe to zagat.com

	FOOD	DECOR	SERVICE	COST

Tamarind ● *Indian* — 25 | 22 | 23 | $51

Flatiron | 41-43 E. 22nd St. (bet. B'way & Park Ave. S.) | 212-674-7400 | www.tamarinde22.com

It "keeps getting better" say fans of this Flatiron "haute Indian" where food "seasoned to perfection" is served by a "gracious" staff in a "chic", "modern" setting; it's "not cheap, but you get what you pay for", and there's a $24 prix fixe lunch as well as an adjacent tearoom offering "lighter, less pricey" options.

Tang Pavilion *Chinese* — 23 | 17 | 21 | $36

W 50s | 65 W. 55th St. (bet. 5th & 6th Aves.) | 212-956-6888

"Not your typical" Chinese, this Midtown "surprise" supplies "subtle", Shanghai-style specialties served "fast and hot"; the "upscale" quarters are "roomier than most", the prices "reasonable" and the staff "efficient" – no wonder it's a "pre-City Center favorite."

Tanoreen Ⓜ *Mediterranean/Mideastern* — 27 | 12 | 22 | $26

Bay Ridge | 7704 Third Ave. (bet. 77th & 78th Sts.) | Brooklyn | 718-748-5600 | www.tanoreen.com

It's "hard to stop eating" at this "extraordinary" Med–Middle Eastern in Bay Ridge that's a "destination" just to see chef-owner Rawia Bishara in action; maybe the "tiny" space "could use a good decorator", but otherwise "everything's fantastic" at this "great value" BYO.

Tao ● *Pan-Asian* — 23 | 27 | 19 | $55

50s | 42 E. 58th St. (bet. Madison & Park Aves.) | 212-888-2288 | www.taorestaurant.com

Brace yourself for "Zensory overload" at this "showy" Midtown Pan-Asian, a "noisy", perennially "packed" place with "larger-than-life" "nightclubby" decor arranged around a great "big Buddha"; although it's "way tao trendy" and pricey for some, the food's "tastier" than you'd expect and the people-watching "inspirational."

Taormina *Italian* — ▽ 24 | 20 | 22 | $46

Little Italy | 147 Mulberry St. (bet. Grand & Hester Sts.) | 212-219-1007

"Real-deal" Italian cooking is yours at this 25-year-old Little Italy vet (rumored to have been "John Gotti's favorite") that's staffed by "old-time waiters" who "know the score"; it's "better if you're a regular" and best if you can snag a sidewalk seat to "watch the street show."

Tarallucci e Vino *Italian* — 19 | 19 | 17 | $37

E Village | 163 First Ave. (10th St.) | 212-388-1190 ●

Flatiron | 15 E. 18th St. (bet. B'way & 5th Ave.) | 212-228-5400

"Simple" grazing is the focus at this Flatiron Italian (and its more "bohemian" East Village sibling) where "great coffee" and pastries in the AM yield to an affordable small-plates menu at night; it's just right for a "casual" light meal in a "comfortable" setting.

Tartine ⊄ *French* — 22 | 14 | 17 | $30

W Village | 253 W. 11th St. (4th St.) | 212-229-2611

On a "charming" West Village corner, this "unpretentious", "tight fit" French bistro serves "straightforward" classics; no reservations, "cheap prices" and a BYO policy with "free corkage" inevitably result in "long lines."

	FOOD	DECOR	SERVICE	COST

NEW Tasca ◐ *Spanish* — ∇ 20 | 18 | 18 | $41

W Village | 130 Seventh Ave. S. (W. 10th St.) | 212-620-6815
Supporters say it's "easy to make a meal" from the "delectable", "reasonably priced" tapas at this "sexy" new Village Spaniard that also offers "dangerously good" sangria; despite "insane crowds" at the bar, some say it "needs more time."

Taste *American* — ∇ 20 | 16 | 19 | $49

E 80s | 1413 Third Ave. (80th St.) | 212-717-9798 | www.elizabar.com
Eli Zabar "knows what he's doing" at this UES cafe-by-day/restaurant-by-night where the perfect "seasonal" New Americana is always "well prepared"; despite its high quality, it's "not that well known", so "table availability" is rarely an issue.

Tasting Room *American* — 22 | 18 | 22 | $62

E Village | 72 E. First St. (bet. 1st & 2nd Aves.) | 212-358-7831 ◐
NoLita | 264 Elizabeth St. (bet. Houston & Prince Sts.) | 212-358-7831 Ⓜ
www.thetastingroomnyc.com
While Colin Alevras' "farmer's market fresh" cuisine is as "inventive" as ever, there's "now room to breathe" since this New American moved to larger digs in NoLita (the East Village original is now a wine bar/cafe); still, some say it's "lost its magic" citing "overpricing", "impersonal" decor and even "uneven cooking" at times.

Taverna Kyclades *Greek/Seafood* — 25 | 12 | 18 | $32

Astoria | 33-07 Ditmars Blvd. (bet. 33rd & 35th Sts.) | Queens | 718-545-8666 | www.tavernakyclades.com
"Off-the-boat fresh" seafood comes at "bargain" tabs at this "casual" Astoria Greek; the "cafeteria" vibe, "small" dimensions and "no reservations" policy are beside the point: the "lines to get in speak for themselves" – to get it "more authentic, go to Athens."

Ⓩ Tavern on the Green *American* — 15 | 24 | 17 | $64

W 60s | Central Park W. (bet. 66th & 67th Sts.) | 212-873-3200 | www.tavernonthegreen.com
"More spectacle than restaurant", this "over-the-top wonderland" in Central Park is best celebrated for its gorgeous garden and "kitschy" "fairy-tale" ambiance by way of "Liberace", not the only "adequate" American eats, "gaping tourists" and "rushed" service; nonetheless, it's capable of doing great parties, and on the right "spring evening", it still may render you "starry-eyed."

Tea & Sympathy *British* — 19 | 16 | 16 | $26

W Village | 108 Greenwich Ave. (bet. 12th & 13th Sts.) | 212-807-8329
www.teaandsympathynewyork.com
"Homesick Brits" tout this West Village "hang-your-hatter" for its "fantasy English food" like bangers and mash plus "daily high tea"; the "tiny", "cramped" digs and slack service may be "sore points", but, no question, this one's an "original."

Tea Box Ⓩ *Japanese* — ∇ 20 | 18 | 19 | $33

E 50s | Takashimaya | 693 Fifth Ave. (bet. 54th & 55th Sts.) | 212-350-0180
After a Midtown "shopping spree", this "oasis" in the Takashimaya basement purveys "delicate", "exquisitely presented" Japanese fare; add "oodles" of tea and "understated" decor, and it's easy to appreciate it

	FOOD	DECOR	SERVICE	COST

...eany 🍴 *Vegan/Vegetarian*
18 | 15 | 17 | $17

...ES | 90 Rivington St. (bet. Ludlow & Orchard Sts.) | 212-475-9190 |
...ww.teany.com

"near endless tea selection" is the draw at this inexpensive, "iPod"-
...ze LES vegan/vegetarian where the "animal-free" menu is "limited"
...ut "not too oppressive"; owned by pop star Moby, it's "worth a shot"
...rovided that you don't mind "weak service" and "plain" decor.

◧◩ Ted's Montana Grill *American*
15 | 15 | 16 | $39

...50s | 110 W. 51st St. (bet. 6th & 7th Aves.) | 212-245-5220 |
...ww.tedsmontanagrill.com

...ed Turner's national franchise famed for its "humongous, fall-off-the-
...un" bison burgers comes to Rock Center; despite "lunchtime
...owds", many say the "novelty wears thin" quickly, citing "mediocre"
...merican eats, "brusque" staffers and a "chain restaurant" look.

◧ Telepan *American*
25 | 20 | 23 | $69

...60s | 72 W. 69th St. (bet. Columbus Ave. & CPW) | 212-580-4300 |
...ww.telepan-ny.com

...ll Telepan – one "heck of a chef" – is the mastermind behind this "bril-
...ant" New American near Lincoln Center, where they "hit the ground
...unning and have just kept going" thanks to an "exceptional", "market-
...riven menu", "pro" service and a "grown-up, non-sceney" setting;
...ore debatable are the "pasture"-colored walls and unneighborly
...bs, but many feel this "triumph" verges on the "transcendent."

...elly's Taverna ◑ *Greek/Seafood*
22 | 14 | 18 | $35

...storia | 28-13 23rd Ave. (bet. 28th & 29th Sts.) | Queens | 718-728-9056 |
...ww.tellytaverna.com

...resh fish is the specialty" of this Astoria taverna where the "grilled,
...ell-seasoned" seafood (at "can't-be-beat" prices) feels like a flight-
...ee "trip to Greece"; the "pleasant" back garden is a calming refuge
...hen the "spacious" dining room gets too "noisy."

...emple Canteen *Indian*
- | - | - | I

...ushing | Hindu Temple Society of North America | 45-57 Bowne St.,
...ownstairs (Holly Ave.) | Queens | 718-460-8493 | www.nyganeshtemple.org

...uthentic South Indian staples draw dosa devotees to this brightly lit
...afeteria in the basement of a Hindu temple in Flushing; decor's at an
...bsolute minimum and you'll bus your own tray, but real-deal eats and
...heap tabs have inspired a cultlike following here.

...empo *Mediterranean*
25 | 23 | 24 | $50

...ark Slope | 256 Fifth Ave. (bet. Carroll St. & Garfield Pl.) | Brooklyn |
...18-636-2020 | www.tempobrooklyn.com

...evotees feel this "highly accomplished" Park Slope Med "should be
...etter known" given its "innovative" kitchen, "gracious" staff and
...ranquil", "bring-the-parents-for-dinner" vibe; it's now prix fixe only,
...ough the same quality "would cost a lot more in Manhattan."

...enzan *Japanese*
23 | 15 | 19 | $32

...70s | 285 Columbus Ave. (73rd St.) | 212-580-7300 ◑
...ensonhurst | 7116 18th Ave. (71st St.) | Brooklyn | 718-621-3238

...lo one comes for the ambiance" – it's the "high quality", "extremely
...esh" sushi sliced in "huge slabs" for modest tabs that keeps these

cross-borough Japanese perpetually "mobbed"; "rush-you-in-rush-you-out" service leads lingerers to opt for "takeout."

Teodora Italian
22 | 16 | 20 | $48

E 50s | 141 E. 57th St. (bet. Lexington & 3rd Aves.) | 212-826-7101
The "atmosphere's relaxed" at this "low-key" Midtown "hideaway" where the Northern Italian food is "delicious" and "upstairs is more comfortable" than down; all right, it's "nothing too exciting" and may be "a little expensive", but at least you're "never rushed."

Terrace in the Sky M French/Mediterranean
22 | 25 | 22 | $67

W 100s | 400 W. 119th St. (bet. Amsterdam Ave. & Morningside Dr.) 212-666-9490 | www.terraceinthesky.com
"Panoramas of Upper Manhattan" are just one of the highlights of this Morningside Heights rooftop French-Med; others are the "excellent food, "romantic" mood and smooth service, so despite the "old fashioned" air, it's a natural for "special occasions" and private parties.

Tevere Italian
▽ 22 | 19 | 21 | $53

E 80s | 155 E. 84th St. (bet. Lexington & 3rd Aves.) | 212-744-0210 | www.teverenyc.com
"If it's romantic and it has to be kosher", amorous observant types are all over this "fine-dining" UES Italian with "tasty" cooking and an ambiance subdued enough to "hear yourself think"; yes, it's "costly" particularly the wines – "but that's to be expected."

Thai Pavilion Thai
▽ 22 | 13 | 22 | $23

Astoria | 37-10 30th Ave. (37th St.) | Queens | 718-777-5546 | www.thaipavilionny.com
"Seriously good food" trumps the "bland" decor at this Astoria Thai where the "authentic", "big portions" come at "cheap" tabs; an "amazingly attentive" staff blunts the need for takeout or delivery (although both are available).

Thalassa Greek/Seafood
22 | 25 | 22 | $63

TriBeCa | 179 Franklin St. (bet. Greenwich & Hudson Sts.) | 212-941-7661 www.thalassanyc.com
For "chic Greek" grazing in TriBeCa, this "stylish" seafooder sells fish "so fresh you'd think they caught it after you ordered it"; service is as "crisp" as the "loftlike", "white-napkin" setting, but by-the-pound entree pricing means it's most economical to stick to the appetizers.

Thalia ◐ American
21 | 20 | 19 | $47

W 50s | 828 Eighth Ave. (50th St.) | 212-399-4444 | www.restaurantthalia.com
A pioneer of the new, "spiffy" Hell's Kitchen, this "spacious", "high-ceilinged" spot decorated with vintage theater posters draws "lively" show-goers with its "quality" New Americana; since it's "well located" and "won't break the bank", it can get a bit "hectic."

Thomas Beisl ◐ Austrian
19 | 16 | 19 | $37

Fort Greene | 25 Lafayette Ave. (Ashland Pl.) | Brooklyn | 718-222-580
"Proximity to BAM" may be the "main advantage" of this Fort Greene Austrian "mainstay", but fans say its "real McCoy" cooking and "value" make it "worth a visit" even if you're not theater-bound; a "delightful outdoor garden" seals the deal.

Thor ● *American* | 18 | 19 | 16 | $59 |

LES | The Hotel on Rivington | 107 Rivington St. (bet. Essex & Ludlow Sts.) | 212-796-8040 | www.hotelonrivington.com

Right off a "trendy" hotel lobby, this "hip" LES New American serves food "on the better side of ok" that plays second fiddle to its "edgy" decor and "loud", party-hearty crowd; "overpricing", "incompetent" service and "way too much scene" are common complaints.

Tía Pol *Spanish* | 24 | 15 | 18 | $38 |

Chelsea | 205 10th Ave. (bet. 22nd & 23rd Sts.) | 212-675-8805 | www.tiapol.com

You'll think you've "died and gone to Barcelona" at this Chelsea Spaniard featuring "adventurous" tapas in a "tiny hallway" of a space; it gets "*muy* cramped" *muy* fast, so prepare to "wait for an eternity for a table" – it's worth it.

Tides ⓂⒻ *Seafood* | ▽ 24 | 23 | 23 | $42 |

ES | 102 Norfolk St. (bet. Delancey & Rivington Sts.) | 212-254-8855 | www.tidesseafood.com

"One of the most unique ceilings in town" – made of bamboo stalks masquerading as sea grass – turns up at this "modern" LES seafooder also known for one of the "best lobster rolls south of Maine"; tabs are "reasonable", and "despite its small footprint, it doesn't seem cramped."

Tierras Colombianas Ⓕ *Colombian* | 22 | 12 | 18 | $23 |

Astoria | 33-01 Broadway (33rd St.) | Queens | 718-956-3012
Jackson Heights | 82-18 Roosevelt Ave. (82nd St.) | Queens | 718-426-8868

A "doggy bag" is a given at these Queens Colombians where the "huge platters" and "heaping" portions at "unbeatable" prices induce many to "eat till they can't walk"; they're a "good change of pace" provided you "bring a Spanish phrase book" and don't mind "diner"-esque digs.

Tintol ● *Portuguese* | ▽ 21 | 16 | 19 | $41 |

W 40s | 155 W. 46th St. (bet. 6th & 7th Aves.) | 212-354-3838 | www.tintol.net

Something different for the Theater District, this "sophisticated" Portuguese provides "interesting" tapas and a "good selection" of wine in "dark" digs; prices can "add up quickly", but for a "chic" bite pre- or post-theater, it's "one of the few acceptable places" around.

Tiramisu ● *Italian* | 20 | 15 | 17 | $35 |

E 80s | 1410 Third Ave. (80th St.) | 212-988-9780

"Quick and easy when you don't feel like cooking", this longtime UES Italian is always a "safe bet" for "families with kids" with its good "basic" grub and "loud" din; "awesome" pizza from the wood-burning oven makes up for "not a lot of warmth from the management."

ⓝ Tocqueville *American/French* | 26 | 24 | 25 | $73 |

Union Sq | 1 E. 15th St. (bet. 5th Ave. & Union Sq. W.) | 212-647-1515 | www.tocquevillerestaurant.com

"Civilized dining for adults" is on the docket at this "oasis of calm" off Union Square where chef Marco Moreira demonstrates his "dexterity" with "serious" French-American cooking yielding "sublime" results; "granted, the "minuscule portions" arrive at "major prices", but in return the place "purrs like a luxury automobile."

	FOOD	DECOR	SERVICE	COST

Todai *Japanese/Seafood*
▽ 18 | 13 | 15 | $31

Murray Hill | 6 E. 32nd St. (bet. 5th & Madison Aves.) | 212-725-1333 | www.todainyc.com

"Eat till you drop, then go back for more" at this Murray Hill "gorgefest" where a "football field–length buffet table" offers hot and cold Japanese seafood for an "affordable flat price"; ok, "Nobu it isn't" (it's "more Wal-Mart"), but it's just the ticket if "quantity is your priority."

Tokyo Pop *Japanese*
20 | 16 | 15 | $31

W 100s | 2728 Broadway (bet. 104th & 105th Sts.) | 212-932-1000

"Above-average" sushi is sliced at this Columbia-area Japanese that's a sibling of French bistro Café du Soleil across the street ("go figure"); "real care" is taken with the food prep and the milieu's "hip", though service careens from "ok" to "lousy."

NEW Toloache *Mexican*
– | – | – | M

W 50s | 251 W. 50th St. (bet. B'way & 8th Ave.) | 212-581-1818 | www.toloachenyc.com

Hell's Kitchen's gentrification continues with the arrival of this spiffy Nuevo Mexicano offering contemporary takes on traditional fare paired with a wide tequila selection; centered around a ceviche/guacamole bar, the split-level setup is decorated with a light touch that conveys a south-of-the-border mood without resorting to kitsch.

Tommaso *Italian*
▽ 23 | 18 | 21 | $45

Dyker Heights | 1464 86th St. (bet. 14th & 15th Aves.) | Brooklyn | 718-236-9883 | www.tommasoinbrooklyn.com

Recalling "dinner at nona's on Sunday", this Dyker Heights "perennial" offers "traditional red-sauce" Italian fare in a "family restaurant" setting; bonus points go to its owner, Thomas Verdillo, who's known to "sporadically break out" into operatic arias.

☑ Tomoe Sushi *Japanese*
26 | 8 | 17 | $41

G Village | 172 Thompson St. (bet. Bleecker & Houston Sts.) | 212-777-9346

"Early or late, you still might wait" at this "flavor"-filled, decor-free Village Japanese where the "no-reservations" policy makes for "ridiculously long lines" at the door; the payoff is "delicious", "just-off-the-boat" sushi sliced in "gigantic" portions for "bargain" bucks – so "get your sleeping bags ready."

Tomo Sushi & Sake Bar ● *Japanese*
20 | 15 | 17 | $26

W 100s | 2850 Broadway (bet. 110th & 111th Sts.) | 212-665-2916

UWS students tout this "reliable", Columbia-convenient Japanese for its "high-quality" sushi and "inexpensive" pricing; all agree it "could use a bit of a face-lift" and probably a service lift as well.

Tom's 🗷⇥ *Diner*
19 | 16 | 24 | $14

Prospect Heights | 782 Washington Ave. (Sterling Pl.) | Brooklyn | 718-636-9738

The "food is good but the love is priceless" at this circa-1936 Prospect Heights diner where "kitsch-explosion" decor, "speed-demon service" and "cheap" checks make for a bona fide Brooklyn "experience"; real egg creams and lime rickeys distract from the fact that it's "closed on Sundays."

ny's Di Napoli *Italian* | 18 | 14 | 18 | $35 |

30s | 1606 Second Ave. (83rd St.) | 212-861-8686
40s | 147 W. 43rd St. (bet. B'way & 6th Ave.) | 212-221-0100 ◗
www.tonysnyc.com

"ulk Hogan–size portions" of "hearty" Italian chow arrive "family-
yle" at this "mobbed", "Carmine's"-esque twosome; "holy cow,
ey're loud", but they're just the ticket "for the right crowd – like rel-
ives you don't really want to hear."

paz Thai *Thai* | 20 | 11 | 15 | $28 |

50s | 127 W. 56th St. (bet. 6th & 7th Aves.) | 212-957-8020

hort stays and high turnover are encouraged" at this Midtown Thai
ar City Center that's good for a "quickie" though some "can't eat as
st as they serve"; "tasty" dishes for "cheap" sums make the "boring
cor" and "tight" quarters tolerable.

sca Café ◗ *Italian* ▽ | 21 | 23 | 19 | $32 |

onx | 4038 E. Tremont Ave. (bet. Miles & Sampson Aves.) | 718-239-3300 |
vw.toscanyc.com

 in Throgs Neck (i.e. the Bronx) lies this "upscale" Italian serving "tra-
:ional favorites" in "dance club"–like digs; "lovely waitresses" and
gendary nightlife at the bar" draw "young" types for "hottie cruising."

ssed *American* | 18 | 7 | 11 | $14 |

atiron | 295 Park Ave. S. (bet. 22nd & 23rd Sts.) | 212-674-6700
40s | 30 Rockefeller Plaza, concourse (bet. 49th & 50th Sts.) |
2-218-2525 ⊠
vw.tossed.com

a "rabbit heaven", this low-budget, "custom-salad" twosome is a
e "create-your-own"-lunch choice offering "unusual ingredient
:rings"; despite "sketchy service" and nearly no decor, it's a "healthy
tion in a sea of temptation."

tonno's Pizzeria Napolitano *Pizza* | 22 | 9 | 14 | $22 |

30s | 1544 Second Ave. (bet. 80th & 81st Sts.) | 212-327-2800
amercy | 462 Second Ave. (26th St.) | 212-213-8800
ney Island | 1524 Neptune Ave. (bet. W. 15th & 16th Sts.) | Brooklyn |
8-372-8606 Ⓜ♔
vw.totonnos.com

eaven-sent" crusts "burnt just right" and sprinkled with "quality"
oppings are the formula for the "old-school" pies plied by this pizzeria
o; they all share "sports bar decor" and "feisty" staffers, but purists
iist the real "Xanadu is in Coney", home of the circa-1924 flagship.

urnesol *French* | 24 | 16 | 20 | $39 |

: | 50-12 Vernon Blvd. (bet. 50th & 51st Aves.) | Queens | 718-472-4355
rench food in Queens is not a punch line" at this LIC bistro that
rves "outstanding" Gallic classics and ups the "authenticity" with
nglish-challenged" staffers; while the "tiny" setup may induce
austrophobia", at these prices nobody minds.

wn *American* | 24 | 24 | 23 | $76 |

50s | Chambers Hotel | 15 W. 56th St. (bet. 5th & 6th Aves.) |
2-582-4445 | www.townnyc.com

ool and sophisticated", Geoffrey Zakarian's Midtown New
nerican draws a "beautiful", "business-oriented" crowd with its

"perfect contemporary" cooking; the "swank" subterranean digs a
equally "enchanting", though the upmarket tariffs cause some to r
serve it as a "special-occasion" place.

Trata Estiatorio Greek/Seafood

21 | 16 | 18 | $54

E 70s | 1331 Second Ave. (bet. 70th & 71st Sts.) | 212-535-3800 |
www.trata.com

"Just caught" fish "served simply" is the hallmark of this UES "neig
borhood" Greek seafooder whose whitewashed setting (and alfres
sidewalk seating) exudes a "taverna feel"; "by-the-pound pricing" ca
make for "expensive" eating, but fans feel it's "worth it."

Trattoria Alba ● Italian

20 | 17 | 22 | $40

Murray Hill | 233 E. 34th St. (bet. 2nd & 3rd Aves.) | 212-689-3200
www.trattoriaalba.com

A "neighborhood restaurant in the best sense", this "longtime
Murray Hill Italian draws "older" folk with a "traditional" menu and
"staff that really cares"; sure, it's "old-fashioned" with "dated" dece
but the modest pricing is fine as is.

Trattoria Dell'Arte ● Italian

22 | 20 | 21 | $55

W 50s | 900 Seventh Ave. (bet. 56th & 57th Sts.) | 212-245-9800 |
www.trattoriadellarte.com

Still "happening" after 20 years, this "high-energy" Midtown Italian
famed for its "affluent" following, super antipasto bar and "surrealis
body parts artwork (there's "always something interesting to look at'
it's "noisy, but a lot of fun" with "proximity to Carnegie Hall a plus."

Trattoria Dopo Teatro ● Italian

16 | 15 | 17 | $41

W 40s | 125 W. 44th St. (bet. B'way & 6th Ave.) | 212-869-2849 |
www.dopoteatro.com

"Surprisingly big", this Theater District Italian draws "madhous
crowds despite an "incredibly average" menu, "lowbrow" decor an
"rushed" service; still, it's "convenient" to Broadway and the "secre
garden room supplies some charm.

❷ Trattoria L'incontro Ⓜ Italian

26 | 19 | 24 | $49

Astoria | 21-76 31st St. (Ditmars Blvd.) | Queens | 718-721-3532 |
www.trattorialincontro.com

Astoria's "glorious, glorified neighborhood restaurant" boasts "ou
standing" Italian cooking from chef Rocco Sacramone and first-ra
service, though it's best known for its "overwhelmingly long list"
daily specials; a new wine bar adjunct dubbed Vino di Vino helps a
sorb the overflow crowds.

Trattoria Pesce & Pasta Italian/Seafood

18 | 14 | 17 | $32

E 50s | 1079 First Ave. (59th St.) | 212-888-7884 ●
E 80s | 1562 Third Ave. (bet. 87th & 88th Sts.) | 212-987-4696 ●
NEW **Garment District** | 536 Ninth Ave. (bet. 39th & 40th Sts.) |
212-594-5408
G Village | 262 Bleecker St. (bet. 6th Ave. & 7th Ave. S.) | 212-645-2993
W 90s | 625 Columbus Ave. (bet. 90th & 91st Sts.) | 212-579-7970
www.pescepasta.com

"Reliable but uninspiring", this "informal" Italian quintet puts o
"consistent" seafood and pastas at "good value"; "casual" settin
and "laid-back service" please those who "don't expect too much."

| | FOOD | DECOR | SERVICE | COST |

Trattoria Romana *Italian*
24 | 17 | 22 | $41

Staten Island | 1476 Hylan Blvd. (Benton Ave.) | 718-980-3113 | www.trattoriaromana.com

Staten Island may have "more Italian restaurants than citizens", but fans say this "authentic" trattoria is particularly "outstanding"; "tight" tables make it "too up close and personal" for some, but "face time with the chef" is "worth the boat trip."

tre dici ⑤ *Italian*
22 | 18 | 19 | $44

Chelsea | 128 W. 26th St. (bet. 6th & 7th Aves.) | 212-243-8183

Parked on an "off-the-beaten-path" stretch of the "Chelsea fur district", this "intimate", modestly priced Italian provides "better than expected" food in modern digs; "far better than the usual neighborhood" spot, it's still "undiscovered" – go figure.

NEW Tree ◐ *French*
▽ 24 | 16 | 19 | $40

E Village | 190 First Ave. (bet. 11th & 12th Sts.) | 212-358-7171 | www.treenyc.com

Instantly "popular", this new East Village bistro is drawing "boisterous" crowds with its "inspired", midpriced takes on "traditional" Gallic grub; the "little" storefront setting makes a vague attempt at "faux French atmosphere", but it plays second fiddle to the "great" back garden.

Trestle on Tenth *American*
19 | 18 | 19 | $49

Chelsea | 242 10th Ave. (24th St.) | 212-645-5659 | www.trestleontenth.com

"Charmingly informal", this Chelsea yearling offers a "meat-centric" array of "Swiss-influenced" New Americana (plus an "original, affordable" wine list) in a "brick-walled", art-lined interior or "lovely" back garden; although its performance can be "spotty", adherents insist it "has potential."

Triangolo ◐ *Italian*
21 | 16 | 22 | $39

E 80s | 345 E. 83rd St. (bet. 1st & 2nd Aves.) | 212-472-4488 | www.triangolorestaurant.com

"Flirtatious waiters" and reasonable prices make for "pleasant" dining at this venerable UES Italian that could be a "model for a neighborhood restaurant"; "solid basics" on the plate and a "no-rush" pace distract from the "elbow-to-elbow" layout.

Tribeca Grill *American*
22 | 21 | 21 | $57

TriBeCa | 375 Greenwich St. (Franklin St.) | 212-941-3900 | www.tribecagrill.com

"Like fine wine", this "original" New American via Drew Nieporent and Robert De Niro just "gets better with time" serving "reliable", albeit pricey, New American food with a side of "celebrity hipness" in "casual" environs; most feel it hasn't lost a beat over the years.

Trinity Place *Eclectic*
▽ 18 | 23 | 19 | $39

Financial District | 115 Broadway (enter on Cedar St., bet. B'way & Trinity Pl.) | 212-964-0939 | www.trinityplacenyc.com

The pub grub may be "fancied up" at this Financial District "hideaway", but it still takes a backseat to the "former bank vault" setting, complete with "huge", 35-ton doors; a very "noisy" weeknight "bar scene" makes it "better for lunch", when you don't have to deposit as much for a meal.

	FOOD	DECOR	SERVICE	COST

Trio ●⑤ Mediterranean
▽ 21 | 17 | 22 | $44

Murray Hill | 167 E. 33rd St. (bet. Lexington & 3rd Aves.) | 212-685-1001 | www.trionyc.com

Although it no longer features Croatian specialties, this "quiet" Murray Hill Med is as "delightful" as ever, ditto the "friendly" staff; while the decor (and clientele) may be "a bit dated", no one minds once the "piano player starts."

Triomphe French
24 | 22 | 23 | $63

W 40s | Iroquois Hotel | 49 W. 44th St. (bet. 5th & 6th Aves.) | 212-453-4233 | www.triomphe-newyork.com

"Largely undiscovered", this "secret little" Theater District rendezvous "deserves to be more crowded" owing to its "fantastic" New French menu and overall "luxurious" air; "quiet in an area where quiet is unusual", it's best when "someone else pays."

Tsampa ● Tibetan
▽ 20 | 20 | 19 | $25

E Village | 212 E. Ninth St. (bet. 2nd & 3rd Aves.) | 212-614-3226

To "get away from it all", try this East Village Tibetan "Zen den" serving a "hard-to-find" cuisine that's both "unusual" and "healthful"; there's "next to no lighting" and the staff can be "a little too relaxed", but no one cares when prices are this low.

Tse Yang Chinese
25 | 23 | 24 | $61

E 50s | 34 E. 51st St. (bet. Madison & Park Aves.) | 212-688-5447

"Extraordinary Peking duck" is the centerpiece of the "gourmet" menu at this "haute" East Midtown Chinese, a longtime supplier of "expertly prepared" cuisine; "upscale" quarters and "attentive but not obtrusive service" help rationalize the "could-it-get-more-expensive?" pricing.

Tupelo Grill ⑤ American
▽ 18 | 16 | 17 | $48

Garment District | 1 Penn Plaza, 33rd St. (bet. 7th & 8th Aves.) | 212-760-2700

When you "don't want a sports bar", this Penn Station–convenient American is an "acceptable" bet before an MSG event; "sparse decor", "expense-account" pricing and just "ok food" don't seem to matter since it's one of the "only games" around.

Turkish Cuisine ● Turkish
20 | 15 | 19 | $31

W 40s | 631 Ninth Ave. (bet. 44th & 45th Sts.) | 212-397-9650 | www.turkishcuisinenyc.com

"Well-prepared", "no-nonsense" cooking is on the docket at this "homey" Hell's Kitchen Turk that's "recently been discovered" and thus can get particularly "crowded" pre-theater; "tired" decor and "slightly pushy" service are trumped by "bargain" tabs and that "funky garden."

Turkish Kitchen Turkish
22 | 19 | 19 | $39

Gramercy | 386 Third Ave. (bet. 27th & 28th Sts.) | 212-679-6633 | www.turkishkitchen.com

"No one goes home hungry" from this "mouthwatering" Gramercy Turk known for its "terrific appetizers" and a "steal" of a Sunday brunch; given the "value" pricing and "cocktail lounge atmosphere", it's "deservedly popular."

	FOOD	DECOR	SERVICE	COST

Turks & Frogs *Turkish*
20 | **18** | **19** | **$40**

TriBeCa | 458 Greenwich St. (bet. Desbrosses & Watts Sts.) | 212-966-4774 | www.turksandfrogs.com

Forget the "middle-of-nowhere" address – this TriBeCa Turk is still handier than "going to Istanbul" and serves appropriately "exotic" fare for "affordable" dough; the "cozy" setting and "hardworking" staff make for "unpretentious", "highly enjoyable" dining.

Turkuaz ● *Turkish*
19 | **20** | **18** | **$33**

W 100s | 2637 Broadway (100th St.) | 212-665-9541 | www.turkuazrestaurant.com

For Turkish cooking "without the jet lag", try this "enormous" Upper Westsider done up in a "deliriously kitschy" "sultan" style, with "tented ceilings" and "hammered tin tables"; the "no-surprises" menu is "tasty" enough, but the "belly dancing" is just plain "delicious" and the service "so friendly you'd think they owed you money."

Turquoise *Seafood*
22 | **18** | **20** | **$55**

E 80s | 240 E. 81st St. (bet. 2nd & 3rd Aves.) | 212-988-4892 | www.turquoiseseafood.com

"Tasty Mediterranean-style" seafood is the hook at this UES fishmonger, a "lively, familial" spot thanks to a "hoot" of an owner who will personally "customize" your order; it's "still pretty secret", but a "must-go" despite "not cheap" pricing.

Tuscan Square ⊠ *Italian*
16 | **18** | **16** | **$44**

W 50s | 16 W. 51st St. (bet. 5th & 6th Aves.) | 212-977-7777 | www.tuscansquare.ypguides.net

"Fine for tourists" and business-lunchers, this moderately priced Rock Center Italian vends "solid" if "average" food in a "formulaic", "Disney-like" setting; it's "largely overlooked at dinnertime", but a hit during the holidays due to its proximity to the "ice skating rink."

Tuscany Grill *Italian*
24 | **19** | **20** | **$44**

Bay Ridge | 8620 Third Ave. (bet. 86th & 87th Sts.) | Brooklyn | 718-921-5633

Those who "know good Italian when they taste it" tout this Bay Ridge standby for when you're in a "romantic" frame of mind; it's "small" but the mood's "intimate", the cooking's "authentic", the prices reasonable and the staff "couldn't be more welcoming."

12th St. Bar & Grill *American*
21 | **19** | **19** | **$35**

Park Slope | 1123 Eighth Ave. (12th St.) | Brooklyn | 718-965-9526

A "true neighborhood eatery" "nestled amid brownstones", this Park Slope "favorite" endears itself to locals with "dependable", "reasonable" New American fare, prix fixe deals and a solid Sunday brunch; better still, a recent redo spruced up its space.

12 Chairs *American/Mideastern*
▽ **19** | **12** | **15** | **$25**

SoHo | 56 MacDougal St. (bet. Houston & Prince Sts.) | 212-254-8640

An eminently "affordable" choice in a neighborhood short on bargains, this "sparse" "little" SoHo cafe specializes in "homey" Middle Eastern-accented American comfort food; if "service lacks" and it can get "crowded", it's "friendly" enough that most don't seem to mind.

	FOOD	DECOR	SERVICE	COST

⚡ 21 Club *American*
22 | 23 | 24 | $71

W 50s | 21 W. 52nd St. (bet. 5th & 6th Aves.) | 212-582-7200 | www.21club.com

This "venerable" onetime speakeasy, a "formidable fixture" in Midtown, delivers "satisfying" Traditional American fare to a "virtual who's who" of "high rollers" in "clubby", jackets-required quarters manned by a "solicitous yet unobtrusive" "formal" crew; to avoid a "shocker" of a tab, "check out the $40 pre-theater prix fixe"; N.B. party-throwers should note there are 10 "lovely" private rooms.

26 Seats Ⓜ *French*
22 | 17 | 20 | $36

E Village | 168 Ave. B (bet. 10th & 11th Sts.) | 212-677-4787 | www.26seats.com

"They're not kidding" about the number of seats at this "popular", "tiny" East Village French where it's easy to feel like you're "dining at the home of a gourmet chef"; "inexpensive" prices seal the deal – so "make a reservation."

Two Boots *Pizza*
18 | 10 | 14 | $15

E 40s | Grand Central | lower level (42nd St. & Vanderbilt Ave.) | 212-557-7992 | www.twoboots.com
E Village | 42 Ave. A (3rd St.) | 212-254-1919 | www.twoboots.com ◑
🆕 **LES** | 384 Grand St. (bet. Norfolk & Suffolk Sts.) | 212-228-8685 | www.twoboots.com
NoHo | 74 Bleecker St. (B'way) | 212-777-1033 | www.twoboots.com ◑
W 40s | 30 Rockefeller Plaza, downstairs (bet. 49th & 50th Sts.) | 212-332-8800 | www.twoboots.com
W Village | 201 W. 11th St. (7th Ave. S.) | 212-633-9096 | www.twoboots.com ◑
Park Slope | 514 Second St. (bet. 7th & 8th Aves.) | Brooklyn | 718-499-3253 | www.twobootsbrooklyn.com

There's a "great marketing scheme" at work at this "nontraditional" pizza chain where the pies come with "cornmeal crusts", "original" toppings and "obscure celeb" names; they are all "extremely child-friendly", especially the separately managed Park Slope branch.

212 ◑ *American*
16 | 16 | 15 | $46

E 60s | 133 E. 65th St. (bet. Lexington & Park Aves.) | 212-249-6565 | www.212restaurant.com

"Euro-fabulous" "twentysomethings" shriek "at each other" and "into their phones" at this Bloomie's-area New American eatery/vodka bar that's best when you "want to be seen but not heard"; "so-so" food, "distracted" service and "pricey" tabs don't dampen the "scene."

202 Cafe *Mediterranean*
21 | 20 | 18 | $33

Chelsea | Chelsea Mkt. | 75 Ninth Ave. (bet. 15th & 16th Sts.) | 646-638-1173

Made for "multitasking", this "comfortable" cafe in Nicole Farhi's Chelsea Market boutique allows diners to "shop for hip clothes in between courses" of "tasty" Med fare; it's popular for a Brit-accented brunch that's happily much more "affordable" than the "designer duds."

2 West *Steak*
▽ 21 | 23 | 24 | $63

Financial District | Ritz-Carlton Battery Park | 2 West St. (Battery Pl.) | 917-790-2525 | www.ritzcarlton.com

When "seeing clients in the Financial District", it's hard to beat this "hidden gem" of a hotel steakhouse in Battery Park that's a "perfect retreat from the hustle and bustle"; "exemplary service" and "elegant, contemporary" environs offset expense account–worthy tabs.

Umberto's Clam House *Italian/Seafood* | 18 | 13 | 17 | $37 |

Little Italy | 386 Broome St. (Mulberry St.) | 212-343-2053 | www.umbertosclamhouse.com ●

Bronx | 2356 Arthur Ave. (186th St.) | 718-220-2526 | www.umbertosclamhousebronx.com

"Taking you back to the heyday of Little Italy", this "infamous" red-sauce "landmark" serves "classic" pasta and fish in a "*Godfather*"-esque milieu; those not "blown away" (as Joey Gallo was) say "leave it to the tourists" and decamp for the "better" Bronx outpost.

Una Pizza Napoletana Ⓜ⇄ *Pizza* | 23 | 10 | 13 | $28 |

E Village | 349 E. 12th St. (bet. 1st & 2nd Aves.) | 212-477-9950 | www.unapizza.com

"Pizza purists" praise this East Villager for its "simply prepared" Neapolitan pies made with "quality" imported ingredients, even if they're "criminally priced" at $21 per 12-inch model; "abysmal" service, no slices and a "limited selection" (four, to be exact) make some wonder if it's "worth the hassle."

Uncle Jack's Steakhouse *Steak* | 23 | 19 | 21 | $67 |

Garment District | 440 Ninth Ave. (bet. 34th & 35th Sts.) | 212-244-0005
Bayside | 39-40 Bell Blvd. (40th Ave.) | Queens | 718-229-1100
www.unclejacks.com

That "old-time steakhouse feel" thrives at this Bayside/Garment District duo where "giant chops" are presented in "boys' club" settings for "high price tags"; maybe they're "not Luger's", but "if steak is a religion, they're good parish churches."

Uncle Nick's *Greek* | 19 | 11 | 15 | $32 |

W 50s | 747 Ninth Ave. (bet. 50th & 51st Sts.) | 212-245-7992

"Rollicking good times" await at this "busy" Hell's Kitchen Hellenic specializing in "delicious" meze and grilled whole fish; it's "nothing fancy" with "rough-and-ready" service, plus an adjoining Ouzaria with much the "same menu" for "leftover laundry money."

☒ Union Square Cafe *American* | 26 | 22 | 26 | $65 |

Union Sq | 21 E. 16th St. (bet. 5th Ave. & Union Sq. W.) | 212-243-4020 | www.unionsquarecafe.com

Voted Most Popular in this Survey, Danny Meyer's New American off Union Square "proves its reputation every time", thanks to Michael Romano's "artfully executed" cuisine, a choice of "well-appointed" spaces and "friendly" service that "never wavers"; true, a reservation can be "problematic", but the walk-in bar area is always available to experience this "definition of comfortable NY dining."

Uno Chicago Grill *Pizza* | 14 | 12 | 14 | $23 |

E 80s | 220 E. 86th St. (bet. 2nd & 3rd Aves.) | 212-472-5656 ●
G Village | 391 Sixth Ave. (bet. 8th St. & Waverly Pl.) | 212-242-5230 ◗
Seaport | Pier 17 | 89 South St. (Fulton St.) | 212-791-7999
W 80s | 432 Columbus Ave. (81st St.) | 212-595-4700 ●
Bay Ridge | 9201 Fourth Ave. (92nd St.) | Brooklyn | 718-748-8667 ◗
Astoria | 37-11 35th Ave. (38th St.) | Queens | 718-706-8800 ◗

(continued)

(continued)

Uno Chicago Grill

Bayside | 39-02 Bell Blvd. (39th Ave.) | Queens | 718-279-4900 ●
Forest Hills | 107-16 70th Rd. (bet. Austin St. & Queens Blvd.) | Queens |
718-793-6700 ●
www.unos.com

"Safe but not exciting" deep-dish pizza is served at this "typical chain"
whose "expanded" menus also include "ordinary" American chow; service is "slow" and decor "bland", but "kids like it" and so will your wallet.

Uskudar *Turkish*

19 | 9 | 17 | $35

E 70s | 1405 Second Ave. (bet. 73rd & 74th Sts.) | 212-988-2641

"Shoebox"-size, this UES Turk tenders "standard" grub that's "reliable" but may "lack subtlety"; still, "cheerful hospitality" and decent
value keep it "crowded all the time" with nonclaustrophobic locals.

Utsav *Indian*

21 | 18 | 19 | $37

W 40s | 1185 Sixth Ave., 2nd fl. (enter on 46th St., bet. 6th & 7th Aves.) |
212-575-2525 | www.utsavny.com

It may be "hard to find", but this "dressy" Theater District Indian is
worth seeking out for its "not-too-spicy, beginner-friendly" food and
"spacious" setting bedecked with "fabric canopies"; any meal here is
a good bet, but the "copious" $15.95 lunch buffet is an especially ap-
pealing introduction for first-timers.

Uva ● *Italian*

21 | 21 | 20 | $37

E 70s | 1486 Second Ave. (bet. 77th & 78th Sts.) | 212-472-4552 |
www.uvawinebarnewyork.com

This UES Italian "hot spot" attracts the "younger set" with "chic" digs,
an "extensive wine list" and "good-looking sommeliers" (the "affordable" food is almost incidental here); the vibe's "bustling bordering on
loud", so insiders head for the quieter "year-round" garden.

Valbella ☒ *Italian*

24 | 24 | 23 | $78

Meatpacking | 421 W. 13th St. (bet. 9th Ave. & Washington St.) |
212-645-7777 | www.valbellany.com

Something "very adult" for the Meatpacking District, this "flawless"
Northern Italian spin-off of the "Greenwich, CT, original" is a "posh"
opportunity to savor "impeccable" food and service in a modern bi-
level setting; maybe the prices soar, but its well-heeled crowd can
easily afford it.

NEW Vamos! *Mexican*

▽ 16 | 17 | 17 | $32

Gramercy | 348 First Ave. (20th St.) | 212-358-7800 |
www.vamosnyc.com

"Underserviced" Stuytown gets a lift with the arrival of this new, low-
budget Mexican brought to you by the "owners of Petite Abeille"; too
bad the food's just "middle of the road", but the "delicious margaritas"
and all that "noise" suggest it "caters more to the bar crowd."

V&T ● *Italian/Pizza*

18 | 9 | 13 | $21

W 100s | 1024 Amsterdam Ave. (bet. 110th & 111th Sts.) | 212-666-8051

Since 1945, this Morningside Heights Italian "that time forgot" has
been a "Columbia student favorite", dishing out "gooey" pizza in
"dingy" digs for "cheap as hell" dough; "snail's pace service" and "bot-
tled salad dressing" are "part of the charm."

Vatan ⓜ *Indian*

Gramercy | 409 Third Ave. (29th St.) | 212-689-5666 | www.vatanny.com

23 | 23 | 22 | $34

For $23.95, "endless plates" keep on coming at this "unique", all-you-can-eat Gramercy Indian vegetarian; the "over-the-top" faux village decor affords one of those transporting experiences that you can't put a price on.

Veniero's ⓞ *Dessert*

E Village | 342 E. 11th St. (bet. 1st & 2nd Aves.) | 212-674-7070 | www.venierospastry.com

23 | 14 | 13 | $15

Since 1894, this "beloved" East Village Italian pastry palace has been a destination for its "creamy cannoli" and other "naughty" desserts; there's "always a line" and the staff could use some "customer service lessons", but ultimately it's "justly celebrated."

Vento ⓞ *Italian*

Meatpacking | 675 Hudson St. (14th St.) | 212-699-2400 | www.brguestrestaurants.com

19 | 19 | 18 | $46

A "great location" in the "happening" Meatpacking District is the bait at Steve Hanson's "lively" Italian featuring an "affordable", small plates–centric menu; though service may need help, it's fun to "sit outside and drool" at the passing "hottie" parade.

ⓩ Veritas *American*

Flatiron | 43 E. 20th St. (bet. B'way & Park Ave. S.) | 212-353-3700 | www.veritas-nyc.com

26 | 22 | 25 | $98

Bolstered by an award-winning wine list, this "outstanding" Flatiron New American continues to impress those seeking "sophisticated", "delicious" dining in "handsome" environs; it's "luxurious from start to finish" with appropriately "first-class" service, though "costly" given the $76 prix fixe-only menu.

Vermicelli *Vietnamese*

E 70s | 1492 Second Ave. (bet. 77th & 78th Sts.) | 212-288-8868 | www.vermicellirestaurant.com

19 | 16 | 18 | $29

Nope, "it isn't Italian" – despite the "odd name", this UES "neighborhood sleeper" offers "flavorful" Vietnamese eats that are "well spiced" and priced; though the ambiance is "unusually calm", many take out the "excellent box lunches" at midday.

Veselka *Ukrainian*

E Village | 144 Second Ave. (9th St.) | 212-228-9682 ⓞ
E Village | First Park | 75 E. First St. (1st Ave.) | 347-907-3317 ⓟ
www.veselka.com

18 | 12 | 14 | $20

"Go hungry and then go nap" after a meal at this bargain East Village Ukrainian where the "rib-sticking" "Eastern European soul food" is served "round the clock" by a "perfunctory" staff; the kiosk satellite features an abbreviated menu and a handful of alfresco tables.

Vespa *Italian*

E 80s | 1625 Second Ave. (bet. 84th & 85th Sts.) | 212-472-2050 | www.barvespa.com

21 | 20 | 20 | $39

"La dolce vita" is alive and well at this "low-key" UES Italian where a chic "Euro vibe" enhances the "delicious", midpriced cooking; the "beautiful" patio is a "wonderful escape" as well as a "romantic refuge."

	FOOD	DECOR	SERVICE	COST

Vezzo *Pizza*
▽ 21 | 16 | 15 | $22

Murray Hill | 178 Lexington Ave. (31st St.) | 212-839-8300

"Fabulous thin-crust" pizza in an underserved part of Murray Hill has made it "hard to get a table" at this Italian yearling; an airy setting and a choice of "any topping you could possibly want" help blunt the "slow service" and "relatively pricey" tabs.

Via Brasil *Brazilian/Steak*
18 | 15 | 18 | $40

W 40s | 34 W. 46th St. (bet. 5th & 6th Aves.) | 212-997-1158 | www.viabrasilrestaurant.com

When "flying to Rio is a little much", there's always this "easygoing" Theater District Brazilian that puts "Ipanema on a platter" via "perfectly marinated" steaks and other "tasty" dishes; though a "recent remodel" gets "low marks", it "comes alive" on "live music nights."

Via Emilia 🗷🐟 *Italian*
21 | 16 | 19 | $36

Flatiron | 47 E. 21st St. (bet. B'way & Park Ave. S.) | 212-505-3072 | www.viaemilia.us

Relocation to "more spacious" digs has some longtime patrons of this Flatiron Italian claiming that it's now "devoid of charm"; but thankfully the "excellent value" and "same great" Emilia-Romagna food remains, along with that "makes-life-difficult" no-plastic policy.

Viand *Coffee Shop*
16 | 8 | 17 | $20

E 60s | 673 Madison Ave. (bet. 61st & 62nd Sts.) | 212-751-6622 🐟
E 70s | 1011 Madison Ave. (78th St.) | 212-249-8250
E 80s | 300 E. 86th St. (2nd Ave.) | 212-879-9425 ◗
W 70s | 2130 Broadway (75th St.) | 212-877-2888 | www.viandnyc.com ◗

There's "no ambiance" at these "quick-in, quick-out" coffee shops, but they remain "NY classics" for their "old-fashioned" vibe, "lightning-fast" service and famous turkey sandwiches "carved right off the bone"; indeed, on many mornings you'll find Mayor Mike breakfasting at the 78th Street branch.

Via Oreto *Italian*
19 | 15 | 18 | $46

E 60s | 1121-23 First Ave. (bet. 61st & 62nd Sts.) | 212-308-0828

"Like dinner at the in-laws' without the stress", this "family-owned" UES Italian exudes a "comfortable", "right-out-of-the-*Sopranos*" vibe with a "caring" staff serving a "solid", midpriced menu of "basics"; "mama's special meatballs" are a revered Sunday/Monday tradition.

Via Quadronno *Italian*
21 | 15 | 16 | $38

E 70s | 25 E. 73rd St. (bet. 5th & Madison Aves.) | 212-650-9880 | www.viaquadronno.com

"Chic" Madison Avenue "art dealers" and "gorgeous Euro moms" patronize this all-day UES Italian for "quick pick-me-ups", particularly the "fab" panini and cappuccinos; "prices are high" for what you get and the "tiny digs ensure you won't stay too long."

ViceVersa 🗷 *Italian*
23 | 21 | 22 | $53

W 50s | 325 W. 51st St. (bet. 8th & 9th Aves.) | 212-399-9291 | www.viceversarestaurant.com

One "reason to go to the Theater District even if you're not seeing a show", this "consistently fine" Italian serves a "first-rate" menu in a

| | FOOD | DECOR | SERVICE | COST |

sunny "modern" setting; service is "friendly" but "professional", and somehow it's "not too touristy in a touristy area."

Vico ●🚭 *Italian* — 21 | 15 | 19 | $59

E 90s | 1302 Madison Ave. (bet. 92nd & 93rd Sts.) | 212-876-2222

It helps "to be known" at this "clubby" Carnegie Hill Italian where "UES Wasps get excited" about the "surprisingly good" menu that really "looks great on the plate"; not as thrilling are the "expensive-for-what-it-is" tabs and "annoying" cash-only policy.

Victor's Cafe ● *Cuban* — 21 | 18 | 20 | $46

W 50s | 236 W. 52nd St. (bet. B'way & 8th Ave.) | 212-586-7714 | www.victorscafe.com

A "touch of Havana" in the Theater District, this palm-decorated "old reliable" has been dishing out "enticing" Cuban food since the early '60s; sure, it's a little "pricey" (maybe "outdated"), but the "ebullient" ambiance and "warm" service keep regulars regular.

Vida 🅼🚭 *Eclectic* — ∇ 20 | 16 | 20 | $34

Staten Island | 381 Van Duzer St. (bet. Beach & Wright Sts.) | 718-720-1501

Featuring an "unusually creative", unusually affordable menu, this Staten Island Eclectic makes locals "feel very much at home – without having to do the dishes"; the only drawback is a "too cozy" setting that's so tiny there's "no privacy at all."

VietCafé 🆂 *Vietnamese* — ∇ 21 | 18 | 19 | $33

TriBeCa | 345 Greenwich St. (bet. Harrison & Jay Sts.) | 212-431-5888 | www.viet-cafe.com

"Haute Vietnamese" food comes to TriBeCa via this "tantalizing" Asian offering "light, delicate" dishes; still, the "small portions" and "high-tech" setting lead some to report there's "no sparkle" here.

View, The *Continental* — 18 | 24 | 19 | $80

W 40s | Marriott Marquis Hotel | 1535 Broadway, 47th fl. (bet. 45th & 46th Sts.) | 212-704-8900 | www.nymarriottmarquis.com

"Still twirlin' after all these years", this hotel Continental is NYC's only "rotating restaurant", with a literally "moving view" of Times Square and beyond; the food's just "so-so" and the prix fixe–only tabs are "pricey", but at least it's "aptly named."

Villa Berulia *Italian* — ∇ 23 | 19 | 24 | $49

Murray Hill | 107 E. 34th St. (bet. Lexington & Park Aves.) | 212-689-1970 | www.villaberulia.com

"Comfortable fine dining" is in store at this venerable Murray Hill Northern Italian known for its "top-quality" cooking and "absolutely delightful" staff; it mostly draws "time travelers" (i.e. "mostly older" types) who don't mind "pricey" tabs and "dated" decor.

Village. *American/French* — 20 | 18 | 19 | $45

G Village | 62 W. Ninth St. (bet. 5th & 6th Aves.) | 212-505-3355 | www.villagerestaurant.com

The mood's "lively" at this "better-than-average" Village bistro where the Franco-American offerings are "consistently good", "especially for the price"; though the "barnlike" back dining room has a "skylight and high ceilings", it could also use a "sound absorber."

	FOOD	DECOR	SERVICE	COST

Villa Mosconi 🖪 *Italian* — 20 | 15 | 22 | $43

G Village | 69 MacDougal St. (bet. Bleecker & Houston Sts.) | 212-673-0390 |
www.villamosconi.com

There's a "dedicated neighborhood following" at this circa-1976
Village Italian, an "old-fashioned" affair with "solid" red sauce on the
menu and "paint-by-numbers paintings" on the walls; "caring" staffers
and modest prices "make you feel like a regular even if you're not."

Vincent's ● *Italian* — 21 | 14 | 18 | $34

Little Italy | 119 Mott St. (Hester St.) | 212-226-8133 |
www.originalvincents.com

For "real Italian, not New Age", try this circa-1904 Little Italy vet famed
for its "secret-formula sauce" served in a "variety of levels of spici-
ness"; it's staffed by a crew of "interesting characters" and decorated
with the "requisite pictures of the *Sopranos* cast members on the wall."

Virgil's Real Barbecue ● *BBQ* — 20 | 13 | 17 | $33

W 40s | 152 W. 44th St. (bet. B'way & 6th Ave.) | 212-921-9494 |
www.virgilsbbq.com

"Monstrous portions" of "lip-smacking", "stick-to-your-ribs ribs"
grace the menu of this "stuff-your-face" BBQ "factory"; the Times
Square location translates into "droves of tourists", "hurried service"
and a general air of "pandemonium"; P.S. "don't forgo the bib."

Vivolo 🖪 *Italian* — 20 | 17 | 20 | $49

E 70s | 140 E. 74th St. (bet. Lexington & Park Aves.) | 212-737-3533 |
www.vivolonyc.com

Set in a "cozy", "wood-paneled" townhouse, this "old-school" UES duplex serves "reliable" Italiana that tastes even better "when the fireplace is lit" in the "inviting" upstairs parlor; it draws "well-dressed
couples of a certain age" with an "outstanding" $26 early-bird.

Vong *French/Thai* — 22 | 23 | 21 | $61

E 50s | 200 E. 54th St. (3rd Ave.) | 212-486-9592 | www.jean-georges.com
The "tableware is as entertaining as the food" at Jean-Georges
Vongerichten's "exotic" Midtown French-Thai where the "artfully prepared" offerings match the "polished" staff and "Asian fantasy" setting; sure, the "tiny portions" come at "splurge"-worthy tabs, but a
$20 "bargain" lunch and $35 pre-theater prix fixes are available.

Vynl *American/Thai* — 17 | 20 | 16 | $25

NEW **E 70s** | 1491 Second Ave. (78th St.) | 212-249-6080
W 50s | 754 Ninth Ave. (51st St.) | 212-974-2003 ●
NEW **W 80s** | 507 Columbus Ave. (bet. 84th & 85th Sts.) | 212-362-1107
www.vynl-nyc.com

"Something for everyone" sums up the menu of this trio of "pretend
diners" known for their "affordable" New American–Thai chow and
"random service"; "tragically kitschy" "music-themed" loos are conversation starters, that is if you can be heard above the "cranking stereo."

Z **NEW** **Wakiya** ● *Chinese* — – | – | – | E

Gramercy | Gramercy Park Hotel | 2 Lexington Ave. (21st St.) | 212-995-1330 |
www.gramercyparkhotel.com

Ian Schrager's trendy rehabbed Gramercy Park Hotel is the setting for
this nouveau Chinese named after star chef Yuji Wakiya, who offers an

exciting 'sharing menu' of hot and cold items as well as dim sum; the long, slender space, done up in red and black, exudes a James Bond vibe (i.e. *Diamonds are Forever*), though pricing is far more modern.

Waldy's Wood Fired Pizza *Pizza*
21 | 11 | 15 | $16

Chelsea | 800 Sixth Ave. (bet. 27th & 28th Sts.) | 212-213-5042 | www.waldyspizza.com

"Highbrow pizza" by way of the "highly inventive" chef Waldy Malouf (Beacon) is yours at this "tiny" Chelsea storefront where "minimal" seating and "fast-food" decor make "delivery a better option"; bonus points go to the "gourmet toppings", especially the fresh herbs.

Walker's ● *Pub Food*
17 | 13 | 16 | $28

TriBeCa | 16 N. Moore St. (Varick St.) | 212-941-0142

Serving "reliable pub grub" long "before TriBeCa was *TriBeCa*", this "neighborhood fixture" has the staples "down pat" with the "most affordable" dining around; expect plenty of "old NY" ambiance and a crowd of "regulars" who tout the burgers and brews.

Wallsé ◐ *Austrian*
26 | 22 | 23 | $66

W Village | 344 W. 11th St. (Washington St.) | 212-352-2300 | www.wallse.com

A "small restaurant with big aspirations", this West Village "charmer" lets you skip the "schlep to Vienna" thanks to chef Kurt Gutenbrunner's "seriously delicious" Austrian cuisine; add "outstanding wines", "gracious service" and "great Julian Schnabel paintings on the wall", and the "high-end" pricing is what you'd expect.

Water Club *American*
20 | 24 | 21 | $62

Murray Hill | East River at 30th St. (enter on 23rd St.) | 212-683-3333 | www.thewaterclub.com

For a "romantic getaway without leaving the city", this "special-occasion" Murray Hill American set on an East River barge "reminds us we're on an island" with its "spectacular views"; maybe it's "expensive" and "out of the way", but the food's "delicious" and the decor appropriately "nautical" at this "unique dining experience"; it's also a great place for a party.

WaterFalls Ⓜ *Italian*
▽ 20 | 19 | 19 | $37

Staten Island | 2012 Victory Blvd. (bet. Bradley & Jewett Aves.) | 718-815-7200 | www.waterfalls-restaurant.com

Offering a "large variety of dishes" at modest prices, this Staten Island Italian is also "pretty" and "tranquil"; though a few find things a bit "cookie-cutter", at least the "consistent" kitchen assures that "you'll get a good meal" here.

Water's Edge Ⓩ *American/Seafood*
23 | 26 | 23 | $60

LIC | East River & 44th Dr. (Vernon Blvd.) | Queens | 718-482-0033 | www.watersedgenyc.com

"Priceless" riverside views of Manhattan are the raisons d'être of this Long Island City New American seafooder that follows through with "tasty" cooking and "prompt" service; despite "free water taxi" service from Midtown, serious tabs make it "not your every-Saturday kind of place."

	FOOD	DECOR	SERVICE	COST

Z NEW Waverly Inn and Garden ● *American* | 18 | 21 | 17 | $57

W Village | 16 Bank St. (Waverly Pl.) | 212-243-7900

The hit of the year, this remake of a circa-1920 West Village tavern produces "reliable", tasty Americana in a lovely, intimate setting that plays to a "celeb-centric" crowd that is mostly friends of owner/*Vanity Fair* editor Grayson Carter; it's virtually "impossible to get a table" without connections, but walk-ins are allowed in the charming front bar; sidewalk tables and the back 'garden room' are bonuses.

wd-50 ● *American/Eclectic* | 23 | 19 | 23 | $82

LES | 50 Clinton St. (bet. Rivington & Stanton Sts.) | 212-477-2900 | www.wd-50.com

"If you're up for an adventure", "go outside the box" at this "unorthodox" Lower East Side American-Eclectic – aka "Molecular Gastronomy Central" – where chef Wylie Dufresne's "envelope-pushing" cuisine induces "love-it-or-hate-it" responses ("outstanding" vs. "outlandish"); there's no debate, however, that it's "expensive" – and "never, ever boring."

West Bank Cafe ● *American* | 20 | 17 | 19 | $44

W 40s | Manhattan Plaza | 407 W. 42nd St. (bet. 9th & 10th Aves.) | 212-695-6909 | www.westbankcafe.com

"Pleasant" is the word on this "off-the-beaten-path" Hell's Kitchen "keeper" with "dependable" New American cooking, a "good price point" and a "quality bar-and-grill atmosphere"; proximity to 42nd Street's Theater Row makes it a natural "hangout for working actors."

Westville *American* | 23 | 12 | 18 | $23

W Village | 210 W. 10th St. (bet. Bleecker & W. 4th Sts.) | 212-741-7971
NEW **Westville East** *American*
E Village | 173 Ave. A (11th St.) | 212-677-2033

"Cheap eats and long lines" sum up this West Village American, a "cult classic" specializing in "fresh greenmarket comfort foods"; the "tight" setup is a bit "less cramped" at the new East Village offspring featuring twice as many seats.

Whole Foods Café *Eclectic/Health Food* | 19 | 9 | 10 | $16

NEW **LES** | 95 E. Houston St., 2nd fl. (Bowery) | 212-420-1320
Union Sq | 4 Union Square S. (bet. B'way & University Pl.) | 212-673-5388
W 60s | Time Warner Ctr. | 10 Columbus Circle, downstairs (60th St. at B'way) | 212-823-9600
www.wholefoods.com

There's "variety aplenty" at these "self-serve" cafeteria adjuncts to the "foodie grocery stores", where the Eclectic offerings include a plethora of "multicultural" items as well as "huge salad bars"; despite "long check-out lines", "not enough seating" and an "every-man-for-himself" ambiance, fans "never tire of it."

Whym *American* | 21 | 18 | 19 | $41

W 50s | 889 Ninth Ave. (bet. 57th & 58th Sts.) | 212-315-0088 | www.whymnyc.com

"Trendy people too lazy to go Downtown" like this "stylish" Hell's Kitchen New American for its "industrial", "nightclublike" look and "positive energy"; its "upscale aspirations" are reflected in the "jazzed-up comfort-food" menu, not the "middle-class prices."

subscribe to zagat.com

	FOOD	DECOR	SERVICE	COST

'wichcraft *Sandwiches*

20 | 11 | 15 | $17

Chelsea | Terminal Warehouse | 224 12th Ave. (bet. 27th & 28th Sts.) | 212-780-0577
E 40s | 555 Fifth Ave. (46th St.) | 212-780-0577 🈂
NEW **Flatiron** | 11 E. 20th St. (bet. B'way & 5th Ave.) | 212-780-0577
G Village | 60 E. Eighth St. (Mercer St.) | 212-780-0577
NEW **Murray Hill** | Equinox | 1 Park Ave. S. (33rd St.) | 212-780-0577
SoHo | Equinox | 106 Crosby St. (Prince St.) | 212-780-0577
TriBeCa | 397 Greenwich St. (Beach St.) | 212-780-0577
W 40s | Bryant Park | Sixth Ave. (bet. 40th & 42nd Sts.) | 212-780-0577
www.wichcraftnyc.com

The "sandwich as art" is the philosophy of this breakfast-and-lunch chainlet from Craft's Tom Colicchio that creates "ambitious combos" via "high-quality ingredients"; though service can be "slow" and it costs "a lot of dough for not much bread", most admit to being under its "spell."

Wild Ginger *Thai*

19 | 18 | 17 | $25

W Village | 51 Grove St. (bet. Bleecker St. & 7th Ave. S.) | 212-367-7200 | www.wildginger-ny.com

"Amazingly affordable" for such a "prime Village location", this "pleasant" Thai serves a "well-prepared" menu that's "not too fusiony"; it's also invitingly "atmospheric", with a "dimly lit", bamboo-heavy setting and "friendly" service.

NEW Wild Salmon *Seafood*

▽ 21 | 20 | 18 | $59

E 40s | 622 Third Ave. (40th St.) | 212-404-1700 | www.chinagrillmgt.com

Like the name says, this new Midtown seafooder from restaurateur Jeffrey Chodorow focuses on salmon with "nearly everything on the menu flown in from the Pacific Northwest" – hence the "pricey" tabs; the "soaring" setting is now festooned with a copper mobile of flying fish.

Willie's Steak House ● *Steak*

▽ 23 | 16 | 19 | $26

Bronx | 1832 Westchester Ave. (bet. Taylor & Thieriot Aves.) | 718-822-9697 | www.williessteakhouse.com

An "extensive menu" of steaks and Latin dishes makes for "authentic", Spanish-style dining at this longtime Bronx chop shop that's well priced and well served for the genre; live jazz performances on Wednesdays and Saturdays are equally appealing.

Wo Hop ●⊅ *Chinese*

21 | 6 | 14 | $17

Chinatown | 17 Mott St. (Canal St.) | 212-267-2536

Right "out of a Woody Allen movie", this 70-year-old Chinatown vet serves "old-fashioned" Cantonese chow at "ridiculously low prices" in a "basement-from-hell" setting; though formerly open 'round the clock, it's now 21/7, closed daily from 7-10 AM.

Wolfgang's Steakhouse *Steak*

25 | 20 | 20 | $71

Murray Hill | 4 Park Ave. (33rd St.) | 212-889-3369
TriBeCa | 409 Greenwich St. (bet. Beach & Hubert Sts.) | 212-925-0350
www.wolfgangssteakhouse.com

"Masters of the universe" who "don't want to make the trip to Brooklyn" vow that these "Luger copy" steakhouses are "as good" as the original, and at least "take credit cards"; while the "mobbed" Murray Hill outpost is more atmospheric with its "vaulted ceilings",

| | FOOD | DECOR | SERVICE | COST |

it's much "noisier" than the "roomier" TriBeCa branch, but either way, "if the cholesterol doesn't stop your heart, the prices will."

Wollensky's Grill ● *Steak* `23` `17` `20` `$51`
E 40s | 201 E. 49th St. (3rd Ave.) | 212-753-0444 | www.smithandwollensky.com

"Less formal" (and "more fun") than its next-door "big sister", Smith & Wollensky, this handsome East Midtown grill serves the same "great steaks and burgers" at "better prices"; night owls say the biggest draw is its "late hours" – "where else can you eat this good after midnight?"

NEW Wombat ●⑰ *Australian* ▽ `21` `14` `22` `$25`
Williamsburg | 613 Grand St. (bet. Leonard & Lorimer Sts.) | Brooklyn | 718-218-7077 | www.thewombatbar.com

"Tiny" and "funky", this "surprisingly good" Williamsburg newcomer features a low-priced variety of hearty Australian dishes served till 2 AM; if the late-night carousing gets to you, there's also a hair-of-the-dingo brunch, available daily.

Wondee Siam *Thai* `22` `7` `16` `$21`
NEW E 80s | 1429 Third Ave. (bet. 80th & 81st Sts.) | 212-772-1494
W 50s | 792 Ninth Ave. (bet. 52nd & 53rd Sts.) | 212-459-9057 ⑰
W 50s | 813 Ninth Ave. (bet. 53rd & 54th Sts.) | 917-286-1726

"Authentic Thai" at prices that will "make you think you're in Minneapolis, not Manhattan", keep the customers coming to this "simple" Hell's Kitchen trio; forget the "total lack of decor" and "spotty" service: "what's really special here is the taste"; N.B. the UES satellite opened post-Survey.

WonJo ● *Korean* ▽ `20` `12` `14` `$32`
Garment District | 23 W. 32nd St. (bet. B'way & 5th Ave.) | 212-695-5815

Do-it-yourself types like cooking their Korean BBQ over "real charcoal" at this "bustling" Garment District spot where the "not-so-good" service is trumped by gentle pricing and a 24/7 open-door policy; those sensitive to "smoke" say the "downstairs seating is better."

Woo Lae Oak *Korean* `23` `21` `18` `$51`
SoHo | 148 Mercer St. (bet. Houston & Prince Sts.) | 212-925-8200 | www.woolaeoaksoho.com

One of NYC's "hippest Koreans", this "fashionable" SoHo grill is set in "sleek" digs, tended by an "eye-candy staff" and priced "on the expensive side"; more typical of the genre, it features "cook-it-yourself" dining.

Wu Liang Ye *Chinese* `21` `12` `16` `$29`
E 80s | 215 E. 86th St. (bet. 2nd & 3rd Aves.) | 212-534-8899
Murray Hill | 338 Lexington Ave. (bet. 39th & 40th Sts.) | 212-370-9648
W 40s | 36 W. 48th St. (bet. 5th & 6th Aves.) | 212-398-2308

"Not for the faint of stomach", this Szechuan trio purveys "adventurous" eats made from "zesty" ingredients – "very spicy means *very spicy*" here – so for best results, go with "someone who knows how to order"; "aging" decor and "impersonal" service are offset by "moderate prices."

Xing ● *Asian Fusion* `21` `21` `19` `$41`
W 50s | 785 Ninth Ave. (52nd St.) | 646-289-3010 | www.xingrestaurant.com

Something "different" for Hell's Kitchen, this "contempo" Asian fusion practitioner features a "novel" menu that works well with the "sleek", "upscale" design built around a "huge" aquarium; "killer cocktails" fuel the place's "high energy" and distract from its "pricey" tabs.

K.O. ⊄ *Chinese* | 18 | 9 | 12 | $17 |

Chinatown | 148 Hester St. (bet. Bowery & Elizabeth St.) | 212-965-8645
Chinatown | 96 Walker St. (bet. Centre & Lafayette Sts.) | 212-343-8339

If you like it "quick" and "cheap", these Hong Kong–style Chinatown cafes are just the ticket, featuring all-day dim sum and menus almost "too long to read" ("what *don't* they have?"); "indifferent" service and "dumpy" digs are the downsides.

Xunta ● *Spanish* | 19 | 12 | 13 | $29 |

E Village | 174 First Ave. (bet. 10th & 11th Sts.) | 212-614-0620 | www.xuntatapas.com

"Crowds of college students" cram into this "rowdy", low-budget East Village Spaniard where the "sangria flows" so freely that the "night is a blur" for most; still, a few remember "*qué bueno*" tapas, "uncomfortable" barrel seating and "absurdly loud" acoustics.

⦻ Yakitori Totto ● *Japanese* | 26 | 18 | 20 | $43 |

W 50s | 251 W. 55th St., 2nd fl. (bet. B'way & 8th Ave.) | 212-245-4555

Bringing an "authentic yakitori experience to the Big Apple", this "unique" Midtowner's grilled skewers are a particular "favorite of Japanese expats"; some menu items may be a "bit much" for Westerners – "chicken knees, anyone?" – but that's not stopping it from being "always full."

Yama *Japanese* | 24 | 13 | 17 | $39 |

E 40s | 308 E. 49th St. (bet. 1st & 2nd Aves.) | 212-355-3370 Ⓢ
Gramercy | 122 E. 17th St. (Irving Pl.) | 212-475-0969 Ⓢ
G Village | 38-40 Carmine St. (bet. Bedford & Bleecker Sts.) | 212-989-9330 Ⓢ
G Village | 92 W. Houston St. (bet. La Guardia Pl. & Thompson St.) | 212-674-0935 ●Ⓜ
www.yamarestaurant.com

Ok, the "obscenely big" pieces of sushi served at this Japanese chainlet "ain't subtle", but they are "fresher than fresh" and extremely "well priced"; if the "absurd" waits and "lame decor" are off-putting, insiders say the 49th Street branch is the most "serene" with the "shortest lines."

York Grill *American* | 23 | 20 | 22 | $48 |

E 80s | 1690 York Ave. (bet. 88th & 89th Sts.) | 212-772-0261

"Traditional" is the word for this Yorkville "neighborhood" spot where a "civilized" "older crowd" savors "old-fashioned" Americana in "quiet", "clubby" environs; trendy types wish it were "more inventive", but still feel it's "consistently excellent" and not that expensive.

Yuca Bar ● *Pan-Latin* | 21 | 14 | 16 | $30 |

E Village | 111 Ave. A (7th St.) | 212-982-9533 | www.yucabarnyc.com

"Divine sangria" and "kick-ass mojitos" keep the mood "festive" at this East Village Pan-Latin that attracts the young with "great value"; it's most memorable, however, as a "primo people-watching location", directly opposite Tompkins Square Park.

	FOOD	DECOR	SERVICE	COST

Yuka *Japanese* | 21 | 11 | 19 | $26

E 80s | 1557 Second Ave. (bet. 80th & 81st Sts.) | 212-772-9675

"Bargain sushi hunters" are all over the $19 all-you-can-eat deal at this longtime UES Japanese; sure, the seating's "tight", the service "rushed" and the setting "informal" (verging on "worn"), but they "slice a generous piece of fish" and "for the price, you can't complain."

Yuki Sushi ◑ *Japanese* | 21 | 14 | 20 | $31

W 90s | 656 Amsterdam Ave. (92nd St.) | 212-787-8200

"Unassuming" yet "pleasant", this UWS Japanese is a "good neighborhood option" for "casual" dining if "not a life-changing experience"; the fish is "prepared with care" for an "affordable" price, while "sweet service" compensates for the "not-much-to-look-at" decor.

NEW Yushi *Japanese* | – | – | – | I

E 40s | 245 Park Ave. (enter on E. 47th St., bet. Park & Lex. Aves.) | 212-687-1900 🅂

Financial District | 4 World Financial Ctr. | 250 Vesey St. (West St.) | 212-945-3096

www.yushi.com

Be prepared to wait in line at these Japanese siblings in Midtown and the Financial District thanks to their fresh, affordable array of grab-and-go sushi and sashimi; cool design touches like steel tabletops and mod pod chairs help working stiffs overlook the canteen-style setting.

Yuva *Indian* | ▽ 24 | 19 | 23 | $38

E 50s | 230 E. 58th St. (bet. 2nd & 3rd Aves.) | 212-339-0090 | www.yuvanyc.com

"Delicious" dining is the deal at this East Midtown Indian where the dishes display "creative finesse" and the decor sports modern-rustic touches; the latest arrival on 58th Street's "high-end Indian Row", this "worthwhile" venue "ain't your average curry mill."

Zabar's Cafe ⊅ *Deli* | 20 | 6 | 11 | $16

W 80s | 2245 Broadway (80th St.) | 212-787-2000 | www.zabars.com

Backers brave bizarre service, white Formica digs and plenty of "pushy NYers" just for the bagels, lox and other "great" noshables at this UWS deli/cafe hitched to the famed gourmet market; what's more, even kvetchers concede prices here "can't be beat" for what you get.

Zarela *Mexican* | 21 | 15 | 17 | $42

E 50s | 953 Second Ave. (bet. 50th & 51st Sts.) | 212-644-6740 | www.zarela.com

Still "buzzing" on the East Side, Zarela Martinez's split-level "winner" shows what "true" Mexican cooking should be; "powerful" margaritas and modest prices are catalysts for the fiesta scene downstairs (upstairs is "more tranquil").

Zaytoons *Mideastern* | 22 | 13 | 17 | $18

Carroll Gardens | 283 Smith St. (Sackett St.) | Brooklyn | 718-875-1880

Fort Greene | 472 Myrtle Ave. (bet. Hall St. & Washington Ave.) | Brooklyn | 718-623-5522

www.zaytoonsrestaurant.com

"Nothing fancy", just "generous" helpings of "dependably delicious" dishes are the stock in trade of these "ever-reliable" Middle Eastern

	FOOD	DECOR	SERVICE	COST

BYOs in Carroll Gardens and Fort Greene; "quick" service and "super-competitive" pricing easily override the modest settings.

Za Za ● *Italian*   20 | 15 | 19 | $37

E 60s | 1207 First Ave. (bet. 65th & 66th Sts.) | 212-772-9997 | www.zazanyc.com

Filling Italiana that "doesn't taste generic" is the calling card of this Eastsider that also comes across with "friendly" service and "reasonable" tabs; perhaps there's "no decor" on the inside, but the "amazing" garden out back certainly "increases the enjoyment."

Zebú Grill *Brazilian*   21 | 16 | 20 | $38

E 90s | 305 E. 92nd St. (bet. 1st & 2nd Aves.) | 212-426-7500 | www.zebugrill.com

Marrying "homestyle cooking" with a "comforting" ambiance and "gracious" service, this "charming" UES Brazilian lures a "loyal crowd" with "basic" but reliably "wonderful" fare; regulars attest "you really get your money's worth" here.

NEW Zenkichi Ⓜ *Japanese*   ▽ 23 | 26 | 24 | $48

Williamsburg | 77 N. Sixth St. (Wythe Ave.) | Brooklyn | 718-388-8985 | www.zenkichi.com

A single orange light marks the entrance to this "elaborately designed" Williamsburg *izakaya*, a "dark", "mazelike" space "out of a David Lynch movie"; the "delicious" Japanese small plates on offer may be "not very filling", but the wide variety of sakes will take care of that.

Zen Palate *Vegetarian*   19 | 16 | 17 | $27

NEW Financial District | 104 John St. (Cliff St.) | 212-962-4208
Union Sq | 34 Union Sq. E. (16th St.) | 212-614-9291
W 40s | 663 Ninth Ave. (46th St.) | 212-582-1669
www.zenpalate.com

"Meatless isn't so scary" at this vegetarian trio that does "amazing things" with "dressed-up" tofu- and soy-based dishes served in "meditative" digs; still, "hard-core carnivores" balk at the "mock meat" eats, saying "how about a bit of flavor?"

Zerza ● *Moroccan*   ▽ 22 | 20 | 18 | $38

E Village | 304 E. Sixth St. (bet. 1st & 2nd Aves.) | 212-529-8250 | www.zerza.com

"Terrific" tagines and other "standout" Moroccan specialties fill out the modestly priced menu of this "cozy", split-level East Villager oddly parked on Sixth Street's Curry Row; the "staff tries very hard", ditto the Saturday night belly dancer.

NEW Zest Ⓜ *American*   ▽ 26 | 23 | 20 | $47

Staten Island | 977 Bay St. (Willow Ave.) | 718-390-8477

The ambiance is more "212" than Staten Island at this new "fine-dining" arrival serving "excellent" French-accented New Americana "in the sticks" of Rosebank; indeed, the garden is so "lovely" that some "feel like they're in Brooklyn."

Zeytin *Turkish*   19 | 17 | 17 | $38

W 80s | 519 Columbus Ave. (85th St.) | 212-579-1145 | www.zeytinny.com

Upper Westsiders seeking "novel flavors" and "decent" prices find their way to this "pleasant", "no-frills" Turk; true, the food is more

| | FOOD | DECOR | SERVICE | COST |

"solid" than spectacular and the "appetizers better than the entrees", but for a "change of pace", it's "just what the neighborhood needed."

Zip Burger ● *Hamburgers* | 18 | 9 | 12 | $13 |

E 50s | 300½ E. 52nd St. (bet. 1st & 2nd Aves.) | 212-308-1308 | www.zipburger.com

You can build your own "quality" burger at this Eastsider that also doles out "fab" Belgian fries along with "delish" shakes in "not-much-to-look-at" digs; there's also a "great" array of toppings for those who don't mind "packing on the calories."

Zócalo *Mexican* | 20 | 15 | 17 | $38 |

E 40s | Grand Central | lower level (42nd St. & Vanderbilt Ave.) | 212-687-5666
E 80s | 174 E. 82nd St. (bet. Lexington & 3rd Aves.) | 212-717-7772
www.zocalonyc.com

"Killer" margaritas help fuel the "daunting" din at this Upper East Side "designer Mexican" where the food is as "contemporary" as the "under-30" crowd; the Midtown spin-off can be as "busy as Grand Central at rush hour– wait, it *is* Grand Central at rush hour."

Zoë *American* | 20 | 18 | 19 | $47 |

SoHo | 90 Prince St. (bet. B'way & Mercer St.) | 212-966-6722 | www.zoerestaurant.com

SoHo-cialites still drop into this area "fixture" that's as "zestful" as ever, supplying "throngs" of shoppers with "consistently good" New American cooking bolstered by "attentive" service; it's not cheap, but devotees don't seem to mind.

NEW Zoë Townhouse *American* | – | – | – | E |

E 60s | 135 E. 62nd St. (bet. Lexington & Park Aves.) | 212-752-6000 | www.zoerestaurant.com

The owners of the erstwhile Jovia have brightened up this bi-level UES townhouse and turned it into a satellite of Zoë, their SoHo New American; while the prices won't faze affluent locals, bargain-seekers gravitate to its all-day 'pizza bar' menu.

NEW Zoma *Ethiopian* | ▽ 23 | 22 | 23 | $27 |

Harlem | 2084 Frederick Douglass Blvd. (113th St.) | 212-662-0620 | www.zomanyc.com

Standing apart from other Ethiopians, this "classy" Harlem newcomer is "blessedly unkitschy" featuring "candlelight" and "spare", stylishly sleek appointments; menuwise, look for "well-spiced", well-priced renditions of classic savory stews eaten with spongy injera flatbread.

Zona Rosa ⊠ *Mexican* | 18 | 16 | 17 | $46 |

W 50s | 40 W. 56th St. (bet. 5th & 6th Aves.) | 212-247-2800 | www.zonarosarestaurant.com

Favored for the "great" guacamole leading off its south-of-the-border lineup, this "upscale" Midtown Mexican attracts *amigos* with "attentive" service and "tasty" preparations; the less impressed tag it "overpriced" and opt for their "powerful" drinks.

Zucco Le French Diner ● *French* | ▽ 22 | 17 | 20 | $29 |

LES | 188 Orchard St. (bet. Houston & Stanton Sts.) | 212-677-5200
A "hidden gem" on Orchard Street, this "quirky" LES French cafe in a "pint-sized" setting turns out totally "legit", sometimes "excellent"

Gallic fare for an attractive price; owner Zucco's accent is almost as "priceless" as watching those "beautiful people not eating what they've ordered."

Zum Schneider ⊄ German

FOOD	DECOR	SERVICE	COST
18	17	16	$27

E Village | 107 Ave. C (7th St.) | 212-598-1098 | www.zumschneider.com

"Hearty" German chow provides stomach lining for the crowds "pounding brews" from "humongous" steins at this East Village Bavarian, a "magnet" for those who want "Oktoberfest" every day; zum say the scene's too "rowdy", but others say "that's the point."

Zum Stammtisch German

FOOD	DECOR	SERVICE	COST
22	17	19	$34

Glendale | 69-46 Myrtle Ave. (bet. 69th Pl. & 70th St.) | Queens | 718-386-3014 | www.zumstammtisch.com

Even if the "trek to Glendale makes Germany seem closer", this inexpensive, "old-school" Bavarian werkhorse remains the "gold standard" for "terrific", "heavy" meals paired with "refreshing" brews; fans say the faux "alpine" setting is similarly *"wunderbar."*

Zutto Japanese

FOOD	DECOR	SERVICE	COST
21	17	20	$39

TriBeCa | 77 Hudson St. (Harrison St.) | 212-233-3287 | www.sushizutto.com

When you can't get a table at Nobu", consider this TriBeCa Japanese "staple" for its "fresh" sushi and "soothing" setting; that it's still a "secret" after 28 years in business is a mystery, especially considering its "best-buy" prices and "interesting" specials.

INDEXES

LOCATION MAPS

Cuisines

Includes restaurant names, locations and Food ratings. ⊠ indicates place
with the highest ratings, popularity and importance.

AFGHAN

Afghan Kebab | **multi.**	19

AFRICAN

Bouillabaisse 126 | **Carroll Gdns**	22
Les Enfants | **LES**	19

AMERICAN (NEW)

Aesop's Tables | **SI**	21
🆕 Alchemy | **Park Slope**	18
Alice's Tea Cup | **multi.**	19
🆕 Almond Flower | **L Italy**	23
⊠ Annisa | **G Vill**	27
applewood | **Park Slope**	25
Arabelle | **E 60s**	21
Aspen | **Flatiron**	20
⊠ Aureole | **E 60s**	27
⊠ Bar Americain | **W 50s**	23
barmarché | **NoLita**	19
🆕 Bar Martignetti | **L Italy**	18
Battery Gdns. | **Financial**	18
Beacon | **W 50s**	22
BG | **W 50s**	20
Bistro Ten 18 | **W 100s**	20
Black Duck | **Gramercy**	20
🆕 BLT Market | **W 50s**	–
BLT Prime | **Gramercy**	24
⊠ Blue Hill | **G Vill**	26
⊠ Blue Ribbon | **multi.**	25
Blue Ribbon Bakery | **G Vill**	24
Boathouse | **E 70s**	16
Bouchon Bakery | **W 60s**	23
Bridge Cafe | **Financial**	22
Bruckner B&G | **Bronx**	21
Bull Run | **Financial**	18
Butter | **E Vill**	19
CamaJe | **G Vill**	23
Caviar Russe | **E 50s**	24
Chestnut | **Carroll Gdns**	23
Chop't Creative | **multi.**	20
Cibo | **E 40s**	20
Clinton St. Baking | **LES**	24
Cocotte | **Park Slope**	20
⊠ Compass | **W 70s**	22
Cornelia St. Cafe | **G Vill**	19
Country | **Gramercy**	23
⊠ Craft | **Flatiron**	25
Craftbar | **Flatiron**	22
⊠ davidburke/dona. | **E 60s**	25
David Burke/Bloom. | **E 50s**	18
Deborah | **G Vill**	21

🆕 Dennis Foy | **TriBeCa**	24
Devin Tavern | **TriBeCa**	18
Diner | **W'burg**	22
District | **W 40s**	20
Ditch Plains | **G Vill**	17
D'twn Atlantic | **Boerum Hill**	19
Dressler | **W'burg**	24
Duane Park | **TriBeCa**	24
DuMont | **W'burg**	23
Eatery | **W 50s**	19
elmo | **Chelsea**	15
Essex | **LES**	20
Etats-Unis | **E 80s**	25
Farm/Adderley | **Ditmas Pk**	23
57 | **E 50s**	22
5 Front | **Dumbo**	21
5 Points | **NoHo**	22
🆕 Flatbush Farm | **Park Slope**	19
Food Bar | **Chelsea**	16
44/X Hell's Kit. | **W 40s**	21
Fred's at Barneys | **E 60s**	20
Freemans | **LES**	21
⊠ Garden Cafe | **Prospect Hts**	27
Gilt | **E 50s**	25
Giorgio's/Gramercy | **Flatiron**	22
good | **W Vill**	22
⊠ Gotham B&G | **G Vill**	27
⊠ Gramercy Tavern | **Flatiron**	27
Greenhouse Café | **Bay Ridge**	19
⊠ Grocery | **Carroll Gdns**	26
Harrison, The | **TriBeCa**	24
🆕 Hawaiian Tropic | **W 40s**	16
Hearth | **E Vill**	25
Henry's End | **Bklyn Hts**	25
Hope & Anchor | **Red Hook**	18
HQ | **SoHo**	19
🆕 Hudson R. Café | **Harlem**	–
Ici | **Ft Greene**	22
🆕 Inn LW12 | **Meatpacking**	19
Isabella's | **W 70s**	20
Jack the Horse | **Bklyn Hts**	20
Jane | **G Vill**	21
Josephina | **W 60s**	18
Josie's | **E 80s**	19
Kings' Carriage | **E 80s**	21
🆕 Klee Brass. | **Chelsea**	21
Knickerbocker | **G Vill**	20
Lady Mendl's | **Gramercy**	22
Landmark Tavern | **W 40s**	18
Lever House | **E 50s**	22

Little D | **Park Slope**	20
Little Giant | **LES**	22
Little Owl | **W Vill**	24
Magnolia | **Park Slope**	19
NEW Mantra | **E 50s**	–
Mas | **G Vill**	25
Mercer Kitchen | **SoHo**	22
Metrazur | **E 40s**	20
☑ Modern, The | **W 50s**	26
Momofuku Ssäm | **E Vill**	24
Monkey Bar | **E 50s**	–
Morgan | **Murray Hill**	20
Morrell Wine Bar | **W 40s**	19
New Leaf | **Wash. Hts**	20
NEW Noble Food | **NoLita**	–
NoHo Star | **NoHo**	18
Norma's | **W 50s**	25
North Sq. | **G Vill**	22
Oceana | **E 50s**	26
One | **Meatpacking**	18
☑ One if by Land | **G Vill**	23
101 | **multi.**	19
Orchard, The | **LES**	24
☑ Ouest | **W 80s**	25
Paloma | **Greenpt**	19
NEW Park Avenue | **E 60s**	–
Patroon | **E 40s**	21
NEW Perilla | **G Vill**	–
Perry St. | **W Vill**	24
☑ Per Se | **W 60s**	28
Philip Marie | **W Vill**	20
Place, The | **W Vill**	21
NEW p*ong | **G Vill**	21
Pop Burger | **Meatpacking**	19
Prune | **E Vill**	24
Quaint | **Sunnyside**	20
Quality Meats | **W 50s**	24
Queen's Hideaway | **Greenpt**	20
Rachel's American | **W 40s**	17
Red Cat | **Chelsea**	24
Redeye Grill | **W 50s**	20
Regency | **E 60s**	18
Relish | **W'burg**	22
Tiingo | **E 40s**	19
River Café | **Dumbo**	26
Riverdale Gdn. | **Bronx**	24
Roebling | **W'burg**	21
Rose Water | **Park Slope**	25
Salt | **multi.**	21
Saul | **Boerum Hill**	27
Savoy | **SoHo**	24
Seven | **Chelsea**	18
NEW Solace | **E 60s**	–
Sorrel | **Prospect Hts**	23
NEW Spitzer's | **LES**	–

NEW STK | **Meatpacking**	20
Stone Park Café | **Park Slope**	24
Sweetwater | **W'burg**	21
☑ Tabla | **Gramercy**	25
Taste | **E 80s**	20
Tasting Rm. | **multi.**	22
☑ Telepan | **W 60s**	25
Thalia | **W 50s**	21
Thor | **LES**	18
☑ Tocqueville | **Union Sq**	26
Tossed | **multi.**	18
Town | **W 50s**	24
Trestle on 10th | **Chelsea**	19
Tribeca Grill | **TriBeCa**	22
12th St. B&G | **Park Slope**	21
212 | **E 60s**	16
☑ Union Sq. Cafe | **Union Sq**	26
☑ Veritas | **Flatiron**	26
Village | **G Vill**	20
Vynl | **multi.**	17
Water's Edge | **LIC**	23
wd-50 | **LES**	23
West Bank Cafe | **W 40s**	20
Whym | **W 50s**	21
York Grill | **E 80s**	23
NEW Zest | **SI**	26
Zoë | **SoHo**	20
NEW Zoë Townhouse | **E 60s**	–

AMERICAN (TRADITIONAL)

Algonquin | **W 40s**	16
Alias | **LES**	23
American Girl | **E 40s**	13
American Grill | **SI**	20
Angus McIndoe | **W 40s**	16
Annie's | **E 70s**	18
Barking Dog | **multi.**	15
NEW Borough Food | **Flatiron**	–
Brooklyn Diner | **multi.**	17
Brown Café | **LES**	25
Bryant Park | **W 40s**	17
Bubba Gump | **W 40s**	14
Bubby's | **multi.**	18
NEW Cafe Cluny | **W Vill**	19
Cafeteria | **Chelsea**	18
Chadwick's | **Bay Ridge**	22
Chat 'n Chew | **Union Sq**	16
Coffee Shop | **Union Sq**	15
Comfort Diner | **multi.**	16
Cookshop | **Chelsea**	23
Corner Bistro | **W Vill**	22
Dirty Bird | **W Vill**	17
Dylan Prime | **TriBeCa**	24
NEW East Village Yacht | **E Vill**	–
E.A.T. | **E 80s**	19

Edward's | **TriBeCa**	16
EJ's Luncheonette | **multi.**	15
Elaine's | **E 80s**	13
Elephant & Castle | **G Vill**	17
ESPN Zone | **W 40s**	12
Fairway Cafe | **multi.**	18
Fraunces Tavern | **Financial**	15
Friend of a Farmer | **Gramercy**	17
Good Enough/Eat | **W 80s**	20
Grand Tier | **W 60s**	19
Hard Rock Cafe | **W 40s**	13
Heartland | **multi.**	14
HK | **Garment**	16
Home | **G Vill**	20
Houston's | **multi.**	20
Hudson Cafeteria | **W 50s**	19
Jackson Hole | **multi.**	17
Joe Allen | **W 40s**	17
Lodge | **W'burg**	16
Mama's Food | **E Vill**	20
Moran's | **Chelsea**	18
Odeon | **TriBeCa**	19
O'Neals' | **W 60s**	17
Penelope | **Murray Hill**	21
Pershing Sq. | **E 40s**	15
Popover Cafe | **W 80s**	18
NEW Public House | **E 40s**	-
Revival | **Harlem**	19
Rock Ctr. | **W 50s**	19
Sarabeth's | **multi.**	20
S'mac | **E Vill**	19
Soda Shop | **TriBeCa**	19
NEW Spotlight Live | **W 40s**	-
Swifty's | **E 70s**	18
☑ Tavern on Green | **W 60s**	15
NEW Ted's Montana | **W 50s**	15
Tupelo Grill | **Garment**	18
12 Chairs | **SoHo**	19
☑ 21 Club | **W 50s**	22
Uno Chicago | **multi.**	14
View, The | **W 40s**	18
Walker's | **TriBeCa**	17
Water Club | **Murray Hill**	20
NEW ☑ Waverly Inn | **W Vill**	18
Westville | **multi.**	23

ARGENTINEAN

Azul Bistro | **LES**	22
Buenos Aires | **E Vill**	21
NEW Caminito | **Harlem**	-
NEW Catch 22 | **W'burg**	-
Chimichurri Grill | **W 40s**	21
NEW Estancia | **TriBeCa**	21
NEW Gaucho | **W 50s**	-
Hacienda/Argentina | **E 70s**	21
Industria | **TriBeCa**	20

Novecento | **SoHo**	22
Sosa Borella | **W 50s**	21

ASIAN

☑ Asia de Cuba | **Murray Hill**	23
China Grill | **W 50s**	22
Chino's | **Gramercy**	22
Citrus B&G | **W 70s**	20
East Buffet | **Flushing**	20
Hispaniola | **Wash. Hts**	21

ASIAN FUSION

☑ Buddakan | **Chelsea**	23
☑ Buddha Bar | **Meatpacking**	19
Chow Bar | **W Vill**	21
JJ's Asian Fusion | **Astoria**	25
Nana | **Park Slope**	21
Roy's NY | **Financial**	25
Xing | **W 50s**	21

AUSTRALIAN

Bondi Rd. | **LES**	21
8 Mile Creek | **L Italy**	20
NEW Sheep Sta. | **Park Slope**	19
NEW Wombat | **W'burg**	21

AUSTRIAN

Blaue Gans | **TriBeCa**	20
Café Sabarsky | **E 80s**	22
Cafe Steinhof | **Park Slope**	19
☑ Danube | **TriBeCa**	26
Thomas Beisl | **Ft Greene**	19
Wallsé | **W Vill**	26

BAKERIES

Amy's Bread | **multi.**	23
Blue Ribbon Bakery | **G Vill**	24
Bouchon Bakery | **W 60s**	23
City Bakery | **Flatiron**	21
Clinton St. Baking | **LES**	24
Columbus Bakery | **W 80s**	18
D'twn Atlantic | **Boerum Hill**	19
Ferrara | **L Italy**	22
La Bergamote | **Chelsea**	24
La Flor Bakery | **Woodside**	24
Le Pain Q. | **multi.**	19
Once Upon a Tart | **SoHo**	22
Provence/Boite | **Carroll Gdns**	20

BARBECUE

Blue Smoke | **Gramercy**	22
Brother Jimmy's | **multi.**	16
☑ Daisy May's | **W 40s**	24
Dallas BBQ | **multi.**	15
Dinosaur BBQ | **Harlem**	22
NEW Fette Sau | **W'burg**	19
NEW Georgia's/BBQ | **LES**	-

NEW Hill Country | **Chelsea**	–
NEW Johnny Utah | **W 50s**	–
Rack & Soul | **W 100s**	20
RUB BBQ | **Chelsea**	20
NEW Smoke Joint | **Ft Greene**	23
Virgil's Real BBQ | **W 40s**	20

BELGIAN

Café de Bruxelles | **W Vill**	21
Le Pain Q. | **multi.**	19
Markt | **Flatiron**	19
Petite Abeille | **multi.**	19
NEW Resto | **Gramercy**	–

BRAZILIAN

Cafe Colonial | **NoLita**	20
Casa | **W Vill**	22
Churrascaria | **multi.**	23
Circus | **E 60s**	20
Coffee Shop | **Union Sq**	15
Green Field | **Corona**	19
Malagueta | **Astoria**	26
Porcão | **Gramercy**	21
Rice 'n' Beans | **W 50s**	19
Samba-Lé | **E Vill**	19
SushiSamba | **multi.**	22
Via Brasil | **W 40s**	18
Zebú Grill | **E 90s**	21

BRITISH

ChipShop | **multi.**	18
Spotted Pig | **W Vill**	22
Tea & Sympathy | **W Vill**	19

BURMESE

Mingala Burmese | **multi.**	20

CAJUN

Bayou | **SI**	22
Delta Grill | **W 40s**	19
Great Jones Cafe | **NoHo**	19
Jacques-Imo's | **W 70s**	17
Mara's | **E Vill**	19
NEW NoNO | **Park Slope**	19
107 West | **multi.**	18

CALIFORNIAN

Michael's | **W 50s**	21

CAMBODIAN

NEW Kampuchea | **LES**	20

CARIBBEAN

NEW Cafe & Wine | **W 100s**	–
Don Pedro's | **E 90s**	23
Ideya | **SoHo**	20
Ivo & Lulu | **SoHo**	22
Mo-Bay | **Harlem**	21

CAVIAR

Caviar Russe | **E 50s**	24
Petrossian | **W 50s**	24

CHEESE STEAKS

Carl's Steaks | **multi.**	22
99 Mi. to Philly | **E Vill**	18

CHINESE

(* dim sum specialist)

NEW Amazing 66 | **Chinatown**	23
Au Mandarin | **Financial**	20
Big Wong | **Chinatown**	22
Café Evergreen* | **E 60s**	20
Chef Ho's | **E 80s**	22
Chiam | **E 40s**	23
China Chalet | **multi.**	19
China Fun* | **multi.**	16
Chinatown Brass.* | **NoHo**	21
Chin Chin | **E 40s**	22
Congee | **multi.**	21
Dim Sum Go Go* | **Chinatown**	20
Dumpling Man | **E Vill**	19
East Manor* | **Flushing**	19
Empire Szechuan | **multi.**	15
Evergreen* | **Murray Hill**	19
Excellent Dumpling* | **Chinatown**	21
Flor de Mayo | **multi.**	20
Fuleen | **Chinatown**	24
Ginger | **Harlem**	21
Golden Unicorn* | **Chinatown**	20
Goodies | **Chinatown**	20
Grand Sichuan | **multi.**	22
HSF* | **Chinatown**	20
Jing Fong* | **Chinatown**	19
Joe's Shanghai | **multi.**	22
King Yum | **Fresh Meadows**	17
Lili's Noodle | **multi.**	16
Mandarin Court* | **Chinatown**	20
Mee Noodle | **multi.**	18
Mr. Chow | **multi.**	20
Z Mr. K's | **E 50s**	23
Mr. Tang | **multi.**	19
New Bo-Ky | **Chinatown**	22
New Green Bo | **Chinatown**	22
NoHo Star | **NoHo**	18
Ollie's | **multi.**	16
Oriental Gdn.* | **Chinatown**	24
Our Place | **multi.**	20
NEW Pacificana* | **Sunset Pk**	24
Peking Duck | **multi.**	22
Philippe | **E 60s**	23
Phoenix Gdn. | **E 40s**	24
Pig Heaven | **E 80s**	19
Ping's Sea.* | **multi.**	22
Rickshaw Dumpling | **multi.**	18

Shanghai Cuisine	Chinatown	21
Shanghai Pavilion	E 70s	21
Shun Lee Cafe*	W 60s	21
Shun Lee Palace	E 50s	24
Shun Lee West	W 60s	23
Spicy & Tasty	Flushing	23
Sweet-n-Tart*	Flushing	20
Tang Pavilion	W 50s	23
Tse Yang	E 50s	25
NEW Z Wakiya	Gramercy	-
Wo Hop	Chinatown	21
Wu Liang Ye	multi.	21
X.O.*	Chinatown	18

COFFEEHOUSES

Cafe Lalo	W 80s	19
Edgar's Cafe	W 80s	18
Edison	W 40s	15
Ferrara	L Italy	22
French Roast	multi.	14
Le Pain Q.	multi.	19
Omonia Cafe	multi.	19
Once Upon a Tart	SoHo	22

COFFEE SHOPS/DINERS

Brooklyn Diner	multi.	17
Burger Heaven	multi.	16
Chat 'n Chew	Union Sq	16
Clinton St. Baking	LES	24
Comfort Diner	multi.	16
Diner	W'burg	22
Edison	W 40s	15
EJ's Luncheonette	multi.	15
Empire Diner	Chelsea	15
Hope & Anchor	Red Hook	18
Junior's	multi.	18
La Taza de Oro	Chelsea	18
Tom's	Prospect Hts	19
Veselka	E Vill	18
Viand	multi.	16

COLOMBIAN

Tierras	multi.	22

CONTINENTAL

Battery Gdns.	Financial	18
Café Pierre	E 60s	23
Cebu	Bay Ridge	21
Z Four Seasons	E 50s	25
Gin Lane	Chelsea	17
Grand Tier	W 60s	19
Jack's Lux.	E Vill	24
Lake Club	SI	21
Park Place	Bronx	20
Petrossian	W 50s	24
Russian Samovar	W 50s	19
NEW Russian Tea	W 50s	19

Sardi's	W 40s	1
View, The	W 40s	1

CREOLE

Bayou	SI	2
Delta Grill	W 40s	1
Jacques-Imo's	W 70s	1
Mara's	E Vill	1
NEW NoNO	Park Slope	1

CUBAN

Z Asia de Cuba	Murray Hill	2
Cafecito	E Vill	2
Cafe Con Leche	multi.	1
Café Habana/Outpost	multi.	2
Cuba	G Vill	2
Cuba Cafe	Chelsea	1
Cubana Café	multi.	2
Guantanamera	W 50s	2
Havana Alma	W Vill	2
Havana Central	multi.	1
NEW Socialista	W Vill	-
Son Cubano	Meatpacking	2
Victor's Cafe	W 50s	2

DELIS

Artie's Deli	W 80s	1
Barney Greengrass	W 80s	2
Ben's Kosher	multi.	1
Z Carnegie Deli	W 50s	2
Ess-a-Bagel	multi.	2
Katz's Deli	LES	2
Leo's Latticini	Corona	2
Liebman's	Bronx	1
Mill Basin Deli	Mill Basin	2
Pastrami Queen	E 70s	1
PicNic Market	W 100s	2
Sarge's Deli	Murray Hill	1
Stage Deli	W 50s	2
Zabar's Cafe	W 80s	20

DESSERT

Cafe Lalo	W 80s	1
Café Sabarsky	E 80s	2
ChikaLicious	E Vill	2
Chocolate Rm.	Park Slope	2
Edgar's Cafe	W 80s	1
Ferrara	L Italy	2
Junior's	multi.	1
NEW Kyotofu	W 40s	2
La Bergamote	Chelsea	2
Lady Mendl's	Gramercy	2
L & B Spumoni	Bensonhurst	2
Max Brenner	multi.	1
Omonia Cafe	multi.	1
Payard Bistro	E 70s	2
NEW p*ong	G Vill	2

subscribe to zagat.co

Serendipity 3	**E 60s**	18
Soda Shop	**TriBeCa**	19
Sweet Melissa	**multi.**	21
NEW Tailor	**SoHo**	-
Veniero's	**E Vill**	23

DOMINICAN

Cafe Con Leche	**multi.**	18
El Malecon	**multi.**	21
Hispaniola	**Wash. Hts**	21

EASTERN EUROPEAN

Sammy's Roum.	**LES**	19

ECLECTIC

NEW Aloe	**E Vill**	-
NEW BarFry	**G Vill**	-
Z Bouley, Upstairs	**TriBeCa**	26
Carol's Cafe	**SI**	26
NEW Chez Lola	**Clinton Hill**	-
Colors	**E Vill**	19
NEW Crave	**E 50s**	-
East Buffet	**Flushing**	20
East of 8th	**Chelsea**	16
NEW Fireside	**E 50s**	21
Ninth	**Meatpacking**	19
NEW FR.OG	**SoHo**	21
NEW Gold St.	**Financial**	15
Good Fork	**Red Hook**	26
Grand Café	**Astoria**	17
NEW Grayz	**W 50s**	-
Harry's	**Financial**	22
Hudson Cafeteria	**W 50s**	19
Josie's	**multi.**	19
Little D	**Park Slope**	20
Native	**Harlem**	19
Nook	**W 50s**	22
Public	**NoLita**	23
Punch	**Flatiron**	19
NEW Revel	**Meatpacking**	-
Rice	**multi.**	19
NEW Saucy	**E 70s**	-
NEW savorNY	**LES**	-
Schiller's	**LES**	18
Stanton Social	**LES**	23
Trinity Place	**Financial**	18
Vida	**SI**	20
d-50	**LES**	23
Whole Foods	**multi.**	19

ETHIOPIAN

Awash	**multi.**	22
Ethiopian Rest.	**E 80s**	17
Ghenet	**NoLita**	22
Meskerem	**multi.**	20
NEW Zoma	**Harlem**	23

EUROPEAN

A.O.C. Bedford	**G Vill**	23
August	**W Vill**	23
Bette	**Chelsea**	19
Z Cru	**G Vill**	26
Employees Only	**W Vill**	18
NEW E.U., The	**E Vill**	20
NEW Klee Brass.	**Chelsea**	21
Knife + Fork	**E Vill**	23
NEW Stella Maris	**Seaport**	-

FILIPINO

Cendrillon	**SoHo**	20
Kuma Inn	**LES**	24

FRENCH

Arabelle	**E 60s**	21
Z Asiate	**W 60s**	24
NEW Babouche	**multi.**	20
Barbès	**Murray Hill**	22
NEW Bistro 33	**Astoria**	-
Bouchon Bakery	**W 60s**	23
Bouillabaisse 126	**Carroll Gdns**	22
Z Bouley	**TriBeCa**	28
Breeze	**W 40s**	20
Brick Cafe	**Astoria**	20
NEW Cafe & Wine	**W 100s**	-
Z Café Boulud	**E 70s**	27
Z Café des Artistes	**W 60s**	22
Café du Soleil	**W 100s**	19
Cafe Gitane	**NoLita**	20
Café Pierre	**E 60s**	23
Z Carlyle	**E 70s**	21
Z Chanterelle	**TriBeCa**	27
Cocotte	**Park Slope**	20
Danal	**E Vill**	22
Z Daniel	**E 60s**	28
Degustation	**E Vill**	26
Demarchelier	**E 80s**	17
Django	**E 40s**	20
Elephant, The	**E Vill**	21
Z Eleven Madison	**Gramercy**	26
Fleur de Sel	**Flatiron**	25
Frederick's	**multi.**	19
NEW FR.OG	**SoHo**	21
NEW Z Gordon Ramsay	**W 50s**	25
Ici	**Ft Greene**	22
Indochine	**E Vill**	20
Ivo & Lulu	**SoHo**	22
Jack's Lux.	**E Vill**	24
Z Jean Georges	**W 60s**	28
Jolie	**Boerum Hill**	20
Kitchen Club	**NoLita**	22
La Baraka	**Little Neck**	21
La Bergamote	**Chelsea**	24
La Boîte en Bois	**W 60s**	21

☒ La Grenouille | **E 50s**	27
☒ L'Atelier/Robuchon | **E 50s**	27
☒ Le Bernardin | **W 50s**	28
Le Cirque | **E 50s**	23
L'Ecole | **SoHo**	23
Le Colonial | **E 50s**	20
Le Grainne Cafe | **Chelsea**	19
Le Pain Q. | **multi.**	19
Le Perigord | **E 50s**	24
Le Refuge Inn | **Bronx**	24
Le Rivage | **W 40s**	19
Les Enfants | **LES**	19
Loft | **W 80s**	17
NEW Maze | **W 50s**	23
Mercer Kitchen | **SoHo**	22
Métisse | **W 100s**	19
☒ Modern, The | **W 50s**	26
Once Upon a Tart | **SoHo**	22
Park Terrace | **Inwood**	22
Pascalou | **E 90s**	22
☒ Per Se | **W 60s**	28
Petrossian | **W 50s**	24
☒ Picholine | **W 60s**	27
PicNic Market | **W 100s**	20
René Pujol | **W 50s**	22
Revival | **Harlem**	19
NEW Safran | **Chelsea**	20
Sapa | **Flatiron**	22
Savann | **W 70s**	19
718 | **Astoria**	21
Terrace in the Sky | **W 100s**	22
☒ Tocqueville | **Union Sq**	26
Triomphe | **W 40s**	24
26 Seats | **E Vill**	22
Vong | **E 50s**	22
Zucco | **LES**	22

FRENCH (BISTRO)

Alouette | **W 90s**	20
A.O.C. | **W Vill**	20
Bandol Bistro | **E 70s**	19
Belleville | **Park Slope**	18
Bistro Cassis | **W 70s**	20
Bistro Citron | **W 80s**	21
Bistro du Nord | **E 90s**	18
Bistro Les Amis | **SoHo**	21
Bistro Le Steak | **E 70s**	17
Bistro 61 | **E 60s**	20
NEW Cafe Cluny | **W Vill**	19
Cafe Joul | **E 50s**	18
Cafe Loup | **G Vill**	18
Cafe Luluc | **Cobble Hill**	20
Cafe Luxembourg | **W 70s**	20
Cafe Un Deux | **W 40s**	16
CamaJe | **G Vill**	23
Capsouto Frères | **TriBeCa**	24

Casimir | **E Vill**	19
NEW Chat Noir | **E 60s**	18
Chez Jacqueline | **G Vill**	18
Chez Josephine | **W 40s**	20
NEW Chez Lola | **Clinton Hill**	–
Chez Napoléon | **W 50s**	20
Chez Oskar | **Ft Greene**	19
Cornelia St. Cafe | **G Vill**	19
Cosette | **Murray Hill**	21
☒ db Bistro Moderne | **W 40s**	25
Deux Amis | **E 50s**	19
Félix | **SoHo**	16
Flea Mkt. Cafe | **E Vill**	19
Florent | **Meatpacking**	20
French Roast | **multi.**	14
Gascogne | **Chelsea**	22
Gavroche | **W Vill**	19
Jack Bistro | **G Vill**	17
Jean Claude | **SoHo**	22
JoJo | **E 60s**	24
Jubilee | **E 50s**	22
Jules | **E Vill**	19
La Bonne Soupe | **W 50s**	18
La Goulue | **E 60s**	20
La Lunchonette | **Chelsea**	22
La Mangeoire | **E 50s**	19
La Mediterranée | **E 50s**	19
La Mirabelle | **W 80s**	22
Landmarc | **multi.**	23
La Petite Aub. | **Gramercy**	20
La Ripaille | **W Vill**	23
NEW Le Barricou | **W'burg**	–
Le Bilboquet | **E 60s**	20
Le Boeuf/Mode | **E 80s**	21
Le Gamin | **multi.**	19
Le Gigot | **G Vill**	24
Le Jardin Bistro | **NoLita**	18
Le Madeleine | **W 40s**	20
Le Monde | **W 100s**	17
L'Entrecote | **E 50s**	19
NEW Le Petit Bistro | **Chelsea**	–
NEW Le Petit Marché | **Bklyn Hts**	22
Le Refuge | **E 80s**	21
Les Halles | **multi.**	20
Le Singe Vert | **Chelsea**	19
Le Tableau | **E Vill**	24
Le Veau d'Or | **E 60s**	17
L'Express | **Flatiron**	17
Loulou | **Ft Greene**	22
Lucien | **E Vill**	21
Lucky Strike | **SoHo**	17
Madison Bistro | **Murray Hill**	18
Mon Petit Cafe | **E 60s**	18
Montparnasse | **E 50s**	19
Moutarde | **Park Slope**	18

subscribe to zagat.co

Nice Matin | **W 70s**	20
Odeon | **TriBeCa**	19
Paradou | **Meatpacking**	19
Paris Commune | **W Vill**	18
Pascalou | **E 90s**	22
Z Pastis | **Meatpacking**	21
Patois | **Carroll Gdns**	21
Payard Bistro | **E 70s**	24
NEW Provence | **SoHo**	21
Provence/Boite | **Carroll Gdns**	20
Quatorze Bis | **E 70s**	21
Quercy | **Cobble Hill**	20
Raoul's | **SoHo**	24
NEW Régate | **LES**	-
Rouge | **Forest Hills**	20
Steak Frites | **Union Sq**	18
Sweetwater | **W'burg**	21
Table d'Hôte | **E 90s**	21
Tartine | **W Vill**	22
Tournesol | **LIC**	24
NEW Tree | **E Vill**	24
Village | **G Vill**	20

FRENCH (BRASSERIE)

Aix Brasserie | **W 80s**	20
Z Artisanal | **Murray Hill**	23
Z Balthazar | **SoHo**	23
Brasserie | **E 50s**	20
Brasserie 8½ | **W 50s**	22
Brasserie Julien | **E 80s**	19
Brass. Ruhlmann | **W 50s**	17
Café d'Alsace | **E 80s**	21
Z Café Gray | **W 60s**	25
Jacques | **multi.**	18
L'Absinthe | **E 60s**	22
Maison | **W 50s**	17
Marseille | **W 40s**	20
NEW Metro Marché | **W 40s**	19
Orsay | **E 70s**	18
Pershing Sq. | **E 40s**	15
Pigalle | **W 40s**	18
Rue 57 | **W 50s**	19

GASTROPUB

NEW Alchemy | **Amer.** | **Park Slope**	18
NEW E.U., The | **Euro.** | **E Vill**	20
NEW Inn LW12 | **Amer.** | **Meatpacking**	19
NEW Nelson Blue | **New Zealand** | **Seaport**	-
NEW Spitzer's | **Amer.** | **LES**	-
Spotted Pig | **British** | **W Vill**	22

GERMAN

Blaue Gans | **TriBeCa**	20
Hallo Berlin | **W 40s**	17

Heidelberg | **E 80s**	17
Killmeyer Bavarian | **SI**	21
Loreley | **LES**	18
Nurnberger Bierhaus | **SI**	21
Rolf's | **Gramercy**	17
Zum Schneider | **E Vill**	18
Zum Stammtisch | **Glendale**	22

GREEK

Agnanti | **multi.**	24
Ammos | **multi.**	22
NEW Anthos | **W 50s**	25
Avra | **E 40s**	24
Cafe Bar | **Astoria**	20
Z Cávo | **Astoria**	21
Demetris | **Astoria**	21
Eliá | **Bay Ridge**	25
Elias Corner | **Astoria**	22
Ethos | **multi.**	22
Greek Kitchen | **W 50s**	19
NEW Gus' Place | **G Vill**	20
Ithaka | **E 80s**	20
NEW Kefi | **W 70s**	23
Kellari Taverna | **W 40s**	23
Kyma | **W 40s**	18
Meltemi | **E 50s**	18
Mezzo Mezzo | **Astoria**	18
Z Milos | **W 50s**	26
Molyvos | **W 50s**	22
Omonia Cafe | **multi.**	19
NEW Ovelia | **Astoria**	21
Periyali | **Flatiron**	23
Pylos | **E Vill**	25
S'Agapo | **Astoria**	20
Snack | **SoHo**	24
Snack Taverna | **W Vill**	22
Stamatis | **Astoria**	22
Symposium | **W 100s**	20
Taverna Kyclades | **Astoria**	25
Telly's Taverna | **Astoria**	22
Thalassa | **TriBeCa**	22
Trata Estiatorio | **E 70s**	21
Uncle Nick's | **W 50s**	19

HAMBURGERS

Better Burger | **multi.**	15
Big Nick's Burger | **W 70s**	17
NEW BLT Burger | **G Vill**	19
Blue 9 Burger | **E Vill**	18
NEW brgr | **Chelsea**	18
Burger Heaven | **multi.**	16
burger joint | **W 50s**	24
Corner Bistro | **W Vill**	22
Cozy | **G Vill**	18
Z db Bistro Moderne | **W 40s**	25
DuMont | **W'burg**	23

NEW Five Guys	**multi.**	⌐
goodburger	**multi.**	18
Hard Rock Cafe	**W 40s**	13
Island Burgers	**W 50s**	22
Jackson Hole	**multi.**	17
J.G. Melon	**E 70s**	21
NY Burger	**Flatiron**	18
P.J. Clarke's	**multi.**	17
Pop Burger	**Meatpacking**	19
Rare B&G	**multi.**	21
Shake Shack	**Flatiron**	24
NEW 67 Burger	**Ft Greene**	21
NEW Stand	**G Vill**	19
Zip Burger	**E 50s**	18

HAWAIIAN

Roy's NY	**Financial**	25

HEALTH FOOD

(See also Vegetarian)

Energy Kitchen	**multi.**	18
Ginger	**Harlem**	21
Josie's	**multi.**	19
Pump Energy	**multi.**	19
Whole Foods	**multi.**	19

HOT DOGS

F & B	**multi.**	18
Gray's Papaya	**multi.**	20
Papaya King	**multi.**	20
Shake Shack	**Flatiron**	23

ICE CREAM PARLORS

L & B Spumoni	**Bensonhurst**	22
Serendipity 3	**E 60s**	18

INDIAN

Adä	**E 50s**	23
Amma	**E 50s**	24
Baluchi's	**multi.**	18
Banjara	**E Vill**	23
Bay Leaf	**W 50s**	19
Bombay Palace	**W 50s**	18
Bombay Talkie	**Chelsea**	20
Bukhara Grill	**E 40s**	20
Cafe Spice	**multi.**	18
NEW Chennai	**E 80s**	⌐
Chennai Gdn.	**Gramercy**	21
ChipShop	**Park Slope**	18
Chola	**E 50s**	23
Curry Leaf	**Gramercy**	20
Dakshin Indian	**E 80s**	20
Darbar	**E 40s**	20
Dawat	**E 50s**	23
Diwan	**E 40s**	21
NEW Earthen Oven	**W 70s**	21
Hampton Chutney	**multi.**	20
Haveli	**E Vill**	23

Indus Valley	**W 100s**	23
Jackson Diner	**Jackson Hts**	22
Jewel of India	**W 40s**	20
Kati Roll Co.	**multi.**	20
Leela Lounge	**G Vill**	22
Mint	**E 50s**	19
Mughlai	**W 70s**	19
Pongal	**multi.**	21
Salaam Bombay	**TriBeCa**	20
Sapphire	**W 60s**	20
Saravanaas	**Gramercy**	23
NEW Spice Fusion	**W 40s**	⌐
Surya	**W Vill**	24
Swagat Indian	**W 70s**	19
Tamarind	**Flatiron**	25
Temple Canteen	**Flushing**	⌐
Utsav	**W 40s**	21
Vatan	**Gramercy**	23
Yuva	**E 50s**	24

IRISH

Landmark Tavern	**W 40s**	18
Neary's	**E 50s**	15

ISRAELI

Azuri Cafe	**W 50s**	25
Hummus Place	**multi.**	23
Miriam	**multi.**	21

ITALIAN

(N=Northern; S=Southern)

Abboccato	**W 50s**	22
Acappella	N	**TriBeCa**	23
NEW Accademia/Vino	**E 60s**	⌐
Acqua	S	**W 90s**	18
Adrienne's Pizza	**Financial**	23
Agata/Valentina	S	**E 70s**	18
☒ Al Di La	N	**Park Slope**	26
Al Forno Pizza	**E 70s**	19
Alfredo of Rome	S	**W 40s**	19
Aliseo Osteria	**Prospect Hts**	23
☒ Alto	N	**E 50s**	26
Ama	S	**SoHo**	23
Amarone	**W 40s**	19
Amorina	**Prospect Hts**	23
Angelina's	**SI**	23
Angelo's/Mulberry	S	**L Italy**	23
Anthony's	S	**Park Slope**	21
Antica Venezia	**W Vill**	23
Antonucci	**E 80s**	20
ápizz	**LES**	24
Areo	**Bay Ridge**	25
Arezzo	N	**Flatiron**	22
Arno	N	**Garment**	20
Aroma	**NoHo**	24
Arqua	N	**TriBeCa**	22
Arté	N	**G Vill**	19

ello | N | **E 60s**	19
ero | **Meatpacking**	20
ick's | **multi.**	24
icola's | **E 80s**	22
ino's | N | **multi.**	21
ocello | N | **W 50s**	21
oodle Pudding | **Bklyn Hts**	24
otaro | N | **Murray Hill**	20
ovitá | N | **Gramercy**	24
ne 83 | N | **E 80s**	21
01 | **multi.**	19
rso | **W 40s**	23
sso Buco | **multi.**	17
steria al Doge | N | **W 40s**	20
steria del Circo | N | **W 50s**	22
steria del Sole | S | **W Vill**	21
steria Gelsi | S | **Garment**	24
steria Laguna | **E 40s**	21
tto | **G Vill**	22
anino'teca | **Carroll Gdns**	18
aola's | **E 80s**	23
appardella | **W 70s**	19
ark Side | **Corona**	24
arma | N | **E 70s**	22
asquale's Rigoletto | **Bronx**	23
asticcio | **multi.**	19
atricia's | **Bronx**	22
atsy's | S | **W 50s**	21
aul & Jimmy's | **Gramercy**	19
easant | **NoLita**	24
ellegrino's | **L Italy**	22
epe | **multi.**	21
epolino | N | **TriBeCa**	24
erbacco | **E Vill**	24
er Lei | **E 70s**	20
escatore | **E 50s**	18
etaluma | **E 70s**	18
ete's Downtown | **Dumbo**	18
iadina | **G Vill**	20
iano Due | **W 50s**	25
iccola Venezia | **Astoria**	25
iccolo Angolo | **W Vill**	25
ietrasanta | **W 40s**	19
ietro's | **E 40s**	23
inocchio | **E 90s**	21
isticci | S | **W 100s**	23
ó | **multi.**	25
omodoro Rosso | **W 70s**	21
onticello | N | **Astoria**	23
ortofino Grille | **E 60s**	19
ortofino's | **Bronx**	19
ositano | S | **L Italy**	21
rimavera | N | **E 80s**	22
rimola | **E 60s**	23
EW PT | **W'burg**	24

CUISINES

Puttanesca | **W 50s**	18
Quattro Gatti | **E 80s**	20
Queen | **Bklyn Hts**	24
Z Rainbow Rm./Grill | N | **W 40s**	19
Z Rao's | S | **Harlem**	22
Regional | **W 90s**	17
Remi | **W 50s**	22
Re Sette | **W 40s**	23
Risotteria | **G Vill**	21
Z **Roberto** | **Bronx**	27
Roberto Passon | **W 50s**	22
Roc | **TriBeCa**	21
Rocco | S | **G Vill**	20
Rossini's | N | **Murray Hill**	23
Rughetta | S | **E 80s**	22
Sac's Place | **Astoria**	21
Sal Anthony's | S | **multi.**	19
Salute! | **Murray Hill**	19
Sambuca | **W 70s**	18
San Domenico | **W 50s**	23
NEW Sandro's | **E 80s**	-
San Luigi | S | **W 70s**	16
San Pietro | S | **E 50s**	24
Sant Ambroeus | N | **multi.**	22
Sapori D'Ischia | **Woodside**	25
Savoia | **Carroll Gdns**	21
Scaletta | N | **W 70s**	21
Scalinatella | **E 60s**	25
Z Scalini Fedeli | N | **TriBeCa**	26
Scarlatto | N | **W 40s**	21
Scottadito | N | **Park Slope**	19
Serafina | **multi.**	18
Sette | **Chelsea**	18
Sette Enoteca | S | **Park Slope**	19
Sette Mezzo | **E 70s**	23
Sfoglia | N | **E 90s**	23
Shelly's Tratt. | **W 50s**	20
Sistina | N | **E 80s**	24
Sosa Borella | **W 50s**	21
Spiga | **W 80s**	21
Spigolo | **E 80s**	25
NEW Spirito | **Park Slope**	-
Supper | N | **E Vill**	24
Taormina | **L Italy**	24
Tarallucci | **multi.**	19
Teodora | N | **E 50s**	22
Tevere | **E 80s**	22
Tiramisu | **E 80s**	20
Tommaso | **Dyker Hts**	23
Tony's Di Napoli | S | **multi.**	18
Tosca Café | **Bronx**	21
Tratt. Alba | N | **Murray Hill**	20
Tratt. Dell'Arte | N | **W 50s**	22
Tratt. Dopo | N | **W 40s**	16
Z Tratt. L'incontro | **Astoria**	26

Tratt. Pesce | **multi.**	18
Tratt. Romana | **SI**	24
tre dici | **Chelsea**	22
Triangolo | **E 80s**	21
Tuscan Sq. | N | **W 50s**	16
Tuscany Grill | N | **Bay Ridge**	24
Umberto's | **multi.**	18
Uva | **E 70s**	21
Valbella | N | **Meatpacking**	24
V&T | **W 100s**	18
Veniero's | **E Vill**	23
Vento | **Meatpacking**	19
Vespa | **E 80s**	21
Via Emilia | N | **Flatiron**	21
Via Oreto | **E 60s**	19
Via Quadronno | N | **E 70s**	21
ViceVersa | **W 50s**	23
Vico | **E 90s**	21
Villa Berulia | N | **Murray Hill**	23
Villa Mosconi | **G Vill**	20
Vincent's | **L Italy**	21
Vivolo | **E 70s**	20
WaterFalls | **SI**	20
Za Za | N | **E 60s**	20

JAMAICAN

Aki | **G Vill**	25
Maroons | **Chelsea**	22
Negril | **multi.**	20

JAPANESE

(* sushi specialist)

Aburiya Kinnosuke | **E 40s**	24
Aki | **G Vill**	25
Aki Sushi* | **multi.**	19
Aquamarine | **Murray Hill**	21
NEW Asiakan* | **W 90s**	19
Z Asiate | **W 60s**	24
NEW BarFry | **G Vill**	-
NEW Bistro 33 | **Astoria**	-
Blue Ginger | **Chelsea**	22
Z Blue Ribbon Sushi* | **multi.**	25
Bond St.* | **NoHo**	25
Butai | **Gramercy**	22
Chanto | **G Vill**	22
China Fun* | **multi.**	16
Chiyono | **E Vill**	23
Cube 63 | **multi.**	21
Dae Dong | **multi.**	18
Donguri | **E 80s**	27
EN Japanese | **W Vill**	22
NEW 15 East* | **Union Sq**	26
Fushimi* | **SI**	26
Z Gari/Sushi* | **multi.**	26
Geisha | **E 60s**	23
Gyu-Kaku | **multi.**	21

Hakata Grill | **W 40s**	2
Haru* | **multi.**	2
Hasaki* | **E Vill**	2
Hatsuhana* | **E 40s**	2
Ichimura* | **E 50s**	2
Ichiro* | **E 80s**	2
Inagiku* | **E 40s**	2
Iron Sushi* | **multi.**	1
Ise* | **multi.**	2
NEW Izakaya 10 | **Chelsea**	
Japonais | **Gramercy**	2
Japonica* | **G Vill**	2
Jewel Bako* | **E Vill**	2
Kai | **E 60s**	2
NEW Kaijou* | **Financial**	
Z Kanoyama* | **E Vill**	2
Katsu-Hama | **E 40s**	2
NEW Ki Sushi* | **Boerum Hill**	
Kitchen Club | **NoLita**	2
Kodama* | **W 40s**	1
Koi* | **W 40s**	2
Korea Palace* | **E 50s**	2
Ko Sushi* | **multi.**	1
Kuruma Zushi* | **E 40s**	2
NEW Kyotofu | **W 40s**	
Lan* | **E Vill**	2
Le Miu* | **E Vill**	2
Z Masa/Bar Masa* | **W 60s**	2
Z Matsuri* | **Chelsea**	2
Z Megu | **multi.**	2
Menchanko-tei | **multi.**	2
Mishima* | **Murray Hill**	2
Mizu Sushi* | **Flatiron**	2
Momoya* | **Chelsea**	2
Monster Sushi* | **multi.**	1
Z Morimoto | **Chelsea**	2
NEW Natsumi | **W 50s**	
Nëo Sushi* | **W 80s**	2
Ninja | **TriBeCa**	1
Nippon* | **E 50s**	2
Z Nobu* | **TriBeCa**	2
Z Nobu 57* | **W 50s**	2
Omen | **SoHo**	2
NEW Omido* | **W 50s**	
Ono* | **Meatpacking**	2
Osaka* | **Cobble Hill**	2
Ota-Ya* | **E 80s**	1
Planet Thailand | **multi.**	2
Z Poke* | **E 80s**	2
Rai Rai Ken | **E Vill**	2
NEW Ramen Setagaya | **E Vill**	1
Riingo | **E 40s**	1
Roppongi* | **W 80s**	2
NEW Rosanjin | **TriBeCa**	2
Rue 57* | **W 50s**	1

subscribe to zagat.co

Sachiko's* | **LES**	25
Sakagura | **E 40s**	24
Sapporo East* | **E Vill**	21
🆕 Sasabune* | **E 70s**	26
🆕 Sense* | **W'burg**	-
Shabu-Shabu 70* | **E 70s**	20
Shabu-Tatsu | **E Vill**	20
Soba Nippon | **W 50s**	22
Soba-ya | **E Vill**	24
🆕 Soto* | **G Vill**	-
🆕 Spoon | **E Vill**	-
☑ Sugiyama | **W 50s**	27
Sushi Ann* | **E 50s**	23
Sushiden* | **multi.**	25
Sushi Hana* | **multi.**	21
SushiSamba* | **multi.**	22
☑ Sushi Seki* | **E 60s**	27
Sushi Sen-nin* | **multi.**	25
Sushiya* | **W 50s**	20
☑ Sushi Yasuda* | **E 40s**	28
Sushi Zen* | **W 40s**	25
🆕 Suteishi* | **Seaport**	25
Takahachi* | **multi.**	24
Tea Box | **E 50s**	20
Tenzan* | **multi.**	23
Todai | **Murray Hill**	18
Tokyo Pop* | **W 100s**	20
☑ Tomoe Sushi* | **G Vill**	26
Tomo Sushi* | **W 100s**	20
☑ Yakitori Totto | **W 50s**	26
ama* | **multi.**	24
uka* | **E 80s**	21
uki Sushi* | **W 90s**	21
🆕 Yushi* | **multi.**	-
🆕 Zenkichi | **W'burg**	23
utto* | **TriBeCa**	21

EWISH

rtie's Deli | **W 80s**	18
arney Greengrass | **W 80s**	23
en's Kosher | **multi.**	17
Carnegie Deli | **W 50s**	21
hickpea | **E Vill**	19
dison | **W 40s**	15
atz's Deli | **LES**	23
ttanzi | **W 40s**	22
ebman's | **Bronx**	19
ill Basin Deli | **Mill Basin**	21
strami Queen | **E 70s**	19
mmy's Roum. | **LES**	19
rge's Deli | **Murray Hill**	19
age Deli | **W 50s**	20

OREAN

(barbecue specialist)

nn | **W 50s**	24
o Dang Gol* | **Garment**	21

Dae Dong* | **multi.**	18
Do Hwa* | **G Vill**	21
Dok Suni's | **E Vill**	21
Gahm Mi Oak | **Garment**	22
Hangawi | **Murray Hill**	23
Kang Suh* | **Garment**	20
Korea Palace* | **E 50s**	18
Kum Gang San* | **multi.**	21
Mandoo Bar | **Garment**	20
Mill Korean | **W 100s**	19
🆕 Moim | **Park Slope**	-
Momofuku Ssäm | **E Vill**	24
WonJo* | **Garment**	20
Woo Lae Oak* | **SoHo**	23

KOSHER

Abigael's | **Garment**	19
Azuri Cafe | **W 50s**	25
Ben's Kosher | **multi.**	17
Caravan/Dreams | **E Vill**	24
🆕 Chennai | **E 80s**	-
Chennai Gdn. | **Gramercy**	21
Le Marais | **W 40s**	20
Levana | **W 60s**	20
Liebman's | **Bronx**	19
Mill Basin Deli | **Mill Basin**	21
Pastrami Queen | **E 70s**	19
Pongal | **multi.**	21
Prime Grill | **E 40s**	22
Sacred Chow | **G Vill**	23
Solo | **E 50s**	22
Tevere | **E 80s**	22

LEBANESE

Al Bustan | **E 50s**	19

MALAYSIAN

Fatty Crab | **W Vill**	21
Nyonya | **multi.**	22

MEDITERRANEAN

Aesop's Tables | **SI**	21
Alta | **G Vill**	23
🆕 Amalia | **W 50s**	21
Amaranth | **E 60s**	20
Barbounia | **Flatiron**	20
Beast | **Prospect Hts**	20
Bello Sguardo | **W 70s**	19
Cafe Bar | **Astoria**	20
Cafe Centro | **E 40s**	20
Café du Soleil | **W 100s**	19
Cafe Ronda | **W 70s**	18
Conviv. Osteria | **Park Slope**	25
Danal | **E Vill**	22
Dee's Pizza | **Forest Hills**	22
Django | **E 40s**	20
Epices/Traiteur | **W 70s**	21

Extra Virgin	W Vill	21
Fig & Olive	multi.	20
5 Points	NoHo	22
Frederick's	multi.	19
NEW Gus' Place	G Vill	20
NEW House	Gramercy	22
Il Buco	NoHo	25
Isabella's	W 70s	20
NEW Island	Astoria	18
Jarnac	W Vill	22
Levana	W 60s	20
Little Owl	W Vill	24
Mangia	multi.	20
Marseille	W 40s	20
Miriam	multi.	21
Moda	W 50s	–
My Moon	W'burg	19
Nice Matin	W 70s	20
Nick & Toni's	W 60s	18
Olea	Ft Greene	20
Olives	Union Sq	22
Park, The	Chelsea	15
NEW Pera	E 40s	22
Z Picholine	W 60s	27
Place, The	W Vill	21
Red Cat	Chelsea	24
Ribot	E 40s	19
Salute!	Murray Hill	19
Savann	W 70s	19
Savoy	SoHo	24
NEW Sea Salt	E Vill	–
Sezz Medi'	W 100s	21
Sharz Cafe	E 80s	21
Solo	E 50s	22
Superfine	Dumbo	18
Taboon	W 50s	24
Z Tanoreen	Bay Ridge	27
Tempo	Park Slope	25
Terrace in the Sky	W 100s	22
Trio	Murray Hill	21
202 Cafe	Chelsea	21

MEXICAN

Alma	Carroll Gdns	20
Blockheads Burritos	multi.	17
Bonita	multi.	19
Café Frida	W 70s	19
Café Habana/Outpost	multi.	22
Centrico	TriBeCa	20
NEW Chiles/Chocolate	Park Slope	18
NEW China de Puebla	Harlem	–
Chipotle	multi.	18
Crema	Chelsea	21
Dos Caminos	multi.	20
El Centro	W 50s	18

El Parador Cafe	Murray Hill
El Paso	G Vill
El Paso Taqueria	multi.
Gabriela's	W 90s
NEW Guadalupe	Inwood
Hell's Kitchen	W 40s
Itzocan	multi.
La Esquina	L Italy
La Flor Bakery	Woodside
La Palapa	multi.
La Taqueria/Rachel	Park Slope
NEW Los Dados	Meatpacking
Mamá Mexico	multi.
Maya	E 60s
Maz Mezcal	E 80s
Mercadito	multi.
Mexicana Mama	multi.
Mexican Radio	NoLita
Mi Cocina	W Vill
Noche Mexicana	W 100s
Pampano	E 40s
Rocking Horse Cafe	Chelsea
Z Rosa Mexicano	multi.
Sueños	Chelsea
NEW Toloache	W 50s
NEW Vamos!	Gramercy
Zarela	E 50s
Zócalo	multi.
Zona Rosa	W 50s

MIDDLE EASTERN

Chickpea	E Vill
Mamlouk	E Vill
Moustache	multi.
Taboon	W 50s
Z Tanoreen	Bay Ridge
12 Chairs	SoHo
Zaytoons	multi.

MOROCCAN

NEW Babouche	multi.
Barbès	Murray Hill
Cafe Gitane	NoLita
Cafe Mogador	E Vill
Park Terrace	Inwood
Zerza	E Vill

NEW ENGLAND

NEW Black Pearl	Chelsea
NEW Ed's Lobster	NoLita
Z Pearl Oyster	G Vill

NEW ZEALAND

| **NEW** Nelson Blue | Seaport |

NOODLE SHOPS

| Bao Noodles | Gramercy |
| Great NY Noodle | Chinatown |

Kelley/Ping	**multi.**	16
Lili's Noodle	**multi.**	16
Mee Noodle	**multi.**	18
Menchanko-tei	**multi.**	20
Momofuku Noodle	**E Vill**	24
New Bo-Ky	**Chinatown**	22
Pho Bang	**multi.**	21
Rai Rai Ken	**E Vill**	22
NEW Ramen Setagaya	**E Vill**	–
Republic	**Union Sq**	18
Soba Nippon	**W 50s**	22
Soba-ya	**E Vill**	24

NORTH AFRICAN

Nomad	**E Vill**	22

NUEVO LATINO

Beso	**Park Slope**	19
Cabana	**multi.**	21
Calle Ocho	**W 80s**	22
NEW Carniceria	**Cobble Hill**	–
Citrus B&G	**W 70s**	20
Esperanto	**E Vill**	20
Luz	**Ft Greene**	24
Paladar	**LES**	18
Sabor	**E 80s**	19

PACIFIC NORTHWEST

NEW Wild Salmon	**E 40s**	21

PAN-ASIAN

Abigael's	**Garment**	19
Aja	**E 50s**	20
Amber	**E 80s**	22
Aquamarine	**Murray Hill**	21
NEW Asiakan	**W 90s**	19
Bluechili	**W 50s**	19
Blue Ginger	**Chelsea**	22
Cendrillon	**SoHo**	20
Chance	**Boerum Hill**	21
Kelley/Ping	**multi.**	16
NEW Mantra	**E 50s**	–
O.G.	**E Vill**	23
Rain	**W 80s**	21
Republic	**Union Sq**	18
Ruby Foo's	**multi.**	19
NEW Spoon	**E Vill**	–
Tao	**E 50s**	23

PAN-LATIN

Boca Chica	**E Vill**	20
Bogota Latin	**Park Slope**	21
NEW Cafe Fuego	**E Vill**	19
NEW Crave	**E 50s**	–
Macy	**Flatiron**	19
NEW Palo Santo	**Park Slope**	25
NEW Rayuela	**LES**	–

Willie's	**Bronx**	23
Yuca Bar	**E Vill**	21

PERSIAN

Pars Grill	**Chelsea**	21
Persepolis	**E 70s**	19

PERUVIAN

Flor de Mayo	**multi.**	20
Lima's Taste	**W Vill**	21
Mancora	**E Vill**	21
Pio Pio	**multi.**	23

PIZZA

Adrienne's Pizza	**Financial**	23
Al Forno Pizza	**E 70s**	19
Amorina	**Prospect Hts**	23
Angelo's Pizza	**multi.**	20
Anthony's	**Park Slope**	21
ápizz	**LES**	24
Arturo's Pizzeria	**G Vill**	21
Baci & Abbracci	**W'burg**	20
Bella Blu	**E 70s**	19
Bella Via	**LIC**	23
Bettola	**W 70s**	21
NEW Cacio e Vino	**E Vill**	21
Cafe Fiorello	**W 60s**	20
Cascina	**W 40s**	18
Coals	**Bronx**	22
Da Ciro	**Murray Hill**	21
Dee's Pizza	**Forest Hills**	22
Denino's	**SI**	25
Z Di Fara	**Midwood**	27
Don Giovanni	**multi.**	17
NEW eleven B.	**E Vill**	–
Fornino	**W'burg**	22
Franny's	**Prospect Hts**	23
Gigino	**multi.**	20
Gonzo	**G Vill**	21
Z Grimaldi's	**Dumbo**	25
NEW Il Brigante	**Seaport**	21
Il Mattone	**TriBeCa**	21
NEW Isabella's Oven	**LES**	–
Joe & Pat's	**SI**	22
Joe's Pizza	**multi.**	23
John's Pizzeria	**multi.**	22
La Bottega	**Chelsea**	18
L & B Spumoni	**Bensonhurst**	22
La Pizza Fresca	**Flatiron**	22
La Villa Pizzeria	**multi.**	21
La Vineria	**W 50s**	20
Lil' Frankie Pizza	**E Vill**	22
Lombardi's	**NoLita**	24
NEW Lucali	**Carroll Gdns**	27
Mediterraneo	**E 60s**	19
Mezzaluna	**E 70s**	19
Naples 45	**E 40s**	17

Nick's | **multi.**	24
Nino's | **E 40s**	21
Otto | **G Vill**	22
Patsy's Pizzeria | **multi.**	20
Pintaile's Pizza | **multi.**	20
Pizza 33 | **multi.**	21
Posto | **Gramercy**	23
Sac's Place | **Astoria**	21
Savoia | **Carroll Gdns**	21
Sezz Medi' | **W 100s**	21
Tiramisu | **E 80s**	20
Totonno Pizza | **multi.**	22
Two Boots | **multi.**	18
Una Pizza | **E Vill**	23
Uno Chicago | **multi.**	14
V&T | **W 100s**	18
Vezzo | **Murray Hill**	21
Waldy's Pizza | **Chelsea**	21

PORTUGUESE

Alfama | **W Vill**	22
Tintol | **W 40s**	21

PUB FOOD

Elephant & Castle | **G Vill**	17
Heartland | **multi.**	14
J.G. Melon | **E 70s**	21
Landmark Tavern | **W 40s**	18
Neary's | **E 50s**	15
Pete's Tavern | **Gramercy**	14
P.J. Clarke's | **multi.**	17
NEW Public House | **E 40s**	–
Walker's | **TriBeCa**	17

PUERTO RICAN

La Taza de Oro | **Chelsea**	18
Sofrito | **E 50s**	22

RUSSIAN

FireBird | **W 40s**	18
Russian Samovar | **W 50s**	19
NEW Russian Tea | **W 50s**	19

SANDWICHES

Amy's Bread | **multi.**	23
Barney Greengrass | **W 80s**	23
Bôi | **E 40s**	19
Bouchon Bakery | **W 60s**	23
Bread | **NoLita**	19
Brennan | **Sheepshead**	19
Chop't Creative | **multi.**	20
Così | **multi.**	16
Dishes | **multi.**	22
DuMont | **W'burg**	23
E.A.T. | **E 80s**	19
Ess-a-Bagel | **multi.**	23
Hale/Hearty | **multi.**	19
Katz's Deli | **LES**	23

Lenny's | **multi.**	19
Liebman's | **Bronx**	19
Nicky's Viet. | **multi.**	22
Panino'teca | **Carroll Gdns**	19
Pastrami Queen | **E 70s**	19
Peanut Butter Co. | **G Vill**	22
Press 195 | **multi.**	22
Roll-n-Roaster | **Sheepshead**	19
Sarge's Deli | **Murray Hill**	19
NEW 67 Burger | **Ft Greene**	22
Stage Deli | **W 50s**	19
Sweet Melissa | **multi.**	22
Tossed | **multi.**	19
'wichcraft | **multi.**	22
Zabar's Cafe | **W 80s**	22

SCANDINAVIAN

AQ Cafe | **Murray Hill**	22
Z Aquavit | **E 50s**	25
Smorgas Chef | **multi.**	21

SEAFOOD

Ammos | **multi.**	22
Z Aquagrill | **SoHo**	
Artie's | **Bronx**	
Z Atlantic Grill | **E 70s**	
Avra | **E 40s**	
Black Duck | **Gramercy**	
NEW Black Pearl | **Chelsea**	
BLT Fish | **Flatiron**	
Blue Fin | **W 40s**	
Z Blue Water | **Union Sq**	
Bond 45 | **W 40s**	
Brooklyn Fish | **Park Slope**	
Bubba Gump | **W 40s**	
Christos | **Astoria**	
City Crab | **Flatiron**	
City Hall | **TriBeCa**	
City Lobster | **W 40s**	
Ditch Plains | **G Vill**	
Docks Oyster | **multi.**	
NEW Ed's Lobster | **NoLita**	
Elias Corner | **Astoria**	
Esca | **W 40s**	
Fish | **G Vill**	
Francisco's Centro | **Chelsea**	
fresh | **TriBeCa**	
Fuleen | **Chinatown**	
NEW Hudson R. Café | **Harlem**	
Ithaka | **E 80s**	
Jack's Lux. | **E Vill**	
Kellari Taverna | **W 40s**	
Lake Club | **SI**	
Z Le Bernardin | **W 50s**	
Lobster Box | **Bronx**	
London Lennie's | **Rego Pk**	

Lure Fishbar | **SoHo** 23
Marina Cafe | **SI** 18
Mary's Fish Camp | **W Vill** 25
McCormick/Schmick | **W 50s** 20
Meltemi | **E 50s** 18
Mermaid Inn | **E Vill** 23
Z Milos | **W 50s** 26
Neptune Rm. | **W 80s** 22
Oceana | **E 50s** 26
Ocean Grill | **W 70s** 23
Oriental Gdn. | **Chinatown** 24
Oyster Bar | **E 40s** 21
Pampano | **E 40s** 25
Z Pearl Oyster | **G Vill** 26
Pearl Room | **Bay Ridge** 23
Pescatore | **E 50s** 18
NEW Petite Crev. | **Carroll Gdns** 24
Ping's Sea. | **multi.** 22
Portofino's | **Bronx** 19
Redeye Grill | **W 50s** 20
Sea Grill | **W 40s** 24
NEW Sea Salt | **E Vill** -
Shaffer City | **Flatiron** 21
Shelly's Tratt. | **W 50s** 20
South Fin Grill | **SI** 20
Stamatis | **Astoria** 22
Taverna Kyclades | **Astoria** 25
Telly's Taverna | **Astoria** 22
Thalassa | **TriBeCa** 22
Tides | **LES** 24
Todai | **Murray Hill** 18
Trata Estiatorio | **E 70s** 21
Tratt. Pesce | **multi.** 18
Turquoise | **E 80s** 22
Umberto's | **multi.** 18
Water's Edge | **LIC** 23
NEW Wild Salmon | **E 40s** 21

SMALL PLATES

(See also Spanish tapas specialist)
Alta | Med. | **G Vill** 23
NEW Bar Stuzz. | Italian | **Flatiron** -
east | Med. | **Prospect Hts** 20
Bellavitae | Italian | **G Vill** 22
Bello Sguardo | Med. | **W 70s** 19
Beyoglu | Turkish | **E 80s** 21
Bocca Lupo | Italian | **Cobble Hill** 21
Butai | Jap. | **Gramercy** 22
NEW Centro Vinoteca | Italian | **W Vill** -
Chino's | Asian | **Gramercy** 22
Degustation | French/Spanish | **E Vill** 26
NEW Dieci | Italian | **E Vill** 23
N Japanese | Jap. | **W Vill** 22
NEW Fireside | Eclectic | **E 50s** 21

Frankies Spuntino | Italian | **multi.** 24
NEW Grayz | Amer. | **W 50s** -
NEW House | Med. | **Gramercy** 22
'inoteca | Italian | **LES** 23
NEW Island | Med. | **Astoria** 18
NEW Izakaya 10 | Jap. | **Chelsea** 19
Kuma Inn | SE Asian | **LES** 24
Z L'Atelier/Robuchon | French | **E 50s** 27
Little D | Eclectic | **Park Slope** 20
NEW Maze | French | **W 50s** 23
Mercadito | Mex. | **multi.** 22
One | Amer. | **Meatpacking** 18
Perbacco | Italian | **E Vill** 24
NEW p*ong | Dessert | **G Vill** 21
Sakagura | Jap. | **E 40s** 24
Samba-Lé | Brazilian | **E Vill** 19
NEW savorNY | Eclectic | **LES** -
NEW Spoon | Asian | **E Vill** -
Stanton Social | Eclectic | **LES** 23
NEW Tailor | Amer. | **SoHo** -
Tarallucci | Italian | **multi.** 19
Tasting Rm. | Amer. | **multi.** 22
Uncle Nick's | Greek | **W 50s** 19
Vento | Italian | **Meatpacking** 19
NEW Zenkichi | Jap. | **W'burg** 23

SOUL FOOD

Amy Ruth's | **Harlem** 22
Charles' Kitchen | **Harlem** 24
NEW Cheryl's | **Prospect Hts** 22
Londel's | **Harlem** 22
Miss Mamie/Maude | **Harlem** 21
Mo-Bay | **Harlem** 21
Pink Tea Cup | **W Vill** 20
Sylvia's | **Harlem** 19

SOUP

Cozy | **G Vill** 18
Hale/Hearty | **multi.** 19
La Bonne Soupe | **W 50s** 18

SOUTH AMERICAN

Cafe Ronda | **W 70s** 18
Don Pedro's | **E 90s** 23
Empanada Mama | **W 50s** 20

SOUTHEAST ASIAN

Cafe Asean | **G Vill** 21
Z Spice Market | **Meatpacking** 22

SOUTHERN

Amy Ruth's | **Harlem** 22
B. Smith's | **W 40s** 19
Charles' Kitchen | **Harlem** 24
Duke's | **multi.** 16
Kitchenette | **multi.** 19
Londel's | **Harlem** 22

Maroons | **Chelsea**	22
Miss Mamie/Maude | **Harlem**	21
Pink Tea Cup | **W Vill**	20
Rack & Soul | **W 100s**	20
River Room | **Harlem**	19
NEW Southern Hosp. | **E 70s**	-

SOUTHWESTERN

Agave | **W Vill**	18
Canyon Road | **E 70s**	19
Cilantro | **multi.**	17
Cowgirl | **W Vill**	16
NEW Johnny Utah | **W 50s**	-
Los Dos Molinos | **Gramercy**	21
Z Mesa Grill | **Flatiron**	24
Miracle Grill | **multi.**	18

SPANISH

(* tapas specialist)

Alcala* | **E 40s**	20
Azafran* | **TriBeCa**	21
Bolo | **Flatiron**	24
Boqueria* | **Flatiron**	23
Cafe Español | **G Vill**	20
Casa Mono | **Gramercy**	25
Degustation | **E Vill**	26
El Charro Español | **G Vill**	22
El Cid* | **Chelsea**	21
El Faro* | **W Vill**	23
El Paso | **G Vill**	-
El Pote | **Murray Hill**	21
El Quijote | **Chelsea**	19
Euzkadi* | **E Vill**	21
Flor de Sol* | **TriBeCa**	20
Francisco's Centro | **Chelsea**	22
La Paella* | **E Vill**	20
Las Ramblas* | **G Vill**	23
NEW Mercat* | **NoHo**	-
Oliva* | **LES**	20
NEW Pamplona* | **Gramercy**	-
Pipa* | **Flatiron**	21
Real Madrid | **SI**	21
Sala* | **multi.**	22
Sevilla | **W Vill**	23
Solera* | **E 50s**	22
Sol y Sombra* | **W 80s**	19
Suba | **LES**	21
NEW Tasca* | **W Vill**	20
Tía Pol* | **Chelsea**	24
Xunta* | **E Vill**	19

STEAKHOUSES

AJ Maxwell's | **W 40s**	22
Angelo & Maxie's | **Flatiron**	21
Artie's | **Bronx**	22
Austin's Steak | **Bay Ridge**	21
Ben & Jack's | **E 40s**	23

Ben Benson's | **W 50s**
NEW Benjamin Steak | **E 40s**
Bistro Le Steak | **E 70s**
Blair Perrone | **E 40s**
BLT Prime | **Gramercy**
BLT Steak | **E 50s**
Bobby Van's | **multi.**
Bond 45 | **W 40s**
Buenos Aires | **E Vill**
Bull & Bear | **E 40s**
NEW Caminito | **Harlem**
Capital Grille | **E 40s**
NEW Carniceria | **Cobble Hill**
Chimichurri Grill | **W 40s**
Christos | **Astoria**
Churrascaria | **multi.**
City Hall | **TriBeCa**
Craftsteak | **Chelsea**
Z Del Frisco's | **W 40s**
Delmonico's | **Financial**
NEW DeStefano's | **W'burg**
Dylan Prime | **TriBeCa**
Embers | **Bay Ridge**
Erawan | **Bayside**
Fairway Cafe | **W 70s**
Frankie/Johnnie | **multi.**
Frank's | **Chelsea**
Gallagher's | **W 50s**
NEW Gaucho | **W 50s**
Green Field | **Corona**
Hacienda/Argentina | **E 70s**
Harry's | **Financial**
Il Bastardo | **Chelsea**
Industria | **TriBeCa**
Jake's | **Bronx**
Keens | **Garment**
Knickerbocker | **G Vill**
NEW Kobe Club | **W 50s**
Le Marais | **W 40s**
Les Halles | **multi.**
Macelleria | **Meatpacking**
Maloney & Porcelli | **E 50s**
MarkJoseph | **Financial**
Michael Jordan's | **E 40s**
Morton's | **E 40s**
Nick & Stef's | **Garment**
Novecento | **SoHo**
Old Homestead | **Meatpacking**
Outback | **multi.**
Z Palm | **multi.**
Patroon | **E 40s**
Z Peter Luger | **W'burg**
Pietro's | **E 40s**
Porcão | **Gramercy**
Porter House NY | **W 60s**

CUISINES

Temple Canteen | **Flushing** -
Vatan | **Gramercy** 23
Zen Palate | **multi.** 19

VENEZUELAN

Caracas | **E Vill** 26
Flor's Kitchen | **G Vill** 16

VIETNAMESE

Bao Noodles | **Gramercy** 20
Bao 111 | **E Vill** 21
Bôi | **E 40s** 19
Doyers Viet. | **Chinatown** 20
Indochine | **E Vill** 20
Le Colonial | **E 50s** 20
NEW Mai House | **TriBeCa** 21

Nam | **TriBeCa** 22
New Bo-Ky | **Chinatown** 22
Nha Trang | **Chinatown** 21
Nicky's Viet. | **multi.** 21
Omai | **Chelsea** 23
Pho Bang | **multi.** 21
Pho Pasteur | **Chinatown** 21
Pho Viet Huong | **Chinatown** 23
NEW Safran | **Chelsea** 20
Saigon Grill | **multi.** 22
Sapa | **Flatiron** 22
NEW Silent H | **W'burg** -
Vermicelli | **E 70s** 19
VietCafé | **TriBeCa** 21

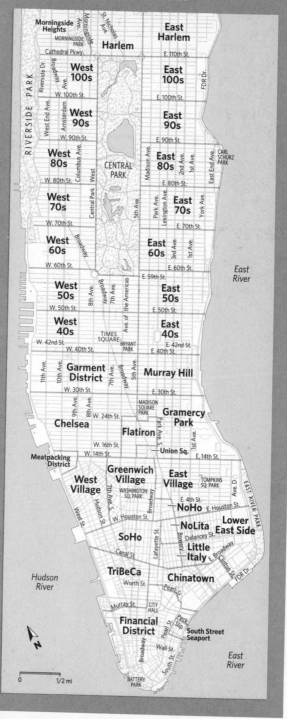

MANHATTAN

Morningside Heights
MORNINGSIDE PARK
Cathedral Pkwy.
Harlem

East Harlem
E. 110th St.

West 100s
W. 100th St.

East 100s
E. 100th St.

West 90s
W. 90th St.

East 90s
E. 90th St.

West 80s
W. 80th St.

CENTRAL PARK

East 80s
E. 80th St.

CARL SCHURZ PARK

West 70s
W. 70th St.

East 70s
E. 70th St.

West 60s
W. 60th St.

East 60s
E. 60th St.

East River

E. 59th St.

West 50s
W. 50th St.

East 50s
E. 50th St.

West 40s
W. 42nd St.

TIMES SQUARE
BRYANT PARK

East 40s
E. 42nd St.

W. 40th St.
E. 40th St.

Garment District
W. 30th St.

Murray Hill
E. 30th St.

MADISON SQUARE PARK

Chelsea
W. 24th St.

Gramercy Park

Flatiron

Meatpacking District

W. 16th St.
W. 14th St.
Union Sq.
E. 14th St.

EAST RIVER PARK

Greenwich Village
WASHINGTON SQ. PARK

East Village
TOMPKINS SQ. PARK
Ave. D

West Village
E. 4th St.

NoHo
E. Houston St.

Lower East Side

NoLita
Delancey St.

SoHo
Canal St.

Little Italy

Hudson River

TriBeCa
Worth St.

Chinatown
Pearl St.

FDR Dr.

Murray St.
CITY HALL

Financial District

Peck Slip
South Street Seaport

Wall St.

East River

BATTERY PARK

0   1/2 mi

MAPS

te at zagat.com

297

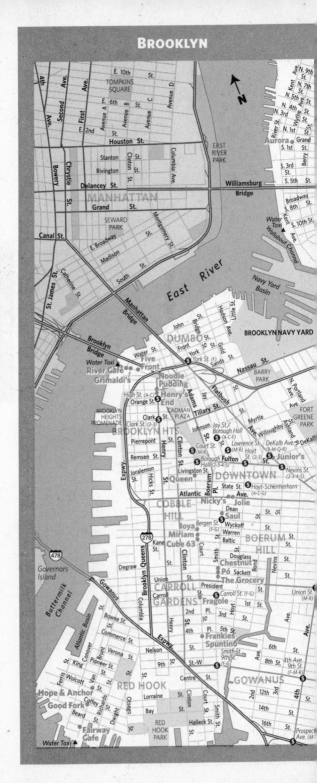

BROOKLYN

N. 10th
N. 8th St.
N. 6th
S. 2nd St.
S. 4th St.
S. 5th St.

Bedford
Ave. (L)
Bamonte's
Frost Ave.
Skillman
Graham
Ave.
Ave.
Olive
St.
Devoe
St.
Grand St. (L)
Waterbury
St.
Morgan
Ave.
Bogart
St.
Ingraham
St.
Varick
Ave.

278

Lorimer
Metropolitan
St. (L)
Ave. (L)
Manhattan
Leonard
Graham
Ave.
Bushwick
Ave.
Stagg
St.
Johnson Ave.
White
Morgan
Ave. (L)
St.
Thames

Metropolitan
DuMont
Burger
Grand
St.
Maujer
Scholes
Meserole
Ave.
Montrose Ave. (L)
St.
Varet
St.
Flushing
Stanwix
Noll

S. 5th
St.
Hewes
St. (J-M)
Broadway
WILLIAMSBURG
Lorimer
St. (G)
Moore
St.
Seigel
St.
Boerum
St.
BUSHWICK

Dressler
Peter
Luger
Roebling
St.
Keap
Hooper
St.
Harrison
Ave.
Marcy
Ave.
(J-M-Z)
Throop
Ave.
Gerry
Ave.
Bartlett
St.
Flushing Ave.
(J-M)
Ellery
Locust
Arion
St.
Beaver St.

S. 9th St.
Division
Ave.
Lee
Ave.
Penn
St.
Middleton
St.
Walton
St.
Ave.
St.
Myrtle Ave. (J-M-Z)
Lewis
Ave.

Clymer
Bedford
St.
Heyward
Wallabout
St.
Flushing
Ave.
Ellery
St.
Throop
Summer
Ave.

Wythe
Ross
Kent
Ave.
Brooklyn
Ave.
Steuben
Flushing
Ave.
Park
Myrtle Ave.
Willoughby Ave. (G)
Tompkins
Ave.
Vernon
Sumner
Ave.

U.S. Naval
Station
Franklin
Kent
Ave.
Myrtle
Nostrand
Hart
St.
DeKalb
Ave.

Flushing
Ave.
Ryerson
Willoughby
Classon
Bedford
Ave.
TOMPKINS
PARK
Van Buren
Ave.

Clinton
Washington
DeKalb
Lafayette
Bedford Ave.
Nostrand Ave. (G)
BEDFORD-
STUYVESANT
Lexington
Gates
Ave.

Clermont
Classon Ave. (G)
Quincy
Franklin
Madison
St.

FORT
GREENE
Ici
Clinton Ave.
Washington Ave. (G)
CLINTON
HILL
Hancock
Macon
St.

Smoke
Joint
Fulton
St.
Greene
Gates
Clinton Ave.
Washington Ave. (C)
Putnam
Ave.
Fulton
Herkimer
Nostrand Ave.
(A-C)
St.

Habana Outpost
Lafayette Ave.
Fulton
Franklin Ave.
(C-S)
St.
Pacific

Brooklyn
Academy
of Music
S. Oxford
Atlantic
Lefferts
Pl.
Dean
New
York
Nostrand

Atlantic Ave.
(B-Q-2-3-4-5)
Pacific St. (D-M-N-R)
Pacific
St.
Vanderbilt
Grand
Classon
St. Marks
Ave.

Convivium
Osteria
Bergen St. (2-3)
Carlton
Dean
Bergen
Franklin
St. Johns Pl.
CROWN
HEIGHTS
Nostrand
Ave. (3)

Pranny's
Garden
Cafe
Prospect
PROSPECT
HEIGHTS
Pl.
Park Pl.
(S)

Chocolate
Room
7th Ave.
(B-Q)
Park
Pl.
Sterling
Tom's
Washington
St. Johns Pl.
Franklin Ave.
(2-3-4-5)

St. Johns Pl.
Lincoln
Berkeley
Flatbush
Ave.
Grand Army Plaza
(2-3)
Lincoln
Eastern
Bedford
Rogers
President
St. (2-5)

Union
Carroll
St.
Eastern Pkwy
Brooklyn Museum
(2-3)
Brooklyn
Museum
President
Crown

Al Di La
Blue Ribbon Sushi
1st
St.
Garfield
Pl.
BROOKLYN
BOTANICAL
GARDEN
Botanic
Garden
(S)
Sullivan
Pl.
Blvd.

Blue
Ribbon
5th
Ave.
PARK
SLOPE
3rd
St.
Flatbush
Empire
Sterling
Bedford
Rd

5th
7th
St.
West
Ave.
Lincoln
Midwood

7th
7th Ave.
(F) St.
Prospect
Fenimore
St.

9th
10th
St.
PROSPECT
PARK
Prospect Park
(B-Q-S)
Ave.

6th
11th
St.

13th
St.
8th
Ave.

15th
St.
15th St.
Prospect Park
(F)
Winthrop
St.

Locations

Includes restaurant names, cuisines and Food ratings. ⚡ indicates places with the highest ratings, popularity and importance.

Manhattan

CHELSEA

(24th to 30th Sts., west of 5th; 14th to 24th Sts., west of 6th)

Amy's Bread	*Sandwich*	23
Bette	*Euro.*	19
Better Burger	*Hamburgers*	15
Biricchino	*Italian*	20
NEW Black Pearl	*Seafood*	17
Blossom	*Vegan/Veg.*	21
Blue Ginger	*Jap./Pan-Asian*	22
Bombay Talkie	*Indian*	20
Bottino	*Italian*	19
NEW brgr	*Hamburgers*	18
⚡ Buddakan	*Asian Fusion*	23
Cafeteria	*Amer.*	18
Cookshop	*Amer.*	23
Craftsteak	*Steak*	22
Crema	*Mex.*	21
Cuba Cafe	*Cuban*	18
Dallas BBQ	*BBQ*	15
Da Umberto	*Italian*	25
⚡ Del Posto	*Italian*	25
Don Giovanni	*Italian*	17
East of 8th	*Eclectic*	16
El Cid	*Spanish*	21
elmo	*Amer.*	15
El Quijote	*Spanish*	19
Empire Diner	*Diner*	15
Energy Kitchen	*Health*	18
F & B	*Hot Dogs*	18
Food Bar	*Amer.*	16
Francisco's Centro	*Spanish*	22
Frank's	*Italian/Steak*	19
Gascogne	*French*	22
Gin Lane	*Cont.*	17
Grand Sichuan	*Chinese*	22
Hale/Hearty	*Sandwich/Soup*	19
NEW Hill Country	*BBQ*	–
Il Bastardo	*Italian/Steak*	19
Intermezzo	*Italian*	18
NEW Izakaya 10	*Jap.*	19
NEW Klee Brass.	*Amer./Euro.*	21
La Bergamote	*Bakery/French*	24
La Bottega	*Italian/Pizza*	18
La Lunchonette	*French*	22
La Taza de Oro	*Diner*	18
Le Grainne Cafe	*French*	19
NEW Le Petit Bistro	*French*	–
Le Singe Vert	*French*	19

Le Zie 2000	*Italian*	21
Maroons	*Jamaican*	22
Mary Ann's	*Tex-Mex*	15
⚡ Matsuri	*Jap.*	23
Momoya	*Jap.*	24
Monster Sushi	*Jap.*	18
Moran's	*Amer.*	18
⚡ Morimoto	*Jap.*	24
Negril	*Carib./Jamaican*	20
Omai	*Viet.*	23
Park, The	*Med.*	15
Pars Grill	*Persian*	21
Patsy's Pizzeria	*Pizza*	20
Pepe	*Italian*	21
Pizza 33	*Pizza*	21
Pongsri Thai	*Thai*	20
Red Cat	*Amer./Med.*	24
Regional Thai	*Thai*	18
Rocking Horse Cafe	*Mex.*	20
Room Service	*Thai*	19
Royal Siam	*Thai*	19
RUB BBQ	*BBQ*	20
NEW Safran	*French/Viet.*	20
Sarabeth's	*Amer.*	20
Sette	*Italian*	18
Seven	*Amer.*	18
Spice	*Thai*	20
Sueños	*Mex.*	2_
Tía Pol	*Spanish*	24
tre dici	*Italian*	2_
Trestle on 10th	*Amer.*	1_
202 Cafe	*Med.*	2_
Waldy's Pizza	*Pizza*	2_
'wichcraft	*Sandwich*	2_

CHINATOWN

(Canal to Pearl Sts., east of B'way

NEW Amazing 66	*Chinese*	2_
Big Wong	*Chinese*	2_
Congee	*Chinese*	2_
Dim Sum Go Go	*Chinese*	2_
Doyers Viet.	*Viet.*	2_
Excellent Dumpling	*Chinese*	2_
Fuleen	*Chinese/Seafood*	2_
Golden Unicorn	*Chinese*	2_
Goodies	*Chinese*	2_
Grand Sichuan	*Chinese*	2_
Great NY Noodle	*Noodles*	2_
HSF	*Chinese*	2_
Jing Fong	*Chinese*	1_
Joe's Shanghai	*Chinese*	2_

Mandarin Court	*Chinese*	20
Mr. Tang	*Chinese*	19
New Bo-Ky	*Noodles*	22
New Green Bo	*Chinese*	22
Nha Trang	*Viet.*	21
Oriental Gdn.	*Chinese/Seafood*	24
Peking Duck	*Chinese*	22
Pho Bang	*Viet.*	21
Pho Pasteur	*Viet.*	21
Pho Viet Huong	*Viet.*	23
Ping's Sea.	*Chinese/Seafood*	22
Pongsri Thai	*Thai*	20
Shanghai Cuisine	*Chinese*	21
Wo Hop	*Chinese*	21
X.O.	*Chinese*	18

EAST 40s

Aburiya Kinnosuke	*Jap.*	24
Alcala	*Spanish*	20
American Girl	*Amer.*	13
Ammos	*Greek*	22
Avra	*Greek*	24
Ben & Jack's	*Steak*	23
NEW Benjamin Steak	*Steak*	23
Blair Perrone	*Steak*	21
Bobby Van's	*Steak*	22
Bôi	*Viet.*	19
Brother Jimmy's	*BBQ*	16
Bukhara Grill	*Indian*	20
Bull & Bear	*Steak*	19
Burger Heaven	*Hamburgers*	16
Burritoville	*Tex-Mex*	16
Cafe Centro	*Med.*	20
Cafe Spice	*Indian*	18
Caffe Linda	*Italian*	18
Capital Grille	*Steak*	23
Chiam	*Chinese*	23
Chin Chin	*Chinese*	22
Chipotle	*Mex.*	18
Cibo	*Amer./Italian*	20
Cipriani Dolci	*Italian*	18
Comfort Diner	*Diner*	16
Darbar	*Indian*	20
Dishes	*Sandwich*	22
Diwan	*Indian*	21
Django	*French/Med.*	20
Docks Oyster	*Seafood*	19
Energy Kitchen	*Health*	18
NEW Fabio Piccolo	*Italian*	–
goodburger	*Hamburgers*	18
Grifone	*Italian*	23
Gyu-Kaku	*Jap.*	21
Hale/Hearty	*Sandwich/Soup*	19
Haru	*Jap.*	21
Hatsuhana	*Jap.*	24
Postino	*Italian*	22

Inagiku	*Jap.*	23
Ise	*Jap.*	22
Junior's	*Diner*	18
Katsu-Hama	*Jap.*	20
Kuruma Zushi	*Jap.*	28
Ⓩ L'Impero	*Italian*	26
Mamá Mexico	*Mex.*	20
Mangia	*Med.*	20
Mee Noodle	*Noodles*	18
Ⓩ Megu	*Jap.*	24
Menchanko-tei	*Noodles*	20
Metrazur	*Amer.*	20
Michael Jordan's	*Steak*	20
Morton's	*Steak*	24
Nanni	*Italian*	24
Naples 45	*Italian*	17
Nino's	*Italian*	21
Osteria Laguna	*Italian*	21
Oyster Bar	*Seafood*	21
Ⓩ Palm	*Steak*	24
Pampano	*Mex./Seafood*	25
Patroon	*Amer./Steak*	21
Pepe	*Italian*	21
NEW Pera	*Med./Turkish*	22
Pershing Sq.	*Amer./French*	15
Phoenix Gdn.	*Chinese*	24
Pietro's	*Italian/Steak*	23
Prime Grill	*Steak*	22
NEW Public House	*Pub*	–
Ribot	*Med.*	19
Riingo	*Amer./Jap.*	19
Sakagura	*Jap.*	24
Sip Sak	*Turkish*	20
Smith & Wollensky	*Steak*	23
Smorgas Chef	*Scan.*	19
Ⓩ Sparks	*Steak*	25
Sushiden	*Jap.*	25
Ⓩ Sushi Yasuda	*Jap.*	28
Two Boots	*Pizza*	18
'wichcraft	*Sandwich*	20
NEW Wild Salmon	*Seafood*	21
Wollensky's	*Steak*	23
Yama	*Jap.*	24
NEW Yushi	*Jap.*	–
Zócalo	*Mex.*	20

EAST 50s

Adä	*Indian*	23
Aja	*Pan-Asian*	20
Al Bustan	*Lebanese*	19
Ⓩ Alto	*Italian*	26
Amma	*Indian*	24
Angelo's Pizza	*Pizza*	20
Ⓩ Aquavit	*Scan.*	25
Baluchi's	*Indian*	18
Bice	*Italian*	20

Blockheads Burritos | *Mex.*	17
BLT Steak | *Steak*	24
Bobby Van's | *Steak*	22
Bottega del Vino | *Italian*	22
Brasserie | *French*	20
Burger Heaven | *Hamburgers*	16
Burritoville | *Tex-Mex*	16
Cafe Joul | *French*	18
Caviar Russe | *Amer.*	24
Cellini | *Italian*	21
Chipotle | *Mex.*	18
Chola | *Indian*	23
Chop't Creative | *Amer.*	20
Così | *Sandwich*	16
NEW Crave | *Pan-Latin*	-
David Burke/Bloom. | *Amer.*	18
Dawat | *Indian*	23
DeGrezia | *Italian*	22
Destino | *Italian*	18
Deux Amis | *French*	19
Dishes | *Sandwich*	22
Dos Caminos | *Mex.*	20
Energy Kitchen | *Health*	18
Ess-a-Bagel | *Deli*	23
F & B | *Hot Dogs*	18
ℤ Felidia | *Italian*	25
57 | *Amer.*	22
NEW Fiorini | *Italian*	-
NEW Fireside | *Eclectic*	21
ℤ Four Seasons | *Cont.*	25
Fresco | *Italian*	23
Giambelli | *Italian*	21
Gilt | *Amer.*	25
goodburger | *Hamburgers*	18
Grand Sichuan | *Chinese*	22
Harry Cipriani | *Italian*	-
Houston's | *Amer.*	20
Ichimura | *Jap.*	24
Il Menestrello | *Italian*	22
Il Nido | *Italian*	23
Jubilee | *French*	22
Korea Palace | *Korean*	18
La Gioconda | *Italian*	20
ℤ La Grenouille | *French*	27
La Mangeoire | *French*	19
La Mediterranée | *French*	19
ℤ L'Atelier/Robuchon | *French*	27
Le Cirque | *French*	23
Le Colonial | *French/Viet.*	20
Lenny's | *Sandwich*	19
L'Entrecote | *French*	19
Le Perigord | *French*	24
Lever House | *Amer.*	22
Maloney & Porcelli | *Steak*	22
NEW Mantra | *Amer./Pan-Asian*	-

Meltemi | *Greek/Seafood*	18
Mint | *Indian*	19
Monkey Bar | *Amer.*	-
Montparnasse | *French*	19
Mr. Chow | *Chinese*	20
ℤ Mr. K's | *Chinese*	23
Neary's | *Pub*	15
Nippon | *Jap.*	22
Oceana | *Amer./Seafood*	26
Our Place | *Chinese*	20
Outback | *Steak*	14
Peking Duck | *Chinese*	22
Pescatore | *Italian/Seafood*	18
P.J. Clarke's | *Pub*	17
Pump Energy | *Health*	19
ℤ Rosa Mexicano | *Mex.*	22
Rothmann's | *Steak*	22
San Pietro | *Italian*	24
Serafina | *Italian*	18
Shun Lee Palace | *Chinese*	24
Sofrito | *Puerto Rican*	22
Solera | *Spanish*	22
Solo | *Med.*	22
Sushi Ann | *Jap.*	23
Taksim | *Turkish*	20
ℤ Tao | *Pan-Asian*	23
Tea Box | *Jap.*	20
Teodora | *Italian*	22
Tratt. Pesce | *Italian/Seafood*	18
Tse Yang | *Chinese*	25
Vong | *French/Thai*	22
Yuva | *Indian*	24
Zarela | *Mex.*	21
Zip Burger | *Hamburgers*	18

EAST 60s

NEW Accademia/Vino | *Italian*	-
Alice's Tea Cup | *Amer.*	19
Amaranth | *Med.*	20
Arabelle | *Amer./French*	21
ℤ Aureole | *Amer.*	27
Bistro 61 | *French*	20
Bravo Gianni | *Italian*	23
Brio | *Italian*	18
Burger Heaven | *Hamburgers*	16
Cabana | *Nuevo Latino*	21
Café Evergreen | *Chinese*	20
Café Pierre | *Cont./French*	23
Canaletto | *Italian*	21
NEW Chat Noir | *French*	18
China Fun | *Chinese*	16
Circus | *Brazilian*	20
Da Filippo | *Italian*	19
ℤ Daniel | *French*	28
ℤ davidburke/dona. | *Amer.*	25

LOCATIONS

Uva | *Italian*	21	Ota-Ya | *Jap.*	20
Vermicelli | *Viet.*	19	Our Place | *Chinese*	20
Viand | *Coffee Shop*	16	Paola's | *Italian*	23
Via Quadronno | *Italian*	21	Papaya King | *Hot Dogs*	20
Vivolo | *Italian*	20	Pig Heaven | *Chinese*	19
Vynl | *Amer./Thai*	17	Pintaile's Pizza | *Pizza*	20

EAST 80s

		Poke | *Jap.*	26
Alice's Tea Cup | *Amer.*	19	Primavera | *Italian*	22
Amber | *Pan-Asian*	22	Quattro Gatti | *Italian*	20
Antonucci | *Italian*	20	Rughetta | *Italian*	22
Baluchi's | *Indian*	18	Sabor | *Nuevo Latino*	19
Beyoglu | *Turkish*	21	Sala Thai | *Thai*	21
Blockheads Burritos | *Mex.*	17	**NEW** Sandro's | *Italian*	-
Brasserie Julien | *French*	19	Sharz Cafe | *Med.*	21
Burger Heaven | *Hamburgers*	16	Sistina | *Italian*	24
Café d'Alsace | *French*	21	Spigolo | *Italian*	25
Café Sabarsky | *Austrian*	22	Sushi Sen-nin | *Jap.*	25
Caffe Grazie | *Italian*	19	Taste | *Amer.*	20
Centolire | *Italian*	20	Tevere | *Italian*	22
Chef Ho's | *Chinese*	22	Tiramisu | *Italian*	20
NEW Chennai | *Indian/Veg.*	-	Tony's Di Napoli | *Italian*	18
Cilantro | *SW*	17	Totonno Pizza | *Pizza*	22
Dakshin Indian | *Indian*	20	Tratt. Pesce | *Italian/Seafood*	18
Demarchelier | *French*	17	Triangolo | *Italian*	21
Divino | *Italian*	18	Turquoise | *Seafood*	22
Donguri | *Jap.*	27	Uno Chicago | *Pizza*	14
E.A.T. | *Amer.*	19	Vespa | *Italian*	21
Elaine's | *Amer./Italian*	13	Viand | *Coffee Shop*	16
Elio's | *Italian*	23	Wondee Siam | *Thai*	22
Erminia | *Italian*	25	Wu Liang Ye | *Chinese*	21
Etats-Unis | *Amer.*	25	York Grill | *Amer.*	23
Ethiopian Rest. | *Ethiopian*	17	Yuka | *Jap.*	21
Firenze | *Italian*	21	Zócalo | *Mex.*	20

		Girasole | *Italian*	20
Giovanni | *Italian*	22	**EAST 90s & 100s**	

(90th to 110th Sts.)

Gobo | *Vegan/Veg.*	22	Barking Dog | *Amer.*	15
Heidelberg | *German*	17	Bistro du Nord | *French*	18
Ichiro | *Jap.*	20	Brother Jimmy's | *BBQ*	16
Ithaka | *Greek/Seafood*	20	Don Pedro's | *Carib./S Amer.*	23
Jackson Hole | *Amer.*	17	El Paso Taqueria | *Mex.*	22
Jacques | *French*	18	Itzocan | *Mex.*	23
Jasmine | *Thai*	19	Jackson Hole | *Amer.*	17
Josie's | *Eclectic*	19	Nick's | *Pizza*	24
Kings' Carriage | *Amer.*	21	Osso Buco | *Italian*	17
Ko Sushi | *Jap.*	19	Pascalou | *French*	22
Land | *Thai*	23	**NEW** Peri Ela | *Turkish*	19
Le Boeuf/Mode | *French*	21	Pinocchio | *Italian*	21
Le Pain Q. | *Bakery/Belgian*	19	Pintaile's Pizza | *Pizza*	20
Le Refuge | *French*	21	Pio Pio | *Peruvian*	23
Lili's Noodle | *Noodles*	16	Sarabeth's | *Amer.*	20
Luca | *Italian*	20	Sfoglia | *Italian*	23
Maz Mezcal | *Mex.*	20	Table d'Hôte | *French*	21
Nicola's | *Italian*	22	Vico | *Italian*	21
One 83 | *Italian*	21	Zebú Grill | *Brazilian*	21

EAST VILLAGE

(14th to Houston Sts., east of B'way, excluding NoHo)

NEW Aloe | Eclectic –
Angelica Kit. | Vegan/Veg. 21
Awash | Ethiopian 22
Baluchi's | Indian 18
Banjara | Indian 23
Bao 111 | Viet. 21
Blue 9 Burger | Hamburgers 18
Boca Chica | Pan-Latin 20
Buenos Aires | Argent. 21
Burritoville | Tex-Mex 16
Butter | Amer. 19
Cacio e Pepe | Italian 22
NEW Cacio e Vino | Italian 21
Cafecito | Cuban 21
NEW Cafe Fuego | Pan-Latin 19
Cafe Mogador | Moroccan 21
NEW Caffe Emilia | Italian –
Caracas | Venez. 26
Caravan/Dreams | Vegan/Veg. 24
Casimir | French 19
Chickpea | Mideast. 19
ChikaLicious | Dessert 24
Chipotle | Mex. 18
Chiyono | Jap. 23
Colors | Eclectic 19
Counter | Vegan/Veg. 22
Cucina di Pesce | Italian 17
Dallas BBQ | BBQ 15
Danal | French/Med. 22
Degustation | French/Spanish 26
NEW Dieci | Italian 23
Dok Suni's | Korean 21
Dumpling Man | Chinese 19
NEW East Village Yacht | Amer. –
Elephant, The | French/Thai 21
NEW eleven B. | Italian/Pizza –
Esperanto | Nuevo Latino 20
NEW E.U., The | Euro. 20
Euzkadi | Spanish 21
Flea Mkt. Cafe | French 19
Frank | Italian 24
NEW Gemma | Italian –
Gnocco Caffe | Italian 21
Grand Sichuan | Chinese 22
Gyu-Kaku | Jap. 21
Hasaki | Jap. 23
Haveli | Indian 23
Hearth | Amer./Italian 25
Holy Basil | Thai 22
Hummus Place | Israeli/Veg. 23
I Coppi | Italian 23
I Bagatto | Italian 23

Indochine | French/Viet. 20
Itzocan | Mex. 23
Jack's Lux. | Cont./French 24
Jewel Bako | Jap. 25
John's/12th St. | Italian 19
Jules | French 19
Z Kanoyama | Jap. 27
Kelley/Ping | Pan-Asian 16
Klong | Thai 19
Knife + Fork | Euro. 23
Lan | Jap. 25
La Paella | Spanish 20
La Palapa | Mex. 20
Lavagna | Italian 24
Le Gamin | French 19
Le Miu | Jap. 25
Le Tableau | French 24
Lil' Frankie Pizza | Pizza 22
Lucien | French 21
Mama's Food | Amer. 20
Mamlouk | Mideast. 23
Mancora | Peruvian 21
Mara's | Cajun/Creole 19
Mary Ann's | Tex-Mex 15
Max | Italian 23
Max Brenner | Dessert 17
Mercadito | Mex. 22
Mermaid Inn | Seafood 23
Mingala Burmese | Burmese 20
Momofuku Noodle | Noodles 24
Momofuku Ssäm | Amer./Korean 24
Moustache | Mideast. 21
Nicky's Viet. | Sandwich 21
99 Mi. to Philly | Cheese Stks. 18
Nomad | African 22
O.G. | Pan-Asian 23
Pepe | Italian 21
Perbacco | Italian 24
Prune | Amer. 24
Pylos | Greek 25
Rai Rai Ken | Noodles 22
NEW Ramen Setagaya | Noodles –
Sal Anthony's | Italian 19
Samba-Lé | Brazilian 19
Sapporo East | Jap. 21
SEA | Thai 20
NEW Sea Salt | Seafood –
Shabu-Tatsu | Jap. 20
S'mac | Amer. 19
Soba-ya | Jap. 24
NEW Spoon | Jap./Pan-Asian –
Supper | Italian 24
Takahachi | Jap. 24
Tarallucci | Italian 19
Tasting Rm. | Amer. 22

LOCATIONS

NEW Tree	*French*	24
Tsampa	*Tibetan*	20
26 Seats	*French*	22
Two Boots	*Pizza*	18
Una Pizza	*Pizza*	23
Veniero's	*Dessert*	23
Veselka	*Ukrainian*	18
Westville	*Amer.*	23
Xunta	*Spanish*	19
Yuca Bar	*Pan-Latin*	21
Zerza	*Moroccan*	22
Zum Schneider	*German*	18

FINANCIAL DISTRICT

(South of Murray St.)

Adrienne's Pizza	*Pizza*	23
Au Mandarin	*Chinese*	20
Battery Gdns.	*Amer./Cont.*	18
Bobby Van's	*Steak*	22
Bridge Cafe	*Amer.*	22
Bull Run	*Amer.*	18
Burritoville	*Tex-Mex*	16
China Chalet	*Chinese*	19
Chipotle	*Mex.*	18
Così	*Sandwich*	16
Delmonico's	*Steak*	22
Fino	*Italian*	20
Fraunces Tavern	*Amer.*	15
Gigino	*Italian*	20
NEW Gold St.	*Eclectic*	15
Hale/Hearty	*Sandwich/Soup*	19
Harry's	*Eclectic/Steak*	22
Ise	*Jap.*	22
Joseph's	*Italian*	21
NEW Kaijou	*Jap.*	–
Lemongrass Grill	*Thai*	17
Lenny's	*Sandwich*	19
Les Halles	*French*	20
Lili's Noodle	*Noodles*	16
Mangia	*Med.*	20
MarkJoseph	*Steak*	24
P.J. Clarke's	*Pub*	17
Roy's NY	*Hawaii Reg.*	25
Smorgas Chef	*Scan.*	19
Trinity Place	*Eclectic*	18
2 West	*Steak*	21
NEW Yushi	*Jap.*	–
Zen Palate	*Veg.*	19

FLATIRON DISTRICT

(14th to 24th Sts., 6th Ave. to
Park Ave. S., excluding Union Sq.)

Angelo & Maxie's	*Steak*	21
Arezzo	*Italian*	22
Aspen	*Amer.*	20
Barbounia	*Med.*	20
NEW Bar Stuzz.	*Italian*	–

Basta Pasta	*Italian*	21
Beppe	*Italian*	23
BLT Fish	*Seafood*	23
Bolo	*Spanish*	24
Boqueria	*Spanish*	23
NEW Borough Food	*Amer.*	–
Chipotle	*Mex.*	18
City Bakery	*Bakery*	21
City Crab	*Seafood*	17
Comfort Diner	*Diner*	16
Così	*Sandwich*	16
☑ Craft	*Amer.*	25
Craftbar	*Amer.*	22
Fleur de Sel	*French*	25
Giorgio's/Gramercy	*Amer.*	22
☑ Gramercy Tavern	*Amer.*	27
Haru	*Jap.*	21
La Pizza Fresca	*Italian*	22
Lenny's	*Sandwich*	19
Le Pain Q.	*Bakery/Belgian*	19
L'Express	*French*	17
Lucy	*Pan-Latin*	19
Mangia	*Med.*	20
Markt	*Belgian*	19
☑ Mesa Grill	*SW*	24
Mizu Sushi	*Jap.*	22
NY Burger	*Hamburgers*	18
Outback	*Steak*	14
Periyali	*Greek*	23
Petite Abeille	*Belgian*	19
Pipa	*Spanish*	21
Planet Thailand	*Thai*	19
Pump Energy	*Health*	19
Punch	*Eclectic*	19
Rickshaw Dumpling	*Chinese*	18
☑ Rosa Mexicano	*Mex.*	22
Sala	*Spanish*	22
Sapa	*French/Viet.*	22
Shaffer City	*Seafood*	21
Shake Shack	*Hamburgers*	23
SushiSamba	*Brazilian/Jap.*	22
Tamarind	*Indian*	25
Tarallucci	*Italian*	19
Tossed	*Amer.*	18
☑ Veritas	*Amer.*	26
Via Emilia	*Italian*	21
'wichcraft	*Sandwich*	20

GARMENT DISTRICT

(30th to 40th Sts., west of 5th)

Abigael's	*Pan-Asian*	19
Aki Sushi	*Jap.*	19
Arno	*Italian*	20
Ben's Kosher	*Deli*	17
Brother Jimmy's	*BBQ*	16
Burritoville	*Tex-Mex*	16

Chipotle | *Mex.*	18
Cho Dang Gol | *Korean*	21
Così | *Sandwich*	16
Dae Dong | *Korean*	18
Frankie/Johnnie | *Steak*	21
Gahm Mi Oak | *Korean*	22
Gray's Papaya | *Hot Dogs*	20
Hale/Hearty | *Sandwich/Soup*	19
Heartland | *Pub*	14
HK | *Amer.*	16
Kang Suh | *Korean*	20
Keens | *Steak*	24
Kum Gang San | *Korean*	21
Mandoo Bar | *Korean*	20
Nick & Stef's | *Steak*	22
Osteria Gelsi | *Italian*	24
Pump Energy | *Health*	19
Tratt. Pesce | *Italian/Seafood*	18
Tupelo Grill | *Amer.*	18
Uncle Jack's | *Steak*	23
WonJo | *Korean*	20

GRAMERCY PARK

(24th to 30th Sts., east of 5th;
14th to 24th Sts., east of Park)

Aki Sushi | *Jap.*	19
A Voce | *Italian*	25
Baluchi's | *Indian*	18
Bao Noodles | *Viet.*	20
Black Duck | *Amer./Seafood*	20
BLT Prime | *Steak*	24
Blue Smoke | *BBQ*	22
Butai | *Jap.*	22
Casa Mono | *Spanish*	25
Chennai Gdn. | *Indian/Veg.*	22
Chino's | *Asian*	22
Coppola's | *Italian*	19
Country | *Amer.*	23
Curry Leaf | *Indian*	20
Dos Caminos | *Mex.*	20
Duke's | *Southern*	16
☑ Eleven Madison | *French*	26
Ess-a-Bagel | *Deli*	23
Friend of a Farmer | *Amer.*	17
NEW House | *Med.*	22
Houston's | *Amer.*	20
Trulli | *Italian*	22
aiya Thai | *Thai*	22
aponais | *Jap.*	20
ady Mendl's | *Amer.*	22
a Petite Aub. | *French*	20
es Halles | *French*	20
os Dos Molinos | *SW*	21
Novità | *Italian*	24
NEW Pamplona | *Spanish*	-
aul & Jimmy's | *Italian*	19

Pete's Tavern | *Pub*	14
Petite Abeille | *Belgian*	19
Pongal | *Indian/Veg.*	21
Pongsri Thai | *Thai*	20
Porcão | *Brazilian/Steak*	21
Posto | *Pizza*	23
Pure Food/Wine | *Vegan/Veg.*	22
NEW Resto | *Belgian*	-
Rice | *Eclectic*	19
Rolf's | *German*	17
Saravanaas | *Indian*	23
☑ Tabla | *Amer.*	25
Totonno Pizza | *Pizza*	22
Turkish Kitchen | *Turkish*	22
NEW Vamos! | *Mex.*	16
Vatan | *Indian*	23
NEW ☑ Wakiya | *Chinese*	-
Yama | *Jap.*	24

GREENWICH VILLAGE

(Houston to 14th Sts., west of
B'way, east of 7th Ave. S.)

Aki | *Jap.*	25
Alta | *Med.*	23
Amy's Bread | *Sandwich*	23
☑ Annisa | *Amer.*	27
A.O.C. Bedford | *Euro.*	23
Arté | *Italian*	19
Arturo's Pizzeria | *Italian*	21
☑ Babbo | *Italian*	27
Baluchi's | *Indian*	18
NEW BarFry | *Eclectic/Jap.*	-
Bar Pitti | *Italian*	22
Bellavitae | *Italian*	22
NEW BLT Burger | *Hamburgers*	19
☑ Blue Hill | *Amer.*	26
Blue Ribbon Bakery | *Amer.*	24
Borgo Antico | *Italian*	19
Cafe Asean | *SE Asian*	21
Cafe Español | *Spanish*	20
Cafe Loup | *French*	18
Cafe Spice | *Indian*	18
CamaJe | *Amer./French*	23
Chanto | *Jap.*	22
Chez Jacqueline | *French*	18
Chipotle | *Mex.*	18
Cornelia St. Cafe | *Amer./French*	19
Così | *Sandwich*	16
Cozy | *Hamburgers/Soup*	18
☑ Cru | *Euro.*	26
Cuba | *Cuban*	21
Cubana Café | *Cuban*	20
Da Silvano | *Italian*	20
Deborah | *Amer.*	21
Ditch Plains | *Seafood*	17
Do Hwa | *Korean*	21

LOCATIONS

El Charro Español | *Spanish*	22
Elephant & Castle | *Pub*	17
El Paso | *Mex./Spanish*	–
Empire Szechuan | *Chinese*	15
Ennio & Michael | *Italian*	21
Fish | *Seafood*	20
Flor's Kitchen | *Venez.*	16
French Roast | *French*	14
Gobo | *Vegan/Veg.*	22
Gonzo | *Italian/Pizza*	21
☑ Gotham B&G | *Amer.*	27
Gradisca | *Italian*	21
Gray's Papaya | *Hot Dogs*	20
NEW Gus' Place | *Greek/Med.*	20
Gusto | *Italian*	22
Home | *Amer.*	20
Hummus Place | *Israeli/Veg.*	23
NEW Hurapan | *Thai*	20
Il Cantinori | *Italian*	22
☑ Il Mulino | *Italian*	27
'ino | *Italian*	24
Jack Bistro | *French*	17
Jane | *Amer.*	21
Japonica | *Jap.*	22
Joe's Pizza | *Pizza*	23
John's Pizzeria | *Pizza*	22
Kati Roll Co. | *Indian*	20
Knickerbocker | *Amer.*	20
La Lanterna | *Italian*	20
La Palapa | *Mex.*	20
Las Ramblas | *Spanish*	23
Leela Lounge | *Indian*	22
Le Gamin | *French*	19
Le Gigot | *French*	24
Lemongrass Grill | *Thai*	17
Lenny's | *Sandwich*	19
Le Pain Q. | *Bakery/Belgian*	19
☑ Lupa | *Italian*	25
Marinella | *Italian*	23
Mas | *Amer.*	25
Maurizio Tratt. | *Italian*	21
Meskerem | *Ethiopian*	20
Mexicana Mama | *Mex.*	23
Minetta Tavern | *Italian*	18
NEW Morandi | *Italian*	19
Negril | *Carib./Jamaican*	20
North Sq. | *Amer.*	22
☑ One if by Land | *Amer.*	23
Osso Buco | *Italian*	17
Otto | *Pizza*	22
Patsy's Pizzeria | *Pizza*	20
Peanut Butter Co. | *Sandwich*	20
☑ Pearl Oyster | *Seafood*	26
NEW Perilla | *Amer.*	–
Piadina | *Italian*	20
Pizza 33 | *Pizza*	21
Pó | *Italian*	25
NEW p*ong | *Dessert*	21
Prem-on Thai | *Thai*	21
Rare B&G | *Hamburgers*	21
Rickshaw Dumpling | *Chinese*	18
Risotteria | *Italian*	21
Rocco | *Italian*	20
Sacred Chow | *Vegan/Veg.*	23
Saigon Grill | *Viet.*	22
NEW Soto | *Jap.*	–
Spice | *Thai*	20
NEW Stand | *Hamburgers*	19
Strip House | *Steak*	25
☑ Tomoe Sushi | *Jap.*	26
Tratt. Pesce | *Italian/Seafood*	18
Uno Chicago | *Pizza*	14
Village | *Amer./French*	20
Villa Mosconi | *Italian*	20
'wichcraft | *Sandwich*	20
Yama | *Jap.*	24

HARLEM/EAST HARLEM

(110th to 157th Sts., excluding Columbia U. area)

Amy Ruth's | *Soul*	22
NEW Caminito | *Argent./Steak*	–
Charles' Kitchen | *Southern*	24
NEW China de Puebla | *Mex.*	–
Dinosaur BBQ | *BBQ*	22
El Paso Taqueria | *Mex.*	22
Ginger | *Chinese*	21
NEW Hudson R. Café | *Amer./Seafood*	–
Londel's | *Southern*	22
Miss Mamie/Maude | *Southern*	21
Mo-Bay | *Carib./Soul*	21
Native | *Eclectic*	19
Papaya King | *Hot Dogs*	20
Patsy's Pizzeria | *Pizza*	20
☑ Rao's | *Italian*	22
Revival | *Amer./French*	19
River Room | *Southern*	19
Sylvia's | *Soul*	19
NEW Zoma | *Ethiopian*	23

LITTLE ITALY

(Canal to Kenmare Sts., Bowery to Lafayette St.)

NEW Almond Flower | *Amer.*	23
Angelo's/Mulberry | *Italian*	23
NEW Bar Martignetti | *Amer.*	18
Da Nico | *Italian*	21
8 Mile Creek | *Australian*	20
Ferrara | *Bakery*	22
Grotta Azzurra | *Italian*	18
Il Cortile | *Italian*	23

Il Fornaio	*Italian*	21
Il Palazzo	*Italian*	23
La Esquina	*Mex.*	21
La Mela	*Italian*	18
Nyonya	*Malaysian*	22
Pellegrino's	*Italian*	22
Pho Bang	*Viet.*	21
Positano	*Italian*	21
Sal Anthony's	*Italian*	19
Taormina	*Italian*	24
Umberto's	*Italian/Seafood*	18
Vincent's	*Italian*	21

LOWER EAST SIDE

(Houston to Canal Sts.,
east of Bowery)

Alias	*Amer.*	23
ápizz	*Italian*	24
Azul Bistro	*Argent./Steak*	22
Bereket	*Turkish*	18
Bondi Rd.	*Australian*	21
Brown Café	*Amer.*	25
Clinton St. Baking	*Amer.*	24
Congee	*Chinese*	21
Cube 63	*Jap.*	21
Essex	*Amer.*	20
Falai	*Italian*	25
Frankies Spuntino	*Italian*	24
Freemans	*Amer.*	21
NEW Georgia's/BBQ	*BBQ*	-
inoteca	*Italian*	23
NEW Isabella's Oven	*Pizza*	-
NEW Kampuchea	*Cambodian*	20
Katz's Deli	*Deli*	23
Kuma Inn	*Filipino/Thai*	24
Les Enfants	*African/French*	19
Little Giant	*Amer.*	22
Loreley	*German*	18
Oliva	*Spanish*	20
NEW Open/Sesame	*Thai*	-
Orchard, The	*Amer.*	24
Paladar	*Nuevo Latino*	18
NEW Rayuela	*Pan-Latin*	-
NEW Régate	*French*	-
Sachiko's	*Jap.*	25
Salt	*Amer.*	21
Sammy's Roum.	*Jewish*	19
NEW savorNY	*Eclectic*	-
Schiller's	*Eclectic*	18
NEW Spitzer's	*Amer.*	-
Stanton Social	*Eclectic*	23
NEW Sticky Rice	*Thai*	19
Suba	*Spanish*	21
Tiany	*Vegan/Veg.*	18
Thor	*Amer.*	18
Tides	*Seafood*	24

Two Boots	*Pizza*	18
wd-50	*Amer./Eclectic*	23
Whole Foods	*Eclectic/Health*	19
Zucco	*French*	22

MEATPACKING DISTRICT

(Gansevoort to 15th Sts.,
west of 9th Ave.)

Z Buddha Bar	*Asian Fusion*	19
Fig & Olive	*Med.*	20
5 Ninth	*Eclectic*	19
Florent	*French*	20
Highline	*Thai*	19
NEW Inn LW12	*Amer.*	19
NEW Los Dados	*Mex.*	-
Macelleria	*Italian/Steak*	21
Nero	*Italian*	20
Old Homestead	*Steak*	23
One	*Amer.*	18
Ono	*Jap.*	21
Paradou	*French*	19
Z Pastis	*French*	21
Pop Burger	*Amer.*	19
NEW Revel	*Eclectic*	-
Son Cubano	*Cuban*	21
Z Spice Market	*SE Asian*	22
NEW STK	*Steak*	20
Valbella	*Italian*	24
Vento	*Italian*	19

MURRAY HILL

(30th to 40th Sts., east of 5th)

Ali Baba	*Turkish*	23
AQ Cafe	*Scan.*	20
Aquamarine	*Pan-Asian*	21
Z Artisanal	*French*	23
Z Asia de Cuba	*Asian/Cuban*	23
Barbès	*French/Moroccan*	22
Barking Dog	*Amer.*	15
Better Burger	*Hamburgers*	15
Blockheads Burritos	*Mex.*	17
Carl's Steaks	*Cheese Stks.*	22
Cosette	*French*	21
Da Ciro	*Italian/Pizza*	21
Duke's	*Southern*	16
El Parador Cafe	*Mex.*	20
El Pote	*Spanish*	21
Ethos	*Greek*	22
Evergreen	*Chinese*	19
Fino	*Italian*	20
Grand Sichuan	*Chinese*	22
Hangawi	*Korean*	23
Iron Sushi	*Jap.*	19
Jackson Hole	*Amer.*	17
Josie's	*Eclectic*	19
La Giara	*Italian*	19

Lemongrass Grill | *Thai* — 17
Madison Bistro | *French* — 18
Mee Noodle | *Noodles* — 18
Mishima | *Jap.* — 23
Morgan | *Amer.* — 20
Notaro | *Italian* — 20
Pasticcio | *Italian* — 19
Patsy's Pizzeria | *Pizza* — 20
Penelope | *Amer.* — 21
Pizza 33 | *Pizza* — 21
Pump Energy | *Health* — 19
Rare B&G | *Hamburgers* — 21
Rossini's | *Italian* — 23
Salute! | *Italian/Med.* — 19
Sarge's Deli | *Deli* — 19
Sushi Sen-nin | *Jap.* — 25
Todai | *Jap./Seafood* — 18
Tratt. Alba | *Italian* — 20
Trio | *Med.* — 21
Vezzo | *Pizza* — 21
Villa Berulia | *Italian* — 23
Water Club | *Amer.* — 20
'wichcraft | *Sandwich* — 20
Wolfgang's | *Steak* — 25
Wu Liang Ye | *Chinese* — 21

NOHO

(Houston to 4th Sts., Bowery to B'way)

Aroma | *Italian* — 24
Bianca | *Italian* — 22
Bond St. | *Jap.* — 25
Chinatown Brass. | *Chinese* — 21
5 Points | *Amer./Med.* — 22
Great Jones Cafe | *Cajun* — 19
Il Buco | *Italian/Med.* — 25
NEW Mercat | *Spanish* — -
NoHo Star | *Amer.* — 18
Rice | *Eclectic* — 19
Sala | *Spanish* — 22
Serafina | *Italian* — 18
Two Boots | *Pizza* — 18

NOLITA

(Houston to Kenmare Sts., Bowery to Lafayette St.)

barmarché | *Amer.* — 19
Bread | *Sandwich* — 19
Cafe Colonial | *Brazilian* — 20
Cafe Gitane | *French/Moroccan* — 20
Café Habana/Outpost | *Cuban/Mex.* — 22
NEW Ed's Lobster | *Seafood* — 23
Ghenet | *Ethiopian* — 22
Jacques | *French* — 18
Kitchen Club | *French/Jap.* — 22
Le Jardin Bistro | *French* — 18

Lombardi's | *Pizza* — 24
Mexican Radio | *Mex.* — 18
NEW Noble Food | *Amer.* — -
Peasant | *Italian* — 24
Public | *Eclectic* — 23
Tasting Rm. | *Amer.* — 22

SOHO

(Canal to Houston Sts., west of Lafayette St.)

Ama | *Italian* — 22
Z Aquagrill | *Seafood* — 26
Aurora | *Italian* — 26
NEW Babouche | *French/Moroccan* — 20
Z Balthazar | *French* — 23
Baluchi's | *Indian* — 18
Barolo | *Italian* — 18
Bistro Les Amis | *French* — 21
Z Blue Ribbon | *Amer.* — 25
Z Blue Ribbon Sushi | *Jap.* — 25
Cendrillon | *Asian/Filipino* — 20
Centovini | *Italian* — 21
Chipotle | *Mex.* — 18
Cipriani D'twn | *Italian* — 20
Dani | *Italian* — 20
Dos Caminos | *Mex.* — 20
Falai | *Italian* — 25
Félix | *French* — 16
Fiamma Osteria | *Italian* — 25
NEW FR.OG | *Eclectic/French* — 21
Giorgione | *Italian* — 23
Hampton Chutney | *Indian* — 20
HQ | *Amer.* — 19
Ideya | *Carib.* — 20
Il Corallo | *Italian* — 22
I Tre Merli | *Italian* — 18
Ivo & Lulu | *Carib./French* — 22
Jean Claude | *French* — 22
Kelley/Ping | *Pan-Asian* — 16
Kin Khao | *Thai* — 22
Z Kittichai | *Thai* — 23
L'Ecole | *French* — 23
Le Pain Q. | *Bakery/Belgian* — 19
Lucky Strike | *French* — 17
Lure Fishbar | *Seafood* — 23
Mercer Kitchen | *Amer./French* — 22
Mezzogiorno | *Italian* — 20
Novecento | *Argent./Steak* — 22
Omen | *Jap.* — 25
Once Upon a Tart | *Coffee* — 22
Peep | *Thai* — 19
Pepe | *Italian* — 21
NEW Provence | *French* — 21
Raoul's | *French* — 24
Salt | *Amer.* — 21

Savoy	*Amer./Med.*	24
Snack	*Greek*	24
NEW Tailor	*Dessert*	-
12 Chairs	*Amer./Mideast.*	19
'wichcraft	*Sandwich*	20
Woo Lae Oak	*Korean*	23
Zoë	*Amer.*	20

SOUTH STREET SEAPORT

Cabana	*Nuevo Latino*	21
Heartland	*Pub*	14
NEW Il Brigante	*Italian*	21
NEW Nelson Blue	*New Zealand*	-
NEW Stella Maris	*Euro.*	-
NEW Suteishi	*Jap.*	25
Uno Chicago	*Pizza*	14

TRIBECA

(Canal to Murray Sts., west of B'way)

Acappella	*Italian*	23
Arqua	*Italian*	22
Azafran	*Spanish*	21
Baluchi's	*Indian*	18
Blaue Gans	*Austrian/German*	20
Z Bouley	*French*	28
Z Bouley, Upstairs	*Eclectic*	26
Bread	*Italian*	19
Bubby's	*Amer.*	18
Burritoville	*Tex-Mex*	16
Capsouto Frères	*French*	24
Carl's Steaks	*Cheese Stks.*	22
Centrico	*Mex.*	20
Z Chanterelle	*French*	27
Churrascaria	*Brazilian*	23
City Hall	*Seafood/Steak*	21
Z Danube	*Austrian*	26
NEW Dennis Foy	*Amer.*	24
Devin Tavern	*Amer.*	18
Duane Park	*Amer.*	24
Dylan Prime	*Steak*	24
Ecco	*Italian*	21
Edward's	*Amer.*	16
NEW Estancia	*Argent./Italian*	21
Gilli Ponte	*Italian*	21
lor de Sol	*Spanish*	20
resh	*Seafood*	24
Gigino	*Italian*	20
Harrison, The	*Amer.*	24
Il Giglio	*Italian*	26
Mattone	*Italian/Pizza*	21
Industria	*Argent./Steak*	20
Kitchenette	*Southern*	19
Landmarc	*French*	23

NEW Mai House	*Viet.*	21
Mary Ann's	*Tex-Mex*	15
Max	*Italian*	23
Z Megu	*Jap.*	24
Mr. Chow	*Chinese*	20
Nam	*Viet.*	22
Ninja	*Jap.*	19
Z Nobu	*Jap.*	27
Odeon	*Amer./French*	19
Pepolino	*Italian*	24
Petite Abeille	*Belgian*	19
Roc	*Italian*	21
NEW Rosanjin	*Jap.*	25
Salaam Bombay	*Indian*	20
Z Scalini Fedeli	*Italian*	26
Soda Shop	*Amer./Dessert*	19
Takahachi	*Jap.*	24
Thalassa	*Greek/Seafood*	22
Tribeca Grill	*Amer.*	22
Turks & Frogs	*Turkish*	20
VietCafé	*Viet.*	21
Walker's	*Pub*	17
'wichcraft	*Sandwich*	20
Wolfgang's	*Steak*	25
Zutto	*Jap.*	21

UNION SQUARE

(14th to 17th Sts., 5th Ave. to Union Sq. E.)

Z Blue Water	*Seafood*	23
Chat 'n Chew	*Amer.*	16
Chop't Creative	*Amer.*	20
Coffee Shop	*Amer./Brazilian*	15
NEW 15 East	*Jap.*	26
Havana Central	*Cuban*	17
Heartland	*Pub*	14
Max Brenner	*Dessert*	17
Olives	*Med.*	22
Republic	*Pan-Asian*	18
Steak Frites	*French*	18
Z Tocqueville	*Amer./French*	26
Z Union Sq. Cafe	*Amer.*	26
Whole Foods	*Eclectic/Health*	19
Zen Palate	*Veg.*	19

WASHINGTON HTS./ INWOOD

(North of W. 157th St.)

Dallas BBQ	*BBQ*	15
El Malecon	*Dominican*	21
Empire Szechuan	*Chinese*	15
NEW Guadalupe	*Mex.*	19
Hispaniola	*Dominican*	21
New Leaf	*Amer.*	20
107 West	*Cajun/Tex-Mex*	18
Park Terrace	*French/Moroccan*	22

AJ Maxwell's | *Steak* — 22
Akdeniz | *Turkish* — 20
Alfredo of Rome | *Italian* — 19
Algonquin | *Amer.* — 16
Amarone | *Italian* — 19
Amy's Bread | *Sandwich* — 23
Angus McIndoe | *Amer.* — 16
Baldoria | *Italian* — 22
Barbetta | *Italian* — 20
Basilica | *Italian* — 19
Ⓩ Becco | *Italian* — 22
Better Burger | *Hamburgers* — 15
Blue Fin | *Seafood* — 22
Bond 45 | *Italian* — 20
Breeze | *French/Thai* — 20
Brooklyn Diner | *Diner* — 17
Bryant Park | *Amer.* — 17
B. Smith's | *Southern* — 19
Bubba Gump | *Amer./Seafood* — 14
Burritoville | *Tex-Mex* — 16
Cafe Un Deux | *French* — 16
Cara Mia | *Italian* — 20
Ⓩ Carmine's | *Italian* — 19
Cascina | *Italian* — 18
Chez Josephine | *French* — 20
Chimichurri Grill | *Argent./Steak* — 21
Chipotle | *Mex.* — 18
Churrascaria | *Brazilian* — 23
City Lobster | *Seafood* — 18
Così | *Sandwich* — 16
Ⓩ Daisy May's | *BBQ* — 24
Dallas BBQ | *BBQ* — 15
Ⓩ db Bistro Moderne | *French* — 25
Ⓩ Del Frisco's | *Steak* — 25
Delta Grill | *Cajun/Creole* — 19
Dervish Turk. | *Turkish* — 19
District | *Amer.* — 20
Don Giovanni | *Italian* — 17
Edison | *Coffee Shop* — 15
Energy Kitchen | *Health* — 18
Esca | *Italian/Seafood* — 25
ESPN Zone | *Amer.* — 12
etc. etc. | *Italian* — 20
FireBird | *Russian* — 18
44/X Hell's Kit. | *Amer.* — 21
Frankie/Johnnie | *Steak* — 21
Ⓩ Gari/Sushi | *Jap.* — 26
Hakata Grill | *Jap.* — 20
Hale/Hearty | *Sandwich/Soup* — 19
Hallo Berlin | *German* — 17
Hard Rock Cafe | *Amer.* — 13
Haru | *Jap.* — 21
Havana Central | *Cuban* — 17
NEW Hawaiian Tropic | *Amer.* — 16

Heartland | *Pub* — 14
Hell's Kitchen | *Mex.* — 23
Jewel of India | *Indian* — 20
Joe Allen | *Amer.* — 17
John's Pizzeria | *Pizza* — 22
Junior's | *Diner* — 18
Kati Roll Co. | *Indian* — 20
Kellari Taverna | *Greek* — 23
Kodama | *Jap.* — 19
Koi | *Jap.* — 23
Kyma | *Greek* — 18
NEW Kyotofu | *Dessert* — 23
La Locanda Vini | *Italian* — 21
La Masseria | *Italian* — 22
Landmark Tavern | *Amer./Irish* — 18
La Rivista | *Italian* — 18
Lattanzi | *Italian*
Le Madeleine | *French* — 20
Le Marais | *French/Steak* — 20
Lenny's | *Sandwich* — 19
Le Rivage | *French* — 19
Marseille | *French/Med.* — 20
Meskerem | *Ethiopian* — 20
NEW Metro Marché | *French*
Monster Sushi | *Jap.*
Morrell Wine Bar | *Amer.*
Ollie's | *Chinese*
Orso | *Italian*
Osteria al Doge | *Italian*
Pam Real Thai | *Thai*
Pietrasanta | *Italian*
Pigalle | *French*
Pongsri Thai | *Thai*
Rachel's American | *Amer.*
Ⓩ Rainbow Room/Grill | *Italian*
Re Sette | *Italian*
Ruby Foo's | *Pan-Asian*
Sardi's | *Cont.*
Scarlatto | *Italian*
Sea Grill | *Seafood*
Shula's | *Steak*
NEW Spice Fusion | *Indian*
NEW Spotlight Live | *Amer.*
Sushiden | *Jap.*
Sushi Zen | *Jap.*
Tintol | *Portug.*
Tony's Di Napoli | *Italian*
Tossed | *Amer.*
Tratt. Dopo | *Italian*
Triomphe | *French*
Turkish Cuisine | *Turkish*
Two Boots | *Pizza*
Utsav | *Indian*
Via Brasil | *Brazilian/Steak*
View, The | *Cont.*

subscribe to zagat.c

Virgil's Real BBQ	*BBQ*	20
West Bank Cafe	*Amer.*	20
'wichcraft	*Sandwich*	20
Wu Liang Ye	*Chinese*	21
Zen Palate	*Veg.*	19

WEST 50s

Abboccato	*Italian*	22
Afghan Kebab	*Afghan*	19
Aki Sushi	*Jap.*	19
NEW Amalia	*Med.*	21
Angelo's Pizza	*Pizza*	20
NEW Anthos	*Greek*	25
Azuri Cafe	*Israeli*	25
Baluchi's	*Indian*	18
Bann	*Korean*	24
Z Bar Americain	*Amer.*	23
NEW Basso56	*Italian*	23
Bay Leaf	*Indian*	19
Beacon	*Amer.*	22
Bello	*Italian*	20
Ben Benson's	*Steak*	24
BG	*Amer.*	20
Blockheads Burritos	*Mex.*	17
NEW BLT Market	*Amer.*	-
bluechili	*Pan-Asian*	19
Bobby Van's	*Steak*	22
Bombay Palace	*Indian*	18
Brasserie 8½	*French*	22
Brass. Ruhlmann	*French*	17
Bricco	*Italian*	19
Brooklyn Diner	*Diner*	17
burger joint	*Hamburgers*	24
Cafe Spice	*Indian*	18
Caffe Cielo	*Italian*	19
Z Carnegie Deli	*Deli*	21
Chez Napoléon	*French*	20
China Grill	*Asian*	22
Così	*Sandwich*	16
Da Tommaso	*Italian*	20
Eatery	*Amer.*	19
El Centro	*Mex.*	18
Empanada Mama	*S Amer.*	20
Gallagher's	*Steak*	20
NEW Gaucho	*Argent./Steak*	-
NEW Z Gordon Ramsay	*French*	25
NEW Grayz	*Eclectic*	-
Greek Kitchen	*Greek*	19
Guantanamera	*Cuban*	22
Hale/Hearty	*Sandwich/Soup*	19
Heartland	*Pub*	14
Hudson Cafeteria	*Amer./Eclectic*	19
Il Gattopardo	*Italian*	23
Il Tinello	*Italian*	26
NEW Insieme	*Italian*	26
Inoue	*Jap.*	22

Island Burgers	*Hamburgers*	22
Joe's Shanghai	*Chinese*	22
NEW Johnny Utah	*BBQ/SW*	-
NEW Kobe Club	*Steak*	20
La Bonne Soupe	*French*	18
La Vineria	*Italian*	20
Z Le Bernardin	*French/Seafood*	28
Le Pain Q.	*Bakery/Belgian*	19
Lili's Noodle	*Noodles*	16
Maison	*French*	17
Mangia	*Med.*	20
Maria Pia	*Italian*	19
NEW Maze	*French*	23
McCormick/Schmick	*Seafood*	20
Mee Noodle	*Noodles*	18
Menchanko-tei	*Noodles*	20
Michael's	*Calif.*	21
Z Milos	*Greek/Seafood*	26
Moda	*Italian/Med.*	-
Z Modern, The	*Amer./French*	26
Molyvos	*Greek*	22
NEW Natsumi	*Italian/Jap.*	-
Nino's	*Italian*	21
Z Nobu 57	*Jap.*	26
Nocello	*Italian*	21
Nook	*Eclectic*	22
Norma's	*Amer.*	25
NEW Omido	*Jap.*	-
Osteria del Circo	*Italian*	22
Z Palm	*Steak*	24
Patsy's	*Italian*	21
Pepe	*Italian*	21
Petrossian	*Cont./French*	24
Piano Due	*Italian*	25
Pump Energy	*Health*	19
Puttanesca	*Italian*	18
Quality Meats	*Amer./Steak*	24
Redeye Grill	*Amer./Seafood*	20
Remi	*Italian*	22
René Pujol	*French*	22
Rice 'n' Beans	*Brazilian*	19
Roberto Passon	*Italian*	22
Rock Ctr.	*Amer.*	19
Rue 57	*French*	19
Russian Samovar	*Cont.*	19
NEW Russian Tea	*Cont./Russian*	19
Ruth's Chris	*Steak*	23
San Domenico	*Italian*	23
Sarabeth's	*Amer.*	20
Serafina	*Italian*	18
Shelly's Tratt.	*Italian*	20
Soba Nippon	*Jap.*	22
Sosa Borella	*Argent./Italian*	21
Stage Deli	*Deli*	20

☑ Sugiyama | *Jap.*	27
Sushiya | *Jap.*	20
Taboon | *Med./Mideast.*	24
Tang Pavilion | *Chinese*	23
NEW Ted's Montana | *Amer.*	15
Thalia | *Amer.*	21
NEW Toloache | *Mex.*	–
Topaz Thai | *Thai*	20
Town | *Amer.*	24
Tratt. Dell'Arte | *Italian*	22
Tuscan Sq. | *Italian*	16
☑ 21 Club | *Amer.*	22
Uncle Nick's | *Greek*	19
ViceVersa | *Italian*	23
Victor's Cafe | *Cuban*	21
Vynl | *Amer./Thai*	17
Whym | *Amer.*	21
Wondee Siam | *Thai*	22
Xing | *Asian Fusion*	21
☑ Yakitori Totto | *Jap.*	26
Zona Rosa | *Mex.*	18

WEST 60s

☑ Asiate | *French/Jap.*	24
Bouchon Bakery | *Amer./French*	23
☑ Café des Artistes | *French*	22
Cafe Fiorello | *Italian*	20
☑ Café Gray | *French*	25
Empire Szechuan | *Chinese*	15
Gabriel's | *Italian*	22
Grand Tier | *Amer./Cont.*	19
☑ Jean Georges | *French*	28
Josephina | *Amer.*	18
La Boîte en Bois | *French*	21
Landmarc | *French*	23
Le Pain Q. | *Bakery/Belgian*	19
Levana | *Med.*	20
☑ Masa/Bar Masa | *Jap.*	27
Nick & Toni's | *Med.*	18
Ollie's | *Chinese*	16
O'Neals' | *Amer.*	17
☑ Per Se | *Amer./French*	28
☑ Picholine | *French/Med.*	27
P.J. Clarke's | *Pub*	17
Porter House NY | *Steak*	22
☑ Rosa Mexicano | *Mex.*	22
Sapphire | *Indian*	20
Shun Lee Cafe | *Chinese*	21
Shun Lee West | *Chinese*	23
☑ Tavern on Green | *Amer.*	15
☑ Telepan | *Amer.*	25
Whole Foods | *Eclectic/Health*	19

WEST 70s

Alice's Tea Cup | *Amer.*	19
Arté Café | *Italian*	18

Bello Sguardo | *Med.*	19
Bettola | *Italian*	21
Big Nick's Burger | *Hamburgers*	17
Bistro Cassis | *French*	20
Burritoville | *Tex-Mex*	16
Café Frida | *Mex.*	19
Cafe Luxembourg | *French*	20
Cafe Ronda | *Med./ S Amer.*	18
'Cesca | *Italian*	23
China Fun | *Chinese*	16
Citrus B&G | *Asian/Nuevo Latino*	20
☑ Compass | *Amer.*	22
Coppola's | *Italian*	19
Così | *Sandwich*	16
Dallas BBQ | *BBQ*	15
NEW Earthen Oven | *Indian*	21
Epices/Traiteur | *Med./Tunisian*	21
Fairway Cafe | *Amer.*	18
☑ Gari/Sushi | *Jap.*	26
Gray's Papaya | *Hot Dogs*	20
Hummus Place | *Israeli/Veg.*	20
Isabella's | *Amer./Med.*	20
Jacques-Imo's | *Cajun/Creole*	1
Josie's | *Eclectic*	1
NEW Kefi | *Greek*	2
La Grolla | *Italian*	2
La Vela | *Italian*	1
Lenny's | *Sandwich*	1
Le Pain Q. | *Bakery/Belgian*	1
Mughlai | *Indian*	1
Nice Matin | *French/Med.*	1
Ocean Grill | *Seafood*	2
Pappardella | *Italian*	1
Pasha | *Turkish*	2
Patsy's Pizzeria | *Pizza*	1
Pomodoro Rosso | *Italian*	2
Ruby Foo's | *Pan-Asian*	2
Sambuca | *Italian*	1
San Luigi | *Italian*	
Savann | *French/Med.*	
Scaletta | *Italian*	
Swagat Indian | *Indian*	
Tenzan | *Jap.*	
Viand | *Coffee Shop*	

WEST 80s

Aix Brasserie | *French*	
Artie's Deli | *Deli*	
Barney Greengrass | *Deli*	
Bistro Citron | *French*	
Brother Jimmy's | *BBQ*	
Cafe Con Leche | *Cuban/Dominican*	
Cafe Lalo | *Coffee/Dessert*	
Calle Ocho | *Nuevo Latino*	
Celeste | *Italian*	

subscribe to zagat.c

Restaurant	Rating
Columbus Bakery	*Bakery*	18
Docks Oyster	*Seafood*	19
Edgar's Cafe	*Coffee*	18
EJ's Luncheonette	*Amer.*	15
Flor de Mayo	*Chinese/Peruvian*	20
French Roast	*French*	14
Good Enough/Eat	*Amer.*	20
Hampton Chutney	*Indian*	20
Haru	*Jap.*	21
Jackson Hole	*Amer.*	17
La Mirabelle	*French*	22
Land	*Thai*	23
Lenny's	*Sandwich*	19
Loft	*French/Italian*	17
Nëo Sushi	*Jap.*	22
Neptune Rm.	*Seafood*	22
Ollie's	*Chinese*	16
☑ Ouest	*Amer.*	25
Popover Cafe	*Amer.*	18
Rain	*Pan-Asian*	21
Roppongi	*Jap.*	19
Sarabeth's	*Amer.*	20
Sol y Sombra	*Spanish*	19
Spiga	*Italian*	21
Sushi Hana	*Jap.*	21
Uno Chicago	*Pizza*	14
Vynl	*Amer./Thai*	17
Zabar's Cafe	*Deli*	20
Zeytin	*Turkish*	19

WEST 90s

Acqua	*Italian*	18
Alouette	*French*	20
NEW Asiakan	*Jap./Pan-Asian*	19
Cafe Con Leche	*Cuban/Dominican*	18
Carmine's	*Italian*	19
El Malecon	*Dominican*	21
Gabriela's	*Mex.*	17
Gennaro	*Italian*	25
Lemongrass Grill	*Thai*	17
Pisca	*Italian*	20
Mary Ann's	*Tex-Mex*	15
Pio Pio	*Peruvian*	23
Regional	*Italian*	17
Roth's Westside	*Steak*	19
Saigon Grill	*Viet.*	22
Pratt. Pesce	*Italian/Seafood*	18
Yuki Sushi	*Jap.*	21

WEST 100s

(See also Harlem/East Harlem)

Awash	*Ethiopian*	22
Bistro Ten 18	*Amer.*	20
NEW Cafe & Wine	*Carib./French*	-
Café du Soleil	*French/Med.*	19

Restaurant	Rating
Empire Szechuan	*Chinese*	15
Flor de Mayo	*Chinese/Peruvian*	20
Havana Central	*Cuban*	17
Indus Valley	*Indian*	23
Kitchenette	*Southern*	19
Le Monde	*French*	17
Mamá Mexico	*Mex.*	20
Max	*Italian*	23
Métisse	*French*	19
Mill Korean	*Korean*	19
Noche Mexicana	*Mex.*	22
Ollie's	*Chinese*	16
107 West	*Cajun/Tex-Mex*	18
PicNic Market	*Deli/French*	20
Pisticci	*Italian*	23
Rack & Soul	*BBQ/Southern*	20
Sezz Medi'	*Med./Pizza*	21
Symposium	*Greek*	20
Terrace in the Sky	*French/Med.*	22
Tokyo Pop	*Jap.*	20
Tomo Sushi	*Jap.*	20
Turkuaz	*Turkish*	19
V&T	*Italian/Pizza*	18

WEST VILLAGE

(Houston to 14th Sts., west of 7th Ave. S., excluding Meatpacking District)

Agave	*SW*	18
Alfama	*Portug.*	22
Antica Venezia	*Italian*	23
A.O.C.	*French*	20
August	*Euro.*	23
Barbuto	*Italian*	22
Burritoville	*Tex-Mex*	16
NEW Cafe Cluny	*Amer./French*	19
Café de Bruxelles	*Belgian*	21
Casa	*Brazilian*	22
NEW Centro Vinoteca	*Italian*	-
Chow Bar	*Asian Fusion*	21
Corner Bistro	*Hamburgers*	22
Cowgirl	*SW*	16
Crispo	*Italian*	23
Da Andrea	*Italian*	24
Dirty Bird	*Amer.*	17
El Faro	*Spanish*	23
Employees Only	*Euro.*	18
Energy Kitchen	*Health*	18
EN Japanese	*Jap.*	22
Extra Virgin	*Med.*	21
Fatty Crab	*Malaysian*	21
Frederick's	*French/Med.*	19
Gavroche	*French*	19
good	*Amer.*	20
Havana Alma	*Cuban*	21
I Tre Merli	*Italian*	18

Jarnac | *Med.*	22
La Focaccia | *Italian*	20
La Ripaille | *French*	23
Le Gamin | *French*	19
Lima's Taste | *Peruvian*	21
Little Owl | *Amer./Med.*	24
Malatesta | *Italian*	21
Maremma | *Italian*	21
Mary's Fish Camp | *Seafood*	25
Mercadito | *Mex.*	22
Mexicana Mama | *Mex.*	23
Mi Cocina | *Mex.*	22
Miracle Grill | *SW*	18
Monster Sushi | *Jap.*	18
Moustache | *Mideast.*	21
Osteria del Sole | *Italian*	21
Papaya King | *Hot Dogs*	20
Paris Commune | *French*	18
Pepe | *Italian*	21
Perry St. | *Amer.*	24
Petite Abeille | *Belgian*	19
Philip Marie | *Amer.*	20
Piccolo Angolo | *Italian*	25
Pink Tea Cup | *Soul/Southern*	20
Place, The | *Amer./Med.*	21
Sant Ambroeus | *Italian*	22
Sevilla | *Spanish*	23
Smorgas Chef | *Scan.*	19
Snack Taverna | *Greek*	22
🆕 Socialista | *Cuban*	-
Spotted Pig | *British*	22
Surya | *Indian*	24
SushiSamba | *Brazilian/Jap.*	22
Tartine | *French*	22
🆕 Tasca | *Spanish*	20
Tea & Sympathy | *British*	19
Two Boots | *Pizza*	18
Wallsé | *Austrian*	26
🆕Ⓩ Waverly Inn | *Amer.*	18
Westville | *Amer.*	23
Wild Ginger | *Thai*	19

Bronx

Artie's | *Seafood/Steak*	22
Beccofino | *Italian*	22
Bruckner B&G | *Amer.*	21
Coals | *Pizza*	22
Dominick's | *Italian*	22
El Malecon | *Dominican*	21
Enzo's | *Italian*	23
F & J Pine | *Italian*	20
Fratelli | *Italian*	21
Jake's | *Steak*	24
Le Refuge Inn | *French*	24
Liebman's | *Deli*	19

Lobster Box | *Seafood*	
Madison's | *Italian*	
Mario's | *Italian*	
Park Place | *Cont.*	
Pasquale's Rigoletto | *Italian*	
Patricia's | *Italian*	
Pio Pio | *Peruvian*	
Portofino's | *Italian/Seafood*	
Riverdale Gdn. | *Amer.*	
Ⓩ Roberto | *Italian*	
Siam Sq. | *Thai*	
Tosca Café | *Italian*	
Umberto's | *Italian/Seafood*	
Willie's | *Steak*	

Brooklyn

BAY RIDGE

Agnanti | *Greek*	
Areo | *Italian*	
Austin's Steak | *Steak*	
Cebu | *Cont.*	
Chadwick's | *Amer.*	
Chianti | *Italian*	
Eliá | *Greek*	
Embers | *Steak*	
Greenhouse Café | *Amer.*	
Omonia Cafe | *Greek*	
101 | *Amer./Italian*	
Pearl Room | *Seafood*	
Ⓩ Tanoreen | *Med./Mideast.*	
Tuscany Grill | *Italian*	
Uno Chicago | *Pizza*	

BENSONHURST

L & B Spumoni | *Dessert/Pizza*	
Tenzan | *Jap.*	

BOERUM HILL

(See map on page 298)

Chance | *Pan-Asian*	
D'twn Atlantic | *Amer.*	
Jolie | *French*	
🆕 Ki Sushi | *Jap.*	
🆕 Lunetta | *Italian*	
Nicky's Viet. | *Sandwich*	
Ⓩ Saul | *Amer.*	

BRIGHTON BEACH

Mr. Tang | *Chinese*	

BROOKLYN HEIGHTS

(See map on page 298)

Caffe Buon Gusto | *Italian*	
Chipotle | *Mex.*	
ChipShop | *British*	
🆕 Five Guys | *Hamburgers*	
Hale/Hearty | *Sandwich/Soup*	

LOCATIONS

ChipShop	*British*	18
Chocolate Rm.	*Dessert*	25
Cocotte	*Amer./French*	20
Conviv. Osteria	*Med.*	25
NEW Flatbush Farm	*Amer.*	19
Joe's Pizza	*Pizza*	23
La Taqueria/Rachel	*Mex.*	19
La Villa Pizzeria	*Italian*	21
Lemongrass Grill	*Thai*	17
Little D	*Amer./Eclectic*	20
Long Tan	*Thai*	19
Magnolia	*Amer.*	19
Miracle Grill	*SW*	18
Miriam	*Israeli/Med.*	21
NEW Moim	*Korean*	-
Moutarde	*French*	18
Nana	*Asian Fusion*	21
NEW NoNO	*Cajun/Creole*	19
NEW Palo Santo	*Pan-Latin*	25
Press 195	*Sandwich*	20
Rose Water	*Amer.*	25
Scottadito	*Italian*	19
Sette Enoteca	*Italian*	19
NEW Sheep Sta.	*Australian*	19
Song	*Thai*	24
NEW Spirito	*Italian*	-
Stone Park Café	*Amer.*	24
Sweet Melissa	*Dessert/Sandwich*	21
Tempo	*Med.*	25
12th St. B&G	*Amer.*	21
Two Boots	*Pizza*	18

PROSPECT HEIGHTS

(See map on page 298)

Aliseo Osteria	*Italian*	23
Amorina	*Pizza*	23
Beast	*Med.*	20
NEW Cheryl's	*Soul*	22
Franny's	*Pizza*	23
Z Garden Cafe	*Amer.*	27
Le Gamin	*French*	19
Sorrel	*Amer.*	23
Tom's	*Diner*	19

RED HOOK

(See map on page 298)

Fairway Cafe	*Amer.*	18
Z Good Fork	*Eclectic*	26
Hope & Anchor	*Diner*	18

SHEEPSHEAD BAY

Brennan	*Sandwich*	19
Roll-n-Roaster	*Sandwich*	19

SUNSET PARK

Nyonya	*Malaysian*	22
NEW Pacificana	*Chinese*	24

WILLIAMSBURG

(See map on page 298)

Aurora	*Italian*	
Baci & Abbracci	*Italian*	
Bamonte's	*Italian*	
Bonita	*Mex.*	
NEW Catch 22	*Argent./Italian*	
NEW DeStefano's	*Steak*	
Diner	*Diner*	
Dressler	*Amer.*	
DuMont	*Amer.*	
NEW Fette Sau	*BBQ*	
Fornino	*Pizza*	
NEW Le Barricou	*French*	
Lodge	*Amer.*	
My Moon	*Med.*	
Z Peter Luger	*Steak*	
Planet Thailand	*Jap./Thai*	
NEW PT	*Italian*	
Relish	*Amer.*	
Roebling	*Amer.*	
SEA	*Thai*	
NEW Sense	*Jap.*	
NEW Silent H	*Viet.*	
Sweetwater	*Amer./French*	
NEW Wombat	*Australian*	
NEW Zenkichi	*Jap.*	

Queens

ASTORIA

Agnanti	*Greek*	
Ammos	*Greek*	
NEW Bistro 33	*French/Jap.*	
Brick Cafe	*French/Italian*	
Cafe Bar	*Greek/Med.*	
Z Cávo	*Greek*	
Christos	*Steak*	
Demetris	*Greek*	
Elias Corner	*Greek/Seafood*	
Ethos	*Greek*	
Grand Café	*Eclectic*	
NEW Island	*Med.*	
JJ's Asian Fusion	*Asian Fusion*	
Malagueta	*Brazilian*	
Mezzo Mezzo	*Greek*	
NEW Momento	*Italian*	
Omonia Cafe	*Greek*	
NEW Ovelia	*Greek*	
Piccola Venezia	*Italian*	
Ponticello	*Italian*	
Sac's Place	*Pizza*	
S'Agapo	*Greek*	
718	*French*	
Stamatis	*Greek/Seafood*	
Taverna Kyclades	*Greek/Seafood*	

lly's Taverna	*Greek/Seafood*	22
ai Pavilion	*Thai*	22
erras	*Colombian*	22
Tratt. L'incontro	*Italian*	26
o Chicago	*Pizza*	14

AYSIDE

n's Kosher	*Deli*	17
affé/Green	*Italian*	21
ae Dong	*Korean*	18
awan	*Thai*	22
ckson Hole	*Amer.*	17
utback	*Steak*	14
ess 195	*Sandwich*	20
acle Jack's	*Steak*	23
no Chicago	*Pizza*	14

OLLEGE POINT

EW Five Guys	*Hamburgers*	-

ORONA

reen Field	*Brazilian*	19
o's Latticini	*Deli/Italian*	28
rk Side	*Italian*	24

LMHURST

utback	*Steak*	14
o Bang	*Viet.*	21
ng's Sea.	*Chinese/Seafood*	22

LUSHING

st Buffet	*Eclectic*	20
st Manor	*Chinese*	19
e's Shanghai	*Chinese*	22
m Gang San	*Korean*	21
o Bang	*Viet.*	21
icy & Tasty	*Chinese*	23
veet-n-Tart	*Chinese*	20
mple Canteen	*Indian*	-

OREST HILLS

aluchi's	*Indian*	18
nn Thai	*Thai*	21
abana	*Nuevo Latino*	21
ee's Pizza	*Med./Pizza*	22
ck's	*Pizza*	24
Thai Bistro	*Thai*	21
uge	*French*	20
no Chicago	*Pizza*	14

RESH MEADOWS

ng Yum	*Chinese*	17

LENDALE

sticcio	*Italian*	19
m Stammtisch	*German*	22

OWARD BEACH

Villa Pizzeria	*Italian*	21

Afghan Kebab	*Afghan*	19
Jackson Diner	*Indian*	22
Jackson Hole	*Amer.*	17
Pio Pio	*Peruvian*	23
Tierras	*Colombian*	22

LITTLE NECK

La Baraka	*French*	21

LONG ISLAND CITY

Bella Via	*Italian*	23
Manducatis	*Italian*	22
Manetta's	*Italian*	22
Tournesol	*French*	24
Water's Edge	*Amer./Seafood*	23

OZONE PARK

Don Peppe	*Italian*	25

REGO PARK

Grand Sichuan	*Chinese*	22
London Lennie's	*Seafood*	21
Pio Pio	*Peruvian*	23

SUNNYSIDE

Quaint	*Amer.*	20

WOODSIDE

La Flor Bakery	*Bakery*	24
Sapori D'Ischia	*Italian*	25
⛾ Sripraphai	*Thai*	26

Staten Island

Aesop's Tables	*Amer./Med.*	21
American Grill	*Amer.*	20
Angelina's	*Italian*	23
Bayou	*Cajun*	22
Bocelli	*Italian*	25
Brioso	*Italian*	25
Caffe Bondi	*Italian*	22
Carol's Cafe	*Eclectic*	26
China Chalet	*Chinese*	19
Da Noi	*Italian*	24
Denino's	*Pizza*	25
Fushimi	*Jap.*	26
Joe & Pat's	*Italian/Pizza*	22
Killmeyer Bavarian	*German*	21
Lake Club	*Cont./Seafood*	21
Marina Cafe	*Seafood*	18
Nurnberger Bierhaus	*German*	21
101	*Amer./Italian*	19
Real Madrid	*Spanish*	21
South Fin Grill	*Seafood/Steak*	20
Tratt. Romana	*Italian*	24
Vida	*Eclectic*	20
WaterFalls	*Italian*	20
NEW Zest	*Amer.*	26

LOCATIONS

e at zagat.com — 319

Special Features

Listings cover the best in each category and include names, locations an■
Food ratings. Multi-location restaurants' features may vary by branch.
🗹 indicates places with the highest ratings, popularity and importance.

Jane	**G Vill**	21	
JoJo	**E 60s**	24	
Le Gigot	**G Vill**	24	
Les Halles	**multi.**	20	
L'Express	**Flatiron**	17	
🗹 Mesa Grill	**Flatiron**	24	
Miracle Grill	**multi.**	18	
Miriam	**Park Slope**	21	
Miss Mamie/Maude	**Harlem**	21	
Mon Petit Cafe	**E 60s**	18	
Nice Matin	**W 70s**	20	
Norma's	**W 50s**	25	
Ocean Grill	**W 70s**	23	
Odeon	**TriBeCa**	19	
Olea	**Ft Greene**	20	
One	**Meatpacking**	18	
🗹 Ouest	**W 80s**	25	
Paris Commune	**W Vill**	18	
🗹 Pastis	**Meatpacking**	21	
Patois	**Carroll Gdns**	21	
Penelope	**Murray Hill**	21	
Petrossian	**W 50s**	24	
Pietrasanta	**W 40s**	19	
Pink Tea Cup	**W Vill**	20	
Pipa	**Flatiron**	21	
Popover Cafe	**W 80s**	18	
Prune	**E Vill**	24	
Public	**NoLita**	23	
Punch	**Flatiron**	19	
🗹 Rainbow Room/Grill	**W 40s**	19	
🗹 River Café	**Dumbo**	26	
Riverdale Gdn.	**Bronx**	24	
Rocking Horse Cafe	**Chelsea**	20	
Rose Water	**Park Slope**	25	
Sarabeth's	**multi.**	20	
Schiller's	**LES**	18	
Sette Enoteca	**Park Slope**	19	
718	**Astoria**	21	
Spotted Pig	**W Vill**	22	
Stanton Social	**LES**	23	
Stone Park Café	**Park Slope**	24	
Sylvia's	**Harlem**	19	
Tartine	**W Vill**	22	
Taste	**E 80s**	20	
Thalia	**W 50s**	21	
Tribeca Grill	**TriBeCa**	22	
Turkish Kitchen	**Gramercy**	22	
Wallsé	**W Vill**	26	
Water Club	**Murray Hill**	20	
Zoë	**SoHo**	20	

BUFFET

(Check availability)

🗹 Aquavit	**E 50s**	25
Arabelle	**E 60s**	21
Bay Leaf	**W 50s**	19

Beacon	**W 50s**	22
Bombay Palace	**W 50s**	18
Brasserie 8½	**W 50s**	22
Bukhara Grill	**E 40s**	20
🗹 Carlyle	**E 70s**	21
Charles' Kitchen	**Harlem**	24
Chennai Gdn.	**Gramercy**	21
Chola	**E 50s**	23
Churrascaria	**multi.**	23
City Bakery	**Flatiron**	21
Dakshin Indian	**E 80s**	20
Darbar	**E 40s**	20
Diwan	**E 40s**	21
East Buffet	**Flushing**	20
Green Field	**Corona**	19
Hudson Cafeteria	**W 50s**	19
Jackson Diner	**Jackson Hts**	22
Jewel of India	**W 40s**	20
🗹 Kittichai	**SoHo**	23
La Baraka	**Little Neck**	21
Lake Club	**SI**	21
Mangia	**multi.**	20
Porcão	**Gramercy**	21
🗹 Rainbow Room/Grill	**W 40s**	19
Roy's NY	**Financial**	25
Salaam Bombay	**TriBeCa**	20
Sapphire	**W 60s**	20
South Fin Grill	**SI**	20
Surya	**W Vill**	24
SushiSamba	**W Vill**	22
Todai	**Murray Hill**	18
Turkish Kitchen	**Gramercy**	22
Turkuaz	**W 100s**	19
2 West	**Financial**	21
Utsav	**W 40s**	21
View, The	**W 40s**	18
Water Club	**Murray Hill**	20
Yuva	**E 50s**	24

BYO

Amy Ruth's	**Harlem**	22
Angelica Kit.	**E Vill**	21
NEW Babouche	**Park Slope**	20
Bereket	**LES**	18
NEW Cafe & Wine	**W 100s**	-
NEW Caffe Emilia	**E Vill**	-
Comfort Diner	**E 40s**	16
Cube 63	**LES**	21
🗹 Di Fara	**Midwood**	27
NEW Georgia's/BBQ	**LES**	-
Hummus Place	**G Vill**	23
Ivo & Lulu	**SoHo**	22
NEW Kaijou	**Financial**	-
La Taza de Oro	**Chelsea**	18
NEW Lucali	**Carroll Gdns**	27
Meskerem	**G Vill**	20

vote at zagat.com

Nook | **W 50s**	22
Peking Duck | **Chinatown**	22
Pho Bang | **multi.**	21
Phoenix Gdn. | **E 40s**	24
Ɀ Poke | **E 80s**	26
NEW Silent H | **W'burg**	-
NEW Spice Fusion | **W 40s**	-
NEW Sticky Rice | **LES**	19
Sweet Melissa | **multi.**	21
Ɀ Tanoreen | **Bay Ridge**	27
Tartine | **W Vill**	22
Wondee Siam | **multi.**	22
X.O. | **Chinatown**	18
Zaytoons | **multi.**	22
Zen Palate | **multi.**	19

CELEBRATIONS

Ɀ Aureole | **E 60s**	27
Beacon | **W 50s**	22
BLT Fish | **Flatiron**	23
BLT Prime | **Gramercy**	24
Bond 45 | **W 40s**	20
Ɀ Bouley | **TriBeCa**	28
Ɀ Buddakan | **Chelsea**	23
Ɀ Café des Artistes | **W 60s**	22
Ɀ Café Gray | **W 60s**	25
'Cesca | **W 70s**	23
Ɀ Cru | **G Vill**	26
Ɀ Daniel | **E 60s**	28
FireBird | **W 40s**	18
Ɀ Four Seasons | **E 50s**	25
Fresco | **E 50s**	23
Gallagher's | **W 50s**	20
Ɀ Gotham B&G | **G Vill**	27
Home | **G Vill**	20
Ɀ La Grenouille | **E 50s**	27
Ɀ Le Bernardin | **W 50s**	28
Le Cirque | **E 50s**	23
Lobster Box | **Bronx**	17
Mas | **G Vill**	25
Ɀ Matsuri | **Chelsea**	23
Ɀ Megu | **TriBeCa**	24
Mercer Kitchen | **SoHo**	22
Ɀ Modern, The | **W 50s**	26
Molyvos | **W 50s**	22
Ɀ Nobu 57 | **W 50s**	26
Odeon | **TriBeCa**	19
Olives | **Union Sq**	22
Ɀ One if by Land | **G Vill**	23
Ɀ Ouest | **W 80s**	25
Ɀ Palm | **multi.**	24
Ɀ Peter Luger | **W'burg**	28
Petrossian | **W 50s**	24
NEW Provence | **SoHo**	21
Ɀ Rainbow Room/Grill | **W 40s**	19

Raoul's | **SoHo**	24
Redeye Grill | **W 50s**	20
Ɀ River Café | **Dumbo**	26
River Room | **Harlem**	19
Rock Ctr. | **W 50s**	19
Rolf's | **Gramercy**	17
Ɀ Rosa Mexicano | **multi.**	22
Ruby Foo's | **multi.**	19
San Domenico | **W 50s**	23
Sea Grill | **W 40s**	24
Ɀ Tavern on Green | **W 60s**	15
Terrace in the Sky | **W 100s**	22
Tratt. Dell'Arte | **W 50s**	22
View, The | **W 40s**	18
Water Club | **Murray Hill**	20
Water's Edge | **LIC**	23

CELEBRITY CHEFS

Julieta Ballesteros	
Crema | **Chelsea**	21
Dan Barber	
Ɀ Blue Hill | **G Vill**	26
Lidia Bastianich	
Ɀ Del Posto | **Chelsea**	25
Ɀ Felidia | **E 50s**	25
Mario Batali	
Ɀ Babbo | **G Vill**	27
Casa Mono | **Gramercy**	25
Ɀ Del Posto | **Chelsea**	25
Esca | **W 40s**	25
Ɀ Lupa | **G Vill**	25
Otto | **G Vill**	22
April Bloomfield	
Spotted Pig | **W Vill**	22
Saul Bolton	
Ɀ Saul | **Boerum Hill**	27
David Bouley	
Ɀ Bouley | **TriBeCa**	28
Ɀ Bouley, Upstairs | **TriBeCa**	24
Ɀ Danube | **TriBeCa**	26
Daniel Boulud	
Ɀ Café Boulud | **E 70s**	26
Ɀ Daniel | **E 60s**	28
Ɀ db Bistro Moderne | **W 40s**	24
Anthony Bourdain	
Les Halles | **Gramercy**	20
Antoine Bouterin	
Le Perigord | **E 50s**	24
Jimmy Bradley	
Harrison, The | **TriBeCa**	23
Red Cat | **Chelsea**	24
Terrance Brennan	
Ɀ Artisanal | **Murray Hill**	23
Ɀ Picholine | **W 60s**	26

avid Burke	**Gabrielle Hamilton**
☑ davidburke/dona. | **E 60s** — 25	Prune | **E Vill** — 24
David Burke/Bloom. | **E 50s** — 18	**Peter Hoffman**
NEW Hawaiian Tropic | **W 40s** — 16	Savoy | **SoHo** — 24
arco Canora	**Daniel Humm**
Hearth | **E Vill** — 25	☑ Eleven Madison | **Gramercy** — 26
NEW Insieme | **W 50s** — 26	**Thomas Keller**
oyd Cardoz	Bouchon Bakery | **W 60s** — 23
☑ Tabla | **Gramercy** — 25	☑ Per Se | **W 60s** — 28
ndrew Carmellini	**Gabriel Kreuther**
A Voce | **Gramercy** — 25	☑ Modern, The | **W 50s** — 26
esare Casella	**Gray Kunz**
Maremma | **W Vill** — 21	☑ Café Gray | **W 60s** — 25
ichael Cetrulo	NEW Grayz | **W 50s** — —
Piano Due | **W 50s** — 25	**Anita Lo**
☑ Scalini Fedeli | **TriBeCa** — 26	☑ Annisa | **G Vill** — 27
n Chalermkittichai	Rickshaw Dumpling | **Flatiron** — 18
☑ Kittichai | **SoHo** — 23	**Michael Lomonaco**
avid Chang	Porter House NY | **W 60s** — 22
Momofuku Noodle | **E Vill** — 24	**Pino Luongo**
Momofuku Ssäm | **E Vill** — 24	Centolire | **E 80s** — 20
ebecca Charles	**Waldy Malouf**
☑ Pearl Oyster | **G Vill** — 26	Beacon | **W 50s** — 22
m Colicchio	Waldy's Pizza | **Chelsea** — 21
☑ Craft | **Flatiron** — 25	**Zarela Martinez**
Craftbar | **Flatiron** — 22	Zarela | **E 50s** — 21
Craftsteak | **Chelsea** — 22	**Sam Mason**
'wichcraft | **multi.** — 20	NEW Tailor | **SoHo** — —
sh DeChellis	**Nobu Matsuhisa**
NEW BarFry | **G Vill** — —	☑ Nobu | **TriBeCa** — 27
arold Dieterle	☑ Nobu 57 | **W 50s** — 26
NEW Perilla | **G Vill** — —	**Henry Meer**
ylie Dufresne	City Hall | **TriBeCa** — 21
wd-50 | **LES** — 23	**Marco Moreira**
dd English	NEW 15 East | **Union Sq** — 26
Olives | **Union Sq** — 22	☑ Tocqueville | **Union Sq** — 26
dette Fada	**Masaharu Morimoto**
San Domenico | **W 50s** — 23	☑ Morimoto | **Chelsea** — 24
ndro Fioriti	**Marc Murphy**
NEW Sandro's | **E 80s** — —	Ditch Plains | **G Vill** — 17
bby Flay	Landmarc | **multi.** — 23
☑ Bar Americain | **W 50s** — 23	**Tadashi Ono**
Bolo | **Flatiron** — 24	☑ Matsuri | **Chelsea** — 23
☑ Mesa Grill | **Flatiron** — 24	**Charlie Palmer**
ea Gallante	☑ Aureole | **E 60s** — 27
☑ Cru | **G Vill** — 26	Metrazur | **E 40s** — 20
ex Garcia	**David Pasternack**
Calle Ocho | **W 80s** — 22	Esca | **W 40s** — 25
NEW Catch 22 | **W'burg** — —	**François Payard**
NEW Gaucho | **W 50s** — —	Payard Bistro | **E 70s** — 24
rt Gutenbrunner	**Zak Pelaccio**
Blaue Gans | **TriBeCa** — 20	NEW Borough Food | **Flatiron** — —
Café Sabarsky | **E 80s** — 22	Fatty Crab | **W Vill** — 21
Wallsé | **W Vill** — 26	

Don Pintabona
Dani | **SoHo** _20_

Alfred Portale
🄩 Gotham B&G | **G Vill** _27_

Michael Psilakis
NEW Anthos | **W 50s** _25_
NEW Kefi | **W 70s** _23_

Gordon Ramsay
NEW 🄩 Gordon Ramsay | **W 50s** _25_
NEW Maze | **W 50s** _23_

Mary Redding
Brooklyn Fish | **Park Slope** _23_
Mary's Fish Camp | **W Vill** _25_

Cyril Renaud
Fleur de Sel | **Flatiron** _25_

Eric Ripert
🄩 Le Bernardin | **W 50s** _28_

Joël Robuchon
🄩 L'Atelier/Robuchon | **E 50s** _27_

Michael Romano
🄩 Union Sq. Cafe | **Union Sq** _26_

Marcus Samuelsson
🄩 Aquavit | **E 50s** _25_

Aarón Sanchez
Centrico | **TriBeCa** _20_
Paladar | **LES** _18_

Mark Strausman
Coco Pazzo | **E 70s** _22_

Noriyuki Sugie
🄩 Asiate | **W 60s** _24_

Gari Sugio
🄩 Gari/Sushi | **multi.** _26_

Nao Sugiyama
🄩 Sugiyama | **W 50s** _27_

Masayoshi Takayama
🄩 Masa/Bar Masa | **W 60s** _27_

Bill Telepan
🄩 Telepan | **W 60s** _25_

Sue Torres
NEW Los Dados | **Meatpacking** _–_
Sueños | **Chelsea** _23_

Laurent Tourondel
NEW BLT Burger | **G Vill** _19_
BLT Fish | **Flatiron** _23_
NEW BLT Market | **W 50s** _–_
BLT Prime | **Gramercy** _24_
BLT Steak | **E 50s** _24_
Brass. Ruhlmann | **W 50s** _17_

Alex Ureña
NEW Pamplona | **Gramercy** _–_

Tom Valenti
🄩 Ouest | **W 80s** _25_

Jean-Georges Vongerichten
🄩 Jean Georges | **W 60s** _28_

JoJo | **E 60s**
Mercer Kitchen | **SoHo**
Perry St. | **W Vill**
🄩 Spice Market | **Meatpacking**
Vong | **E 50s**

Yuji Wakiya
NEW 🄩 Wakiya | **Gramercy**

David Waltuck
🄩 Chanterelle | **TriBeCa**

David Walzog
Strip House | **G Vill**

Jonathan Waxman
Barbuto | **W Vill**

Michael White
🄩 Alto | **E 50s**
🄩 L'Impero | **E 40s**

Jody Williams
NEW Morandi | **G Vill**

Roy Yamaguchi
Roy's NY | **Financial**

Naomichi Yasuda
🄩 Sushi Yasuda | **E 40s**

Orhan Yegen
NEW Sea Salt | **E Vill**
Sip Sak | **E 40s**

Patricia Yeo
Monkey Bar | **E 50s**

Geoffrey Zakarian
Country | **Gramercy**
Town | **W 50s**

Galen Zamarra
Mas | **G Vill**

CHEESE TRAYS

🄩 Artisanal | **Murray Hill**
🄩 Babbo | **G Vill**
🄩 Café Gray | **W 60s**
🄩 Chanterelle | **TriBeCa**
🄩 Craft | **Flatiron**
🄩 Daniel | **E 60s**
🄩 Eleven Madison | **Gramercy**
NEW 🄩 Gordon Ramsay | **W 50s**
🄩 Gramercy Tavern | **Flatiron**
'inoteca | **LES**
🄩 Jean Georges | **W 60s**
🄩 La Grenouille | **E 50s**
🄩 Modern, The | **W 50s**
Morrell Wine Bar | **W 40s**
Otto | **G Vill**
🄩 Per Se | **W 60s**
🄩 Picholine | **W 60s**

CHEF'S TABLE

Abigael's | **Garment**
🄩 Aquavit | **E 50s**

Bao 111	**E Vill**	21	London Lennie's*	**Rego Pk**	21
Barbuto	**W Vill**	22	Miss Mamie/Maude	**Harlem**	21
Brasserie Julien	**E 80s**	19	Nick's	**multi.**	24
Ⓩ Café Gray	**W 60s**	25	Ninja	**TriBeCa**	19
Country	**Gramercy**	23	Peanut Butter Co.	**G Vill**	20
Ⓩ Daniel	**E 60s**	28	Pig Heaven	**E 80s**	19
NEW Ⓩ Gordon Ramsay	**W 50s**	25	Rack & Soul*	**W 100s**	20
NEW House	**Gramercy**	22	Rock Ctr.*	**W 50s**	19
Il Buco	**NoHo**	25	Rossini's	**Murray Hill**	23
Maloney & Porcelli	**E 50s**	22	Sammy's Roum.	**LES**	19
Ⓩ Megu	**TriBeCa**	24	Sarabeth's	**multi.**	20
NEW Mercat	**NoHo**	–	Savoia	**Carroll Gdns**	21
Olives	**Union Sq**	22	Shake Shack	**Flatiron**	23
NEW Palo Santo	**Park Slope**	25	Soda Shop	**TriBeCa**	19
NEW Park Avenue	**E 60s**	–	NEW Spotlight Live	**W 40s**	–
Patroon	**E 40s**	21	Sylvia's*	**Harlem**	19
Remi	**W 50s**	22	Ⓩ Tavern on Green*	**W 60s**	15
NEW Resto	**Gramercy**	–	Tony's Di Napoli	**multi.**	18
Smith & Wollensky	**E 40s**	23	Two Boots*	**multi.**	18
Turks & Frogs	**TriBeCa**	20	View, The*	**W 40s**	18
Valbella	**Meatpacking**	24	Virgil's Real BBQ*	**W 40s**	20
Yuva	**E 50s**	24	Whole Foods	**multi.**	19
Zoë	**SoHo**	20	Zum Stammtisch*	**Glendale**	22

CHILD-FRIENDLY

(See also Theme Restaurants;
* children's menu available)

Alice's Tea Cup*	**W 70s**	19
American Girl	**E 40s**	13
Amy Ruth's*	**Harlem**	22
Annie's	**E 70s**	18
Antica Venezia	**W Vill**	23
Artie's Deli*	**W 80s**	18
Barking Dog*	**multi.**	15
Beso	**Park Slope**	19
Blue Smoke*	**Gramercy**	22
Boathouse*	**E 70s**	16
Brennan	**Sheepshead**	19
Bubby's*	**multi.**	18
Cafe Un Deux	**W 40s**	16
Ⓩ Carmine's	**W 40s**	19
Chat 'n Chew*	**Union Sq**	16
Columbus Bakery	**W 80s**	18
Comfort Diner*	**multi.**	16
Cowgirl*	**W Vill**	16
Dallas BBQ*	**multi.**	15
Da Nico*	**L Italy**	21
EJ's Luncheonette*	**multi.**	15
ESPN Zone*	**W 40s**	12
Friend of a Farmer*	**Gramercy**	17
Gargiulo's	**Coney Is**	21
Good Enough/Eat*	**W 80s**	20
Hard Rock Cafe*	**W 40s**	13
Jackson Hole*	**multi.**	17
Junior's*	**multi.**	18
L & B Spumoni*	**Bensonhurst**	22

COMMUTER OASES

Grand Central

Ammos	**E 40s**	22
Bobby Van's	**E 40s**	22
Brother Jimmy's	**E 40s**	16
Burger Heaven	**E 40s**	16
Cafe Centro	**E 40s**	20
Cafe Spice	**E 40s**	18
Capital Grille	**E 40s**	23
Cipriani Dolci	**E 40s**	18
Dishes	**E 40s**	22
Django	**E 40s**	20
Docks Oyster	**E 40s**	19
Hale/Hearty	**E 40s**	19
Hatsuhana	**E 40s**	24
Junior's	**E 40s**	18
Menchanko-tei	**E 40s**	20
Metrazur	**E 40s**	20
Michael Jordan's	**E 40s**	20
Morton's	**E 40s**	24
Nanni	**E 40s**	24
Oyster Bar	**E 40s**	21
Patroon	**E 40s**	21
Pepe	**E 40s**	21
Pershing Sq.	**E 40s**	15
NEW Public House	**E 40s**	–
Ⓩ Sushi Yasuda	**E 40s**	28
Two Boots	**E 40s**	18
Zócalo	**E 40s**	20

Penn Station

Chipotle	**Garment**	18
Gray's Papaya	**Garment**	20

SPECIAL FEATURES

Nick & Stef's | **Garment** 22
Uncle Jack's | **Garment** 23
Port Authority
  Angus McIndoe | **W 40s** 16
  Better Burger | **W 40s** 15
  Chez Josephine | **W 40s** 20
  Chimichurri Grill | **W 40s** 21
  Dallas BBQ | **W 40s** 15
  Don Giovanni | **W 40s** 17
  Esca | **W 40s** 25
  ESPN Zone | **W 40s** 12
  etc. etc. | **W 40s** 20
  HK | **Garment** 16
  John's Pizzeria | **W 40s** 22
  Le Madeleine | **W 40s** 20
  Marseille | **W 40s** 20
  NEW Metro Marché | **W 40s** 19
  Rachel's American | **W 40s** 17
  Shula's | **W 40s** 20
  West Bank Cafe | **W 40s** 20

COOL LOOS

Bette | **Chelsea** 19
Brasserie | **E 50s** 20
Butter | **E Vill** 19
Z Compass | **W 70s** 22
ESPN Zone | **W 40s** 12
NEW Z Gordon Ramsay | **W 50s** 25
NEW Kobe Club | **W 50s** 20
Z Matsuri | **Chelsea** 23
Z Megu | **TriBeCa** 24
Z Modern, The | **W 50s** 26
Z Morimoto | **Chelsea** 24
Ono | **Meatpacking** 21
Paradou | **Meatpacking** 19
Z Pastis | **Meatpacking** 21
Peep | **SoHo** 19
P.J. Clarke's | **multi.** 17
Prem-on Thai | **G Vill** 21
Sapa | **Flatiron** 22
Schiller's | **LES** 18
SEA | **W'burg** 20
Z Tao | **E 50s** 23
Vynl | **multi.** 17
wd-50 | **LES** 23

CRITIC-PROOF

(Gets lots of business despite so-so food)

Algonquin | **W 40s** 16
Angus McIndoe | **W 40s** 16
Barking Dog | **multi.** 15
Better Burger | **multi.** 15
Boathouse | **E 70s** 16
Brother Jimmy's | **multi.** 16
Bubba Gump | **W 40s** 14

Burger Heaven | **multi.** 16
Burritoville | **multi.** 16
Cafe Un Deux | **W 40s** 16
Chat 'n Chew | **Union Sq** 16
China Fun | **multi.** 16
Coffee Shop | **Union Sq** 15
Comfort Diner | **multi.** 16
Così | **multi.** 16
Cowgirl | **W Vill** 16
Dallas BBQ | **multi.** 15
Duke's | **multi.** 16
East of 8th | **Chelsea** 16
Edison | **W 40s** 15
EJ's Luncheonette | **multi.** 15
Elaine's | **E 80s** 13
elmo | **Chelsea** 15
Empire Diner | **Chelsea** 15
Empire Szechuan | **multi.** 15
ESPN Zone | **W 40s** 12
Fraunces Tavern | **Financial** 15
French Roast | **multi.** 14
Hard Rock Cafe | **W 40s** 13
Heartland | **multi.** 14
Kelley/Ping | **multi.** 16
Lili's Noodle | **multi.** 16
Mary Ann's | **multi.** 15
Ollie's | **multi.** 16
Outback | **multi.** 14
Park, The | **Chelsea** 15
Pershing Sq. | **E 40s** 15
Pete's Tavern | **Gramercy** 14
Sardi's | **W 40s** 16
Z Tavern on Green | **W 60s** 15
Tratt. Dopo | **W 40s** 16
212 | **E 60s** 16
Uno Chicago | **multi.** 14
Viand | **multi.** 16

DANCING

Z Cávo | **Astoria** 21
Z Rainbow Room | **W 40s** 19
River Room | **Harlem** 19
Z Tavern on Green | **W 60s** 15

ENTERTAINMENT

(Call for days and times of performances)

Alfama | fado | **W Vill** 22
Algonquin | cabaret | **W 40s** 16
Blue Fin | jazz | **W 40s** 22
Blue Smoke | jazz | **Gramercy** 22
Z Blue Water | jazz | **Union Sq** 23
Café Pierre | piano/vocals | **E 60s** 23
Chez Josephine | piano | **W 40s** 20
Cornelia St. Cafe | varies | **G Vill** 19
Delta Grill | varies | **W 40s** 19

ireBird | harp/piano | **W 40s** 18
lor de Sol | flamenco | **TriBeCa** 20
deya | jazz | **SoHo** 20
ules | varies | **E Vill** 19
Knickerbocker | jazz | **G Vill** 20
a Lanterna | jazz | **G Vill** 20
a Lunchonette | accordion/vocals | **Chelsea** 22
ondel's | varies | **Harlem** 22
Rainbow Room | orchestra | **W 40s** 19
River Café | piano | **Dumbo** 26
on Cubano | Cuban/DJs | **Meatpacking** 21
ylvia's | varies | **Harlem** 19
Tavern on Green | varies | **W 60s** 15
ommaso | varies | **Dyker Hts** 23
Valker's | jazz | **TriBeCa** 17

FIREPLACES

adä | **E 50s** 23
Agave | **W Vill** 18
Alta | **G Vill** 23
pplewood | **Park Slope** 25
Aspen | **Flatiron** 20
NEW Benjamin Steak | **E 40s** 23
eppe | **Flatiron** 23
istro Ten 18 | **W 100s** 20
lack Duck | **Gramercy** 20
ruckner B&G | **Bronx** 21
Caffé/Green | **Bayside** 21
NEW Catch 22 | **W'burg** –
ebu | **Bay Ridge** 21
Cornelia St. Cafe | **G Vill** 19
Cucina di Pesce | **E Vill** 17
Danal | **E Vill** 22
Dee's Pizza | **Forest Hills** 22
Delta Grill | **W 40s** 19
evin Tavern | **TriBeCa** 18
mployees Only | **W Vill** 18
7 | **E 50s** 22
ireBird | **W 40s** 18
NEW Fireside | **E 50s** 21
rankie/Johnnie | **Garment** 21
raunces Tavern | **Financial** 15
riend of a Farmer | **Gramercy** 17
ieisha | **E 60s** 23
iorgione | **SoHo** 22
NEW Grayz | **W 50s** –
Greenhouse Café | **Bay Ridge** 19
Hacienda/Argentina | **E 70s** 21
NEW House | **Gramercy** 22
ci | **Ft Greene** 22
Trulli | **Gramercy** 22
eens | **Garment** 24

Kelley/Ping | **E Vill** 16
Lady Mendl's | **Gramercy** 22
Z La Grenouille | **E 50s** 27
Lake Club | **SI** 21
La Lanterna | **G Vill** 20
Landmark Tavern | **W 40s** 18
La Ripaille | **W Vill** 23
Lattanzi | **W 40s** 22
Le Refuge Inn | **Bronx** 24
Lobster Box | **Bronx** 17
Lumi | **E 70s** 19
Manducatis | **LIC** 22
Manetta's | **LIC** 22
Marco Polo | **Carroll Gdns** 20
Mezzo Mezzo | **Astoria** 18
Moran's | **Chelsea** 18
Notaro | **Murray Hill** 20
Nurnberger Bierhaus | **SI** 21
Z One if by Land | **G Vill** 23
NEW Ovelia | **Astoria** 21
Paola's | **E 80s** 23
Park, The | **Chelsea** 15
Patois | **Carroll Gdns** 21
Pearl Room | **Bay Ridge** 23
Z Per Se | **W 60s** 28
Piccola Venezia | **Astoria** 25
Portofino Grille | **E 60s** 19
Public | **NoLita** 23
Quality Meats | **W 50s** 24
René Pujol | **W 50s** 22
Riverdale Gdn. | **Bronx** 24
Savoy | **SoHo** 24
Serafina | **NoHo** 18
Shaffer City | **Flatiron** 21
NEW Sheep Sta. | **Park Slope** 19
NEW STK | **Meatpacking** 20
Z Telepan | **W 60s** 25
Telly's Taverna | **Astoria** 22
Terrace in the Sky | **W 100s** 22
Tiramisu | **E 80s** 20
Tosca Café | **Bronx** 21
Triomphe | **W 40s** 24
Z 21 Club | **W 50s** 22
Uncle Jack's | **Garment** 23
Vivolo | **E 70s** 20
Water Club | **Murray Hill** 20
Water's Edge | **LIC** 23
NEW Z Waverly Inn | **W Vill** 18
wd-50 | **LES** 23
NEW Zoë Townhouse | **E 60s** –

GRACIOUS HOSTS

Angelina's | *Angelina Malerba* | **SI** 23
Angus McIndoe | *Angus McIndoe* | **W 40s** 16

SPECIAL FEATURES

NEW Anthos | *Donatella Arpaia* | **W 50s**	25
Barbetta | *Laura Maioglio* | **W 40s**	20
☑ Blue Hill | *Franco Serafin* | **G Vill**	26
Bricco | *Nino Cituogno* | **W 50s**	19
☑ Chanterelle | *Karen Waltuck* | **TriBeCa**	27
Chez Josephine | *Jean-Claude Baker* | **W 40s**	20
Chin Chin | *James Chin* | **E 40s**	22
☑ Danube | *Walter Kranjc* | **TriBeCa**	26
☑ davidburke/dona. | *Donatella Arpaia* | **E 60s**	25
Degustation | *Grace & Jack Lamb* | **E Vill**	26
Deux Amis | *Bucky Yahiaoui* | **E 50s**	19
Due | *Ernesto Cavalli* | **E 70s**	22
Eliá | *Christina & Pete Lekkas* | **Bay Ridge**	25
☑ Four Seasons | *Julian Niccolini, Alex von Bidder* | **E 50s**	25
Fresco | *Marion Scotto* | **E 50s**	23
☑ Garden Cafe | *Camille Policastro* | **Prospect Hts**	27
☑ Jean Georges | *P. Vongerichten* | **W 60s**	28
Jewel Bako | *Grace & Jack Lamb* | **E Vill**	25
Kitchen Club | *Marja Samsom* | **NoLita**	22
La Baraka | *Lucette Sonigo* | **Little Neck**	21
☑ La Grenouille | *Charles Masson* | **E 50s**	27
La Mirabelle | *Annick Le Douaron* | **W 80s**	22
Le Cirque | *Sirio Maccioni* | **E 50s**	23
Le Perigord | *Georges Briguet* | **E 50s**	24
Le Zie 2000 | *Claudio Bonotto* | **Chelsea**	21
Loulou | *Christine & William Snell* | **Ft Greene**	22
Luca | *Luca Marcato* | **E 80s**	20
Neary's | *Jimmy Neary* | **E 50s**	15
Nino's | *Nino Selimaj* | **E 70s**	21
Paola's | *Paola Marracino* | **E 80s**	23
Piccolo Angolo | *R. Migliorini* | **W Vill**	25
Pig Heaven | *Nancy Lee* | **E 80s**	19
Primavera | *Nicola Civetta* | **E 80s**	22
☑ Rao's | *Frank Pellegrino* | **Harlem**	22
San Domenico | *Tony May* | **W 50s**	23

San Pietro | *Gerardo Bruno* | **E 50s**	24
Shaffer City | *Jay Shaffer* | **Flatiron**	21
Sistina | *Giuseppe Bruno* | **E 80s**	24
Spigolo | *Heather Fratangelo* | **E 80s**	25
Tamarind | *Avtar & Gary Walia* | **Flatiron**	25
Tasting Rm. | *Renée Alevras* | **E Vill**	22
☑ Tocqueville | *Jo-Ann Makovitzky* | **Union Sq**	26
Tommaso | *Thomas Verdillo* | **Dyker Hts**	23
☑ Tratt. L'incontro | *Rocco Sacramone* | **Astoria**	26
Tratt. Romana | *V. Asoli, A. Lobianco* | **SI**	24
Turquoise | *Sam Marelli* | **E 80s**	22

HISTORIC PLACES

(Year opened; * building)

1762 | Fraunces Tavern | **Financial**	15
1794 | Bridge Cafe* | **Financial**	22
1853 | Morgan* | **Murray Hill**	20
1864 | Pete's Tavern | **Gramercy**	14
1868 | Landmark Tavern* | **W 40s**	18
1868 | Old Homestead | **Meatpacking**	23
1875 | Harry's* | **Financial**	22
1880 | Veniero's* | **E Vill**	23
1884 | P.J. Clarke's | **E 50s**	17
1885 | Keens | **Garment**	24
1887 | Peter Luger | **W'burg**	28
1888 | Katz's Deli | **LES**	23
1890 | Walker's* | **TriBeCa**	17
1892 | Ferrara | **L Italy**	22
1896 | Rao's | **Harlem**	22
1900 | Bamonte's | **W'burg**	23
1902 | Algonquin | **W 40s**	16
1902 | Angelo's/Mulberry | **L Italy**	23
1904 | Sal Anthony's* | **E Vill**	19
1904 | Trinity Place* | **Financial**	18
1904 | Vincent's | **L Italy**	21
1907 | Gargiulo's* | **Coney Is**	21
1908 | Barney Greengrass | **W 80s**	23
1908 | John's/12th St. | **E Vill**	19
1910 | Wolfgang's* | **Murray Hill**	25
1913 | Oyster Bar* | **E 40s**	21
1917 | Café des Artistes | **W 60s**	22
1919 | Mario's | **Bronx**	22
1920 | Leo's Latticini | **Corona**	28
1920 | Waverly Inn* | **W Vill**	18
1921 | Sardi's | **W 40s**	16
1922 | Rocco | **G Vill**	20
1922 | Tosca Café | **Bronx**	21

1924 | Totonno Pizza | **Coney Is**	22
1925 | El Charro Español | **G Vill**	22
1926 | Frankie/Johnnie | **W 40s**	21
1926 | Palm | **E 40s**	24
1927 | Diner* | **W'burg**	22
1927 | El Faro | **W Vill**	23
1927 | Gallagher's | **W 50s**	20
1929 | Empire Diner* | **Chelsea**	15
1929 | John's Pizzeria | **G Vill**	22
1929 | Russian Tea* | **W 50s**	19
1929 | 21 Club | **W 50s**	22
1930 | Carlyle | **E 70s**	21
1930 | El Quijote | **Chelsea**	19
1931 | Café Pierre | **E 60s**	23
1932 | Pietro's | **E 40s**	23
1933 | Patsy's Pizzeria | **Harlem**	20
1934 | Papaya King | **E 80s**	20
1934 | Rainbow Room/Grill | **W 40s**	19
1936 | Monkey Bar* | **E 50s**	–
1936 | Tom's | **Prospect Hts**	19
1937 | Carnegie Deli | **W 50s**	21
1937 | Denino's | **SI**	25
1937 | Le Veau d'Or | **E 60s**	17
1937 | Minetta Tavern | **G Vill**	18
1937 | Stage Deli | **W 50s**	20
1938 | Brennan | **Sheepshead**	19
1938 | Heidelberg | **E 80s**	17
1938 | Wo Hop | **Chinatown**	21
1939 | L & B Spumoni | **Bensonhurst**	22
1941 | Sevilla | **W Vill**	23
1944 | Patsy's | **W 50s**	21
1945 | Gino | **E 60s**	21
1945 | V&T | **W 100s**	18
1946 | Lobster Box | **Bronx**	17
1950 | Junior's | **Downtown Bklyn**	18
1952 | Lever House* | **E 50s**	22
1953 | King Yum | **Fresh Meadows**	17
1953 | Liebman's | **Bronx**	19
1954 | Pink Tea Cup | **W Vill**	20
1954 | Serendipity 3 | **E 60s**	18
1954 | Veselka | **E Vill**	18
1957 | Arturo's Pizzeria | **G Vill**	21
1957 | Giambelli | **E 50s**	21
1957 | La Taza de Oro | **Chelsea**	18
1957 | Moran's | **Chelsea**	18

HOTEL DINING

Affinia Dumont	
Barking Dog | **Murray Hill**	15
Alex Hotel	
Riingo | **E 40s**	19

Algonquin Hotel	
Algonquin | **W 40s**	16
Amsterdam Court Hotel	
NEW Natsumi | **W 50s**	–
Blakely Hotel	
Abboccato | **W 50s**	22
Bowery Hotel	
NEW Gemma | **E Vill**	–
Bryant Park Hotel	
Koi | **W 40s**	23
Carlton Hotel	
Country | **Gramercy**	23
Carlyle Hotel	
Z Carlyle | **E 70s**	21
Chambers Hotel	
Town | **W 50s**	24
City Club Hotel	
Z db Bistro Moderne | **W 40s**	25
Club Quarters Hotel	
Bull Run | **Financial**	18
Cosmopolitan Hotel	
Soda Shop | **TriBeCa**	19
Dream Hotel	
Serafina | **W 50s**	18
Edison Hotel	
Edison | **W 40s**	15
Elysée Hotel	
Monkey Bar | **E 50s**	–
Embassy Suites	
Lili's Noodle | **Financial**	16
Flatotel	
Moda | **W 50s**	–
Four Seasons Hotel	
57 | **E 50s**	22
Z L'Atelier/Robuchon | **E 50s**	27
Gansevoort Hotel	
Ono | **Meatpacking**	21
Gramercy Park Hotel	
NEW Z Wakiya | **Gramercy**	–
Helmsley Middletowne	
Diwan | **E 40s**	21
Hilton Garden Inn Times Sq.	
Pigalle | **W 40s**	18
Hotel on Rivington	
Thor | **LES**	18
Hudson Hotel	
Hudson Cafeteria | **W 50s**	19
Inn at Irving Pl.	
Lady Mendl's | **Gramercy**	22
Iroquois Hotel	
Triomphe | **W 40s**	24
Le Parker Meridien	
burger joint | **W 50s**	24
Norma's | **W 50s**	25

Le Refuge Inn
  Le Refuge Inn | **Bronx**   24
London NYC
  NEW Z Gordon Ramsay | 25
  W 50s
  NEW Maze | **W 50s**   23
Lowell Hotel
  Post House | **E 60s**   23
Mandarin Oriental Hotel
  Z Asiate | **W 60s**   24
Maritime Hotel
  La Bottega | **Chelsea**   18
  Z Matsuri | **Chelsea**   23
Marriott Financial Ctr.
  Roy's NY | **Financial**   25
Marriott Marquis Hotel
  View, The | **W 40s**   18
Mercer Hotel
  Mercer Kitchen | **SoHo**   22
Michelangelo Hotel
  NEW Insieme | **W 50s**   26
Morgans Hotel
  Z Asia de Cuba | **Murray Hill**   23
Muse Hotel
  District | **W 40s**   20
NY Palace Hotel
  Gilt | **E 50s**   25
Omni Berkshire Place Hotel
  NEW Fireside | **E 50s**   21
Park South Hotel
  Black Duck | **Gramercy**   20
Pierre Hotel
  Café Pierre | **E 60s**   23
Plaza Athénée Hotel
  Arabelle | **E 60s**   21
Pod Hotel
  Montparnasse | **E 50s**   19
Regency Hotel
  Regency | **E 60s**   18
Ritz-Carlton
  NEW BLT Market | **W 50s**   –
Ritz-Carlton Battery Park
  2 West | **Financial**   21
San Carlos Hotel
  Mint | **E 50s**   19
Shelburne Murray Hill Hotel
  Rare B&G | **Murray Hill**   21
Sherry Netherland
  Harry Cipriani | **E 50s**   –
60 Thompson
  Z Kittichai | **SoHo**   23
Surrey Hotel
  Z Café Boulud | **E 70s**   27
Trump Int'l Hotel
  Z Jean Georges | **W 60s**   28

Waldorf-Astoria
  Bull & Bear | **E 40s**   19
  Inagiku | **E 40s**   23
Washington Square Hotel
  North Sq. | **G Vill**   22
Westin NY Times Sq.
  Shula's | **W 40s**   20
W Times Sq.
  Blue Fin | **W 40s**   22
W Union Sq.
  Olives | **Union Sq**   22

JACKET REQUIRED

(* Tie also required)
Café Pierre | **E 60s**   23
Z Carlyle | **E 70s**   21
Z Daniel | **E 60s**   28
Z Four Seasons | **E 50s**   25
NEW Z Gordon Ramsay | 25
  W 50s
Z Jean Georges | **W 60s**   28
Z La Grenouille | **E 50s**   27
Z Le Bernardin | **W 50s**   28
Le Cirque | **E 50s**   23
Z Modern, The | **W 50s**   26
Z Per Se | **W 60s**   28
Z Rainbow Room/Grill | **W 40s**   19
Z River Café | **Dumbo**   26
San Domenico | **W 50s**   23
Z 21 Club* | **W 50s**   22

JURY DUTY

(Near Foley Sq.)
Acappella | **TriBeCa**   23
Arqua | **TriBeCa**   22
Big Wong | **Chinatown**   22
Blaue Gans | **TriBeCa**   20
Z Bouley | **TriBeCa**   28
Z Bouley, Upstairs | **TriBeCa**   26
Bread | **TriBeCa**   19
Carl's Steaks | **TriBeCa**   22
Centrico | **TriBeCa**   21
City Hall | **TriBeCa**   21
Dim Sum Go Go | **Chinatown**   20
Doyers Viet. | **Chinatown**   20
Duane Park | **TriBeCa**   24
Ecco | **TriBeCa**   21
Excellent Dumpling | **Chinatown**   21
fresh | **TriBeCa**   24
Fuleen | **Chinatown**   24
Golden Unicorn | **Chinatown**   20
Goodies | **Chinatown**   20
Great NY Noodle | **Chinatown**   22
HSF | **Chinatown**   20
Jing Fong | **Chinatown**   19
Mandarin Court | **Chinatown**   20
Mary Ann's | **TriBeCa**   15

Nam | **TriBeCa**	22
New Bo-Ky | **Chinatown**	22
New Green Bo | **Chinatown**	22
Nha Trang | **Chinatown**	21
Odeon | **TriBeCa**	19
Oriental Gdn. | **Chinatown**	24
Peking Duck | **Chinatown**	22
Petite Abeille | **TriBeCa**	19
Pho Pasteur | **Chinatown**	21
Pho Viet Huong | **Chinatown**	23
Ping's Sea. | **Chinatown**	22
Pongsri Thai | **Chinatown**	20
Shanghai Cuisine | **Chinatown**	21
Soda Shop | **TriBeCa**	19
Takahachi | **TriBeCa**	24
Wo Hop | **Chinatown**	21

LATE DINING

(Besides most diners and delis;
weekday closing hour)

Agave | 1 AM | **W Vill**	18
Arturo's Pizzeria | 1 AM | **G Vill**	21
☑ Balthazar | 1 AM | **SoHo**	23
Bao 111 | 2 AM | **E Vill**	21
Baraonda | 2 AM | **E 70s**	18
NEW Bar Martignetti | 2 AM | **L Italy**	18
Bereket | 24 hrs. | **LES**	18
Bette | 1 AM | **Chelsea**	19
Big Nick's Burger | varies | **W 70s**	17
Blue 9 Burger | varies | **E Vill**	18
☑ Blue Ribbon | varies | **multi.**	25
☑ Blue Ribbon Sushi | varies | **SoHo**	25
NEW Borough Food | 2 AM | **Flatiron**	–
Brennan | 1 AM | **Sheepshead**	19
Cafe Lalo | 2 AM | **W 80s**	19
Cafe Mogador | 1 AM | **E Vill**	21
Cafeteria | 24 hrs. | **Chelsea**	18
☑ Carnegie Deli | 3:30 AM | **W 50s**	21
☑ Cávo | 2 AM | **Astoria**	21
Cebu | 3 AM | **Bay Ridge**	21
NEW Centro Vinoteca | 2 AM | **W Vill**	–
Chez Josephine | 1 AM | **W 40s**	20
Chickpea | varies | **E Vill**	19
Coffee Shop | varies | **Union Sq**	15
Congee | varies | **multi.**	21
Corner Bistro | 3:30 AM | **W Vill**	22
Così | 1 AM | **G Vill**	16
Cozy | 24 hrs. | **G Vill**	18
Demetris | 1 AM | **Astoria**	21
Ditch Plains | 2 AM | **G Vill**	17
DuMont | 2 AM | **W'burg**	23
Edgar's Cafe | 1 AM | **W 80s**	18

Edward's | 1 AM | **TriBeCa**	16
Elaine's | 2 AM | **E 80s**	13
El Malecon | varies | **Wash. Hts**	21
El Paso Taqueria | 1 AM | **multi.**	22
Empire Diner | 24 hrs. | **Chelsea**	15
Empire Szechuan | varies | **multi.**	15
Employees Only | 3:30 AM | **W Vill**	18
Florent | 24 hrs. | **Meatpacking**	20
Frank | 1 AM | **E Vill**	24
French Roast | 24 hrs. | **multi.**	14
Fuleen | 3 AM | **Chinatown**	24
Gahm Mi Oak | 24 hrs. | **Garment**	22
NEW Gold St. | 24 hrs. | **Financial**	15
Grand Café | 1 AM | **Astoria**	17
Gray's Papaya | 24 hrs. | **multi.**	20
Great NY Noodle | 4 AM | **Chinatown**	22
Grotta Azzurra | 1 AM | **L Italy**	18
NEW Hawaiian Tropic | 1 AM | **W 40s**	16
HK | 1 AM | **Garment**	16
NEW House | 3 AM | **Gramercy**	22
NEW Inn LW12 | 3 AM | **Meatpacking**	19
'ino | 2 AM | **G Vill**	24
'inoteca | 3 AM | **LES**	23
NEW Isabella's Oven | 1 AM | **LES**	–
Jackson Hole | varies | **multi.**	17
J.G. Melon | 2:30 AM | **E 70s**	21
Joe's Pizza | 5 AM | **G Vill**	23
NEW Johnny Utah | 2 AM | **W 50s**	–
Kang Suh | 24 hrs. | **Garment**	20
Kati Roll Co. | varies | **G Vill**	20
Knickerbocker | 1 AM | **G Vill**	20
Kum Gang San | 24 hrs. | **multi.**	21
La Esquina | 2 AM | **L Italy**	21
La Lanterna | 3 AM | **G Vill**	20
La Mela | 2 AM | **L Italy**	18
Lan | 1 AM | **E Vill**	25
Landmarc | 2 AM | **multi.**	23
L'Express | 24 hrs. | **Flatiron**	17
Lil' Frankie Pizza | 2 AM | **E Vill**	22
Lucien | 1 AM | **E Vill**	21
Lucky Strike | varies | **SoHo**	17
Macelleria | 1 AM | **Meatpacking**	21
Maison | 24 hrs. | **W 50s**	17
Mas | 4 AM | **G Vill**	25
Neary's | 1 AM | **E 50s**	15
NEW Nelson Blue | 2 AM | **Seaport**	–
Odeon | 1 AM | **TriBeCa**	19
Ollie's | varies | **W 100s**	16
Omonia Cafe | 4 AM | **multi.**	19

Ⓩ Pastis | varies | **Meatpacking** 21
Ping's Sea. | varies | **Elmhurst** 22
P.J. Clarke's | varies | **multi.** 17
Pop Burger | varies | **Meatpacking** 19
Rai Rai Ken | 2:30 AM | **E Vill** 22
Raoul's | 1 AM | **SoHo** 24
NEW Resto | 1 AM | **Gramercy** —
Roebling | 1 AM | **W'burg** 21
Roll-n-Roaster | 1 AM | **Sheepshead** 19
Sabor | 2 AM | **E 80s** 19
Sahara | 2 AM | **Gravesend** 20
NEW Sandro's | 2 AM | **E 80s** —
Sarge's Deli | 24 hrs. | **Murray Hill** 19
Schiller's | 1 AM | **LES** 18
NEW Southern Hosp. | 2 AM | **E 70s** —
NEW Spitzer's | 4 AM | **LES** —
NEW Spoon | varies | **E Vill** —
Spotted Pig | 2 AM | **W Vill** 22
Stage Deli | 2 AM | **W 50s** 20
Stamatis | varies | **Astoria** 22
Stanton Social | 3 AM | **LES** 23
NEW STK | 1 AM | **Meatpacking** —
SushiSamba | varies | **multi.** 22
Ⓩ Sushi Seki | 3 AM | **E 60s** 27
NEW Tasca | 2 AM | **W Vill** 20
Tosca Café | 1 AM | **Bronx** 21
Trio | 1 AM | **Murray Hill** 21
Two Boots | varies | **multi.** 18
Umberto's | 4 AM | **L Italy** 18
Uno Chicago | varies | **multi.** 14
Uva | 2 AM | **E 70s** 21
Veselka | varies | **E Vill** 18
Viand | varies | **multi.** 16
Vincent's | 1:30 AM | **L Italy** 21
Walker's | 1 AM | **TriBeCa** 17
West Bank Cafe | 1 AM | **W 40s** 20
Wollensky's | 2 AM | **E 40s** 23
NEW Wombat | 2 AM | **W'burg** 21
WonJo | 24 hrs. | **Garment** 20

MEET FOR A DRINK

(Most top hotels, bars and the following standouts)

Aix Brasserie | **W 80s** 20
Algonquin | **W 40s** 16
Amaranth | **E 60s** 20
Arno | **Garment** 20
Ⓩ Artisanal | **Murray Hill** 23
Aspen | **Flatiron** 20
Ⓩ Atlantic Grill | **E 70s** 22
Aurora | **W'burg** 26
NEW Babouche | **SoHo** 20
Ⓩ Balthazar | **SoHo** 23
Bandol Bistro | **E 70s** 19

Barbounia | **Flatiron**
Beast | **Prospect Hts**
Blue Fin | **W 40s**
Ⓩ Blue Water | **Union Sq**
Boathouse | **E 70s**
Bond St. | **NoHo**
Boqueria | **Flatiron**
Brick Cafe | **Astoria**
Bryant Park | **W 40s**
Ⓩ Buddakan | **Chelsea**
Ⓩ Buddha Bar | **Meatpacking**
Bull & Bear | **E 40s**
NEW Cafe Fuego | **E Vill**
Ⓩ Café Gray | **W 60s**
Cafe Luxembourg | **W 70s**
Cafe Steinhof | **Park Slope**
NEW Centro Vinoteca | **W Vill**
City Hall | **TriBeCa**
Ⓩ Compass | **W 70s**
Country | **Gramercy**
Ⓩ Daniel | **E 60s**
Demarchelier | **E 80s**
Devin Tavern | **TriBeCa**
Ditch Plains | **G Vill**
Django | **E 40s**
Dos Caminos | **multi.**
Dressler | **W'burg**
NEW East Village Yacht | **E Vill**
Edward's | **TriBeCa**
8 Mile Creek | **L Italy**
Employees Only | **W Vill**
NEW Fette Sau | **W'burg**
NEW Flatbush Farm | **Park Slope**
Ⓩ Four Seasons | **E 50s**
Freemans | **LES**
Geisha | **E 60s**
NEW Gold St. | **Financial**
Ⓩ Gotham B&G | **G Vill**
Ⓩ Gramercy Tavern | **Flatiron**
NEW Grayz | **W 50s**
Harry's | **Financial**
NEW Hawaiian Tropic | **W 40s**
HK | **Garment**
NEW House | **Gramercy**
Houston's | **multi.**
NEW Hudson R. Café | **Harlem**
Il Bastardo | **Chelsea**
'inoteca | **LES**
NEW Island | **Astoria**
Ⓩ Jean Georges | **W 60s**
Keens | **Garment**
Kellari Taverna | **W 40s**
Koi | **W 40s**
Landmarc | **W 60s**
Le Cirque | **E 50s**

Le Colonial | **E 50s**	20
☑ L'Impero | **E 40s**	26
Lucky Strike | **SoHo**	17
Luz | **Ft Greene**	24
Maloney & Porcelli | **E 50s**	22
Markt | **Flatiron**	19
☑ Masa/Bar Masa | **W 60s**	27
☑ Matsuri | **Chelsea**	23
NEW Maze | **W 50s**	23
NEW Mercat | **NoHo**	–
Michael Jordan's | **E 40s**	20
☑ Modern, The | **W 50s**	26
☑ Morimoto | **Chelsea**	24
NEW Natsumi | **W 50s**	–
NEW Nelson Blue | **Seaport**	–
NEW Noble Food | **NoLita**	–
☑ Nobu 57 | **W 50s**	26
Odeon | **TriBeCa**	19
NEW Omido | **W 50s**	–
One | **Meatpacking**	18
O'Neals' | **W 60s**	17
☑ Ouest | **W 80s**	25
Park, The | **Chelsea**	15
☑ Pastis | **Meatpacking**	21
Patroon | **E 40s**	21
NEW Pera | **E 40s**	22
Piano Due | **W 50s**	25
Porcão | **Gramercy**	21
NEW PT | **W'burg**	24
Quaint | **Sunnyside**	20
NEW Rayuela | **LES**	–
NEW Revel | **Meatpacking**	–
Room Service | **Chelsea**	19
Sala | **NoHo**	22
Samba-Lé | **E Vill**	19
Sapa | **Flatiron**	22
NEW Silent H | **W'burg**	–
☑ Spice Market | **Meatpacking**	22
Stanton Social | **LES**	23
NEW STK | **Meatpacking**	20
Stone Park Café | **Park Slope**	24
☑ Tao | **E 50s**	23
Thor | **LES**	18
Town | **W 50s**	24
212 | **E 60s**	16
NEW Vamos! | **Gramercy**	16
Wollensky's | **E 40s**	23

NATURAL/ORGANIC

(Places specializing in organic,
local ingredients)

Angelica Kit. | **E Vill**	21
applewood | **Park Slope**	25
Better Burger | **multi.**	15
Blossom | **Chelsea**	21
NEW BLT Market | **W 50s**	–

☑ Blue Hill | **G Vill**	26
NEW Borough Food | **Flatiron**	–
Brown Café | **LES**	25
Candle | **E 70s**	23
Caravan/Dreams | **E Vill**	24
Chennai Gdn. | **Gramercy**	21
Chestnut | **Carroll Gdns**	23
Cho Dang Gol | **Garment**	21
Chop't Creative | **Union Sq**	20
City Bakery | **Flatiron**	21
Clinton St. Baking | **LES**	24
Cookshop | **Chelsea**	23
Counter | **E Vill**	22
☑ Craft | **Flatiron**	25
Dirty Bird | **W Vill**	17
☑ Eleven Madison | **Gramercy**	26
Employees Only | **W Vill**	18
57 | **E 50s**	22
FireBird | **W 40s**	18
5 Front | **Dumbo**	21
5 Points | **NoHo**	22
NEW Flatbush Farm | **Park Slope**	19
Fornino | **W'burg**	22
☑ Four Seasons | **E 50s**	25
Frankies Spuntino | **multi.**	24
Franny's | **Prospect Hts**	23
fresh | **TriBeCa**	24
Friend of a Farmer | **Gramercy**	17
NEW FR.OG | **SoHo**	21
Gabriel's | **W 60s**	22
Geisha | **E 60s**	23
Ginger | **Harlem**	21
Gobo | **multi.**	22
☑ Grocery | **Carroll Gdns**	26
Home | **G Vill**	20
Ivo & Lulu | **SoHo**	22
Josephina | **W 60s**	18
Josie's | **multi.**	19
L'Ecole | **SoHo**	23
Le Pain Q. | **Flatiron**	19
Mas | **G Vill**	25
New Leaf | **Wash. Hts**	20
Once Upon a Tart | **SoHo**	22
☑ One if by Land | **G Vill**	23
☑ Per Se | **W 60s**	28
PicNic Market | **W 100s**	20
Popover Cafe | **W 80s**	18
Pure Food/Wine | **Gramercy**	22
Rose Water | **Park Slope**	25
Sacred Chow | **G Vill**	23
☑ Saul | **Boerum Hill**	27
Savoy | **SoHo**	24
NEW Silent H | **W'burg**	–
NEW 67 Burger | **Ft Greene**	21
Superfine | **Dumbo**	18

SPECIAL FEATURES

Tasting Rm. | **E Vill** — 22

☑ Tocqueville | **Union Sq** — 26

Tsampa | **E Vill** — 20

Vento | **Meatpacking** — 19

Whole Foods | **multi.** — 19

Zebú Grill | **E 90s** — 21

Zen Palate | **multi.** — 19

NOTEWORTHY NEWCOMERS (234)

(* not open at press time, but looks promising)

Accademia/Vino | **E 60s** — _

Adour* | **E 50s**

Ago* | **TriBeCa**

A La Turka | **E 70s** — 18

Alchemy | **Park Slope** — 18

Allen & Delancey* | **LES**

Almond Flower | **L Italy** — 23

Aloe | **E Vill** — _

Amalia | **W 50s** — 21

Amazing 66 | **Chinatown** — 23

Anthos | **W 50s** — 25

Asiakan | **W 90s** — 19

Babouche | **multi.** — 20

Back Forty* | **E Vill**

Bar Blanc* | **G Vill**

Bar Boulud* | **W 60s**

BarFry | **G Vill** — _

Bar Martignetti | **L Italy** — 18

Bar Milano* | **Flatiron**

Bar Tano* | **Park Slope**

Bar Stuzz. | **Flatiron** — _

Basera* | **W 50s**

Basso56 | **W 50s** — 23

Belcourt* | **E Vill**

Benjamin Steak | **E 40s** — 23

Bistro Benoit* | **W 50s**

Bistro 33 | **Astoria**

Black Pearl | **Chelsea** — 17

Blossom Cafe* | **W 80s**

BLT Burger | **G Vill** — 19

BLT Market | **W 50s** — _

Blue Ribbon Sushi B/G* | **W 50s**

Bobo* | **W Vill**

Borough Food | **Flatiron** — _

Brasserie Cognac* | **W 50s**

brgr | **Chelsea** — 18

Broadway East* | **LES**

Bun* | **SoHo**

Cacio e Vino | **E Vill** — 21

Cafe & Wine | **W 100s** — _

Cafe Cluny | **W Vill** — 19

Cafe Fuego | **E Vill** — 19

Cafe Tango* | **W 90s**

Caffe Emilia | **E Vill** — _

Cambodian Cuisine* | **E 90s**

Caminito | **Harlem** — _

Cantina* | **E Vill** — _

Carniceria | **Cobble Hill** — _

Catch 22 | **W'burg** — _

Centro Vinoteca | **W Vill** — _

Chat Noir | **E 60s** — 18

Chennai | **E 80s** — _

Cheryl's | **Prospect Hts** — 22

Chez Lola | **Clinton Hill** — _

Chiles/Chocolate | **Park Slope** — 18

China de Puebla | **Harlem** — _

Co.* | **Chelsea**

Community Food* | **W 100s**

Crave | **E 50s** — _

Delicatessen & Mac Bar* | **SoHo**

Dennis Foy | **TriBeCa** — 24

DeStefano's | **W'burg** — _

Dieci | **E Vill** — 23

Dovetail* | **W 70s**

Earthen Oven | **W 70s** — 21

East Village Yacht | **E Vill** — _

Ed's Lobster | **NoLita** — 23

eighty one* | **W 80s**

eleven B. | **E Vill** — _

El Quinto Pino* | **Chelsea**

Estancia | **TriBeCa** — 21

E.U., The | **E Vill** — 20

Fabio Piccolo | **E 40s** — _

Fette Sau | **W'burg** — 19

15 East | **Union Sq** — 26

Fiorini | **E 50s** — _

Fireside | **E 50s** — 21

Five Guys | **multi.** — _

Flatbush Farm | **Park Slope** — 19

FR.OG | **SoHo** — 21

Gallo Nero* | **W 40s**

Gaucho | **W 50s** — _

Gemma | **E Vill** — _

Georgia's/BBQ | **LES** — _

Gold St. | **Financial** — 15

☑ Gordon Ramsay | **W 50s** — 25

Gottino* | **G Vill**

Graffiti Bistro* | **E Vill**

Grange Hall* | **W Vill**

Grayz | **W 50s** — _

Greenwich Grill* | **TriBeCa**

Guadalupe | **Inwood** — 19

Gus' Place | **G Vill** — 20

Hakata Ippudo* | **E Vill**

Hawaiian Tropic | **W 40s** — 16

Hill Country | **Chelsea** — _

House | **Gramercy** — 22

Hudson R. Café | **Harlem** — _

Hurapan | **G Vill** — 20

SPECIAL FEATURES

subscribe to zagat

SPECIAL FEATURES

Fresco | **E 50s** — 23
Gallagher's | **W 50s** — 20
Gilt | **E 50s** — 25
☑ Gotham B&G | **G Vill** — 27
Harry's | **Financial** — 22
☑ Jean Georges | **W 60s** — 28
Keens | **Garment** — 24
☑ La Grenouille | **E 50s** — 27
☑ Le Bernardin | **W 50s** — 28
Le Cirque | **E 50s** — 23
Lever House | **E 50s** — 22
Michael's | **W 50s** — 21
☑ Nobu | **TriBeCa** — 27
☑ Nobu 57 | **W 50s** — 26
Norma's | **W 50s** — 25
Patroon | **E 40s** — 21
☑ Peter Luger | **W'burg** — 28
☑ Rao's | **Harlem** — 22
Regency | **E 60s** — 18
NEW Russian Tea | **W 50s** — 19
Sant Ambroeus | **multi.** — 22
Smith & Wollensky | **E 40s** — 23
Solo | **E 50s** — 22
☑ Sparks | **E 40s** — 25
☑ 21 Club | **W 50s** — 22
NEW ☑ Wakiya | **Gramercy** — –
NEW ☑ Waverly Inn | **W Vill** — 18

PRIVATE ROOMS/ PARTIES

(Restaurants charge less at off times; call for capacity)
Arabelle | **E 60s** — 21
Barbetta | **W 40s** — 20
Battery Gdns. | **Financial** — 18
Beacon | **W 50s** — 22
Ben & Jack's | **E 40s** — 23
BLT Fish | **Flatiron** — 23
BLT Prime | **Gramercy** — 24
BLT Steak | **E 50s** — 24
☑ Blue Hill | **G Vill** — 26
Blue Smoke | **Gramercy** — 22
☑ Blue Water | **Union Sq** — 23
☑ Buddakan | **Chelsea** — 23
☑ Café Gray | **W 60s** — 25
Capital Grille | **E 40s** — 23
Cellini | **E 50s** — 21
Centolire | **E 80s** — 20
City Hall | **TriBeCa** — 21
☑ Compass | **W 70s** — 22
Country | **Gramercy** — 23
☑ Craft | **Flatiron** — 25
☑ Daniel | **E 60s** — 28
☑ Danube | **TriBeCa** — 26
☑ Del Frisco's | **W 40s** — 25
Delmonico's | **Financial** — 22

☑ Del Posto | **Chelsea**
☑ Eleven Madison | **Gramercy**
EN Japanese | **W Vill**
ESPN Zone | **W 40s**
☑ Felidia | **E 50s**
Fiamma Osteria | **SoHo**
F.illi Ponte | **TriBeCa**
FireBird | **W 40s**
☑ Four Seasons | **E 50s**
Fresco | **E 50s**
Gabriel's | **W 60s**
Geisha | **E 60s**
☑ Gramercy Tavern | **Flatiron**
NEW Grayz | **W 50s**
Il Buco | **NoHo**
Il Cortile | **L Italy**
'inoteca | **LES**
☑ Jean Georges | **W 60s**
Keens | **Garment**
☑ La Grenouille | **E 50s**
Landmark Tavern | **W 40s**
☑ Le Bernardin | **W 50s**
Le Cirque | **E 50s**
Le Perigord | **E 50s**
Lever House | **E 50s**
Le Zie 2000 | **Chelsea**
☑ L'Impero | **E 40s**
Maloney & Porcelli | **E 50s**
☑ Matsuri | **Chelsea**
☑ Megu | **TriBeCa**
Michael's | **W 50s**
Mi Cocina | **W Vill**
☑ Milos | **W 50s**
☑ Modern, The | **W 50s**
Moran's | **Chelsea**
Mr. Chow | **E 50s**
☑ Mr. K's | **E 50s**
☑ Nobu | **TriBeCa**
☑ Nobu 57 | **W 50s**
Oceana | **E 50s**
Park, The | **Chelsea**
Patroon | **E 40s**
Periyali | **Flatiron**
☑ Per Se | **W 60s**
☑ Picholine | **W 60s**
Redeye Grill | **W 50s**
Remi | **W 50s**
Re Sette | **W 40s**
Riingo | **E 40s**
☑ River Café | **Dumbo**
Rock Ctr. | **W 50s**
Sambuca | **W 70s**
Shun Lee Palace | **E 50s**
Solo | **E 50s**
☑ Sparks | **E 40s**

pice Market | **Meatpacking** 22
abla | **Gramercy** 25
ao | **E 50s** 23
avern on Green | **W 60s** 15
ace in the Sky | **W 100s** 22
Massa | **TriBeCa** 22
ocqueville | **Union Sq** 26
eca Grill | **TriBeCa** 22
1 Club | **W 50s** 22
| **E 60s** 16
to | **Meatpacking** 19
er Club | **Murray Hill** 20

BS/MICROBREWERIES

(e Zagat NYC Nightlife)

us McIndoe | **W 40s** 16
dwick's | **Bay Ridge** 22
Shop | **Bklyn Hts** 18
ner Bistro | **W Vill** 22
ile Creek | **L Italy** 20
E.U., The | **E Vill** 20
rtland | **multi.** 14
Inn LW12 | **Meatpacking** 19
kson Hole | **multi.** 17
Melon | **E 70s** 21
Allen | **W 40s** 17
meyer Bavarian | **SI** 21
dmark Tavern | **W 40s** 18
eals' | **W 60s** 17
's Tavern | **Gramercy** 14
Clarke's | **multi.** 17
Public House | **E 40s** -
tted Pig | **W Vill** 22
ker's | **TriBeCa** 17
lensky's | **E 40s** 23

ICK BITES

orina | **Prospect Hts** 23
y's Bread | **multi.** 23
ri Cafe | **W 50s** 25
eket | **LES** 18
er Burger | **multi.** 15
BLT Burger | **G Vill** 19
9 Burger | **E Vill** 18
nnan | **Sheepshead** 19
ritoville | **multi.** 16
acas | **E Vill** 26
J's Steaks | **Murray Hill** 22
na Fun | **multi.** 16
Shop | **Park Slope** 18
p't Creative | **multi.** 20
Bakery | **Flatiron** 21
ls | **Bronx** 22
umbus Bakery | **W 80s** 18
i | **multi.** 16
y | **G Vill** 18

Daisy May's | **W 40s** 24
David Burke/Bloom. | **E 50s** 18
Dishes | **E 40s** 22
Dumpling Man | **E Vill** 19
Ess-a-Bagel | **multi.** 23
F & B | **Chelsea** 18
Fresco | **E 50s** 23
goodburger | **E 40s** 18
Good Enough/Eat | **W 80s** 20
Gray's Papaya | **multi.** 20
Hale/Hearty | **multi.** 19
Hampton Chutney | **SoHo** 20
'ino | **G Vill** 24
Island Burgers | **W 50s** 22
Joe's Pizza | **multi.** 23
Kati Roll Co. | **multi.** 20
La Esquina | **L Italy** 21
Leo's Latticini | **Corona** 28
Morgan | **Murray Hill** 20
Nicky's Viet. | **multi.** 21
99 Mi. to Philly | **E Vill** 18
NEW Omido | **W 50s** -
Once Upon a Tart | **SoHo** 22
Papaya King | **multi.** 20
Pastrami Queen | **E 70s** 19
Peanut Butter Co. | **G Vill** 20
Press 195 | **Park Slope** 20
Pump Energy | **multi.** 19
Rice 'n' Beans | **W 50s** 19
Rickshaw Dumpling | **Flatiron** 18
Risotteria | **G Vill** 21
Shake Shack | **Flatiron** 23
NEW Silent H | **W'burg** -
NEW Spice Fusion | **W 40s** -
Tossed | **multi.** 18
Two Boots | **multi.** 18
Westville | **W Vill** 23
Whole Foods | **multi.** 19
'wichcraft | **TriBeCa** 20
Zabar's Cafe | **W 80s** 20
Zip Burger | **E 50s** 18

QUIET CONVERSATION

Alto | **E 50s** 26
Arabelle | **E 60s** 21
Aroma | **NoHo** 24
Asiate | **W 60s** 24
Café Pierre | **E 60s** 23
Chanterelle | **TriBeCa** 27
NEW Dieci | **E Vill** 23
El Paso | **G Vill** -
Fleur de Sel | **Flatiron** 25
Giovanni | **E 80s** 22
Il Gattopardo | **W 50s** 23
Jarnac | **W Vill** 22
Jean Georges | **W 60s** 28

SPECIAL FEATURES

Kai	**E 60s**	25
Kings' Carriage	**E 80s**	21
Knife + Fork	**E Vill**	23
NEW Kyotofu	**W 40s**	23
Z La Grenouille	**E 50s**	27
NEW Le Barricou	**W'burg**	–
Z Le Bernardin	**W 50s**	28
Lumi	**E 70s**	19
Z Masa/Bar Masa	**W 60s**	27
Z Mr. K's	**E 50s**	23
North Sq.	**G Vill**	22
Z Per Se	**W 60s**	28
NEW Petite Crev.	**Carroll Gdns**	24
Petrossian	**W 50s**	24
Z Picholine	**W 60s**	27
Provence/Boite	**Carroll Gdns**	20
NEW PT	**W'burg**	24
NEW Rosanjin	**TriBeCa**	25
NEW savorNY	**LES**	–
Sfoglia	**E 90s**	23
Sorrel	**Prospect Hts**	23
Terrace in the Sky	**W 100s**	22
Z Tocqueville	**Union Sq**	26
NEW Tree	**E Vill**	24
Tsampa	**E Vill**	20
12 Chairs	**SoHo**	19
NEW Zenkichi	**W'burg**	23

RAW BARS

American Grill	**SI**	20
Angus McIndoe	**W 40s**	16
Z Aquagrill	**SoHo**	26
Z Atlantic Grill	**E 70s**	22
Baldoria	**W 40s**	22
Z Balthazar	**SoHo**	23
Z Bar Americain	**W 50s**	23
Ben & Jack's	**E 40s**	23
NEW Black Pearl	**Chelsea**	17
BLT Fish	**Flatiron**	23
bluechili	**W 50s**	19
Blue Fin	**W 40s**	22
Z Blue Ribbon	**multi.**	25
Blue Smoke	**Gramercy**	22
Z Blue Water	**Union Sq**	23
Bond 45	**W 40s**	20
Brooklyn Fish	**Park Slope**	23
City Crab	**Flatiron**	17
City Hall	**TriBeCa**	21
City Lobster	**W 40s**	18
Craftsteak	**Chelsea**	22
Ditch Plains	**G Vill**	17
Docks Oyster	**multi.**	19
East Buffet	**Flushing**	20
NEW East Village Yacht	**E Vill**	–
NEW Ed's Lobster	**NoLita**	23
Employees Only	**W Vill**	18

NEW E.U., The	**E Vill**	
Fish	**G Vill**	
Gin Lane	**Chelsea**	
Giorgione	**SoHo**	
Jack's Lux.	**E Vill**	
Le Singe Vert	**Chelsea**	
London Lennie's	**Rego Pk**	
Lure Fishbar	**SoHo**	
Markt	**Flatiron**	
McCormick/Schmick	**W 50s**	
Mercer Kitchen	**SoHo**	
Mermaid Inn	**E Vill**	
Metrazur	**E 40s**	
NEW Natsumi	**W 50s**	
Neptune Rm.	**W 80s**	
Ocean Grill	**W 70s**	
Olea	**Ft Greene**	
Oyster Bar	**E 40s**	
P.J. Clarke's	**E 50s**	
NEW Provence	**SoHo**	
San Luigi	**W 70s**	
Shaffer City	**Flatiron**	
Shelly's Tratt.	**W 50s**	
Shula's	**W 40s**	
South Fin Grill	**SI**	
NEW Spitzer's	**LES**	
NEW Stella Maris	**Seaport**	
Thalia	**W 50s**	
Tides	**LES**	
Todai	**Murray Hill**	
Trata Estiatorio	**E 70s**	
Umberto's	**multi.**	
Uncle Jack's	**Garment**	
Water Club	**Murray Hill**	
Water's Edge	**LIC**	
NEW Wild Salmon	**E 40s**	

ROMANTIC PLACES

Aix Brasserie	**W 80s**	
Algonquin	**W 40s**	
Alma	**Carroll Gdns**	
Alta	**G Vill**	
Z Asiate	**W 60s**	
Z Aureole	**E 60s**	
Z Balthazar	**SoHo**	
Barbetta	**W 40s**	
Barolo	**SoHo**	
Battery Gdns.	**Financial**	
Z Blue Hill	**G Vill**	
Blue Ribbon Bakery	**G Vill**	
Boathouse	**E 70s**	
Bottino	**Chelsea**	
Z Bouley	**TriBeCa**	
Z Café des Artistes	**W 60s**	
Café Pierre	**E 60s**	
Caffé/Green	**Bayside**	

SPECIAL FEATURES

☑ Felidia | **E 50s**	
NEW Fiorini | **E 50s**	
Gallagher's | **W 50s**	25
Giovanni | **E 80s**	20
Grifone | **E 40s**	22
Il Nido | **E 50s**	23
☑ Il Tinello | **W 50s**	23
☑ Jean Georges | **W 60s**	26
La Bonne Soupe | **W 50s**	28
La Goulue | **E 60s**	18
La Mangeoire | **E 50s**	20
La Mediterranée | **E 50s**	19
La Mirabelle | **W 80s**	19
La Petite Aub. | **Gramercy**	22
Lattanzi | **W 40s**	20
Le Boeuf/Mode | **E 80s**	22
Le Marais | **W 40s**	21
Le Perigord | **E 50s**	20
Levana | **W 60s**	24
Lusardi's | **E 70s**	20
MarkJoseph | **Financial**	24
Montparnasse | **E 50s**	24
☑ Mr. K's | **E 50s**	19
Nicola's | **E 80s**	23
Nippon | **E 50s**	22
Pastrami Queen | **E 70s**	22
Paul & Jimmy's | **Gramercy**	19
Piccola Venezia | **Astoria**	19
Pietro's | **E 40s**	25
Ponticello | **Astoria**	23
Primola | **E 60s**	23
Quattro Gatti | **E 80s**	23
Rao's | **Harlem**	20
René Pujol | **W 50s**	22
☑ River Café | **Dumbo**	22
Rossini's | **Murray Hill**	26
Rughetta | **E 80s**	23
NEW Russian Tea | **W 50s**	22
Sal Anthony's | **E Vill**	19
San Pietro | **E 50s**	19
Sardi's | **W 40s**	24
☑ Saul | **Boerum Hill**	16
Scaletta | **W 70s**	27
Shun Lee West | **W 60s**	21
☑ Tavern on Green | **W 60s**	23
12 Chairs | **SoHo**	15
	19

SINGLES SCENES

Angelo & Maxie's | **Flatiron**	21
☑ Asia de Cuba | **Murray Hill**	23
Aspen | **Flatiron**	20
☑ Atlantic Grill | **E 70s**	22
Baraonda | **E 70s**	18
Blue Fin | **W 40s**	22
☑ Blue Ribbon | **multi.**	25
☑ Blue Water | **Union Sq**	23

Boca Chica | **E Vill**	
Brasserie 8½ | **W 50s**	—
Brother Jimmy's | **multi.**	
Bryant Park | **W 40s**	
☑ Buddakan | **Chelsea**	
☑ Buddha Bar | **Meatpacking**	
Butter | **E Vill**	
Cabana | **multi.**	
Canyon Road | **E 70s**	
Chinatown Brass. | **NoHo**	
Citrus B&G | **W 70s**	
Coffee Shop | **Union Sq**	
Dos Caminos | **multi.**	
East of 8th | **Chelsea**	
NEW East Village Yacht | **E Vill**	
Elephant, The | **E Vill**	
elmo | **Chelsea**	
Employees Only | **W Vill**	
Essex | **LES**	
Félix | **SoHo**	
Flor de Sol | **TriBeCa**	
Freemans | **LES**	
NEW Gold St. | **Financial**	
Heartland | **multi.**	
Houston's | **multi.**	
Hudson Cafeteria | **W 50s**	
Ideya | **SoHo**	
'inoteca | **LES**	
Isabella's | **W 70s**	
NEW Island | **Astoria**	
Jane | **G Vill**	
Japonais | **Gramercy**	
Joya | **Cobble Hill**	
NEW Kobe Club | **W 50s**	
Koi | **W 40s**	
La Esquina | **L Italy**	
La Goulue | **E 60s**	
Lure Fishbar | **SoHo**	
Maloney & Porcelli | **E 50s**	
Markt | **Flatiron**	
☑ Mesa Grill | **Flatiron**	
Monkey Bar | **E 50s**	
One | **Meatpacking**	
Otto | **G Vill**	
Pam Real Thai | **W 40s**	
☑ Pastis | **Meatpacking**	
Peep | **SoHo**	
Pete's Tavern | **Gramercy**	
Pipa | **Flatiron**	
Punch | **Flatiron**	
Ruby Foo's | **multi.**	
Schiller's | **LES**	
☑ Spice Market | **Meatpacking**	
NEW STK | **Meatpacking**	
Suba | **LES**	

SPECIAL FEATURES

Piccolo Angolo | W Vill — 25
Picholine | W 60s — 27
Prune | E Vill — 24
River Café | Dumbo — 26
Solo | E 50s — 22
Tratt. Dell'Arte | W 50s — 22
Tribeca Grill | TriBeCa — 22
Union Sq. Cafe | Union Sq — 26
Water Club | Murray Hill — 20
Zoë | SoHo — 20

TASTING MENUS

($ minimum)

Alto | $115 | E 50s — 26
Amma | $50 | E 50s — 24
Annisa | $68 | G Vill — 27
Anthos | $85 | W 50s — 25
applewood | $55 | Park Slope — 25
Aquavit | $115 | E 50s — 25
Asiate | $125 | W 60s — 24
Aureole | $95 | E 60s — 27
Babbo | $70 | G Vill — 27
Blue Hill | $72 | G Vill — 26
Café Boulud | $125 | E 70s — 27
Café Gray | $135 | W 60s — 25
Chanterelle | $125 | TriBeCa — 27
Country | $135 | Gramercy — 23
Cru | $110 | G Vill — 26
Daniel | $155 | E 60s — 28
Danube | $90 | TriBeCa — 26
davidburke/dona. | $85 | E 60s — 25
Dawat | $65 | E 50s — 23
Del Posto | $120 | Chelsea — 25
Donguri | $85 | E 80s — 27
Eleven Madison | $145 | Gramercy — 26
Esca | $75 | W 40s — 25
Falai | $80 | LES — 25
Felidia | $85 | E 50s — 25
15 East | $120 | Union Sq — 26
Fleur de Sel | $89 | Flatiron — 25
Four Seasons | $135 | E 50s — 25
fresh | $75 | TriBeCa — 24
Gari/Sushi | $70 | multi. — 26
Gilt | $105 | E 50s — 25
Gordon Ramsay | $120 | W 50s — 25
Gramercy Tavern | $110 | Flatiron — 27
Grocery | $75 | Carroll Gdns — 26
Hearth | $75 | E Vill — 25
Insieme | $85 | W 50s — 26
Jack's Lux. | $50 | E Vill — 24
Jean Georges | $128 | W 60s — 28
Jewel Bako | $95 | E Vill — 25
JoJo | $65 | E 60s — 24

Kittichai | $65 | SoHo
Knife + Fork | $45 | E Vill
Kuruma Zushi | $250 | E 40s
La Grenouille | $130 | E 50s
L'Atelier/Robuchon | $190 | E 50s
Le Bernardin | $135 | W 50s
Le Miu | $55 | E Vill
L'Impero | $110 | E 40s
Mas | $95 | G Vill
Masa | $400 | W 60s
Maze | $75 | W 50s
Modern, The | $125 | W 50s
Morimoto | $120 | Chelsea
Nobu | $100 | TriBeCa
Oceana | $110 | E 50s
Payard Bistro | $72 | E 70s
Per Se | $250 | W 60s
Piano Due | $85 | W 50s
Picholine | $110 | W 60s
Pó | $50 | multi.
River Café | $115 | Dumbo
Rosanjin | $150 | TriBeCa
Rose Water | $54 | Park Slope
Sasabune | $70 | E 70s
Saul | $85 | Boerum Hill
Scalini Fedeli | $90 | TriBeCa
Spigolo | $70 | E 80s
Sugiyama | $86 | W 50s
Sushi Seki | $70 | E 60s
Tabla | $79 | Gramercy
Telepan | $64 | W 60s
Tempo | $55 | Park Slope
Tocqueville | $90 | Union Sq
Town | $95 | W 50s
Wallsé | $70 | W Vill
Zenkichi | $88 | W'burg

TEA SERVICE

Alice's Tea Cup | multi.
American Girl | E 40s
BG | W 50s
Café Pierre | E 60s
Danal | E Vill
Kings' Carriage | E 80s
Lady Mendl's | Gramercy
NEW Maze | W 50s
Morgan | Murray Hill
North Sq. | G Vill
Payard Bistro | E 70s
Sant Ambroeus | multi.
Sarabeth's | multi.
Soda Shop | TriBeCa
Sweet Melissa | multi.
Tea & Sympathy | W Vill
Tea Box | E 50s

teany | **LES** 18
202 Cafe | **Chelsea** 21

THEME RESTAURANTS

Brooklyn Diner | **multi.** 17
Bubba Gump | **W 40s** 14
Cowgirl | **W Vill** 16
ESPN Zone | **W 40s** 12
Hard Rock Cafe | **W 40s** 13
NEW Hawaiian Tropic | **W 40s** 16
NEW Johnny Utah | **W 50s** -
Ninja | **TriBeCa** 19
Shula's | **W 40s** 20

TRANSPORTING EXPERIENCES

☒ Asiate | **W 60s** 24
☒ Balthazar | **SoHo** 23
Boathouse | **E 70s** 16
☒ Buddakan | **Chelsea** 23
☒ Buddha Bar | **Meatpacking** 19
☒ Café des Artistes | **W 60s** 22
Chez Josephine | **W 40s** 20
FireBird | **W 40s** 18
Fraunces Tavern | **Financial** 15
Il Buco | **NoHo** 25
Keens | **Garment** 24
☒ La Grenouille | **E 50s** 27
Le Colonial | **E 50s** 20
☒ Masa/Bar Masa | **W 60s** 27
☒ Matsuri | **Chelsea** 23
☒ Megu | **TriBeCa** 24
Ninja | **TriBeCa** 19
☒ One if by Land | **G Vill** 23
☒ Per Se | **W 60s** 28
☒ Rainbow Room/Grill | **W 40s** 19
☒ Rao's | **Harlem** 22
Soda Shop | **TriBeCa** 19
uba | **LES** 21
☒ Tao | **E 50s** 23
☒ Tavern on Green | **W 60s** 15
atan | **Gramercy** 23
Water's Edge | **LIC** 23

VIEWS

lma | **Carroll Gdns** 20
ntica Venezia | **W Vill** 23
☒ Asiate | **W 60s** 24
attery Gdns. | **Financial** 18
G | **W 50s** 20
oathouse | **E 70s** 16
ouchon Bakery | **W 60s** 23
ryant Park | **W 40s** 17
ubby's | **Dumbo** 18
abana | **Seaport** 21
Café Gray | **W 60s** 25

Caffé/Green | **Bayside** 21
Cipriani Dolci | **E 40s** 18
Fairway Cafe | **Red Hook** 18
F.illi Ponte | **TriBeCa** 21
Gigino | **Financial** 20
Heartland | **Seaport** 14
Hispaniola | **Wash. Hts** 21
NEW Hudson R. Café | **Harlem** -
NEW Kaijou | **Financial** -
Lake Club | **SI** 21
Le Refuge Inn | **Bronx** 24
Lobster Box | **Bronx** 17
Marina Cafe | **SI** 18
Metrazur | **E 40s** 20
Michael Jordan's | **E 40s** 20
☒ Modern, The | **W 50s** 26
☒ Per Se | **W 60s** 28
Pete's Downtown | **Dumbo** 18
P.J. Clarke's | **Financial** 17
Porter House NY | **W 60s** 22
Portofino's | **Bronx** 19
☒ Rainbow Room/Grill | **W 40s** 19
☒ River Café | **Dumbo** 26
River Room | **Harlem** 19
Rock Ctr. | **W 50s** 19
Sea Grill | **W 40s** 24
South Fin Grill | **SI** 20
NEW Suteishi | **Seaport** 25
☒ Tavern on Green | **W 60s** 15
Terrace in the Sky | **W 100s** 22
2 West | **Financial** 21
View, The | **W 40s** 18
Water Club | **Murray Hill** 20
Water's Edge | **LIC** 23

VISITORS ON EXPENSE ACCOUNT

NEW Anthos | **W 50s** 25
☒ Bouley | **TriBeCa** 28
☒ Carlyle | **E 70s** 21
☒ Chanterelle | **TriBeCa** 27
☒ Craft | **Flatiron** 25
Craftsteak | **Chelsea** 22
☒ Daniel | **E 60s** 28
☒ Del Frisco's | **W 40s** 25
☒ Del Posto | **Chelsea** 25
☒ Four Seasons | **E 50s** 25
☒ Gari/Sushi | **W 40s** 26
NEW ☒ Gordon Ramsay | **W 50s** 25
Harry Cipriani | **E 50s** -
Harry's | **Financial** 22
☒ Il Mulino | **G Vill** 27
☒ Jean Georges | **W 60s** 28
NEW Kobe Club | **W 50s** 20
Kuruma Zushi | **E 40s** 28
Le Cirque | **E 50s** 23

☑ Masa/Bar Masa | **W 60s**	27
☑ Megu | **TriBeCa**	24
☑ Milos | **W 50s**	26
☑ Nobu | **TriBeCa**	27
☑ Nobu 57 | **W 50s**	26
☑ One if by Land | **G Vill**	23
☑ Per Se | **W 60s**	28
Petrossian | **W 50s**	24
Roy's NY | **Financial**	25
NEW Russian Tea | **W 50s**	19
NEW ☑ Wakiya | **Gramercy**	–

WATERSIDE

Alma | **Carroll Gdns**	20
Battery Gdns. | **Financial**	18
Boathouse | **E 70s**	16
Cabana | **Seaport**	21
Lake Club | **SI**	21
Marina Cafe | **SI**	18
Pete's Downtown | **Dumbo**	18
Portofino's | **Bronx**	19
☑ River Café | **Dumbo**	26
River Room | **Harlem**	19
South Fin Grill | **SI**	20
Water Club | **Murray Hill**	20
Water's Edge | **LIC**	23

WINNING WINE LISTS

NEW Accademia/Vino | **E 60s**	–
Aix Brasserie | **W 80s**	20
Alfama | **W Vill**	22
☑ Alto | **E 50s**	26
☑ Annisa | **G Vill**	27
☑ Aquavit | **E 50s**	25
Arno | **Garment**	20
☑ Artisanal | **Murray Hill**	23
☑ Asiate | **W 60s**	24
☑ Aureole | **E 60s**	27
A Voce | **Gramercy**	25
☑ Babbo | **G Vill**	27
☑ Balthazar | **SoHo**	23
Barbetta | **W 40s**	20
Barolo | **SoHo**	18
☑ Becco | **W 40s**	22
Ben Benson's | **W 50s**	24
BLT Steak | **E 50s**	24
☑ Blue Hill | **G Vill**	26
☑ Blue Ribbon | **multi.**	25
Bottega del Vino | **E 50s**	22
☑ Bouley | **TriBeCa**	28
☑ Café Boulud | **E 70s**	27
☑ Café Gray | **W 60s**	25
Capital Grille | **E 40s**	23
Casa Mono | **Gramercy**	25
'Cesca | **W 70s**	23
☑ Chanterelle | **TriBeCa**	27

Chiam | **E 40s**	23
City Hall | **TriBeCa**	21
☑ Compass | **W 70s**	22
Conviv. Osteria | **Park Slope**	25
Counter | **E Vill**	22
Country | **Gramercy**	23
☑ Craft | **Flatiron**	25
☑ Cru | **G Vill**	26
☑ Daniel | **E 60s**	28
☑ Danube | **TriBeCa**	26
☑ db Bistro Moderne | **W 40s**	2
Del Frisco's | **W 40s**	2
Del Posto | **Chelsea**	25
☑ Eleven Madison | **Gramercy**	2
Falai | **LES**	2
Fatty Crab | **W Vill**	2
☑ Felidia | **E 50s**	2
Fiamma Osteria | **SoHo**	2
Fleur de Sel | **Flatiron**	2
Gabriel's | **W 60s**	2
Gilt | **E 50s**	2
☑ Gotham B&G | **G Vill**	2
☑ Gramercy Tavern | **Flatiron**	2
Harrison, The | **TriBeCa**	2
Hearth | **E Vill**	2
Il Buco | **NoHo**	2
'ino | **G Vill**	2
'inoteca | **LES**	2
I Trulli | **Gramercy**	2
☑ Jean Georges | **W 60s**	2
Landmarc | **multi.**	2
La Pizza Fresca | **Flatiron**	2
Lavagna | **E Vill**	2
☑ Le Bernardin | **W 50s**	2
Le Cirque | **E 50s**	2
☑ L'Impero | **E 40s**	2
☑ Lupa | **G Vill**	2
Mas | **G Vill**	2
☑ Megu | **TriBeCa**	2
Michael Jordan's | **E 40s**	2
Michael's | **W 50s**	2
☑ Milos | **W 50s**	2
☑ Modern, The | **W 50s**	2
Morrell Wine Bar | **W 40s**	
Nice Matin | **W 70s**	
Nick & Stef's | **Garment**	
Oceana | **E 50s**	
Orsay | **E 70s**	
Osteria del Circo | **W 50s**	
Otto | **G Vill**	
☑ Ouest | **W 80s**	
☑ Per Se | **W 60s**	
☑ Picholine | **W 60s**	
Post House | **E 60s**	
NEW PT | **W'burg**	

Raoul's | **SoHo**	24	Tasting Rm. | **multi.**	22
Ruth's Chris | **W 50s**	23	☑ Telepan | **W 60s**	25
San Domenico | **W 50s**	23	☑ Tocqueville | **Union Sq**	26
San Pietro | **E 50s**	24	Tommaso | **Dyker Hts**	23
Scalini Fedeli | **TriBeCa**	26	Town | **W 50s**	24
Sea Grill | **W 40s**	24	Tribeca Grill | **TriBeCa**	22
Scottette Enoteca | **Park Slope**	19	Tse Yang | **E 50s**	25
Sharz Cafe | **E 80s**	21	☑ 21 Club | **W 50s**	22
Smith & Wollensky | **E 40s**	23	☑ Union Sq. Cafe | **Union Sq**	26
Solera | **E 50s**	22	Uva | **E 70s**	21
Sparks | **E 40s**	25	☑ Veritas | **Flatiron**	26
Strip House | **G Vill**	25	Wallsé | **W Vill**	26
Supper | **E Vill**	24	West Bank Cafe | **W 40s**	20
Tabla | **Gramercy**	25	Zoë | **SoHo**	20

SPECIAL FEATURES

Wine Vintage Chart

This chart, based on our 0 to 30 scale, is designed to help you se wine. The ratings (by **Howard Stravitz,** a law professor at University of South Carolina) reflect the vintage quality and the wi readiness to drink. We exclude the 1991–1993 vintages because t are not that good. A dash indicates the wine is either past its pea too young to rate. Loire ratings are for dry white wines.

Whites	88	89	90	94	95	96	97	98	99	00	01	02	03	04	05
French:															
Alsace	-	25	25	24	23	23	22	25	23	25	27	25	22	24	25
Burgundy	-	23	22	-	28	27	24	22	26	25	24	27	23	27	26
Loire Valley	-	-	-	-	-	-	-	-	24	25	26	23	24	27
Champagne	24	26	29	-	26	27	24	23	24	24	22	26	-	-	-
Sauternes	29	25	28	-	21	23	25	23	24	24	28	25	26	21	26
California:															
Chardonnay	-	-	-	-	-	-	-	-	24	23	26	26	25	27	29
Sauvignon Blanc	-	-	-	-	-	-	-	-	-	-	27	28	26	27	26
Austrian:															
Grüner Velt./ Riesling	-	-	-	-	25	21	26	26	25	22	23	25	26	25	26
German:	25	26	27	24	23	26	25	26	23	21	29	27	24	26	28

Reds	88	89	90	94	95	96	97	98	99	00	01	02	03	04	05
French:															
Bordeaux	23	25	29	22	26	25	23	25	24	29	26	24	25	24	27
Burgundy	-	24	26	-	26	27	25	22	27	22	24	27	25	25	27
Rhône	26	28	28	24	26	22	25	27	26	27	26	-	25	24	25
Beaujolais	-	-	-	-	-	-	-	-	-	24	-	23	25	22	28
California:															
Cab./Merlot	-	-	28	29	27	25	28	23	26	22	27	26	25	24	24
Pinot Noir	-	-	-	-	-	-	24	23	24	23	27	28	26	25	24
Zinfandel	-	-	-	-	-	-	-	-	-	-	25	23	27	24	23
Oregon:															
Pinot Noir	-	-	-	-	-	-	-	-	-	-	-	27	25	26	27
Italian:															
Tuscany	-	-	25	22	24	20	29	24	27	24	27	20	25	25	22
Piedmont	-	27	27	-	23	26	27	26	25	28	27	20	24	25	26
Spanish:															
Rioja	-	-	-	26	26	24	25	22	25	24	27	20	24	25	26
Ribera del Duero/Priorat	-	-	-	26	26	27	25	24	25	24	27	20	24	26	26
Australian:															
Shiraz/Cab.	-	-	-	24	26	23	26	28	24	24	27	27	25	26	24
Chilean:	-	-	-	-	-	-	24	-	25	23	26	24	25	24	26

subscribe to zagat.c

ZAGATMAP

Manhattan Subway Map

Most Popular Restaurants

Map coordinates follow each name. Sections A–H lie south 34th Street (see adjacent map). Sections I–P lie north of 34th Street (see reverse side of map).

1. Union Square Cafe (B-4)
2. Gramercy Tavern (B-4)
3. Le Bernardin (O-3)
4. Babbo (C-3)
5. Jean Georges (N-3)
6. Daniel (M-5)
7. Gotham Bar & Grill (C-4)
8. Peter Luger (E-7)
9. Bouley (F-4)
10. Balthazar (E-4)
11. Blue Water Grill (B-4)
12. Eleven Madison Park (B-4)
13. Nobu (F-3)
14. Per Se* (N-3)
15. Rosa Mexicano (B-4, N-3, N-6)
16. Modern, The (O-4)
17. Aureole (N-5)
18. Del Posto (C-2)
19. Four Seasons (O-5)
20. Café Boulud (L-4)
21. Atlantic Grill (L-5)
22. Spice Market (C-2)
23. Buddakan (C-2)
24. Picholine (N-3)
25. Artisanal (A-4)
26. Il Mulino (D-4)
27. Telepan (M-3)
28. Chanterelle (F-3)
29. Tabla (B-4)
30. Aquavit (N-5)
31. Palm (O-3, P-5, P-5)
32. Carmine's (K-2, P-3)
33. Becco (O-3)
34. Café des Artistes (M-3)
35. davidburke & donatella (N-
36. Del Frisco's (O-4)
37. Aquagrill (E-3)
38. Lupa (D-4)
39. Bar Americain (O-3)
40. Pastis (C-2)
41. Felidia (N-5)
42. Mesa Grill (C-4)
43. Craft (B-4)
44. One if by Land, Two if by Sea
45. Blue Hill (D-3)
46. L'Impero (P-6)
47. Sparks (O-5)
48. Nobu 57 (N-4)
49. db Bistro Moderne (P-4)
50. Ouest* (K-2)

*Indicates tie with above